CULT IN CONTEXT

Reconsidering Ritual in Archaeology

CULT IN CONTEXT

Reconsidering Ritual in Archaeology

Edited by

David A. Barrowclough
and Caroline Malone

OXBOW BOOKS

Published by
Oxbow Books, Oxford, UK

© Oxbow Books and the individual authors, 2007
Paperback reprint 2010

ISBN 978-1-84217-964-2

A CIP record for this book is available from the British Library

This book is available direct from

Oxbow Books, Oxford, UK
(Phone: 01865-241249; Fax: 01865-794449)

and

The David Brown Book Company
PO Box 511, Oakville, CT 06779, USA
(Phone: 860-945-9329; Fax: 860-945-9468)

or from our website
www.oxbowbooks.com

Front cover: View looking out of the Ġgantija Temple, Gozo. (Photo: Simon Stoddart)

Back cover: A selection of illustrations from the volume.

Printed in Great Britain by
Short Run Press
Exeter

CONTENTS

LIST OF CONTRIBUTORS

MARK ALDENDERFER
Department of Anthropology
University of Arizona
Tucson
AZ 85721-0030
aldender@u.arizona.edu

SILVIA ALFAYÉ
Institute of Archaeology
36 Beaumont Street
Oxford
OX1 2PG
silvia.alfaye@arch.ox.uk

MICHAEL ANDERSON
Department of Classics
San Francisco State University
1600 Holloway Avenue
San Francisco
CA 94132
wpiw3wt@gmail.com
maa35@sfsu.edu

DAVID A. BARROWCLOUGH
McDonald Institute for Archaeological Research
Cambridge University
Downing Street
Cambridge
CB2 3ER
dab32@cam.ac.uk

PETER F. BIEHL
Department of Archaeology
Cambridge University
Downing Street
Cambridge
CB2 3DZ
pfb27@cam.ac.uk

ANTHONY BONANNO
Department of Classics and Archaeology
University of Malta
Msida MSD 06
Malta
anthony.bonanno@um.edu.mt

CLIVE J. BOND
Department of Archaeology
Faculty of Social Sciences
The University of Winchester
West Hill
Winchester
Hampshire
SO22 4NR
clivejbond@aol.com

RICHARD BRADLEY
Department of Archaeology
University of Reading
Whiteknights
PO Box 218
Reading
RG6 2AA
r.j.Bradley@reading.ac.uk

CAMILLA BRIAULT
McDonald Institute for Archaeological Research
Cambridge University
Downing Street
Cambridge
CB2 3ER
cb490@cam.ac.uk

LETIZIA CECCARELLI
Department of Archaeology
Cambridge University
Downing Street
Cambridge
CB2 3DZ
lc368@cam.ac.uk

GABRIEL COONEY
School of Archaeology
University College Dublin
Newman Building
Belfield
Dublin 4
Ireland
gabriel.cooney@ucd.ie

TIMOTHY DARVILL
Archaeology and Historic Environment Group
School of Conservation Sciences
Bournemouth University
Fern Barrow
Poole
Dorset
BH12 5BB
tdarvill@bournemouth.ac.uk

PIOTR DRAG
Institute of Archaeology
36 Beaumont Street
Oxford
OX1 2PG
piotr.drag@arch.ox.ac.uk

GEORGE EOGAN
59 Brighton Road
Rathgar
Dublin 6
Ireland
eogan@eircom.net

DRAGOS GHEORGHIU
Department of Research
National University of Arts
Bucharest
gheorghiu_dragos@yahoo.com

REUBEN GRIMA
Heritage Malta
National Museum of Archaeology
Republic Street
Valletta
VLT 04
reuben.grima@gov.mt

ROBIN HARDIE
8 Abbeville Road
London
SW4 9NJ
robin.hardie@ecosse.net

MATTHEW HAYSOM
Leventis Fellow
British School at Athens
Odhós Souidhías 52
10676 Athens
Greece
matthew.haysom@bsa.ac.uk

DAVID ILAN
Nelson Glueck School of Biblical Archaeology
Hebrew Union College-Jewish Institute of Religion
13 King David St.
Jerusalem 94101
Israel
dilan@huc.edu

TIMOTHY INSOLL
Archaeology
School of Arts, Histories, and Cultures
University of Manchester
Oxford Road
Manchester
M13 9PL
tim.insoll@manchester.ac.uk

LILIANA JANIK
Department of Archaeology
Cambridge University
Downing Street
Cambridge
CB2 3DZ
lj102@cam.ac.uk

SIMON KANER
Sainsbury Institute for the Study of Japanese Arts and
Cultures
SOAS
Russell Square
London
WC1H 0XG
s.kaner@sainsbury-institute.org

PATRICK MCCAFFERTY
Irish and Celtic Studies
9 University Square
Belfast
BT7 1NN
pmccafferty03@qub.ac.uk

LAMBROS MALAFOURIS
Department of Archaeology
Cambridge University
Downing Street
Cambridge
CB2 3DZ
lm243@cam.ac.uk

CAROLINE MALONE
McDonald Institute for Archaeological Research,
Cambridge, and School of Geography, Archaeology and
Palaeoecology
Queen's University Belfast
Belfast
BT7 1NN
catm20@cam.ac.uk

JON P. MITCHELL
Arts C254
University of Sussex
Falmer
Brighton
BN1 9QN
j.p.mitchell@sussex.ac.uk

IAIN MORLEY
McDonald Institute for Archaeological Research
Cambridge University
Downing Street
Cambridge
CB2 3ER
irm28@cam.ac.uk

HOLLEY MOYES
Dept. of Anthropology
University of Arizona
Tucson
AZ 85721-0030
hmoyes@email.arizona.edu

GOCE NAUMOV
University of Skopje
Institute for History of Art and Archaeology
Kiro Krstevski Platnik 11 – 2/7
1000 Skopje
Republic of Macedonia
gonaumov@mail.net.mk

BLAZE O'CONNOR
Humanities Institute Post-Doctoral Fellow
School of Archaeology
Newman Building
University College Dublin
Belfield
Dublin 4
Ireland
blaze.oconnor@ucd.ie

MUIRIS O'SULLIVAN
School of Archaeology
Newman Building
University College Dublin
Belfield
Dublin 4
Ireland
muiris.osullivan@ucd.ie

ALAN PEATFIELD
School of Classics
Newman Building
University College Dublin
Belfield
Dublin 4
Ireland
alan.peatfield@ucd.ie

SARAH RALPH
Network Archaeology
22 High Street
Buckingham
MK18 1NU
sarahr@netarch.co.uk

COLIN RENFREW
Department of Archaeology
Cambridge University
Downing Street
Cambridge
CB2 3DZ
des25@cam.ac.uk

YORKE M. ROWAN
Jordanian-American Commission for Educational
Exchange (JACEE)
(aka The Binational Fulbright Commission in Jordan)
PO Box 850215
Amman 11185
Jordan
yrowan@nd.edu

ROBIN SKEATES
Department of Archaeology
Durham University
South Road
Durham
DH1 3LE
robin.skeates@durham.ac.uk

KATE SPENCE
McDonald Institute for Archaeological Research
Cambridge University
Downing Street
Cambridge
CB2 3ER
kes1004@cam.ac.uk

SIMON STODDART
Department of Archaeology
Downing Street
Cambridge
CB2 3DZ
ss16@cam.ac.uk

KATYA STROUD
Curator, World Heritage Sites
Heritage Malta
National Museum of Archaeology
Republic Street
Valletta
VLT 04
katya.stroud@gov.mt

CHRISTOPHER TILLEY
Department of Anthropology
University College London
Gower Street
London
WC1E 6BT
c.tilley@ucl.ac.uk

ANDREW TOWNSEND
Bristol and Region Archaeological Services
Bristol's City Museum and Art Gallery
Queen's Road
Bristol
BS8 1RL
apjttowns@yahoo.co.uk

DAVID TRUMP
87 de Freville Avenue
Cambridge
CB4 1HP
trump@defrave.freeserve.co.uk

NICHOLAS VELLA
Department of Classics and Archaeology
University of Malta
Msida MSD 06
Malta
nicholas.vella@um.edu.mt

RUTH D. WHITEHOUSE
Institute of Archaeology
University College London
31–34 Gordon Square
London
WC1H 0PY
ruthataccordia@ntlworld.com

Chapter 1

INTRODUCTION

Caroline Malone, David A. Barrowclough and Simon Stoddart

Religion is the frozen thought of men, out of which they build temples. Jiddu Krishnamurti 1928

God is as myghtye in the stable as in the temple. Thomas More 1529

Introduction

This volume arose out of a conference held at Magdalene College, Cambridge in December 2006. The meeting of more than a hundred participants and over forty contributors was made possible by the award of a research grant from the Templeton Foundation within a wider programme of investigation entitled 'Becoming Fully Human: Social Complexity and Human Engagement with the Natural and Supernatural World'. Our specific project was entitled 'Explorations into the conditions of spiritual creativity in Prehistoric Malta' and focused on the ritual, art and architecture of that Mediterranean archipelago.

In designing our research proposal, we were acutely aware that our interpretation of the Maltese evidence for religious ritual was part of a wider archaeological endeavour aimed at developing a contextual methodology for understanding religion and cult through material culture. It was therefore appropriate that at the centre of our project lay an interdisciplinary conference which brought together not only other scholars engaged in research on Malta and the Mediterranean, but also those working elsewhere that shared our central concern of putting *Cult in Context*.

The aim was to set our work in the wider context of current archaeological research, to assess theory and method, and to enrich and exchange the interpretations that we had of one cultural context with the ideas of many others. The outcome is this collection of studies and discussions which demonstrate the vigour and interest in how a contextual archaeology investigates the challenging subjects of ritual, religion and cult. The results as seen in the following pages, is a wealth of material and approaches that tackle a variety of different concerns about how cult

and ritual can be recognised, recovered, interpreted and understood.

It might be wise to start with a definition of what is meant by these terms so that the interpretations of them that follow build on some essential understanding. This is the approach adopted in several of the papers that follow. Colin Renfrew more particularly addresses the central concern of how we define ritual, cult and religion, revisiting his earlier work (1985; 1994). If we define religion as systems of notions about the supernatural and the sacred, about life after death and related themes, then rituals are the social processes which give a concrete expression to these notions (cf. Morley, this volume). Very generally, we may suggest that rituals are rule-bound often public events which in some way or other thematise the relationship between the earthly and the spiritual realms.

Ritual is important because it is a synthesis of several levels of social reality: the symbolic and the social, the individual and the collective; and it usually brings out, and tries to resolve, at a symbolic level, contradictions in society. One major contradiction, that between life and death, is addressed almost universally by religion. Many peoples have notions about an after-life, which represent an idealised version of life here and now, devoid of its problems and frustrations. Notions of the afterlife can give an impression of continuity and serve to demystify death. These notions translate into a universal interest in the cycle of life whose interpretation can vary to a considerable degree cross-culturally (Bradley, Stoddart, this volume).

Many non-literate societies pay great attention to ancestors and ancestral spirits. This focus clearly deals with the problem of continuity, both in society and in the individual lifespan, when a life is suddenly stopped. In an article on ancestral cults in Africa, Kopytoff (1971) observed that there is not necessarily a sharp distinction between living humans and ancestral spirits. The living become wiser, 'drier' and less mobile the older they become; the ancestors are thus perceived as extremely wise, dry and immobile persons. There is no rigid boundary between life and death in this scheme, rather a gradual transition to another phase, which begins long before death.

Cult may be defined as 'a particular form of religious worship that implies devotion to a particular person or thing' and the variety of cult is explored in a number of papers. Some papers focus on cults which relate the living and the dead (Barrowclough, Drag, Naumov, Stoddart, this volume); one paper introduces the cult of fire (Gheorghiu this volume) and another that of the severed human head (Ralph, this volume). Two other papers, having distinguished cult from other forms of religious activity, take our reconsideration of definitions onto a another stage with analysis of totems, ancestors and animism (Insoll, this volume; and also Janik, this volume). Once again, what appear familiar and straightforward terms, when analysed, take on a complexity of their own. The conclusion is that the interpretation of such terms in the singular is 'flawed and instead interpretive plurality is required' (Insoll, this volume).

This brings us neatly to discussion of context. Like ritual, religion and cult, context is a word frequently applied to the archaeological record, often uncritically. In a volume dedicated to *Cult in Context* it is worthwhile considering the implications of context as specifically applied to archaeological investigation of the numinous. The use of symbols (including material culture) is central to religious cult rituals. Studies of ritual symbols must therefore not merely investigate which symbols (artefacts) are being used, but must also look into their mutual relationship and their meaning.

Context is important because symbols are polysemic. Contrary to the work of Durkheim (1965 [1912]) and Malinowski (1966 [1935]; 1974 [1948]), Leach (1954) shows that rituals positively encourage instability within society, since they offer themselves to conflicting interpretations. It was Turner (1967) who identified how symbols can be multivocal, where several meanings can be read into a symbol. The major insight in Turner's work is that symbols have to be multivocal or ambiguous in order to create solidarity, and since people are different, the symbols must be capable of meaning different things to different people. Maurice Bloch asserted that 'rituals are events that combine the properties of statements and actions. It is because of this combination that their analysis has proved endlessly elusive' (Bloch 1986, 181) shows this inherent complexity that makes archaeological interpretation so challenging and explains why context must be at the heart of our study.

The precise context, be it a cave, a mountainside, a building or a domestic shrine, and its intrinsic sense of place within the wider environment, is where the archaeological exploration of ritual begins. This context of ritual activity, the arena in which action was played out, where offering, veneration, display and ceremony were focused, surely holds structural, material and spatial clues to past

activity that has potential still to inform and enlighten modern inquiry.

For far too long, the notion that the place of ancient ritual should be the primary focus of attention has been overshadowed by the dominance of the study of ritual art and image. This approach has been with archaeology ever since objects began to be seen as important indicators of culture, chronology, style and technology over a century ago. The many catalogues of so-called 'ritual objects', figurines, offering bowls, etc. that fill library shelves, are invariably objects out of context, and rarely re-connected with their archaeological association or findspot. The result has been a dominance of object type over its relationship with what made it meaningful in the first place. Such objects have been re-described, reformatted and re-valued into something quite different, as indeed, have sacred pictures hanging in art museums, or objects displayed in rows in glass cases. Decontextualised, such material has little hope of informing us about what role it played in the rituals and cult beliefs of early religion unless described in contemporary literary sources.

The combination of place, context and its related paraphernalia has rarely been tackled as the genuine evidence of religion, although this logical approach should have been the fundamental starting point for archaeology. New archaeological work has the benefit of hindsight, so that current projects (for example Çatalhöyük – Hodder 2006) have set out explicitly with the aspiration of discovering context furnished with ritual material. But all is not lost, studies of old records, revisited sites, systematic studies of symbols, place and context can reignite understanding and show us aspects of early belief systems and the cults and rituals that were played out in at sites. There is much that the archive can offer (Barrowclough, Anderson and Stoddart, this volume).

Over the last twenty-five years post-processual archaeology, liberated from concerns with chronology and other fundamental knowledge of the past, has become increasingly interested in reaching beyond the obvious and descriptive, and exploring the symbolic and cognitive dimensions of past societies. It has become important within the scholastic environment, as well as in popular archaeological presentation to show people of the past as thinking creative communities, with beliefs and values that echo aspects of our own, regardless of their chronological remoteness. Constrained by archaeological methods and resources, most archaeologists have tended to emphasise, the extremes, the micro or the macro scale of context, from the individual pit or artefact to the entire landscape, which appear to be definable aspects that reveal the past. This approach is often at the expense of understanding or even acknowledging the actual site and its structure and layout. These days it is less common to consider the actual site and its many component parts and instead to consider the whole landscape of Stonehenge, for example, or to identify ritual deposits in a ditch terminal. Neither extreme of scale truly presents sufficient context of cult practice and ritual behaviour to take us further. Some of the studies presented here (in particular, Goseck – Biehl; Stonehenge – Darvill; Malta – Malone, Barrowclough, Stroud, and Grima; the Sweet Track – Bond) focus on this elementary contextual relationship between setting, site and individual contexts showing that even well-known material still has much to explore, by exploring linkage.

Defining and recognising convincing ritual context has often been problematic given the fragmentary nature of much archaeology, so rarely has an understanding of space and place been considered together with material objects and images. Emphasis on one has often distorted the value or association of the other. Rather than an integrated and holistic approach to the archaeological cult context in its entirety (as might be expected for the study of a 'traditional' society where ritual is embedded within all aspects of life), researchers have tended to separate or conflate the components that survive from a once rich cosmological and ceremonial environment. The results for prehistory have been inadequate or extreme, with scholars either playing down the possibilities of accessing the spiritual and ceremonial world, or overplaying the interpretation of isolated elements, be they 'structured depositions', figurines, sacrifices, altars or whatever, into an amalgam of uninformed discourse. This volume explores how contextual archaeologists are approaching the task of interpreting ritual and cult in the archaeological record by re-establishing integration.

Caves, landscapes, seascapes and mountain peaks provide special arenas for experience and sensation, some of which are influenced by seasonal or diurnal changes of light and atmosphere, making certain contexts special places for cult. Several papers (Whitehouse, Skeates, Bradley, Tilley, Peatfield, Haysom, Grima, Aldenderfer, and Bond, this volume) explore the experience that particular types of context have on provoking ritual and cult responses. Issues about death (Ralph, this volume), territory (Grima, this volume), cosmology (Bond, this volume) and the workings of the human brain (Malafouris, this volume) provide much stimulus for discussion. The influence of catastrophic change in the environment and the resulting impact on societies has often been used to explain extreme or unexpected cult expression. Two papers address this contentious topic through investigations of drought (Moyes, this volume) and comets (McCafferty, this volume), and the possible impact these may have had on already marginal societies, resulting in cultic responses.

Malta provides one of the best documented cases of prehistoric ritual (Figure 1.1). A core group of papers investigates the development and change of prehistoric and later ritual and cult within this specific context. The studies include a review of the antecedents of pre-temple ritual (Trump, this volume) and a deconstruction of the speculation about the origins of the label 'Temple' (Stroud, this volume). Explorations of how the temples may have functioned as ritual space are a principal focus of two papers (Malone; Anderson and Stoddart, this volume) which demonstrate how old records, when combined with new methodologies, allow us to formulate new interpretations of built spaces. Precise spatially contextualised mortuary data from the Maltese islands, reported in detail elsewhere (Malone *et al.* 2007), are placed in the scaled temporal contexts of the cycle of life (Stoddart, this volume), alerting us to the importance of temporal as much as spatial context.

One of the central problems that face archaeologists when working with artefacts and sites excavated before the advent of scientific archaeology is the de-contextualisation of one from another, which sometimes re-examination of records can illuminate. In the case of the Maltese Temples at Tarxien it has been possible to re-contextualise site and artefact thanks to the careful recording of the early twentieth century excavations by their director Themistocles Zammit. Using the Zammit diaries it is possible to generate new insights into where reliefs, figurines and portable objects were placed in the temple and to see their relationship to one another, from which an understanding of their role may be proposed (Malone *et al.* in prep).

Three papers anticipate this work by employing archival material from the 1920s and 1930s. The first has reinterpreted the deposition of miniature greenstone axes within the Temple, and offers a detailed pilot study of the potential (Barrowclough, this volume). The second makes a first assessment of the visibility and accessibility of artefacts from the perspective of the celebrants (Anderson and Stoddart, this volume). Old records and new ideas thus provide enlightenment in long abandoned material. This is a theme very much in keeping with a further paper which introduces us to the 'lost' archive of Italian archaeologist Luigi Ugolini who had proposed, as long ago as the early 1930s, to attempt to study the artefacts excavated from the Maltese Temples in the context of those structures (Vella, this volume). Events prevented the completion of these scholars' work which is only now being attempted once again.

Precise spatial context is not everything. Broader social context is equally important. One of the Maltese papers (Townsend, this volume) focuses on a particular social class of artefact, the Maltese figurines, exploring the depiction of obesity and leading the author to speculate on what the significance of this might have been. Figurative art on Malta and elsewhere, as presented in the conference, provided an important linking theme for this paper.

It is easy for the prehistoric period to dominate interpretations of Maltese archaeology. Little linkage or chronological consideration has been given before to the

Figure 1.1. The archipelago of Malta (the larger island) and Gozo with the location of the Temple Period sites indicated. Image courtesy of M. Anderson.

ritual world of later Malta, but papers here addressed both the later prehistoric and Phoenician ritual landscape (Bonanno, this volume), and the adaptation of Jewish ritual to Roman Malta (Drag, this volume). These two papers show how ritual landscapes are palimpsets of monumental activity.

Discussions broadened from the case study of Malta to embrace theoretical approaches to cult contexts in the wider Mediterranean. The first (Whitehouse, this volume) is a revisit to an earlier approach for the identification of religion and cult in the archaeological record (Whitehouse 1992). Here she proposes a role for phenomenological, sensory, experience in the interpretation of Italian cult sites. The notion that there is a role for experience in interpretation is another linking theme between papers. The theme underlies the study of Maltese caves (Skeates, this volume), the analysis of Minoan Peak Sanctuaries (Peatfield, this volume) and the comparative perspective on visual imagery between Maltese and Irish temples (Tilley, this volume).

A group of papers focused on Northern Europe, and particularly Ireland, are indicative of the rich archaeological

record, and a testament to the scholarly tradition of the contextual recording of its prehistory. Firstly, a study of the emergence of the Irish Passage Tombs from the perspective of the beginnings of megalith builders and megalithic art, exemplifies the expression of a new religious cult which originated in the Boyne Valley (Eogan, this volume). The significance of stone, as a symbolic resource as much as a building material, is the focus of current debate which came to the fore in one particular discussion of the construction of Neolithic monuments. As 'the processes that channel material actions in working stone are always embedded in a broader symbolic system' (Cooney, this volume) they rightly fit in our discussion of ritual. The point is reinforced by a reappraisal of that most iconic archaeological monument, Stonehenge, which takes into account 'its construction sequence, materials, arrangement, structure, associations, and related folklore in a way that relates architecture and form to ritual and meaning' (Darvill, this volume). The paper argues that by focusing on 'context, sequence and association' there is still much to be learnt from that most familiar landmark. The same can be said of the Mound of Hostages, Tara, where a contextual approach (O'Sullivan, this volume) to the deposition of human bone allows the tracking of changes in funerary practice over time. This permits the identification of changes in attitudes towards the dead from which something of the religious cult beliefs of the community can be inferred. The notion of a 'cult place' is central to another paper (Biehl, this volume), which develops a methodology for a contextual appreciation of places where religious ceremonies were held, and which has utility beyond the Neolithic of Europe.

Stone also figures in another paper on the nature of megalithic art and stone carving in general, in the creation of individual and group identity (O'Connor, this volume). This work underscores our earlier point that symbols are polysemic and can only be interpreted after the careful reconstruction of context. Rock art studies are also central to another study of ritual beliefs, although a little further afield (Janik, this volume). Utilising her fieldwork on Lake Baikal in Siberia Janik develops a theoretical approach to the interpretation of religious cult, based on the notion of 'embodied realism, a concept propounded by Lakoff and Johnson in their work on cognitive processes of the human brain'. This discussion provides a further linking strand within the volume.

Cognitive approaches, taken at their broadest, link two papers (Janik; Malafouris, this volume) whose focus is on archaeology and neuroscience, and another two papers (Bradley; Morley, this volume) whose cognitive interest is influenced by Pascal Boyer (2001), who argue that 'religious belief is a consequence of the workings of the human mind' (Bradley, this volume). Both these papers consider the cyclical nature of events and the possible religious and cultic interpretations for them. In the first case (Morley, this volume) it takes the form of a wide-ranging examination of time cycles, cosmology and ritual behaviour. In the second case (Bradley, this volume) the paper focuses on explanation of the relationship between diurnal and seasonal cycles, and the landscape and beliefs in later Bronze Age Scandinavia, seen through iconography.

In fact the theme of the life cycle, writ large, unites the two dimensions of ritual context: the spatial and the temporal. The established emphasis on the spatial context of ritual has been fuelled by the increasing accuracy of excavation records, and this is implicit in key archaeological contributions in the recognition of ritual (Renfrew 1985; 1994). More recently, temporality (Bradley 2002) in all its dimensions from the individual life history, through the history of the descent group to the trajectory of the individual civilisation, has been given greater emphasis. However, it is only very recently that scientific advances have permitted the pinpointing of time in the life cycle. Work on the biological life cycle as read from human bones still needs further calibration, but effective implementation of radiocarbon dating can now situate ritual within broader schemes of temporality with considerable precision (Whittle et al. 2007). These combinations of informed theory with advanced methodology will lead to major advances in our understanding of ritual, as in all the case studies presented here.

Time and with it issues of continuity and discontinuity underlie the discussion of Jomon Japan (Kaner, this volume). Kaner suggests that a possible 'defining characteristic of cult is the presence within a community of "a group having an exclusive ideology and ritual practices centred on sacred symbols"'. In Jomon, these symbols were timber posts, but as we have seen in the case of Ireland and Britain, elsewhere they may have been stone. A prominent case of the importance of stone is in Tibet where the discussion focuses on the *rdo-ring* (long stones) of the Tibetan plateau (Aldenderfer, this volume). These alignments of standing stones pose a problem for archaeologists keen to offer an interpretation for them. They prompt the exploration of alternative theoretical approaches out of which develops an approach which combines perspectives 'melded together via a pragmatic approach' (Aldenderfer, this volume) in which context is to the fore.

The theme of ritual diversity underlies another group of papers. The study of the Chalcolithic Levant (Rowan and Ilan, this volume) explores how power and changing social relations may be reflected in the funerary rituals and symbolic and recurring use of artefacts. The use of material culture as an expression of individual funerary identity was presented in another paper (Naumov, this volume), using figurative burial vessels from the Balkans. In a further paper, fire cults, houses, and house models provide a base for understanding cult behaviour on tell sites (Gheorghiu, this volume). The transformation of personal identity through male and female figurative art is explored in relation to gender, particularly maleness, and to the nature of context in the final prehistoric paper (Hardie, this volume). Unlike many funerary or ritual contexts that produce figurines, much of the material from the Balkans is from explicitly domestic contexts, implying that ritual embraces all aspects of life.

The transition to the historical world in many respects, offers an alternative chance of understanding cult and ritual, given the textual evidence and survival of traditions that permit a more internalised ethnographic analysis. Egypt especially, offers indications of what ritual and cult meant within dynastic society, but nevertheless, many archaeological elements still remain obscure and poorly understood, particularly in the arena of domestic cult (Spence, this volume). The study of Minoan religion has a long tradition, supported not only by the privileged location in the Greek world, but also by a wealth of evidence of practice from special sites such as peak sanctuaries and shrines (Briault; Haysom; Peatfield, this volume). Whilst related material from the Aegean undoubtedly stimulated Renfrew's celebrated discussion of the recognition of Cult (Renfrew 1985) the evidence is reviewed and progressed in this volume. The European Iron Age is frequently quoted for its grisly rituals and a paper on the cult of severed heads (Ralph, this volume) offers an insight into the curious prestige and power of the human head and its images. Contemporary cults in Spain suggest that there is a rich body of data to be retrieved and studied there, and another Iron Age paper (Alfayé, this volume) shows how the study of context has progressed an understanding of the Celtic ritual world south of the Pyrenees. The documented complexity of rituals and cults in the later Classical world is beyond the realms of this volume, but one paper (Ceccarelli, this volume), which focused on the specific rituals that took place in the early Latin city of Ardea, indicates how the use of historical sources may complement the archaeological record. The different shrines and temples are now sufficiently well known for interpretations of ritual significance and symbolism to be developed from both an understanding of practice (from archaeological evidence) and from reported textual meanings.

Our archaeological approaches to cult and ritual are informed from different sources: history, art and especially anthropology, and much use of analogy is made in order to demonstrate the possibilities of what otherwise can seem improbable and extreme forms of human behaviour as interpreted from the archaeological record. The final paper (Mitchell, this volume) records the thirty-year anniversary of a tradition opened by Edmund Leach (1977). Whereas Leach closed archaeologists into a metaphorical black box (Leach 1973), the anthropological commentator in this volume is refreshingly open to the possibilities offered by ritual practice from archaeology. This pooled experience is enhanced by the scenery of Malta, shared both by his fieldwork (Mitchell 2002) and by Malta-based archaeologists providing a core of the papers presented here. The view from the bridge painted by Leach was that of an anthropological captain steering his ship through the dangerous reefs of archaeological experience, at a time of divergence between social anthropology and archaeology. The newly constructed bridge (Mitchell, this volume) is one linking two traditions which, now at a time of greater convergence, permit a shared interest in ritual practice and material culture. Malta is one of a number of rich contexts where the interlinked cycles of ritual, archaeological and anthropological, can be assembled together to provide a seven thousand year history of ritual experience (Stoddart 1992).

The discussion by Renfrew drew the conference to a close, but here opens our discussions in print with a review of how our notions of Cult as opposed to Ritual have been defined and refined. It is right to be questioning of definitions of words such as cult and temple, but the problem is more pressing if one is still embedded in a Western Graeco-centric perspective. In many of the societies studied in this volume, ritual of varying formality, reaching even the level of cult activity, was embedded in daily practice. In exceptional cases, the level of that formality achieves a pitch, exceptionally evident in the case of Malta, such that the cult place can authoritatively draw upon the Roman (dare we say Etruscan rather than Greek) concept of *templum,* which above all emphasises the sense of place. Anyone who has entered a Maltese ritual monument has witnessed that sense of constructed place, summarised as scale and axiality, but containing much more as ongoing research reveals. Renfrew remains sceptical, even taking up the role of Leach, diplomatically relinquished by the anthropologist (Mitchell, this volume), while neglecting his anthropological mantle, about how far archaeology can go into these still mysterious areas of the past (Renfrew, this volume). However, we the editors feel that these are terms, issues and discussions that should remain open, lively and heated for the foreseeable future. It is by taking an anthropologically informed position, and one not too influenced by Western values of Graecocentricity or monotheism, as Renfrew rightly maintains, that advances are to be made. We thank all those who participated and for the excellent contributions that have been presented here and which advance in precisely a direction no longer dependent on textbound classical models.

Acknowledgements

We would like to thank the following for their help in making this conference and its resulting publication possible: The Templeton Foundation, Cambridge University (McDonald Institute for Archaeology), the Master and Fellows of Magdalene College Cambridge, Heritage Malta, Oxbow Books, and the many helpers and assistants who managed the conference events so efficiently. Victoria Blennerhassett, Mary Chester-Kadwell, Katherine Cooper, Naomi Farrington, Francesca Fulminante, Holly Hardisty, Elisabeth Rutherford, Robin Whaley, Alice Whitmore.

Caroline Malone, as Principal Investigator of the recent research in Malta and this Conference wishes to acknowledge with thanks the award by the Templeton Foundation of Biocomplexity Grant no. 1093 which has supported this publication, and the preceding conference. Thanks also to Sarah Monks of Oxbow Books for typesetting the volume.

References

Bloch, M. 1986. *From Blessing to Violence: history and ideology in the circumcision ritual of the Merina of Madagascar.* Cambridge, Cambridge University Press.
Boyer, P. 2001. *Religion Explained.* London, Heinemann.
Bradley, R. 2002. *The Past in Prehistoric Societies.* London – New York, Routledge.

Durkheim, É. 1965 [1912]. *The Elementary Forms of Religious Life* Translated by Swain, J. W. New York, Free Press.

Hodder, I. 2006. *The Leopard's Tale: Revealing the Mysteries of Çatalhöyük*. London, Thames and Hudson.

Kopytoff, I. 1971. Ancestors as elders in Africa. *Africa* 41(2), 128–142.

Krishnamurti, J. 1928. Sayings of the Week. (From essay "Life the Goal") *Observer* 22 April 1928.

Leach, E. R. 1954. *Political systems of Highland Burma: a study of Kachin social structure*. London, G. Bell – London School of Economics and Political Science.

Leach, E. 1973. Concluding Address. In A. C. Renfrew (ed.). *The Explanation of Culture Change: Models in Prehistory*. London, Gerald Duckworth and Co. Ltd, 7761–7771.

Leach, E. 1977. A view from the Bridge. In M. Spriggs (ed.). *Archaeology and Anthropology: areas of mutual interest*. BAR Supplementary Series 19. Oxford, British Archaeological Reports, 161–176.

Malinowski, B. 1966 [1935]. *Coral Gardens and their Magic*. Second edition. London, Allen and Unwin.

Malinowski, B. 1974 [1948]. *Magic, science and religion, and other essays*. London, Souvenir Press.

Malone, C. A. T., Stoddart, S. K. F., Trump, D., Bonanno, A. and Pace, A. (eds). 2007. *Mortuary ritual in prehistoric Malta. The Brochtorff Circle excavations (1987–1994)*. Cambridge, McDonald Institute.

Malone, C. A. T. and Stoddart, S. K. F. (in preparation). *Art, cult and context: a study of prehistoric ritual in early Malta*.

More, T. 1529. *A dyaloge of syr Thomas More knyghte: one of the counsayll of oure souerayne lorde the kyng [and] chauncellour of hys duchy of Lancaster. Wherin be treated dyuers maters, as of the veneration [and] worshyp of ymages [and] relyques, prayng to sayntys, [and] goyng o[n] pylgrymage. Wyth many othere thyngys touching the pestylent sect of Luther and Tyndale, by the tone bygone in Saxony, and by tother laboryed to be brought in to Englond*. London, Johannes Rastell.

Mitchell, J. P. 2002. *Ambivalent Europeans. Ritual memory and the Public Sphere in Malta*. London, Routledge.

Renfrew, A. C. 1985. Towards a framework for the Archaeology of Cult Practice. In Renfrew, A. C. (ed.). *The Archaeology of Cult. The Sanctuary at Phylakopi*. London, Thames and Hudson – The British School of Archaeology at Athens, 11–26.

Renfrew, A. C. 1994. The archaeology of religion. In A. C. Renfrew and E. Zubrow, (eds). *The Ancient Mind. Elements of Cognitive Archaeology*. Cambridge, Cambridge University Press, 47–54.

Stoddart, S. K. F. 1992. Towards a historical ethnology of the Mediterranean. *Current Anthropology* 33(5), 599–560.

Turner, V. W. 1967. *The forest of symbols: aspects of Ndembu ritual*. Ithaca, Cornell University Press.

Whitehouse, R. D. 1992. *Underground religion. Cult and culture in prehistoric Italy*. London, Accordia Research Centre.

Whittle, A. W. R., Barclay, A., Bayliss, A., McFadyen, L., Schulting, R. and Wysocki, M. 2007. Building for the Dead: events, processes and changing worldviews from the thirty-eighth to the thirty-fourth centuries cal. BC in Southern Britain. *Cambridge Archaeological Journal* 17(1 (supplement)), 123–147.

Chapter 2

RITUAL AND CULT IN MALTA AND BEYOND: TRADITIONS OF INTERPRETATION

Colin Renfrew

The following observations were offered not at the start of this interesting Conference, but after two days' worth of very stimulating papers. They take as their starting point some of the points raised in those papers. Underlying them, however, is an acute awareness that while the architectural remains of the Neolithic 'temples' of Malta and the finds associated with them are exceptionally rich, their interpretation has so far proved problematic. I shall argue that they share this uneasy situation with many other categories of find and monument in prehistory, where explanations and interpretations initially developed many decades ago have often been followed rather unquestioningly by generations of later scholars. Indeed it is possible in some cases to identify traditions of interpretation reaching back through several layers and generations of scholarship to scholarly inventions advanced in early times, often with little sustaining evidence. The range of papers in the present Conference allows some of these traditions to be identified and questioned.

First of all, the papers of the first day, which I think did set the scene very well, introduced matters of ritual. Then we had a wonderful second day devoted primarily to the antiquities of Malta, starting with David Trump's excellent introduction, and taking us on through the millennia right on to Phoenician and Jewish catacombs, Jewish hypogea, and to the symbolism to be seen in them.

There are a couple of preliminary remarks to be made. It soon became apparent that we should not really have been having a conference entitled 'Cult in Context' so much as 'Ritual in Context.' The distinction, of course, is that 'cult' implies a religious context while 'ritual' can have much wider connotations. Most of the things we were talking about at the Conference could undoubtedly arise from the practice of ritual, but it is very much open to debate, as we shall see, how many of them may be judged clearly to arise from cult.

This brings me to a second and central point, namely the pervasive influence of traditions of presentation. We all know that it is not always easy, on the basis of the material

evidence, to talk about prehistoric religion (or prehistoric cult which may be taken to be more or less synonymous). I don't want to get too lost in definitions, although I will to clarify below a little what I mean by those terms. It is, however, interesting to note that most of the conclusions we reach start from our own *a priori* standpoint, which forms a point of departure. Our point of departure here, for instance is to follow a long-standing convention, and to talk about the 'Temples' in Malta. I am uncertain who was the first scholar to speak, early in the last century or even earlier, in this context of 'temples'. But they certainly have much to answer for. Nobody, I think, during the first two days of our Conference questioned the term 'temple', since it is perhaps difficult to think of a better one. Yet the word 'temple' is deeply rooted in traditions of understanding, perhaps referring primarily to Greek temples. Indeed, a great deal of our discussion about religion is clouded by a terminology that rests to some extent upon the experience of the specific religion, with which most of us are acquainted, which is one of monotheism. Very few of us (although we may have some Hindu followers in our midst) are acquainted with religions beyond the monotheistic. This carries with it a number of inherent limitations. So, for instance, it is easy to speak of the 'cult of the dead' in the Jewish case which we were discussing earlier. But if you are taking a broader view, the Jewish cult in question is more accurately to be considered a cult *for* the dead not a cult *of* the dead. For if you speak of a cult 'of' something you are usually speaking of supplication toward some divine or transcendental agency. In the Jewish case that agency is none other than the (one and only) Lord. The prayers offered in those funerary chambers were in reality offered to the good Lord Jehovah on behalf, as it were, of the dead. They were certainly not offered *to* the dead (as a 'cult of the dead' in other contexts would imply) but *for* the dead. Such a conclusion does not follow at all however, when Christopher Tilley, for instance, sees the Neolithic inhabitants of Ireland as invoking all kinds of material agency to ensure that the dead stay safely within their realm, located within some megalithic tomb. There he really is talking about veneration of the dead, in effect a cult of the ancestors, and it is the dead who are felt to have agency, (although it remains to be discussed whether those dead themselves are thought to be subordinate to some more powerful agency or deity). These, then are some of the issues that arise when we are talking about cult.

Without being too tedious about definitions – and everyone is entitled to their own – it is interesting to centre a little more upon the word 'ritual', whose meaning is, effect. very close to the word 'ceremonial', used by one or two people at this meeting. Ritual and ceremonial are very closely related. Partly through the work of Evangelios Kyriakidis I have come to realise that to speak of the 'Archaeology of Cult' as I once did in a book of that title requires a little more caution, for a good part of it is, in reality, an archaeology of ritual rather than archaeology of cult. So what then is ritual? There could be all kinds of definitions and I formulated one recently, which probably comes close to many: 'Inception or repetition of conventional programmes of expressive action'. Ritual thus involves the production of performative actions that are situated in time and are repeated, and it has clearly has a performative element. But the definition makes no statement about the belief system which underlies the ritual, nor does it imply a religious motivation. The notion of expressive or performative action avoids the problem of repeated, mundane actions in daily life. If you were on a production line in some company making motorcars you would go through repeated actions. But in general they would not be regarded as expressive actions. Expressive action carries the implication that either there is a situation where there is an actor and spectators or, alternatively, one with a group of actors who are performing expressively to each other, or indeed both.

It was extremely useful to have Ruth Whitehouse amongst us, for many reasons. In particular her very clear expression of a standpoint of atheism at the outset was extremely helpful in encouraging us to develop this emerging perspective of ritual without a necessary accompanying religious component. For instance in our own society we do have burial rituals that can operate with complete propriety in a context where no deity is being invoked. Those would still be rituals pertaining to death. We need not go into the details, but we have all been to crematoria and witnessed funerary ceremonies conducted in a non-religious context, yet they are still performative, or usually so. There are still proprieties to be maintained, and respect and solemnity have to be shown. In such a case it may not be appropriate to use the word cult.

Definitions may vary, but I would regard cult as the practice of worship within a religious context. Inevitably we need to discuss next what one might mean by religion, which is notoriously difficult to define. One of the most convenient definitions of religion involves consideration of transcendental or supernatural forces and of the sense of the numinous. If we wish to make the discussion more subjective, in terms of personal experience, as Christopher Tilley might advocate, we may wish to emphasise the sense of the numinous. This stand close to religious experience and may perhaps include visions of the transcendental, and the awareness of powers which are exterior to oneself and of powers superior to one's own.

It does seem to be a safe generalisation, however, that all cult involves ritual. All religious performance certainly involves ritual. But, conversely, not all ritual involves cult, as I hope I have made clear.

Most burials involve do indeed involve ritual performative conventions. But, as we have seen, it is not at all clear that most burials involve cult. It is important to be aware of that. We really don't know much about these performative rituals in many prehistoric communities, and in the case of Malta our concern is mainly with the prehistoric communities of the island. Much of the discussion during the Conference was of societies that may be broadly described as non-state societies, and therefore non-literate societies.

Some anthropologists do speak of a cult of the ancestors and it seems to me that they do that with two meanings. One refers to performative rituals involving religious beliefs in which the burial of the deceased takes place. The Jewish case associated with the Maltese hypogea has been mentioned and there are many others where we could discuss the burial customs operating within established religions. But there is the other case which has not yet been dealt with systematically here: the cult of the ancestors. Here one is actually invoking the ancestors, inviting the ancestors to return as a living presence, and even worshipping them as ancestors. That is really what the notion of the cult of the ancestors ultimately can mean and in this context should mean. It is entirely reasonable to ask in what instances in prehistory this may have been the case, and to suggest that the enormous effort of monumentality seen in the megalithic monuments of north-western Europe in which the dead clearly played a central role involves giving the dead a central place within the belief system in society.

It may be appropriate now to consider the question of religion a little further. My own thinking about the archaeology of cult came through my experience of excavating the sanctuary at Phylakopi in Melos. There I had to consider various definitions of religion. I found the Oxford dictionary definition quite convenient:

> Action or conduct indicating a belief in or reverence for and desire to please a divine ruling power.

One might perhaps put the reference to 'a divine ruling power' in the plural and then proceed to define what is meant by the divine, and consider the notion of the transcendental or supernatural.

It is interesting that some of the most distinguished anthropologists have chosen deliberately to avoid the transcendental, to dodge the supernatural column, so to speak. Durkheim's definition of religion is:

> a unified system of beliefs and practices: that is sacred things: that is to say, things set apart and forbidden – beliefs and practices which unite into one single moral community called a Church, all those who adhere to them. (Durkheim 1915, 47)

Durkheim uses the word 'sacred' and then his definition of sacred is: 'set apart and forbidden'. He does not speak of the transcendental which is a conspicuous, and no doubt deliberate, omission.

Geertz likewise offers a very strange definition of religion:

> a system of symbols which acts to establish powerful, pervasive and long-lasting moods and motivations in men by formulating conceptions of a general order of existence, and clothing these conceptions with such an order of factuality that the moods and motivations seem uniquely realistic. (Geertz 1966, 4)

One can see how most religions would fall within the definition, but it did dawn upon me with great clarity that the concept of money could also fit Geertz's definition very neatly. If I had a hundred pound note in my pocket and offered it to the audience I think you would see exactly what I mean.

Geertz too is here seen dodging the transcendental column. He deliberately avoids the concept of the transcendental in his definition of religion. But I think the transcendental column is not so easy to dodge, although I am aware that if one goes to a Taoist shrine you have to be rather careful how you define the transcendental.

To turn now more specifically to Malta, the meeting has usefully reminded us that by modern standards the great excavations in Malta of Zammit and his predecessors remain to some extent unpublished excavations. Indeed I think the greatest fruit of all the work that we have been hearing about, beyond the excavation and publication of the Xagħra Brochtorff Circle itself, will be the detailed publication at last of the data that are available whether from the early work of Ugolini or from the notebooks of Zammit. We really shall know then something about context at a level which is not currently available.

We heard earlier about the Ġgantija and the belief that giants erected the Maltese Temples. That reminded me of one of the names that was given to Stonehenge in the eighteenth century: *Choreum Giganteum*, the dancing place of the giants. That is a useful reminder of a very early interpretive tradition, and that the term choreography has recently and usefully been brought into the discussion in considering the performative aspects of the rituals that might be associated with the temples. Katya Stroud was

one of those who indicated that line of thought in her paper.

The impact of different traditions of interpretation is well illustrated by the decorated 'altar' from Ħaġar Qim (Evans 1971, figure 47) first published, I believe, by Mayr. He was working and publishing before the excavations of Sir Arthur Evans at Knossos in Crete were comprehensively published. He wrote instead under the influence of Sir Arthur Evans's earlier work on the Mycenaean Tree and Pillar cult (Evans 1901). Inevitably, perhaps, he assumed Aegean influence upon Malta: that was a diffusionist context although not yet a Minoan diffusionist context. And even when, many years later, the first radiocarbon dates became available, as David Trump has reminded us, the comparison between Maltese spirals and Mycenean or (by then) then the earlier Minoan spirals was utilised in order to seek some chronological placing of the Maltese temples. It wasn't until the calibration of radiocarbon that it became clear that this association had to be abandoned. From the same early period of interpretation came the thinking which goes back, I think, to Bachofen, several generations before Gimbutas, that the figures, the plump figures, of Malta should be assimilated to the view that there had been a pan-Mediterranean Great Earth Mother, a goddess of fertility. Early authors considered that she was to be associated with the cities of western Asia Minor, where she was allegedly documented in classical times. All this now seems a little extraordinary because even the notion of Artemis of the Ephesians has to be read now in an Indo-European context, with the realisation that all of the languages of western Anatolia in classical times were in fact Indo-European languages. Nineteenth century scholars and many of their twentieth century successors claimed a divergence between the Asiatic religions (with the notional Earth Mother) on the one hand, and the Indo-European religions on the other. Their deities were supposed to have very different characteristics. It is ironic therefore that the type cases of the 'Asiatic' religions, originally drawn from western Anatolia, came from a context that has now been shown to be Indo-European, so that the purported dualism disappears.

As any of us that visit Malta – or indeed Çatalhöyük – realise we may be buttonholed at any time by devotees of the Great Earth Mother. They may have linked up with devotees of the Chalice and the Blade. If you are skilful you may escape what I now recognise as a Neo-Californian cult, but it does require some skill. Their interpretive tradition is certainly a compelling one.

There is another tradition, popular in the nineteenth century, which I think has largely disappeared now. It chose to think of the temples of Malta as essentially 'megalithic', laying emphasis upon the general manner of their construction, and seeing them as the handiwork of 'the megalith builders'. No doubt these buildings *are* megalithic in the sense that they are constructed of large stones. But they are no longer felt to be part of some unified movement which led also to the construction of the megalithic tombs of north-western Europe.

Traditions of interpretation persist. Another is to speak rather easily of 'chiefdoms' when considering monumental constructions in prehistoric societies. I was guilty of that myself when I suggested that the territories of Malta might be compared with the chiefdom territories of Easter Island. I now agree with those critics who suggest that the term 'chiefdom' is not really a very helpful one in Malta, even if one still has to explain how the mobilisation of labour that produced these great structures was achieved. I would make by way of excuse the point that at the time I was writing *Before Civilisation* the aim was to try to make explicable, in a general sense, some of the most striking phenomena of European prehistory. This had now to be undertaken in the light of the radiocarbon revolution, while avoiding the *ex oriente lux* position of diffusionist explanation which had prevailed in earlier decades.

There are other traditions of interpretation, some of much more recent origin. These days whenever anybody finds a few animal bones in a pit there is a tendency to start talking of feasting. Over the last five years everybody has been having a terrific time feasting in all these places where ritual or cult may be suspected. Similarly in one or two papers at the Conference there was an invocation of shamanism, another recently fashionable explanatory theme. I have nothing against shamanism as such, except that it has recently been applied so widely as to become almost a universal explanation when some arcane ritual is to be elucidated. Shamanism has of late achieved a very widespread application as an explanation in symbolic and structural archaeology which has come to rival the convenient universality of the Great Earth Mother. Perhaps the two could be made to merge so that, like plus and minus, like positron and electron, they could disappear altogether in a puff of smoke!

Another concept recently introduced to the discussion, and not yet to be categorised as a 'tradition', is the notion of regeneration. I very much enjoyed Simon Stoddart's interpretation of the splendid pair of seated figures from Xaghra, in which a small figure seated in the lap of a larger one, was seen as a small infant. This allowed reference to the notion of fertility and indeed of regeneration. I could however suggest another and different convention of interpretation which would tend to assume that when a large figure holds a very small figure the scene might well be taken rather as representing a patron deity holding a diminutive human. The small scale would be the human scale and the divine scale would be larger. I found Caroline Malone's paper one of the most encouraging of the entire Conference because of the excellent work that is being done in recognising pattern. Pattern sometimes does fall into dichotomies as she showed so admirably.

Just three weeks before the Conference I was in Turkmenia at the site of Gonur Tepe. Here again I found myself in presence of modes of interpretation, which are well formulated and reasonably satisfying, and yet ultimately questionable. It is a wonderful site, brilliantly excavated by Victor Sarianidi. He regards the entire site as a cult centre. The site is fortified and boasts also an inner fortification. The excavator has found it possible to ascribe uses to different areas of the site, just as Sir Arthur Evans felt able to define the 'king's megaron' and the 'queen's megaron' at the palace of Knossos. The site has been extensively excavated, and then interpreted, in a manner not unlike that applied to the palace at Knossos, perhaps a shade intuitively. There have been those who have likewise argued that the entire palace of Knossos is a cult centre, yet there are many others who have emphasised that with peak sanctuaries and caves functioning as cult places in Minoan Crete, you do not need in addition the whole palace at Knossos to serve as a cult centre. Sarianidi identified Gonur Tepe with its alleged fire temples and the use of the drug ephedra (which may be the *soma* that one reads about in the hymns of the Rig Vega) as a cult centre. But one may question whether it is appropriate to see the entire walled area of Gonur Tepe as a cult centre in this way. The alternative would be to see the site as an urban centre (a city), no doubt containing cult places and altars, but nonetheless dedicated mainly to those urban functions which we see in other early cities of western Asia. This very issue is relevant in a general way to the Maltese case. If we view the entire urban centre (at Gonur Tepe) or the totality of the remaining architectural remains (in Neolithic Malta) as dedicated to cult, what is available for the other functions of society?

There are questions to be posed about these frameworks of interpretation. Again they take off from a well-defined starting point and develop a terrific coherence. But there are problems. Conversely to do without any recognised religious centre is a problem, which the student of the Indus valley civilisation faces, to choose another interesting example. I don't want to say much here about the cult practices of state societies, but it is the case that most state societies of which we have knowledge do indeed have a religious system which is reflected in their material remains. This often results in a clear differentiation on the ground, so to speak. So that very often in a settlement serving as a central place in a state society you can distinguish between a sanctuary and other non-holy places – a point made effectively in York Rowan and David Ilan's paper for the Conference on the Chalcolithic in the Levant. There remains the troubling problem in the Indus valley civilisation that we have no clear indications at all of clearly identified locations for the public practice of cult. That is a very interesting question.

It is appropriate now to return to the general topic of

ritual. We have already defined ritual as repeated conventional programmes of expressive action. It is worth reflecting further upon the circumstances when and where ritual occurs. Clearly, it occurs very widely throughout life, as any anthropological consideration will show. Let us further ask when and where does indications of ritual practice enter the archaeological record. That is a matter of formation processes. One obvious example is through deliberate burial: through the burial of the dead, or the burial of valuables in hoards or of material in pits, which has recently been the focus of much work in British prehistory. Those are deliberate depositions which may well be accompanied by ritual practices. But one can easily envisage other deliberate depositions which are not accompanied by ritual. There can be deposition when you store (you dig a hole and store things in it), a process that may or may not be accompanied by ritual.

Of course there are other ways in which ritual is documented in the archaeological record, other than by deliberate burial. One may also have evidence of ritual when there is a product, the result of a ritual process, which is endlessly repeated. One may find that in iconography, in redundant iconography. Another area where ritual may be inferred is often in association with monumentality. Indeed most cases of monumentality to be found in the prehistoric period were probably associated with ritual.

Iain Morley reminded us during the Conference of the importance of time structuring. Time is a very good way to approach the notion of ritual performance. There may be calendric performances based on the day, the year, cycles of 56 years, or even an era, as in the Maya civilisation, where a great deal of attention and elaborate ritual was assigned to the ending of an era. Or the cycles of time may work in a personal sense, by birth or maturity or ephebism, or marriage, or the birth of offspring or other rites of passage. Or there may be rituals of social representation: rituals associated with a ruler, such as the accession to throne rituals or the appearances of the Egyptian pharaoh, or with other collective rituals pertaining to the society. That must certainly be true of those societies in Ireland or Malta which had considerable powers of mobilisation and therefore of organisation but which did not necessarily have chiefly persons. One sees similar phenomena for instance in the periodic games of the Greek city states which were accompanied by significant rituals. There may be commercial rituals, that is to say rituals associated with commercial practices such as periodic markets, and there are certainly religious rituals which are marked by their own periodicity. The society we are talking of in Malta may have had many such practices. So we really do have to step away a little from the notion of the temple, if to use that term restricts the range of the possibilities which we are able to consider.

One could scarcely deny that the so-called temples of Malta were indeed places where ritual must indeed have been practised. But why should we assume it to be always to have been religious in nature? It is a very peculiar feature of Malta (though perhaps it's a feature we do find echoed in the megalithic monuments of north-western Europe), that we know much about the monuments themselves and yet very little about the domestic habitations of their builders. That differs from the surviving remains in most societies where there are indeed temples and ritual monuments, but also surviving evidence for houses. Where are the domestic remains in Malta? David Trump's work at Skorba is still one of the best indicators. Perhaps like the dwellings associated with the megalithic monuments of north-western Europe the houses were not so well built, or perhaps they were not permanently inhabited.

Perhaps one could say that such monuments were occupied by the dead and permanently used by the living. These are factors to be considered when we address the monuments of Malta. To call them ritual or ceremonial centres is probably more appropriate than to regard them as cult centres. To say that is not, however, to exclude their use for cult purposes.

In Orkney, to choose another intriguing case, one sees the emergence of ritual centres even if we don't know a great deal of what went on. Again there has been a tendency to regard them as cult centres, and one of reasons for this is the emphasis which we may infer on the movement of the sun and moon. For when we talk of cult and religion we are often moving towards cosmology, towards a total world view, which while not necessarily centring upon the sun and the moon and other celestial bodies, must necessarily include them. It is interesting that while in Ireland we don't recognise such places of assembly as the henge monuments of England and Scotland, yet there is the phenomenon of Newgrange, and with it the other orientations of passage graves which remind us of the interest in the solar and lunar directions.

But I think I have said enough. In the case of Malta, I would say that we need to be more explicit about ritual practices broadly defined. One may perhaps conclude that there were rituals involving the dead, possibly but not necessarily a cult of the ancestors. With these figurations at Xagħra and at the Ħal Saflieni Hypogeum it is plausible that we have a system involving deities, or something like that, so this may be not just a ritual of the dead but also indeed a cult for the dead.

It did occur to me to wonder that one might think a little more about different functionalities. Is it impossible that the island of Malta, or indeed Malta with Gozo, constituted a single territory in the Tarxien phase? If so, is it not interesting that at Ħaġar Qim we have a notable concentration of figures and at Tarxien a wonderful sequence of spirals and also figures. Other 'temple' sites had different resources and one could develop a model where the different monumental sites had different functions. Tarxien, in particular, does resemble a stage set – a location which may have had ritual functions and may have had cultic functions. But perhaps in one's interpretation one does not have to rely exclusively on these aspects. One does however have to marvel at the deliberate monumentality of the presentation.

It is important also not to omit the Hypogeum of Ħal Saflieni from the discussion. Here in the provision for the dead they used elements of architecture which they were using above ground in the rituals for the living.

The many uncertainties in the above discussion suggest to me that we are still at an early stage in the long quest for a valid understanding of the prehistoric monuments of Malta. It is more than ever abundantly clear that they offer one of the richest examples in world prehistory of a very early society, non-literate and non-urban, yet with a wealth of architectural and symbolic complexity. The excavations in the so-called Brochtorff Circle at Xagħra, discussed here, together with the more detailed documentation of the data from earlier excavations now becoming available, serve to emphasise that richness. But our interpretive models and our frameworks of inference are as yet insufficiently developed. As I have sought to show, we still rely heavily upon frameworks of interpretation which require critical scrutiny, and which often rest upon untested assumptions. The study of the archaeology of ritual and of cult is still at an early stage. The case of prehistoric Malta will continue to have an important place in that developing study.

References

Durkheim, E. 1915. *The Elementary Forms of Religious Life.* London, Allen and Unwin.

Evans, A. J. 1901. The Mycenaean tree and pillar cult and its Mediterranean relations. *Journal of Hellenic Studies* 21, 99–204.

Evans, J. D. 1971. *Prehistoric Antiquities of the Maltese Islands.* London, Athlone Press.

Geertz, C. 1966. Religion as a cultural system. In M. Banton (ed.). *Anthropological Approaches to the Study of Religion* (A.S.A. Monographs 3). London, Tavistock Press, 1–46.

Chapter 3

MALTESE TEMPLE CULT:
THE ANTECEDENTS

David Trump

In the absence of written records, cult can only be reconstructed from the material remains, if then. Everything beyond that is more or less conjectural. It is for this reason that Malta, with its wealth of religious architecture and statuary in the Temple Period, both encouraged by the magnificent local stone, has such an important role to play. For earlier periods on the islands, however, the evidence is much scantier, and for long was thought not to exist.

Sixty years ago, it was unthinkable that the temples and their contents could have a purely local origin. Instead, antecedents were sought in Mycenean Greece or Atlantic Europe. Better still, if they came from the east, they could have been passed on to the west, providing an origin for the latter's megalithic architecture too. Failing all else, there was always Atlantis, or some other so far unidentified source. At that time, diffusion was called upon to explain everything.

In the early 1950s, John Evans (1953) brought together a number of significant points. Firstly, although all three areas built in blocks of stone of large size, and made female figurines, though not many of these in the west, the details of architecture and statuary in the three areas under consideration had very little in common. Later, radiocarbon finally severed those suggested links.

At the Hypogeum of Ħal Saflieni, while the core of the site was clearly closely related to the above-ground temples, its uppermost storey, patently the earliest part of the site, was both much simpler and more irregular. Applying the same principle to the temples, Evans postulated a typological sequence from a vaguely lobed plan, to trefoil, to five-apse, to four-apse, and finally to six-apse. He was much encouraged to find, when this was compared to his new pottery sequence, which was in turn confirmed by excavated stratigraphy, that the first three stages of temple plan fell within the earlier Ġgantija phase of his sequence, the last two into the later Tarxien phase.

That would still not explain where the first temple plans came from, since they looked quite unlike anything in Greece or the Atlantic seaboard. Instead, he compared it with the plan of the lobed chambers of the rock-cut tombs he had excavated at Xemxija, St Paul's Bay, especially tombs 1, 2 and 5, which chronologically preceded the first of the temples. Though admittedly somewhat speculative, it offered a better solution than any other, particularly since Ħal Saflieni had already demonstrated a close link between temples and tombs, with implications for cult beliefs, if not necessarily practices.

Then in the early 1960s, a new factor came to light in the excavations at Skorba, Zebbieh (Trump 1966). Alongside the two temples there, of typical Ġgantija (three-apse) and Tarxien (four-apse) form, two oval chambers of much earlier date came to light. They measured 8.4 × 5.4 m and 5.6 × 3.2 m, and were built on massive foundations of medium-sized, certainly not megalithic, blocks, though their fill showed that their superstructures had been of mudbrick. It was the use of mudbrick, perhaps, which prevented the realisation of their full implications at the time.

Already there was plenty of evidence that this building had a religious function. The south room had no doorway, and neither had any hearth. The floor of both was natural bedrock, with no attempt to level up or smooth off its marked irregularities. Although the sherds of many high quality pottery vessels were suggestive of cult use, they were not in themselves conclusive. More so were two goat skulls, complete with their horns, perhaps also twenty cow digitals, their proximal ends ground smooth so that they could be stood up on end like chess pawns, though for what purpose is by no means clear. Nine fragmentary female figurines were even more explicit. There had been none in domestic deposits behind the temples. All this was sufficient for these chambers to be interpreted as shrines, given the strong hint of animal sacrifice and fertility symbolism, although 'shrine' is admittedly a fairly vague term. Compared with the later temples, there is nothing further here to suggest cult practices or beliefs.

Reconsidering the matter later (Trump 2002), Skorba strengthens John Evans's suggestion of independent development. Here was evidence for religious architecture nearly a millennium before the first known temple. Given the influence of the lobed tomb plan, we have an even more convincing ancestor for those temples. Surely we no longer need to look outside Malta for their origin.

A similar story can be made out for the statuary. Leaving aside the argument for a world-wide, or at least pan-European, Great Mother Goddess, Skorba has yielded Maltese female figurines in both ceramic and in one case stone, again well before their appearance in the temples. Unlike the buildings, we even have two examples to bridge that millennium gap, from Ta' Trapna, Żebbuġ, and the Xagħra Circle, admittedly unlike either the earlier or later ones, but attesting to a tradition of carved stone figurines.

So we can now make a strong case for indigenous antecedents for both the architecture of the extraordinary temples of Malta, and at least some of their paraphernalia, those sophisticated statuettes. For cult practices, we still have to rely almost entirely on the much more detailed evidence of the temple period, with no reason to doubt that that too goes back to origins in the earlier phases of Maltese prehistory.

References

Evans, J. D. 1953. The prehistoric culture sequence of the Maltese archipelago. *Proceedings of the Prehistoric Society* 19: 41–94.

Malone, C. A. T., Stoddart, S. K. F., Trump, D., Bonanno, A. the late Gouder, T. and Pace, A. (eds). 2007. *Mortuary ritual in prehistoric Malta. The Brochtorff Circle excavations (1987–1994)*. Cambridge, McDonald Institute.

Trump, D. H. 1966. *Skorba: Excavations Carried out on Behalf of the National Museum of Malta 1961–1963*. Oxford, Reports of the Research Committee of the Society of Antiquaries of London XXII.

Trump, D. H. 2002. *Malta Prehistory and Temples*. Valletta: Midsea Books.

Chapter 4

OF GIANTS AND DECKCHAIRS: UNDERSTANDING THE MALTESE MEGALITHIC TEMPLES

Katya Stroud

The interpretation of the Maltese Megalithic Temples has ranged from the seventeenth century belief that the massive monuments dotting the Maltese landscape were buildings constructed by giants, to that which proposed they were Phoenician sanctuaries dedicated to the seven *Cabiri*, to the popular twentieth century interpretation which has dubbed them 'temples'.

This paper looks at the discovery and excavation of the Maltese Megalithic Temples as well as the history of their understanding and interpretation. It looks at how the interpretation of these sites has changed through their discovery and how their interpretation has played a central role in the way they have been managed. It is evident that the management, as well as the physical conservation and restoration of these prehistoric monuments, have been driven by the way they were understood and interpreted. As a result, past interpretation and approaches to these Megalithic Temples have directly influenced the physical remains that we are trying to understand today.

To the medieval eye

Many of the monuments which commanded the Maltese Neolithic landscape remained visible and therefore attracted attention and curiosity well beyond the time when they fell into disuse. To the medieval eye, these mysterious buildings constructed in gigantic stone blocks, which occasionally yielded some curious object, took on mystical proportions.

Little documentary evidence has survived to indicate early interpretation, although some of the sites' names have embodied popular interpretations of the seventeenth and eighteenth century. At the time, these monuments were attributed to giants, hence the name 'Ġgantija' ('of giants' or 'pertaining to giants') for the most impressive of the sites visible at the time.

Further indications come from one of the systematic descriptions of the Maltese Islands from this period; the 'Della Descrittione di Malta' by Giovanni Francesco Abela,

Vice-Chancellor of the Order of the Knights of St. John, published in 1647. Abela gives a factual and historical description of the Maltese Islands and includes brief descriptions of several megalithic sites. He in fact recognised that these buildings predated the Phoenicians and Romans and, following popular beliefs of the time, says that they were constructed by a race of giants which, he believed, had inhabited Malta before the Flood. Abela (1647, 145–146) adopts a scientific approach to this popular interpretation and presents material evidence to support it saying that apart from the sheer size of the buildings themselves, which in itself attests to this theory, large bones and teeth belonging to this race had been found on the Islands. As a historian, Abela is here referring to popular beliefs for his interpretation and corroborates it with scientific evidence. The bones he refers to were most probably Quarternary fossils of elephants and hipopotami.

In the late eighteenth century Jean Houel, engraver to King Louis the sixteenth, visited a number of the Megalithic Temples during his travels in the Mediterranean. However, unlike preceding authors, Houel attributes these sites to the Phoenicians (Houel 1787, CCLX); an attribution which will last until the beginning of the twentieth century. His illustrations of Ġgantija and Ħaġar Qim provide us with a unique opportunity of seeing these sites from an eighteenth century observer's point of view, depicting what the remains actually looked like at the time (Figure 4.1). Houel's plate of Ħaġar Qim is invaluable in this respect as it shows us the depth to which the site was buried before its excavation in the nineteenth century. It is also precious in that it records the interaction of early visitors with the site at the time as it depicts figures holding up objects and others engaged in deep conversation, indicating that these megalithic sites were a focus for curiosity and debate for locals and visitors alike.

> It is to the Phoenicians that I am inclined to attribute the erection of this monument... (Vance 1842, 234)

This is further confirmed by Vance, an officer of the Royal Engineers who first excavated Ħaġar Qim in 1839. He records;

> The assemblage of huge perpendicular stones which still remain unshaken in their original position, have for some time been objects of peculiar attention, and have not failed to awaken that degree of interest and curiosity which the mind is wont to be affected with, when contemplating the relics of antiquity, and investigating the manners of people who lived in an age of darkness and superstition. (Vance 1842, 227)

In his report of the Ħaġar Qim excavations, Vance again attributes the site to the Phoenicians and suggests that these megalithic buildings were;

> ...raised for the purpose of tracing with greater accuracy the motions of the different planets. (Vance 1842, 233)

The excavation of Ħaġar Qim Temples which took place between November 1839 and January 1840, included the removal of infill material from within the thickness of the walls of the outer apses of the larger building. The only excavations conducted at a Megalithic Temple up to the time were those at Ġgantija in 1827. Therefore, not having any prior information about the architecture of these monuments, Vance interprets these intra-mural areas as chambers (Figure 4.2). Comparison with other sites and a better understanding of the architecture of these monuments now tends to suggest that these spaces were originally filled in with soil and rubble and would not have been accessible in prehistory.

An interesting aspect of Vance's interpretation of the remains is that he discusses them in view of other finds in England, Egypt and ritual practices in India but makes no reference to the archaeology of geographically neighbouring areas such as Sicily or Italy. This aspect of nineteenth century interpretation of the Megalithic Temples was probably dictated by the Islands' new political scenario through which Malta and Gozo were divorced from their regional context and introduced to the networks of the British Empire.

The introduction of the Maltese Islands to this new political scenario also helped solidify the popular interpretation that the monuments were originally Phoenician. One of the beliefs of British nineteenth century archaeology was that the Phoenicians had reached Britain and settled there. Therefore this common Phoenician ancestry helped provide the impression of an ancient kinship between the Maltese and the new British governors, legitimising the new political status.

The finds collected from Ħaġar Qim during Vance's excavation fuelled the now politically-supported interpretation of the monuments' Phoenician origins and in 1876 Dr Cesare Vassallo proposes that Ħaġar Qim was in fact dedicated to the seven *Cabiri* since seven stone statuettes of seated obese figures were found within its chambers (Vassallo 1876, 23–25).

In time this interpretation came to influence directly the actual remains of one of the Megalithic Temples. In June 1885 a proposal was made to build a rubble wall around Ħaġar Qim, but since the extent of the remains here had never been ascertained, excavation works were carried out before the construction of this boundary wall. To this effect, additional excavations were carried out at Ħaġar Qim in 1885 under the direction of A. A. Caruana, Librarian of the Government Public Library who was also in charge of the Museum of the Public Library. Excavations were followed by extensive restoration works, which Caruana recorded by means of colour-coded plans. They included the restoration of what Caruana calls the 'temenos' enclosing the forecourt

Figure 4.1. Jean Houel's drawing of Ħaġar Qim Temples, 1787.

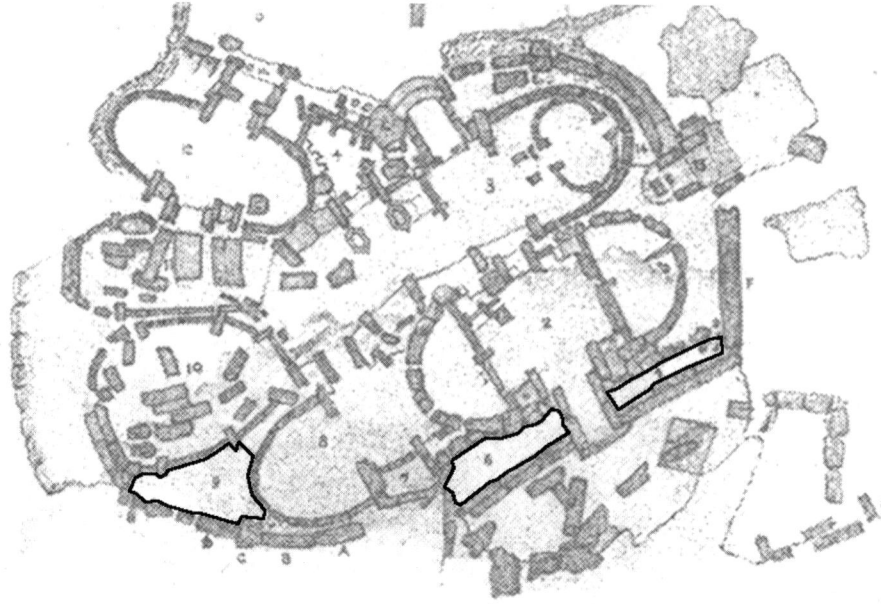

Figure 4.2. Intra mural 'chambers' excavated by J. G. Vance in 1839.

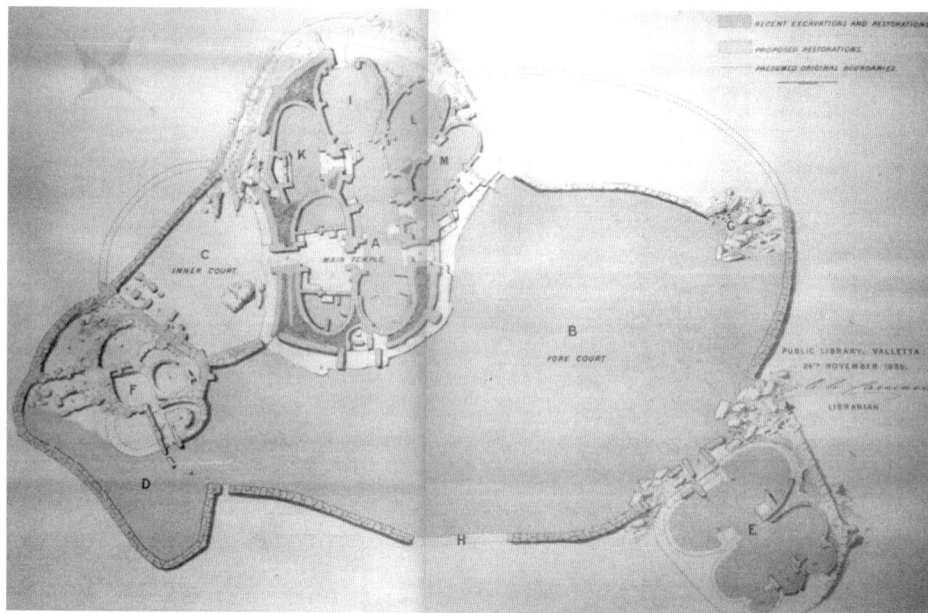

Figure 4.3. The 'temenos' at Ħaġar Qim restored by A. A. Caruana in 1885.

and the court to the rear of the main building. Caruana says that these walls were built on ancient foundations which clearly followed the typical Phoenician formula of having temple grounds enclosed within a boundary wall (Figure 4.3). However, investigations carried out by Ashby in 1910 disproved the authenticity of these walls and they were subsequently dismantled in 1949 (Ashby *et al.* 1913, 64–65 and Baldacchino 1950, I). It is interesting to note that by the 1910 investigations and restoration works at Ħaġar

Qim, the Megalithic Temples were no longer believed to be Phoenician and were therefore being studied through a different lens.

Creating boundaries

The end of the nineteenth century saw a transformation in the approaches and attitudes towards the management of these megalithic sites. A campaign of expropriation and fencing off of these monuments was started, with their management coming directly in the hands of government. The fences and walls raised around these sites did not follow contours or field boundaries but cut across fields forming an artificial boundary between the site and its landscape context. In addition, although on the one side the walls protected the monuments from souvenir seekers, on the other side the walls kept the landowners and farmers, the original protectors and managers of the sites, outside. Foci of popular local curiosity and debate were suddenly turned into exclusive government properties.

The results of this exclusivity can still be seen today as the major part of the Maltese population views the megalithic sites as purely government properties, or at best, tourist destinations. The vandalism at Mnajdra Temples in 1996 when the letters 'RTO', which normally denote land reserved for hunting, were sprayed across the threshold of the South Temple, epitomises this relationship (Figure 4.4).

In addition, since archaeological investigation up to the nineteenth century had focused exclusively on the monuments themselves, significant features in their surroundings and areas of potential archaeological value, were excluded from this expropriation exercise. As a result, these areas were subjected to a radically different management policy to the detriment of possible additional information about these sites.

Setting dates

The beginning of the twentieth century saw a major revolution in the understanding of the Maltese Temples. A fresh and more systematic approach to the study of the Maltese Megalithic Temples was undertaken by Dr Albert Mayr, a German archaeologist who conducted a study tour of the Islands in 1897–98. During this visit Mayr catalogued and studied all the prehistoric remains known at the time and in so doing, ascertained that the monuments dated to some time earlier than the Phoenicians (Mayr 1908, 42–47). The discovery and excavation of the Ħal Saflieni Hypogeum in 1903 confirmed this new interpretation, whilst the excavation of the newly-discovered megalithic complex of Tarxien in 1909 presented the opportunity of addressing the issue of chronology through the study of stratigraphy.

Following the Second World War a grant from the Inter-University Council for Higher Education in the Colonies gave the opportunity for a detailed re-examination of the prehistoric evidence in Malta. In 1952 John D. Evans was given the responsibility of co-ordinating this new survey, which gave the opportunity for new sondage excavations tying the monuments to an emerging cultural sequence.

Eventually, the excavation of Skorba between 1961 and 1963 provided the opportunity to refine this culture sequence and provide absolute dates for the chronology of the Maltese Neolithic, which not only confirmed their pre-Phoenician origins but set them as the oldest megalithic buildings discovered to date.

Recognising a unique phenomenon

As the monuments were slowly being identified with their pre-Phoenician origins, concerns started being expressed as to their preservation. Extensive restoration and conserva-

Figure 4.4. 'RTO', normally denoting land reserved for hunting and trapping, was sprayed on the threshold of Mnajdra Temples in 1996.

tion works were carried out at Ħaġar Qim and Mnajdra in 1910. These works were conducted with a strong sense for authenticity so that relocation of megaliths was carried out in areas where there was clear evidence for their original location, whilst additions to indicate missing original architecture were constructed in small stone blocks making the intervention visually distinctive from the original.

At Tarxien, Temi Zammit made proposals for a shelter to be constructed over the site so that,

> ...this most important Neolithic monument be protected as to have it preserved for future generations as it is; the weathering of the stones since their discovery is seriously deteriorating the monument. (Letter from Sir T. Zammit (Director of Museums) to the Minister of Education, 30th August 1929, Ministry of Public Works registry file, MW 755/29)

Such an intervention, although aesthetically invasive, would have remained distinct from the original megaliths and would not have involved any direct intervention on the monument itself. However, after Zammit's death in November 1935 this option was not considered further.

The end of the Second World War was also accompanied by a programme of restoration of a number of sites. It is during this campaign of restoration that some sites underwent the most drastic aesthetic changes. This is especially evident at Tarxien, where funds provided by the

Carnegie Corporation, originally earmarked for the shelter mentioned above, enabled extensive restoration works in cement to a large number of megaliths, and especially to the entrance.

This is more so evident at Ħaġar Qim where the transformation of the façade gave it the impressive monumental appearance that we are familiar with today. The monumentalisation of the facades of these sites may have been partly the result of the new-found recognition amongst scholars that the Maltese Megalithic Temples are in fact a unique phenomenon, and therefore worthy of aesthetic grandeur. This recognition may also have gone as far as influencing town planning in the 1950s. At the time the Reconstruction Scheme for Tarxien included new buildings in the area of Tarxien Temples. Housing in the area was in high demand as the naval docks continued to provide an attractive prospect of employment. As the development approached Tarxien Temples, the Victorian street grid system was adjusted and buildings circled the site turning it into a physical focal point where the site itself is buffered by gardens (Figure 4.5). This project appears to have been implemented in its entirety except for the encroachment into the buffer green areas by the cemetery and football grounds, which in their nature still offer some breathing space for the site.

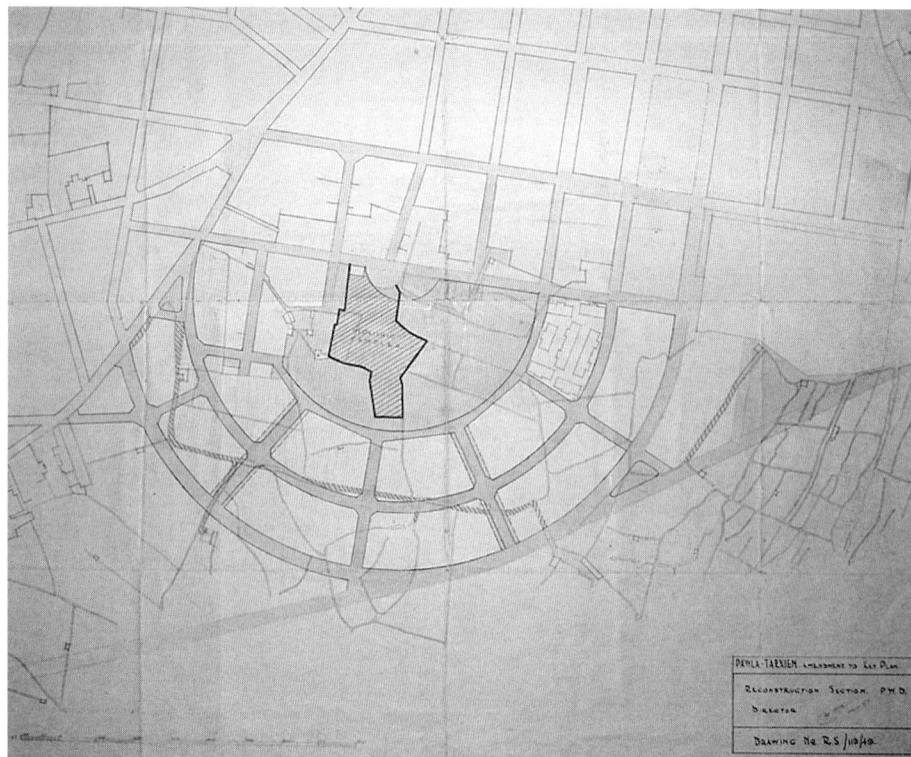

Figure 4.5. 1950s roads scheme for Paola and Tarxien turned Tarxien Temples into a physical focal point within an urban landscape.

'Older than the Pyramids of Egypt or Stonehenge'

As the realisation of the distinctiveness of the Megalithic Temples and the fact that they are 'older than the Pyramids of Egypt or Stonehenge' (as found in numerous websites advertising Malta as a tourist destination) spread, their allure as tourist destinations and their economic potential started playing a part in the tourism economy, the main source of income for the Islands. The Megalithic Temples not only feature in adverts for the Maltese Islands, but also in adverts for Maltese local beer, banks, various restaurants and hotels.

In 1966 as the development of one of the main tourist areas on the Islands, Bugibba, was well underway, restoration works were carried out on the entrance of the Buġibba Temple. It is not clear who conducted these restoration works since no mention of them is made in the Museums Department records for the site. However, the works were contemporary with plans for the construction of an extensive high class hotel in the immediate vicinity of the temple. The Dolmen Hotel was opened in March 1968, and despite attempts by the Secretary of the Ministry of Education, Culture and Tourism to persuade the proprietors of the hotel to change its name to something more in keeping with the nature of the monument on the site, the hotel still holds this misleading name to this day (Reference made in a letter from Mallia (Curator of Archaeology) to the Secretary for the Minister of Education, Culture and Tourism, 14th March 1968, Museums Department registry file MUS 92/63). The hotel building encloses the landward side of the monument and has integrated it within its swimming pool areas, at best transforming it into a curious pool-side conversation piece, or more likely a rock-garden in the background (Figure 4.6).

In December 2001 a proposal was made for extensive rock-cutting to take place within the area of the hotel so as to develop a Marina within its grounds, which according to the architects would 'create a waterfront for patrons to enjoy, allowing them to sit out and have a coffee, or walk directly by the sea' (Quoted by Galea Debono 2001, 3). According to this proposal, the Buġibba Temple would apparently become part of this seaside stroll, being permanently separated from its landscape context and having its conservation compromised due to the close proximity to the sea. Thanks to the timely intervention of the Museums Department, this proposal was never developed.

What will be inherited?

Fortunately the majority of the Maltese Megalithic Sites have not suffered this dire fate but the concept of their solely being tourist attractions and economic commodities, is still dangerously prevalent. In contrast with these views and modes of interaction with the sites, worthy of note, are those of the 'goddess movement'. This movement, which is ever increasing, has adopted the Maltese Megalithic Temples as a focal point for its beliefs and principles. Unfortunately, the movement's interpretation of the sites and finds do not always originate from the archaeological evidence itself, and interaction with the monuments does not always give priority to their preservation.

Figure 4.6. Buġibba Prehistoric Temples incorporated within the pool area of the Dolmen Hotel in 1968.

This quick look at the history of the understanding of the Maltese Megalithic Temples clearly illustrates the close ties between the scholarly interpretation of these sites, approaches to their management and restoration, as well as popular attitudes and feelings towards them. Past interpretation has therefore directly influenced the nature and extent of the archaeological evidence that we are trying to understand, and in turn, what is passed on to the future may indeed be shaped by the way we interpret these sites today.

References

1929, Ministry of Public Works registry file, MW 755/29

1963, Museums Department registry file, MUS 92/63

Abela G. F. 1647. *Della Descrittione di Malta: Isola nel mare Siciliano con le sue antichità, ed altre notittie*. Facsimile of the Malta 1647 edition, 1984. Valletta, Midsea Books.

Ashby T., Bradley R. N., Peet T. E., Tagliaferro N. 1913. 'Excavations in 1908–11 in Various Megalithic Buildings in Malta and Gozo' *Papers of the British School at Rome*, vol.6 no.1, 43–109.

Baldacchino J. G. 1950. *Annual Report on the Working of the Museum Department, 1949–50*. Malta, Government Printing Office.

Galea Debono F. 2001. 'Tumas Group wants to create inlet at New Dolmen'. *The Times of Malta*, 3, 12/12/2001. Malta.

Houel J. 1787. *Voyage Pittoresque des Isles de Sicile, de Malte et de Lipari*. Paris.

Mayr A. 1908. *The Prehistoric Remains of Malta*. Printed for private circulation, Malta.

Vance J. G. 1842. 'Description of an Ancient Temple near Crendi, Malta'. *Archaeologia*, vol. 29, Society of Antiquaries of London, 227–240.

Vassallo C. 1876. *Dei Monumenti Antichi del Gruppo di Malta*. Stamperia del Governo. Malta.

Chapter 5

RITUAL, SPACE AND STRUCTURE –
THE CONTEXT OF CULT IN MALTA AND GOZO

Caroline Malone

The purpose of this paper is twofold: an examination of a richly designed and embellished archaeological context that implies ritual use; and, an exploration of symbolic structure and ritual action that reflect universal ritual values.

The megalithic temples of prehistoric Malta present some of the most sophisticated, designed architectural ritual spaces furnished with symbolic iconography and material culture in early western Europe. Contemporary with later Neolithic megalithic structures such as Stonehenge, the unparalleled Maltese temples of the late IV and earlier III millennia BC offer a hint of highly structured ceremonial ritual practice and cosmology which perhaps reflected an equally complex social structure. Long interpreted as the focus of a Mother Goddess or fertility cult (e.g. Gimbutas 1974; 1989; 1991), the built complexes may represent the remnants of practices and beliefs which are far more interesting and wide reaching than simply fertility.

The methodological and theoretical apparatus for dealing with archaeological ritual and cult is poorly developed, in spite of some twenty-five years of discussion within post-processual and cognitive frameworks. Anthropological warnings (Leach 1966; 1976) and archaeological reticence (Hawkes 1954) meant archaeologists, recognising their limitations, stepped carefully and verbally around the problem of dealing with ritual and belief in the archaeological record. At the heart of the problem is the recognition of what evidence constitutes 'ritual', be it structured deposits, hoards and artefacts, intentional breakage, odd associations and non-domestic structures or entire landscapes of 'monuments in close proximity' (Harding and Lee 1987). Focus on key landscapes/sites such as Stonehenge (Whittle 1997; Darvill 2006) reveal that with sufficient archaeological knowledge, meaning and significance is justifiably gleaned from prehistoric remains. Burial remains offer insight into an early society's concerns and beliefs, but few prehistoric sites really preserve structured space and context that is similarly intact or interpretable. The definition of ritual space (context) at whatever scale (landscape, site or individual feature) is

fundamental for archaeologists, unlike anthropologists who have mostly ignored spatial context to focus on the rich verbal, cognitive and visual body of data they encounter in living societies. Rare studies (e.g. Turner 1967; 1969) acknowledged ritual space and action in showing how classifications of space and body underpinned notions and rituals concerned with life, death and liminality (Van Gennep 1909). The promising beginnings of ethnoarchaeology, post-processual and cognitive theory, which demonstrated the intentionality and significance of deposition, structure and context in living societies has not been sustained or applied effectively to archaeology (Hodder 1982a; 1982b; 1987; Moore 1982; Richards and Thomas 1984). For example Moore's study of the Marakwet revealed how 'generative rules' of gender, age, polarity, pollution and fertility underpinned the spatial placement of structures and their use, with important implications for interrogating archaeological residues.

Renfrew's compilation of eighteen 'criteria' for recognising cult (Renfrew 1985), introduced a rigorous checklist and potential methodology for the identification of 'ritual' in archaeology (2004 this volume) and this starts with the cult place itself. Key attributes of a cult place (or perhaps we should now say 'ritual' place – see Renfrew, this volume) include attention focusing devices, the presence of the transcendent and its symbolic form, the special aspects of a liminal zone, and evidence of participation and offering (sacrifice, libation etc.). In the anthropological study of ritual and religion, interest focuses on the transformation of everyday routine into the mystical and spiritual through multifaceted action, performance, participation, communication, knowledge and emotion (Bell 1992; Bowie 2006, 140–3). The media for those transformations are expressed through a repetition of symbols, rigidity, formality and fusion. For some scholars (especially with a Marxist agenda) ritual offers a means of resolving disruption and conflict, whether at a personal or wider societal level, through ordered, institutional, repetitious, explanatory action that legitimises the social order. The continual reassertion of a world view embodied in ritual is seen to maintain relations of dominance in small scale societies (Tilley 1984, 114–6), by 'the elaboration of symbolic forms which allude to social reality not by presenting it or expressing it, but by presenting it as other than it really is by characterising society as a unitary, harmonious whole'. Indeed, ritual could be interpreted as a deliberate distortion of reality in order to gain power, knowledge, dominance and legitimacy. Tilley (1984, 116) in particular, asserts that rituals become embedded in social life to provide an 'anchoring point for the affirmation of power... and the legitimisation of the social order'. Rites of passage and the successive tripartite stages identified by Van Gennep (1909) of separation, liminality and reincorporation/reaggregation involve a middle stage (liminal) where normal social relations are nullified, and where ritual is often played out, before return to the normal order. The ritual action is usually formalised, repetitive and makes use of symbols in special places which potentially leave recognisable archaeological material remains.

In essence, two broad types of public or institutional ritual exist: 1) rites of passage and 2) time-related or calendrical rites, both of which may have impact on the archaeological context that is the theme of this paper. The former relate to individuals who are always elevated from one social status to another, whilst the latter calendrical rites are associated with fertility/the seasons, and may involve status reversal (Turner 1969, 168–70; Tilley 1984, 115). Additional subdivisions (Bell 1997, 94) expand the categories to: 3) exchange and communication rites, 4) rites of affliction and health, 5) rites of feasting, fasting and festivals, 6) political rituals, and are all likely to be bound up with 1) and/or 2).

Ritual action and meaning thus has many levels of significance and function, which for archaeology represents a challenge, when prehistoric societies are so remote and little understood. The question is whether any context remains sufficiently complete for interpretation today.

Malta and its temples

The 'temples' of Malta are some of the most impressive built structures from European prehistory, and there is a long history of clearance, study and interpretation (Cilia 2004; Trump 2002). They emerged in the earlier fourth millennium BC, but the present elaborate if ruined forms mainly date from c. 3300–2450 BC. Most accounts do not challenge the designation 'temple' and the identification of ritual focus (Renfrew 1973). The megalithic buildings are essentially repetitive forms, based around an open forecourt leading into a central corridor, from which open lobed semi-circular spaces forming a 'clover-leaf' floor plan of numerous apses. The entrances are oriented out towards specific cardinal points or distinct horizons, and temples are located in prominent, often elevated, positions. The interiors were furnished with paved or plastered floors, plastered wall surfaces, and a series of individual offering and display places marked by altars, benches, libation holes, hearths and bowls. Shelves, cupboards, small hidden rooms concealed ritual specialists and so-called 'oracle' holes provided areas for the storage of artefacts and statues. Steps and thresholds separated the spaces, narrow doorways with moveable barriers controlled access both from the outside, and between different spaces within. Some later sites incorporated adjoining structures, and access was formed between them (Ħaġar Qim, Tarxien) but in essence, the interior was maintained as a series of distinct spaces, roofed and enclosed – almost an artificial 'cave'. The external space was apparently an unrestricted public arena for participation, performance and display, and there is no evidence for controlled access and no evident barriers or walls around it. Instead, investment was put into forming extensive public open areas (Ġgantija, Mnajdra, Kordin III and Ħaġar Qim). 'Libation' holes were set into the thresholds and stone kerbs surrounding the temples, 'oracle' holes penetrated from the outside to the interior, and tethering stones may have secured animals for sacrifice (e.g. at Ħaġar Qim, Tarxien). Material retrieved from the temple sites includes quantities of animal bone, offering bowls, stone tools, ornaments, figurative artefacts, statues, carved stones and art. Of the thirty or so known temple structures, only two complexes have reasonable excavation records (Skorba and Tarxien) so much of the potential detailed information on context and association is lost.

In parallel to the temples above ground, subterranean funerary hypogea represent another form of ritual space in Malta. Two only are known, the Brochtorff Circle, Xagħra and Ħal Saflieni, the Hypogeum. The first, the subject of recent study (Malone et al. 2007) records precise placement of objects, fitments and burials within a clearly defined ritual space, whilst the second, located over a century ago, was cleared of its contents without systematic record. Ħal Saflieni consists of thirty or more intentionally carved sophisticated pseudo-architectural spaces, whilst Brochtorff Circle, Xagħra, is quite the reverse in structure and appearance, a rugged natural cave, later modified and elaborated with imported megalithic stones to form a burial hypogeum. Both have produced an astounding array of figurative objects (over half of all known Neolithic art from the islands) and prehistoric valuables from deeply hidden locations within the funerary spaces. Our study (Malone et al. 2007; Stoddart et al. 1993) at Xagħra reveals archaeological patterns and associations of ritual material in structural context. By inference with Tarxien's record (Figure 5.1), we can suggest that Temple ritual and cult practice is reflected in patterns of deliberate design and deposition at many sites. Ritual symbolism is apparent in the specific locations, the repetition and redundancy we

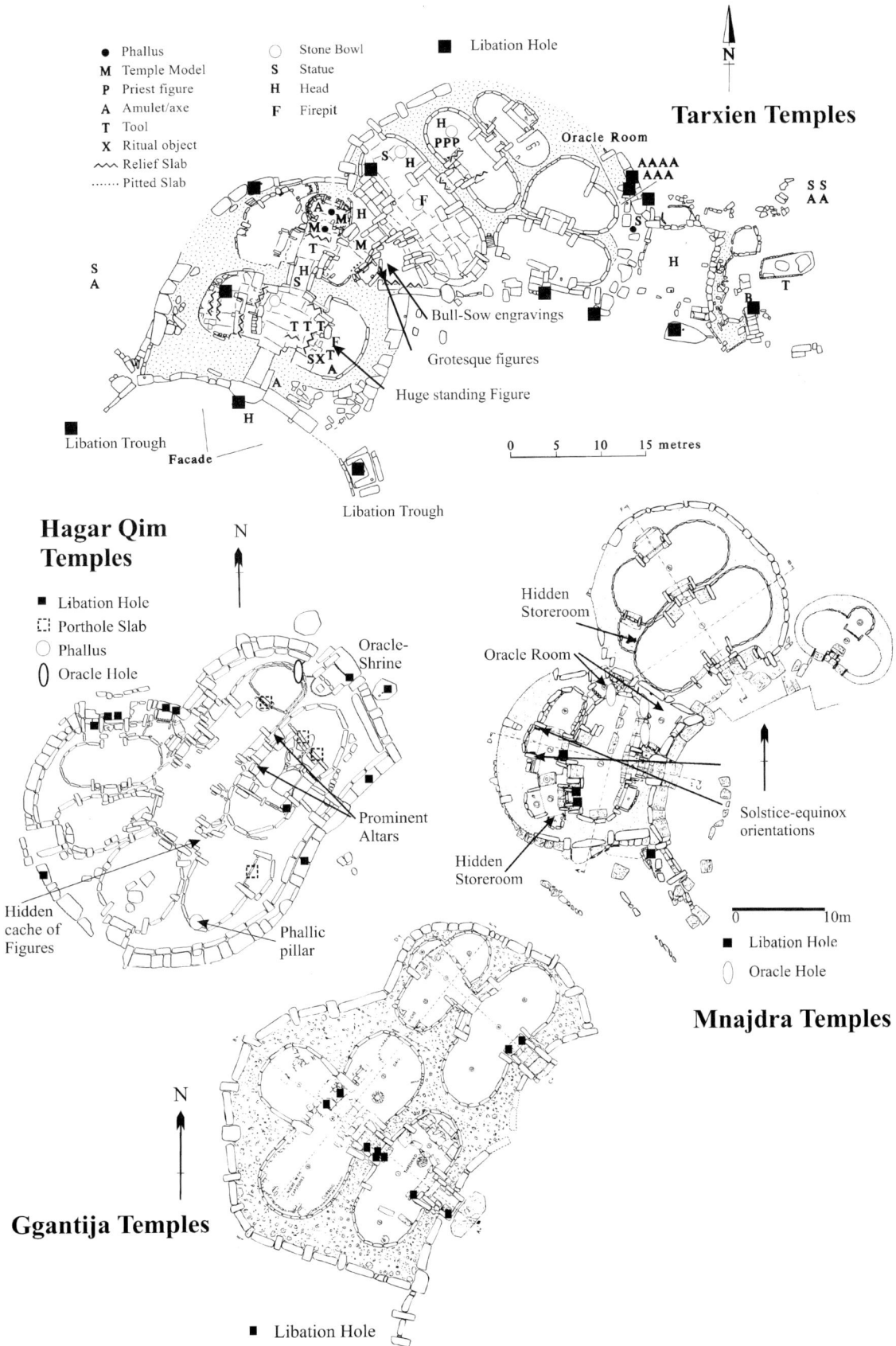

Figure 5.1. Tarxien ground plan of fixtures and fitments, Mnajdra, Brochtorff, Hal Saflieni, Hagar Qim.

observe in both the temples of the living and the dead. However, can we gain insight into ritual action and meaning in context from these rich data?

The architecture arrangement of the Maltese structures, both temple and hypogea, share repetitive characteristics, from orientation and position to the built elements noted above (statues, phallic objects, hearths, bowls, feasting residues, caches of ritual equipment and panels of relief art and textured pattern). The variety of material, surface and layout were significant in the sensory experience that a ritual place engendered (Whittle 1997). Firstly, orientation of the majority of central corridors in the temples face between southwest and southeast (Ventura 2004), and in twenty temples where an orientation can be measured, fifteen have a principal corridor-axis aligned to the distant horizon, of which fourteen face SE–SSW over an arc of 78.5° (Figure 5.2). Only one temple axis (Mnajdra S) faces directly east towards the Equinox sunrise and the Pleiades star cluster visible from Malta in *c.* 3000 BC. The remaining temples orientate too far south to observe sun/ moon movements, although were well placed to observe the stars of the Southern Cross, when in *c.* 3000 BC, this cluster was visible in the northern hemisphere. These stars could have assisted navigation, so directionality and external origins may have been significant stimuli for temple orientation in some cases (Stoddart *et al.* 1993). Both funerary sites appear to be oriented in respect of celestial bodies. New evidence from Hal Saflieni shows that a trilithon doorway in the upper zone led to the original west-facing entrance, orientated on the summer solstice sunset and the moon at its most northerly position, with potential light illumination of lower levels. Likewise, the (destroyed) megalithic entrance to the Brochtorff Circle, Xaġhra, faced directly east, towards sunrise and Ġgantija Temples, whilst the access down to burials and the ancestors was approached facing directly west, but possibly illuminated by low level sunlight at dawn (Figure 5.2). Much symbolism can be generated about life and death, sunrise and sunset, from this apparent intentionality, supporting ideas that the temples-hypogea functioned within time-related and calendrical rituals as well as death rituals.

As noted above, the distinction between internal and external space is quite explicit in temple structures. Enclosure, either temple walls or hypogea outer walls (Brochtorff Circle), controlled physical access and visibility, and symbolically contained spiritual powers. The theme of visibility and concealment informs our understanding of the internal structural arrangements and potentially how they functioned. Firstly, views into temples were limited to the central corridor, from entrance threshold to prominent altars ahead and areas immediately left and right. Notions of laterality seem to play a significant role in the ritual action inside the temple sites. Views for most participants

were along, and to right and left of, the stage-like corridor, framed by trilithon doorways dramatically backed by altars and fires, against which the action was played out by ritual specialists (Figure 5.4). Areas to either side of this central view were hidden, unless access to the interior of the temple was permitted. It seems likely that dramatic revelation and concealment were employed during ceremonies, one moment performing to a wide audience in the forecourt, another closing the action to all but selected initiates.

From this first study, it seems that patterns of specific placement for important ritual apparatus were repeated at many Maltese temple sites, suggesting the ceremonies demanded adherence to formal ritual behaviour which frequently respected lateral positions. Table 5.1 summarises the different positions of the most prominent, in built and intact structural features and fitments that we have recorded in the surviving temples.

Regular patterns are seen in a variety of fitments. Hearths and firepits were placed directly ahead or just out of public view on the right side, whilst large stone bowls were placed on the left. Internal libation holes are along central corridors on thresholds (usually placed left or centre) or situated externally around the perimeter of temples, where a procession could have accessed them in turn. Pyramid-shaped stone stoppers may have sealed in the offering. 'Phallic' pillars are mostly on the left (Figure 5.3 and 5.6), and similarly, portal stones, which involved stooping in order to pass through them, are predominantly left sided. Oracle holes, penetrating outside walls are found located in hidden areas on the right side. Flamboyant decoration and ascetic restraint appear to be organised laterally with highly elaborated and carved temples/rooms located on the SW or left-hand side of the main temple complex (Tarxien, Ġgantija, Mnajdra), and sometimes organised to face opposite built features on the right. For instance, an elaborate carved, stepped altar (Tarxien, SW temple, L-side) is associated with a stone basin and friezes of animals (male animals progressing to the right, female/ unsexed animals progressing to the left) (Figure 5.4). This arrangement opposes a large statue (Figure 5.4) and altar-table on the right. The deeper spaces of Tarxien contain additional bowls/basins on the left, and central/right sided hearths (Figure 5.1) which also occurs at Ġgantija. Hidden spaces, cupboards, niches, including a secret room containing carved reliefs of two bulls and a sow with piglets (Figure 5.4), are mostly located on the right side. The adherence to right and left is striking, and seemingly significant within the ritual space.

Portable objects, typically obese un-gendered figurines, valuables, ornaments, tools, vessels, amulets and animal bones were stored, displayed and used in the temple-hypogea spaces. The canon of anthropomorphic art includes skirted standing figures in a formal pose, usually with distinct hair styles, belts and flounced, gathered skits, seated

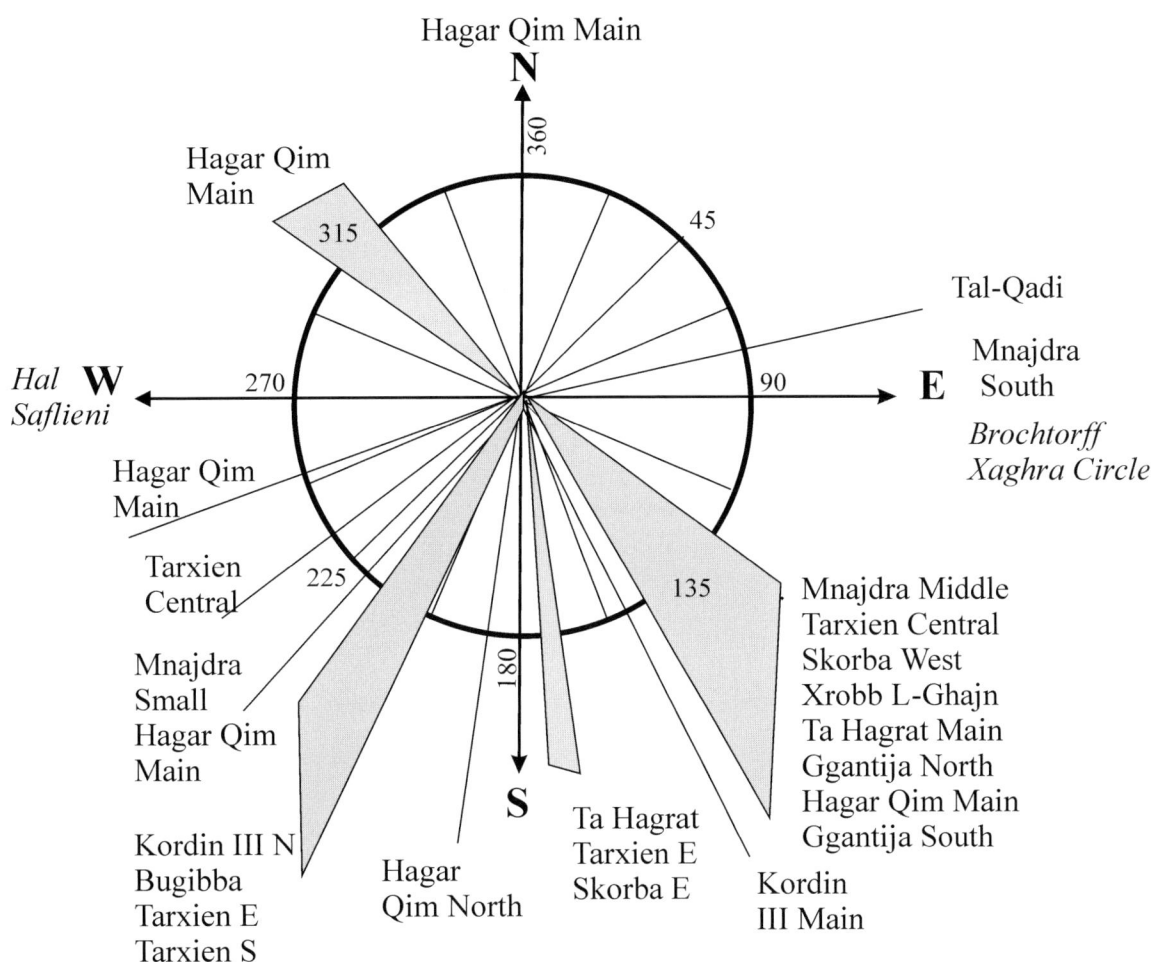

Azimuths of the main Maltese Temples, measured through the central corridor or main axis indicate the orientation of the structures. Note: the funerary hypogea are shown in italics.

Figure 5.2. Maltese Temple orientations and azimuths.

and squatting figures and a few lying figures, sometimes on beds/couches (Figure 5.3). They vary from crude, spontaneous, exaggerated creations to sophisticated carved objects made of stone and terracotta. Some figurines are explicitly gendered with exaggerated female features, penis-stomachs, breasts, 'V' marked genitalia, clay twists (considered to represent foetuses) and figurines marked with incisions and impressions that might suggest sympathetic medicine magic or witchcraft (Vella Gregory 2005, 106–115), with ritual deposition concentrated in altar-areas set on the right side at both Tarxien and Mnajdra. Generally, object placements range from very prominent visible locations for larger statues (displayed on benches and altars) to hidden secret places for small

personal or 'magic' objects and amulets. These were secreted close to areas furnished with apparatus for ceremonial action in the funerary ritual (such as the Shaman's bundle of six rectangular-stick figures/heads, three head/animal figures, and the seated paired figure found at the Brochtorff Circle, adjacent to the large stone bowl). Not only were such objects deliberately placed in structured positions in the temples, but they also demonstrate formal postures in respect of right and left. For example, the majority of figurines portrayed have the right hand outstretched or uppermost, perhaps emphasising conformity to traditional practices and a set of beliefs that symbolise the relationship with the world around the body.

Feature	Left	Centre	Right	External
Hearths and firepits		Tarxien	Tarxien, Ggantija, Ħaġar Qim N	
Bowls	Tarxien × 3 Skorba Kordin 111 Brochtorff Ħal Saflieni Mnajdra – altar bowls		Ħaġar Qim N	Tarxien
Phallic pillars	Ħaġar Qim Mnajdra S, Brochtorff, ?Ħal Saflieni Kordin 1, Kordin II, Kordin III	Tarxien central altar area × 4 small	Tarxien – pitted pyramid behind large statue, Ggantija = snake stone + pillar stone	Tarxien, Ħaġar Qim
Portal stones	Ħal Saflieni, Mnajdra, Brochtorff, Ħaġar Qim	Mnajdra, Ħal Saflieni	Ħaġar Qim, Mnajdra, Tarxien,Ggantija S	Tarxien
Oracle holes			Tarxien, Ħaġar Qim, Mnajdra, Brochtorff, Ħal Saflieni, Ggantija	Tarxien, Ħaġar Qim
Libation Holes	Tarxien, Ggantija, Ta Hagrat, Kordin III, Ħaġar Qim	Kordin III, Skorba, Mnajdra, Ħaġar Qim, Ggantija Tarxien E	Ggantija	Tarxien, Ħaġar Qim
Animal	Tarxien –friezes, sheep/goat Brochtorff – sheep, pig		Tarxien – bulls, sow, lizard in altar, Ggantija – snake	Tarxien = several animal terracottas in field rubble
Human figures	Tarxien = 6 Priest figs = 3 Brochtorff = small Terracottas 45 Seated pair Cache = 6	Tarxien = 4 Brochtorff = 1 large	Tarxien = 1, face bead Grotesques = Mnajdra =11	Tarxien = 4 – dumps Ħaġar Qim – dumps
Architectural models	Ħaġar Qim (cache = 5) Mnajdra – engraving		Tarxien – temple amulet	Tarxien – 2 figs in niche/oracle room, Ta Hagrat – location uncertain

Table 5.1 Relative positions of the structural features of the Maltese Temples.

Bodies and ritual meaning

Anthropology has long been aware of the manner in which some cultures emphasise the human body in relation to the world (Bell 1992, 94–117). Structural oppositions and much of the thinking of structuralism takes root from such concepts, although that perspective can be mechanistic and inevitable, rather than culturally constructed and symbolic. Whatever the theoretical position, humans project themselves from their bodily perspective – above-below, right-left, in front-behind, inside-outside, visible-invisible, male-female, young-old; and then to the world beyond, wild-tame, dead-alive, black-white and so on. Such oppositions neatly envelope many concerns and notions that lie at the heart of the ritual process, transforming people from one condition to another through symbolic mnemonic, posture, context and association. Ceremonial action within ritual spaces is expressed through specific posture, gesture and positions of laterality and polarity, and may signify certain values and beliefs and reinforce them through repetition. Most world religions are conducted according to strict regulations concerning placement and position, and the relationship of a participant to those positions. For example, Buddhists process around a stupa

Skorba libation holes in threshold

Kordin Trough

Mnajdra Oracle Hole

Multi-hole libation trough
at Tarxien

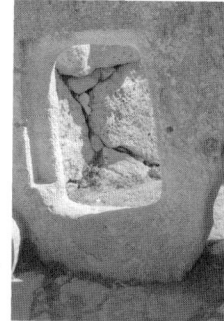

Porthole slab,
Hagar Qim

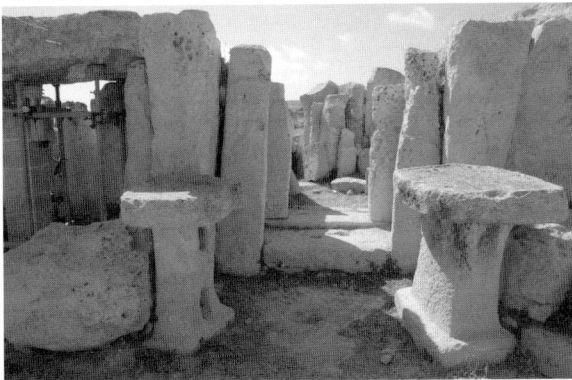

Altar tables in Hagar Qim

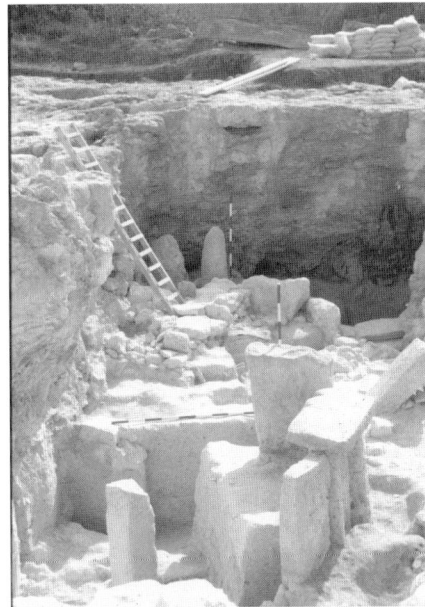

Phallic Betyl, Brochtorff Xaghra Circle

External Phallic shrine at Hagar Qim

Tarxien bowl

Figure 5.3. Fitments and in-built elements designed for 'Ritual' in Maltese sites (Photos: Templeton Project).

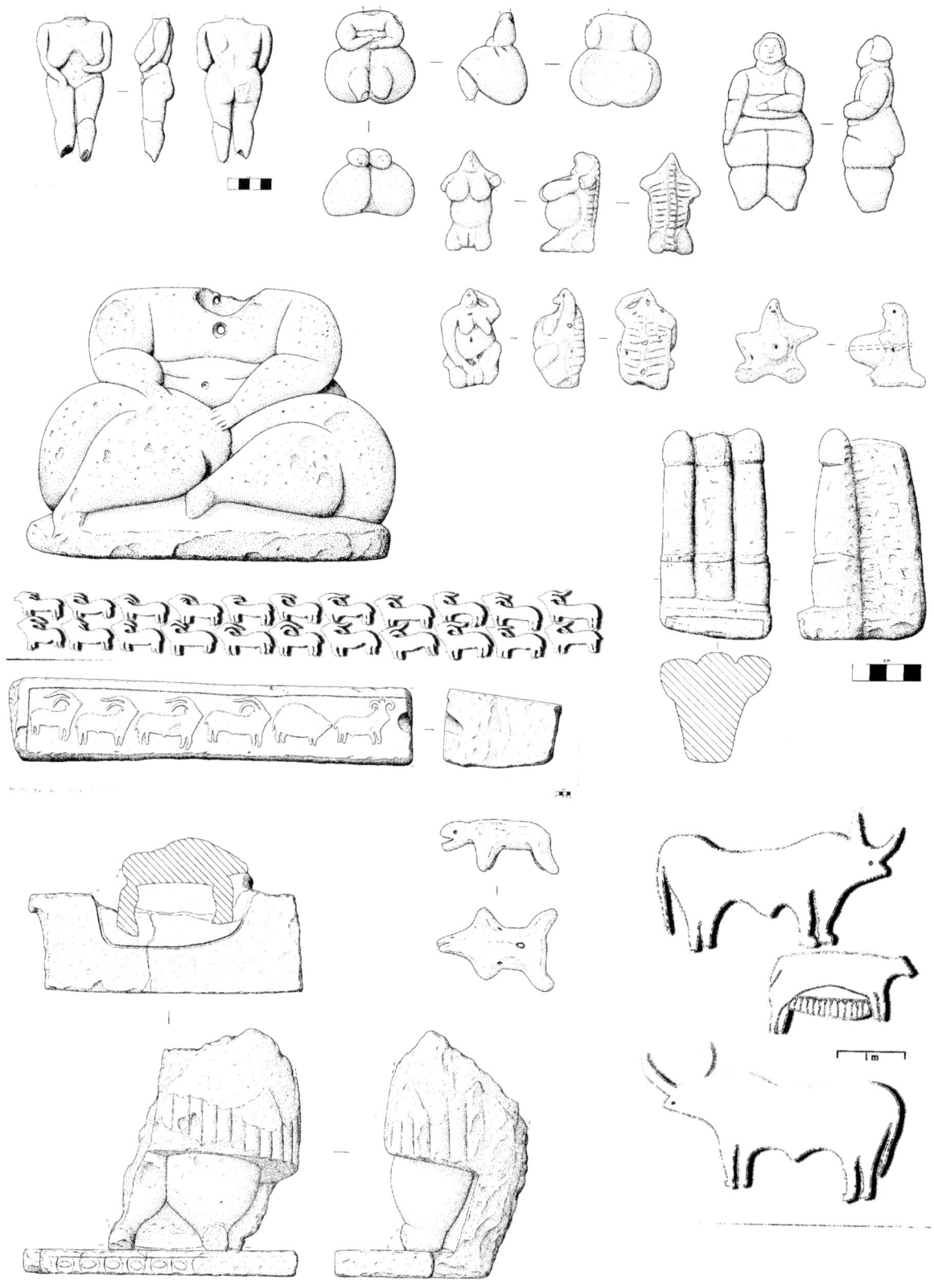

Figure 5.4. Figurative art from Maltese sites. Tarxien [5, 8, 9, 10, 13], Mnajdra [3], Ħal Saflieni [2, 4, 12], Ħaġar Qim [1, 7].

with their right side facing the stupa. Many Asian cultures eat only with right hand (which is considered pure) and use their left for polluting activities such as defecation. The examples are numerous, but right and left are fundamental notions in the way people must act out ritual (see Needham 1973). Robert Hertz's essay (Hertz 1973) on the 'The pre-eminence of the right hand: a study in religious polarity' stimulated considerable anthropological interest in the past. Hertz explored the variety of cultural values attached to the importance of the right-hand, showing that across many cultures, the right was considered the benevolent and virtuous (Figure 5.5) whilst the left was the reverse of these values. In particular, females, weakness, pollution and death were associated with the left. Other studies (Needham 1973), employing structuralism further assert these almost universal values. The question for archaeology is whether such notions extend into the prehistoric past, and whether we can them assign such values to spatial and structural placement in the Maltese temples.

The fitments and features of temples and hypogea in prehistoric Malta appear to have regularity, rigidity even, and architectural components occur in predictable locations in several sites. Altars for the making or receiving of offerings are either visible and central, or hidden to left or right. Those on the right invariably seem to be associated with cooking, hearths and feasting. At the Brochtorff Circle, animal remains predominate on the right of the entrance, yet the majority of body parts were left-sided at a ratio of 1:3 (see Figure 5.6). Elsewhere, deep inside the burial caves, right-sidedness or centrality (trophy heads) appear to be more significant, and we may construe that across Maltese sites, body parts were intentionally selected and symbolically placed (Malone *et al.* 2007), and this laterality has certainly been identified at other sites (West Kennet enclosure where up to 80% of some cattle and pig bones were from the right side, Edwards and Horne 1997, 125–7). The liquid offering of libation (water, blood, brew etc.), poured into specific cavities in and around temples was demanded either at intervals externally, or on crossing the threshold to inner spaces (Figures 5.1, 5.3), and some thresholds contain several holes. An immense libation hole occurs on the right of the central altar at Ggantija S, in full view of all who might have peered along the central corridor, but its position is an exception to a rule. Oracle holes also symbolise offering (with posted objects collected inside the hidden spaces presumably occupied by a ritual specialist (see Barrowclough this volume)), but they could also represent the giving and receiving of knowledge, between participant and specialist. Potentially, since some societies perceive knowledge as strong and male, the right side may be significant.

Notions of pollution and cleanliness are recurrent themes in ritual, since washing, burning, colour and smell reflect concerns about purity and dirt. The presence of fire pits and hearths set prominently in several sites suggest not only cooking and feasting, but also the cleansing of pollution through fire. The presence of the huge stone bowls/basins on the left opposite the right-sided fire pits may symbolise these fundamental opposites, fire and water. In Hertz's argument, the perception that the left is weak and the right is strong are apparently emphasized here (see Figure 5.5). Could the Maltese evidence indicate parallel notions of belief and ritual, with the placement of cleansing apparatus on the left, and purification apparatus on the right? At Brochtorff Circle, a stone portal slab was placed so that access to the bowl also required passing through the portal – bending low, demeaning and lowering, before being purified and enabled to participate in ritual. Other notions of opposition also may be reflected in body placement, with predominantly female/infant burials clustered around the left-side stone bowl at Brochtorff Circle, whilst pre-dominantly male burials were placed in a pit on the right side of the entrance threshold, possibly signifying ancestral identities, but perhaps also the universal notions of strength, life, maleness and ancestors (see Stoddart, this volume).

The relative role and identity of male and female in early Malta is a vexed subject with a long history and some crazy theories, which have developed from the unparalleled images. But, far from the majority of the figurines representing females (as asserted by Gimbutas and her adherents, Gimbutas 1991) very few Maltese images are specifically gendered, and when they are, their character-istics are quite explicit! Females are shown figuratively or represented by triangles, triangular stones and perhaps libation holes, males are phallic, reduced to symbolic inset relief panels or large carved pillar stones, sometimes associated with triangular slabs set in front or behind, or as explicit animal representations. At Ħaġar Qim, to the right of the main east entrance, a shrine set into the exterior wall displays a pillar stone behind a triangular stone, beside an oracle hole (Figure 5.3). However, once inside the temple, the laterality reverses, and a large pillar stone is found in the apse directly to the left (Figures 5.1, 5.3). A similar location is encountered inside the east cave of the Brochtorff Circle, where a finely worked pillar stone (or Betyl) (Figures 5.1, 5.3) is placed deep inside, with a triangular stone set some distance in front, but still retaining a potentially male/female relationship. Similar settings are recorded at other sites, although their present positions may not be as reliable. These are the exceptions, and most figurative objects are un-gendered, and unrealistically shown in idealised abundance, suggesting idealised ancestors rather than deities or individuals.

In Maltese temple and burial hypogea, the redundancy of ritual action and image seems undeniable. Excavation has been too little, too late, to be sure of the patterns we identify, but hints there are, and in abundance, unmoved and built in. Ritual action appears to be highly structured,

Hertz's DUALISTIC scheme of Right and Left

<table>
<tr><td valign="top">

LEFT

FEMALE

WEAK
DIRTY
POLLUTED
DEATH
BAD
DARK
•NORTH/WEST
INFERTILE
IGNORANCE
NIGHT
LOW
BELOW
BEHIND
PROFANE
HELL
OUTSIDE
</td><td valign="top">

RIGHT

MALE

STRONG
CLEAN
PURE
LIFE
GOOD
LIGHT
EAST/SOUTH
FERTILE
KNOWLEDGE
DAY
HIGH
ABOVE
IN FRONT
SACRED
HEAVEN
INSIDE
</td></tr>
</table>

Model for Prehistoric Malta

<table>
<tr>
<td valign="top">

LEFT

WEST - SUNSET=
DEATH
LIBATION
OFFERING
PURIFICATION
BOWL=WASHING
GENDER
PRIEST IMAGE
ANIMAL
AMULETS &
FIGURINES
PORTAL HOLES=
LOW
 ABASEMENT
HIDDEN
</td>
<td valign="top">

OFFERING
ALTARS
FIGURES
STATUES
FIRE
DECORATION

VISIBLE
AHEAD

CENTRE
</td>
<td valign="top">

RIGHT

EAST-SUNRISE=
LIFE
SACRIFICE-MEAT
FEASTING
FIRE - CLEANSED
BULLS-MALES
UNGENEDERED
ORACLE HOLES
= KNOWLEDGE
GROTESQUES =
MEDICAL-
MAGICAL
-POWERS
 RAISED STEPS
HIDDEN
</td>
</tr>
</table>

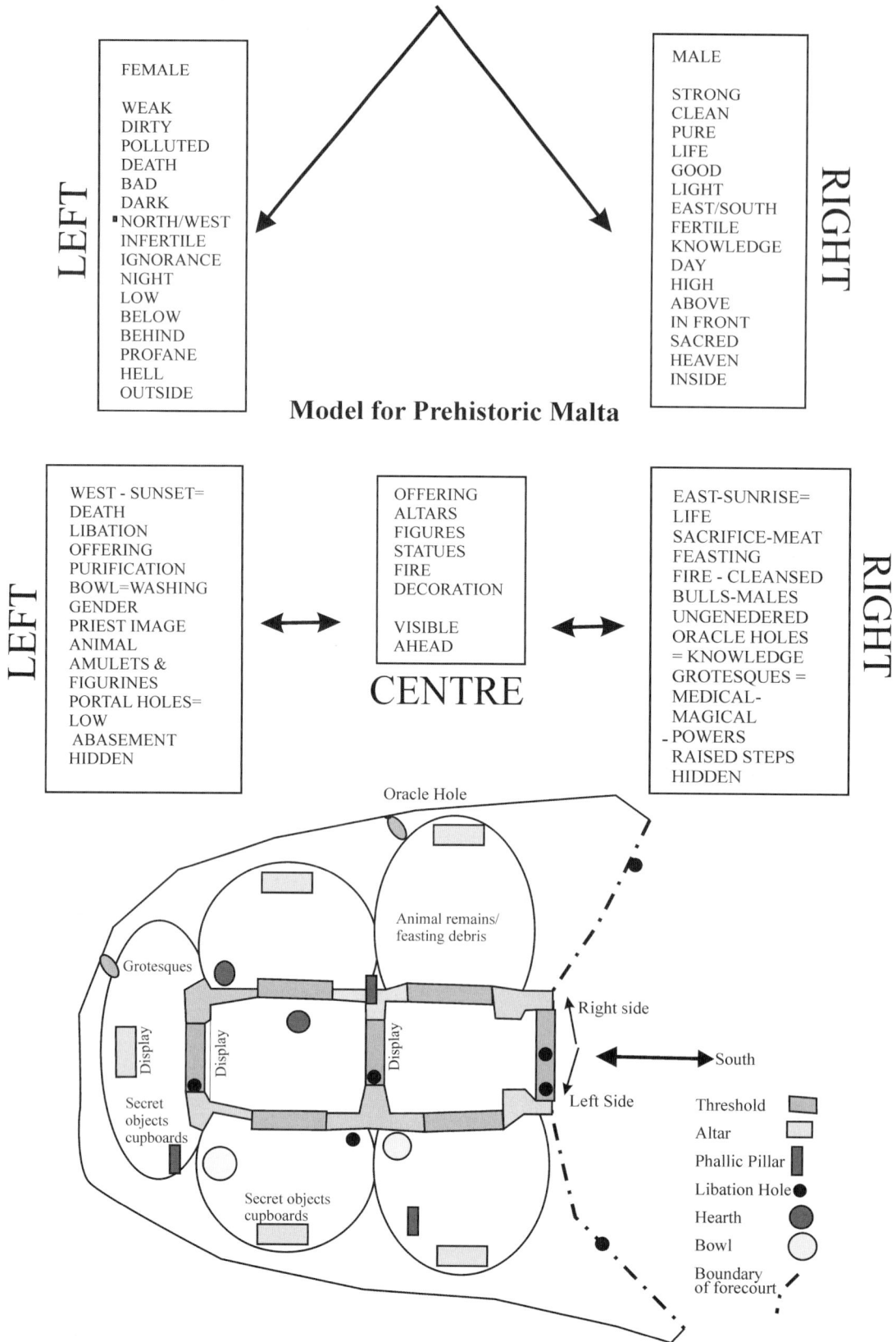

Figure 5.5. Hertz scheme – left-right – Malta model.

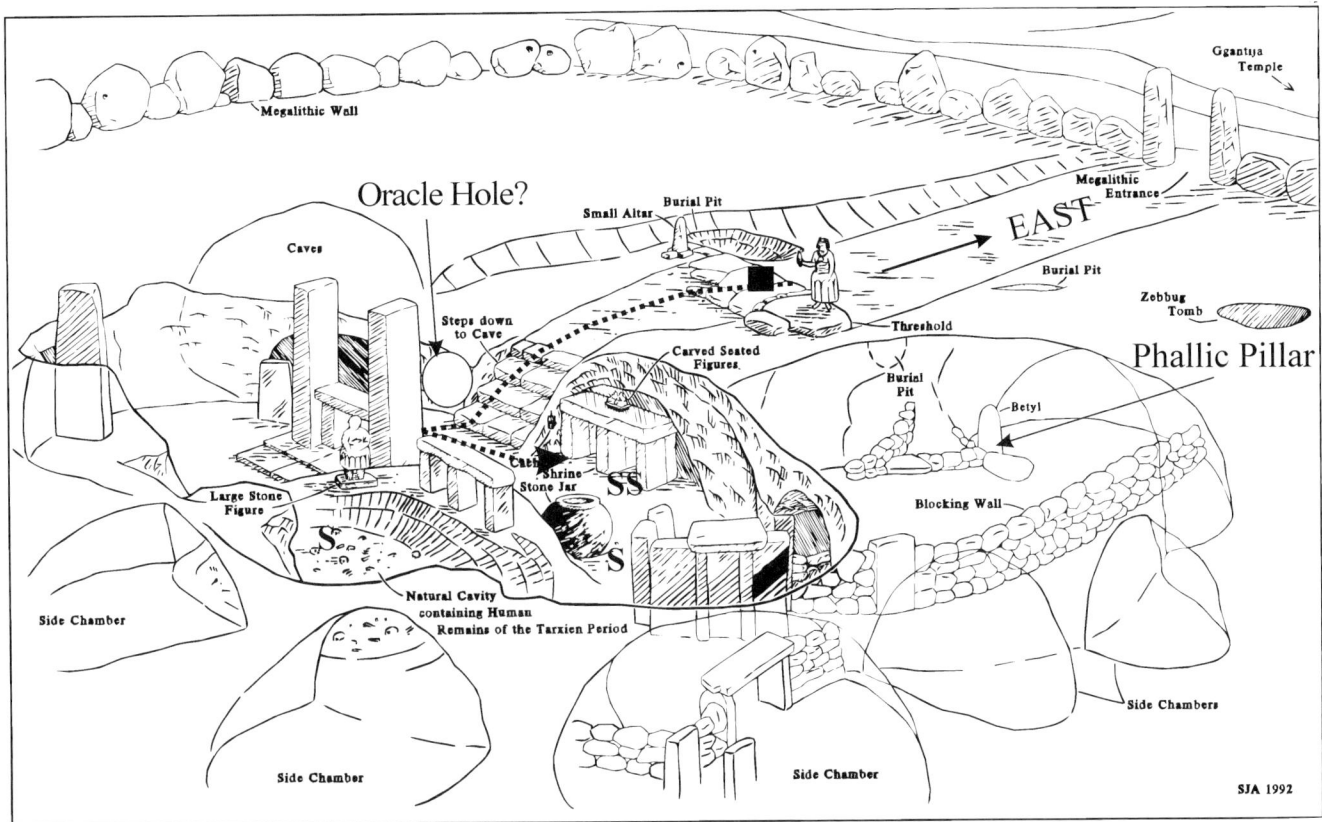

Figure 5.6. Reconstruction of the Brochtorff-Xaghra Circle showing fitments and likely access routes (drawn by Steven Ashley).

controlled, mediated, and conducted within strict rules of behaviour. The significance of the Maltese evidence and its spatial context is that it informs on a society, its ritual and iconography in the third millennium BC, graphically and richly (Malone *et al.* in prep.), which appears to have ritual notions that occur in many societies. Potentially we can construct a cosmology and ritual tradition from archaeological materials, allowing for a methodology of accurate record and interpretation to penetrate prehistoric cult and religion in a secure context.

Acknowledgements

I wish to thank the Templeton Foundation for the support that Research Grant 1093 provided for the fieldwork and study leave which gave rise to this paper. I also wish to thank Sharon Sultana and Suzannah Depasquale and their helpful staff in the National Museum of Archaeology in Valletta, and the assistance of my team in Malta (D. Barrowclough, K. Cooper, M. Anderson, D. Redhouse, F. Sturt, M. Brudenell, J. Gibbons and L. Prestell).

References

Bowie, F. 2006. *The Anthropology of Religion, an Introduction.* Oxford, Blackwell.

Bell, C. 1992. *Ritual Theory Ritual Practice.* Oxford, Oxford University Press.

Bell, C. 1997. *Ritual Perspectives and Dimensions.* Oxford, Oxford University Press.

Cilia, D. 2004. *Malta Before History: the world's oldest free-standing architecture.* Sliema, Miranda Publishers.

Darvill, T. 2006. *Stonehenge: biography of a landscape.* Stroud, Tempus.

Douglas, M. 1975. *Implicit Meanings.* London, Routledge and Kegan Paul.

Edwards, A., and Horne, M. 1997. In A. Whittle (ed.). *Sacred Mound Holy Ring: Silbury Hill and the West Kennet palisade complex in north Wiltshire.* Oxford, Oxbow Monograph 74, 117–29.

Gimbutas, M. 1974. *The Gods and Goddesses of Old Europe 7000–3500 B.C.* London, Thames and Hudson.

Gimbutas, M. 1989. *The Language of the Goddess.* San Fransisco, Harper Row.

Gimbutas, M. 1991. *The Civilisation of the Goddess: the world of old Europe.* San Fransisco, Harper Row.

Harding, A. F. and Lee, G. E. 1987 Henge monuments and related sites of Great Britain. British Archaeological Reports, British series no. 175, Oxford.

Hawkes, C. 1954. Archaeological theory and method: some suggestions from the Old World. *American Anthropologist* 56, 155–68.

Hertz, R. 1973. The pre-eminence of the right hand: a study in religious polarity. In R. Needham (ed.). *Right and Left: Essays on Dual Symbolic Classification*. London, University of Chicago Press.

Hodder, I. 1982a. *Symbols in Action*. Cambridge, Cambridge University Press.

Hodder, I. 1982b. *Symbolic and Structural Archaeology*. Cambridge, Cambridge University Press.

Hodder, I. 1987. *The Archaeology of Contextual Meanings*. Cambridge, Cambridge University Press.

Kyriakidis, E. Forthcoming. Introduction to the 2004 Third Corsen Advanced Seminar in The Archaeology of Ritual, UCLA.

Leach, E. 1966. Ritualisation in man. *Philosophical Transactions of the Royal Society*, Series B 251, 403–8.

Leach, E. 1976. *Culture and Communication : the logic by which symbols are connected*. Cambridge, Cambridge University Press.

Malone, C., Stoddart. S., Trump, D., Bonnano, A., the late Gouder, T. and Pace, A. (eds) 2007. *Mortuary Ritual on Gozo: Excavations at the Brochtorff Circle, Xaghra, Gozo 1987–94*. Cambridge, McDonald Institute Monographs.

Malone, C. and Stoddart, S. In preparation. *Art, cult and content: a study of prehistoric ritual in early Malta*.

McCaulay, R. N. and Lawson, E. T. 2002. *Bringing Ritual to Mind: Psychological Foundations of Cultural Forms*. Cambridge, Cambridge University Press.

Moore. H. 1981. Spatial patterning in settlement residues. In I. Hodder 1982b. *Symbolic and Structural Archaeology*. Cambridge, Cambridge University Press, 74–9.

Needham, R. 1973 (ed.). *Right and Left: Essays on Dual Symbolic Classification*. London, University of Chicago Press.

Pace, A. 2004. Hal Saflieni. In D. Cilia, *Malta Before History: the world's oldest free-standing architecture*. Sliema, Miranda Publishers, 77–92.

Renfrew, C. 1985. *The Archaeology of Cult. The sanctuary at Phylakopi*. Supplementary volume 18, The British School at Athens. London, Thames and Hudson.

Renfrew, C. 1973. The world's first stone Temples. In C. Renfrew. *The Emergence of Civilisation*. Harmondsworth, Penguin, 161–182.

Renfrew, C. 2004. Abstract for Problems in theorizing an Archaeology of Ritual: The Aegean Case. In A. Kyriakidis (ed.). Forthcoming. *The Archaeology of Ritual*. Los Angeles, UCLA, The Third Cotsen Seminar.

Richards, C. and Thomas, J. 1984. Ritual activity and structured deposition in later Neolithic Wessex. In R. Bradley and J. Gardner (eds). *Neolithic Studies*. Oxford, British Archaeological Reports 133, 189–218.

Shanks, M. and Tilley, C. 1982. Ideology, symbolic power and ritual communication: a reinterpretation of Neolithic mortuary practices. In I. Hodder (ed.). *Symbolic and Structural Archaeology*. Cambridge, Cambridge University Press, 129–54.

Stoddart, S., Bonanno, A., Gouder, T., Malone, C. and Trump, D. 1993. Cult in an Island Society: Prehistoric Malta in the Tarxien period. *Cambridge Journal of Archaeology* 3 (1), 3–19.

Tambiah, S. 1969. Animals are good to think with and good to prohibit. *Ethnology*, 8, 423–59.

Tilley, C. 1984 Ideology and the legitimation of power in the Middle Neolithic of Southern Sweden. In D. Miller and C. Tilley (eds). *Ideology, Power and prehistory*. Cambridge, Cambridge University Press, 111–46.

Turner, V. 1967. The forest of symbols. Ithaca, New York, Cornell University Press.

Turner, V. 1969. The Ritual Process. Penguin, Harmondsworth.

Trump, D. H. 2002. *Malta: prehistory and temples: Malta's living heritage*. Malta, Midsea Books.

Van Gennep, A. 1909 (1960). *The Rites of Passage*. London, Routledge and Kegan Paul.

Vella Gregory, I. 2005. *The human form in Neolithic Malta*. Malta, Midsea Books.

Whittle, A. 1997. Remembered and imagined belongings: Stonehenge and its traditions and structures of meaning. In B. Cunliffe and C. Renfrew (eds). *Science and Stonehenge*. Proceedings of the British Academy 92, 145–66. London.

Ventura, F. 2004. Temple Orientations. In Cilia, D. (ed.). *Malta Before History: the world's oldest free-standing architecture*. Sliema, Miranda Publishers, 307–25.

Chapter 6

LANDSCAPE AND RITUAL IN LATE NEOLITHIC MALTA

Reuben Grima

Debates on cult, religion and ritual in Late Neolithic Malta have inevitably focussed on the well-known monumental buildings of this period, which have attracted the interest of researchers for centuries. Their landscape setting, by contrast, has received much less attention. Here it will be argued that a better understanding of how these buildings relate to the landscape will shed light on their purpose and significance.

A substantial body of ethnographic evidence suggests that in many cultures, the landscape setting in which ritual occurs is often an integral part of its meaning. The position of ritual sites and buildings is often carefully chosen to locate them meaningfully in the landscape (Evans 1999). Conversely, architectural space is often designed to represent the environment or even the world as understood by its builders (Parker Pearson and Richards 1994). Over the past decade, archaeological interpretations of ritual sites have increasingly paid attention to the reciprocal relationship between site and landscape, which has become generally recognized as a fundamental consideration when trying to understand how people in the past used ritual to engage with the world that they inhabited (see for instance Aldenderfer, this volume). Against this background, the question of how the monumental sites of Late Neolithic Malta relate to their landscape setting is not only a pressing one, but also one that promises interesting answers. The present chapter is based on the results of some recent work addressing this question (Grima 2005).

The 'multi-scalar nature' of cult places has been repeatedly emphasised (Biehl, this volume). Here the relationship between site and landscape is investigated using two very different but complementary methods, applied at two different scales of analysis. The first examines where monumental buildings are placed in the landscape, using GIS-based statistical analysis. The second approach examines spatial order within monumental buildings, by examining how architectural spaces and images are deployed within these buildings.

Some characteristics of the Maltese archipelago

A useful starting point is to outline some of the key characteristics that shaped and defined the Maltese landscape during the Late Neolithic. The archipelago is made up of two main islands and several minor ones, with a present-day total area of around 316 square kilometres. All the sites discussed here are located on the two principal islands. The geological stratigraphy of the archipelago is composed of a sedimentary sequence of Tertiary limestones and marls. The lowermost visible formation is Lower Coralline Limestone, characterized by its durability. The next formation is the much softer Globigerina Limestone, widely exploited in building and sculpture because of its workability. Above this lies the Blue Clay formation, critical for the hydrology of the archipelago, because it is the only impermeable layer in the sequence. The Blue Clay is followed by the Greensands formation. The entire sequence is capped by the harder Upper Coralline Limestone formation (Earlier work reviewed in Pedley *et al.* 1976). Coralline Limestone and Globigerina Limestone present a sharp contrast in appearance, hardness, texture, and workability, but both are widely used in Neolithic megalithic structures.

The topography of the archipelago is closely controlled by geological structure, faulting and erosion (Dewdney 1961). These factors have created a highly fragmented landscape (Bowen-Jones and Dewdney 1961). Different geological formations outcrop in different parts of the archipelago, giving them their distinctive topography. Their variable resistance to erosion has resulted in highly selective erosion patterns. Where Globigerina Limestone outcrops, it forms the gently rolling plains that characterise south-eastern Malta and part of southern Gozo. Upper Coralline Limestone outcrops form the perched plateaux that dominate western and northern Malta, and most of Gozo. The edges of the Upper Coralline outcrops are characterized by steep slopes that form with the slumping of the underlying clay. Erosion and faulting act on this essentially horizontal stratigraphy to create a more rugged relief. Pleistocene valley systems have furthermore incised deep wadis through the limestone formations.

Another important factor that has shaped the islands' topography is faulting. The archipelago is located in a tectonically active region, which has resulted in a series of dramatic fault systems (Illies 1981; Alexander 1988; Dart *et al.* 1993). One fault system has broken up north-western Malta into a series of horsts and grabens, which form a succession of parallel and sharply defined ridges and valleys. Another fault system has created the vertical cliffs that today characterize the south coast of Gozo and the south-western coast of Malta.

Processes of erosion and sedimentation are closely controlled by geology and topography. Erosion is most evident in the more perched, karst environments that form on the Upper Coralline Limestone plateaux, the exposed outcrops of the plastic clay deposits, and the deeply-incised storm-water courses. The low-lying plains that form on the Globigerina Limestone and on the floors of graben basins favour the deposition of material eroded out of more exposed areas having steeper gradients (Hunt 1996, 108).

Soils on the karst landscapes on the Upper Coralline Limestone plateaux are dominated by terra soils, while slopes that descend from the Upper Coralline plateaux to the Globigerina plains are dominated by carbonate raw soils (Lang 1961; Schembri 1996). These often lie on steep slopes that require terracing in order to permit cultivation (Lang 1961, 94). The plains on the Globigerina outcrops and in the graben basins in northern Malta are characterized by xerorendzinas. The properties of these soils, together with the low gradients where they usually occur, provide favourable conditions for agriculture without requiring the extremely labour-intensive building and maintaining of terraced fields.

The archipelago has no rivers or reserves of surface water, and the valley system that drains the islands of rainwater runoff runs dry during the summer. Groundwater reserves were therefore vital to make the islands habitable. The geological structure of the islands consists mostly of a succession of porous limestones that retain a body of fresh water at sea level, which across most of the archipelago lies deep beneath the ground. Where the impervious clay layer is present, it creates another, perched aquifer which supplies a large number of perennial springs (Newbery 1968).

Where are monumental buildings placed in the landscape?

Two principal categories of monumental site have been recognized for late Neolithic Malta. The first comprises monumental buildings raised above ground, generally referred to as 'temples' in the literature. The second comprises underground funerary sites, carved into the rock. The focus of this chapter is monumental buildings raised above ground, of which more examples are known, making them more suitable for statistical analysis.

GIS-based statistical analysis was used in order to test the relationship between the location of monumental buildings and different variables in the landscape. A 50 m digital elevation model (DEM) of the archipelago, obtained from the Malta Environment and Planning Authority, formed the basis of the analysis. The geographical analysis was conducted in ArcView 3.2.

The landscape variables considered here are of two types, best addressed using different bivariate techniques. The first are measured at the nominal scale, while the second are measured at the ratio scale (see discussion in Shennan 1997, 8–12). Relationships with discontinuous variables measured at the nominal scale, such as surface geology or aspect, were tested with a χ^2 (chi-squared) test. Continuous variables measured at the ratio scale, such as slope, elevation, or distance from a resource, were tested using a Kolmogorov-Smirnov (K-S) test. K-S testing compares the cumulative distribution curves of the two variables under consideration, and determines the statistical likelihood of a given deviation between the two curves (Shennan 1997, 57–61). In this manner, the test determines whether relationships between site distribution and a given variable are statistically significant. For the values in the present instance, the most appropriate tables are those given by Miller (Miller 1956, 113), using the Kolmogorov approximation (Kim and Jennrich 1973, 84–86). The one-sample K-S test makes it possible to use the entire population that is being considered, rather than a random sample of points in the landscape. This is statistically desirable because a total sample makes the test more robust (Kvamme 1990).

The location of monumental buildings was analysed in relation to a number of variables, including surface geology, elevation, slope of terrain, aspect (direction of slope), distance from plains, accessibility from the sea, and hydrology. Results varied considerably. The location of monumental buildings showed no preference for any particular type of solid surface geology. Likewise, there was no particular preference to position sites at a higher or lower elevation (Figure 6.1, top left), regardless whether this was measured in absolute terms or in relation to the immediate surroundings. No preference was detected for sites with a steeper or shallower gradient (Figure 6.1, top right). On the other hand, the direction of slope, or aspect, appears to have been an important consideration, as most monumental buildings are positioned on slopes facing south and, to a lesser extent, west. A strong relationship was also noted with plains where deeper soil accumulated on shallower gradients. Most sites were positioned near the edges of these plains (Plate 1). Another very specific relationship was that with the sea. No pattern that could be

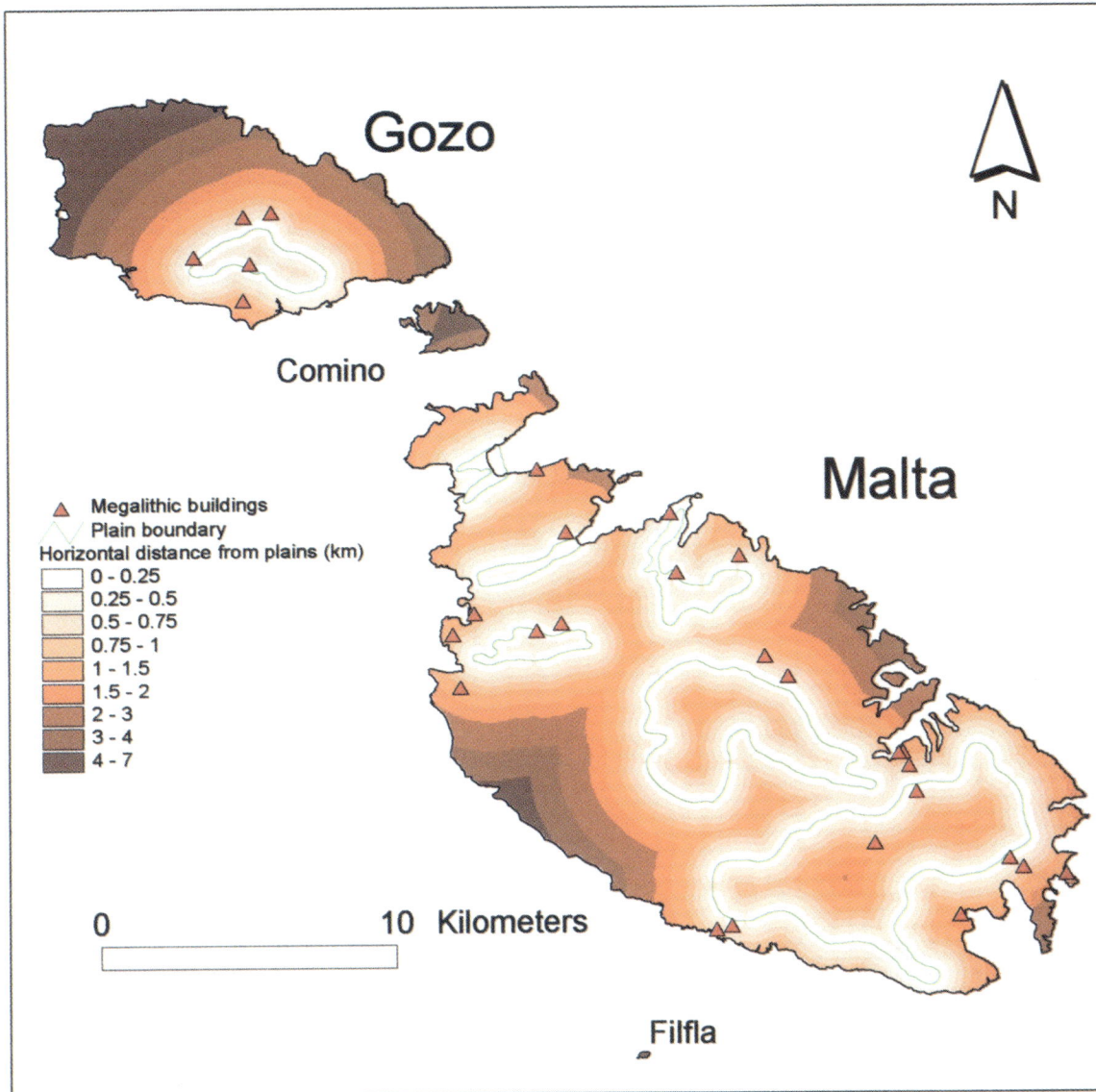

Plate 1. Map showing location of megalithic buildings plotted against horizontal distance from plain boundaries.

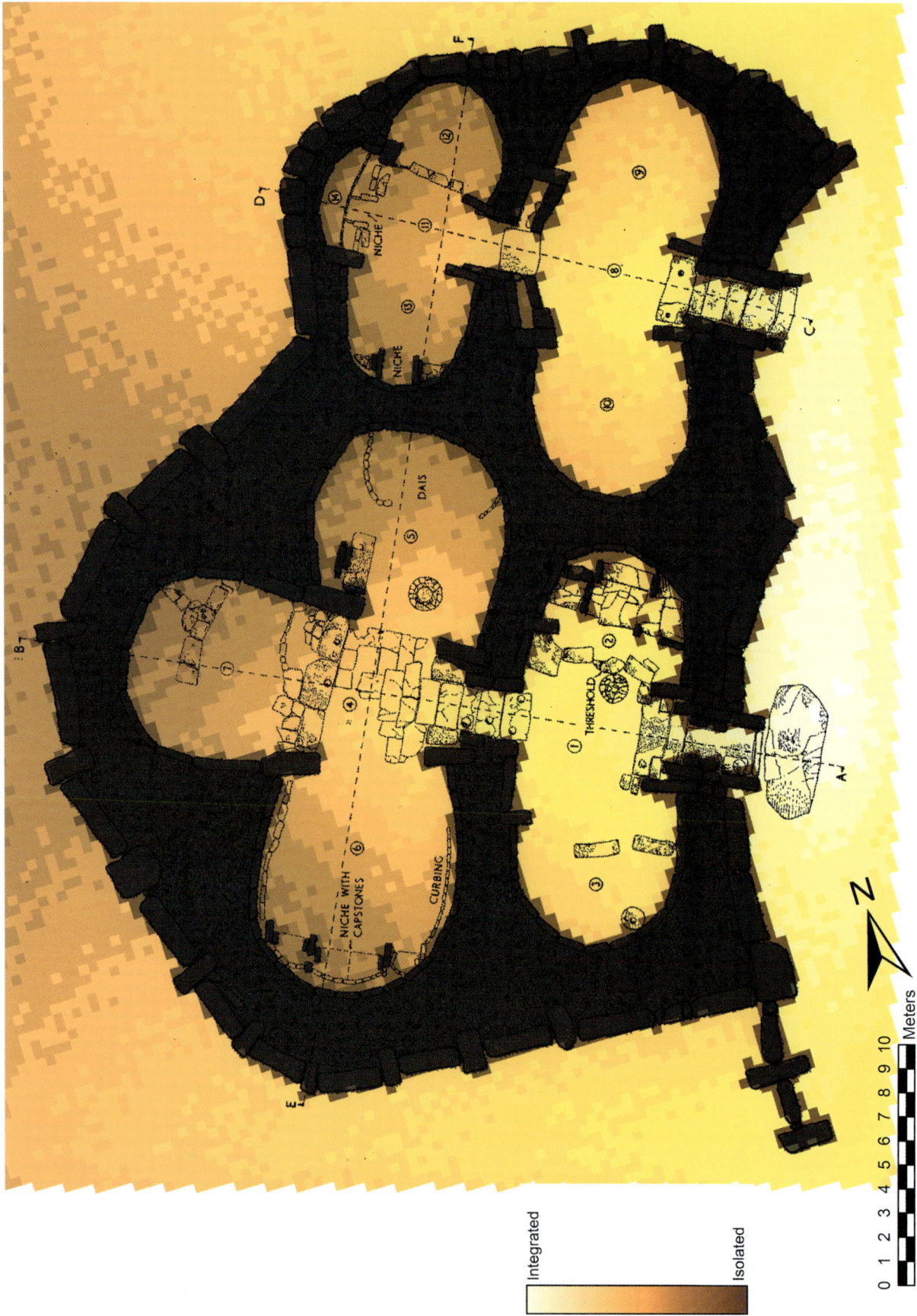

Plate 2. Access map of the Ġgantija temple.

Integrated

Isolated

0 1 2 3 4 5 6 7 8 9 10
Meters

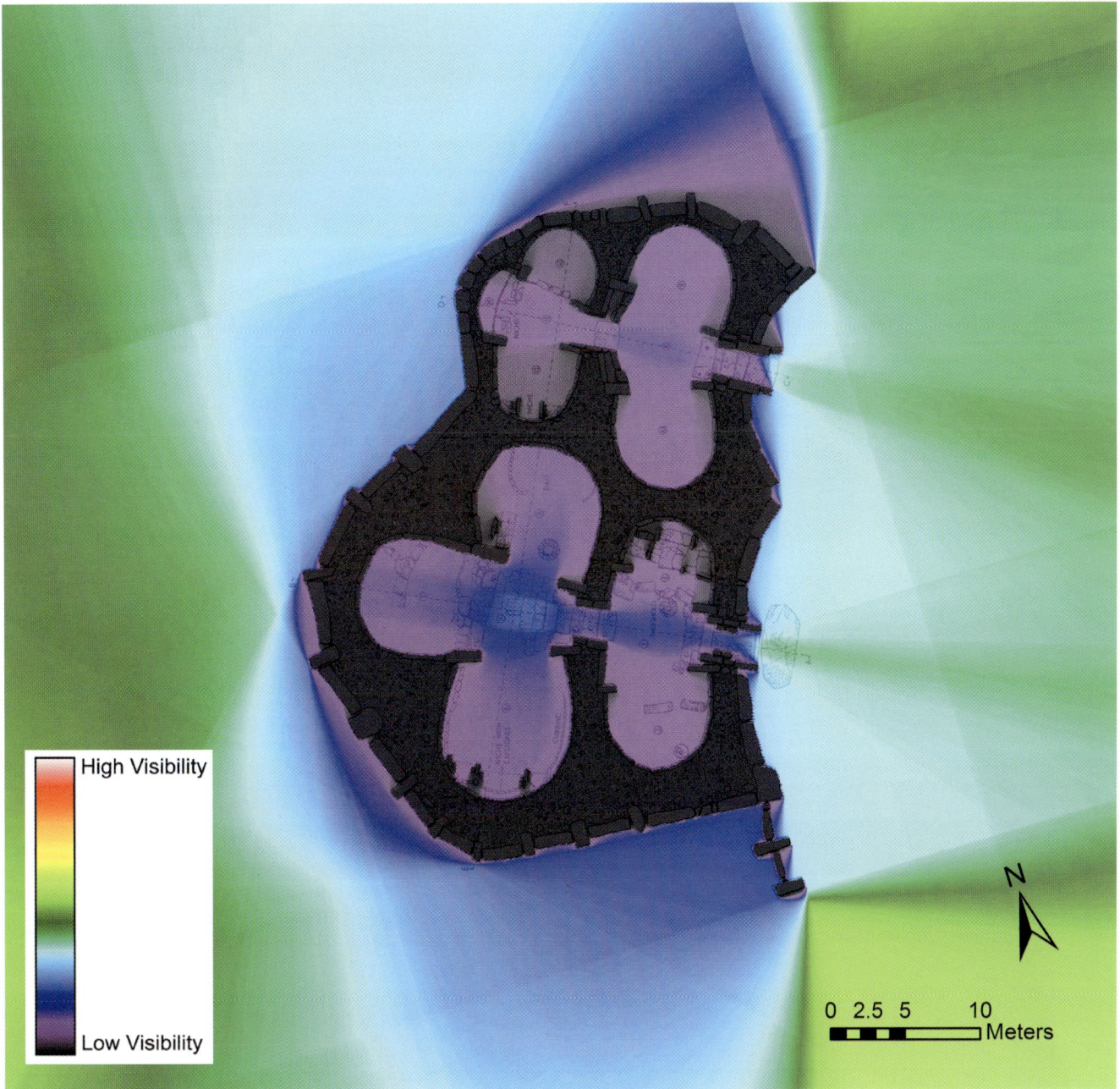

Plate 3. Visibility map of the Ġgantija temple.

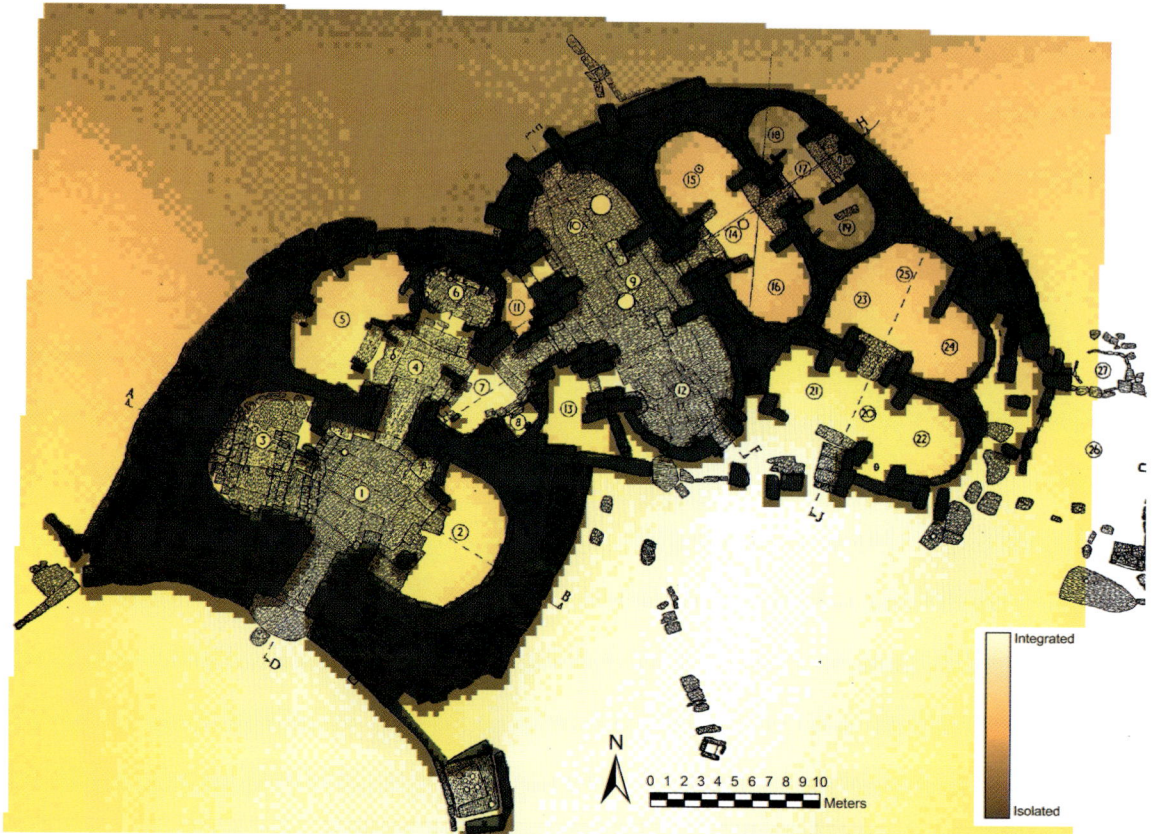

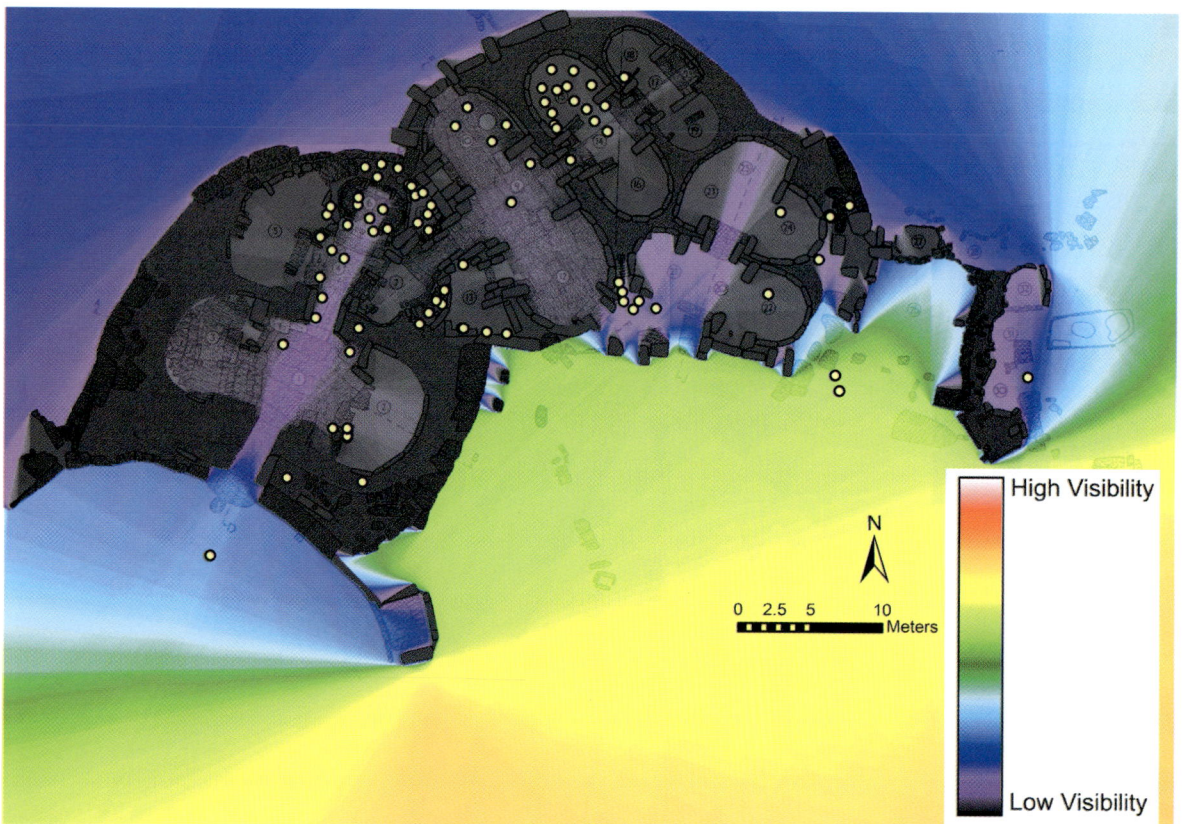

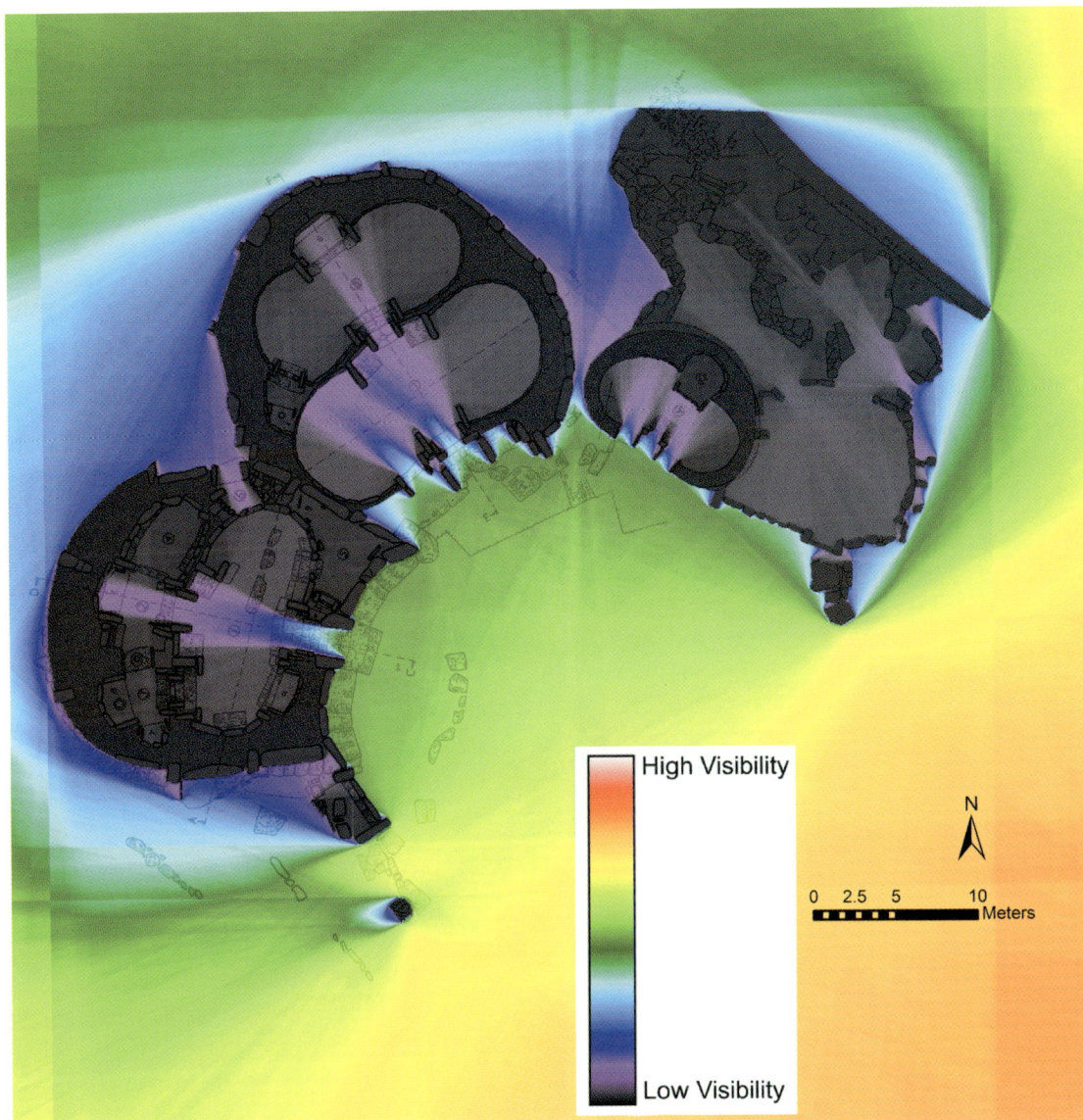

Plate 6. Visibility map of Mnajdra temples.

High Visibility

Low Visibility

N

0   2.5   5   10
                    Meters

Opposite:

Plate 4 (top). Access map of the Tarxien temples.

Plate 5 (bottom). Visibility map of the Tarxien temples, with location of major finds from the Zammit archive.

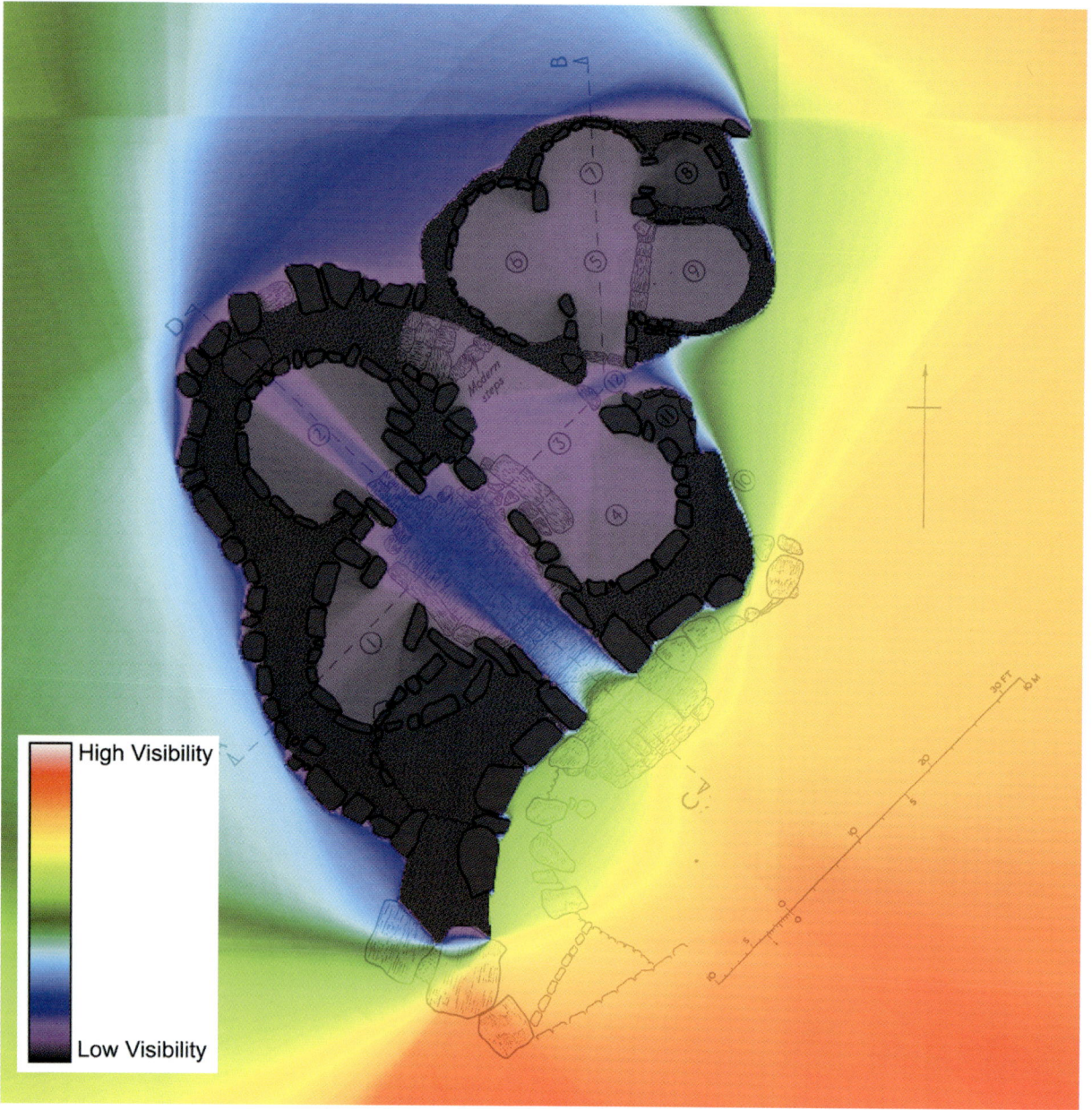

Plate 7. Visibility map of Ta' Hagrat temple.

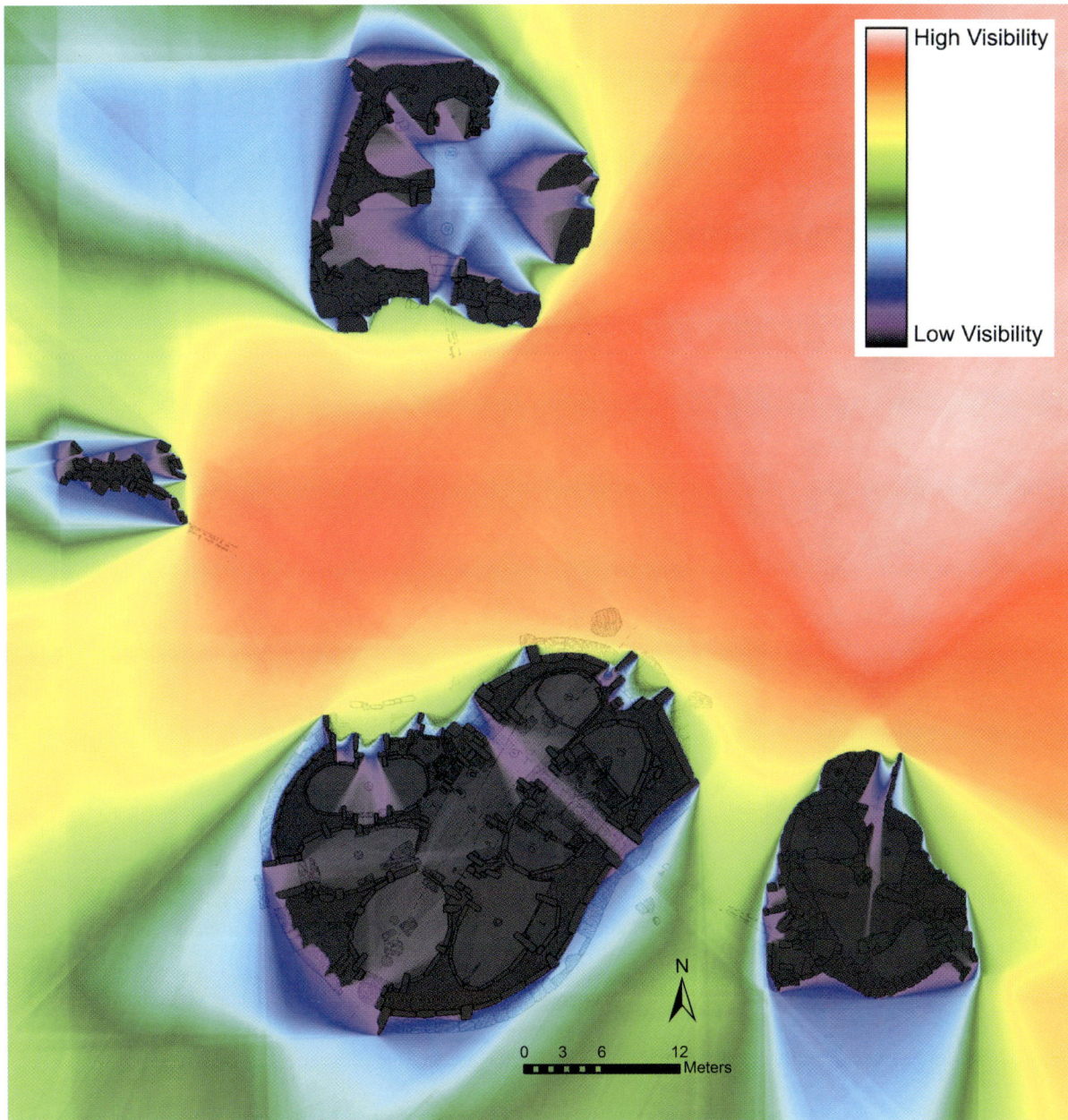

Plate 8. Visibility map of Ḥaġar Qim temples.

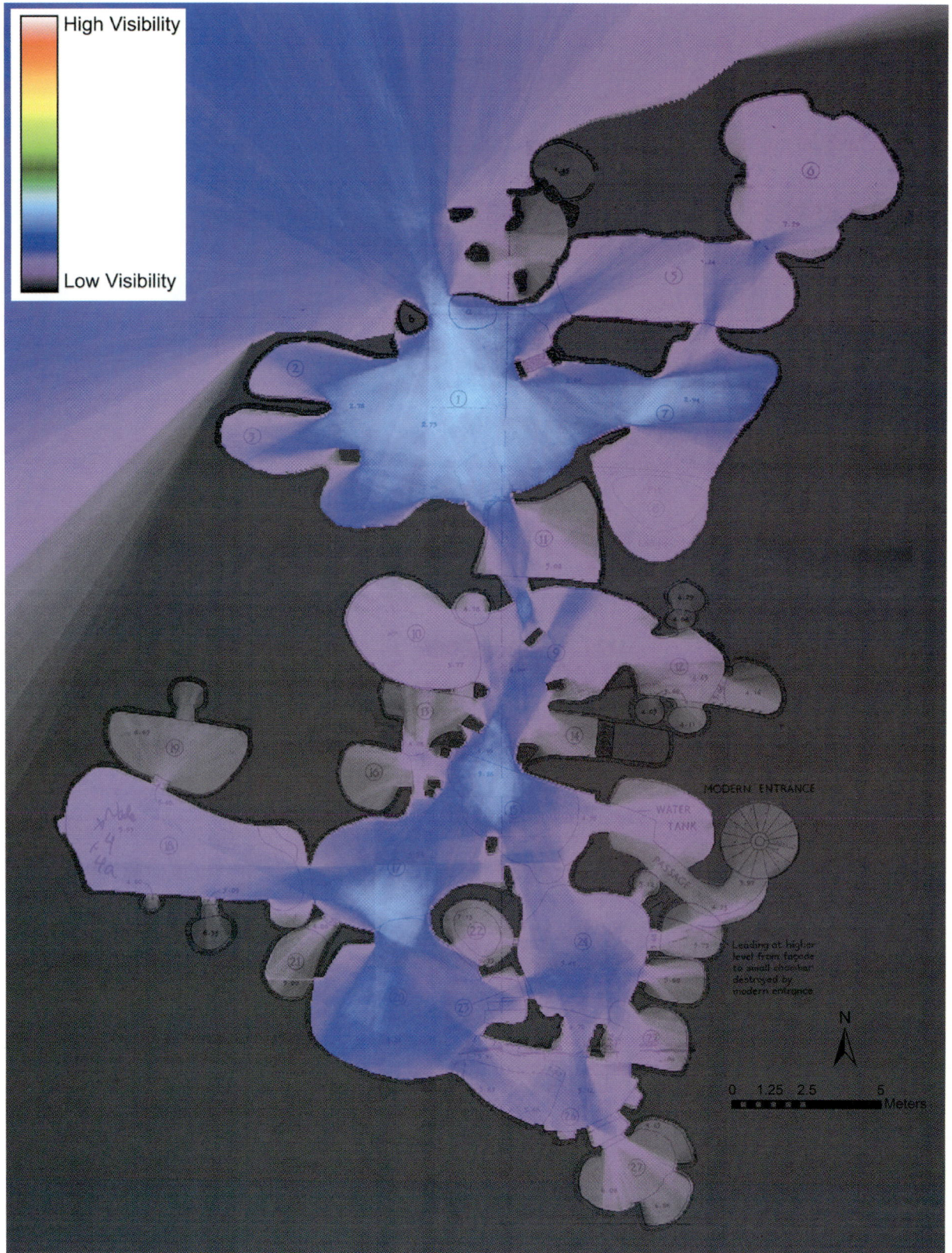

Plate 9. Visibility map of Hal Saflieni.

usefully generalized was detected for visibility to or from the sea. In sharp contrast, the location of monumental buildings showed a marked preference for locations that enjoyed better access to the sea. Another variable for which a strong relationship could be demonstrated was hydrology. Using the known repertoire of medieval toponyms referring to springs (Wettinger 2000), it was possible to demonstrate a marked preference for areas closer to freshwater springs.

Multivariate analysis was used to confirm that there were no high levels of interdependence between the landscape variables, as these may give misleading results. Also using multivariate analysis, the different variables that showed a relationship to site location could be combined to model which parts of the archipelago were considered more favourable and appropriate for a monumental building. For instance, for each parcel of land that makes up a cell of the DEM, the distance from plain boundaries, cost distance from freshwater springs and

distance from embarkation points could be added to give a new value to that cell. The closer the cell is to all three resources, the more favourable it is for the siting of a monumental building. In the resulting map, a number of more favourable zones are readily apparent. When the distribution of monumental buildings was tested against this map, it was found to have considerable explanatory power. 67% of monumental buildings were found to be located within the 'most favourable' 24% of the archipelago's surface (Figure 6.1, bottom left). Factoring in aspect and surface geology further strengthens the predictive power of the model. 50% of sites were found to lie within the most favourable 7.6% of the land area. A 100% of the sites are located within the most favourable 43% of the land area. In other words, the model identified 57% of the land area as very unsuitable for monumental buildings (Figure 6.1, bottom right).

In view of the dense interplay of different attributes in a

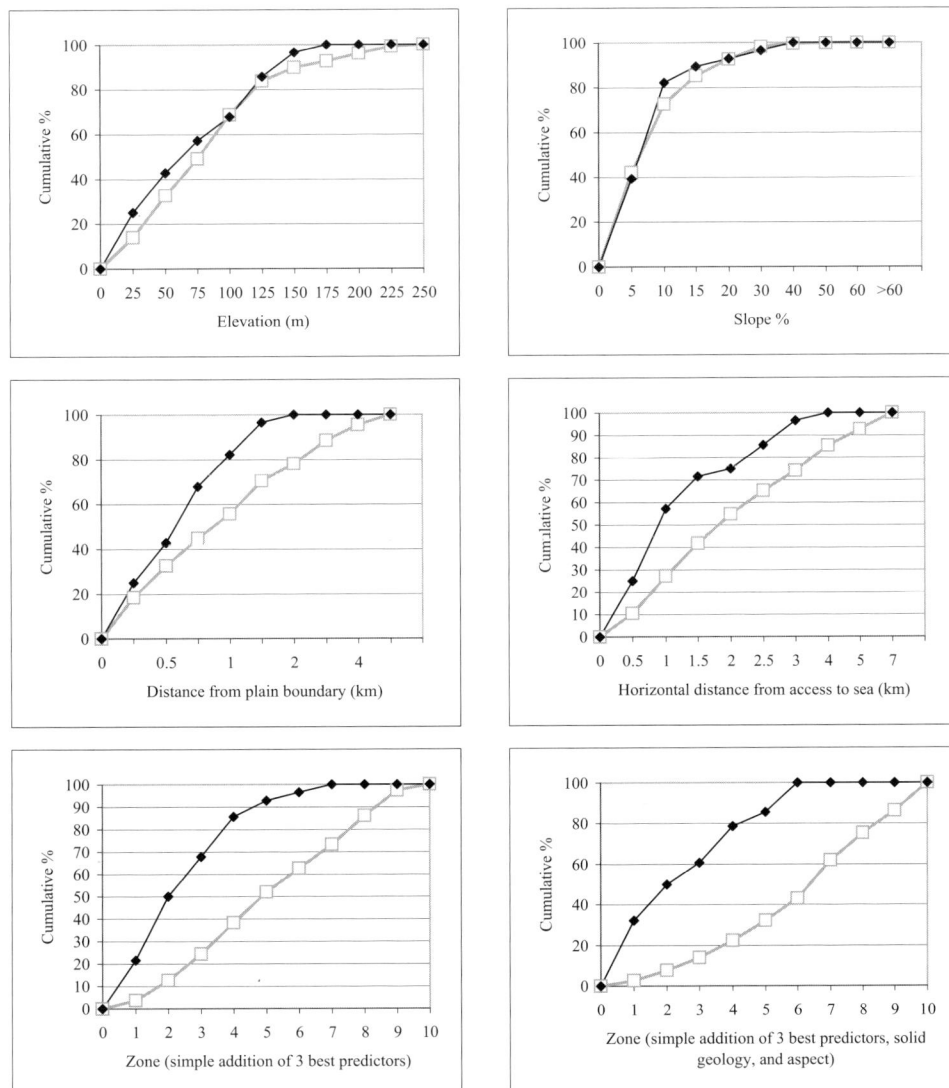

Figure 6.1. A selection of cumulative distribution curves showing the relationship of site location to different landscape variables. The black line with solid diamonds shows the cumulative distribution of megalithic buildings. The grey line with white squares shows the distribution of land area, ordered by different variables. In both graphs at the top of the figure, the graph for site distribution closely follows that for land distribution, showing that the variable being considered did not have a significant influence on site location. The two graphs in the middle of the page, on the other hand, show a considerable departure between the two graphs, which when measured statistically, demonstrates that proximity to plain boundaries and proximity to embarkation points were both significant considerations. Finally, the two graphs at the bottom show two examples of multivariate analysis, where the combination of different variables increases the explanatory power of the model.

restricted and variable landscape, these are very powerful results, suggesting that the model is representing decisions about site location quite reliably. In spite of the small scale of the archipelago, they demonstrate that meaningful patterns may be detected in the archaeological record of the site distribution of monumental buildings, shedding light on how different parts of the landscape were perceived and organized. These patterns allow us to begin to locate monumental buildings in an inhabited landscape, in order to gain fresh insight into their role in the cultural construction and appropriation of that landscape.

The variables that appear to influence the choice of location of monumental buildings are all closely tied to strategies for subsistence and survival in a small island context. Proximity to the fertile plains that provided the most favourable conditions for agriculture, proximity to freshwater springs, as well as the preference for south-facing slopes, are very much the same considerations that would have determined which areas were more attractive for settlement. The same may be said of the preference for locations with ready access to the sea, which was so important for connectivity within and beyond the archi-pelago, and a complementary source of subsistence. The fact that monumental buildings show a strong relationship with all of these variables strongly suggests that they formed an integral part of the taskscapes of everyday life.

Monumental buildings are often located on sites that had been in use for several centuries before they were constructed (Trump 1966; Evans 1971). The choice of location is not, therefore, dictated primarily by the physical suitability of the site for a monumental building, but rather by a preference for sites that were already significant places for the inhabitants. The evidence from Skorba (Trump 1966) is particularly eloquent here, as it clearly shows that monumental buildings stood side by side with domestic huts. Monumental buildings were evidently not remote places to be approached on rare occasions, but were at the focus of the daily life of the community.

A close relationship has been observed between the location of monumental buildings and areas that afforded access to key resources, suggesting that these more favourable areas were recognized and exploited. Pockets in the landscape that afforded optimal conditions appear to have shaped organizational units. The building of monu-ments appears to have played an important role in this appropriation of the landscape. Monumental buildings do not appear to have been 'central places' located in the middle of these pockets. Instead, their relationship to site attributes suggests they may have been located near the boundaries of these zones. The relationship to maritime connectivity suggests that one of their purposes may have been that of ceremonial gateways between land and sea, mediating interaction between communities in different parts of the archipelago, and with the outside world.

Invoking the landscape

The observations made above make a compelling case that the megalithic buildings of Neolithic Malta have a very specific relationship with their landscape context. This relationship may be explored further by considering evidence at a different scale, that of the buildings themselves.

The buildings typically consist in an external forecourt and a number of circular chambers (usually referred to as apses in the literature) arranged around one or more internal courts. The boundaries between these different spaces are emphasised using a number of devices, such as monumental doorways and thresholds, changes in level, different types of paving, apertures and stone screens that separate chambers from courts. Sculpture is also widely used in these spaces. Here it will be argued that the use of sculpture follows set rules, using different modes of representation for different subjects, and representing different subjects in different parts of the building. It will be further argued that one of the uses of sculpture is to invoke the island environment within the architectural spaces of the building, ordering those spaces according to a schematic programme.

Two of the principal media that are used to create the images found in the Maltese megalithic buildings are low-relief sculpture, and sculpture in the round. One remark-able, but often overlooked fact about the way these different modes of representation are used is that they are used for different subjects. The human form is invariably represented in the round or in high-relief sculpture, which is a variation of sculpture in the round. On the other hand, the human form never makes an appearance in the known repertoire of low-relief sculpture. Some of the subjects represented in low-relief sculpture are readily recognizable, such as quadrupeds or fish. Other representations are more open to interpretation, such as motifs that have often been described as 'tree-like', or series of spirals that have sometimes been interpreted as representations of water or the sea.

The carved elements from the Maltese megalithic buildings have been largely treated in isolation, as individual works of art. Here it will be argued that their spatial context and the relationships and juxtapositions between different sculptures are meaningfully constituted, and that they are critical to our understanding of the significance of the spaces where they are found, as well as of the sculptures themselves. The low-relief panels are almost invariable carved from the exposed faces of substantial megaliths that have been found *in situ*, permitting very precise inferences about the position that each panel was created for, as well as the way it related to other low-relief panels.

Some interesting patterns may be observed, allowing a tantalising glimpse into the grammar of the system of representation of which they form part. Specific motifs appear to be associated with specific spaces within the buildings, and it would appear that certain rules are respected throughout the repertoire of known sites across the archipelago. The distinction between court and apse appears to be a key factor. The low-relief panels from Tarxien showing quadrupeds were placed at the far end of a circular apse, while the reliefs of fish from Buġibba were found in the central court of the building. The tree-like motif from Tarxien was found on a block immediately adjacent to one of the panels showing quadrupeds. On the other hand, reliefs showing a repetitive sequence of spiral motifs are found around the courts, as borne out by examples from Tarxien, Ġgantija, and Buġibba. At Buġibba, they are positioned immediately adjacent to the block carrying reliefs showing fish (Figure 6.2).

One rule that all the relief panels respect is that different motifs are not mixed within the same panel, or even on different panels on the same megalith. Several megaliths carry more than one low-relief panel, but invariably, they all represent the same motif. Witkin's work on representational codes (Witkin 1995) strongly suggests that we are dealing here with a haptic system of representation, where the megalith itself 're-presents', or makes present, the subject of the low-reliefs it carries. Applying Witkin's terms, a megalith carved with low-reliefs is not simply a picture of its subject, but an invocation that stands in for the subject. Furthermore, relationships between different subjects are represented through the spatial ordering of the blocks that invoke them. The evidence suggests a spatial division

between terrestrial motifs and maritime motifs. At Tarxien, a block carrying three panels with a tree-like motif is located immediately next to another block showing quadrupeds, at the inner end of an apse. At Buġibba, a block carrying two low-reliefs of spirals was found immediately adjacent to the block carrying two reliefs of fish, in the court (Figure 6.2). This prompts the suggestion that the tree-like motif from Tarxien does in fact represent a plant or tree, while the running spirals associated with the courts may be an invocation of the sea. Low-reliefs around courts therefore appear to be making references to the maritime environment, while low-reliefs within apses appear to be making references to the terrestrial environment.

We may now return to the question posed by the absence of the human form from the low-relief panels, which may provide an important key to understanding the representational codes that are being employed. It is suggested that sculpture in the round is being deliberately used for representations of the human form, in order to place them on a different plane of representation to the low-relief panels. The distinction between these planes of representation is perhaps best explained in terms borrowed from the world of theatre. The low-relief panels invoke elements from the islandscape in order to conjure up the terrestrial environment and the marine environment in different parts of the building. They provide a scenographic frame of reference that assigns significance to the architectural spaces where they are located, comparable to theatre

Figure 6.2. Buġibba. Excavation photograph dated June 1928, showing the low-reliefs in the central court shortly after discovery. (National Museum of Archaeology)

'props', so called because they define the properties of the stage. Representations of the human form, on the other hand, bodily occupy the stage-set defined by the low-reliefs, on the same plane as living humans entering those spaces. In this sense, they are also actors and performers. The above observations suggest that the system of representation that is employed here is one that relied heavily on performance. It is not a merely a series of images to be looked at, but a scenographic system that needs to be enacted.

Conclusion

The two lines of analysis at two different scales outlined above tell parts of the same story, that of how the Neolithic islanders perceived, organized, inhabited and appropriated their world, and allow us glimpses of the cosmological belief systems and ritual practices that they used to this end. The positioning of the megalithic buildings in natural gateways between land and sea, noted at the first scale of analysis, is echoed in the scenographic representation of the maritime and the terrestrial environments, separated by elaborate threshold arrangements, observed at the second scale of analysis. The contextual relationships and characteristics that have been noted suggest that the use of images in Maltese megalithic buildings made extensive references to the environment, while ritual performances within the buildings appear to have invoked the islanders' engagement with that environment. In this light, the landscape context of the megalithic buildings was not simply the geographical context in which ritual and monumental activity took place, but appears to have formed the basis of a cosmological frame of reference that was integral to the ritual practices themselves.

References

Alexander, D. 1988. A review of the physical geography of Malta and its significance for tectonic geomorphology. *Quaternary Science Reviews* 7, 41–53.

Bowen-Jones, H. and Dewdney, J. C. 1961. Agricultural regions. In H. Bowen-Jones, J. C. Dewdney and W. B. Fisher (eds). *Malta: Background for Development*, 235–288. Durham, University of Durham.

Dart, C. J., Bosence, D. W. J. and McClay, K. R. 1993. Stratigraphy and structure of the Maltese graben system. *Journal of the Geological Society* 150, 1153–1166.

Dewdney, J. C. 1961. Relief and landforms. In H. Bowen-Jones, J. C. Dewdney and W. B. Fisher (eds). *Malta: Background for Development*, 34–42. Durham, University of Durham.

Evans, C. 1999. Cognitive maps and narrative trails: Fieldwork with the Tamu-mai (Gurung) of Nepal. In P. J. Ucko and R. Layton (eds). *The Archaeology and Anthropology of Landscape: Shaping Your Landscape* 439–457. London, Routledge.

Evans, J. D. 1971. *The Prehistoric Antiquities of the Maltese Islands: A Survey*. London, Athlone Press.

Grima, R. 2005. *Monuments in Search of a Landscape: the Landscape Context of Monumentality in Late Neolithic Malta*. Unpublished PhD thesis, University of London.

Hunt, C. O. 1996. Quaternary deposits in the Maltese Islands: a microcosm of environmental change in Mediterranean lands. *GeoJournal* 41, 101–109.

Illies, J. H. 1981. Graben formation – The Maltese Islands – A case history. *Tectonophysics* 73, 151–168.

Kim, P. J. and Jennrich, R. I. 1973. Tables of the exact sampling distribution of the two-sample Kolmogorov-Smirnov criterion. In *Selected Tables in Mathematical Statistics*. Providence, American Mathematical Society.

Kvamme, K. L. 1990. One-sample tests in regional archaeological analysis. *American Antiquity* 55, 367–381.

Lang, D. 1961. Soils. In H. Bowen-Jones, J. C. Dewdney and W. B. Fisher (eds). *Malta: Background for Development* 83–98. Durham, Department of Geography, University of Durham.

Miller, L. H. 1956. Table of percentage points of Kolmogorov statistics. *Journal of the American Statistical Association* 51, 111–121.

Newbery, J. 1968. The perched water table in the upper limestone aquifer of Malta. *Journal of the Institution of Water Engineers* 22, 551–570.

Parker Pearson, M. and Richards, C. 1994. Ordering the world: Perceptions of architecture, space and time. In M. Parker Pearson and C. Richards (eds). *Architecture and Order: Approaches to Social Space* 1–37. London, Routledge.

Pedley, H. M., House, M. R. and Waugh, B. 1976. The geology of Malta and Gozo. *Proceedings of the Geological Association* 87, 325–341.

Schembri, P. J. 1996. The Maltese Islands: climate, vegetation and landscape. *GeoJournal* 41, 115–125.

Shennan, S. 1997. *Quantifying Archaeology*. 2nd edn. Edinburgh, University Press.

Trump, D. H. 1966. *Skorba*. Oxford, Society of Antiquaries.

Wettinger, G. 2000. *Place-Names of the Maltese Islands Ca. 1300–1800*. Malta, PEG.

Witkin, R. 1995. *Art and Social Structure*. Cambridge, Polity Press.

Chapter 7

MAPPING CULT CONTEXT:
GIS APPLICATIONS IN MALTESE TEMPLES

Michael Anderson and Simon Stoddart

Introduction

Other papers in this volume make the case for the ritual use and context (Malone, this volume), and even the cultural landscape (Grima, this volume) of the prehistoric Temples of Malta, so it is hardly necessary to reiterate the case for the importance or the historical significance of these remarkable structures for our understanding of the prehistory of the Mediterranean region. Whatever else may be said about the Temples, it is certain that the structures represent a significant social and economic investment in labour, time and resources (Clark 2004). There can be little doubt that they were of central importance in the social rituals and religious ceremonies of the associated populations which created them. However, although considerable evidence for ancient Maltese ritual and religion exists in a variety of different artefacts ranging from bowls and horn cores, to *steatopygous* figurines, carved decoration, small finds and pottery fragments, these do not present a transparent gloss on the nature or function of the rituals and ceremonies from which they must ultimately derive.

This paper presents an overview of the development of an idea first conceived by the two authors in Cambridge. The fieldwork and computerised analysis were executed by Michael Anderson (funded by the Templeton Foundation in a project headed by Caroline Malone). The methodology was that implemented in his PhD, supervised by Simon Stoddart, and originally applied to the investigation of Roman houses in Pompeii. The Maltese results were first presented, prior to fieldwork, at a conference in Cambridge in 2005, and then implemented during fieldwork in Malta in 2006, to achieve the microanalysis necessary to situate these elements of art within the liturgical and mortuary spaces created by the Maltese megaliths. In order to accomplish this, it was necessary to examine the information presented by the temples themselves more closely (Zammit 1930), considering the effects of the spatial arrangements of the monuments upon activities which could have taken place within and surrounding them. The monuments present a sophisticated and complex internal organisation comprised of a variety of different elements. Certainly we may imagine that the great effort and precision which went into the creation of the temples would not have been done without careful consideration as to their eventual use. While it may be impossible to reconstruct every detail of the religious practices associated with the temples, it is certainly possible to examine and quantify some of the experiential qualities of the buildings and with these observations to make better informed suggestions about the rituals which may have taken place inside them.

The Sample and the GIS Process

The total sample for our research consisted of eleven structures (Evans 1971). Nine of these are normally considered to be 'temples:' Ta' Ħagrat, Tarxien, Skorba, Ħaġar Qim, Mnajdra and the three temples at Kordin on the island of Malta and Ġgantija on Gozo, whilst two are clearly 'mortuary structures:' the hypogeum on Malta and the Brochtorff Circle at Xagħra on Gozo (Malone, *et al.* 2007). Because of the realities of incomplete preservation or later destruction, several of these temples played only an ancillary role from the visual-spatial analysis which inevitably centres upon the more complete examples. Each temple was subjected to two analyses designed to interrogate and summarize quantitatively two of the most important aspects through which humans experience the built environment – movement and visibility.

Movement within structures is most strongly influenced by the access provided to the various spaces they contain. Some spaces are isolated within the spatial organisation of a building and are therefore on average difficult to reach (asymmetric), whilst other spaces will tend to coordinate and facilitate movement through the building by interconnecting other spaces and providing traffic flow (integrated). A method of examining this aspect of the built environment has been developed by the spatial syntax school of architectural theory over the past thirty years (Hanson 1998; Hillier and Hanson 1984). By counting the number of steps between spaces in a building it is possible to identify those spaces which are the most isolated from other spaces. More importantly, by averaging the distances travelled between rooms, one may speak of movement within the house in general – identifying those areas which tend to be isolated from traffic and those which will tend to channel it. Expanding this analysis to a finer level of detail, it has been possible to examine which parts of each space function in these ways. The work presented in this paper builds on earlier spatial syntax analysis of the temples by one of the two authors (Bonanno, *et al.* 1990) and the unpublished work by Christopher Hayden (1990).

The procedure followed in the course of this research involved producing a digitized image of the floor plan of each temple – a grid of squares forming the movement steps. A specially designed program which one of us, Michael Anderson, wrote during the course of his PhD in the Perl scripting language was then employed to process these images over a period of many hours. This work produced an 'access map' for each monument in which darker gold represents those areas that are remote and private, and lighter gold to white interconnected areas which would have generally experienced a greater degree of traffic as people moved throughout the building (Plate 2).

The method used to examine visibility in the research made use of geographical information systems (GIS) software. A small scale terrain grid (DEM) was created within the GIS for each temple so that standing walls would block visibility whilst openings, doorways and open space would not block line of sight.

The sum of views from a single point could then be calculated by tracing lines in every direction from that point until an obstacle was reached. This representation of visibility is generally called a viewshed or isovist. In order to examine the total effect however, it was necessary to consider the views from every location simultaneously.

This was achieved by means of a one metre interval grid of points that was placed over each temple within the GIS software. These points provided the locations from which each view was calculated and then layered. Many intersecting viewsheds indicate that as movement throughout the building occurs an area is generally rather visible, whilst a low number suggests a state of privacy and visual isolation. A 'visibility map' was generated for each of the temples with red and yellow areas indicating high potential visibility and blue to black areas denoting low visibility (Plate 3).

Results

Comparison of the temples, differences and similarities

Examining the cumulative viewshed and access analyses for the temples in the sample immediately suggests a number of observations. While on the one hand the monuments do display a number of similar characteristics, particularly in access and movement, idiosyncrasies can also be observed in the particular way in which each arranges its own spatio-visual appearance.

For access analysis, the pattern visible at Ġgantija (Plate 2) is generally representative; revealing a rather simple arrangement of movement possibilities with two groups of apsidal rooms located side by side which open onto a shared open courtyard area. This court is the most accessible location in the structure and simultaneously has the greatest potential for reaching all other locations. The only truly difficult areas to access are the deepest areas of the building (perhaps exactly what we might expect). The temple which contrasts most starkly with these two temples is that at Tarxien, probably because its final phase seems to have developed from the complicated combination of a number of earlier structures. Tarxien presents possibilities for unmonitored movement through its interconnected corridors which are much more complicated than that of the other temples, a fact which must have had great significance for ritual performance there (Plate 4).

Visually, the temples display greater individualistic patterning. Tarxien presents a very structured view from its main court (Plate 5), directly upon a focal point at the end of its main axis through rooms 1, 4, and 6, but also contains a number of extremely remote and private areas. Other temples such as Ġgantija tend to be much more freely inter-visible and focus and control the viewer's vista much less aggressively (Plate 3). Significantly, Mnajdra (Plate 6), Ta' Ħagrat (Plate 7) and Ħaġar Qim (Plate 8), despite their very different structural arrangements, all manage to provide a very similar vista to the outside viewer. This effect, which must have been deliberately created, causes the viewer to witness a visual replication of the opening facade located further inside the temple. In fact, the view from the south of Mnajdra and the north of Ħaġar Qim can be said to be nearly identical.

On the other hand, a clear distinction may be observed between the temples and mortuary complexes. Because the Brochtorff Circle at Xagħra is not preserved in enough detail (or completely excavated enough) it is not possible to say exactly how closely it mirrors Ħal Saflieni, but the hypogeum is certainly in a class of its own with respect to the Temples. Despite having a large number of architectural motifs in common, such as oval shaped spaces, *trilithon*, inward sloping roofs and square openings cut through stones, the spatial arrangement of these visual motifs produces an entirely different visual effect (Plate 9).

Ritual uses, revelations; rope holes – staged openings

Revelations about the possibilities presented by the Maltese temples for the performance of ritual suggested by the results are no less interesting. Every temple creates numerous areas of low visibility in close proximity to areas of high accessibility. This arrangement will have facilitated sudden movement from the 'hidden' areas to regions of 'display.' The temples therefore seem to be purpose-built for the process of revelation or epiphany; perhaps rituals involved the unveiling aspects of cult or secret attributes of the deity or deities of the temples.

The clearest example of this arrangement is the temple at Ta' Ħagrat, where emphasis upon the central, sunken area eclipses all other zones in the complex. Priests bearing objects stored in these rooms could easily have appeared from these areas in order to allow for the epiphany to take place to an audience outside. Further emphasizing the 'epiphanic' nature of temples is the suggestion that doorways within the structure could be closed or opened with some manner of door or screen. 'Rope holes' and single 'post holes' have been identified in a number of the doorways of these structures implying that either a symbolic or physical barrier could be erected barring access and/or visibility to deeper areas of the structure. The dramatic revelation of mysteries to an audience located on the platform outside of the temple might have been a component of the rituals for which these temples were designed (Hayden 1990; Tilley and Bennett 2004) and may follow a principle similar to that proposed for Minoan tripartite doors (Hitchcock 1994).

Artefacts – private locations; deposition, ritual, visibility and the taphonomic process

From the start it was the intention of the Templeton project to coordinate all of the research resulting from the project through a single spatially related database using geographical information systems (GIS). Each of these locations was coordinated within a geo-referenced database of the islands including a digital elevation model (DEM). This is important because it allows for the comparison of our results between all of the sites and because it means that the results of work of various team members can now be brought together for combined analysis.

This has been the case particularly for the archival work carried out by David Barrowclough on the find spots of artefacts recovered from the temples at Mnajdra, Ħaġar Qim and most especially Tarxien using the original day books of Zammit and other authors. By assigning each of the objects a 'visual index' on the basis of the grid viewshed polygon in which it is located within the GIS model, it was possible to quantify exactly how 'visible' a given object would have been. (In this process exact precision with regard to the location of the objects has only been possible in Tarxien, where Zammit's precise records permit a more accurate reconstruction of find spots. Elsewhere, an average based on the visibility of the room from which the objects were recovered was assigned. Nevertheless, the more generalised results from Mnajdra and Ħaġar Qim support the more detailed results from Tarxien.)

The most striking observation to be made about the objects is their nearly universally low visibility index – in nearly all cases less than 10 per cent of the observed points offered visibility (Plate 5). Only especially visible artefacts, such as several recovered from temple forecourt areas and the engraving of the temple found in the north temple at Mnajdra break this trend. Initial examination of the differences between these visually remote objects however, suggests that stone objects or tools, flint flakes, pottery scatters, bowls and cones might be somewhat more visible, whilst moveable statues and statue fragments, horn cores, bones, and temple models are the most invisible. Perhaps this suggests a hierarchy of importance within the sample, with more important objects stored safely out of view whilst more common or functional objects were discarded within general view. Certainly stone flakes could easily have been neglected and permanently placed stone bowls would have been more difficult to move. It seems likely that the patterning of the artefact distribution with regard to visibility derives from a variety of depositional and post-depositional factors including ease of transport, intrinsic value and a variety of culturally patterned values such as significance or meaning. We must also remember that the assemblage examined in this research speaks most strongly to the post-Temple period abandonment process of the sites which may have involved a closure ritual (Stoddart this volume) that is seen in a number of early monumental sites (Piggott 1962; Schmidt 2006). These are the objects which were not taken away from the site or disposed of in the final phases of its use. Surely the lack of visibility of these objects played a role in their survival into modern times. This conclusion is supported by the fact that the most visible artefacts are those which could not be moved (such as decoration or built-in features). The power of spatio-visual characteristics upon formulation of the archaeological record and taphonomic processes is perhaps the most interesting result from this analysis and was an entirely unexpected bonus in our research.

Conclusions

It has not been the purpose of this paper to suggest aspects of meaning or to present a symbolic interpretation of the rituals performed in the temples, but rather to suggest what types of performance rituals would have been likely given the structural arrangement of the monuments themselves and to situate the possibilities for liturgical action within the Maltese megaliths as far as such actions related to motion and visibility. The strongest initial conclusions in this regard relate control of display to the relatively high visual seclusion of the find spots of objects within them. In the interpretation of these objects we must therefore consider their liturgical use for 'revelation' and their possible associations with 'hidden' or secret components of the deity or the practice of worship within the temples.

The megalithic temples of Malta are complex and multi-faceted monuments, which were clearly designed to perform a number of different ritual functions. No doubt there were components of the daily ritual life of the temples which are not related to the spatial qualities we have examined, but certainly the shapes and arrangements of the stones suggest that it was a very important component of their purpose. The research presented by this paper suggests that continued quantification and examination of the phenomenological effects created by the buildings, rather than simply depending on individual experience, may reveal even more aspects of the use of these monuments and the intentions of their builders.

Acknowledgements

We wish to thank Caroline Malone for the opportunity to contribute to this valuable project of research; and David A. Barrowclough for his work on the Zammit archive; and the Templeton and Leverhulme Foundations for supporting the research.

References

Bonanno, A., Gouder, T., Malone, C. and Stoddart, S. 1990. Monuments in an island society: the Maltese context. *World Archaeology* 22(2), 190–205.

Clark, D. 2004. Building logistics. In D. Cilia (ed.). *Malta Before History*. Malta: Miranda, 367–377.

Evans, J. D. 1971. *The prehistoric antiquities of the Maltese islands: a survey*. London: Athlone Press.

Hanson, J. 1998. *Decoding Homes and Houses*. Cambridge: Cambridge University Press.

Hayden, C. 1990. *The Social Organisation of Space in Buildings of the Temple Period of the Maltese Islands*. BSc thesis, University College, London.

Hillier, B. and Hanson, J. 1984. *The Social Logic of Space*. Cambridge: Cambridge University Press.

Hitchcock, L. A. 1994. The Minoan Hall System: Writing the Present out of the Past. In M. Locock, (ed.). *Meaningful Architecture: Social Interpretations of Buildings*. Worldwide Archaeology Series. Aldershot, Hampshire, Avebury, 14–43.

Malone, C. A. T., Stoddart, S. K. F., Trump, D., Bonanno, A. and Pace, A. (eds) 2007. *Mortuary ritual in prehistoric Malta. The Brochtorff Circle excavations (1987–1994)*. Cambridge: McDonald Institute.

Piggott, S. 1962. *The West Kennet Long Barrow*. London: HMSO.

Schmidt, K. 2006. *Sie bauten die ersten Tempel. Das rätselhafte Heiligtum der Steinzeitjäger*. Munich: C. H. Beck Verlag.

Tilley, C. Y. and Bennett, W. 2004. *The materiality of stone: explorations in landscape phenomenology*. Oxford: Berg.

Zammit, T. 1930. *Prehistoric Malta, the Tarxien Temples*. Oxford-London: Oxford University Press.

Chapter 8

PUTTING CULT IN CONTEXT: RITUAL, RELIGION AND CULT IN TEMPLE PERIOD MALTA

David A. Barrowclough

Introduction

Recently there has been renewed interest in the archaeological study of religion. This follows the recognition of a lacuna in our understanding of symbolic behaviour. A number of publications concerned with religion have appeared (e.g. Cauvin 1994; Lewis-Williams 2002; Insoll 2004). Despite this there still remains a gap in our understanding of the relationship between ritual, religion and cult. This paper suggests a different approach to this relationship using elements of the Maltese Neolithic Temple Period cultural assemblage as a case study to offer some new insights into the problem.

In what follows emphasis is placed upon a contextual approach, based upon study of actual find spots within the archipelago, where there are indications that cult observances may have been carried out. In order to establish this, rules of procedure for the identification of prehistoric ritual, religion, and cult from the archaeological remains have to be laid out. In the next section definitions of ritual, religion and cult, together with their archaeological correlates, will be considered further, before the contextual analysis of the Maltese evidence for this symbolic activity is undertaken, and some tentative conclusions offered.

Definitions

Consideration has to be given to how we define ritual, religion and cult, identifying the key distinction between each, before we can turn to their recovery from the archaeological record (see Introduction, this volume). Here, as with discussion of Neolithic Malta, the intention is not to produce a definitive review of the existing literature; space will not allow for this. Instead the approach is to focus on producing working definitions, which can usefully be deployed as tools in distinguishing between each category.

Ritual suggests repetition of a custom, habit or practice of a group or class of people. Importantly for the present discussion it can refer to both secular and religious activities. The ceremonies associated with, for example, student gradations or admission into certain professions, although ritualised (see Douglas 1996 [1970], 1–20), they are structured customs, are not dependent upon religious belief, nor need they involve any form of religious observance. In order to understand the difference between different types of ritual we need to distinguish between religious activity and secular activity.

The definition of religion has been the subject of much debate (Tylor 1873; Durkheim 1947 [1912]; Geertz 1973) recently reviewed by Insoll (2004, 6–8). As Colin Renfrew has pointed out, attempts at a single definition have often failed (Renfrew 1994 and revisited in this volume), while Insoll's conclusion that it is 'in many respects indefinable' (2004, 7), although understandable, does not advance the present discussion. I must therefore offer a working definition, recognising that it will inevitably prove to be less than perfect: religion can be understood as the formalised recognition of some higher, unseen, divine power as having control over human destiny, and as a consequence is worthy of reverence, obedience and organised worship.

What then of the distinction between religion and cult? Cult should be distinguished from religion. For some writers the two have seemed interchangeable. This is implied by Insoll who says that he finds the term to be 'weak' (Insoll 2004, 5), because it has connotations of the 'marginal' and 'freakish' (cf. Pfeiffer 1957, 55). He prefers the term 'religion' implying that it can be adopted as an alternative term. Similarly, Renfrew, this volume, retreats from his earlier use of 'cult' (Renfrew 1985) saying that he now prefers to use the word 'religion'. Cult is not synonymous with religion. I define it as a particular form of religious worship that implies devotion to a particular person or thing. For me it does suggest something that is less than a religion, and to that extent I agree with Insoll, if that is what he meant by the word marginal. I disagree that it is necessarily 'freakish', that is to interpret cult through modern eyes, where the term is often applied to contemporary fringe beliefs. Certainly, in the case of Classical Greece where cult worship was widespread, there was nothing 'freakish' about the practice. It is perhaps better to think of cult as small-scale, perhaps local. Whilst the cult rite may be elaborate, in comparison to religion, which is larger in scale and in contemporary society national/supranational, cult is less systemic. In the case of Classical Greece cult worship was widespread, and yet its scale was small. At the level of the individual, of the household and of the community the practice was both personal, in the case of ancestor veneration, and small scale, at the level of the temple and the City State.

Rather than a weakness, it is the *strength* of the term 'cult' that it allows one to distinguish between religion and other forms of worship, which may either exist independently, or lie within a mainstream religion as a sub-set of beliefs. It is also important because occasionally from small scale localised beliefs develop larger mainstream religions. This relationship is exemplified by the case of the Jewish cult that surrounded the historical Jesus, out of which grew the religion of Christianity. In that instance, the first cult was peripheral, 'marginal' to use Insoll's language, to mainstream Jewish belief. Cults may be the building blocks upon which later religions are founded, but equally, cults may emerge out of larger pre-existing religions. There is therefore an important relationship between cult and religion, but the two are distinct.

In summary, both religion and cult involve ritual practices, but because ritual has both secular and religious aspects it need involve neither religion nor cult. Religion, as the organised worship of a divine power, may be based upon an original cult and/or may have within it cult activity. Cult is therefore something less in terms of scale and of complexity than a religion, whilst maintaining close affinities to religion, sharing as it does elements of worship.

The problem: distinguishing between religion and cult ritual

How do we distinguish between ritual, religion and cult in the archaeological record? Ruth Whitehouse (1992, Chapter 4, and revisited in this volume) identified religious ritual based on site form and location. Inaccessible locations suggested ritual use when associated with natural features such as stalactites, wall paintings, burials and 'special' deposits such as food, miniature artefacts and exotic items. Colin Renfrew first addressed the problem of separating ritual from other types of activity, and in particular, of identifying religious ritual activity from other activities, by suggesting his 'Archaeological Indicators of Ritual' (Renfrew and Bahn 1991, 390–91 repeated and expanded upon in Renfrew 1994, 51–52). He suggested sixteen indicators, separated into four classes, identified as: the existence of attention focusing devices, the existence of a

boundary zone between this world and the next, evidence for the presence of a deity, and evidence for the participation in worship and making of offerings. This approach assumes that religious ritual employs a range of material culture specific to that activity, and relies upon detailed contextual analysis (see Introduction this volume for discussion) of the archaeological assemblage in order to identify this class of object/monument. It is open to the criticism that to a greater or lesser extent religious and secular life may be combined (see Robertson Smith 1889, 29), in which case clear distinctions between one and the other may not exist (*contra* Durkheim 1947 [1912]). With that caveat in mind I suggest that Renfrew's indicators of religious ritual are a sensible place to begin when considering how one may go about distinguishing between religion and cult activity in the archaeological record.

Having adopted a contextual analysis (see also Biehl this volume) to data in order to establish that a site is first of a ritual nature and then that the ritual was religious in character, it is necessary to ask whether we can distinguish between cult activity and religion. Whether or not this will be possible will be dependent upon the nature and extent of the archaeological record. In many cases data will not facilitate this fine-grained analysis, but in others it may be possible.

A key difference between cult and religion is the degree and extent of structured worship. Religion is formalised belief expressed through organised worship at a scale beyond the level of the household or community. In order to investigate the extent of organisation and structure, and thus distinguish between cult and religion, what are required are comparable data sets from a series of sites within a geographic region where religious ritual has already been identified. Comparison between these sites should reveal the extent to which they share similar material culture. The more features that different sites have in common, the more likely it is that organised religion was taking place across a region. If, for example, the attention focusing devices follow a similar design, are located in similar positions within a building and that the buildings share similar floor plan then it may be argued that a formalised religion exists. If on the other hand the archaeological assemblage for a region, although pointing to the existence of religious ritual, perhaps because of significant redundancy (see Rappaport 1979, 175; Briault this volume), is markedly different between sites the existence of a formalised religion may be doubted, and instead it may be argued that that it points to a series of localised cults. It stands that if one were to find a combination of the two, a high degree of formalised structure across the majority of sites, but with an occasional deviant from the norm, one may suggest that what has been found is a system of religious belief within which was operating a cult. In the case study that follows I will explore the possibility that this approach offers for understanding the relationship between ritual religion and cult in practice.

Investigating religion and cult, the case of Neolithic Malta

The Maltese archipelago was the location for megalithic activity on a large scale during the Neolithic (Evans 1971). The so-called temples number twenty-eight, five of which are on the smaller island of Gozo, with the remainder on the mainland of Malta (Figure 1.1). In addition are two hypogea complexes, at Ħal Saflieni on Malta and at Xagħra on Gozo. The communities that built these structures were also responsible for elaborate material culture: pottery, carved statues and ornament (e.g. Figures 5.4 and 11.1–5). These objects and structures are what most distinguishes the Maltese Neolithic from other Neolithic cultures in the Mediterranean. Yet the whole notion of a prehistoric Maltese religion still stands in need of critical re-evaluation.

What is missing in existing studies of Maltese prehistory is an awareness of the structural relationships between people, objects and places, and the material dimensions of these relations in social practices that enable a distinction to be drawn between ritual, religion and cult. Recent research in Malta (Malone *et al.* in prep.), made possible a detailed analysis of the Temple Period monuments and their associated material culture. In particular working with the original excavation diaries of Sir Themistocles Zammit (Zammit unpublished) a contextual analysis of the relationship between individual finds and monuments was possible. For the first time (but see Vella this volume) the significance of particular artefacts could be studied on the basis of patterns of association documented by their exact find context. Using these data the following questions were addressed.

Was there a Maltese religion? That is to say, was there at any time during the Neolithic a sufficient degree of uniformity in religious ritual practice within the island archipelago to warrant our speaking of a single 'religion', or are we better to think of ritual activity in terms of individual cult practices? If the latter is true, what were the regional variations at any given time during the Neolithic of cult practices within the Maltese islands?

Monuments as temples, identifying ritual

As Katya Stroud has pointed out (this volume) the association between monument and religion has become entrenched in the term temple, which is now the most popular and widespread interpretation for these archaeological monuments. But what evidence do we have that they served a religious function? We need to critically reassess this interpretation before our understanding of them can go further.

The approach is to test data against the Archaeological Indicators of Religion (Renfrew 1994, 51–52). Taking each monument in turn the various criteria suggested by Renfrew were applied to determine the extent to which they fit the definition of ritual in a religious context. The results, summarised in Table 8.1, reveal a strong correlation between the key indicators of religious ritual and the material culture of the Maltese megaliths. It is therefore felt appropriate to continue to use the term 'temple' in the discussion that follows as convenient shorthand, although this is not to imply that the practices performed in these buildings necessarily bore any relation to those of contemporary religions.

Cult in the Maltese context

Previous discussion of the Neolithic megaliths has been satisfied with an uncritical interpretation of them as temples (e.g. Renfrew 1973, Chapter 8), the locus for some poorly understood, yet clearly identifiable religious activity. As such there has been an implicit assumption that the structures were part of a single Maltese religion. The focus has been on using this idea as the basis for hypothetical territorial reconstruction (Renfrew 1973, 168, figure 33). Although Grima's approach (Grima this volume and 2005) was somewhat different, his focus was on the environment, placing the temples in their landscape setting, the assumption remained, that they were part of a religion that spanned the archipelago. This interpretation requires critical evaluation.

What distinguishes religion from cult is the recurrence of a structured form of worship across a region. This will be evident from close examination of the ritual monuments. In the case of Malta even a cursory glance at the site plans for the various temples (e.g. Figure 5.1) reveals that no two are identical. Ħaġar Qim for example, is circular in form with a clear line of site through the central passage, which is very different to the other temples, which have a single entrance/exit facing onto a ceremonial forecourt. Ta Haġrat has a different axis to other temples. It consists of two connected structures. The larger building lies on an axis running south-east to north-west and the small building south-south-west to north-north-east. Within temples which appear to be similar there are subtle differences. Mnajdra and Ġgantija appear at first similar. Both have the form of a paired of lobed structures with large forecourts off which each of the entrances to the two temples run. But this apparent similarity is masked by considerable differences. Temple A at Mnajdra has a raised platform off which runs the entrance, which takes the form of a double or possibly triple doorway, whereas all other temples have single doorways leading into them. At Tarxien the lobed format is extended through a series of phases linking three temples into a single structure. At Ħaġar Qim the 'ancillary

	Tarxien	Ħaġar Qim	Mnajdra	Skorba	Kordin III	Ġgantija	Ta Ħaġrat	Buġibba	Ħal Saflieni	Xagħra Circle
Special building	*	*	*	*	*	*	*	*	*	*
Altars	*	*	*	*	*	*	*	*		*
Benches	*	*	*			*		*	*	
Ritual vessels	*	*	*	*	*	*	*	*	*	*
Redundancy in symbols	*	*	*	*		*		*		
Public arena – Forecourt	*	*	*	*	*	*	*	*	*	*
Private areas – Chambers	*	*	*	*	*	*	*	*	*	*
Basins	*	*	*		*		*		*	*
Representation of deity	*	*	*	*		*	*	*	*	*
Iconography of animals	*	*		*			*	*	*	
Restricted movement – Rope holes	*	*	*	*	*	*	*	*	*	
Sacrifice of animals	*	*	*	*		*	*			*
Offerings of food and drink	*	*	*	*	*	*	*	*	*	*
Votive offerings	*	*	*	*	*	*	*	*	*	*
Investment in buildings	*	*	*	*	*	*	*	*	*	*
Investment in offerings	*	*	*	*	*	*	*	*	*	*
Human Bone									*	*
Threshold	*	*	*	*	*	*	*	*	*	*

Table 8.1. Archaeological Indicators of Religion for Maltese Neolithic monuments. This table highlights considerable evidence pointing toward the ritual religious use of Maltese megaliths. Using Renfrew's framework of the Archaeological Indicators of Ritual the megalithic buildings contain all the major elements associated with religious ritual. They employ a series of attention focusing devices, including altars and hearths, located along site lines, and often richly decorated with repeated symbols and motifs. A boundary zone between this world and the next is incorporated within the monuments in the form of elaborate raised thresholds set into entrance passageways, which separate external courtyard areas, apparently designed for conspicuous public display, from more private interior chambers and niches where exclusive mysteries may have been revealed. Thresholds between one and the other are marked by steps, and often decoration, and delimited by ropes or bars that would have been fixed in notches cut into the passage walls. Concepts of cleanliness and pollution are reflected in the existence of large numbers of libation holes and basins, which were located at entrances and at the sides of altars. The presence of the deity is represented by ritualistic symbols, statues and carvings of human figures may relate iconographically to the deities worshipped and to their associated myth. Animal symbolism, particularly of sheep/goat and bulls, reflected in art, together with evidence for their sacrifice and consumption is widespread. All this suggests considerable investment of wealth, not only in terms of sacrifice, but also in the rich decoration and paraphernalia of objects found within the monuments, and in the resources invested in their construction. The evidence points to the monuments having first ritual and second religious function, as such the term 'temple' may well seem appropriate.

building' represent the possible remains of two other temples, which were not connected together. The structures of Ħal Saflieni and Xagħra Circle have always been considered separately to the temples, because they are subterranean and were the only structures to enclose human remains. These differences mask considerable similarities between hypogea and temples: the corbelled roof, niches, ceramic assemblages suggest that they should not be considered in isolation but as another variant within the corpus of Neolithic monuments.

The differences in structure are matched by analysis of the archaeological assemblages recovered from the temples. In the past, emphasis has been placed upon similarities between these. The emphasis has been on the presence of corpulent, asexual figurines, the large amounts of pottery and the frequency of animal bone, were all taken as evidence for a unified religion. More instructive are the differences in material culture identified through re-analysis of the Zammit archives.

The most iconic of the Neolithic artefacts are site specific. The Sleeping Lady and other sleeping figures are unique to Ħal Saflieni, the Seated Pair are unique to Xagħra Circle (Figure 11.3; Malone *et al.* 2007), the Venus figure is unique to Skorba (Trump 1966), Tarxien has unique Priest Figures and animal carvings, and Buġibba has a unique fish carving. In fact, upon close examination, the material culture of each temple begins to take on a unique flavour, and as a consequence, I question the notion that there was a single unifying Maltese religion. Instead what we may be witnessing is evidence of a number of different cult centres, each dedicated to a different deity as represented by the iconography of the temple.

If this is so we need to re-evaluate our model for Maltese society. Rather than applying a familiar 'Christian' mode of religion to the past, we should look to alternative models that better represent cult beliefs, for example the cults of Classical Greece. Reinterpreting Maltese ritual in terms of cult would help explain one of the problems that current interpretations encounter, that temples while widely spaced around the island, tend also to be found in small clusters: in pairs or triplets (Figure 1.1). Thus, Kordin I, II and III are found close together, and not far from Ħal Saflieni and Tarxien. Mnajdra and Ħaġar Qim are likewise found close together. These groupings are problematic to interpretations that see each temple as a territorial centre. 'Why each territory should contain two temples...is not at first clear, but this pairing in the spatial distribution of the temples must surely reflect some aspect of prehistoric Maltese social organization' (Renfrew 1973, 168).

If we adopt an interpretation of temples as cult shrines the problem of clustering dissolves. The population of a territory may have had split allegiances between different cults, or may have worshipped different gods, at different times, for different reasons. This would explain why temples

could be found close together. Adopting a cult ritual explanation also accounts for the problem of the 'missing' dead. At present only two hypogea are known, whilst each contains many thousands of body parts, together they still account for only a small percentage of the estimated ancient population. This poses a problem: if Malta were subject to an overarching religious belief that required the dead to be buried in hypogea, where are the remainder of the population? This problem disappears if one accepts that there is no overarching religion. Instead there were a series of cults, some of which adopted burial in hypogea, while others adopted less archaeologically visible methods.

Greenstone axe pendants – cult amulets?

Space prevents me from discussing all forms of evidence that support this view. Instead I propose to focus in detail upon a single example. I have selected greenstone axes because their study will complement discussion of other aspects of Temple Period Malta found elsewhere in this volume (Trump; Stroud; Grima; Anderson and Stoddart; Malone; Stoddart; Skeates; Tilley; Townsend). There is no need for me to dwell upon aspects of landscape, burial or monumentality at any length when they have already been covered so thoroughly. Instead I wish to focus attention on the cult practices of fragmentation and accumulation associated with this particular form of material culture, stone pendants, in the context of Maltese ceremonial buildings, as a means to say something new about a cult practice through which social relations were created and maintained within the island archipelago during the Neolithic.

Pendants, pierced stones, often but not exclusively fashioned from greenstone (Figure 8.1) have been considered elsewhere (Skeates 1995, 279–301; Leighton and Dixon 1992, 179–200; Leighton 1989, 135–159). They indicate contact with the world beyond the archipelago. The metamorphic rock, from which they are made, is best represented in Calabria. A few are of basaltic rock from volcanic deposits in the area of Mount Etna, and one (from Xagħra Circle) is of jadeite traced to the Alps (Malone *et al.* 2007, and pers. comm.). They all originate outside the island context.

The distribution of pendants (Table 8.2) reveals that whilst they are found at a limited number of places, these include both temple, particularly Tarxien (12 examples) and hypogea contexts (53 and 201 examples). This may confirm my earlier suggestion that the distinction between temple and hypogea is not as clear cut as we might imagine. Factors other than the presence or absence of human burials may have been important in categorising sites in the Neolithic. Where greenstone axe pendants are found it is often in large numbers, either in a cache as at Tarxien, or in the hypogea, where they were found in large numbers from necklaces.

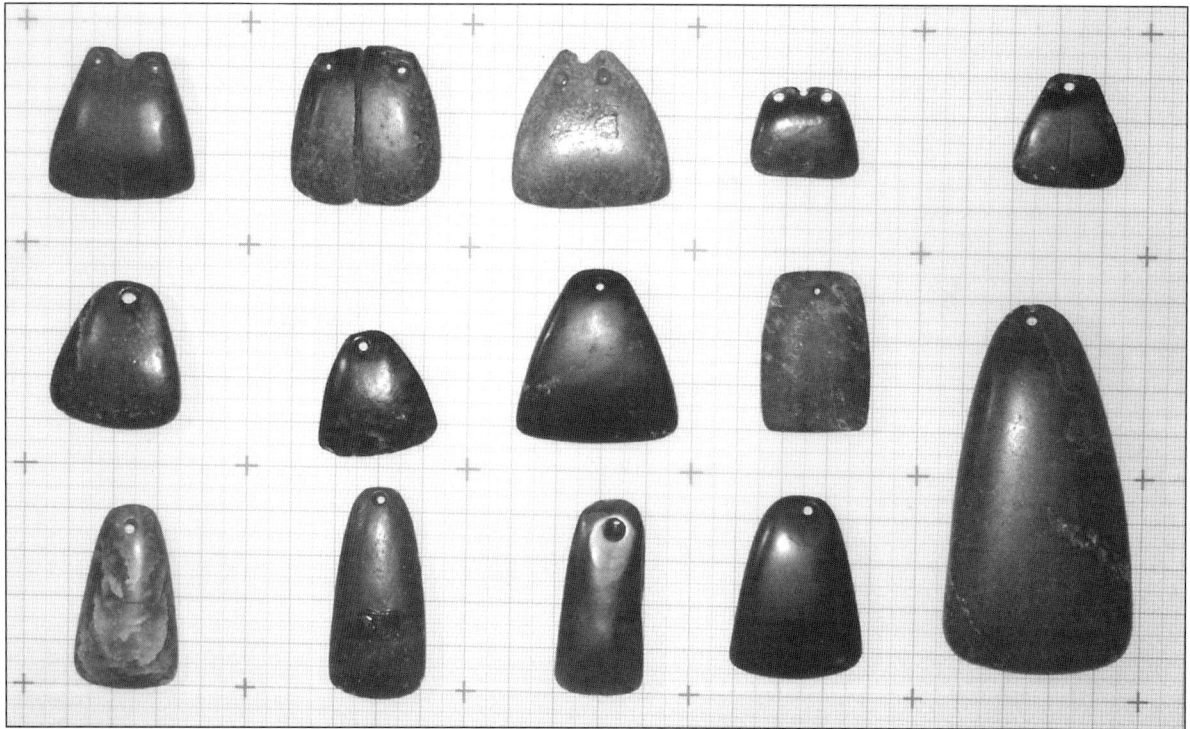

Figure 8.1. Examples of greenstone axe pendants from Neolithic sites within the Maltese archipelago (with thanks to the National Museum of Archaeology of Malta).

Site	Reference	Number
Ta Ħaġrat	Mg/S4	1
Kordin I	K1/S2	1
Kordin II	Lost	1
Mnajdra	Mn/S3	1
Skorba	SKPC71962/2 & SKRD2/1963/1	2
Tarxien	T/S43-6	12
Xagħra Circle	Various	53
Ħal Saflieni	S/S2, 26-30	201
Xemxija Tomb 5	Xe5/S1	2
Għar Dalam	GD/S8a & GD/S8b	2
Unprovenanced	UN	1
	Total	289

Table 8.2. Distribution of greenstone axe pendants within the Maltese archipelago. Source Evans 1971, Malone et al. 2007.

If we accept that greenstone axe pendants were amulets, worn by adherents of a cult, we may begin to understand their distribution. I postulate that Tarxien was the site of this cult. It was there that these comparatively rare, imported, objects were bestowed upon initiates. Adherents wore the amulets about their neck, during life and were buried with them. The funerary rite of this cult required burial in hypogea. This explains the limited distribution of these objects, but to be more than mere speculation it requires evidence which may be gleaned through careful analysis of the Zammit diaries.

The greenstone axe pendants were found in a cache (Table 8.3), in and around a peculiar area which Zammit called the Oracle Room (Figure 8.2). The Oracle Room

Find Location	Reference	Number
Oracle Room	T/S 43	4
Oracle Room	T/S 44	2
Oracle Room	T/S 45	1
Unknown	T/S 46	5

Table 8.3. Find location of greenstone axe pendants, Tarxien Temple. Source Zammit unpublished and 1920, 194.

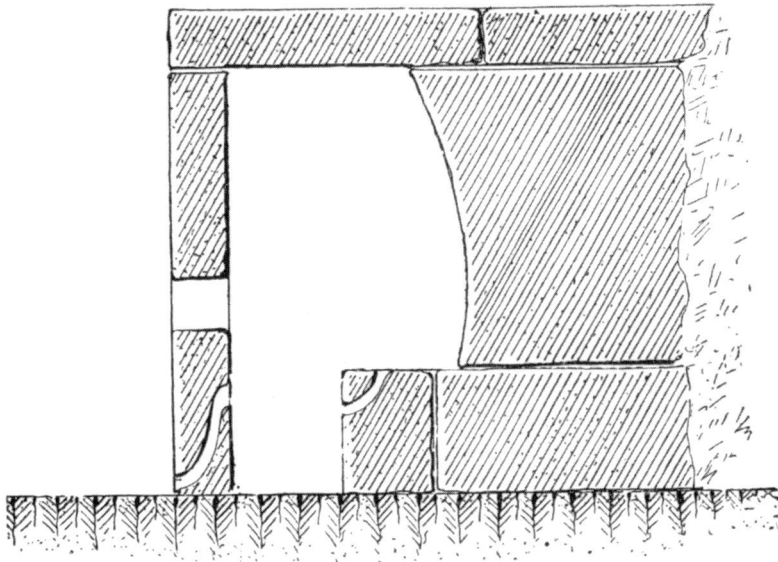

Figure 8.2. Section through Oracle Room, Tarxien Temple. Source Zammit 1920, 182.

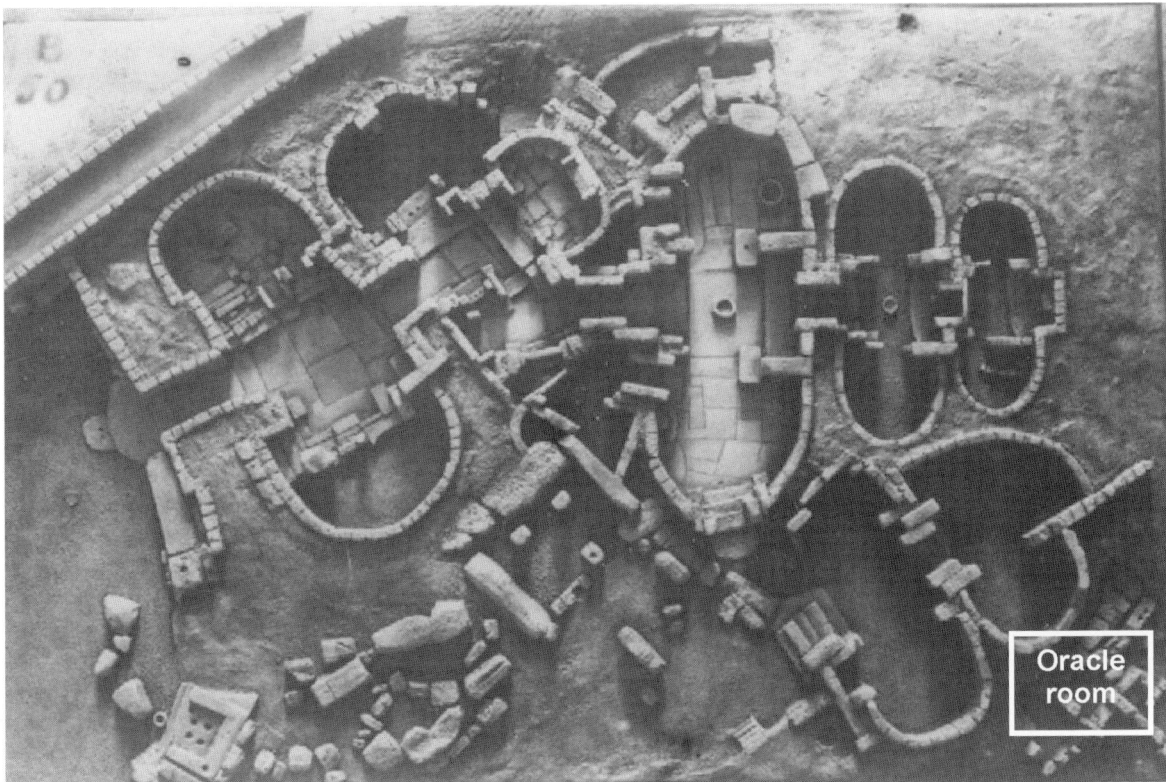

Figure 8.3. Model of Tarxien Temple with the location of the Oracle Room where 12 greenstone axe pendants were excavated marked. National Museum, Malta.

Figure 8.4. Fragmentation: the different stages of division of axe pendants. The original pendant (left) still retains part of its original single perforation, through which has been marked a dividing line, whilst two new holes have been drilled to either side. In the second photograph (centre) the process of division has begun. Finally, the axe is completely divided (right) creating two new smaller lozenge shaped pendants, one of which is shown in the photograph. (With thanks to the National Museum of Archaeology of Malta.)

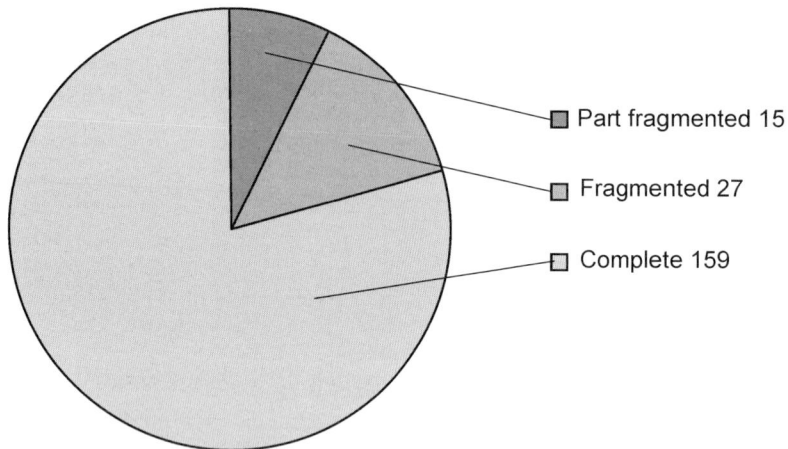

☐ Part fragmented 15

☐ Fragmented 27

☐ Complete 159

Figure 8.5. Fragmentation of greenstone axe pendants, Ħal Saflieni N=201.
In this analysis of the Ħal Saflieni pendants we can begin to see just how common the practice was. Of 201 pendants recorded from the site fifteen were part fragmented. There were a further twenty-seven fragments of axe pendant, that is of broken pieces. There remain 159 complete pendants, this number includes the products of early sub-divisions.

consisted of a stone chamber connected to one of the main apses by a small window like aperture and a sinuous channel. Zammit suggested that small objects, such as pendants could be dropped through the channel by a priest-like figure to worshippers (Figure 8.3).

In addition to data linking axe pendants to a specific ritual site there is evidence that the people who wore the ornaments were closely linked to one another through them. The pendants form the basis of enchained relationships through fragmentation that unite members of the cult. The mechanism for the creation of relationships through fragmentation has been described by John Chapman (2000) and can be explained as follows: the two people who wish to establish a social relationship through cult membership, the priest and the initiate, agree on a specific artefact, in this case the greenstone pendant, and break it in two parts, each keeping one as a token of the relationship. In turn, each part of the object may itself be further broken and passed to a third party, the next initiate. In this way a chain

of relationships between people and objects is created which binds the members of the cult together. The fragments of the object are then worn as an amulet until death. Reconstitution of the parts occurs in death when the individual members of the cult are buried in a structured way within hypogea with the amulets about their neck.

In the Maltese Neolithic we can see evidence for this type of fragmentation with the best evidence coming from Ħal Saflieni (Figure 8.5). In Figure 8.4 we see a number of examples of axe pendants that are in the process of fragmentation. It is difficult to be certain how frequently, or in what proportion, axes had been divided. Once split, and the parts polished, it is difficult to trace it back to its parent or even grand-parental pendant, and this is not strictly necessary. The important point is that the practice of fragmentation was a significant aspect of the repro-duction of cult in Neolithic Malta. The Tarxien cult is a structured way of connecting cultural material to the ancestors and their living kin.

Conclusion

Greenstone pendants were a means of strengthening the relationship between persons and objects, and the temple. The enchained relationships that linked members of the cult depended upon objects whose values were created out of an abstract value, ritual cult meaning. The cult involving the greenstone pendants was but one of several cults that I believe to have co-existed during the Neolithic. Adopting a contextual approach to data offers the potential to distinguish between ritual, religion and cult from which new insights into Maltese prehistoric symbolic activity can be gained, thus putting 'cult in context'.

Acknowledgements

The author acknowledges with thanks the support provided by the Templeton Foundation which enabled participation on the project as research assistant, the stimulus and encouragement provided by Caroline Malone, for introducing me to the archaeology of Malta and whose research on Maltese axes suggested the idea for this paper, and to Cynthianne Spitieri for her transcription of the Zammit Diaries. Thanks also to the staff of Heritage Malta and the National Museum of Archaeology, Valletta, for their unstinting help.

References

Biehl, P. 2007. Enclosing Places: a contextual approach to cult and religion in Neolithic Central Europe. In D. A. Barrowclough and C. A. T. Malone (eds). *Cult in Context, Reconsidering Ritual in Archaeology*. Oxford, Oxbow Books.

Briualt, C. 2007. The Ultimate Redundancy Package: routine, structure and the archaeology of ritual transmission. In D. A. Barrowclough and C. A. T. Malone (eds). *Cult in Context, Reconsidering Ritual in Archaeology*. Oxford, Oxbow Books.

Cauvin, J. 2000. *The Birth of the Gods and the Origins of Agriculture*. Cambridge, Cambridge University Press.

Chapman, J. 2000. *Fragmentation in Archaeology: people, places and broken objects in the prehistory of south-eastern Europe*. London, Routledge.

Douglas, M. 1996 [1970] Natural Symbols (2nd edn). London, Routledge.

Durkheim, E. 1947 [1912 edit. Trans. J. Swain]. *The Elementary Forms of the Religious Life*. London, Allen and Unwin.

Evans, J. D. 1971. *The Prehistoric Antiquities of the Maltese Islands*. London, The Athlone Press.

Geertz, C. 1973. The Interpretation of Cultures. New York, Basic Books.

Grima, R. 2005. *Monuments in Search of a Landscape: the landscape context of monumentality in late Neolithic Malta*. London, unpublished PhD thesis, Institute of Archaeology.

Grima, R. 2007. The cultural construction of the landscape in Late Neolithic Malta. In In D. A. Barrowclough and C. A. T. Malone (eds). *Cult in Context, Reconsidering Ritual in Archaeology*. Oxford, Oxbow Books.

Insoll, T. 2004. *Archaeology, Ritual, Religion*. London, Routledge.

Leighton, R. 1989. Ground stone tools from Serra Orlando (Morgantina) and stone axe studies in Sicily and Southern Italy. *Proceedings of the Prehistoric Society* 55, 135–159.

Leighton, R. and Dixon, J. E. 1992. Jade and greenstone in the prehistory of Sicily and Southern Italy. *Oxford Journal of Archaeology* 11(2), 179–200.

Lewis-Williams, D. 2002. *The Mind in the Cave*. London, Thames and Hudson.

Malone, C. 2007. Space, structure and ritual in prehistoric Malta. In D. A. Barrowclough and C. A. T. Malone (eds). *Cult in Context, Reconsidering Ritual in Archaeology*. Oxford, Oxbow Books.

Malone, C., Stoddart, S., Trump, D., Bonanno, A., the late Gouder, T. and Pace, A. 2007. In press. *Mortuary Ritual on Gozo: excavations at the Brochtorff Circle at Xaġhra (1987–1994)*. Cambridge, McDonald Institute for Archaeological Research.

Malone, C. and Stoddart, S. in prep. *Art, Cult and Context: a study of prehistoric ritual in early Malta*.

Pfeiffer, R. H. 1957. *Books of the Old Testament*. London, Black.

Rappaport, R. 1979. *Ecology, Meaning and Religion*. Berkeley, North Atlantic Books.

Renfrew, A. C. 1973. *Before Civilization: the radiocarbon revolution and prehistoric Europe*. London, Penguin Books.

Renfrew, A. C. 1985. *The Archaeology of Cult*. London: Thames and Hudson.

Renfrew, A. C. and Bahn, P. 1996. *Archaeology: Theories, Methods and Practice* (2nd edn). London, Thames and Hudson, 390–91.

Renfrew, A. C. 1994. The archaeology of religion. In A. C. Renfrew and E. B. W. Zubrow (eds). *The Ancient Mind, Elements of Cognitive Archaeology*. Cambridge, Cambridge University Press.

Robertson Smith, W. 1889. *The Religion of the Semites*. Edinburgh, A and C Black.

Skeates, R. 1995. Animate objects: a biography of prehistoric 'axe-amulets' in the central Mediterranean region. *Proceedings of the Prehistoric Society* 61, 279–301.

Stoddart, S. 2007. Maltese funerary cult in context. In D. A. Barrowclough and C. A. T. Malone (eds). *Cult in Context Conference* proceedings. Oxford, Oxbow Books.

Stroud, K. 2007. Forthcoming. Of giants and deckchairs: understanding the Maltese Temples. In D. A. Barrowclough and C. A. T. Malone (eds). *Cult in Context, Reconsidering Ritual in Archaeology*. Oxford, Oxbow Books.

Trump, D. H. 1966. *Skorba* (Reports of the Research Committee of the Society of Antiquaries of London, no. 22). London, Society of Antiquaries.

Trump, D. H. 2007. Maltese temple cult: the antecedents. In D. A. Barrowclough and C. A. T. Malone (eds). *Cult in Context, Reconsidering Ritual in Archaeology*. Oxford, Oxbow Books.

Tylor, H. B. 1873. *Primitive Culture*. London, Murray.

Whitehouse, R. D. 1992. *Underground Religion. Cult and Culture in Prehistoric Italy*. London, Accordia Specialist Studies on Italy 1.

Whitehouse, R. D. 2007. Underground Religion Revisited. In D. A. Barrowclough and C. A. T. Malone (eds). *Cult in Context, Reconsidering Ritual in Archaeology*. Oxford, Oxbow Books.

Zammit, T. 1920. Third report on the Hal-Tarxien excavations, Malta. *Archaeologia* 70, 1918–20, 181–200.

Zammit, T. Unpublished. Diaries of the excavations at Tarxien. Valletta, National Museum Archive. DAG.16.100 MSS 22, 24, 25, 26, 27.

Chapter 9

THE MALTESE DEATH CULT
IN CONTEXT

Simon Stoddart

Introduction

The cycle of life underwrites much ritual. In many comparative social studies, the social conception of the life cycle does not map directly onto the biological life cycle defined by science (Geertz 1966; 1973; Kopytoff 1971). The cycle of life is woven into a series of cycles extending back and forward in time, within a container of cosmological time. This short essay proposes to situate the expanding scale of the Maltese cult of death in this broader cyclical and cosmological framework, using the recently completed study of the Brochtorff Circle at Xagħra (Malone, *et al.* 2007). This ia a site which combines an unparalleled range of evidence of one phase in the life cycle, its closure, yet related so clearly to the broader cycles of time of this prehistoric society.

The funerary ritual was a performance by the living employing the material culture occasioned by the dead. This Maltese ritual has been situated elsewhere in its landscape, sensory and cosmological context (Stoddart 1999; 2002a; 2002b; Stoddart, *et al.* 1999). Performance was clearly enhanced by the full emersion of the individual in a sensory experience of space, sight, sound, taste (with closely associated smell) and time. The aim here is to integrate the different scales of time implicit in the articulation of the interrelated cycles of life (cf. Stoddart 2004): the individual, the descent group and the identity of the island population.

The chronological setting

The period between *c.* 4100 BC and 2400 BC in the Maltese islands forms a clear cycle of ritual development (Stoddart 1992). In the Żebbuġ phase (*c.* 4100/3800 BC), evidence is restricted to funerary ritual which was small scale and compartmentalised in small chambered tombs. In the Ġgantija phase (*c.* 3600–3000 BC), a new scale of public community space was added to an unchanged scale of funerary activity. In the final Tarxien phase (*c.* 3000–2400

BC), the public community space for life rituals was paralleled by a corresponding scale of public community space for death ritual. At the end of this ritual cycle, the public community spaces of life ritual appear to have been intentionally closed down and ritual activity restricted to a funerary ritual of a very different character (Tarxien Cemetery phase). This paper will concentrate on the two funerary phases prominent in the evidence recently investigated in the Brochtorff Circle at Xagħra: Żebbuġ and Tarxien.

Żebbuġ phase

The Żebbuġ funerary activity at the Circle comprised one and, almost certainly two, rock-cut chambered tombs, an open niche and most probably some single inhumations close to bedrock. The core funerary activity of the Żebbuġ phase was the small scale ritual of a descent group inserting deceased individuals within the bounds of a chambered tomb, as has been consistently identified in the two key sites of Ta' Trapna, Żebbuġ (Baldacchino and Evans 1954) and the main chambered tomb at the Brochtorff Circle at Xagħra (Malone, *et al.* 1995). In this core ritual, the individual life cycle was inserted within the longer life cycle of several generations of ancestors.

To confirm the scale of the contributing population to the ritual we can make an upper and lower estimate based on ranges of a) number of interred individuals, b) estimated age expectancy at birth and c) estimated period of use of the chambered tomb. The most problematic of these estimates is the estimated age expectancy at birth because the number of interred pre-adults is only 25% a figure that is almost certainly an under-representation of the total figure which should probably approach 50% for such populations (Chamberlain 1997). These upper and lower estimates are presented in Table 9.1, employing the standard formula for estimating the contributing population (Boddington 1987: 184):

$$P = \frac{e(0) \ B^1}{t}$$

where P is the estimated size of the contributing population, e(0) is the estimated age of death at birth, B^1 is the number of burials, and t is the length of use.

	Length of use (years): t	Number of burials (including pre-adult): B'	Expected age of death at birth: e(0)	Estimated size of contributing population: P
Upper estimate	300	72	45	10.8
Probable estimate	300	72	25	6
Lower estimate	700	65	25	2.3

Table 9.1. Gross estimates of the size of the contributing population to the Zebbug tomb.

As can be seen, these population estimates lie within the range of a single family over several generations. The other burial practices on the Xagħra site give an indication of where the younger members of the family were interred – in an open niche – and where other stages in the burial process may have taken place – in the form of single inhumations close to bedrock.

From this overall pattern we can infer that the main burial practice was the insertion of family members over a cycle of several generations into a family tomb. The burial practice was probably many staged. In some cases single inhumations took place outside the tomb and when a new body was introduced, it is highly probable that larger, indeed more individualised parts such as skull and long bones, were removed to make way for the new interment, since these bones are relatively under-represented. The younger members of the family were also under-represented and, from limited available evidence elsewhere on the site appear to have been interred or disposed of separately.

The Ġgantija phase

The burial practices of the intervening Ġgantija phase are very difficult to judge on the basis of current evidence. However, the available human bone assemblages from Xemxija and Xagħra, in the absence of clear stratigraphy from Ħal Saflieni, indicate a broad continuity of Żebbuġ practice. The life cycle of the individual was inserted within the life cycle of the family unit, by the repeated practice of insertion of the deceased in a family tomb. This was in contradistinction to the expanded scale of community ritual materialised in the elaborate monuments, generally designated 'temples'.

The Tarxien phase (c. 3000–2400 BC)

The final Tarxien phase undoubtedly represented the incorporation of the funerary cult into the scale of a community ritual. The precise scale is difficult to calibrate since the vast majority of the skeletons recovered were disarticulated. Some 190,000 fragments of human bone were found in Tarxien levels, with minimum numbers headed by skulls (823) and femora (735). Accurate estimates of the interred population are thus difficult.

Nevertheless, even if we accept these uncertainties and apply the same formula applied to the Żebbuġ data, it is clear that there could have been a between eighteen and ten fold increase in the contributing population (Table 9.2). This suggests minimally the involvement of a grouping of families, most probably of related descent groups. Furthermore the 'burying group' paralleled much more closely the expected life table of the 'dying group'. Not only was there a broad matching of the sexes (with the exceptions remarked on below), but also as much as 50% of the buried population was pre-adult at death, as might have been expected in an early agricultural population (Chamberlain 1997), although representation of the very young was at the lower end of the expected range (c. 18%) (Rega 1997). In spite of these greatly increased figures, the numbers fall short of the estimated prehistoric population for Gozo of between 1400 and 1800 (Clark 2004) and suggest either that the Circle served merely a village community on the Xagħra plateau or simply the elite portion of the population of the wider island. If the Circle served a village community there might have been as many as seven such communities on Gozo to complete the demographic picture. Alternatively, since the Ġgantija cluster of ritual structures was clearly pre-eminent on the island, it is entirely possible that some form of hegemony was practised over other parts of the same community with an accompanying privileged access to the burial rite.

The burial rite itself, on the completion of the biological life cycle, comprised a series of performance cycles after the primary deposition of any individual body. Some deposits (primarily the foundation deposits deeply seated within the stratigraphy of the site) remained broadly

	Length of use (years): t	Number of burials (including pre-adult): B'	Expected age of death at birth: e(0)	Estimated size of contributing population: P
Upper estimate	500	2103	45	189.2
Probable estimate	600	2103	25	87.6
Lower estimate	700	823	20	23.5

Table 9.2. Gross estimates of the size of the contributing population to the Tarxien burials.

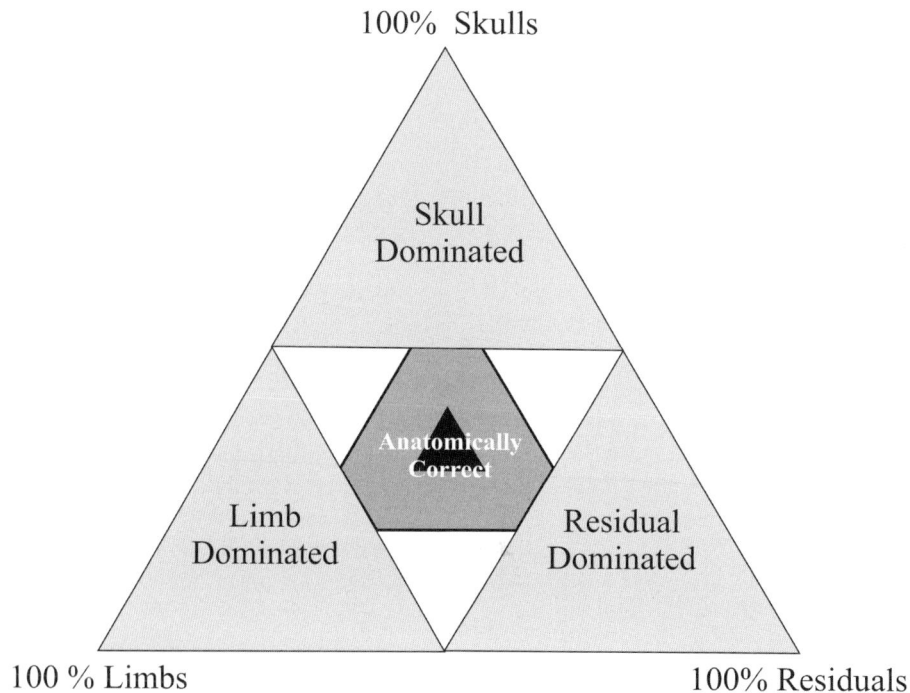

Figure 9.1. The relative proportion of skulls, long bones and residual bones in the archaeological deposit.

anatomically intact. Most of the performance cycles, however, sought to annihilate individual presence and transform individuals into a collective identity. The majority of deposits are consequently not intact. Some deposits (most notably the largest open display deposit) had disproportionate numbers of residual bones (that is primarily extremities) suggesting that these deposits had lost skulls and limb bones to other deposits. Correspondingly other deposits had larger numbers of limbs, and still others larger proportion of skulls (Figure 9.1). In part, this process may have been a natural consequence of graveyard management, the taphonomical effects of redigging of deposits, but the structured nature of some special deposits suggests that there was also a deliberate and intentional placing of parts together.

The importance of male memory in an enclosed space

An important characteristic of the remaining intact articulated bodies was both that a) they initiated and thus *founded* stratigraphic sequences of deposit and b) that (although in relatively low frequency) they were exclusively *male*. Three prominent instances occur of hidden males (Figure 9.2). The *first* is to the right of the threshold at the entrance to the site where a crouched male was placed at the foot of a pit filled with a sequence of skeletal remains culminating in a group of predominantly male skulls, most probably dating to an earlier period than the male at the start of the sequence. The *second* is at the base of the sacristy shrine in the heart of the site. A group of four males are succeeded by a further male and only then by a female bundle burial. This sequence forms the base of

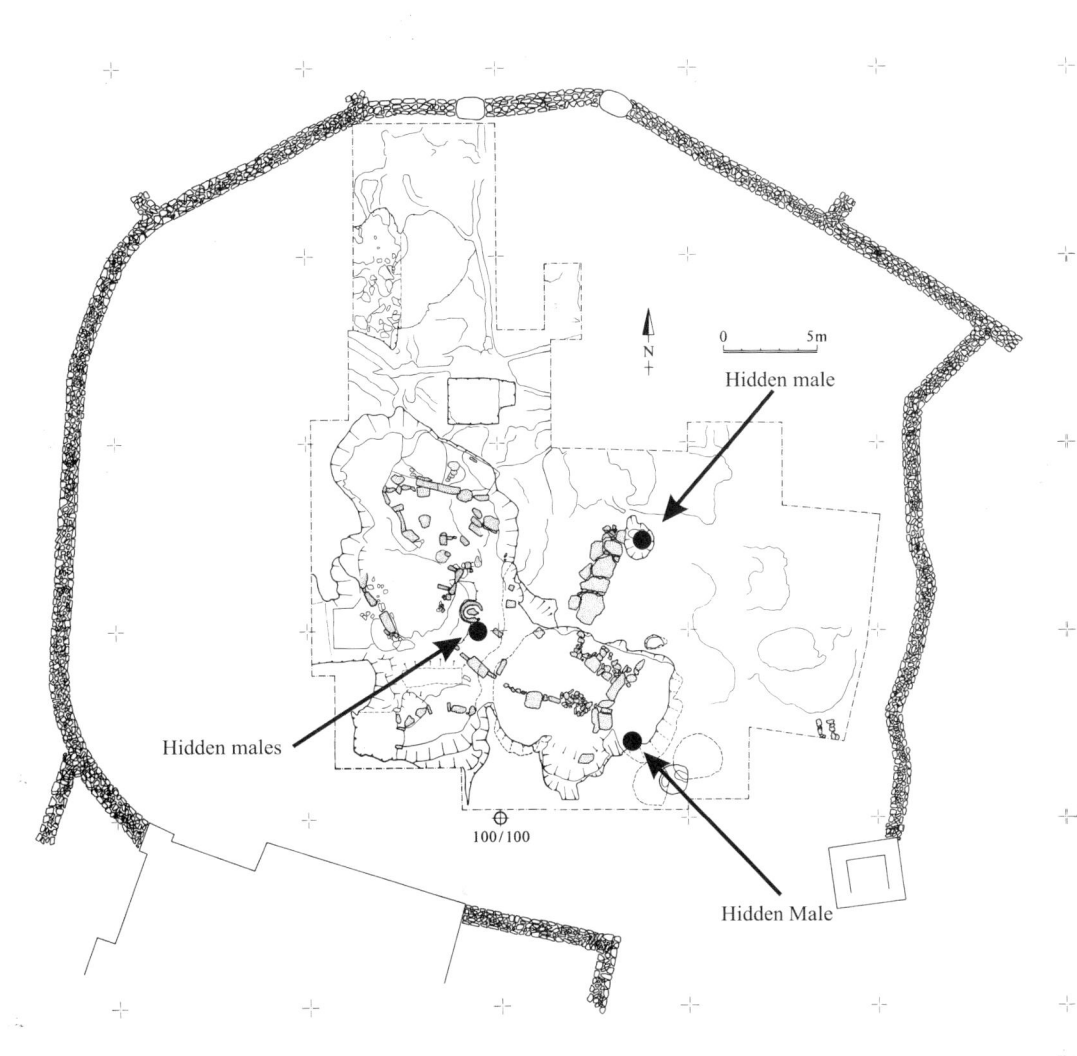

Figure 9.2. The location of hidden intact males (Brochtorff, Xagħra Circle).

sacristy shrine in which some of the most precious ritual objects were found at a higher level (see discussion of the symbolism of the life cycle below). The *third* is the foundation deposit of the innermost part of the inner cave where a male forms the basal deposit accompanied with little interruption by a female. All these microstratigraphies show the primacy of the male in ordering cycles of burial performance. The available radiocarbon dating also hints at complexities of re-arrangement to produce sometimes inverted chronologies that only a systematic dating programme will elucidate, but already strengthen the appearance of intentionality.

The whole cemetery was closely guarded by a megalithic enclosure marked originally by two uprights. The dead were thus symbolically bounded. The skeletal deposits show no signs of exposure either to the elements or to the depredation of wild animals. The males were the most guarded of the skeletal material as a consequence of their deep insertion within the stratigraphic deposit, a point that is analysed in more detail elsewhere (Malone and Stoddart, in press).

The symbolism of the life cycle

The emphasis on the life cycle was strengthened by the symbolism of the prominent material culture from the shrine sacristy which appears to be redolent with the rhythms of the life cycle (Figure 9.3). *Firstly*, stick figurines from the cache of ritual objects are in different stages of production. These not only stress the performative nature of the craft production, but quite plausibly represent frozen stages of the life cycle. At one extreme, there is the rough-

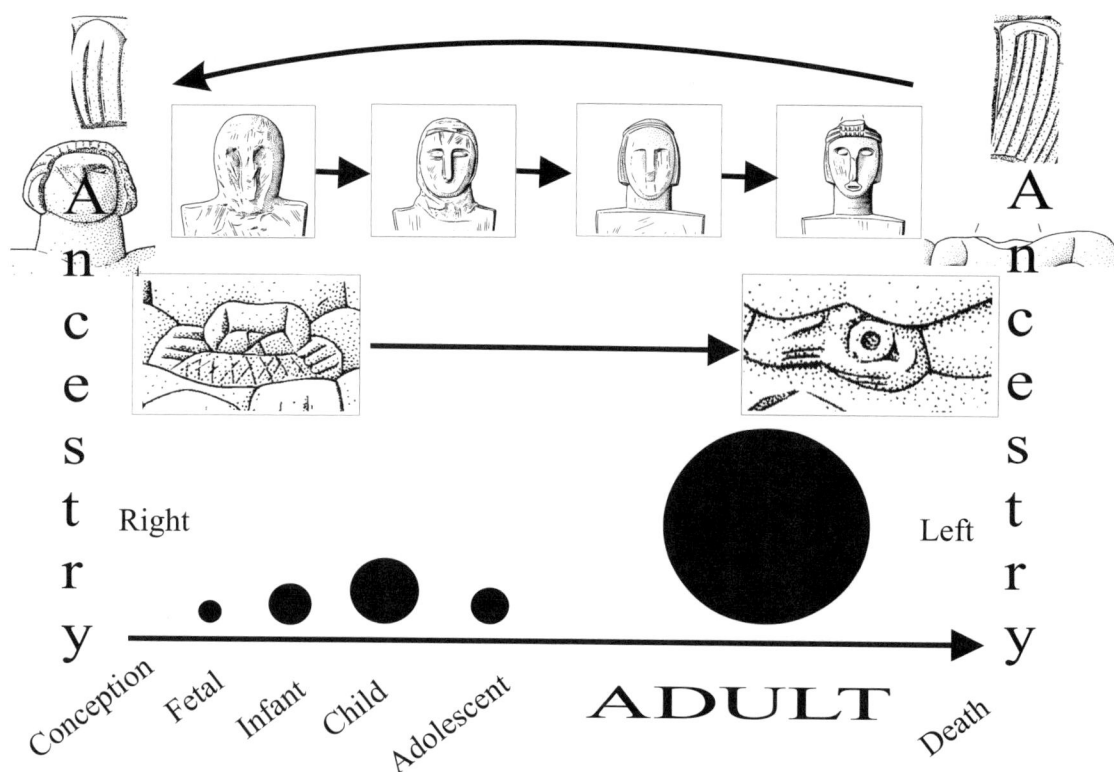

Figure 9.3. The symbolism of the life cycle.

out. From this, the other figures emerge in increasingly refined stages, with an enhanced, yet impersonalised, identity of the facial features, ending in a complete, but damaged figure. These may represent the development, formation, and dissolution of an individual cycle in a stylised format that was transferable between individuals (as they died) in a repetitive continuity that merges with the longer life cycle of the descent group symbolised by distinctive Tarxien skirts. *Secondly*, the three figures on the couch can be variously interpreted and indeed the multivalency of interpretation may be part of the message of this group of figures. Some have interpreted this grouping as some form of sacred family. Others have emphasised the femininity of the images, associating the production of the child metaphorically with the production of the pot (Mitchell pers. comm.); both require the combination of distinct elements, the moulding, shaping and then gestation of the constituent parts in a specially prepared chamber. All these interpretations are embedded in one particular stage of the life cycle namely regeneration. An alternative framework is to stress the binary nature of the group of figures. The figures on the right (large figure and child), cross-culturally the positive side of the group (Hertz 1960), appear to represent the beginning of the life cycle. It is this group that is dominant since its style of skirt encompasses the figure to its left. The figure on the (sinister) left, appears

to represent the end of the life cycle since it holds the pot that was offered to the deceased or which contained the ochre used to daub the bones of the dead. This same figure has lost its head. When viewed as a constellation of symbols, all these elements, whatever their detailed interpretation, appear to point to regeneration or repetition of the life cycle through the generations, given once again ancestral continuity by the Tarxien style of the skirt that decorates both the corpulent as well as stick figures.

Closure of the ritual cycle

The three phases of Żebbuġ, Ġgantija and Tarxien form an interconnected ritual cycle of increasing intensity over 1800 years. The most intense, Tarxien, phase appears to have come to a state of closure and completion in about 2400 BC according to the latest radiocarbon dating. In at least two sites, Tas-Silġ and and Brochtorff Circle at Xagħra the closure appears to have been a deliberate act of completion. The first example is stratigraphically more difficult to interpret and could relate either to a ritual iconoclasm of subsequent Bronze Age date (Vella 1999) or to a Tarxien period action. However, the closure of the ritual cycle at Xagħra appears more clearly to be Tarxien in at least two regards, and Tarxien Cemetery in terms of a memorial or recognition of what preceded. Firstly, the upper fill of the

Level	Definition	Occupants	Material culture
Upper	Celestial	Exotic ancestors and divine	Stars, exotic materials
Middle	Mundane	The living	Temples, houses
Lower	Spirits	The dead	Mortuary complexes

Table 9.3. Levels of Maltese cosmology.

sacristy/shrine appears to be an intentional backfilling with ritual paraphernalia, suggesting a deliberate closure of the focal screened area of the site containing the washing bowl. Secondly, a presiding statue appears to have been deliberately broken up and its identity (its head) removed or obliterated. Both these two acts seem to be Tarxien in date. A similar breaking up of a shrine may have taken place near the entrance threshold. Finally, during the Tarxien Cemetery phase the limits of the burial caves to the east and west were 'respected' by the deposit of Tarxien Cemetery type vessels. If the first phase of closure was a deliberate completion by the ritual specialists, this would not be a unique occurrence, since such deliberate blocking of ritual activity can occur in societies as disparate as the Neolithic of southern England (Piggott 1962), northern Mesopotamia (Schmidt 2006) and ancient Egypt (Kemp pers. comm.). In these cases, a natural site formation process can be excluded even though this has been suggested for some prehistoric sites in Scotland (Ralston pers. comm.)

The cosmic cycle

The funerary cult did not take place in isolation. These funerary activities which provided the cultural marking of the end of the biological life cycle were most probably mapped onto particular loci in the horizontal and vertical landscape. A bipartite multi-dimensional mapping is typical of the cosmological arrangement of space in pre-urban societies (Oknuki-Tierney 1972).

The horizontal landscape of the Xaġhra plateau contained monument markers – the mortuary circle and the temples – mediating the living and the dead, the world of the island and the world of the Mediterranean. Cyclical processions (Stoddart and Malone in press) would most probably have interconnected these monument markers and associated freshwater springs, passing naturally along the line of the contours. Monuments would have provided the enclosed and secure nodal points for negotiating dangerous transitions from world outside the island (temples) and to the world outside life (the burial circle) (cf. Grima this volume).

The vertical landscapes were most probably demarcated into three zones (Stoddart 2002b) (Table 9.3). The lowest level comprised the cemeteries below ground, the enclosed area of the dead and their spirits, the location of one ritual cycle. The middle level comprised the temples and the houses of the living, the location of another ritual cycle that ran in parallel and interacted with the first. The upper level comprised the celestial, including stars, ancestors and the divine, an all encompassing cycle that transcended the two earthly cycles, and yet the annual celestial cycle would also have interacted with the alignment of the monuments, linking the various levels of the vertical landscape into one coherent framework.

Conclusion: Nested cycles of cult

The cult of the dead thus formed not only one element which closed the individual biological life cycle, but also a component within a wider range of nested cycles relating to the development of the descent group and the wider identity of the island population. The cyclicity of the death cult interacted with the cyclicity of the life rituals which in turn situated themselves within the broader ancestral ritual cycle of Zebbug–Ġgantija–Tarxien which had its own rhythms of foundation, maturity, expansion, florescence and closure. The causes of this closure remain controversial. Was the closure caused by the pre-ordained cultural fulfilment of a ritual cycle (Sahlins 1981), by an iconoclastic reaction against the long-standing stable ritual structures, by some dissatisfaction with the efficacy of the religion, by some ecological perturbation or by some external hostile impact? Only further research will define the probabilities within these possibilities.

Acknowledgements

The author wishes to thank the Leverhulme Trust for supporting this research.

References

Baldacchino, J. G. and Evans, J. D. 1954. Prehistoric tombs near Zebbug, Malta. *Papers of the British School at Rome* 22, (n.s. 9), 1–21.

Malone, C. A. T. and Stoddart, S. K. F. in press. Caves of the Living. Caves of the Dead. Experiences above and below ground in prehistoric Malta. In H. Moyes (ed.). *Journeys into the Dark Zone: A Cross Cultural Perspective on Caves as Sacred Spaces.* Boulder, University Press of Colorado.

Boddington, A. 1987. From bones to population: the problem of numbers. In A. Boddington, A. N. Garland and R. C. Janaway (eds). *Death, decay and reconstruction. Approaches to archaeology and forensic science.* Manchester, Manchester University Press, 180–197.

Chamberlain, A. T. 1997. Commentary: missing stages of life – towards the perception of children in archaeology. In J. Moore and E. Scott (eds). *Invisible people and processes: writing gender and childhood into European Archaeology.* Leicester, Leicester University Press, 248–250.

Clark, D. 2004. Building logistics. In D. Cilia (ed.). *Malta Before History.* Malta, Miranda, 367–377.

Geertz, C. 1966. *Person, time, and conduct in Bali: an essay in cultural analysis.* New-Haven, Yale University Press.

Geertz, C. 1973. Person, time, and conduct in Bali. In C. Geertz (ed.). *The interpretation of cultures; selected essays.* New York, Basic Books, 360–411.

Hertz, R. 1960. *Death and the Right Hand.* London, Cohen and West.

Kopytoff, I. 1971. Ancestors as elders in Africa. *Africa* 41 (2), 128–142.

Malone, C. A. T., Stoddart, S. K. F., Bonanno, A., Gouder, T. and Trump, D. 1995. Mortuary ritual of fourth millennium BC Malta: the Zebbug tomb from the Brochtorff Circle (Gozo). *Proceedings of the Prehistoric Society* 61, 303–345.

Malone, C. A. T., Stoddart, S. K. F., Trump, D., Bonanno, A., the late T. Gouder and Pace, A. (eds) 2007. *Mortuary ritual in prehistoric Malta. The Brochtorff Circle excavations (1987–1994).* Cambridge, McDonald Institute.

Oknuki-Tierney, E. 1972. Spatial concepts of the Ainu of the north-west coast of Southern Sakhalin. *American Anthropologist* 74: 426–457.

Piggott, S. 1962. *The West Kennet Long Barrow.* London, HMSO.

Rega, E. 1997. Age, gender and biological reality in the Early Bronze Age cemetery at Mokrin. In J. Moore and E. Scott (eds). *Invisible People and processes: writing gender and childhood into European Archaeology.* London, Leicester University, 229–247.

Sahlins, M. 1981. *Historical metaphors and mythical realities: structure in the early history of the Sandwich Islands kingdom.* Ann Arbor, University of Michigan Press.

Schmidt, K. 2006. *Sie bauten die ersten Tempel. Das rätselhafte Heiligtum der Steinzeitjäger.* Munich, C. H. Beck Verlag.

Stoddart, S. K. F. 1992. Towards a historical ethnology of the Mediterranean. *Current Anthropology* 33(5), 599–560.

Stoddart, S. K. F. 1999. Mortuary customs in prehistoric Malta. In A. Mifsud and C. Savona-Ventura (eds), *Facets of Maltese Prehistory.* Mosta, Prehistoric Society of Malta, 183–190.

Stoddart, S. K. F. 2002a. Monuments in the prehistoric landscape of the Maltese islands: ritual and domestic transformations. In B. David and M. Wilson (eds). *Inscribed Landscapes: Marking and making place.* Honolulu, University of Hawaii Press, 176–186.

Stoddart, S. K. F. 2002b. The Xaghra shaman? In G. Carr and P. A. Baker (eds). *New Approaches to Medical Archaeology and Medical Anthropology: Practitioners, practices and patients.* Oxford, Oxbow Books, 125–135.

Stoddart, S. K. F. 2004. Cycles of Life or eternity: new light on prehistoric Maltese funerary ritual from the Brochtorff Circle at Xaghra *2003 Conference in Malta (CD-ROM).* Sarasota, Florida, EMPTC.

Stoddart, S. K. F. and Malone, C. A. T. in press. Changing beliefs in the Maltese body. In D. Boric and J. Robb (eds). *Past Bodies.* Oxford, Berghahn.

Stoddart, S. K. F., Wysocki, M., Burgess, G., Barber, G., Duhig, C., Malone, C. A. T. and Mann, G. 1999. The articulation of disarticulation. Preliminary thoughts on the Brochtorff Circle at Xaghra (Gozo). In J. Downes and A. Pollard (eds). *The loved body's corruption: archaeological contributions to the study of human mortality.* Glasgow, Cruithne Press, 94–105.

Vella, N. C. 1999. "Trunkess legs of stone": debating ritual continuity at Tas-Silg, Malta. In A. Mifsud and C. Savona-Ventura (eds). *Facets of Maltese Prehistory.* Malta, The Prehistoric Society of Malta, 225–239.

Chapter 10

FROM *CABIRI* TO GODDESSES: CULT, RITUAL AND CONTEXT IN THE FORMATIVE YEARS OF MALTESE ARCHAEOLOGY

Nicholas Vella

1985 is a date certainly familiar to most of us who have gathered in Cambridge to discuss interdisciplinary approaches to the study of cult and ritual. Colin Renfrew's archaeological report of the Phylakopi sanctuary on the island of Melos was published, proposing a methodology for the recognition of the archaeological manifestations of religious ritual (Renfrew 1985). Also in that year, a gathering of scholars was convened on Malta to discuss the theme of Archaeology and Fertility Cult in the Ancient Mediterranean (Bonanno 1986). The conference was intended to cast a wide net, analysing the theme diachronically throughout the Mediterranean to include also the Classical period. Although explicit cross-cultural comparisons and multidisciplinary approaches were notably few during the eclectic gathering, the conference showed the complexities and diversities of the archaeological record related to ancient Mediterranean religion. This was a point made by Renfrew (1986) in his intervention when he reiterated the argument made years earlier by archaeologists for debunking the myth of a pan-European, pan-Mediterranean goddess, and the need for a clear framework of inference in archaeology. But for the doyen of Goddess studies, Marija Gimbutas, who was present at the conference, such caution was anathema to a belief that she consciously felt she had to preach, especially after the summer of 1985 – when she had 'to fight with the boys' about the Goddess (Noble 1989, 6). 'I don't say I can prove on paper that this is the owl goddess', Gimbutas retorted to a remark from Renfrew as to whether she intended to test her hypotheses. 'I shall not prove [this] to many of the archaeologists of modern times but I think that mythologists or historians of religions will believe. We are divorced from each other and archaeologists cannot see', she concluded to the applause of like-minded followers.

It is not the intention here to look at on-going debates dealing with the Goddess movement or contemporary meanings of Maltese prehistoric goddesses. Recent publications (Rountree 1999; 2002) have done just that, exploring social contexts and helping to trace the cultural biographies of objects that continue to be potent symbols of Maltese prehistory in the present. It is towards a consideration of the spatial context of three-dimensional anthropomorphic representations from Late Neolithic Malta that this paper is geared. It is inspired by work in progress related to the study of unpublished works on Maltese prehistory by the Italian archaeologist Luigi Ugolini (1895–1936). In 2000 the archive was traced in the Museo Nazionale Preistorico Etnografico 'L. Pigorini' in Rome (Pessina and Vella 2005). Ugolini's work, undertaken in the early 1930s, had consisted of a thorough description of the megalithic monuments and of all the objects that had been excavated over the previous century and which could be located in the showcases and stores of the Valletta museum. A study of these papers shows that Ugolini intended to study the objects in the context of spatial distribution and other artefactual associations. One of the volumes, the largest, was to build on Themistocles Zammit's seminal work at the Tarxien complex for it is here that Ugolini saw the potential of moving from contextual descriptions to interpretation. Ugolini's work was not only based on a close reading of Zammit's interim publications but, more importantly, on his notebooks and on questions Ugolini could ask the aged gentleman before Zammit passed away in 1935.

An appraisal of Ugolini's survey methodology got me to explore the extent to which an explicit attention to context to guide interpretation was a novel approach during the formative years of Maltese archaeology. In particular, I was interested to see the extent to which interpretation of prehistoric anthropomorphic representations was tempered by contextual information. This paper considers this matter after a brief prelude on the significance of context in archaeology.

The significance of context

That anthropomorphic representations – figurines, statuettes, statues – were evocative, expressive objects, potent tools to the men, women and children who used them in the past has long been recognised in the archaeological literature. Interpretation was sometimes considered as counter-intuitive, the context providing the right clues, as when Robertson Smith (1927, 208) remarked in one of his seminal lectures on the religion of the Semites dealing with Phoenician sacred representations that 'an image in like manner [i.e. with accompanying inscription] declares its own meaning better than a mere pillar, but the chief idol of a great sanctuary did not require to be explained in this way; its position showed what it was without either figure or inscription'. But in prehistoric studies generally, interpretation and explanation of anthropomorphic representations has set scholars at opposing ends of the discipline: from those supporting totalising narratives (of the Goddess type, for instance) to those who acknowledge that it is naïve to assume that archaeologists can reconstruct *the* meaning when ethnography tells us that society might have entertained several. Bailey (2005), for example, has argued that the paradox of figurine meaning is that several proposed interpretations could be correct and incorrect. He considers two levels of meaning for prehistoric figurines, one relating to particularities associated with use and function, in which the original archaeological context of individual figurines matters for the interpretative exercise, and a second one where meaning is related to the contemporary social context and may have nothing to do with archaeological findspot. In this case, Bailey is interested in the reactions of people to visual representations, in particular the body with its significance as a cultural, social and political object.

The recognition of two levels of contextual analysis was explicitly made by Schiffer more than thirty years ago, although in a manner that was predominantly concerned with the problems inherent in identifying patterns related to site formation processes through formalized middle range verification (Schiffer 1972; 1987). For Schiffer, the distinction between archaeological and systemic contexts was necessary in order to understand the life history of artefacts, from the time of discard to the moment they are recovered by archaeologists. Although this useful approach has been criticized for ignoring, for example, the 'issue of whether discard is meaningfully constituted' (Hodder 1992, 5), it is clear that rigorous studies of formation processes on a site – how layers and objects come to be – are essential for interpretation, not least on sites where ritual activity is suspected (e.g. Hill 1995). In putting into practice apparently diverging principles, archaeological theoreticians converge when they infer ritual activity from the archaeological evidence. Whether we are dealing with Flannery's (1976) or Renfrew's (1985) contextual analysis of ritual paraphernalia at Oaxaca or Melos respectively using a proclaimed hypothetico-deductive method (dubbed 'essentially inductive' by one reviewer – Warren (1986) on Renfrew), or Hodder's hermeneutic spiral at Haddenham (1992, 213–40; 1999, 34–40) and reflexive method at Çatalhöyük (1997), the majority of research excavation reports go to great lengths to provide a thorough description of contextual data. Detailed and painstaking plotting of macro- and micro-artefacts is often followed by quantification within and across contexts in an effort to see how artefact patterns might have been affected by formation processes. A rich narrative often written by the project director, explores the cross-cutting relationships between artefacts, even of different classes, and the deposits which contained them. Such integrated analyses make possible the interpretation of the materials recovered and allow different levels of meaning to be explored. As an example of such work I can single out the archaeological report of the Runnymede Bridge (London) research excavations by Needham and Spence (1996) which explored the formation of refuse and the meaning of midden deposits. In a résumé of their work they make it clear that a definition of ritual depends on context: '[...] insights into the frequency of certain kinds of deposits, their regularity or otherwise, the way material was treated prior to incorporation, ultimately the balance between the commonplace and the unusual' (Needham and Spence 1997, 86).

I want to come back to figurines, in particular those from Malta's Late Neolithic. I would like to show that in studying figurines as bounded entities there has been a strikingly general lack of attention to the spatial context in which they have been found. In what follows I suggest reasons for this state of affairs and explore the resultant implications.

Discoveries and definitions

Malta's megalithic monuments have long been the subject of antiquarian interest. A long list of local and foreign historians, antiquarians, naturalists, surveyors, clerics, and visitors more generally has been perplexed by the ruins, offering explanations for their origins well before the idea of prehistory had been accepted in the early twentieth century (Leighton 1989). Several left notes, letters, or full-blown accounts of what they observed; few engaged artists to depict the ruins and their landscape setting and had drawings, woodcuts or lithographs made to illustrate their travelogues (Attard Tabone 1999; Bonello 1996; Grima 2004). As stories of giants and diluvial theories associated with the monoliths at Ħaġar Qim (Abela 1647, 145) were gradually dropped, eventually in the face of new palaeontological discoveries, Phoeniciomania crept in as an alternative. Ġgantija, excavated between 1821 and 1823, visited by de la Marmora in January 1834 and reported in a letter to the superintendent of antiquities in the Bibliothèque in Paris, was described as a temple dedicated to a goddess of nature, Astarte, or to a moon goddess. A tapering monolith found there could conceivably be associated with the aniconic representation of Astarte at Paphos in Cyprus (de la Marmora 1836, 11). The association of other similar monuments with a female divinity was sustained by discoveries made in 1839 during excavations at Ħaġar Qim by J. G. Vance.

In what is, I believe, the first lengthy account of an excavation of a Maltese megalithic building, accompanied by a plan and several elevated views prepared by Lieutenant William Foulis of the 59th (2nd Nottinghamshire Regiment) of Foot stationed in Malta, Vance takes the reader carefully through the reasons why he believed the building to be the remains of a place of worship (Vance 1842). The narrative is exacting and sequential as most reports read to the Society of Antiquaries in London, like this one, had to be (cf. Hodder 1989). Indeed, I see here much of the rigour in formulating interpretations on the basis of contextualized evidence which is characteristic of modes of archaeological writing of the 1980s and 1990s to which reference was made above. Vance knew that without inscriptions he had to rely on what he found to explain the relics of antiquity, and although he looked at other sites in Malta to look for similarities (including Ġgantija and Mnajdra) he refrained from pressing too far comparisons with Avebury and Stonehenge in Wiltshire and Carnac in France because the Maltese monuments were 'quite unique and dissimilar to any discovery hitherto treated of' (Vance 1842, 231). He was careful to identify unwarranted interpretation of the monuments as conjecture and thought that 'the interior arrangement [...], the style of the altars, and other appendages to a place of worship [...] are the only guides by which we may hope to unravel their history' (1842, 231). He interpreted two 'rudely cut tablets' located in the northern division of the building, at the entrance of chamber No. 4, as altars for sacrifices on account of the evidence for fire and the traces of bones and ash discovered there in great quantities, especially in chamber No. 12 (1842, 229). The southern division exhibited no signs of fire, 'but contained nine images, (five of which were lying near the foot of the altar), and four in the semicircular chamber adjoining), also many fragments of very ancient pottery in the shape of bowls, small jugs, lamps, and other utensils' (1842, 229) (Figure 10.1). Vance identified the headless limestone statuettes with deities or mythological heroes, suggesting that the heads could be changed 'according to the innumerable forms under which a polytheistic people might wish to picture their deities or heroes' (1842, 231). He concluded that the heads may have been broken off by their possessors – the Phoenicians – with a view of preserving their worship in other countries. Another representation, in terracotta, of a naked upright figurines

of a beautiful shape was identified with 'Venus Urania', the goddess adored by the Phoenicians. Vance interpreted this area of the building, chamber No. 2, with its 'peculiar' doorways cut out of the centre of large blocks, with that entirely devoted to the vocal adoration of the deities (1842, 232); a conical hole cut in a stone slab opposite the altar 'doubtless connected in some way with the service of the altar, but for what purpose I can form no idea, except that of containing a libation', he wrote (1842, 237).

Even if it is a far cry from modern reports, the text is crisp and rigorous and I think that later archaeologists were particularly unkind in describing the report 'extremely inadequate' and the images 'poorly executed' (Evans 1971, 81). The narrator is present in the text, toing-and-froing between ideas and contextualised data as he moves about the monument, explores the spaces, and enters some of them through holes with a moderate inclination of the head and back; the method of inference is clear and the reader can accept or refute his ideas, hypotheses and conclusions. The report contains many descriptive labels and interpretations that more than a century and a half later are still found in the literature on Maltese prehistory. Only the labels changed over the years: for successive public librarians (Vassallo 1853, 222; 1872, 5–6; Caruana 1882, 11–13), dilettanti (Furse 1869, 412) and travellers (Tallack 1861, 117), the pantheon included the grotesque *cabiri*, gods described by Herodotus (III, 37), which became Phoenician through a mix of legendary genealogy and myth (cf. Perrot and Chipiez 1885, 315). When the idea of prehistory was belatedly accepted in Malta by Albert Mayr and others in the early twentieth century (Vella and Gilkes 2001, 355–6), the statuettes were identified with anonymous, fat, obese, steotypagus, sometimes female or asexual and genderless deities. The challenging and novel interpretation of the 'temples' as tombs with ceremonial halls for celebrating the dead (Fergusson 1872, 425–6) and aniconic pillars or betyls representing them (Evans 1901, 200), or as abodes for princes and chiefs (Riccio 1951, 111) did not have any consequences of note.

Although Ugolini resurrects Vance's Venus (Ugolini 1931), taking care to regard its temporal context that was often ignored by Venus theorists (cf. Antonielli 1925), the infatuation which Europeans had with the Goddess (Hutton 1997) failed to find a home in Malta, perhaps because the sexual attributes of the stone and clay representations were rarely unambiguous. Zammit, the excavator of the Tarxien megalithic complex, remained cautious in his publications: the Ħaġar Qim statuettes were identified with '"fat" deities' in his guide to the Valletta museum (Zammit 1919, 29) and in his Tarxien monograph he wrote of a divinity cult without specifying the gender of the transcendent (1930, 15). He identified numerous clay and stone figurines with miniature representations of corpulent deities. Their gesture was telling: 'a ritual attitude with one forearm bent on the chest

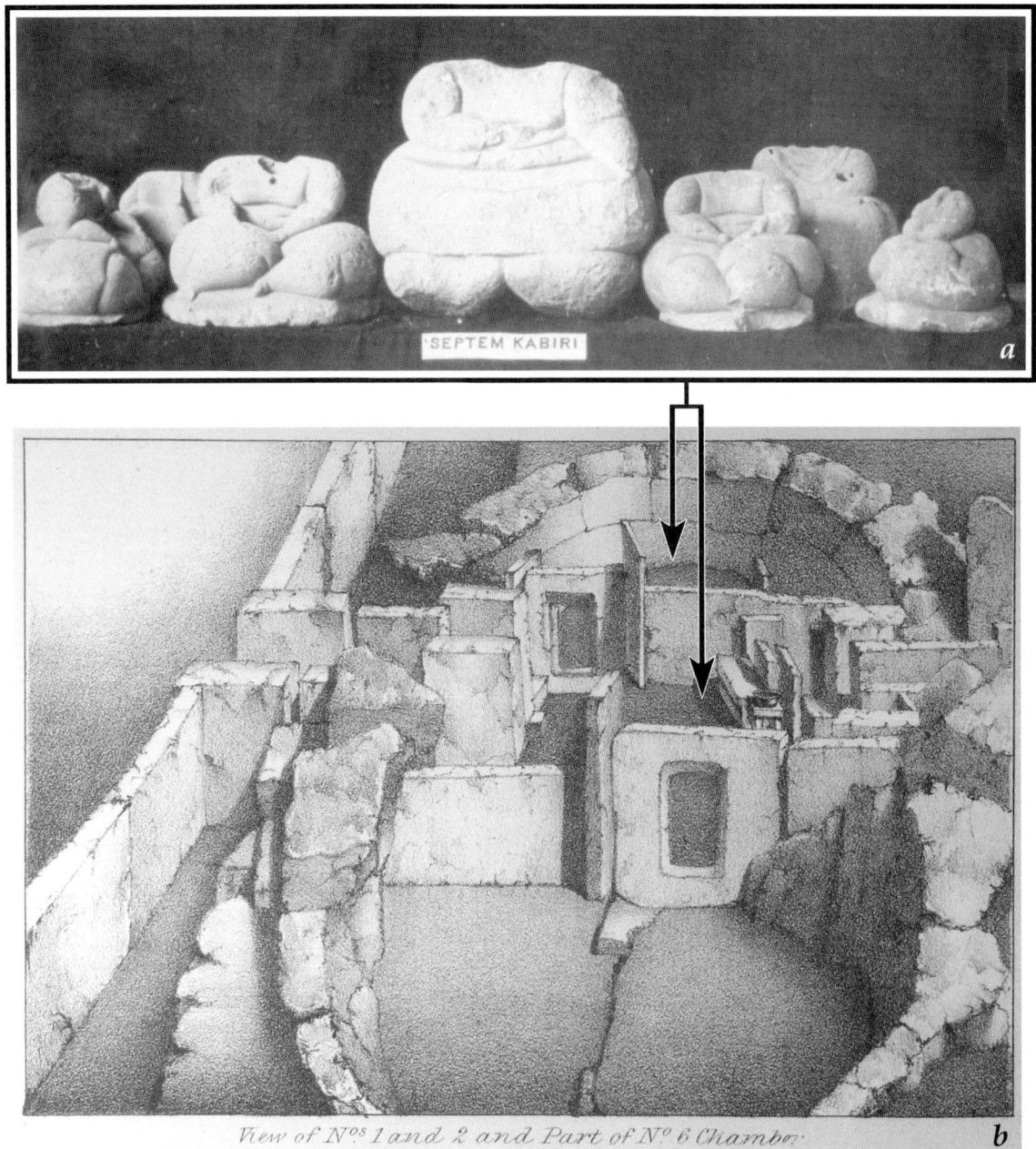

Figure 10.1. The findspot of the limestone statuettes recovered at Ħaġar Qim in 1839: (a) the 'septem kabiri' photographed for an album Antiquitates Phoeniciae in Insulis Melitae et Gaulos *compiled by the Society of Archaeology, History and Natural Sciences of Malta in 1868 (courtesy of the National Library of Malta); (b) elevated view of the chamber No. 2 at Ħaġar Qim from a litograph prepared for J. G. Vance (1842: plate 24).*

and the other hanging by the side' (1930, 44). His framework of inference to identify the purpose of the buildings in which they were found – sanctuaries of the Stone Age period' – was made clear for all to follow (1930, 42–44). Although he kept abreast with major publications of his day and was in touch with numerous foreign scholars, he was careful in seeking comparisons with sites abroad even if explanatory models at the time were largely

diffusionistic. Parallels sought with Arthur Evans's Neolithic Crete, for instance, were made in passing, posing questions 'for the future to answer' (Zammit and Singer 1924, 78) while a note on the pleated skirts and posture of Sumerian or Chaldean priest figures was jotted down in an unpublished notebook in order 'to compare with the clay statuettes from Tarxien' (Zammit 1906–1921); when he made use of the information he did not press the connection

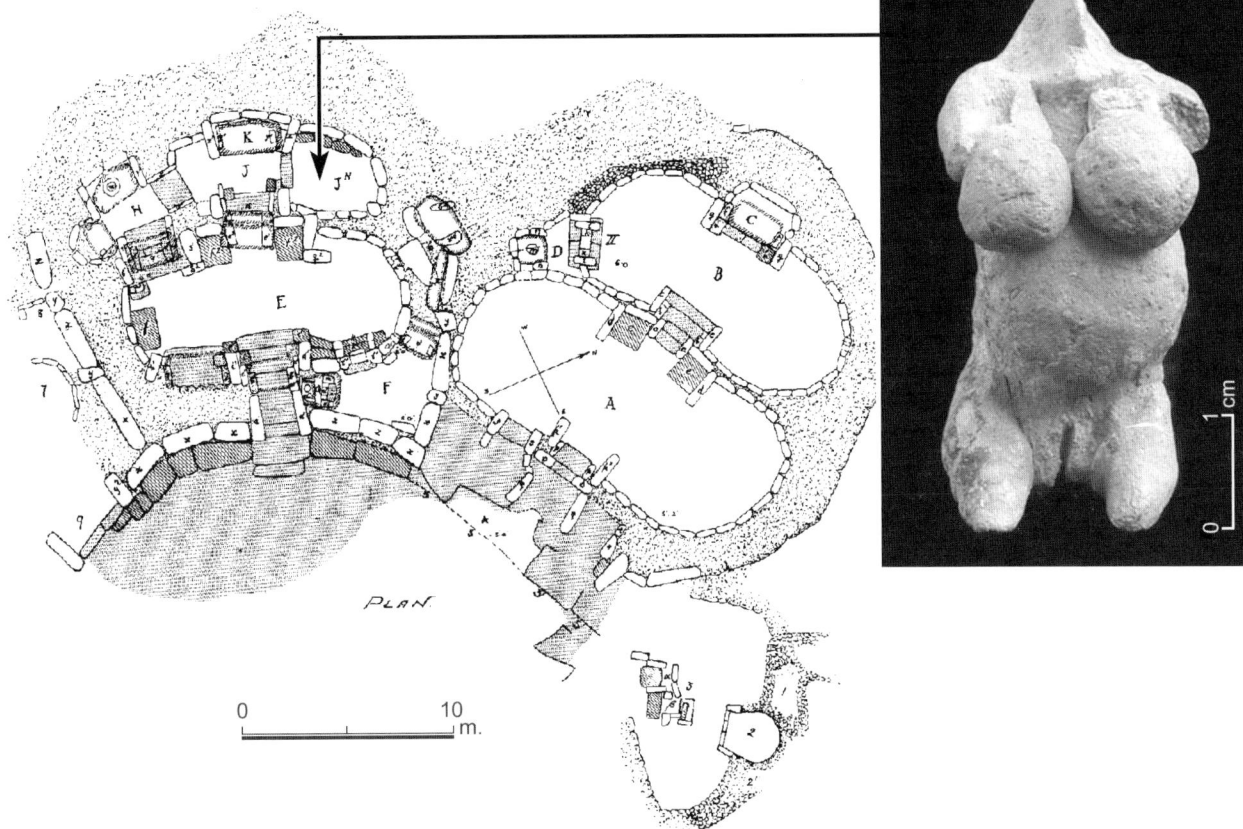

Figure 10.2. A terracotta figurine recovered with other terracotta figurines in 1910 from within the floor of apse J^N by T. Ashby. The photo is reproduced courtesy of D. Cilia; the plan is from Ashby et al. *(1914: plate 20).*

(Zammit 1930, 97) even though the label 'priests' for the object has stuck in the literature raising the ire of feminists who prefer to see female equivalents and replace a reconstructed flat chest with a pair of breasts (Biaggi 1989). Given his medical training, Zammit was confident in giving an accurate description of the human form, also identifying abnormalities – extreme fatness, swollen abdomen, enlarged groin – with pathological conditions (Zammit and Singer 1924, 72 and 76). Mnajdra, where one such terracotta figurine was found in 1910 together with clay representations of the diseased part of the human body, was home, in his opinion, to a cult of a healing deity (Zammit 1919, 31) (Figure 10.2).

Displacement and display

The deadlock reached in offering interpretations of the anthropomorphic representations was compounded, in my opinion, by three facts. I look at them in turn before I conclude.

First, excepting the investigations at Mnajdra in 1910, one excavation after another at minor megalithic sites –

Xewkija (1904), Kordin (1908–1909), Santa Verna (1911), Xrobb il-Għaġin (1913), Ħal Ġinwi (1917), Borġ in-Nadur (1921–1923; 1926–1927), Ta' Ħaġrat (1923; 1925–1926), Tal-Qadi (1927), Buġibba (1928), Kunċizzjoni (1938) (details in Evans 1971; Pace 2004b) – failed to uncover figurines that could have offered an interpretative challenge to the excavators, in their majority anything but prehistorians by training. By the time that new discoveries were made – in 1949 at Ħaġar Qim (Baldacchino 1951) and in 1964 at Tas-Silġ (Mallia 1965) – the Mother Goddess view was upheld in Hawkes's seminal work on European prehistory (1940, 153) and later in the work of Gimbutas (1989) and her followers (Biaggi 1986). Archaeologists working in Malta remained reticent to use the label despite seeing a clear connection between the statuettes and a fertility cult (Evans 1959, 143; cf. Crawford 1957, 49). The real challenge only came about as a result of the 1985 cult conference held in Malta when a joint Anglo-Maltese team agreed to start research excavations at the Xagħra Circle in Gozo (Malta) to explore the archaeological context of prehistoric art objects (Stoddart *et al.* 1993, 3).

Second, in describing, drawing and photographing

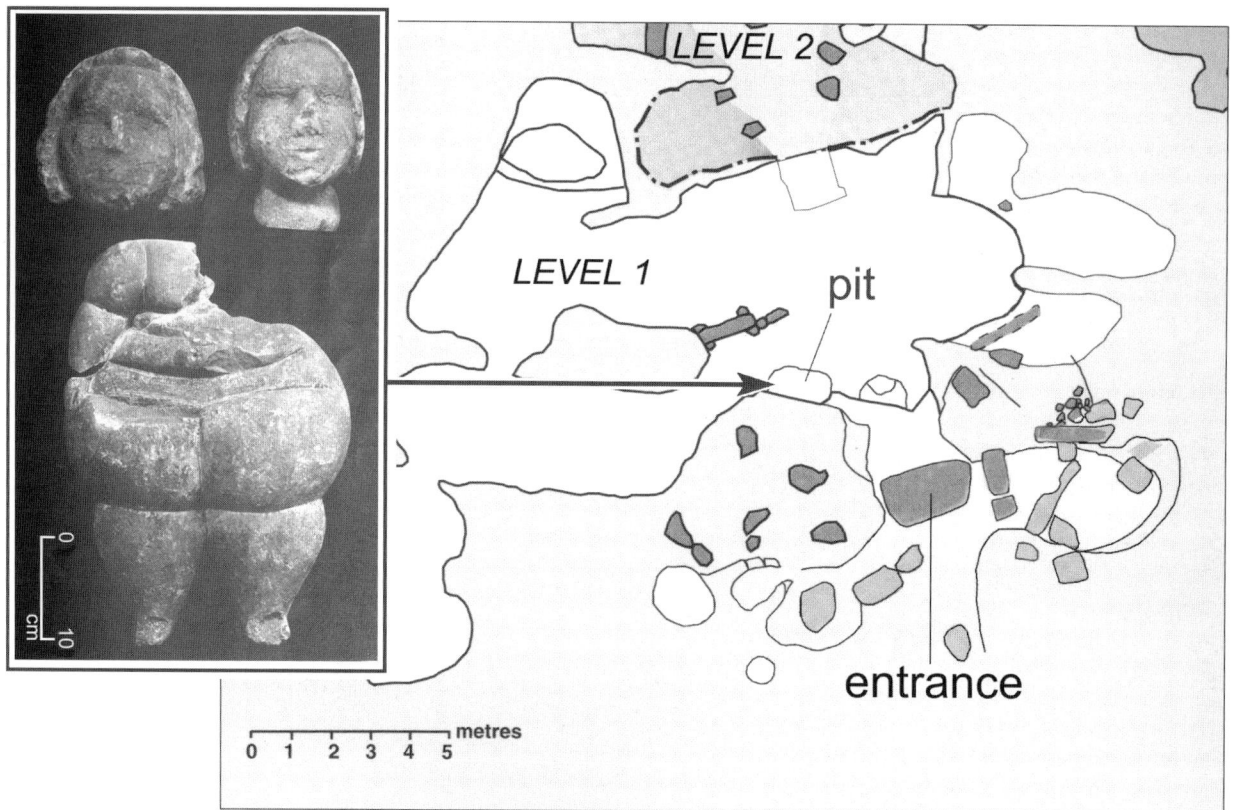

Figure 10.3. The limestone statue and two heads recovered from a rock-cut pit in the upper level of the Ħal Saflieni hypogeum. The plan is adapted from Pace (2004a); the photograph was published in Zammit (1926).

single objects according to type or material – the most common of archaeological practices (cf. Conolly 2000) – the unity of the archaeological context was pulled apart, often when the scale of analysis shifted from a spatial unit to an entire site. In their catalogue of Neolithic representations of the human form, for instance, Zammit and his medic friend from University College London, Charles Singer, failed to appreciate the interpretation tempered by a consideration of context which Vance gave for the Ħaġar Qim statuettes. Instead they erroneously take him to task for 'failing to tell us in what part of the building they were found' (1924, 71). The inconsistency with which the importance of an object's archaeological context was recognised can be seen in the case of the damaged limestone statue found in the Ħal Saflieni hypogeum in 1908 (Figure 10.3). Whereas, in a note in the museum annual report for the same year Zammit made it clear that the statue was found in a rock-cut floor pit in association with two limestone heads (Zammit 1909, E4), in the catalogue of small objects from the site (Zammit *et al.* 1912, 5) and in the guidebook to the hypogeum (Zammit 1926), this important datum disappears. The objects were published against a black background, a non-space, continuing a tradition that started in 1868 when the Society of

Archaeology of Malta compiled an album of photographs which it presented at the International Congress of Prehistoric Archaeology held in Norwich that year (Furse 1869, 411). Compelling interpretations of these objects were made years later, even by Zammit (Zammit and Singer 1924, 75), when this singular association was taken into account, and in most cases the explanations are not dissimilar from Vance's (e.g. Vella Gregory 2005, 162). It is clear that the removal of body parts, especially the head with the gaze and the power of looking, may have been a significant act in Late Neolithic Malta.

The practice of singling out objects for archaeological study brings me to my third point: the display of objects now and in prehistory. In transferring objects from sites to museum showcases, a practice that flourished in the second half of the nineteenth century and was often inspired by nascent forms of nationalisms (cf. Skeates 2005), curators robbed the figurines of that vital spatial context which often allowed the first level interpretation to take place. Over a century that context has often been forgotten, indeed, physically changed in the case of Ħaġar Qim's chamber No. 2 (Figure 10.4). Today's encounter with these figurines occurs generally through books and the displays at the National Museum of Archaeology in Valletta. In different

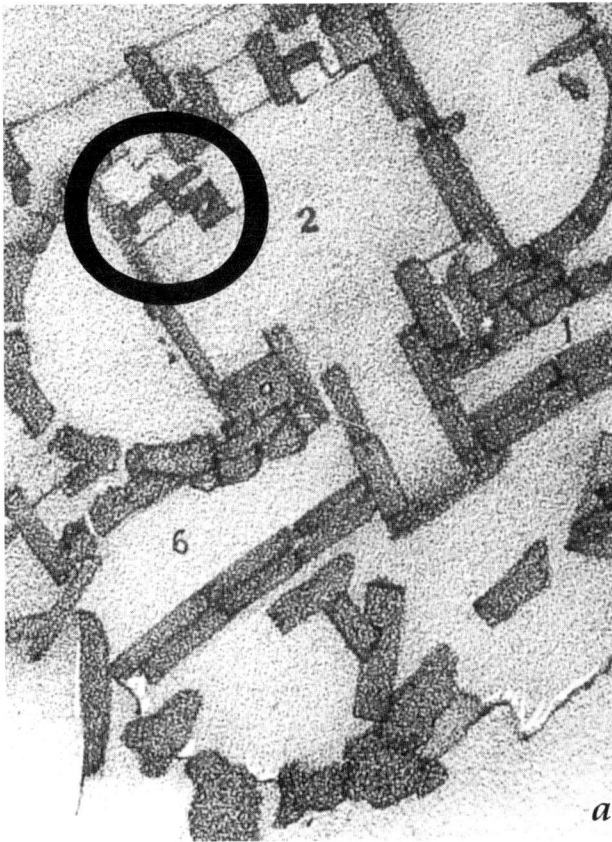

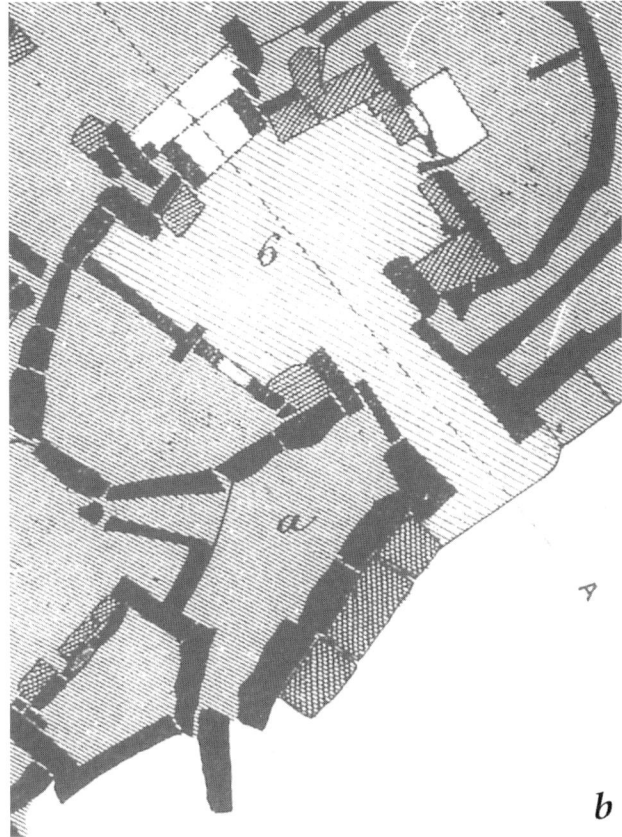

Figure 10.4. The 'altar' and decorated slab at Ħaġar Qim: (a) set-up (circled) as shown in a lithographed plan appended to J. G. Vance's report (1842: plate 23); (b) set-up missing from a plan of the same area prepared by the Society of Archaeology, History and Natural Sciences of Malta and reproduced by one of its members (Adams 1870: plate 5); view of the 'altar' and slab in a lithograph (Vance 1842: plate 27); (d) view of the altered set-up with copies of the 'altar' and slab, 2006.

rooms visitors see displays of objects that have been separated from other objects with which they were originally found. The Temple-period displays favour a breakdown of prehistory in terms of themes with relevant classes of materials: pottery, lithics, anthropomorphic representations (including body parts), zoomorphic representations, low relief sculpture, architectural models (cf. Camilleri 2001, 122). Except for the 'Sleeping Lady', the figurines, statuettes, and statues have all been placed in the same room dedicated to the 'Human Form' some carefully propped up because they lack body parts, with no indication where exactly in a monument – burial hypogeum or 'temple' – they were found (though as I write plans are unfolding to change this situation). The heads recovered during excavations are placed in a separate showcase, one next to the other in a line, some with their characteristic upturned gaze. Certainly, the objects have exhibition value but quite what message the curators wanted to convey here is not clear to me, other than the fact that the juxtaposition of different heads can allow visitors to appreciate better symmetrical appropriations of form, more generally qualities of craftsmanship, aesthetic and cultural achievement. A provoking critique of museum displays has pointed out that '"aesthetic" exhibitions' assume that

> our visual perception is a somehow coherent, even objective process, as if all that is necessary is 'to see properly', without taking any account of how complicated and problematic a process "seeing" is, nor how easy it is to misconstrue even the most elementary kinds of visual experience. (Vergo 1989, 49)

Such assumptions pose problems relevant to this study. Hayden (1998) and Grima (1999) have argued that particular codes of representing the human figure in Malta several millennia ago may be different from those with which we are accustomed today. For Grima, for instance, the curvilinear proportions associated with several of Malta's prehistoric figurines may have less to do with oft-quoted qualities of fatness, obesity and fertility – qualities which some would like to see acknowledged in the museum's display (e.g. Rountree 1990, 218) – and more to do with representations of perceptual sensations and physical sense-experiences. One could argue that such an explanation would probably require an over-contexualised display, laden with texts that viewers are ill-prepared to read. It is nonetheless frustrating that the display does not extend a helping hand to the viewer eager to make sense of this class of objects even if it is to elicit questions or to suggest that gesture and body might have been fundamental to figurine function in prehistory. I have already made reference above to one archaeological context where the unequivocal connection between heads and body exits. Zammit noted that one of the heads from the Ħal Saflieni entrance pit fitted into the cavity of the statue (Zammit and Singer 1924, 87). Recently the body and the second head

have been joined together in several photographs (Vella Gregory 2005, figure on p. 45) and reproduced in a recent guidebook to the museum (Sultana 2006, 27). The association between the finds would be clearer if the museum display were to place the objects *together* – as Zammit had done years ago (1919, 28) – rather than in separate showcases.

This plea for re-contextualising anthropomorphic representations in the museum can be extended to the group of four limestone statuettes which Baldacchino found grouped below the largest step leading to a raised apse at Ħaġar Qim in 1949 (Baldacchino 1951) – an intentional cache, as most concur (Malone *et al.* 1995, 9) not objects forgotten by the original excavators below 'modern steps' as has been suggested (Evans 1959, 143; 1993, 54) (Figure 10.5).

Museum displays bring this paper to a close by way of a final thought. It has been noted that display of objects is not a post-Renaissance phenomenon, originating only in cabinets of curiosities (Pearce 1992, 89–91). Gosden (2004) has in fact argued that in British prehistory a complex dialectic between concealment and display, between hiding and revealing things, including artefacts and human bodies, may have existed as a vital basis for social power. It is a short step to complement this suggestion with the possibility that older, prehistoric forms of display can be recognised also in Malta if we start considering categories of objects in the context of the structured space of the megalithic buildings, not least Tarxien for which we have the contextual data: for instance, large (or miniature) ceramic and stone containers or caches of cattle bone and horn. In this view, anthropomorphic representations in clay, stone and exotic alabaster become one part of several expressive, technically-enchanting (to follow Gell 1992)) objects that may have been displayed prior to deposition and concealment inside the megalithic monuments: in pits, below floors, below thresholds, behind screens – spatial contexts recovered archaeologically. Phenomenal engagements with megalithic buildings can go beyond narratives elicited by experience structured mainly by empty space (e.g. Tilley 2004) to include also the symbolic potential of the material world, portable objects now housed in museum displays or in storage. The potential has already been explored by Grima with exciting insights related to how an island cosmology may have been embodied in the megalithic structures people built in the Late Neolithic (Grima 2001; 2003). Moreover, Turnbull has provided us with a definition of the Maltese megalithic monuments – '"theatres of knowledge" in which the Neolithic Maltese knowledge traditions were performed' (Turnbull 2002, 137) – that can challenge stereotyped labels, including the ubiquitous 'temples'. Looked at in terms of the esoteric knowledge associated with transforming raw materials into objects (e.g. taking ceramic pyrotechnology to new limits; cf. Bailey

Figure 10.5. The findspot of three limestone statuettes discovered by J. G. Baldacchino below steps leading to an elevated chamber at Ḥaġar Qim: (a) the statuettes, courtesy of D. Cilia; (b) the original steps as they appear in a photograph taken by L. Ugolini in the early 1930s (courtesy of the Museo "Pigorini", Rome); (c) the same area photographed in 2006 showing the replaced steps; (d) photograph from the Sunday Times of Malta *of 30th October 1949 showing J. G. Baldacchino looking over the spot where the statuettes were discovered.*

2005, 5) or the regenerative power often attributed to animal bones (cf. Helms 1998, 29), the varieties of definitions and values that can be attached to objects increase. We can start moving beyond archaeological contexts to explore multiple meanings, which is what this conference did, a lasting gift from its organisers.

Acknowledgements

This paper has grown out of a project that will see the publication of the Luigi Ugolini archive held in Rome, jointly with Andrea Pessina. I am grateful to Caroline Malone and to David A. Barrowclough for extending a timely invitation to deliver a paper at the Cult in Context conference, to Simon Stoddart for his practical help and encouragement, and to David and Bridget Trump for kindly hosting me in Cambridge. I am grateful to Anthony Bonanno for readily making available the tape recordings of the 1985 Archaeology and Fertility Cult conference he organised at the University of Malta. Others have helped me by providing references or useful source material, often at very short notice. I wish to thank them all: Anton Bugeja, Patricia Camilleri, Daniel Cilia, Chris Gemmell and Andrew Townsend.

References

Abela, G. F. 1647. *Della descrittione di Malta isola nel mare siciliano con le sve antichita, ed altre notitie.* Malta, Paolo Bonacota.

Adams, A. L. 1870. *Notes of a Naturalist in the Nile Valley and Malta.* Edinburgh, Edmonston and Douglas.

Antonielli, U. 1925. Una statuette feminile di Savignano sul Panàro e il problema delle figure dette "steatopigi", *Bullettino di paletnologia italiana* 45, 35–61.

Attard Tabone, J. 1999. The Gozo stone circle rediscovered. In A. Mifsud and C. Savona Ventura (eds). *Facets of Maltese Prehistory.* Malta, The Prehistoric Society of Malta, 169–81.

Bailey, D. W. 2005. *Prehistoric Figurines: Representation and Corporeality in the Neolithic.* London, Routledge.

Baldacchino, J. G. 1951. *Annual Report on the Working of the Museum Department 1949–1950.* Malta, Government Printing Office.

Biaggi, C. 1986. The significance of the nudity, obesity and sexuality of the Maltese goddess figures, in A. Bonanno (ed.), 131–40.

Biaggi, C. 1989. The priestess figure of Malta. In I. Hodder (ed.). *The Meaning of Things: Material Culture and Symbolic Expression.* London: Harper Collins Academic, 103–21.

Bonanno, A. (ed.) 1986. *Archaeology and Fertility Cult in the Ancient Mediterranean.* Amsterdam, B. R. Grüner Publishing Co.

Bonello, G. 1996. The Gozo megalithic sites: early visitors and artists. In A. Pace (ed.), *Maltese Prehistoric Art 5000–2500 BC.* Malta, Patrimonju Publishing, 19–29.

Camilleri, P. 2001. *L'analisi strutturale: verso una semiologia museale.* MA thesis, University of Malta.

Caruana, A. A. 1882. *Report on the Phoenician and Roman Antiquities in the Group of the Islands of Malta.* Malta, Government Printing Office.

Conolly, J. 2000. Çatalhöyük and the archaeological 'object'. In I. Hodder (ed.). *Towards reflexive method in archaeology: the example at Çatalhöyük:.* Cambridge, British Institute of Archaeology at Ankara, McDonald Institute of Archaeological Research, 51–56.

Crawford, O. G. S. 1957. *The Eye Goddess.* London, Phoenix House Ltd.

Flannery, K. V. 1976. Contextual analysis of ritual paraphernalia from Formative Oaxaca. In K. V. Flannery (ed.). *The Early Mesoamerican Village.* Florida: Academic Press Inc, 329–33.

Furse, P. 1869. On the prehistoric monuments in the islands of Malta and Gozo. In *Transactions of the International Congress of Prehistoric Archaeology, Third Session.* London, Longman, Green and Co, 407–17.

Evans, A. J. 1901. Myceanean tree and pillar cult and its Mediterranean relations, *Journal of Hellenic Studies* 21, 99–204.

Evans, J. D. 1959. *Malta.* London, Thames and Hudson.

Evans, J. D. 1971. *The Prehistoric Antiquities of the Maltese Islands: a Survey.* London, The Athlone Press.

Evans, J. D. 1993. Religion and life in ancient Malta. *F[ranco]M[aria]R[icci]* 61, 52–62.

Fergusson, J. 1872. *Rude Stone Monuments in all countries; their ages and uses.* London, John Murray.

Gell, A. 1992. The technology of enchantment and the enchantment of technology. In J. Coote and A. Shelton (ed.), *Anthropology, Art and Aesthetics.* Oxford, Clarendon Press, 40–63.

Gimbutas, M. 1989. *The Language of the Goddess: Unearthing the Hidden Symbols of Western Civilization.* London, Thames and Hudson.

Gosden, C. 2004. Making and display: our aesthetic appreciation of things and objects. In C. Renfrew, C. Gosden and E. DeMarrais (ed.). *Substance, Memory, Display: Archaeology and Art.* Cambridge: McDonald Institute for Archaeological Research, 35–45.

Grima, R. 1999. Waking up to the Sleeping Lady, *Malta Archaeological Review* 3, 3–8.

Grima, R. 2001. An iconography of insularity: a cosmological interpretation of some images and spaces in the Late Neolithic Temples of Malta, *Papers from the Institute of Archaeology* 12, 48–65.

Grima, R. 2003. Image, order and place in Late Neolithic Malta. In J. B. Wilkins and E. Herring (ed.). *Inhabiting symbols: symbol and image in the ancient Mediterranean.* London, Accordia Research Institute, University of London, 29–41.

Grima, R. 2004. *The Archaeological Drawings of Charles Frederick de Brocktorff.* Malta, Midsea Books Ltd and Heritage Malta.

Hawkes, C. F. C. 1940. *The Prehistoric Foundations of Europe to the Myceanean Age.* London, Methuen and Co Ltd.

Hayden, C. 1998. Monuments, hierarchy and obesity: perceptions of size in Temple Period Malta. *Archaeological Review from Cambridge* 15/1, 49–74.

Helms, M. W. 1998. *Access to Origins: Affines, Ancestors and Aristocrats.* Austin, University of Texas Press.

Hill, J. D. 1995. *Ritual and rubbish in the Iron Age of Wessex: a study on the formation of a specific archaeological record.* Oxford, British Archaeological Reports.

Hodder, I. 1989. Writing archaeology: site reports in context. *Antiquity* 63, 268–74.

Hodder, I. 1992. *Theory and Practice in Archaeology.* London, Routledge.

Hodder, I. 1997. 'Always momentary, fluid and flexible': towards a reflexive excavation methodology. *Antiquity* 71, 691–700.

Hodder, I. 1999. *The Archaeological Process: An Introduction.* Oxford, Blackwell.

Hutton, R. 1997. The Neolithic great goddess: a study in modern tradition. *Antiquity* 71, 91–99.

Leighton, R. 1989. Antiquarianism and prehistory in west Mediterranean islands. *The Antiquaries Journal* 69, 183–204.

Mallia, F. S. 1965. Prehistoric Finds, in *Missione archeologica italiana a Malta. Rapporto preliminare della Campagna 1964.* Roma, Università di Roma, 73–78.

Malone, C. A. T., S. K. F. Stoddart and A. Townsend. 1995. The landscape of the Island Goddess? A Maltese perspective of the central Mediterranean. *Caeculus* 2, 1–15.

Marmora, A. de la. 1836. Lettre à Monsieur Raoul Rochette, membre de l'Institut archéologique, sur le Temple de l'Isle de Gozo dit La Tour des Géants. *Nouvelles annales publiées par la section française de l'Institut archéologique* 1, 1–33.

Needham, S. P. and A. J. Spence. 1996. *Refuse and Disposal at Area 16 East Runnymede.* London, British Museum Press.

Needham, S. P. and A. J. Spence. 1997. Refuse and the formation of middens. *Antiquity* 71, 77–90.

Noble, V. 1989. Marija Gimbutas: Reclaiming the Great Goddess. *Snake Power* 1, 5–7.

Pace, A. 2004a. *The Hal Saflieni Hypogeum, Paola.* Malta, Heritage Books in association with Heritage Malta.

Pace, A. 2004b. The sites. In D. Cilia (ed.). *Malta before History: the world's oldest free-standing stone architecture.* Malta: Miranda Publications, 42–227.

Pearce, S. M. 1992. *Museums, Objects and Collections.* Washington DC, Smithsonian Institution Press.

Perrot, G. and C. Chipiez. 1885. *History of Art in Phoenicia and its Dependencies*, vol. I. London, Chapman and Hall Ltd.

Pessina, A. and N. Vella. 2005. *Luigi Maria Ugolini: Un archeologico italiano a Malta/An Italian Archaeologist in Malta.* Malta, Midsea Books.

Renfrew, C. 1985. *The Archaeology of Cult: The Sanctuary of Phylakopi.* London, The British School of Archaeology at Athens and Thames and Hudson.

Renfrew, C. 1986. The prehistoric Maltese achievement and its interpretation. In A. Bonanno (ed.), 118–30.

Riccio, M. 1951. *Civiltà megalitica dell'arcipelago maltese.* Roma, Università di Roma, Istituto di Paetnologia.

Rountree, K. 1999. Goddesses and monsters: contesting approaches to Malta's Neolithic past, *Journal of Mediterranean Studies* 9, 201–31.

Rountree, K. 2002. Re-inventing Malta's Neolithic temples: contemporary interpretations and agendas. *History and Anthropology* 13, 31–51.

Schiffer, M. B. 1972. Archaeological context and systemic context. *American Antiquity* 37, 156–65.

Schiffer, M. B. 1987. *Formation Processes of the Archaeological Record.* Albuquerque, University of New Mexico Press.

Skeates, R. 2005. Museum archaeology and the Mediterranean cultural heritage. In E. Blake and A. B. Knapp (ed.). *The Archaeology of Mediterranean Prehistory.* Oxford, Blackwell Publishing, 303–20.

Smith, W. Robertson. 1927. *Lectures on the Religion of the Semites: The Fundamental Institutions.* 3rd edition. London, A. and C. Black Ltd.

Stoddart, S., A. Bonanno, T. Gouder, C. Malone and D. Trump. 1993. Cult in an island society: prehistoric Malta in the Tarxien period. *Cambridge Archaeological Journal* 3, 3–19.

Sultana, S. 2006. *The National Museum of Archaeology: the Neolithic period.* Insight Heritage Guides. Malta, Heritage Books in association with Heritage Malta.

Tallack, W. 1861. *Malta under the Phoenicians, Knights and English.* London, A. W. Bennett and Houlstone and Wright.

Tilley, C. 2004. *The Materiality of Stone: Explorations in Landscape Phenomenology.* Oxford, Berg.

Turnbull, D. 2002. Performance and narrative, bodies and movement in the construction of places and objects, spaces and knowledges: the case of the Maltese megaliths. *Theory, Culture and Society* 19, 125–43.

Ugolini, L. 1931. La venere preistorica di Malta. *Dedalo* 11, 1281–86.

Vance, J. G. 1842. Description of an ancient temple near Crendi, Malta. In a letter from J. G. Vance, Esq. to Nicholas Carlisle, Esq. K.H., F.R.S., Secretary. *Archaeologia* 29, 227–40.

Vassallo, C. 1853. Phoenician and Egyptian Monuments in Malta. *The Art-Journal* 5: 221–24.

Vassallo, C. 1872. *A Guide to the Museum or The Ancient Monuments of Malta preserved in the Museum of the Public Library.* Malta, Government Printing Office.

Vergo, P. 1989. The reticent object. In P. Vergo (ed.). *The New Museology.* London, Reaktion Books, 41–59.

Vella, N. and Gilkes, O. 2001. The lure of the antique: nationalism, politics and archaeology in British Malta (1880–1964). *Papers of the British School at Rome* 69, 353–84.

Vella Gregory, I. 2006. *The Human Form in Neolithic Malta.* Malta, Midsea Books.

Warren, P. 1986. Review of C. Renfrew (1986). *Antiquity* 60, 155–56.

Zammit, T. 1906–1921. *Notes Connected with the Language and the History of Malta taken from Books Read I.* Unpublished manuscript.

Zammit, T. 1909. *Annual report of the Museum Department, 1908-1909.* Malta, Government Printing Office.

Zammit, T. 1919. *Guide to the Valletta Museum with a historical summary.* Malta, Government Printing Office.

Zammit, T. 1926. *The Hal-Saflieni Neolithic Hypogeum.* 2nd edn. Malta, Empire Press.

Zammit, T. 1930. *Prehistoric Malta: the Tarxien Temples.* Oxford, Oxford University Press.

Zammit, T., Peet, T. E. and Bradley, R. N. 1912. *The Small Objects and Human Skulls found in the Hal-Saflieni Prehistoric Hypoguem at Casal Paula, Malta.* 2nd Report. Malta.

Zammit, T. and Singer, C. 1924. Neolithic representations of the human form the islands of Malta and Gozo. *The Journal of Royal Anthropological Institute of Great Britain and Ireland* 54, 67–100.

Chapter 11

EPHEBISM IN MALTESE PREHISTORIC ART?

Andrew Townsend

Introduction

This paper explores the premise that form and symbol, as represented by the anthropomorphic imagery of the Maltese Temple Period (*c.* 4100–2500 BC), expressed an ideal surrounding the primacy of life of both males *and* females. The term adopted for this notion is ephebism. The notion of ephebism, as expressed in art, was pioneered by Yale art historian Robert Thompson in his 1970s critique of Yoruba art of sub-Saharan Africa (Thompson 1973). Thompson (*op. cit.*) employed the term not singularly for male or female but for 'people', considering it the most important aspect of his exposition. For Thompson, ephebism was, essentially, the artistic rendition of people in the prime of their life.

In terms of its Greek origin, ephebism is strictly speaking a male-orientated term. Its use, therefore, for the male and female tense, as undertaken by Thompson (*op. cit.*) and in the present paper, would be incorrect without some explication. The *Oxford English Dictionary* (Simpson and Weiner 1989, 321) defines ephebe as:

> Among the Greeks, a young citizen from
> eighteen to twenty years of age, during which he
> was occupied chiefly with garrison duty.

And where e'phebic is defined as:

> of or pertaining to an ephebus, or to early manhood.

Youthfulness, strength and well-being are thus implied to be the qualities that, in terms of their totality, make for the idealized male. Thompson's dual-sex application of ephebism, divorced from its Classical tense and usage, serves as a convenient heuristic device to denote the primacy of life whether male or female. It is suggested in this paper that the artists of prehistoric Malta used the asexual human form in what artistically may be termed an 'unnaturalistic' way and embellished it with symbolism that signified the primacy of life. In this way, images were created that signified an ideal state of being in the world.

The Temple Period of Malta

The Temple Period of the Maltese islands is generally considered to commence in the Żebbuġ phase (*c.* 4100–3700 BC) although it is only with the Ġgantija phase (*c.* 3600–3200 BC) that the first temples appear (Bonanno *et al.* 1990). In addition to the above-ground temples, subterranean complexes for the deceased (hypogea) were also constructed although only two examples have been discovered to date (Malone *et al.* forthcoming; Pace 2000; 2004). Regrettably, there is at present a noticeable and problematic shortage of settlement evidence on the islands (Malone *et al.* 1988).

Through time, the temple architecture appears to have undergone a process of elaboration, not only in terms of configuration, but also with the incorporation of elaborate artistic schemes (Stoddart *et al.* 1993). At Tarxien, considered to be the most elaborate of all the temples, stone slabs are carved in relief with spirals and others with rows of animals (Evans 1971, plate 18.3). The image of a snake was found at Ġgantija (Evans 1971, figure 61) and fish at Buġibba (Evans 1971, plates 13.2 and 3). Such temple embellishments constitute, in part, the fixed or static component of the artistic element in the temples. There is, in addition, a repertoire of portable art objects including anthropomorphic figures, containers, altars, niches and even models of temples (Evans 1971, plates 33.11 and 12). While acknowledging the considerable scope and variation of Temple Period art it is specifically the production of the anthropomorphic form and related symbolism which is the central focus of the ephebism model proposed in this paper.

Anthropomorphic imagery of the Temple Period

The anthropomorphic imagery of the Temple Period is probably one of its most outstanding features and is primarily represented three-dimensionally, although some pottery surface-designs are thought to represent the anthropomorphic form. By way of contrast, zoomorphic and 'abstract' imagery is generally found carved in relief on large blocks.

In the Żebbuġ phase (c. 4100–3700 BC) the anthropomorphic image was manifested in the form of small 'menhirs' of which to date only two examples are known (Evans 1971, plates 61.7 and 8; Malone et al. 1995a, figure 17), and possible surface-designs on pottery (Malone et al. 1995a, figure 12a).

The proliferation of temple construction in the Ġgantija phase (c. 3600–3200 BC) heralds an episode of intense artistic expression lasting over one millennium, reaching its zenith in the Tarxien phase (c. 3150–2500 BC). It is probably fair to say that this somewhat abstruse phase of the islands' prehistoric trajectory boasts evidence for ritual and ceremonial activities on an unprecedented scale and for which the anthropomorphic image appears to have been an essential component.

A frame of reference for Temple Period anthropomorphic imagery has been devised by Malone et al. (1995b). Three portability-factored categories of object are proposed: statues (fixed), statuettes (portable) and figurines (portable). The usefulness of the model is partly in the way it helps forge a pathway of understanding for the way in which objects of different physical scale (statues, statuettes, figurines) were possibly used and functioned in different site contexts or 'domains' (temple, hypogeum [?]settlement). Beyond this observable disparity in physical scale, however, is also a raft of symbolic elements that appear to bridge between the objects and thus cut across scale and context. These 'social aspects of the human body' (Polhemus 1978) include: hairstyle/headdress, skirt design, posture, colouration, abstract symbols (see Figure 11.1) and, no doubt, others awaiting discovery.

At present there is quantitatively insufficient data to facilitate patterning formulation or other type of analysis from the Malta assemblage. A number of the symbolic elements, however, betray definite structuration of design which attend to some level of inference. Examples of figurative work excavated at the Xagħra Circle in the 1990s incorporate the symbolic elements included in Figure 11.1. First, fragments of what was originally a large skirted anthropomorphic figure of the statue class of object (Figure 11.2). Not enough of the object survives to permit detailed discussion. Important to note, however, is the distinct design of the skirt and standing posture. Second, a limestone twin-seated figure of the statuette class (Figure 11.3). In terms of its sheer symbolic content, this is probably the most elaborate and complex of all the figures excavated on the Maltese islands to date. One of the people depicted holds what appears to be a child while the other (head missing) appears to be clasping a small container. Although

one of the heads is missing, traces on the torso suggest that both people originally incorporated a distinct hairstyle or headdress. Abstract symbolism is represented in the form of 'Tarxien Spirals' on the bed (Beck 1993) or bench on which the people are seated. The top of the bench and bulbous legs of the two people are also embellished with red ochre. It is interesting to note that the object appears to have been created in order to be seen from all angles, including the base which is carved with an elaborate fretwork design. What appears to be structuration in design is to be found on the skirt element of the figure. At least three different skirt designs are depicted but do not give the impression of being indiscriminately applied. What might be considered to be an expression of bipolarity is symbolised on the back of the object by the use of two distinct skirt designs which happen to meet exactly at the juncture of the two seated people. The entire front of the object, however, incorporates only a single skirt design. The figure holding the infant or child has been interpreted as a mother holding her child and is thus female; by implication the second figure has been seen as of the male sex. Close examination, however, reveals that no biological sex is overtly depicted. Nevertheless, even if the representation of biological sex was originally intended there is nothing depicted that would allow us to make a firm attribution. In terms of physical scale, the figure appears to be a smaller version of a truncated statue of the same configuration built into the walls at Ħaġar Qim (Vella Gregory 2005, figure 179). Third, a group of six staff figures of the statuette category accompanied by three limestone figurines and a miniature pot bearing traces of red ochre (Figure 11.4). All six staff figures are anthropomorphic in form while the figurines comprise two anthropomorphs and a zoomorph (?pig or dog). Familiar symbolic elements are present on the anthropomorphic figures including the depiction of distinct hairstyles/headdresses and Tarxien skirts. The tapering block configuration of the upper torso of the figures appears to be symbolic and is also present in the form of megaliths at the temples and Xagħra Circle (Evans 1971, plate 9.1). In a not dissimilar way, statuette representations of the phallus (Evans 1971, plate 51.1) may refer to statue-size betyls such as that at Ħaġar Qim (Trump 2002, 76). A puzzling aspect of the anthropomorphic figures is their different stages of completeness (Stoddart et al. 1993). Had the figures been recovered from a workshop context this might then be explained without too much difficulty, but a mortuary context find spot presents us with a far greater puzzle to solve. There is no indication as to the biological sex of the figures although their angularity of form gives the impression of being male (McElroy 1954). Fourth, over twenty figurine-class objects, mostly ceramic (Figure 11.5) were recovered from the Xagħra Circle. The majority of the objects were recovered from a carefully demarcated

Hairstyle/Headdress
(Hallpike 1969)

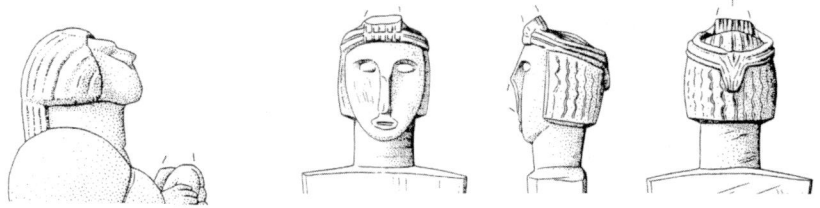

'Skirt' Design

Posture
(Hewes 1955, 1957)

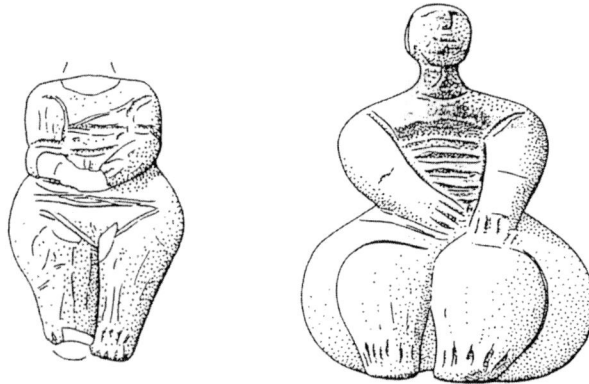

Colouration
(Gage *et al.* 1999)

Abstract Designs

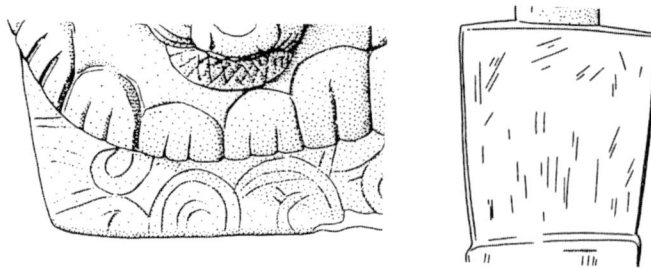

Figure 11.1. Common symbols employed on prehistoric Maltese anthropomorphic figures. (Drawn by Steven Ashley.)

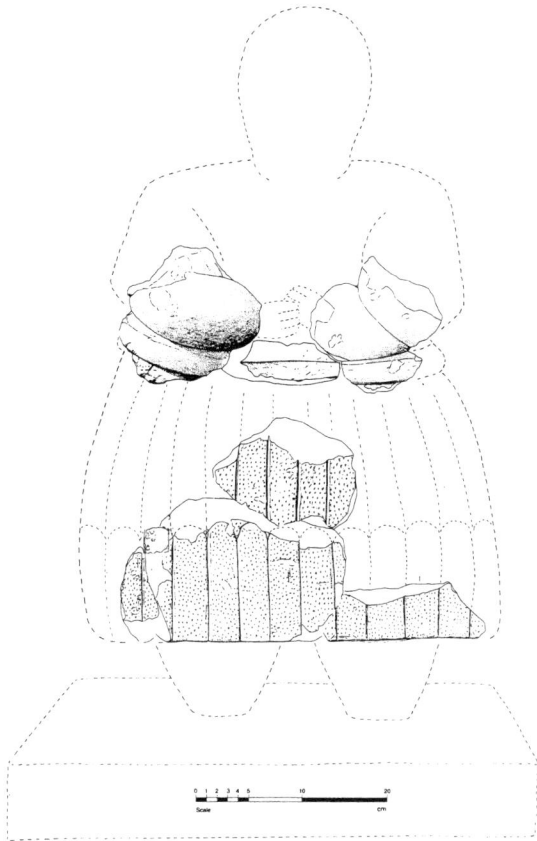

Figure 11.2 (left). Reconstruction of an anthropomorphic statue based on limestone fragments excavated at the Xaġhra Circle, Gozo. (Drawn by Ben Plumridge.)

Figure 11.3 (below). Triple anthropomorphic statuette carved from limestone, excavated at the Xaġhra Circle, Gozo. (Drawn by Steven Ashley.)

Figure 11.4. Selection from group (N=6) of staff figurines carved from limestone excavated at the Xagħra Circle, Gozo. (Drawn by Steven Ashley.)

area containing many human burials (known on site as 'the bone pit'). While none of the objects appears to be 'dressed' they do show variation in terms of the type of posture depicted. Some also incorporate rudimentary hairstyles. The apparent 'nudity' of the figures may also be symbolic (Townsend forthcoming). An upper torso and head fragment of one of the figures incorporates what appears to be deliberate incisions on one upper arm and the abdomen. Whether these markings represent meaningful symbols, possibly tattoos, has not been agreed upon to date. Similarly, there is no agreement as to which biological sex (if any) is being depicted, although many have been indiscriminately labelled as female (and, by implication, representations of the Mother Goddess).

A

B

C

D

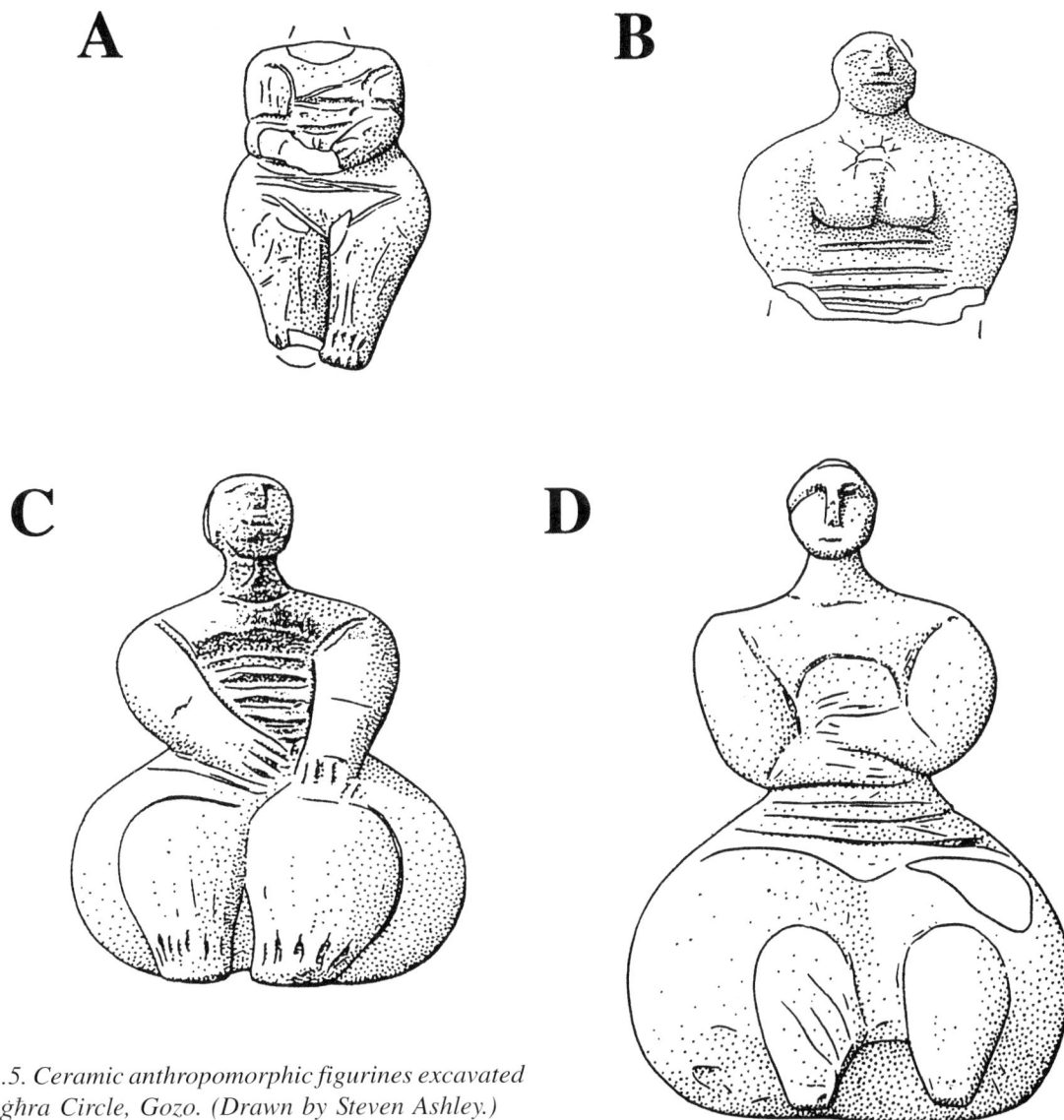

Figure 11.5. Ceramic anthropomorphic figurines excavated at the Xagħra Circle, Gozo. (Drawn by Steven Ashley.)

Assessing the symbolism of Temple Period anthropomorphic imagery

The visual evidence at hand demonstrates that a complex raft of symbols was incorporated in the anthropomorphic imagery of the Temple Period of the Maltese islands. This includes the overt (e.g. hairstyle/headdress) to the less overt (e.g. human posture).

A problem exists, however, when it comes to the attribution of biological sex to the figures. There are examples modelled with definite female attributes such as breasts (Evans 1971, plate 40.10) where a female attribution would appear to be safe. Yet the majority are generally ambiguous, bearing no readily identifiable sexual attributes whatsoever. Given this situation, it is surprising that the vast majority of known figures have been passively accepted as female representations.

What can be gleaned from this quandary concerning depicted symbolism and sexual ambiguity? Are we indeed fooling ourselves in attempting to attribute specific sex to the figures when it is possible that this was never intended by their makers?

It is apparent that much of the symbolism discussed in this paper tends to cut across the range of anthropomorphic images (figurine, statuette, statue) and also appears with other cultural manifestations such as temple/hypogeum elements (e.g. tapering megaliths, spiral motifs). The use of symbolic elements was not the only artistic device employed in the production of figures. In addition, a convention of physical scale was clearly employed as evidenced by the statue, statuette and figurine categories of object. The use of scale as a communicative device appears to have been omnipresent in Temple Period Malta. Not only is it found employed with figurines and statuary but in a number of other circumstances. Thus we find small temple-model amulets, models of temples, engravings of temples and the full life-size temples themselves. There are also miniature pots, 'standard' pots and massive carved-stone bowls. A combination of form and scale clearly played an important symbolic role in artistic creativity during the Temple Period and appears to be yet another device used in the ratification of ritual and ceremonial performance (Townsend 1999).

Ephebism: towards a better understanding of prehistoric Maltese art

If one problematic area had to be identified in prehistoric Maltese art studies, the attribution of biological sex to anthropomorphic imagery would stand as a good candidate. The images have all too often fallen prey to mis-interpretation on a grand scale mainly on the assumption that, unless patently otherwise, they are representations of the female. The firmly entrenched Mother Goddess or Great Earth Mother hypothesis is partly the product of such reasoning (Gimbutas 1974; 1991) (Figure 11.6). Yet, even

Figure 11.6. The 'Goddess Matrix'.

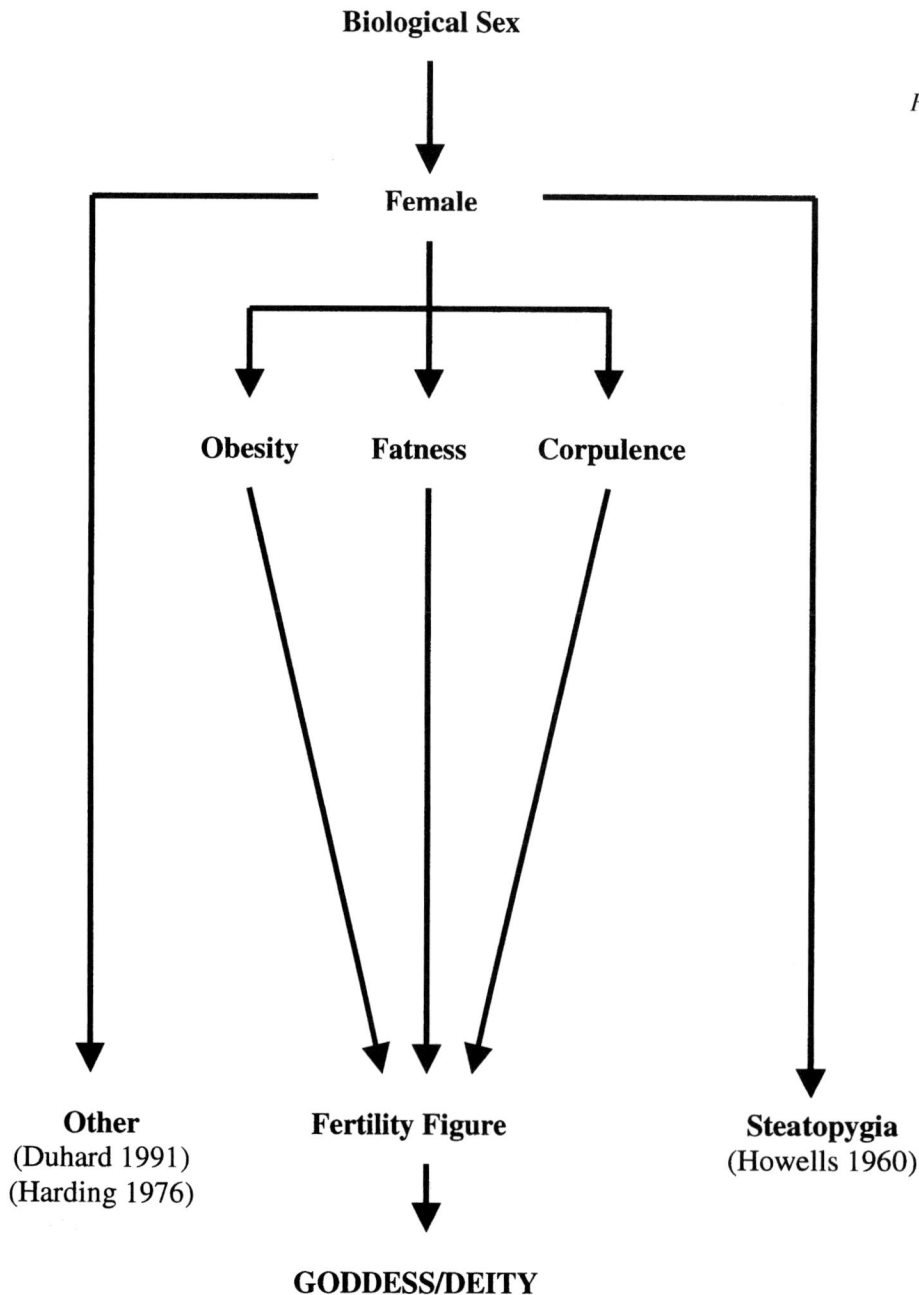

a cursory glance at the known images suggests that sexual ambiguity appears to predominate. The notion of producing imagery that is sexually ambiguous may be further elucidated to by the fact that some figures were made with removable (?interchangeable) heads (Evans 1971, plate 39.20).

A model of ephebism, as proposed here, allows us to break away from the obsession of attributing biological sex to the figures. Instead, an idealised state of the person is seen as that depicted in the art (Figure 11.7). Symbolic attributes such as hairstyle/headdress or skirt designs may represent participation in ceremonial engagement rather than sexual markers and could apply to male or female alike. An important observation in this respect is that symbols such as the 'Tarxien Skirt' are seen employed on different forms of object and across physical scale (statuette, statue). Other symbols such as the tapering block and spiral were employed for the embellishment of statuettes and also used as architectural components in the temples and surface decoration in the hypogea. In this respect the symbols may be viewed as neutral in that they do not appear to indicate biological sex but rather a common value, possibly that relating to a state of well-being or primacy of people in general.

The idea of ephebism in Temple Period art is based on the notion that primacy of life, well-being of the individual and longevity of society as a whole were important ideals for society and naturally applied equally to both sexes. Can it therefore be reasoned that the ideal state of people was expressed in the art neutrally, devoid of sexual affiliation?

Ceremonial activities enacted within the temples and hypogea (Evans 1976–77; 1996) may have entailed separate male and female elements of order and space, but it was possibly an ideal common to both sexes that ultimately prevailed. In the small-scale Temple society of Malta and Gozo such an ideal could be readily upheld through cult practices. An ideology concerning the primacy of life may have been the product of ever-changing dynamics taking place within a *relatively* isolated island environment where demographic factors and the reliability on the physical environment played important roles. External factors, possibly involving trade networks in the central Mediterranean and beyond, may also have played their part.

Contrary to popular belief, it is often when societies are under stress or even threatened by extinction that artistic expression and creativity come to the fore (Taçon 1983; Wolf 1999). This is accompanied by ritual practices entailing the use of cultic paraphernalia. A not dissimilar situation may have prevailed on Temple Period Malta. Thus, the ideology surrounding ephebism may be perceived as a social mechanism for coping with the strains resulting from social perturbations. There is indeed ample evidence on the Maltese islands for ritual and ceremonial practices to support this suggestion (Evans 1976–77).

Conclusion

It is partly the task of archaeology to interpret the material evidence of past human activities. In the absence of historical accounts or description prehistorians in particular are faced with an archaeological 'black box' (Leach 1973). Cognisant of the theoretical hurdles posed by prehistoric data (Hawkes 1954) it is apparent that there is, nevertheless, a universe of symbolism waiting to 'speak' to us, provided we are prepared to accept numerous shortcomings in terms of what can be achieved. Put simply, we have to accept that some of the intent and meaning of the objects is now lost to us for ever.

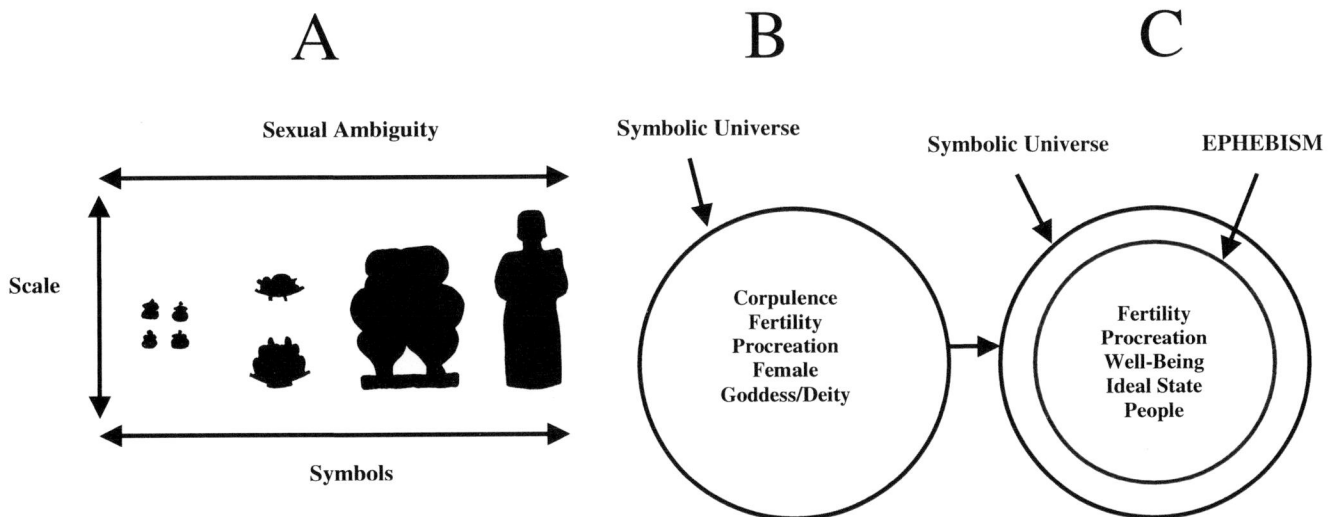

Figure 11.7. Ephebism model for Maltese prehistoric anthropomorphic imagery.

This paper has attempted to retrieve a degree of meaning from Temple Period art of the Maltese islands, albeit based on a notion derived from modern-day observations of tribal art in West Africa. The symbolism overtly, and less overtly, displayed in the Temple Period anthropomorphic imagery, it is suggested, represents an idealized state of being irrespective of biological sex.

A model of ephebism, essentially, paves the way for argumentation that is free from the fetters of sexual bipolarity or sexual dominance. It considers 'people', female and/or male, in an idealised state of existence. The prime of life of individuals, female or male, is an ideal that may have been central to the beliefs of a small island society that are the Maltese islands. If, by the end of the Temple Period, society was experiencing some form of stress, this is likely to have been the end result of ongoing cumulative effects rather than sudden unexpected events, although the latter should not be ruled out. In such a social environment, ideals may have been at the forefront of expression played out through ritual and ceremony (Shils 1966). Nudity itself may also have played an important role in this respect (Townsend, forthcoming).

The question must be asked: if we are indeed looking at renditions of the human ideal in Temple Period art was this then an inversion of social reality?

Acknowledgements

I should like to thank Drs Caroline Malone and Simon Stoddart for allowing me access to the Xagħra Circle material, including the artwork by Steven Ashley.

References

Beck, P. 1993. Early Bronze Age 'Bed-Models' Reconsidered. *Tel Aviv* 20 (1), 33–40.

Biaggi, C. 1986. The Significance of the Nudity, Obesity and Sexuality of the Maltese Goddess Figures. In A. Bonanno (ed.). *Archaeology and Fertility Cult in the Ancient Mediterranean. Papers Presented at the First International Conference on Archaeology of the Ancient Mediterranean. The University of Malta 2–5 September 1985.* Amsterdam, B.R. Grüner Publishing Co., 131–140.

Biaggi, C. 1989. The Priestess Figure of Malta. In I. Hodder (ed.). *The Meanings of Things: Material Culture and Symbolic Expression.* London, Unwin Hyman Ltd, 103–121.

Duhard, J-P. 1991. The Shape of Pleistocene Women. *Antiquity* 65 (248), 552–561.

Bonanno, A., Gouder, T., Malone, C. and Stoddart, S. 1990. Monuments in an Island Society: The Maltese Context. *World Archaeology* 22 (2), 190–205.

Evans, J. D. 1971. *The Prehistoric Antiquities of the Maltese Islands: A Survey.* London, The Athlone Press.

Evans, J. D. 1973. Islands as Laboratories for the Study of Culture Process. In, Renfrew, C. (ed.). *The Explanation of Culture Change: Models in Prehistory.* London, Gerald Duckworth and Co. Ltd, 517–520.

Evans, J. D. 1976–77. Archaeological Evidences for Religious Practices in the Maltese Islands During the Neolithic and Copper Ages. *Kokalos* 22–23 (1), 130–146.

Evans, J. D. 1977. Island Archaeology in the Mediterranean: Problems and Opportunities. *World Archaeology* 9 (1), 12–26.

Evans, J. D. 1984. Maltese Prehistory – A Reappraisal. In, W. H. Waldren, R. Chapman, J. Lewthwaite and R-C. Kennard (eds). *The Deya Conference of Prehistory. Early Settlement in the Western Mediterranean Islands and Their Peripheral Areas. Part ii.* Oxford, BAR IS 229 (ii), 489–497.

Evans, J. D. 1996. What Went on in a Maltese Megalithic Temple? In A. Pace (ed.). *Maltese Prehistoric Art 5000–2500 BC.* Fondazzjoni Patrimonju Malti in Association with The National Museum of Archaeology. Valletta, Patrimonju Publishing Limited, 39–44.

Gage, J., Barber, E. J. W., Bradley, R., Jones, A., Spence, K. and Taçon, P. S. C. 1999. What Meaning Had Colour in Early Societies? *Cambridge Archaeological Journal* 9 (1), 109–126.

Gimbutas, M. 1974. *The Gods and Goddesses of Old Europe 7000–3500 BC: Myths, Legends and Cult Images.* London, Thames and Hudson Ltd.

Gimbutas, M. 1991. *The Civilization of the Goddess: The World of Old Europe.* San Francisco, Harper San Francisco.

Gregory, I. V. 2005. *The Human Form in Neolithic Malta.* Malta, Midsea Books Ltd.

Hallpike, C. R. 1969. Social Hair. *Man* (New Series) 4 (2), 256–264.

Harding, J. R. 1976. Certain Upper Palaeolithic 'Venus' Statuettes Considered in Relation to the Pathological Condition Known as Massive Hypertrophy of the Breasts. *Man* 11, 271–272.

Hawkes, C. 1954. Archaeological Theory and Method: Some Suggestions from the Old World. *American Anthropologist* 56 (2.1), 155–168.

Hayden, C. 1998. Monuments, Hierarchy and Obesity: Perceptions of Size in Temple Period Malta. *Archaeological Review from Cambridge (The Archaeology of Perception and the Senses)* 15 (1), 49–74.

Hewes, G. W. 1955. World Distribution of Certain Postural Habits. *American Anthropologist* 57 (2), 231–244.

Hewes, G. W. 1957. The Anthropology of Posture. *Scientific American* 196 (2), 122–132.

Howells, W. W. 1960. The Distribution of Man. *Scientific American* 203 (3), 113–127.

Leach, E. 1973. Concluding Address. In C. Renfrew (ed.). *The Explanation of Culture Change: Models in Prehistory.* London, Gerald Duckworth and Co. Ltd, 761–771.

Malone, C. 1998. God or Goddess: The Temple Art of Ancient Malta. In L. Goodison and C. Morris (eds). *Ancient Goddesses: The Myths and the Evidence.* London, The British Museum Press, 148–163.

Malone, C., Bonanno, A., Gouder, T., Stoddart, S. and Trump, D. 1993. The Death Cults of Prehistoric Malta. *Scientific American* 269 (6), 76–83.

Malone, C. and Stoddart, S. 1995. Discoveries at the Brochtorff Circle. *Treasures of Malta* 1 (2), 15–19.

Malone, C. and Stoddart, S. 1998. The Conditions of Creativity for Prehistoric Maltese Art. In S. Mithen (ed.). *Creativity in Human Evolution and Prehistory*. London, Routledge, 241–259.

Malone, C., Stoddart, S., Bonanno, A., Gouder, T. and Trump, D. 1995a. Mortuary Ritual of 4th Millennium BC Malta: The Żebbuġ Period Chambered Tomb from the Brochtorff Circle at Xagħra (Gozo). *Proceedings of the Prehistoric Society* 61, 303–345.

Malone, C., Stoddart, S. and Townsend, A. 1995b. The Landscape of the Island Goddess? A Maltese Perspective of the Central Mediterranean. *Caecvlvs* II. Papers on Mediterranean Archaeology, Archaeological Institute, Groningen University, 1–15.

Malone, C., Stoddart, S. and Trump, D., 1988. A House for the Temple Builders: Recent Investigations on Gozo, Malta. *Antiquity* 62, 297–301.

Malone, C., Stoddart, S., Trump, D., Bonanno, A. the late Gouder, T., and Pace, A. forthcoming. *Excavations at the Brochtorff Xagħra Circle, Gozo, 1987–1994*. Cambridge, McDonald Institute Monographs.

Marshack, A. 1981. On Paleolithic Ochre and the Early Uses of Color and Symbol. *Current Anthropology* 22 (2), 188–191.

McElroy, W. A. 1954. A Sex Difference in Preferences for Shapes. *British Journal of Psychology* (General Section) XLV, 209–216.

Pace, A. 1994. Prehistoric Art Forms from Megalithic Malta. *Treasures of Malta* 1 (1), 39–43.

Pace, A. (ed.), 2000. *The Ħal Saflieni Hypogeum 4000 B.C. – 2000 A.D.* Malta, National Museum of Archaeology.

Pace, A. 2004. *The Ħal Saflieni Hypogeum, Paola*. Insight Heritage Guides Series No. 3. Malta, Heritage Books.

Polhemus, T. (ed.) 1978. *Social Aspects of the Human Body: A Reader of Key Texts*. Harmondsworth, Penguin Books Ltd.

Robb, J. 2001. Island Identities: Ritual, Travel and the Creation of Difference in Neolithic Malta. *European Journal of Archaeology* 4 (2), 175–202.

Shils, E. 1966. Ritual and Crisis. *Philosophical Transactions of the Royal Society of London* (Series B) 251, 447–450.

Simpson, J. A. and Weiner, E. S. C. 1989. *The Oxford English Dictionary, Volume V*. Second Edition. Oxford, Oxford University Press.

Stoddart, S., Bonanno, A., Gouder, T., Malone, C. and Trump, D. 1993. Cult in an Island Society: Prehistoric Malta in the Tarxien Period. *Cambridge Archaeological Journal* 3 (1), 3–19.

Taçon, P. 1983. An Analysis of Dorset Art in Relation to Prehistoric Culture Stress. *Études/Inuit/Studies* 7 (1), 41–65.

Thompson, R. F. 1973. Yoruba Artistic Criticism. In W. D'Azevedo (ed.). *The Traditional Artist in African Societies*. Bloomington and London, Indiana University Press, 19–61.

Townsend, A. P. J. 1997. The Materially-Structured Social Environment of the Maltese Islands During the Temple Building Phase. In G. Nash (ed.). *Semiotics of Landscape: Archaeology of Mind*. BAR IS 661. Oxford, Archaeopress, 89–104.

Townsend, A. P. J. 1999. The Social Context of Maltese Prehistoric Art. In A. Mifsud and C. Savona-Ventura (eds). *Facets of Maltese Prehistory*. Malta, The Prehistoric Society of Malta, 117–135.

Townsend, A. P. L. (forthcoming). *Ritualized Nudity in Prehistoric Malta?*

Trump, D. H. 1963. A Prehistoric Art Cycle in Malta. *The British Journal of Aesthetics* 3 (3), 237–244.

Trump, D. H. 1996. Art in Pottery. In A. Pace (ed.) *Maltese Prehistoric Art 5000–2500 BC*. Fondazzjoni Patrimonju Malti in Association with The National Museum of Archaeology, 31–37. Valletta, Patrimonju Publishing Limited.

Trump, D. H. 2002. *Malta: Prehistory and Temples*. Malta, Midsea Books Ltd.

Wolf, E. R. 1999. *Envisioning Power: Ideologies of Dominance and Crisis*. London, University of California Press, Ltd.

Wreschner, E. E.1980. Red Ochre and Human Evolution: A Case for Discussion. *Current Anthropology* 21 (5), 631–644.

Zammit, T. and Singer, C. 1924. Neolithic Representations of the Human Form from the Islands of Malta and Gozo. *Journal of the Royal Anthropological Institute* LIV, 67–100.

Chapter 12

GENDER TENSION IN FIGURINES
IN SE EUROPE

Robin Hardie

This paper is a first attempt to show that cross-cultural patterns are visible in diachronic changes in representations of maleness (including phallic imagery) and female sensuality (i.e. erotic aspects of female imagery) in Neolithic and Chalcolithic figurines across southeast Europe. These previously unremarked patterns may reveal a gender dynamic inherent in the Neolithic cultural model which spread northwards from Greece.

Allied to notions of agency and contestation these patterns suggest a shift away from a perceived and possibly resented female prominence in ritual and perhaps society which was associated with and partly expressed by the representation of sensuality. If views that the status of women is higher in societies where there is less division between the domestic and public spheres (Sanday 1973) and that 'some small-scale foraging and horticultural societies are among the most socially and sexually egalitarian societies in the world' (Lepowski 1990, 177) are correct these patterns could indicate that some elements of Gimbutas' perspective were not entirely fantastic. It may also be relevant that current explanations for the emergence of male ideology and chiefdoms at the start of the Bronze Age are lacking in depth of time. It would not be surprising if these developments were at least partly enabled by changes in the Chalcolithic, themselves possibly stretching back into the Neolithic. Any indications of a shift towards maleness in these horizons may therefore be of wider interest.

The ideas outlined here are the result of broader research into representations of maleness in figurine cultures in central and SE Europe and the Mediterranean. These representations often show more variation than female figurines and fall into categories that seem to hold across different cultures and horizons. Moreover, they appear to have a recurring and almost predictable relationship with, in particular, the sensuality of female figurines.

I will first address some of the theoretical issues raised by the approach taken – notably regarding gender, sensuality and cross-cultural comparisons – before turning

to the different types of maleness in figurines in southeast Europe and finally to specific gender patterns in figurines in the southern and central Balkans and in the Chalcolithic Tripolye culture in Moldavia and the Ukraine.

Recent research on figurines has focused largely on abstract concepts of identity and representation. Amongst others, Biehl (1996 *et al.*) has written on symbolic designs, Chapman (2000) on fragmentation, Talalay (2004) on decapitation and Bailey (2005) on the mechanisms of social homogenization. There are frequent citations of Butler's theory of performativity and the construction of personal and group identities through figurines. These directions of research may be works in progress but they have yet to yield real dividends, at least for the non-specialist. A Cambridge conference in 2005 ('Image and Imagination: Material Beginnings. The Global History of Figurative Representation' at The McDonald Institute, 13–17 September 2005) struggled to identify new perspectives offering more than just marginal progress.

These are restricted by two limitations which archaeologists currently impose on themselves. Both concern existing and readily available data which, if the thesis of this paper is in any way correct, could substantially increase our understanding of these horizons and the role that figurines played in them. These limitations are contextual particularism and what I call the PG syndrome – post-Gimbutas. It seems that transgressing either could be professionally hazardous because it rarely happens.

The combination of contextual particularism (as a theoretical approach) and geographical specialization (as a professional constraint) discourages comparative analysis of prehistoric figurines from different cultures and horizons. In this context it is possible that potentially significant similarities and patterns are overlooked and even unwanted. However, it is at least plausible to posit that the various traditions are connected in some ways, starting with their origins. None maintains that figurines in the Ukraine or Moravia sprang up spontaneously with no connection to the traditions in SE Europe. Indeed, it seems they all derive from Greece where figurines appeared with the rest of the Neolithic package which was already fully formed (Perles 2001).

Aspects of their use and meaning must have differed across cultures and horizons – and even villages – but their principal context (domestic), material (clay), subject (the body) and size (miniaturized) are relatively constant. There can be variance in one of these factors, such as the bone figurines from Kodzadermen and the figurines in graves in Hamangia, but rarely, if ever, in two. This suggests a broad, underlying coincidence.

A proposed connection between the various traditions is supported by the relatively sudden (by archaeological standards) and still unexplained reduction or outright disappearance of figurines in most cultures by or in the Chalcolithic. The cause is not obviously external. One could postulate influence from the Pontic steppes but how then could we explain the rich, and late, traditions of Cucuteni and Tripolye in the Chalcolithic itself? These cultures lie exactly between the steppes and SE Europe. If the cause was internal it might be suggested in the figurines themselves, reflecting – and partly constituting – a dynamic tension in these early farming societies, which led to a similar result in nearly every case: the disappearance of figurines, often without their replacement by other material signs of cult. The existence both of common attributes in the early figurines of different traditions and of similar patterns in their later evolution would support this thesis. If cult and everyday life in these horizons were indeed intimately enmeshed, these might allow us to glimpse changes in both.

The second limitation, the PG syndrome, concerns gender. The retreat from an interest in gender in figurines after (and in reaction to?) the publication of Gimbutas' books was, ironically, encouraged by feminist writers. They warned that an emphasis on female figurines or any suggestion of female goddesses could undermine the goals of feminist archaeology and even feminism itself by promoting the essentialist view of the 'elevated status of women …[as]…due to their reproductive capabilities' (Talalay 1994, 173). Since the late 1980s most writing on figurines has been gender-neutral or even -neutered. In the excavation report on Selevac by Tringham and Krstić (1990) the words 'male' and 'female' are practically restricted to the chapter on animals. Bailey (1994 et al.) and others have stressed the large number of figurines which are ungendered. With some exceptions (e.g. Talalay 2000; 2005) gender is incidental to most current theoretical concerns.

Two potentially useful types of data – neither, as it happens, eschewed by Gimbutas – can be missed as a result. The first is representations of maleness (whether in male figurines, phalli or phallic forms) which have rarely been addressed outside the culture-historical tradition (Gimbutas 1982 et al., Karageorghis 1991). Possible reasons are that

male figurines and phalli are relatively uncontroversial to identify but the attribution of a phallic form is epistemologically problematic. The consideration of phalli also still seems to be tainted with our Victorian legacy. Moreover, the amount of maleness in figurines would have to be radically revised if long necks (including the entire cruciform canon in Cyprus, for example) were to become recognized as phallic. All of these have discouraged a more direct approach to this topic.

The second type of overlooked data is the sensuality of figurines. Attribution of eroticism may seem highly subjective and culturally bound but the phallus is a universal symbol of male sexual arousal – and possibly of arousal in either gender as there is no comparably visual female equivalent. Buttocks are widely and carefully modelled in various figurine cultures and may also be a near-universal erotic symbol. I cannot, however, cite any academic research to support this.

Nevertheless, traditional reserve among prehistorians is breaking down. Inspired by Butler's theorizing (1990 et al.) and following Yates' widely cited article on Scandinavian rock art (1993) which addressed depictions of phalli, Meskell (1996 et al.) and Joyce (2000 et al.) are leading the way in establishing sexually embodied subjects as a focus of archaeological analysis. A joint summary of their work is titled 'Phallic Culture' (Meskell and Joyce 2003). Joyce's article on male sexuality and the ancient Maya was notable for both the images and the archaeological novelty of her approach: 'a consideration of sexuality…as the play of desire' (2000, 264). Meskell has written on female sexuality in New Kingdom Egypt (2000) and called for more attention to maleness and to male and phallic figurines at Catalhöyük and elsewhere (Meskell and Nakamura 2005). Bailey has also stressed sexuality in his recent book on figurines (2005).

What patterns, then, can be seen in maleness and sensuality in figurines? The most intriguing figurines lie at the start of many European figurine traditions. I call them 'phallic females' as the phallic form is incorporated into the neck, torso and buttocks of otherwise female figurines and only becomes evident when they are viewed from the rear. All these figurines have large buttocks, some exuberant. Examples from various cultures are shown in Figure 12.1. These figurines were first highlighted by Gimbutas although this is rarely recognized by other writers. Knapp and Meskell wrote on similar figurines from Chalcolithic Cyprus, suggesting that the phallic elements represent 'characterizations of the individual self' (1997, 195) and the emergence of individuals in Cypriot prehistory. Their view may have been influenced by their interpretation of the Bronze Age in Cyprus 'where representations of the self seem to be highly visible' (1997, 191) and I do not know if they would apply it to early Neolithic European figurines.

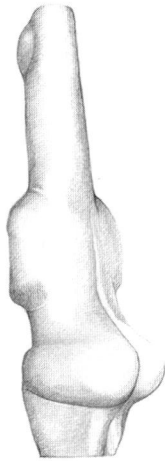

a) Attica, Proto-Sesklo
after Gimbutas 1982

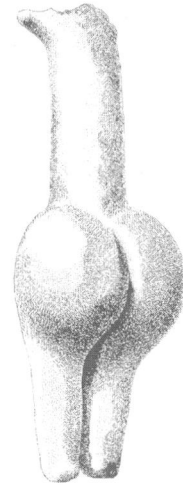

b) Bakonycserny, Lengyel *c*.4500 BC
Reproduced by permission of
Archaeolingua, from Kalicz 1998

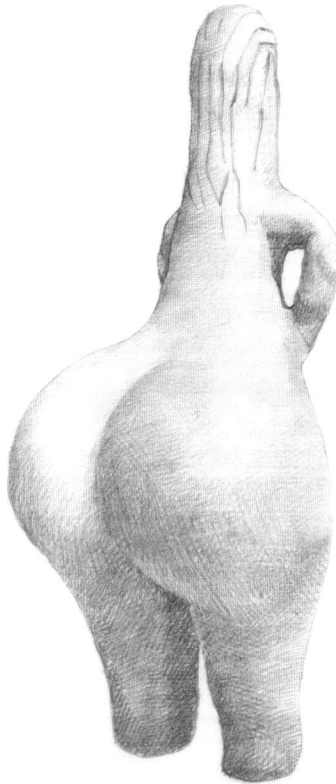

c) Donja Branjevina, Starčevo
c.6000 BC; H *c*.30cm
after photo by M. Trninic

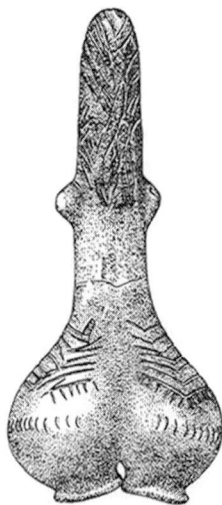

d) Endrőd-Szujoskereszt, Körös
c.5500 BC; H *c*.19cm
Reproduced by permission of Thames
& Hudson, from Gimbutas 1989

e) Poduri-Dealul Ghîndaru
pre-Cucuteni *c*.4800 BC; H *c*.8cm
after photo by G. Dumitriu

Figure 12.1. Phallic females.

I agree with the main, gynocentric conclusions of Kokkinidou and Nikolaidou's frequently cited article (1997) on these figurines except for the authors' emphasis on fertility as opposed to sensuality and for their rejection of any potency of phallic imagery in its own right as suggested by their statement that phallic-shaped objects were 'especially appropriate' for use as pedagogic items (1997, 103). Whittle (2003, 56; 1998a, 473–4) has described these figurines as strongly phallic and suggested that 'this fascinating combination…lies at the heart of the lifestyle' of these cultures without, unfortunately, elaborating further. These figurines are therefore well-known but have not, perhaps, been put in a wider, diachronic context.

In early Neolithic Starčevo we see possibly phallic figurines which are cylindrical or have very long necks but without a lower body. Long necks on female figurines in neighbouring Greece become almost ubiquitous in the middle Neolithic and are widespread in other cultures as has often been noted. Male figurines with long necks are, however, extremely rare in either horizon. If interpretations by Kokkinidou and Nikolaidou (1997) and Whittle (1998b) of long necks as phallic are correct these are a more formalized and less sensual image than the earlier full-bodied phallic females. A similar progression can be seen in Chalcolithic Cucuteni where the necks on female figurines become significantly shorter over time.

Phalli themselves appear in most cultures and in different periods, including the early phase, although without any obvious pattern. However, in the miniaturized world of figurines, phalli are the only objects that are commonly lifesize, and often larger than figurines themselves. Two striking examples of apparently vivified phalli from early Neolithic Greece and Starčevo indicate clear comfort with sexual imagery (see Gimbutas 1982, 135, figure 94 and 1982, 217 figure 168). They do not seem disembodied or cases of *pars pro toto* but to have been given being in their own right. These various observations support the notion that the sensuality of figurines in different cultures was at its height in the earliest phases when, with rare exceptions, there are no clearly male figurines. These tend to appear only in the middle or later periods.

The key criterion of maleness for most writers is a penis although it may be safer to view a penis as representing maleness (on figurines which may or may not be primarily or exclusively male) rather than as a redundant criterion. Male figurines can also be placed into three broad categories – informal, ritual and realistic – two of which, informal and realistic, are significantly more common in male than in female figurines and therefore of potential interest.

The most troublesome term is 'informal'. It is imprecise, relative and in this context new but nevertheless, I believe, useful. It stands in contrast to 'ritual' for figurines that are asymmetrical, sitting on the ground, more roughly finished

or less decorated. Figurines such as the thinker from Tîrpeşti (see Gimbutas 1982, 233, plate 251–252), which is seated on the ground but with the hands on each side of its face, possess formal ambiguity – a combination of both formal and informal elements. In the famous couple from Cernavoda (see Gimbutas 1982, 232, plate 247–248) the symmetrical male figurine seated on a stool is more formal (and active, in its thinking) than the female, which is asymmetrical and sitting on the ground. Neither, however, is 'ritual' because of their realism and lack of decoration. The vast majority of ithyphallic figurines and a significant proportion of all male figurines are informal and suggest a certain ritual exclusion – perhaps the main inference of this category. If this exclusion had a perceived social parallel it would not be surprising if the resulting tension was reflected in figurines. The ithyphallic figure from Larisa (see Theocaris 1973, figure 55) is the largest figurine in either horizon in Europe and an example of seemingly outright contestation. Seated on a stool but in an asymmetrical posture with one hand holding what was probably an enormous phallus and the other on its face the figurine is formally ambiguous. If one understands material culture as being more of an argument than a conversation this was a very loud statement.

Formal, 'ritual' male figurines are uncommon and may have differing interpretations. A series of seated figurines with penises from a restricted area in Neolithic Thessaly (see Gimbutas 1982, 231, plates 244–245, and Gallis and Orphanidis 1996) shows their legs depicted as the front legs of a curved stool. They have been remarked on (see Talalay 2000, 5–7) but not yet studied and have a clear formality in their posture and symmetry. The indisputably feminine breasts on one of them (see Gallis and Orphanidis 1996, figure 45) make it the inverse – or imitation – of the earlier phallic females. There, a predominantly female form incorporates a male phallus. Here, a predominantly male form incorporates female breasts. This unusual and localized series suggests a challenge to elsewhere predominantly female ritual imagery. The so-called 'sickle god' from Szegvar-Tuzkoves in middle Neolithic Tisza in eastern Hungary (see Gimbutas 1982, 84, plate 46–47) might be interpreted differently. It is symmetrical (apart from the sickle) and seated on a chair but the seated female figurines from the same site (see Gimbutas 1982, 211, plate 210–211) are more decorated and I take them to have more central ritual importance. The female figurines are also depicted without a head. This example seems one of acceptance of male ritual representation and participation, albeit in a subsidiary role, rather than contestation.

The third category of male figurines is realistic and seen particularly in heads. Figure 12.2 shows some of the first lifelike sculpted heads in Europe. They have also not been studied and have yet to be given importance in either archaeology or art-history. (Lifelike engraved heads in the

a) Domokos, Thessaly H 6.7cm
after Gallis and Orphanidis 1996

b) Drama, Karanovo VI H 4.3cm
after Költsch *et al.* 1988

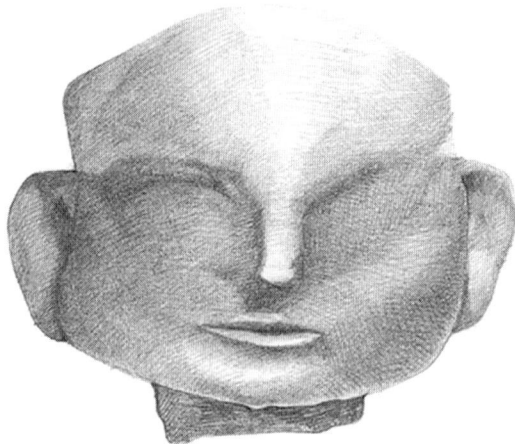

c) Gabarevo, Karanovo VI H 7cm
after Költsch *et al.* 1988

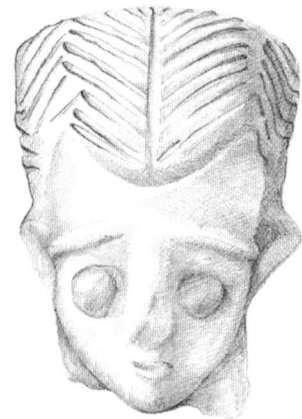

d) Butmir, late Neolithic H *c.*5cm
after Benac *et al.* 1979

Figure 12.2. Realistic Heads.

Upper Palaeolithic have a similarly low academic profile. See Roussot 1997, figure 33 for images of the heads in the cave of La Marche.) I take them to be male by the shape of the jaw, especially in profile, since few, if any, female figurines have a similarly pronounced jaw or chin. Even semi-realistic female heads are rare in European figurines and none compare in terms of detail. This apparent taboo and its (possibly indirect) transgression only in male figurines suggest that rituals centered on female representations were cultic and not just social. The appearance of these realistic male heads towards the end of various traditions implies change in the established cultic and social practices relating to figurines.

I will now look briefly at specific gender patterns in three figurine traditions to illustrate possible applications of the approach outlined above. I have sketched the progression in early Neolithic Greece from full-bodied phallic females to less sensual elongated necks and the appearance of different types of male figurine. How do we account for the limited canon in the succeeding Rachmani culture in the Chalcolithic of acrolithic figurines with flat, painted torsos and an apparent emphasis on heads which

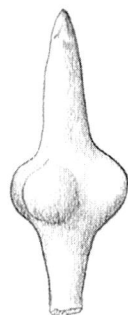

a) Golerkany, early Tripolye H *c.*7cm

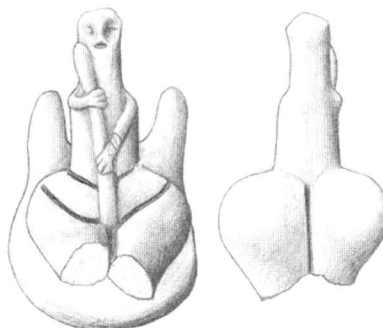

b) Sabatinovka, early Tripolye H *c.*8cm

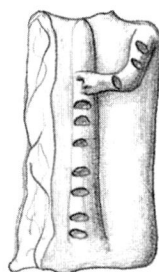

c) Lenkovcy, early Tripolye
H *c.*6cm

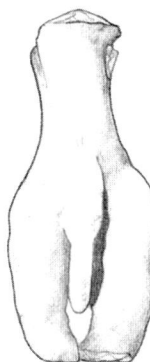

d) Luka Vrubleveckaja, mid
Tripolye H *c.*9cm

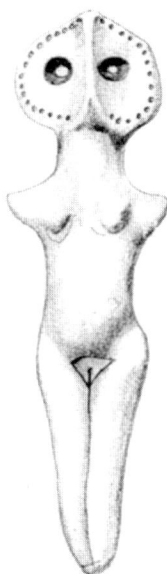

e) Vychvatincy, late
Tripolye H *c.*13cm

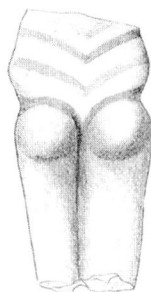

f) Zalesciki, mid Tripolye H *c.*10.4cm

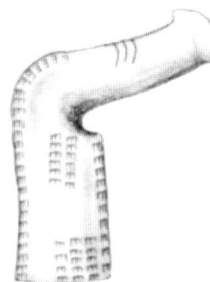

g) Usatovo, final Tripolye H *c.*7cm

Reproductions by permission of Beiträge zur Allgemeinen
und Vergleichenden Archäologie from Pogoševa 1985

Figure 12.3. Tripolye.

lack any facial features? One interpretation taking this whole trajectory into account could be that a gender-based contestation of the early Neolithic female and sexualized imagery led to the elimination of *all* gendered representations in favour of a new and sexually more conservative iconography. One result of this playing out of gender tensions through ritual was the removal of female imagery not just from a position of apparent dominance but from the entire corpus. If sensuality was associated with perceived – and resented – female dominance, the Rachmani figurines may not be as gender-neutral as they appear.

Further north in the central Balkans the overt sensuality of Starčevo figurines was completely eradicated in the succeeding Vinča culture whose figurines are amongst the most decorated and dressed of any European culture. Large buttocks, phallic necks or torsos and separate phalli are almost non-existent and there are few clear indications of gender. There is a small number of male figurines in all three of the categories identified earlier and figurines drop off sharply in the Chalcolithic Baden culture. Throughout its long duration the Vinča aversion to sexual imagery was almost complete and suggests that a perception of sensuality in the preceding Starčevo culture is not just subjective.

Finally, Cucuteni's sister culture of Tripolye constitutes the last of the figurine traditions in Europe and an intriguing case (see examples in Figure 12.3). Highly sensual semi-abstract figurines appear at the very start of the tradition and an obvious and seemingly refined sensuality persists until the final stage of the culture. Female buttocks are often pronounced and heavily decorated and become more realistic in the later period with a shift towards young people of both sexes. There are two examples of ritual male figurines, both from the early period. The seated female figurine from Sabatinovka holding a rod is well-known. The rod is often considered to be phallic although the figurine itself is also phallic. However, two other, less well-known figurines (one of them considerably larger) holding a similar rod appear to be male. They are more decorated than the figurine from Sabatinovka and the notches on their arms and rods indicate greater formality and a more central ritual role.

As would be expected from other traditions (although female Tripolye figurines also become more realistic over time), informal and realistic male figurines appear in the middle and late periods, possibly representing elements of disruption since some seem grotesque. In the final, Usatovo phase both realism and variety give way to a single form that is ungendered apart from a curious phallic neck and head. The early appearance of ritual male figurines, the persistence of sensuality and the extension of sensuality and realism to figurines of both genders all suggest that the Tripolye culture negotiated and maintained a gender

balance more successfully than many of its predecessors and almost to the end.

In conclusion, within discrete developments in different European figurine traditions there seem to be elements of a possibly generalized (though not uniform) pattern of increasing contestation of the relative dominance and sensuality of early female figurines. These elements might reflect the playing out of gender tensions inherent in the ritual and structural model of the Neolithic package in SE Europe which spread northwards from Greece – tensions which may ultimately have contributed to the as yet unexplained disappearance of figurines themselves. More detailed studies of individual cultures and including other aspects such as mortuary data (abundant in some cases although scant in most) may help to assess the validity of the ideas presented here. The possibility that depictions of (in particular, female) sensuality indicate a greater prominence and latitude for women that diminished over time should also be addressed. Whatever the merits of particular interpretations in this paper, however, I hope to have persuaded some readers of the wider potential of analysing representations of both maleness and sensuality in these horizons.

Acknowledgements

This paper is based on research undertaken for the MPhil. in Archaeology at St. John's College Cambridge in 2006.

References

Bailey, D. W. 1994 Reading prehistoric figurines as individuals. *World Archaeology* 25(3), 322–331.

Bailey, D. W. 2005 *Prehistoric Figurines. Representation and Corporeality in the Neolithic.* New York, Routledge.

Biehl, P. F. 1996. Symbolic communication systems. Symbols on anthropomorphic figurines in Neolithic and Chalcolithic Southeast Europe. *Journal of European Archaeology* 4, 153–176.

Butler, J. 1990. *Gender Trouble: Feminism and the Subversion of Identity.* London, Routledge.

Chapman, J. 2000. *Fragmentation in Archaeology. People, places and broken objects in the prehistory of south-eastern Europe.* London, Routledge.

Gallis, K. and Orphanidis, L. 1996. *Figurines of Neolithic Thessaly. Volume 1.* Academy of Athens Research Centre for Antiquity, Monograph 3.

Gimbutas, M. 1982. *The Goddesses and Gods of Old Europe 6500–3500 BC. Myths and Cult Images.* London, Thames and Hudson.

Joyce, R. A. 2000. Male Sexuality among the Ancient Maya. In R. A. Schmidt and B. L. Voss (eds). *Archaeologies of Sexuality.* New York and London, Routledge.

Karageorghis, V. 1991. *The Coroplastic Art of Ancient Cyprus I. Chalcolithic-Late Cypriote I.* Nicosia, A. G. Leventis Foundation.

Knapp, B. A. and Meskell, L. M. 1997. Bodies of Evidence on Prehistoric Cyprus. *Cambridge Archaeological Journal* 7(2), 183–204.

Kokkinidou, D. and Nikolaidou, M. 1997. Body imagery in the Aegean Neolithic: ideological implications of anthropomorphic figurines. In J. Moore and E. Scott (eds). *Invisible People and Processes*. London, Leicester University Press, 88–112.

Lepowsky, M. 1990. Gender in an Egalitarian Society. In P. R. Sanday and R. G. Goodenough (eds). *Beyond the Second Sex. New Directions in the Anthropology of Gender*. Philadelphia, University of Pennsylvania Press, 171–223.

Meskell, L. M. 1996 The Somatization of Archaeology: Institutions, Discourses, Corporeality. *Norwegian Archaeological Review* 29(1), 1–16.

Meskell, L. M. 2000 Sexuality in New Kingdom Egypt. In R. A. Schmidt and B. L. Voss (eds). *Archaeologies of Sexuality*. New York and London, Routledge.

Meskell, L. M. and Joyce, R. M. 2003. Phallic Culture. In L. M. Meskell and R. Joyce *Embodied Lives*. New York and London, Routledge.

Meskell, L. M. and Nakamura, C. 2005. Figurines and Miniature Clay Objects. In *Catalhöyük 2005 Archive Report*: www.catalhoyuk.com/archive_reports/2005

Perlès, C. 2001. *The Early Neolithic in Greece: the First Farming Communities in Europe*. Cambridge, Cambridge University Press.

Pogoševa, A. P. 1985. Die Statuetten der Tripolie-Kultur. *Beiträge zur Allgemeinene und Vergleichenden Archäologie* 7, 95–242.

Roussot, A. 1997. *L'art prehistorique*. Bordeaux, Editions Sud Ouest.

Sanday, P. R. 1973. Toward a Theory of the Status of Women. *American Anthropologist* 75, 1682–1700.

Talalay, E. L. 1994. A Feminist Boomerang: The Great Goddess of Greek Prehistory. *Gender and History* 6(2), 165–183.

Talalay, E. L. 2000. Archaeological Ms.conceptions: Contemplating Gender and Power in the Greek Neolithic. In M. Donald and L. Hurcombe (eds). *Representations of Gender from Prehistory to the Present*. London, Macmillan.

Talalay, E. L. 2004. Heady Business: Skulls, Heads and Decapitation in Neolithic and Greece. *Journal of Mediterranean Archaeology* 17,139–163.

Talalay, E. L. 2005. The Gendered Sea: Iconography, Gender and Mediterranean Prehistory. In E. Blake and A. B. Knapp (eds). *The Archaeology of Mediterranean Prehistory*. Oxford, Blackwell.

Theocaris, D. R. 1973. *Neolithic Greece*. Athens, National Bank of Greece.

Tringham, R. and Krstić, D. 1990. *Selevac. A Neolithic Village in Yugoslavia*. Los Angeles, Institute of Archaeology, University of California.

Whittle, A. 1998a. Beziehungen zwischen Individuum und Gruppe: Fragen zur Identität im Neolithikum der ungarischen Tiefebene [trans: Connections between the individual and the group: questions of Neolithic identity in the Hungarian Plains]. *Ethnographische-Archäologische Zeitschrift* 39, 465–87.

Whittle, A. 1998b. Fish, faces and fingers: presences and symbolic identities in the Mesolithic-Neolithic transition in the Carpathian basin. *Documenta Praehistorica* 25, 133–150.

Whittle, A. 2003. *The Archaeology of People: dimensions of Neolithic life*. London, Routledge.

Yates, T. 1993. Frameworks for an archaeology of the body. In C. Tilley (ed.) *Interpretive Archaeology*. Oxford, Berg, 31–72.

Chapter 13

RELIGIOUS EXPERIENCE IN THE PREHISTORIC MALTESE UNDERWORLD

Robin Skeates

Introduction: making sense of caves

Caves present a significant potential to be re-considered in terms of the embodied human experience of their powerful multi-sensory environments, sensed, appropriated and modified during the course of dwelling, visiting, working, performing and thinking. Indeed, people and their bodies can be regarded as constituting part of cave environments. The main aim of this paper is, therefore, to re-conceptualise and explore the materiality of a range of caves in terms of human experience and perception, and to explore trans-formations in their sensory environments, with particular reference to the development of underground burial complexes during the Temple Period in Malta.

My perspective is informed by the emergent inter-disciplinary field of sensual culture studies (e.g. Feld and Basso 1996; Finnegan 2002; Howes 2005; Rodaway 1994). These explore peoples' multi-sensory experiences and perceptions of the lived-in world, both in the past and in the present, and their construction of culturally diverse sensory values and orders. Such multi-disciplinary studies characteristically relate the embodied senses to the material world, and to conceptions of supernatural power, human communicating, social rankings and ideologies, cultural diversity, and historical transformations. Caution is certainly required, for the prehistorian attempting to enter this field faces many problems, including the fragmentary nature of the archaeological evidence, and the current lack of an agreed methodology for an archaeology of the senses (e.g. Insoll 2004, 85–92). However, I do believe that this perspective helps archaeologists interpret past cultures in a fresh manner, by encouraging us: to adopt a comprehensive viewpoint, to become deeply immersed in the realities of the archaeological evidence, to distance ourselves from our own cultural bias, and to ask new questions.

Some research combining the study of caves with thinking about sensory culture has already been undertaken by Central Mediterranean prehistorians. In particular, research by Ruth Whitehouse and others, working on religious significance, ritual experience and cultural

transformation of prehistoric caves, has begun to explore how the fantastic atmospheres of these multi-sensory underground spaces were physically and psychologically experienced by people, and how such embodied encounters contributed to the construction of social identities and cultural categories in the past (e.g. Whitehouse 1992; Skeates in press; Betts 2003). Their work refers to themes such as access, movement, sound, darkness, strangeness, secrecy, fear and sensory deprivation. Independently, British landscape archaeologists have also begun to reconsider the ways in which caves may have been experienced in prehistory, with particular reference to their landscape settings, their 'architecture', their sacred character, acts of ritual deposition within them, and their relationship with other forms of monument (e.g. Barnatt and Edmonds 2002; Bradley 2000). Other research projects with other agendas have also touched upon the multi-sensory dimensions of underground sites in prehistoric Malta. For example, the artistry and visual symbolism of the elaborate underground architecture, portable artworks and red ochre-stained mortuary deposits have been the subject of numerous studies (e.g. Malone 1998). The extraordinary acoustic properties of the 'Oracle Chamber' in the Ħal Saflieni hypogeum are much noted (e.g. Marler 2000; Topp 1960, 45). (These are, however, unlikely to have been intentionally created by the hypogeum's builders, and are certainly enhanced today by the fact that the complex has been almost totally cleared of deposits, which would have originally reduced the resonance of low-pitched voices in the chambers.) The smell of decomposing bodies in the 'foul, reeking caves of the dead' has also captured the imagination of some archaeologists (e.g. Malone *et al.* 1993, 82; Tagliaferro 1911, 150). More recently, the kinaesthetic experience of carefully controlled bodily movement through the interior spaces of the hypogea has been considered (e.g. Stoddart 2002b, 133), together with the smooth feel of two highly tactile alabaster figurines from Ħal Saflieni (Vella Gregory 2005, 46). The sixth sense has even been alluded to with reference to caves, which 'with their hidden, cool atmosphere, stalagmites, stalagtites, and underground streams, exude a mysterious quality' (Gimbutas 1999, 60). These observations highlight the significant potential of the naturally cave-rich landscape of the Maltese islands to be explored further, with particular reference to religious experiences and transformations of their multi-sensory underground environments throughout prehistory.

Dwelling, ritual and the other world: 5200–4400 BC

The earliest well-defined human use of caves in Malta can be assigned to the period dated to between around 5200 and 4400 BC, known as the Earlier Neolithic or Għar Dalam phase. In addition to dwelling in farmsteads composed of a few houses built in the open, a few natural caves were appropriated for occupation during this period by colonising groups of early farmers originating in Sicily for whom cave-use was a long-established tradition. Examples include Għar Il-Mixta on Gozo, and Għar Dalam and Il-Latmija on Malta.

The human occupation of these caves has generally been interpreted by archaeologists in terms of convenient dwelling places or habitations adopted by newly arrived Sicilian Neolithic settlers, whose domestic life is recorded in the remains of hearths, trampled earth, and decorated pottery vessels, tools, sling-stones, body ornaments, animal bones and mollusc shells deposited in them (e.g. Bonanno 1987, 4; Pace 2004, 30).

An alternative ritual and symbolic interpretation has been championed by Marija Gimbutas. She asserted that caves such as Għar Dalam (and Grotta Scaloria in SE Italy) 'probably housed rituals of regeneration. Pottery left in these caves incorporates regenerative designs, such as eggs, snakes and plant shoots' (Gimbutas 1999, 71), and that caves 'exude a mysterious quality perhaps equated to the regeneration of life itself: the enclosed spaces of caves symbolize the birth canal and womb of the goddess' (1999, 60).

There is, in fact, some archaeological evidence of small-scale ritual practices having been performed in Għar Dalam. A first hint is provided by the presence of scant and scattered human remains in the Holocene and Pleistocene deposits, at least some of which are likely to date to the Earlier Neolithic (e.g. Baldacchino 1933–4, xxiii; Caton Thompson 1923, 12; Despott 1917, 297). A second and stronger hint of ritual practice, apparently overlooked by previous commentators, comes from the first layer of Giuseppe Despott's Trench II, 34 m in from the cave entrance, particularly towards the left side of the cave (Despott 1918, 220). Here, the 30–45 cm thick 'rich red soil' contained a noteworthy deposit with: numerous small stones; signs of burning; part of a human skull, some teeth, several phalanges, some metacarpal and metatarsal bones;

some bones of cow, pig, sheep/goat and red deer; three lower portions of a naturally decorated tortoise shell; fragments of pottery decorated with incised designs; a 3.2 cm high 'terracotta bull's head' (probably part of a zoomorphic vessel handle – Evans 1959, 47), with schematic but symbolically powerful horns, eyes, muzzle, nostrils, mouth and linear decorations that Despott interpreted as 'the animal's head trappings'; a 'very highly polished' miniature dark greenstone axe-blade; a 'very neatly worked and highly polished' borer made from a bird humerus, and another 'well-worked' fragment of a possible bone borer; three perforated canine teeth of a canid; and some bi-conical sling-stones of globigerina limestone. (In addition, a second, similar, decorated animal head of terracotta, 6 cm high, was found by Despott (1923, 23) at a comparable level in an adjacent excavation trench.) This deposit, which contained not only human remains but also a concentration of unusual, finely made, visually distinctive and culturally significant objects, can, I think, be interpreted as a 'special deposit' of things, gathered together and placed there as part of a ritual performance, and left relatively undisturbed until its archaeological excavation.

There is, then, just about enough archaeological evidence to suggest, from an anthropologically informed perspective, that the repeated performance of rituals in the deeper parts of caves in the Central Mediterranean at around 5000 BC does reflect a widespread religious perception of the underworld as an ambiguous liminal boundary and point of contact with 'the other world' (Skeates 1991, 127–9). In Malta, this belief might have framed the multi-sensory experiences of dwelling and ritual in Għar Dalam, and contributed to its incorporation within one part of the newly domesticated landscape.

The placing of the dead: 4400–3600 BC

The next phase of Maltese prehistory dates to between around 4400 and 3600 BC. It can be described as the Final Neolithic. A notable development in this phase is the repeated formal burial and accumulation of the corpses of a cross-section of the population in clusters of artificial mortuary chambers, carved out of the soft Maltese limestone, in prominent locations away from settlements on the sides and crests of hills. Examples include: Ta' Trapna, Buqana, Ħal Saflieni and San Pawl Milqi on Malta, and the Xagħra Circle and North Cave on Gozo (e.g. Malone et al. 1995).

The religious and social significance these mortuary structures and their ritual symbolism have been the subject of varied interpretations. John Evans (1959, 62, 135–6) wrote of an ancestor cult, originally brought from Sicily by the first colonizers of Malta, which was slowly elaborated to take the form of 'some kind of propitiation of the spirits of the dead', involving offerings of animal bones, the use of red ochre to symbolize blood and life, and vague anthropomorphic representations of the spirit or goddess of fertility. Anthony Bonanno (1987, 9) has, likewise, described the Ta' Trapna and Xagħra stone idols as representing a divinity or spiritual being connected with death, or an ancestral image, and has commented that their stylistic affinities indicate a degree of homogeneity in religious beliefs between the islanders of Malta and Gozo. He also states that the ritual 'must have been in response to preconceived ideas of the relationship between the dead and the living and, possibly, of an afterlife' (*ibid.* 2004, 280). Simon Stoddart and Anthony Pace have extended this social dimension by suggesting that the tombs were used by rival extended families over several generations, who may have emphasised their cumulative and collective nature: to assert a sense of the past, to maintain kinship ties, and to suppress individual identity (Pace 1997; Stoddart *et al.* 1993, 7). This can be linked to a broader contemporary social concern in the Central Mediterranean region at around 4000 BC with: defining the (separate) place of the dead, caring for them, and maintaining good relations with them, as ancestral members of enduring kin-groups (Skeates 2005, 134). This concern was expressed through the performance of mortuary rites in sanctified ancestral places, set apart from but overlooking the cultural landscape of the living, which provided visual reference-points in the landscape for establishing and remembering the distinct histories and territories of those groups. A somewhat different interpretation has been promoted by Marija Gimbutas (1989, 151–3 and 218), who regarded the oval form and blood-red ochre staining of the rock-cut tombs of Malta, Sicily and Sardinia as a symbolic womb (or egg or kidney) of the mother goddess, in which burial of the deceased in a foetal position would have been thought of in terms of a process of regeneration in which new life emerged from the old, analogous to a seed being planted in the earth. More recently, Christopher Tilley (2004, 140–3) has asserted that red ochre was a rare and exotic cultural product imported across the dangerous sea from ancestral Sicily, and that it provided an obvious metaphor for the blood of life and death, and a potent symbol associated with ancestral creation and the past. As such, it was regarded as a transformative substance, and therefore painted onto the living and sprinkled over the dead to nourish them and to induce changes in the human body, ritual states and individual identity.

Overall, I think that we can, at least, identify some of the general themes that informed funerary rites of transition enacted at rock-cut tombs in the Central Mediterranean region at around 4000 BC. They can be summarised as those of life, death and regeneration, and of a past and present social landscape populated by inter-dependent kin-groups, ancestors and supernatural forces. In the Maltese islands, cast away in the middle of the sea, these practices and beliefs helped people to stay connected across significant distances of space and time.

The elaboration of underground religion: 3600–2500 BC

The next major phase of Maltese prehistory dates to between around 3600 and 2500 BC. It is commonly known as the Temple Period. An increased number and variety of cave sites were now exploited alongside the continued use of established underground sites, and at the same time as a proliferation in surface monuments.

Some natural caves were probably used as temporary shelters during the course of primarily subsistence-related activities. Ghar in-Nghaġ, for example, which is situated at the inland end of the small Wied il-Mixta ravine, close to the south-west coast of Malta, offered a rock-shelter and cave (11 m long and 2–3 m wide) that appears to have been used for 'habitation (or perhaps for temporary shelter)' (Evans 1971, 21). Indications of its use as, at least, a seasonal base-camp for herding, hunting and gathering come from its second stratigraphic layer, which contained numerous pottery sherds (assigned mainly to the Temple Period but also to the Bronze Age). Here, a hearth contained the charred bones of sheep/goat and pig and the shells of edible molluscs. Four bone points were also found in this layer.

Other caves were used as burial places. Bur Mgħez, is the most obvious example, located on the Luqa plateau in east-central Malta, just a few hundred metres from the contemporary Id-Debdieba megalithic building. This cave comprises three narrow fissures in the Globigerina Limestone. The largest fissure (19 m long and 2–4 m wide), excavated by Napoleon Tagliaferro, was filled to within 30 cm of its ceiling by a Pleistocene layer overlain by a rich Temple Period mortuary deposit. The second fissure, excavated by George Sinclair, was smaller (6 m long, 4 m wide), but also contained a similar mortuary deposit.

Other natural caves may have served a different ritual purpose. Ghar ta-Gheiżu, in particular, located only a few hundred metres upslope from the Ġgantija temple complex on Gozo's Xagħra plateau, is a modified natural cave (14 m long and 6 m wide) that may have been used as a repository or dump for ritual deposits cleared periodically from the temples (Bonanno *et al.* 1990, 201–1). Its fill, sealed by a thin stalactitic layer, contained an exceptionally large number of Ġgantija-style pottery fragments, including part of a small bowl, and a sherd decorated with a large cross-shaped human figure applied in relief.

Previously established rock-cut tombs were re-used and only modified on a small scale. At the Xagħra Circle rock-cut tomb, for example, the shaft was re-opened in the Ġgantija phase, the entrance to Chamber 1 enlarged, deposits at the front of this chamber cleared, and a single burial placed in this space together with some bowls, before the entrance and shaft were re-sealed by stones for the last time (Malone *et al.* 1995).

New rock-cut chamber tombs also tended to conform to tradition. At another site in Xagħra, for example, a small and simple tomb was dug, probably also in the Ġgantija phase, with a conical shaft (0.9 m deep), a roughly square entrance at the bottom sealed by a square stone slab, and a circular chamber with a domed ceiling (1.7 m in diameter and 0.7 m high) (Zammit 1926–7).

At a few sites, however, the chambers of rock-cut tombs were enlarged, multiplied, interconnected and elaborated. The most notable example is the mortuary site of Xemxija. Here, however, a group of six somewhat larger and more elaborate rock-cut structures were created, with relatively large kidney-shaped chambers (3.1–5.6 m long), two expanded by a series of lobed spaces divided by protruding supports (Tombs 1 and 5), one sub-divided by a raised sill (Tomb 2), two interconnected by a short passage (Tombs 1 and 2), and two with their entrance shafts preceded by shallow rock-cut steps (Tombs 2 and 4) (Evans 1971, 112–6).

Hypogea evolved gradually and locally from these rock-cut tombs, combining and extending various aspects of their traditional and innovative architectural forms, together with elements derived from the ritual architecture of the contemporary above-ground temples, particularly during the Tarxien phase, after around 3200 BC. Three examples are known so far: at Ħal Saflieni, Santa Luċija, and the Xagħra Circle.

In the hypogea, it is clear that an expanded range of highly symbolic resources, including architectural spaces, ornamented human bodies (both living and dead) and special artefacts, were produced, used and embellished in more elaborate rituals, particularly during the Tarxien phase. Primary and secondary burial rites and initiation rites may have been enacted in the hypogea, repeatedly and with reference to tradition. Such rites of passage, separation, transition and transformation could have represented a journey through life and death to the afterlife. Like the above-ground temple rituals, they would have been performative, embodied and multi-sensory in nature (e.g. Stoddart *et al.* 1999, 98–9; Tilley 2004, 131–3 and 143; Turnbull 2002). As such, it is possible to imagine them in some detail.

They may have involved groups of ritual participants making their way between the temples and hypogea, and through the artificial underground structures, in a choreographed sequence of movement. They would have walked, stooped and even crawled along pathways, across boundaries and down steps, descending down into and climbing up out of the underworld, via a disorienting series of voluminous and confined spaces.

They would also have experienced the aesthetic impact of the sacred and symbolic temple-like architecture, and the almost animate figurative representations, abstract patterns and strong colours that they encountered there. This impact would have been heightened by contrasts between beams of natural sunlight filtering in from above (most strongly during the afternoon and sunset hours around the summer solstice), the use of dim, shadowy and flickering artificial lights, and the creepy half-light or darkness of the innermost spaces. Some things would have been illuminated and seen clearly, but others would have been controlled and concealed, with the vision of the spectators often intentionally obstructed. The visitors would also have kept an eye on each other, their bodies communicating through blurred facial expressions, gestures, postures and proximities.

Like non-sighted persons, any impoverishment of their sense of sight would have been compensated for by an enhancement of their other senses and their visual imaginations. They would have felt their way through the gloom, some with confidence, others holding hands, their bodies occasionally bumping into obstacles and each other, as they tripped or fell. They would have felt contrasts, between roughly carved walls and smoothed or drilled surfaces of Globigerina Limestone, between the damp ceilings and dry walls, between the living and the dead, and between flesh and bones. They would have carried things, ranging from heavy corpses to hand-held tools, and would have handled, even caressed, some highly tactile sacred objects. They would also have sensed the size and shape of the different chambers that they entered, and the strange airless humidity of the underground environment, surrounded by rock. They would have made and heard sounds that reverberated through those underground spaces: communicating in the dark with the sound of their breathing, footsteps, whispers, sighs, sobs, announcements, shouts, chants, and ceremonial instruments. They would also have smelt the invisible and unfamiliar odour of decomposing human bodies that characterised this inadequately ventilated place, as well as the familiar smell of close kin and friends. The smell of some bodies might have been so repugnant that they had to be avoided, while others might have smelt less foul and hence been deemed ready for reburial.

The visitors might have sensed the haunting presence of spirits of the dead and supernatural forces, announced by flashes of sight or conspicuous sounds or smells in these fantastic dream-spaces. These senses would have triggered a range of emotions, with the stress, shock and fear of the uninitiated perhaps ultimately being replaced by an educated sense of security in the minds of those most familiar with the rites of passage through the underworld, particularly knowing that they, too, would be at home and well cared for here when their time came to join their ancestors. Then, safely above ground, they would have relived their experiences, through countless verbal accounts, memories and legends of the underworld.

The rich symbolism of the rites was dominated by references to the bodies of living and dead people, as well those of other living things (Stoddart in press). From a religious perspective, their rites may have expressed and celebrated the cycle of life, death and regeneration. Recurrent juxtaposed themes and ideals may have included: the desirability of abundant food, health, productivity, sociability and energy; the inevitability of pain, sickness and biological death; the fear and negation of social death; altered human and animal states of being; return journeys across land, sea and sky to a world beyond; the maintenance of reciprocal relations with potentially dangerous and benign ancestors, spirits and deities; and the regeneration of an eternal island life. From a social perspective, the rites may also have addressed people's social identities and transitions in them from one kind to another. Here, a dominant theme appears to have been the dialectic relationship of the individual and the corporate social group. On the one hand, the lavish architecture and rites demonstrated and celebrated the achievements, unity and immortality of the community of living and dead persons to which each hypogeum belonged, and sought to fully incorporate individuals within it. On the other hand, the rites enabled differences of social status and power to be established between the living participants and even between the deceased. Experienced ritual specialists, in particular, would have guided, taught and controlled the ways in which the sacred resources of the underworld were accessed by their companions – physically, visually and conceptually. Archaeological talk of 'priest-chiefs' may be slightly overstated, even if community leaders also acted as ritual specialists, but the exuberance of the hypogea does make it possible to speak of a mobilised religious fervour and commitment, and of the emergence of a 'cult of the dead', in the Tarxien phase (e.g. Malone *et al.* 1993, 78–81; Pace 2004, 33; Tilley 2004, 98; Whittle 1996, 321).

Of course, these interpretations of the religious experience and symbolism of the hypogea leave many questions unanswered. How specialised was architectural and artistic production, and to what extent did it form part of the ritual process? If initiation rites were performed, did they comprise an integral part of the mortuary rites, or were they enacted on separate occasions? Were all deceased persons buried in underground burial caves and hypogea, or only a selection of the population? What kind of communities did they belong to, and to what extent were they in competition with each other? To what degree did the underground rituals and their meanings differ from those established above-ground in the temples, and to what extent did both serve as a model of and for society? How many and what kinds of people would have participated in the rites? Just how dark would it have been underground?

How disgusting was the smell of the decomposing bodies? To what extent was the ritual experience intended to be frightening and disorienting? How controlled was access and knowledge underground, and was it used for the good of all or misappropriated by a few? How complex were their religious beliefs, and to what extent were they doubted?

To sum up, the elaboration of sacred places, ritual experiences and religious beliefs in the Temple Period clearly evolved out of previously established traditions. For example, the long-established concept of the underworld as a liminal point of contact with the other world was open to diversification. The performance of traditional underground rites of transition, which explored life, death and regeneration and a past and present social landscape populated by living communities, ancestors and supernatural forces, were equally open to embellishment. Perhaps one of the most striking aspects of this religious transformation is the way in which it fed the local population's belief in their sense of permanence and belonging to an island world (Robb 2001), to such an extent that they did increasingly become cast adrift in the sea.

Conclusion

In general, one might say that caves in prehistoric Malta were perceived by successive generations of islanders as underground passageways in which the living, the ancestors and supernatural forces cohabited and communicated using all of their senses. Over time, they were culturally transformed from dwellings to places of intense social and religious experience and back again. In particular, they became known as a distinct kind of sensescape, with a characteristic combination of features, including: restrictions of light and air, abnormal coolness and humidity, disorientating bodily movements and inaccessibility, evocative visual forms and colours that shifted in and out of focus, conspicuous reverberating sounds, contrasting textures, unfamiliar and lingering smells, and haunting supernatural forces. These multi-sensory dimensions triggered personal and shared emotions, ranging from anxiety, fear, shock and disgust to feelings of hope, security and vitality. They also contributed to the construction of a wide variety of meanings and values that helped groups of islanders make sense of their place in the world. Caves, however, cut across so many physical and conceptual boundaries, some binary others more complex: lying both above ground and underground, outside and inside, in this world and in the underworld, between culture and nature, the domesticated and the wild, life and the afterlife, the transitory and the immortal, the mundane and the sacred, the good and the bad, the seen and the invisible, the real and the represented, the safe and the polluting, the ordered and the unpredictable, the communal and the individual, the unified and the disconnected, the known and the secret, etc. As a consequence, their place was always liminal, their cultural status frequently ambiguous, their sensory order rarely mundane and often uncertain.

References

Baldacchino, J. G. 1933–34. Ghar Dalam. *Annual Report on the Working of the Museum Department*, 1933–34, xxii–iv.

Barnatt, J. and Edmonds, M. 2002. Places Apart? Caves and Monuments in Neolithic and Earlier Bronze Age Britain. *Cambridge Archaeological Journal*, 12/1, 113–29.

Betts, E. 2003. The sacred landscape of Picenum (900–100 B.C.): towards a phenomenology of cult places. In J. B. Wilkins and E. Herring (eds*). Inhabiting Symbols: Symbol and Image in the Ancient Mediterranean*. London, Accordia Research Institute, 101–120.

Bonanno, A. 1987. *Malta: an Archaeological Paradise*. Malta, M. J. Publications.

Bonanno, A., Gouder, T., Malone, C. and Stoddart, S. 1990. Monuments in an island society: the Maltese context. *World Archaeology*, 22/2, 190–205.

Bradley, R. 2000. *An Archaeology of Natural Places*. London, Routledge.

Caton Thompson, G. 1923. Ghar Dalam. In M. A. Murray, *Excavations in Malta. Part I*. London, B. Quaritch, 6–13.

Despott, G. 1917. The Excavations Conducted at Ghar Dalam (Malta) in July 1916. *Report of the British Association for the Advancement of Science*, 86, 294–302.

Despott, G. 1918. Excavations Conducted at Ghar Dalam (Malta) in the Summer of 1917. *Journal of the Royal Anthropological Institute of Great Britain and Ireland*, 48, 214–21.

Despott, G. 1923. Excavations at Ghar Dalam (Dalam Cave), Malta. *The Journal of the Royal Anthropological Institute of Great Britain and Ireland*, 53, 18–35.

Evans, J. D. 1959. *Malta*. London, Thames and Hudson.

Evans, J. D. 1971. *The Prehistoric Antiquities of the Maltese Islands: a Survey*. London, The Athlone Press, University of London.

Feld, S. and Basso, K. H. (eds) 1996. *Senses of Place*. Santa Fe, New Mexico, School of American Research Press.

Finnegan, R. 2002. *Communicating: the Multiple Modes of Human Interconnection*. London, Routledge.

Gimbutas, M. 1989. *The Language of the Goddess*. London, Thames and Hudson.

Gimbutas, M. 1999. *The Living Goddesses*. Berkeley, CA, University of California Press.

Howes, D. (ed.) 2005. *Empire of the Senses: the Sensual Culture Reader*. Oxford, Berg.

Insoll, T. 2004. *Archaeology, Ritual, Religion*. London, Routledge.

Malone, C. 1998. 'God or Goddess: the Temple Art of Ancient Malta'. In L. Goodison and C. Morris (eds). *Ancient Goddesses: the Myths and the Evidence*. London, British Museum Press, 148–63.

Malone, C., Bonanno, A., Gouder, T., Stoddart, S. and Trump, D. 1993. The Death Cults of Prehistoric Malta. *Scientific American*, December 1993, 76–83.

Malone, C., Stoddart, S., Bonanno, A., Gouder, T. and Trump, D. (eds) 1995. Ritual of 4th Millennium BC Malta: the Zebbug Period Chambered Tomb from the Brochtorff Circle at Xaghra (Gozo). *Proceedings of the Prehistoric Society*, 61, 303–45.

Marler, J. 2000. 'The Ħal Saflieni Hypogeum', album notes accompanying *ReTurning: Recorded in the Oracle Chamber in the Hypogeum at Ħal Saflieni, Malta*. CD. Albany, CA, Edge of Wonder Records.

Pace, A. 1997. The Archaeology of Collectivity. Cognitive Design Processes: the Case of Maltese Prehistoric Funerary Sites (4000–2500 B.C.). *Malta Archaeological Review*, 2, 14–19.

Pace, A. 2004. Malta during Prehistory: an Overview. In K. Gambin (ed.). *Malta: Roots of a Nation. The Development of Malta from an Island People to an Island Nation*. Valletta, Malta, Heritage Malta, 25–44.

Robb, J. 2001. Island Identities: Ritual, Travel and the Creation of Difference in Neolithic Malta. *European Journal of Archaeology*, 4/2, 175–202.

Rodaway, P. 1996. *Sensuous Geographies: Body, Sense and Place*. London, Routledge.

Skeates, R. 1991. Caves, Cult and Children in Neolithic Abruzzo, Central Italy. In P. Garwood, D. Jennings, R. Skeates and J. Toms (eds). *Sacred and Profane: Proceedings of a Conference on Archaeology, Ritual and Religion. Oxford, 1989*. Oxford, Oxford University Committee for Archaeology, 122–34.

Skeates, R. 2005. *Visual Culture and Archaeology: Art and Social Life in Prehistoric South-East Italy*. London, Duckworth.

Skeates, R. In press. Constructed caves: transformations of the underworld in prehistoric Southeast Italy. In H. Moyes (ed.). *Journeys into the Dark Zone: a Cross Cultural Perspective on Caves as Sacred Spaces, Volume I*. Boulder, CO, University Press of Colorado.

Stoddart, S. 2002b. The Xagħra Shaman? In P. A. Barker and G. Carr (eds). *Practitioners, Practices and Patients: New Approaches to Medical Archaeology and Anthropology. Proceedings of a Conference held at Magdalene College, Cambridge, November 2000*. Oxford, Oxbow Books, 125–35.

Stoddart, S. In press. Changing Beliefs in the Human Body in Prehistoric Malta, 5000–1500 B.C. In J. Robb and D. Boric (eds). *Past Bodies*. Oxford, Berghahn.

Stoddart, S., Bonanno, A., Gouder, T., Malone, C. and Trump, D. 1993. Cult in an Island Society: Prehistoric Malta in the Tarxien period. *Cambridge Archaeological Journal*, 3/1, 3–19.

Stoddart, S., Wysocki, M. and Burgess, G. 1999. The Articulation of Disarticulation: Preliminary Thoughts on the Brochtorff Circle at Xaghra (Gozo). In J. Downes and T. Pollard (eds). *The Loved Body's Corruption: Archaeological Contributions to the Study of Human Mortality*. Glasgow, Cruithne Press, 94–105.

Tagliaferro, N. 1911. Prehistoric Burials in a Cave at Bur-Megħez, Near Mkabba, Malta. *Man*, 11, 147–50.

Tilley, C. 2004. *The Materiality of Stone: Explorations in Landscape Phenomenology*. Oxford, Berg.

Topp, C. 1960. *Pre-Historic Malta and Gozo*. Valletta, Malta, Progress Press.

Turnbull, D. 2002. Performance and Narrative, Bodies and Movement in the Construction of Places and Objects, Space and Knowledges: the Case of the Maltese Megaliths. *Theory, Culture and Society*, 19/5–6, 125–43.

Vella Gregory, I. 2005. *The Human Form in Neolithic Malta*. Malta, Midsea Books Ltd. and Heritage Malta.

Whitehouse, R. D. 1992. *Underground Religion: Cult and Culture in Prehistoric Italy*. London, Accordia Research Centre.

Whittle, A. 1996. *Europe in the Neolithic: the Creation of New Worlds*. Cambridge, Cambridge University Press.

Zammit, T. 1926–27. Rock-Tombs. *Annual Report on the Working of the Museum Department*, 1926–27, iii.

Chapter 14

UNDERGROUND RELIGION REVISITED

Ruth D. Whitehouse

Introduction

In 1992 I published a book entitled *Underground Religion. Cult and Culture in Prehistoric Italy,* in which I identified a widespread phenomenon of ritual activity in 'underground' sites during the Neolithic and Copper Age of peninsular Italy and Sicily. Since it was published, the book has been subject to several critiques; also new theoretical approaches have come to the fore in archaeology and some new discoveries have been made on the ground. Above all much new work has been done in adjacent areas, especially the Maltese archipelago – work celebrated in the 'Cult in Context' conference, held in Cambridge in December 2006, from which the present volume derives. The time and the context seem appropriate for a re-assessment of the study.

In this paper I address the critiques and look at new theoretical approaches to ritual practice, especially experiential aspects, and assess what they may add to our understanding of the sites in question.

Original thesis

The study was devoted to an exploration of religion and religious ritual in peninsular Italy and Sicily during the period approximately 6500 to 2500 cal. BC (Figure 14.1). It started from an analysis of a range of 'underground' sites, which I argued were used for cult purposes. The sites included natural caves, rock-shelters, rock-cut tombs and other artificial rock-cut structures (Figure 14.2). I looked at a sample of 33 sites in some detail, with a particular emphasis on the large natural caves and a detailed analysis of the wall paintings in one of them: Grotta di Porto Badisco (Figure 14.3).

There are a number of reasons for regarding the sites as used primarily for ritual purposes. These include the form of the sites and their topographical locations (remote, hidden, difficult to access and restricted in space) and the incorporation of remarkable natural formations, often involving stalactites, stalagmites and pools of stillicide water; sometimes there is evidence of particular ritual attention being paid to these features. Other evidence of ritual use includes the presence of wall-paintings, human burials and the deposition of foodstuffs; we find also depositions of a range of artefacts that can be considered 'special' in one sense or another (unusual or rare in type; miniaturised versions of more common artefacts; versions made of special materials or finished with unusual care or both). Details of all these aspects and the associated argumentation can be found in the original book (Whitehouse 1992, Chapter 4).

I employed a number of approaches to interpreting the sites, the rites carried out in them and the meanings of the symbolism involved. I identified three major ritual themes, which could be taken to represent major cultural values of the societies in question and thus provide an entrée into an understanding of their cosmology and general 'world view'. (Whitehouse 1992, Chapter 6). I labelled them the secrecy theme, the hunting cult and the cult of 'abnormal' water. Of these, secrecy is the primary theme, relating to the hidden locations of the sites, their difficulty of access and their dark, restricted spaces. Not only are the sites themselves difficult to find, but within them the areas of maximum cult activity are usually found in the zones most difficult to reach and furthest from daylight. Hunting seems to have been a second major focus of ritual attention, manifested both in the cave paintings of Grotta di Porto Badisco and a few other sites, and in the deposition of faunal remains of wild animals and birds, both associated with human burials and separately, as most notably, in the rock-cut structure of Ipogeo Manfredi at Santa Barbara. This focus on hunting occurs, perhaps surprisingly, in the context of communities of settled farmers, for whom hunting contributed only a minor part of their diet. The third theme relates to cult connected with 'abnormal' water, by which I mean water occurring in forms different from everyday forms, such as rivers and rainfall. The most common manifestations of 'abnormal' water were those

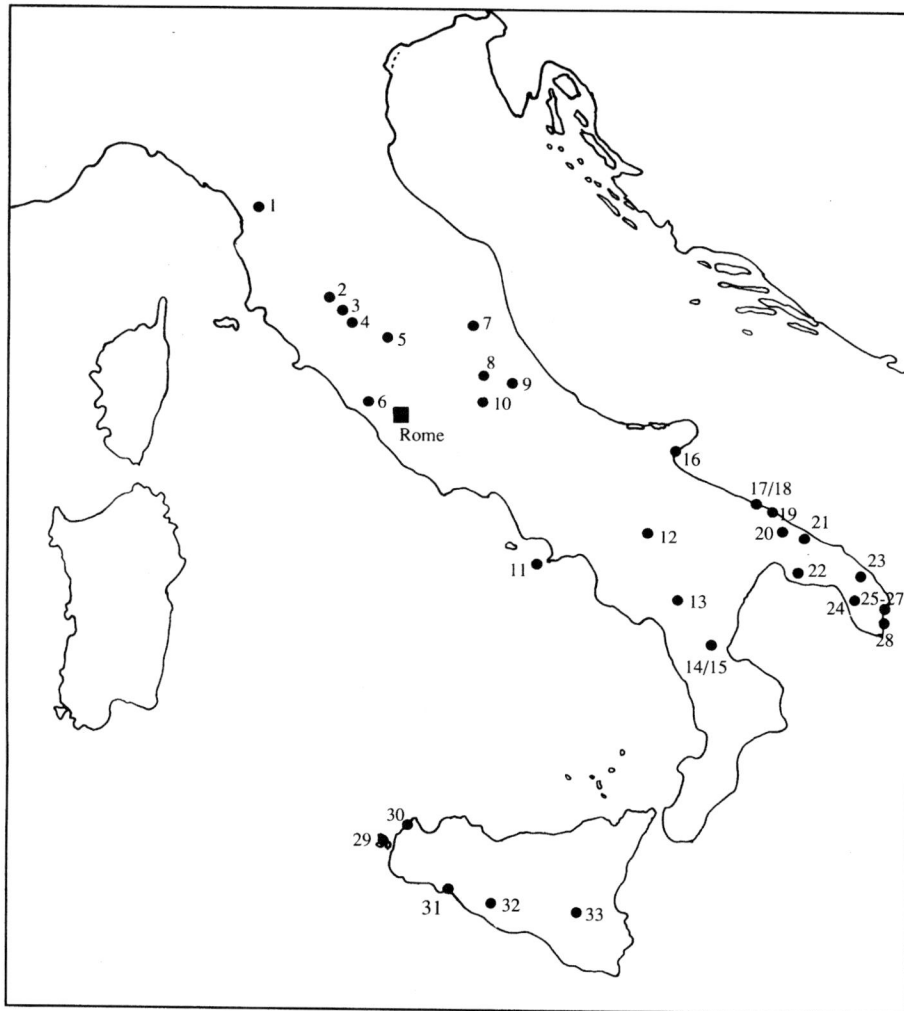

Figure 14.1. Map of sites discussed in 1992 book.
Key: *1 Grotta del Leone; 2 Grotta del Beato Benincasa; 3 Grotta dell'Orso; 4 Grotta Lattaia; 5 Pozzi della Piana; 6 Grotta Patrizi; 7 Grotta Sant'Angelo (Civitella del Tronto); 8 Grotta delle Marmitte; 9 Grotta dei Piccioni; 10 Grotta Continenza; 11 Grotta delle Felci; 12 Riparo Ranaldi; 13 Grotte Latronico; 14 Grotta di Sant'Angelo III (Cassano Ionio); 15 Grotta Pavolella; 16 Grotta Scaloria; 17 Grotta di Cala Scizzo; 18 Grotte di Cala Colombo; 19 Ipogeo Manfredi, Santa Barbara; 20 Grotta Pacelli; 21 Grotta di Sant'Angelo (Ostuni); 22 Caverna dell'Erba; 23 Arnesano; 24 Grotta Cappuccini; 25 Grotta di Porto Badisco; 26 Grotta Cosma; 27 Grotta dei Diavoli; 28 Grotta Zinzulusa; 29 Grotta dei Cervi, Levanzo; 30 Grotta dei Cavalli; 31 Grotta di San Calogero; 32 Cozzo Busonè; 33 Palikè.*

related to stalactites and stalagmites ('solid' water), but there is also evidence of cult associated with steam (gaseous water), waterfalls (rapidly moving water) and possibly at one site where water in a small lake bubbles with naturally occurring carbon dioxide.

I interpreted the cult using four different analytical approaches, relating to different aspects of the cult: structural meaning (Chapter 7), social function (Chapter 8), long term historical development (Chapter 9) and what in 1992 I called psychological meaning, though I would now prefer to label it 'experiential' rather than 'psychological' (Chapter 10).

The discussion of structural meaning was based on traditional structuralist understanding, derived from the work of Claude Lévi-Strauss (e.g. Lévi-Strauss 1966) and also Edmund Leach (e.g. Leach 1976). I started by comparing the secular and sacred worlds, represented respectively by settlement sites and cult sites, which I presented as a set of structured contrasts (Table 14.1). I argued that these could be equated with the fundamental contrast of structuralist analysis, between *culture* and *nature*. In relation to the three main ritual themes, the structural meaning of the secrecy theme shows culture to be defined as open, accessible and light, while nature,

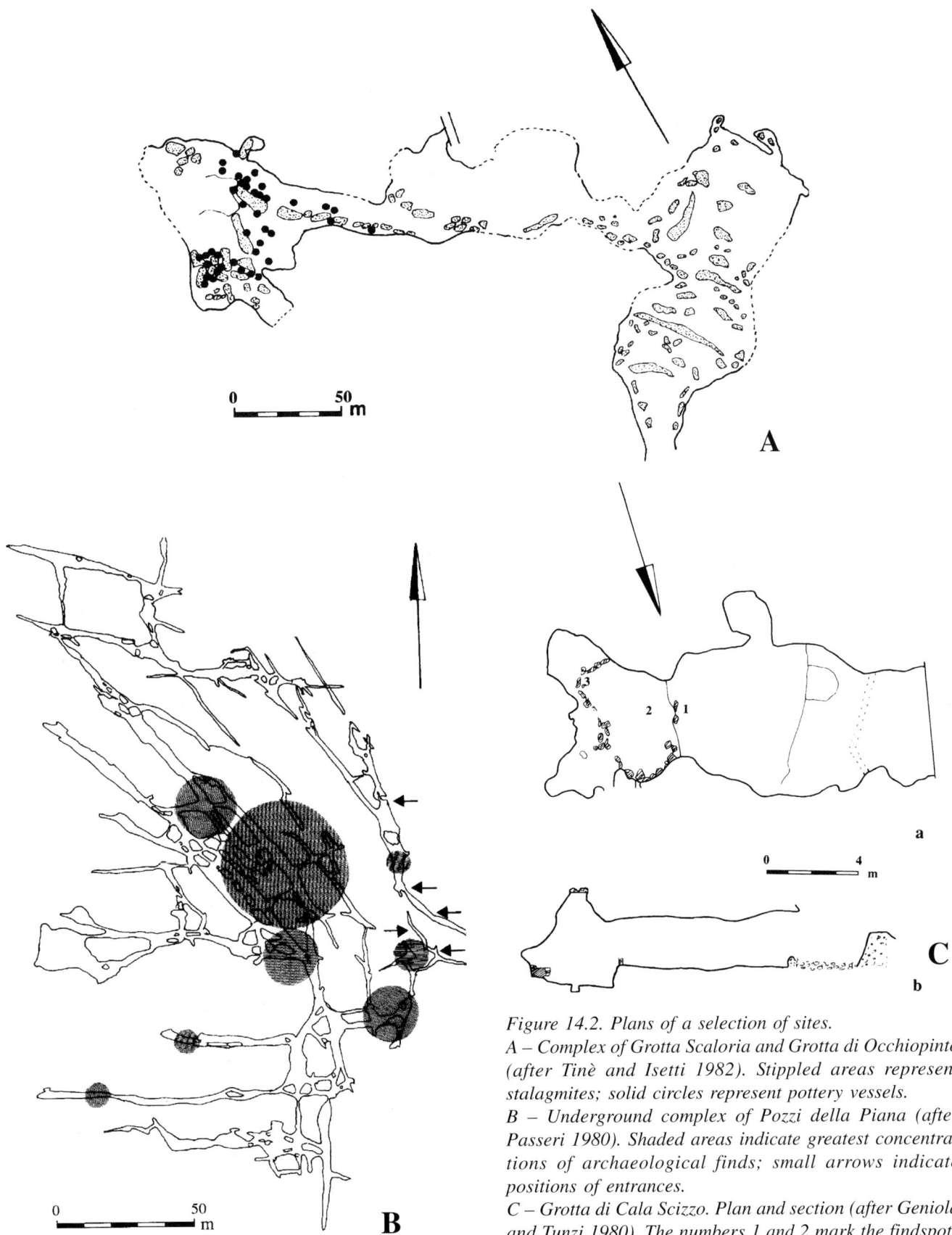

Figure 14.2. Plans of a selection of sites.
A – Complex of Grotta Scaloria and Grotta di Occhiopinto (after Tinè and Isetti 1982). Stippled areas represent stalagmites; solid circles represent pottery vessels.
B – Underground complex of Pozzi della Piana (after Passeri 1980). Shaded areas indicate greatest concentrations of archaeological finds; small arrows indicate positions of entrances.
C – Grotta di Cala Scizzo. Plan and section (after Geniola and Tunzi 1980). The numbers 1 and 2 mark the findspots of painted pebbles, 3 of a clay head.

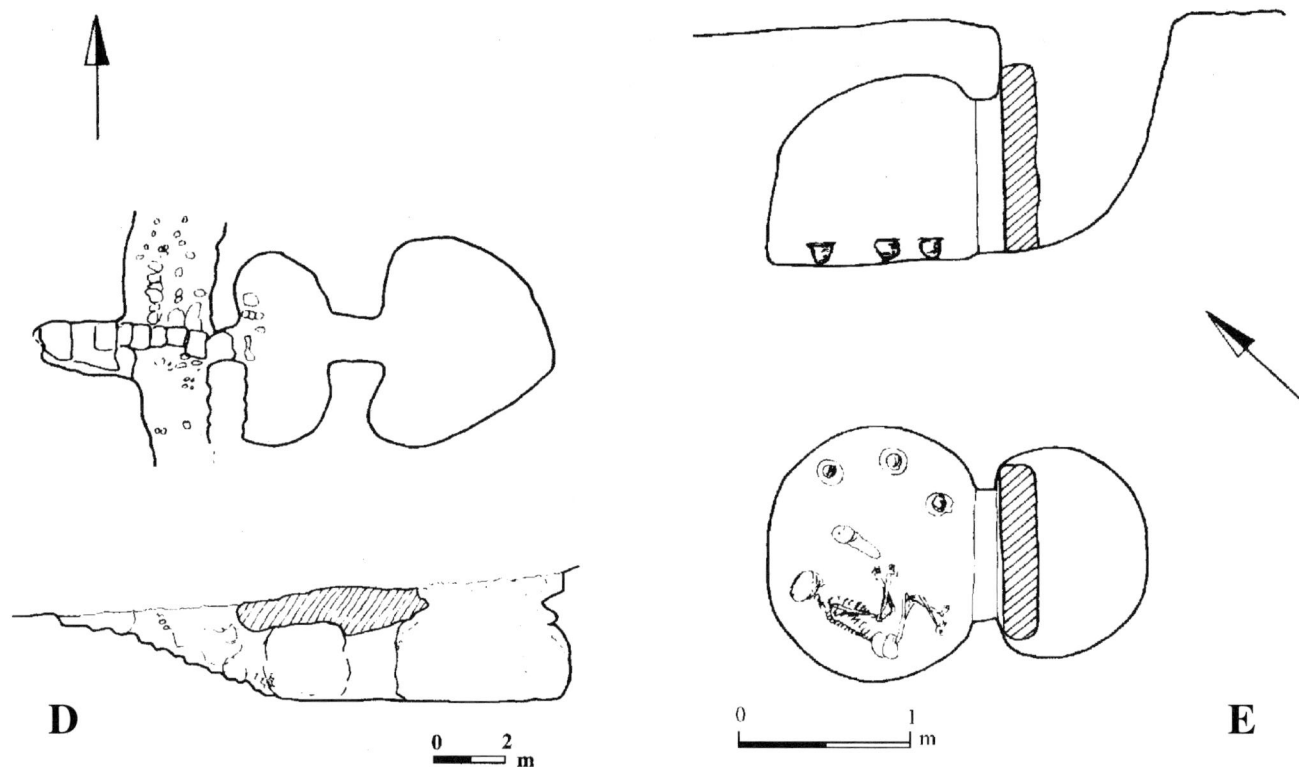

Figure 14.2. Plans of a selection of sites (cont.)
D – Ipogeo Manfredi, Santa Barbara. Plan and section (after Geniola 1987).
E – Arnesano rock-cut tomb. Plan and section (after Lo Porto 1972).

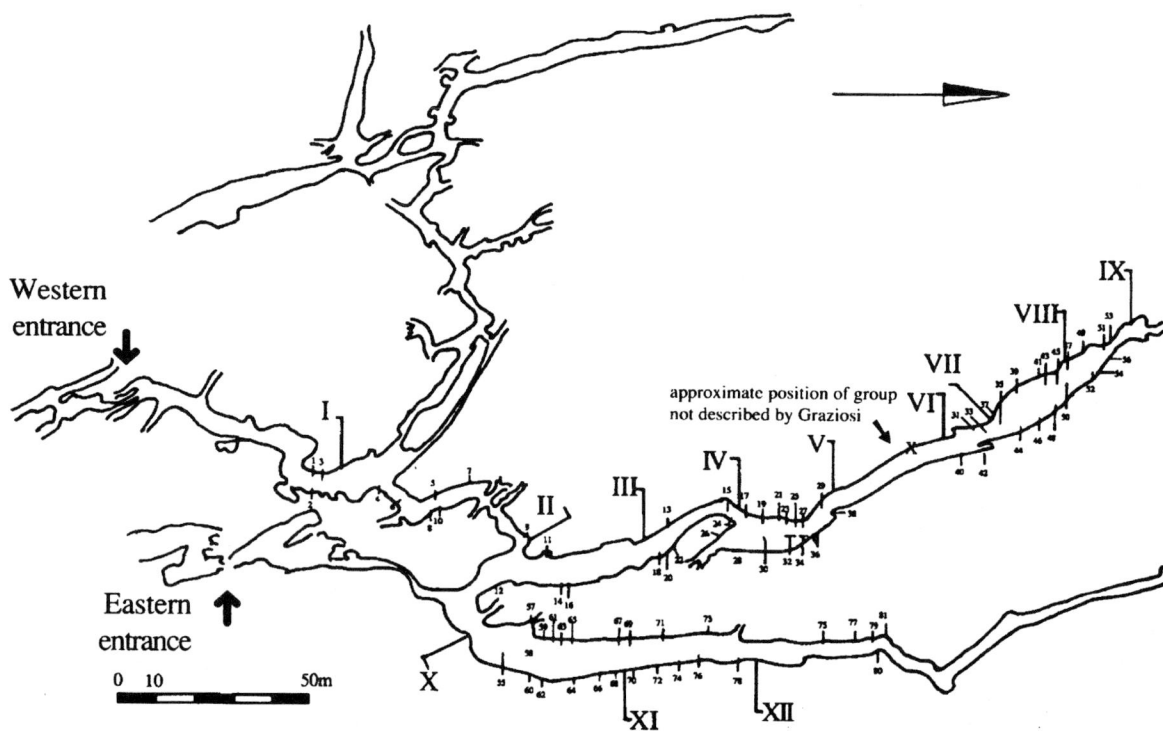

Figure 14.3. Plan of Grotta di Porto Badisco (after Graziosi 1980). Roman numbers indicate zones of the cave; Arabic numbers indicate areas of wall paintings.

Characteristic	Secular sphere (settlement sites)	Sacred sphere (cult sites)
Location	above ground; open	underground; hidden
Accessibility	easy	difficult
Illumination	light	dark
Space	abundant	restricted
Animals	domesticated	wild
Plants	domesticated	wild?
Mode of exploitation	farming	hunting (and gathering?)
Water	'normal': cold, liquid, moving	'abnormal': hot, gaseous, solid, still
Artefacts	everyday materials, utilitarian	special materials, non-utilitarian
Context of artefact discard	domestic rubbish	deliberate deposition
Condition of artefacts	worn, broken	unused, complete

Table 14.1. Table showing structural contrasts in Neolithic Italy.

associated with the sacred, is deep, dark and dangerous. In terms of the hunting cult, culture is associated with the domestic, nature with the wild. In relation to the cult of abnormal water, culture is associated with water flowing in rivers or as rainfall, while nature is associated with water in 'abnormal' forms, for instance steam or even apparently solid (stalactites and stalagmites). I went on to reconstruct the cosmology of the Neolithic communities on the assumption that one of the prime functions of cult is to create and re-create the categories of culture through symbolic action in repetitive ritual practice. Moreover particular ritual attention would be addressed to boundaries, the ambiguous and dangerous areas between one category and another: in our case, between light and dark, overground and underground, domestic and wild, normal water and abnormal water. In general terms the rituals carried out in the cult sites would have served to defend the boundaries of culture ('this world') from the dangerous forces of nature ('the other world'). We may deduce that the 'other world' of the Neolithic communities was located underground, associated with darkness, wildness and abnormal water.

My analysis of the social function of the cult was based on a different strand of anthropological theorising, starting with the pioneering work of Émile Durkheim (1912) and focusing particularly on that of 'Neo-Durkheimian' Mary Douglas (e.g. Douglas 1966; 1970). Adopting the sociological orientation of these scholars' approaches, I argued

that religious ritual was one basis of social power in the Neolithic communities of Italy. The underlying assumptions are that in these small-scale societies the *sources* of power were access to the supernatural and control of cosmological knowledge, while the *means* of exercising power was through control of ritual practice. From the detailed analysis of the cult sites, I argued that they were used for rites of passage and that some of the large natural caves, particularly the Grotta di Porto Badisco, were used for rites of initiation into religious knowledge. Based on the evidence of the hunting cult and on analysis of gendered figures in the paintings of the Grotta di Porto Badisco, I argued that this cult was probably restricted to males. Drawing on the rich ethnographies of secret male cults from New Guinea and Melanesia, I suggested that the power system was based on the control of men over women and older men over younger ones.

The analysis of the historical development of the cult, which I developed further in a later article (Whitehouse 1996), is concerned with continuity in ritual practice from the Upper Palaeolithic into the Neolithic. Apart from general traits, such as the use of caves for cult purposes, a number of specific features such as painted pebbles and depictions of hybrid human-bird figures, demonstrate remarkable long term continuity (Table 14.2). Since the time span involved runs across the transition from hunting and gathering to farming, usually regarded as one of the most important changes in human social development, I

Characteristic	Upper Pal. Early	Upper Pal. Late	Meso. (Epipal.)	Neolithic Early	Neolithic Late	Copper Age	Bronze Age
Cult use of caves a) Burials in caves	✓	✓	✓	✓	✓	✓	✓
b) Cave art	✓	✓	✓ (?)	✓	✓	✓ (?)	
Use of red ochre	✓	✓	✓	✓	✓	✓	
Human figurines	✓			✓	✓	✓	✓
Hunting cult	✓	✓	✓	✓	✓	?	
Men-bird figures		✓	?	?	✓		
Painted and incised pebbles		✓	✓	✓	✓		
Cult of 'abnormal' water				✓	✓	✓	✓
Rock-cut tombs and hypogea					✓	✓	✓

Table 14.2. Table showing continuity in cult practice in prehistoric Italy.

argued that it was unlikely that the meaning of the ritual symbolism, particularly that of the hunting cult, remained unchanged throughout. Instead the *meaning* would have changed, while the *form* of the ritual remained more or less the same – an adaptive tradition developing within a framework of continuity. In this way, long-lived religious symbolism, familiar from repeated practice and sanctioned by ancestral authority, would have provided a reassuringly traditional backdrop to changing cultural meanings.

In my brief discussion of 'psychological' meaning, I addressed individual emotional experience of religious ritual. One approach was through the forms of the sites themselves and their implications for the nature of the rituals carried out in them, which would have involved separation from the community, isolation and sensory deprivation. Another approach was through the nature of some of the symbolism I identified in the cult sites, which referred to bodily substances and functions. Whatever the specific cultural meanings of such symbolism, their reference to universal bodily experiences, would have meant that they carried a powerful emotional load. I develop these ideas further in the 'New approaches' section below.

Critiques

My work has attracted some criticism. Critiques by Italian scholars (e.g. D'Arragon 1996; Grifoni Cremonesi 1994)

are mainly based on rejection of the anthropological orientation of Anglo-American archaeology in favour of more familiar continental historical traditions. There is no answer to these critiques except that I still believe that my approach has something to offer. Criticisms from English and American scholars (most comprehensively by Robin Skeates (1994), but see also Morter and Robb 1998; Pluciennik 1998) have more substance and I shall deal with them briefly here.

One of Skeates' main criticisms is that my work is insufficiently contextual and too generalising and that I therefore miss differences in ritual use between individual sites as well as changes through time. Pluciennik also argues that I overlook possible regional differences in ritual practice. My response to this critique is that it all depends on one's view of appropriate levels of generalisation. I still believe in discussing broad patterns in prehistory, as well as (not instead of) detailed contextual studies. In my original work I tried to make my conclusions appropriate for the level of generalisation I was aiming at, but I recognise that I might not have always succeeded.

Skeates also argues that my use of the New Guinea ethnographic material was inappropriate and was of the 'formal' rather than the 'relational' type as described by Hodder (1982, Chapter 1). However, I would argue that my use of this material *was* relational; in my original search for appropriate analogies I started from the secrecy theme and looked for broad, rather than specific, parallels. The New Guinea material stood out because of the very strong emphasis on secrecy in these societies, although obviously there are many ways in which these communities are unlike those of the south Italian Neolithic (environmental context being one of the most obvious). Moreover my interpretation was not based exclusively on the ethnographic analogies but was also a direct interpretation of the archaeological evidence. I still think that a good case can be made that the Badisco cave at least was used for initiation rites into a secret male cult.

Having criticised my tendency for over-generalisation, Skeates goes on to make some sweeping generalisations of his own about the nature of small-scale agrarian societies. One such generalisation is that in such societies gender relations are usually egalitarian and complementary, rather than hierarchical and coercive, as I suggested for the Italian Neolithic societies. This is a rose-coloured view of small-scale societies and is not supported by the ethnographic evidence. There are many examples of small-scale farming societies that have hierarchical gender systems, the New Guinea ones among them (see Godelier's work on the Baruya for a compelling example that specifically addresses the issue of male domination: Godelier 1986). Having said that, I must add that I do now think my original interpretation of gender relations in the south Italian Neolithic was unbalanced and that I did not consider women's contributions to cult or anything else. Embarassing though it is to admit, I think that I was seduced by the ideology of the male cult and assumed that the values it celebrated were universal in south Italian Neolithic society. It might just have been the male view, with women doing and thinking rather differently, a suggestion made by Morter and Robb (1998). We could interpret the differences in evidence of ritual between the settlement sites and the caves in these terms, with women involved in rituals connected with the everyday concerns of life in the village, while away in their remote and hidden caves men battled to keep the cosmos in order.

In general, while I recognise the validity of some of the criticisms made, I feel that my interpretation of the Italian cult sites still has value, which might be enhanced by the application of some other approaches. The rest of the paper is devoted to a discussion of two such approaches.

New approaches

The two approaches I discuss here both owe much to the work of Chris Tilley. The first approach is that of phenomenology, relating to his 1994 work, *A Phenomenology of Landscape* while the second is metaphor, relating to his 1999 book, *Metaphor and Material Culture*.

Phenomenology – sensory experience

I addressed the relevance of phenomenology to the cult cave sites in an article in 2001 entitled 'A Tale of Two Caves', in which one of the caves described was the Grotta di Porto Badisco. I was struck by the contrast between what Tilley (1994, 16) describes as the starting point for understanding somatic space – 'the upright human body looking out on the world' – with the situation in relation to the caves. Here the human body turns its back on the world, bends down and crawls or slithers into the dark uncomfortable world of the cave. The caves are characterised by many features contrasting with those found in the outside world. These include restriction of light, restriction of movement and the dominance of senses other than vision. This last point is relevant to the criticism sometimes made of phenomenological work, that it concentrates too much on vision in comparison to other senses (e.g. Hamilakis 2002). It is impossible to do this in the caves, where, once one has moved away from the area close to the entrance where daylight penetrates, one is either in total darkness or able to see only with the help of artificial light which, in the case of prehistoric technology, would probably have illuminated only small areas at a time and would have been liable to go out altogether without warning.

As vision diminishes, other senses are sharpened: one becomes very aware of sounds, smells and sensations on the skin, and all these are very different from those experienced in the outside world. Sound behaves strangely in caves: in some places it echoes, bouncing off the walls and surrounding one with repeating but unlocated noise; in other places it is absorbed and travels only very short distances, so one cannot hear another human being only a few metres away in a neighbouring chamber. During prehistory, those in charge of the cave rituals might have manipulated these features to produce impressive, frightening or disorienting effects. It is harder to reconstruct the sense of smell: today the caves smell damp, but clean; in prehistory, when they sometimes at least contained decaying human bodies, the remains of meals as well as living microfauna, the smell must have been strong and probably nauseating.

The sense of touch too is heightened, not just by the restriction of vision, but by the fact that movement is so limited that many parts of the body are touching the cave floor, walls and roof. The sensations are variable: almost everywhere there is hard rock, although this may be smooth or rough-surfaced, with rounded profiles or angled projections, dry or wet. In the areas of stalagmite formations, sharp points may attack the skin. Some areas of the caves are particularly difficult to get into, involving wriggling on all fours or on one's stomach through extremely restricted passages or openings, or twisting one's body round as one negotiates an angled and sloping passage into another chamber, or trying simultaneously to avoid stalactites above and stalagmites below. The movement through the cave would inevitably have involved scratches from stalagmites, minor falls and stumbles, causing some level of pain – which some scholars think should be considered a sense in its own right, rather than a subset of touch.

Assessing the impact of these sensations on the prehistoric users of the caves is not straightforward, given that the sensory world is always interpreted through cultural filters. However, there are also biological universals to sensory experience and I think we may assume that movement through the caves would have been accompanied by emotions of fear and trepidation. This is particularly likely to have been the case if, as I have argued, visits to the caves were relatively rare events, on the occasions of rites of initiation. Indeed, it is possible that the sensations described here might have been enhanced, altered or added to by all kinds of cultural action. Drawing on the rich body of ethnographic documentation of rites of passage in small-scale societies, the participants might have been subjected to physical and verbal humiliation and abuse, dressed in strange clothes or left naked, beaten, fed with poisonous foods or hallucinatory drugs or starved – all adding to feelings of apprehension and fear.

What does the consideration of sensory experience add to our understanding of the use of the cult caves? I would argue that its relevance relates to the nature of rites of passage. Much anthropological discussion is concerned with the sociology of these rites and they way in which they mark changes in social state. However for the individuals concerned, such rites involve not only a change in social category but also an irrevocable change in personhood. This change of identity has to be *lived* as well as taught, hence the need for the elaborate, disorienting, painful, frightening bodily experiences. Roger Keesing, writing about the New Guinea societies, expresses it well:

> no amount of careful sociological analysis and symbol decipherment will tell us what initiation experience is about, why the blood and pain and trauma, as well as the hidden secrets, are needed to turn boys into men. (Keesing 1982, 32)

Metaphor

The second new approach I shall discuss is metaphor. This is also connected with bodies, as both Mary Douglas and Pierre Bourdieu have shown, from rather different, but inter-related, perspectives. Douglas argues that the human body is often considered symbolic of the social body. She spells this out most explicitly in Chapter 5 of *Natural Symbols*, entitled 'The Two Bodies':

> The social body constrains the way the physical body, always modied by the social categories through which it is known, sustains a particular view of society. There is a continual

exchange of meanings between the two kinds of bodily experience so that each reinforces the categories of the other. As a result of this interaction the body itself is a highly restricted medium of expression. (Douglas 1970, 65)

Bourdieu, with his emphasis on practice, has a rather different perspective (Bourdieu 1977; 1990). He moves away from the view of 'society' as something with a separate existence and instead relates the culturally encoded system of symbolic meanings to the lived experience of individuals. One of the useful concepts developed by Bourdieu is *habitus*, which is a non-theoretical knowledge of the world constructed by individuals through habitual action. It works recursively: structures shape the way people behave, but behaviour also creates the structures. Bourdieu tells us that 'bodies take metaphors seriously' (Bourdieu 1990, 71–2). So, human bodies not only experience sensory impressions; they also learn the cultural lessons of spaces structured by myth and ritual. Bourdieu's work was concerned with built space, but his ideas can be applied equally to natural spaces chosen for ritual purposes, such as the Italian cult caves.

I did consider symbolism in my original work, but I concentrated on the structuralist aspect, in which symbols take meaning from their position in a binary contrasting code, rather than from any inherent qualities they might have, or be thought to have (although I did deal a little with the latter in the chapter on 'Psychological Meaning'). The difference between the two ways of thinking about symbols can be thought of as the distinction between digital and analogic logic (Barth 1975, 208; Tilley 1999, 28–31). The analogic way that metaphor works means that the choice of a symbol is not arbitrary, but depends in some way on the characteristics of the object in question, albeit interpreted through a specific cultural filter. This approach has something to offer in analysis of the Italian cult caves and, by way of example, I discuss two aspects here: the form of the caves themselves and the water cult.

Form of the caves

This applies particularly to the large natural caves with their restricted entrances and markedly zoned character, including narrow, low passages that can only be negotiated on all fours. Such caves are metaphorically appropriate for rites of passage. Changes of social category are often considered in terms of death and rebirth, and caves can be considered metaphorically both tombs and wombs (Turner 1967, 99). Another aspect that works metaphorically is the *journey* through the cave. Rites of passage are metaphorical journeys and what could be more appropriate to symbolise this than the difficult physical journey through the cave, across thresholds, through tunnels, passages and chambers to the innermost, most sacred areas and then the return journey back to the everyday world in an irrevocably altered state?

Cult of abnormal water

Originally I concentrated on the structural contrasts between the 'normal' water of everyday life and the 'abnormal' water of the cult sites. Here I focus on the metaphorical aspect of the cult of stalagmites, stalactites and stillicide water. A number of different features are relevant. One of the most obvious is *colour*, which I did discuss in the original book. The high calcium content of stillicide water makes it opaque and whitish in colour. This might have prompted symbolic interpretations in terms of bodily fluids with similar qualities: breast milk or semen, or both. There is no specific archaeological evidence to support this interpretation in the Italian Neolithic or Copper Age. However, colour is almost always involved in documented symbolic systems and references to vital bodily fluids are also very common. Moreover, without reference to any specific psychological theorising, we may assume that bodily metaphors of this sort would carry a heavy emotional load.

Another aspect relevant to metaphorical meaning, not discussed in the original book but addressed in another article (Whitehouse in press), is the *transformational* aspect of stillicide water. Slow though the process of stalagmite formation is, it might nonetheless have been understood and perceived as 'water turning to stone'. This is suggested by the discovery at Grotta Scaloria of stalagmites truncated to create flat surfaces on which painted pottery vessels had been placed – presumably to collect stillicide water dripping from the cave roof (Tinè and Isetti 1982). If this was the case, then it may have been perceived as a powerful and magical transformation, given the 'essential' differences between the elements: liquid water and solid stone. If the cult caves were used for rites of passage, the transformative character of the stillicide water would have been particularly appropriate. Rites of passage are by definition *about* transformation: irreversible changes in the social status, personal identity and embodied experiences of the individuals taking part. Just as I have argued that the physical context of the caves, with their tunnels, passages and corridors to be negotiated and thresholds to be crossed, provided a metaphor for the journey of the rite of passage, so the consumption of water that turns into stone might have symbolised the internal transformation of the participant.

Concluding remarks

The rich data from the Italian cult sites have much further interpretative potential. While I recognise the validity of some of the criticisms of my original study, I remain convinced by the main thesis I developed there. In the present paper I have shown how the development of other ways of looking at the evidence, referring to sensory experience and to metaphor, provide additional inter-pretative layers to our understanding of these sites.

References

Bourdieu, P. 1977. *Outline of a Theory of Practice*. Cambridge, Cambridge University Press.

Bourdieu, P. 1990. *The Logic of Practice*. Cambridge, Polity Press.

D'Arragon, B. 1996. Review of 'Underground Religion. Cult and Culture in Prehistoric Italy'. *Religioni e Società*, 24, 116–9.

Douglas, M. 1966. *Purity and Danger*. London, Routledge and Kegan Paul.

Douglas, M. 1970. *Natural Symbols*. London, Cresset Press.

Durkheim, E. 1912. *Les formes élementaires de la vie religieuse*. Paris, Alcan.

Geniola, A. 1987. Stratigrafia comparata delle grotte cultuali di S. Barbara (Polignano a Mare) e di Cala Colombo e Cala Scizzo (Torre a Mare, Bari). *Atti della XXV Riunione Scientifica dell'Istituto Italiano di Preistoria e Protostoria*. Florence, Istituto Italiano di Preistoria e Protostoria, 279–95.

Geniola, A. and Tunzi, A. M. 1980. Espressioni cultuali e d'arte nella Grotta di Cala Scizzo presso Torre a Mare (Bari). *Rivista di Scienze Preistoriche*, 35, 125–46.

Godelier, M. 1986. *The Making of Great Men. Male Domination and Power among the New Guinea Baruya*. Cambridge, Cambridge University Press.

Graziosi, P. 1980. *Le pitture preistoriche della grotta di Porto Badisco*. Orgines. Florence, Istituto Italiano di Preistoria e Protostoria.

Grifoni-Cremonesi, R. 1994. Observations on the problems related to certain cult phenomena during the Neolithic in the Italian peninsula. *Journal of European Archaeology* 2(2), 153–68.

Hamilakis, Y. 2002. The past as oral history: towards an archaeology of the senses. In Y. Hamilakis, M. Pluciennik and S. Tarlow (eds). *Thinking Through the Body: Archaeologies of Corporeality*. New York, Kluwer.

Hodder, I. 1982. *The Present Past*. London, Batsford.

Keesing, R. M. 1982. Introduction. In G. H. Herdt (ed.). *Rituals of Manhood. Male Initiation in Papua New Guinea*. Berkeley, University of California Press, 1–43.

Leach, E. 1976. *Culture and Communication*. Cambridge, Cambridge University Press.

Lévi-Strauss, C. 1966 (original in French 1962). *The Savage Mind*. London, Weidenfeld and Nicholson.

Lo Porto, F. G. 1972. La tomba neolitica con idolo in pietra di Arnesano (Lecce). *Rivista di Scienze Preistoriche*, 27, 358–72.

Morter, J. and Robb, J. 1998. Space, gender and architecture in the southern Italian Neolithic. In R. Whitehouse (ed.). *Gender and Italian Archaeology: Challenging the Stereotypes*. London, Accordia Research Institute and Institute of Archaeology, 83–94.

Passeri, L. 1970. Ritrovamenti preistorici nei Pozzi della Piana (Umbria). *Rivista di Scienze Preistoriche*, 25, 225–51.

Pluciennik, M. 1998. representations of gender in prehistoric southern Italy. In R. Whitehouse (ed.). *Gender and Italian Archaeology: Challenging the Stereotypes*. London, Accordia Research Institute and Institute of Archaeology, 57–82.

Robb, J. 1994. Gender contradictions, moral coalitions, and inequality in prehistoric Italy. *Journal of European Archaeology*, 2, 20–49.

Skeates, R. 1994. Burial, context and gender in Neolithic South-eastern Italy. *Journal of European Archaeology*, 2, 119–214.

Tilley, C. 1994. *A Phenomenology of Landscape*. Oxford, Blackwell.

Tilley, C. 1999. *Metaphor and Material Culture*. Oxford, Blackwell.

Tinè, S. and Isetti, F. 1982. Culto neolitico delle acque e recenti scavi nella Grotta Scaloria. *Bullettino di Paletnologia Italiana*, 82 (1975–80), 31–70.

Turner, V. 1967. *The Forest of Symbols. Aspects of Ndembu Ritual*. Ithaca and London, Cornell University Press.

Whitehouse, R. D. 1992. *Underground Religion. Cult and Culture in Prehistoric Italy*. London, Accordia Research Centre.

Whitehouse, R. D. 1996. Continuity in ritual practice from Upper Palaeolithic to Neolithic and Copper Age in southern Italy and Sicily. In V. Tinè (ed.). *Forme e tempi della neolitizzazione in Italia meridionale e in Sicilia*. IRACEB/IIAS, Rossano, 385–410.

Whitehouse, R. D. 2001. A tale of Two Caves: the archaeology of religious experience in Mediterranean Europe. In P. F. Biehl and F. Bertemes (eds). *The Archaeology of Cult and Religion*. Budapest, Archaeolingua, 161–7.

Whitehouse, R. D. In press. Water turned to stone: stalagmites and stalactites in cult caves in prehistoric Italy. In F. Stevens (ed.). *The Archaeology of Water: Social and Ritual Dimensions*. Walnut Creek, Left Coast Press and London: Publications of the Institute of Archaeology, University College, London.

Chapter 15

THE PHOENICIANS AND THE MALTESE PREHISTORIC CULTURAL LANDSCAPE

Anthony Bonanno

Introduction

Sometime in the fourth century AD the skeletal remains of two individuals were discovered below the floor of a church in northern Italy. The circumstances of the discovery, especially the quantity of 'blood' (presumably red ochre) covering the original bodies, suggest that they were late Palaeolithic burials. St Ambrose, however, bishop of Milan, inspired by a dream, declared the remains to belong to two early Christian martyrs. Soon the bones proved to be miraculous and their owners were canonised as Saints Protasus and Gervaise (Haldane 1985; Bradley 2002, 112–3).

In Malta, similar early twentieth century discoveries of skeletons in matrices heavily imbued with red ochre, far from being given a religious interpretation, were thought to result from recent murders and were reported to the police (Evans 1971, 6, 190–191). On the other hand, the striking megalithic structures on Gozo, so outstanding in the landscape, conjured up folk tales of a female giant handling gigantic stones with one arm while holding a baby in the other. Maltese place names, the majority of which originate between the Arab period and early modern times, generally dwell on the physical appearance of ancient remains, even the more spectacular ones; only rarely do they attribute religious or cultural connotations to them (Wettinger 2000, xxxv and *passim*).

From early Medieval times onwards, in spite of the availability of building stone, conspicuous remains of prehistoric and ancient buildings were sometimes exploited only for their stone which was re-cut and re-employed without any consideration for the cultural significance of such remains. The best example is the whole of the ancient city of Melite which has been replaced by present day Mdina and part of Rabat. Another example is the site of the sanctuary of Tas-Silġ where several robber trenches have been traced archaeologically on top of lower courses of huge ashlar blocks. Here stone robbing started very early in the history of the site, and it is not easy to tell which stones

were re-cycled for the erection of an early Christian church and which ones were robbed in the sixteenth to eighteenth centuries for use as building material for other secular, or religious, buildings in the surroundings.

The above are a few examples of the diversity of attitudes towards the relics of the past (for other examples from northwest Europe see Bradley 2002). In the following paper I shall try to trace the impact that the prehistoric cultural landscape had on the first historical population of the Maltese islands, the Phoenicians.

The date of the earliest Phoenician settlement on Malta is a hotly debated issue. Claudia Sagona (2002; 2003) places it as early as the tenth century BC, without providing sufficiently stringent evidence, as shown by Nicholas Vella (2005, *passim* especially 442–443) who brings it down to 750 BC or later, on the basis of the available evidence. There is no doubt, however, that the Phoenicians had inserted themselves in the physical and cultural Maltese landscape by the beginning of the seventh century BC (bibl. in Vella 2005, 439; Bonanno 1993, 419–421).

Given the total absence of mineral resources from the geological formation of the Maltese islands – apart from excellent stone for building and clay for pottery making – the major attractions of the latter for the Phoenician seafarers must have been the archipelago's geographical location right in the centre of the Mediterranean and its excellent well-sheltered harbours (Pedley *et al.* 2002). Whatever currents and wind regimes were prevalent in the Mediterranean at the time (Aubet 1997, 155–162, figures 26–29; Atauz 2004, 43–50) the islands were ideally placed as a convenient port of call on the Phoenicians' frequent voyages from their homeland to their western colonies and trading posts (and vice-versa). This view is in keeping with the perception of the ancients as relayed to us by Diodorus Siculus (V. 12).

What was the landscape like that the Phoenicians found there? The landscape, apart from the general geo-morphology (characterized by hilly land with reasonably fertile valleys and sufficient water resources) was very different from the present over-urbanized one, segmented as it is into small handkerchief-size fields by myriads of rubble walls and terraced walls. The tree cover might not have been that different, as has been revealed by current research undertaken by Frank Carroll and Katrin Fenech on deep cores taken from the Marsa flood plain (Carroll *et al.* 2004). What was the impact of this landscape on the Phoenicians and how did they interact with it? The following are just some preliminary observations relating to these questions, concentrating on these oriental sea-traders' interaction with the Maltese *cultural* landscape.

When the Phoenicians set foot on the islands, that landscape was mainly characterized by scattered, naturally defended, settlements on high ridges and flat hills inhabited by the *Borg in-Nadur* and *Baħrija* population of the islands. But the most striking cultural feature standing out in the natural landscape was the complex megalithic buildings of the previous Temple culture (3600–2500 BC). Like their Medieval successors, who left behind a series of place-names referring to these features, the Phoenician settlers were struck by these strange structures, their most tangible impact being on the Tas-Silġ temple complex

Tas-Silġ

The site of Tas-Silġ is now pretty well known even if the Italian excavators are in the process of revising some of their interpretations of the 1960s and 1970s, following current excavations on strategically selected spots (Ciasca and Rossignani 2000). With their resumption of excavations since 1997, they have even extended their direct interest to the prehistoric phases of the site which they had formerly refrained from investigating in the 1960s. Their excavations of the deposits outside the main surviving temple unit, beyond and to the northwest side of the back exit, have revealed not only a significant *Tarxien* phase activity in the area, but also a continuation of use later in the Bronze Age; but not, apparently, in the Phoenician period. As this information is still very provisional, I am limiting my reflections to the accounts of the previous excavations.

The megalithic complex of Tas-Silġ appears to have been quite extensive. Standing megaliths have been encountered even in the recent University of Malta excavations on the south side of the road, some 60 m away from the main temple unit; other megalithic structures had previously surfaced about 20 m to the north and 40 m to the northwest. But the most significant structure remains the main temple unit with its horse-shoe shaped outer wall and as yet undetermined layout of internal spaces. It is this unit which received the major attention from the Phoenician occupation onwards. It is assumed by the excavators that the temple was in a reasonable state of preservation when it was adopted by the Phoenicians as the hub of their own place of worship. I find it hard, however, to accept the

survival of the full elevation of the temple unit as reconstructed in a drawing published by the late Antonia Ciasca (1999) (Figures 15.1 and 15.2). This reconstruction shows a full façade based on the small model found at Tarxien, with a forward monumental extension consisting of two arms ending in two antae with pilasters, each crowned by two superimposed Egyptian cavetto cornices. But even if the surviving elevation of the temple reached only the height of the first course of uprights, as I am inclined to believe, the surviving structure with its peculiar shape was left untouched by the Phoenicians who adapted their ritual architecture to that of the prehistoric temple. They placed a semi-interred altar block (the so-called 'ground altar') in the centre, between the new extended entrance and the original one, and enclosed the whole structure within a rectangular wall.

What is striking here is that the Phoenicians sacrificed the rectangular temple plan typical of all the religions of the Levant and of the few surviving ones of their own, such as the temple of Ashtart in Kition (Aubet 1997, 43, figure 12) and the various Punic temples in Sardinia (Moscati 1968, 109–119). The adoption of the curvilinear plan of the prehistoric temple is quite a unique feature in the Phoenician world.

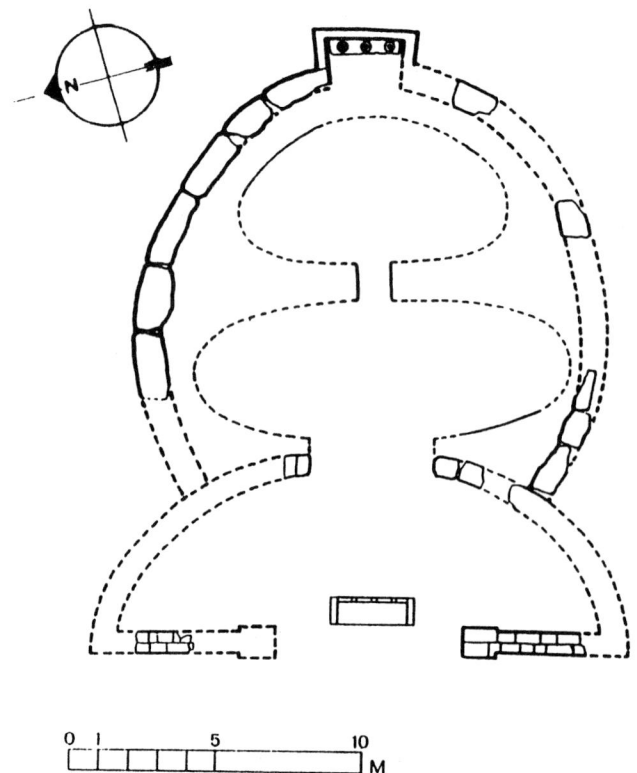

Figure 15.1. Hypothetical reconstruction of the plan of the prehistoric temple with the Phoenician extension.

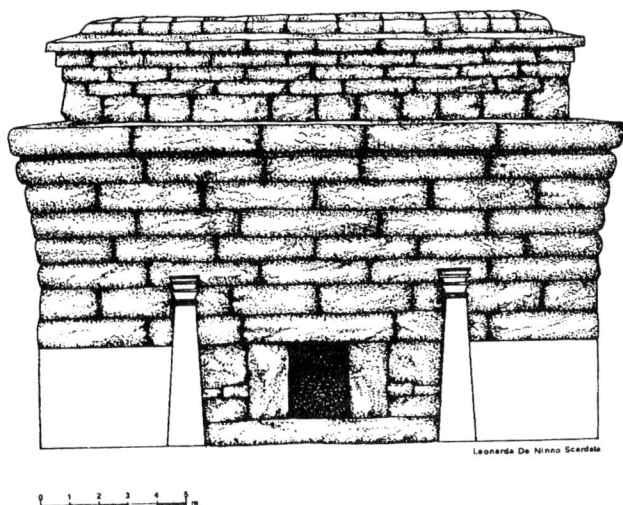

Figure 15.2. Hypothetical reconstruction of the façade of the prehistoric temple with the Phoenician extension (after Ciasca 1999).

Whether they assimilated also the deity worshiped previously in the prehistoric temple, as is often claimed, is another matter. All we know for certain is that the new arrangement was for the worship of their major female goddess Ashtart. Previous claims that this marked a continuity of cult of a female goddess of fertility are, to my mind, unfounded. Apart from the fact that we are not at all sure that the prehistoric deity of the temple period was a female one, even less so that it was a fertility one, this claim does not take into consideration the 18-centuries-long hiatus of the Bronze Age occupation of the site, which might well have been a non-religious one. Had there been a real continuity of cult of a female fertility deity, her successor would have been Ashtart in her fertility role of Aphrodite, as in the case of the sanctuary of Aphrodite of Eryx in western Sicily. Although none of the inscriptions found on the site go back to the earlier two centuries of Phoenician occupation (seventh to sixth centuries), they show unambiguously that the Ashtart of Tas-Silġ was the equivalent of the Greek Hera and Roman Juno, the consort of Zeus/Jupiter. Given the topographical location of the sanctuary and its close and intimate connection with the sea, as revealed also by the remains of offerings found during the excavations in the immediate periphery of the building, Ashtart was most probably revered here as the protectress of mariners.

Other megalithic sites

Phoenician intervention in, or occupation of, prehistoric megalithic temples is not limited to Tas-Silġ, as might

appear to be the case from a first impression. For the purpose of this paper I have tried to find out whether there is any mention of Phoenician-Punic finds in the material unearthed during the excavations, scientific or otherwise, of the other prehistoric sites. For this exercise I have consulted John Evans' *Survey of the Maltese prehistoric antiquities* (1971), which has remained unsurpassed for the thoroughness of its documentation of the various sites and their contents.

Unfortunately, Evans' account does not always mention, or hardly ever refers to, Punic occupation of the prehistoric sites. Out of 56 sites listed and described in his *Survey*, barely eleven mention Punic remains being found in one or another of the stratigraphic units. This cannot reflect the real situation, as I have had the opportunity of verifying when I checked the original account of the Tarxien excavations in Temi Zammit's Field Notebooks, where I met frequent mention of 'Punic pottery' from the very earliest accounts of his 1915 campaign onwards. The only mention of Punic material for Tarxien in Evans is, in contrast, the one relating to the bell-shaped cistern near the entrance of the west temple which contained no material earlier than 'late Punic and Roman' (Evans 1971, 118). For this reason, for a proper survey of Punic occupation of prehistoric sites one cannot rely solely on Evans' accounts. It is necessary to go to the original excavation accounts, as I did for the Tarxien temples. Such a search is further hampered by the unscientific excavations of the major temple complexes (Ġgantija, Ħaġar Qim, and Mnajdra) in the nineteenth century and by the general belief then that these structures were Phoenician. Furthermore, proper excavation documentation for these temples and for the Ħal Saflieni Hypogeum is sadly absent.

Tarxien

It might come as a surprise that in the account of the discovery of the Tarxien temples there is so frequent reference to 'Punic' pottery. From the very first days of his excavation at Tarxien, Zammit came across pottery which he designated as 'Punic'. On 21 July 1915 Zammit noted that the 'proportion of Punic to Neolithic ware [was] about 10 to 1' (Zammit Field Notebook 11, 2). On the same day he came across a 'portion of a very thick early Punic bilychne lamp'.

At Tarxien, there is widespread evidence of quarrying of old building stone. On the upper surface of blocks with missing upper parts there are traces of short channels which served for the insertion of metal wedges used in breaking off building stone. Traces of such use of wedges can also be observed on the upper surface of the remaining lower half of the colossal corpulent figure (N. C. Vella, personal observation). This quarrying activity might be connected with the intensive Punic presence suggested by the abundant quantity of 'Punic' pottery encountered by Zammit in the upper layers during his excavations of 1915–1918.

Assuming that we are right in associating the presence of the Punic pottery with this episode in the biography of the Tarxien temples, this mundane, opportunistic activity contrasts very strongly with the conversion of the Tas-Silġ temple into a Phoenician one. Had there not been any activity at all, one would have interpreted the omission as a possible passive reaction, one of reverence for the surviving physical remains of a sacred (clearly non-secular) building. But actively despoiling the structure of its physical constituent elements surely meant indifference or insensitivity for such sentimental value. This might be taken to show that the remains of the prehistoric sacred building at Tas-Silġ had other qualities that motivated their incorporation into another religious building, qualities that the Tarxien temples lacked. One such quality could be the closer proximity to the sheltered harbour. Besides, it appears that the Marsaxlokk harbour was preferred by the Phoenicians to those on the northern coast of the island (Bonanno 2005, 59–61).

Settlement

The Phoenicians, both in their homeland and in their colonies in the western Mediterranean, followed a fixed pattern in their choice of places for their settlements: a small island in close proximity of the mainland, or a promontory, preferably with a sheltered harbour or anchorage close by. In Malta they made a very conspicuous exception. Although they used extensively the good harbours of the island, especially the south-eastern one, where they even set up a sanctuary, they chose to settle inland, on the tip of an elevated ridge, some ten kilometres from that harbour. It is here, on the headland today occupied by the old city of Mdina, that they set up their abode, eventually consolidating it into the major urban centre. Recent discoveries in various spots of Mdina have revealed very early Phoenician occupation in archaeological strata immediately above Bronze Age ones (Cutajar 2001). If, as it is claimed, these finds provide enough evidence of an extensive Borġ in-Nadur settlement in Mdina (and possibly in Rabat), implying that the spaces in between were also covered with huts like those excavated by David Trump at Borġ in-Nadur, I wonder whether these discoveries can be construed as evidence of proto-urban development which was already in its embryonic stage in the later stages of the Bronze Age and which the Phoenicians merely adopted for their own purposes. This would be very much in line with the Phoenician innate disposition to adapt to circumstances.

Burial

The underground cemeteries of the prehistoric Temple culture must have become invisible and forgotten by the time of the Phoenician colonization. Nevertheless, the Phoenician burial rites reintroduced a tomb typology which was characteristic of the earlier phases of the Temple Period (4100–3600 BC), the rock-cut shaft-and-chamber tomb, rather than the full-scale underground cemetery, typical of the last phase (3000–2500 BC). This burial system, however, was certainly imported from the Phoenician homeland and, apart from Malta, it is found in other Phoenician colonies in the central and western Mediterranean (such as Almuñecar in Spain, the necropoleis of Puig des Molins in Ibiza, Tharros in Sardigna and Carthage itself). This does not exclude the possibility of the occasional discovery and re-use of late Neolithic rock-cut tombs. I am quite sure that on a close examination some of the Phoenician-Punic tombs will turn out to be such re-used shaft-and-chamber tombs; the likeliest being those with a very shallow and circular shaft.

We know for certain that the Phoenicians made use of already existing rock-cut pits in the ground that had a completely different purpose among the previous middle Bronze Age population. Thus, these ancient features were invested with a new meaning. We have several instances, mostly at Mtarfa, a hill close to ancient Melite, where they converted Borġ in-Nadur phase 'silo-pits' into graves. On their own these tombs, as well as others of different shape, suggest that, whereas the Bronze Age settlement on the Mdina promontory might have well been adopted by the Phoenicians as their main urban centre, the Mtarfa one, which had equally been settled on, as evidenced by the multitude of typically Borġ in-Nadur silo-pits, was turned into a cemetery area.

The absence of such rock-cut tombs from within the known boundaries of the ancient city of Melite which had its predecessor in Phoenician-Punic times, and their early concentration in different areas around that city, suggest that, even if they had adopted the major pre-urban settlement that had been established by the Bronze Age settlement, the Phoenicians followed their burial traditions and buried their dead outside their urban centre. Some of the earlier tombs are located on promontories separated from the town by a valley; perhaps not so much the Għajn Qajjet and Għajn Klieb, but certainly the Mtarfa ones. Their position is very suggestive, and could be reminiscent, of the concept of the journey of the soul across the waters, as it appears in a papyrus inscription from Tal-Virtu. This inscription was contained in a Horus-headed bronze amulet that was found in a rock-cut tomb in that locality. From it we learn that the Phoenicians appear to have borrowed from the Egyptians, among other cultural and religious aspects, the belief in a journey that the deceased must undertake across the waters, immediately after their death

(Frendo *et al.* 2005). In Egypt this journey across the water took place over the Nile which separated the world of the living, on the east side of the river, from the world of the dead, on its western side. In the Phoenician world, the cemeteries were also separated from the settlement by a body of water, as in Tyre, Motya, Sulcis, Cadiz and Mogador (Aubet 1997, 253–256).

Maltese geomorphology and hydrology are, of course, quite different. There are no rivers in Malta. At most there are a few perennial springs flowing out from the interface between the upper coralline limestone and the blue clay wherever these are present in the geological formation. Such springs must have been much more numerous and bountiful in antiquity, as evidenced by the old place names, before water extraction by artesian wells became increasingly common since early modern times. The Mdina/Rabat promontory is flanked on two sides by valleys into which such springs flowed more copiously than they do at present. This landscape must have provided the alternative to the body of water that separated the urban settlement from the necropoleis (Frendo *et al.* 2005).

Conclusion

I am presenting this paper not as a result of a career-long piece of research, far from it, but as a new approach to Maltese archaeological studies. It is not even a presentation of work in progress because the work has not even started. All I have done is to explore the potentials of such a field of investigation; an approach which I believe will leave fruitful and rewarding results. I have only scratched the surface. The most pressing investigation should be, in my view, that of the impact of the cultural landscape on the *Tarxien Cemetery* people. A better understanding of their relationship with the structural monuments bequeathed to them by the previous Temple culture seems to be emerging from the recent Italian excavations outside the temple unit at Tas-Silġ. Such an investigation will perhaps help to solve one of the most intriguing problems of Maltese prehistory, the question of continuity or break between the Temple culture and the following Bronze Age one.

References

Atauz, A. D. 2004. *Trade, Piracy and Naval Warfare in the Central Mediterranean: the maritime history and archaeology of Malta.* PhD thesis, Texas A and M University.
Aubet, M. E. 1997. *The Phoenicians and the West: Politics, Colonies and Trade.* Cambridge, University Press
Bonanno, A. 1993. Evidence of Greek, Carthaginian and Etruscan maritime commerce south of the Tyrrhenian: the Maltese case. In T. Hackens (ed.). *Flotte e Commercio Greco, Cartaginese ed Etrusco nel Mar Tirreno / Navies and commerce of the Greeks, the Carthaginians and the Etruscans in the Tyrrhenian sea, Acts of the European Symposium held at Ravello, January 1987,* 417–428. Rixensart: P.A.C.T. 20.
Bonanno, A. 2005. *Malta: Phoenician, Punic, and Roman.* Malta, Midsea Books Ltd.
Bradley, R. 2002. *The Past in Prehistoric Societies.* London and New York, Routledge.
Carroll, F. A., Fenech, K., Bonanno, A., Hunt, C., Jones, A. M., and Schembri, P. J. 2004.The past environment of the Maltese Islands: the Marsa cores. In L. Eneix (ed). *Exploring the Maltese Prehistoric Temple Culture: presentations from the 2003 Conference* (available only in CD) (Sarasota 2004), 10.
Ciasca, A. 1999. Le isole maltesi e il Mediterraneao fenicio. *Malta Archaeological Review* 3, 21–25.
Ciasca, A. and Rossignani, M. P. 2000. Scavi e ricerche della Missione Archeologica Italiana a Malta. *Malta Archaeological Review* 4, 51–67.
Cutajar, N. 2001. Recent discoveries and the archaeology of Mdina. *Treasures of Malta* VIII, 1 (Christmas 2001), 79–85.
Evans, J. D. 1971. *The Prehistoric Antiquities of the Maltese Islands: a Survey.* London, Athlone
Frendo, A. J., de Trafford, A. and Vella, N. C. 2005. Water journeys of the dead: a glimpse into Phoenician and Punic eschatology. In A. Spanò Giammellaro (ed), *Atti del Congresso Internazionale di Studi Fenici e Punici, Marsala-Palermo 2–8 Ottobre 2000,* vol. 1, 427–443. Palermo.
Haldane, J. B. S. 1985. God-makers. In J.B.S. Haldane (ed.). *On Being the Right Size and Other Essays*: 85–100. Oxford, Oxford University Press.
Mifsud-Chircop, M. 1990. Folklore of Gozo. In C. Cini (ed.). *Gozo: the Roots of an Island*: 161–193. Malta, Said International.
Moscati, S. 1968. *Fenici e Cartaginesi in Sardegna.* Milan, il Saggiatore.
Pedley, M., Hughes Clarke, M. and Galea, P. 2002. *Limestone Isles in a Crystal Sea.* Malta, PEG.
Sagona, C. 2002. *The Archaeology of Punic Malta,* Ancient Near Eastern Studies Supplement 9. Leuven, Peeters.
Sagona, C. 2003. *Punic Antiquities of Malta and other ancient artefacts held in ecclesiastical and private collections.* Ancient Near Eastern Studies Supplement 10. Leuven, Peeters.
Vella, N. C. 2002. The lie of the land: Ptolemy's temple of Hercules in Malta. *Ancient Near Eastern Studies* 39, 83–112.
Vella, N. C. 2005. Phoenician and Punic Malta (review article of Sagona 2002 and 2003). *Journal of Roman Archaeology* 18: 436–450.
Wettinger, G. 1976. Some Maltese Medieval placenames of archaeological interest, in *Atti del Colloquio Internazionale di Archeologia Medievale, Palermo-Erice 20–22 Sett. 1974,* 329–365. Palermo.
Wettinger, G. 2000. *Place-Names of the Maltese Islands ca. 1300–1800.* Malta, P.E.G.

Chapter 16

CULT OF THE DEAD OR CULT FOR THE DEAD: STUDIES OF JEWISH CATACOMBS IN MALTA IN CONTEXT

Piotr Drag

Death is written into the life of our human existence on earth. Its unpreventable almighty presence and mysterious perception influence people's beliefs and mark the way different societies carry the memory of the deceased. Burial customs and funerary rites express faith and display social identity, status, gender, and the place of the dead in society. Therefore, the archaeological evidence gained from burial places such as funerary inscriptions and the items preserved in tombs provide data about the mourning customs and burial practices and the material culture of a given period.

The subject of Jewish responses to death and Jewish beliefs about the afterlife has attracted numerous investigators over the past century or so. Almost from the very beginning, the interpretation of this aspect of Jewish culture has been fraught with controversy, which has oscillated around the question of how kosher is the cult of the dead: can one talk at all about a Jewish *cult of* the dead or is this rather a *cult for* the Jewish dead?

The meaning and impact of death on an individual society is an exceptionally multifaceted issue. In its analysis there is a strong need of terminological precision in distinguishing between the terms (and their implications): funerary rites (burial and mourning), mortuary rites (care, feeding, and commemoration), magical mortuary rites (necromancy and exorcism) and the proper definition of the cult of the dead (veneration or worship). In order to delineate the cult of the dead, the paper refers to Emile Durkheim's definition. He sees the cult of the dead as 'repeated standardized practices oriented toward the dead at ritual locations associated with the dead' (1915, 63).

The twentieth century has seen both advocates and opponents of the Jewish death cult. The line of the division between them can be drawn along the different approaches of scholars toward the topic of Jewish responses to the dead. Some have concentrated upon the texts of the Hebrew Bible for their primary data, some upon the importance of cultural parallels to neighbouring practices, while others have emphasized their research upon the archaeological remains of tombs and other funerary structures. Also, at times the scholars' attitudes have been dimmed by current societal attitudes towards archaeological evidence, new finds, and the reinterpretation of Biblical text. Their intention, sometimes influenced by the *zeitgeist*, had its impact on the attempt to (re)establish the singularity and uniqueness of Jews and Judaism among the people and religions of antiquity. Among the advocates of the cult of the dead in Judaism in the twentieth century, following in the footsteps of nineteenth century investigator F. Coulanges, are Sir J. Frazer, G. Quell, J. Pedersen, E. Bickerman, P. Brown, J. N. Lightstone and B. R. McCane. Their point of view was challenged by the opponents of the Jewish cult of the dead: Y. Kaufmann, W. F. Albright, G. E. Wright, R. de Vaux, B. B. Schmidt, R. Albertz and P. S. Johnston. Some of the above scholars shifted their opinions during their life time. For instance, Albright, who began his career in the camp of opponents at the end of fifties, joined the advocates of the cult of dead in Judaism. In 1957 he wrote:

> Biblical references to veneration of heroic shrines (e.g. Rachel and Deborah), cult of departed spirits or divination with their aid, and high places in general add up to a much greater significance for popular Israelite belief in life after death and the cult of the dead than has hitherto appeared prudent to admit. (Albright 1957, 257)

Malta for many reasons is a fascinating territory for research, mainly because of its rich history and location, being a crossing bridge for different people who all have left traces on the island. Malta is a relatively small territory, where the importance of context in the understanding of a particular cult can be fully observed in depth. Studies show that the cult of dead is difficult to interpret due to its complex nature. The context very often brings new insights to analysis of a particular practice, as otherwise it is almost impossible to predict how an individual society will deal with the various aspects of funerary practices and the commemoration of deceased ancestors. This is as much of a challenge for investigators of past cultures as it is for investigators of contemporary cultures where extensive documentation and living informants are still available (cf. Ucko 1969; Humphreys 1982).

This research assumes that Judaism, because of its firmly fortified purity laws, had ambiguous attitudes toward the dead compared to other monotheistic religions in Antiquity. Nonetheless Jews, especially those living in the Mediterranean Diaspora, very often followed the practices of their neighbours, such as burial. The Jewish catacombs in Malta are exemplary of this. They are distinct proof of the existence of a Jewish community there in Antiquity.

Some scholars have dated the Jewish presence in Malta back to the Phoenician time. In the most comprehensive work on this subject entitled *The Jews of Malta*, which was read to the Jewish Historical Society of England in March 1928, Cecil Roth suggested that the Jews, especially the Hebrew seafaring tribes of Zebulun and Asher, would almost certainly have come to Malta with the ancient Phoenicians, whose presence is proved by a Phoenician inscription discovered at the Ggantija temple in Xaghra. Maybe Jews even stayed continually during the time when the island changed its ownership and went from Carthaginian to Roman hands. Unfortunately, this cannot be proved by any literary evidence. Malta in this regard is not different from other parts of the Roman Empire. Although there was a substantial Jewish population in Western Europe from at least the first century BC, literary evidence before the end of the sixth century AD is very sparse, amounting to a few, mainly hostile references by Roman writers and some materials of doubtful historical value in rabbinic or hagiographic sources. For example from the Acts of the Apostles 28, 1–11 one can find out that when the disciple Paul (still a Jew called Saul) was shipwrecked on a tiny rock off the coast of Malta, he dismissed the local inhabitants as being nothing more than βάρβαροι. The word is nominative plural adjective of βάρβαρος and it could be translated as: non-Greek, uncivilised, foreigner, native, but it also could mean that the natives of Malta spoke a native Punic tongue (Buhagiar 1986, 4). During Paul's three-month stay in Malta, unlike his usual custom, he neither met with the Jewish community in Malta, nor with any of its representatives, but this is not sufficient to prove the claim that there was not a Jewish community at the time in Malta.

Thus, knowledge of the Jewish communities of Malta and the Mediterranean area is therefore almost entirely dependent on funerary inscriptions, which contain information about community organization, the use of biblical texts and religious symbols, linguistic habits, naming practices and social status, burial customs and beliefs about life after death. The inscriptions can testify about the Jewish character of the place. It is therefore very important to evaluate each inscription through the context and content, as well as the language and symbols that the inscription might include.

These criteria are very important, as the existence of separate Jewish burial areas before the catacombs seems on the whole fairly unlikely. Jews elsewhere, and Christians in Rome, apparently did not object to sharing burial areas with pagans in the first and second centuries, and Jews in many places adopted the forms of tombs and the methods of commemoration most generally favoured in their cities.

The Maltese Islands are rich in Late Roman and Byzantine burial sites, and it is no surprise that among them distinctively Jewish catacombs can be found. Maltese Catacombs represent the earliest archaeological evidence of a Christian and Jewish presence in Malta. In my research I was able to investigate the catacombs located on the outskirts of the old Roman capital of Melite (today's Mdina), which have been named after St. Paul and St. Agatha. Jewish Catacombs can be found within the St. Paul/St. Agatha Catacombs (the area between St. Paul and St. Agatha Catacombs) and in St. Agatha Catacombs, which were cleared up and investigated in 1894 by A. A. Caruana, the pioneer of archaeology in Malta. In Roman times they were most likely parts of one large burial complex.

They are a typical complex of interconnected, underground Roman cemeteries that were in use from the fourth century AD (Buhagiar 1986, 38). Their locations outside the city walls and their forms match the style of burial from other places in the Roman Empire dated from the same time. Such catacombs are probably a product of an indigenous development which was to a certain extent influenced by similar overseas practices such as a drastic shift in practices during the second century AD, when cremation was replaced by inhumation (Nock 1932, 323–4; Noy 1998, 74–75).

The Maltese catacombs are rather modest in size when compared with those of Rome, Sicily and North Africa. In the Maltese context one ought perhaps to speak in terms of miniature catacombs or simply hypogea. The distinction normally used here between graves and hypogea is that in the latter the tombs and burial chambers are grouped into short galleries or corridors. The smaller hypogea apparently originally had only one gallery. They are never labyrinthine and are mainly dug on one level. Nevertheless, they have rich tomb architecture and a surprising wealth of details.

Among the Maltese Catacombs there are eight different types of tombs: window tomb, arcosolium, loculi, tomba a baldacchino, saddle-back canopied table grave, floor tomb, the burial – cubicles, bench tomb, and table tomb (Buhagiar 1986, 21). There are also other features found in the Catacombs such as: small niches cut into the side walls used to hold an oil lamp to light the whereabouts, mural

Figure 16.1. Agape/Omega Tables (the St. Paul Catacombs).

Figure 16.2. Menora at the Entrance (the St. Agatha Catacombs).

painting, sealing-slabs and other blocking arrangements e.g. monolithic stone doors, the typical for neo-Punic head rest and the very distinct feature of the Maltese Catacombs – the Agape Table (Triclinium) (Figure 16.1).

The Agape Table is a round table hewn out of the live rock about 60 cm above the ground level, about 75 cm in diameter at the upper part, flat and encircled with a rim about 3 cm high. On the front part, a small section of the rim is opened, which gives the impression from above that the table has the form of the last letter of the Greek alphabet Ω (omega). Hereafter the term *Omega Table* instead of *Agape Table* will be used as the term *Agape Table* is a misnomer, because these tables have nothing to do with the early Christian practice of Agape banquets that used to be held after Eucharistic gatherings. Usually the Omega Tables are situated at the entrance to an important gallery or in a hall which may have served for assemblies. This might suggest that they were used for the hosting of some form of commemorative meals during the annual festival of the dead when the rites of burials were renewed. One hypogeum may have more than one table. In some cases it looks like there was a desire to be buried close to the Omega Table. Such a burial would incline the living members of a family to come into the vicinity of their dead during the event for which the place was used.

All of the above discussed features of the Catacombs are present in seemingly Jewish part of the Catacombs except the Omega Tables. They rather occur in a context that is clearly Christian e.g. crosses or Latin inscriptions. This Maltese context becomes a distinct criterion in establishing the Jewish section of the Catacombs.

There are seven catacombs found in Rabat (Malta) that one can consider Jewish. Five of them are located in the St. Paul/St. Agatha Catacombs. In this area the catacombs are numbered 3 to 24, Catacombs 10, 12, 13, 14, 17a are apparently Jewish. This enumeration is rather arbitrary. Two other apparently Jewish catacombs belong to the

complex of St. Agatha Catacombs. Section 1 is a big Jewish section, and section 2 a small Jewish one (Camilleri 2001, 99–103). In other publications these two sections are called ST. AGATHA 17 and 18 (cf. Buhagiar 1986, 29).

The other criterion that proves the Jewish origin of the catacombs is the appearance of the *per excellence* Jewish symbol: the menorah, the candlestick with seven branches. The menorah is one of the symbols that remained strictly Jewish although many Jewish symbols were adopted by the early Christians. Therefore there is sometimes a certain level of difficulty to decide whether a certain symbol, in a rock-cut tomb of the First Centuries AD, is Jewish or Christian (Zammit 1923, 20) (Figure 16.2). In all of these above named seven catacombs, the menorah appears in different places. Mainly it is scratched or deeply engraved above or on the side of the entrance to different hypogeum. It is as if the owners of the catacombs would like to emphasise for the newcomers that this is a Jewish part. The menorah is used in this manner everywhere except in the Catacomb 17a. But, this catacomb possibly was fused with the Jewish Catacomb 14 by an opening which seems to date to the period when the hypogeum was still in use. The menorah also can be found on the side of baldacchino graves (Catacomb 13, 14) and at the head rest (Catacomb 13). The menorahs are of different shapes and sizes. The most original menorahs accompany the Greek inscription from catacomb 17a and Section 1 from the St. Agatha catacombs. In both cases the menorah is well cast under the Greek inscription τόπος Διονυσίας ἡ κέ Εἰρήας—'Tomb of Dionisia call also Irene' (Ferrua 1949). In the first catacomb the menorah has a five-legged base and in the second case it has a four-legged base, which is a rather original way of representing the three-legged based menorah (Figure 16.3).

Figure 16.3. Four legged base Menorah with inscription.

Figure 16.4. Palm leaf entrance.

Figure 16.5a. The benches.

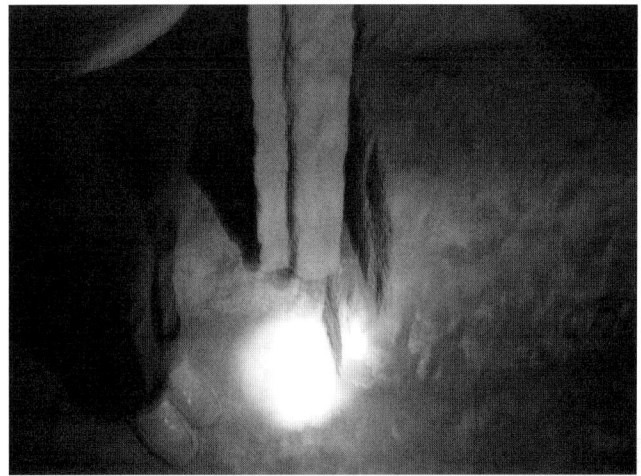

Figure 16.5b. Pivot stone.

The use of Greek is also very common in the Jewish Mediterranean Diaspora. This was proved by extensive comparative studies done on two Jewish catacombs in Rome: Monteverde and Vigna Randanini (Noy 1993). The minimal use of Hebrew/Aramaic could be a survival of Palestinian practices or a late innovation. Sometimes, mixing Greek, Latin and Hebrew could represent a stage in a change from one language to the other, or it could be a consequence of wishing to use expressions for which only one language was regarded as appropriate. One needs to keep in mind that the linguistics mainly can tell us how users wished to present their inscriptions to others. Would they like to be understood by others or not?

The assimilation of the Maltese Jews in the neo-Punic and Christian society is also visible through other symbols such as the boat (e.g. Catacomb 14) and the palm leaf (Lewis 1977, 156). The latter is especially present in

Catacomb 13 and Section 1. It is worthy to notice that after the menorah, which by far is the most distinctive Jewish Symbol, the other very distinct symbols would be the *lulab* or palm leaf (Figure 16.4). This would correspond to the coins from the Romans' time when the palm tree or palm leaf symbol was used with reference to Judea and Israel (Fine 2005, 140–5).

The Jewish identity of particular catacombs is also testified by the lack of the typical features of Maltese Catacombs – the Omega Tables, round stone tables surrounded by typical Roman-style couches for reclining when dining. Nevertheless a Jewish cult of the dead could be proved by the existence of some stone benches within the Jewish hypogea that would permit a visitor a longer stay in the presence of his ancestors. For instance, in Catacomb 10 inside the cubicle the door recess is flanked on either side by a rock-bench, about 43 cm high (Figure

16.5a). These benches are not left accidentally, as one of them is carved in such a way that the larger stone pivot-door which is preserved *in situ* can be freely opened (cf. Zammit 1923, 20) (Figure 16.5b).

The grave for the Jews was an impure place, where one would not like to spend much time. The similarity of the style of the graves would suggest that the Jews were aware of the forms of their neighbours' burial sites. The Omega Tables were associated with some form of meal in the presence of dead ancestors. In Judaism, it would not be permitted to have a meal in the vicinity of dead people or to accommodate Omega Tables. To the puzzle with the benches one can add the fact that the Jews would not recite any prayers while seated unless these were connected with a meal. Could this kind of form be seen as an expression of spiritual creativity in an attempt to assimilate certain practises associated with their neighbours? This question should remain open for further research at this stage.

Conclusion

In none of the above seven Maltese catacombs are the graves orientated/directed towards Jerusalem; this goes against the typical Jewish custom in Antiquity. However, while these graves may not look Jewish, they most certainly are. The Jewish identity of the catacombs found in Rabat (Malta) is evidenced strongly. It is interesting to observe how these early Jews tried to remain faithful to their religious identity while undergoing the process of assimilation with local customs and habits related to the preservation of the dead ancestors' memory. But, this process is very complex and demands extensive investigation.

The Jews had no objection to constructing their catacombs in the same manner and with the use of the same forms of tombs as the neo-Punics and Christians were doing; they placed their catacombs in areas surrounded by those of the non-Jews; but, they did not imitate their non-Jewish neighbours completely, as they distinguished their tombs' entrances by putting menorah signs in visible places and avoiding the use of Omega Tables. However, in all other ways they constructed their catacombs as the others had done, sometimes re-using the shafts and tombs which had been constructed by the Punics before them. Like other religious groups, the Jews used Greek in denoting the names of those buried in the tombs. Likewise, the symbols of the boat and the palm leaf are found on the walls of the Jewish tombs. While the Jews rejected the use of Omega Tables, the appearance of benches possibly marks an evolution towards treating the cult of the dead in a way that would conform to their religious beliefs. This may stand as an example of a shift that may occur over time in the way the Jews treated their dead ancestors.

What today might be a cult for the dead tomorrow might become a cult of the dead.

Would this interest in the dead be connected with potential benefits for the living to which Jews and others were exposed? The extent to which we are able to see this already on the basis of archaeological evidence remains to be answered. The topic being researched is very delicate and complex, though extremely interesting. There are also other places connected with the Jewish presence in Malta, like the inscription from a Jewish necropolis at Mtarfa outside of Rabat (also known as Kibur il-Lhud or the Jewish Grottoes) or the apparently Jewish hypogeum at Tac-Caghqi Secondary School (where the reference to libation rite was found) needs to be once again investigated to learn more about Jewish Diaspora practices and beliefs about death in Antiquity. An in-depth study of these practices could contribute very fruitfully to the study of the Cult in the Maltese context.

Acknowledgments

The earlier parts of this paper have previously been presented at the Roman Discussion Forum Seminar series at the Institute of Archaeology, at Oxford University 2006 and the Institute for Advanced Studies, Hebrew University, 2006, the Interdisciplinary Conference, Cult in Context, Cambridge University, 2006. On all of these occasions and in the process of writing, I have benefited greatly from the questions and comments of others. Especially I would like to express my gratitude for their contribution to: Prof. Colin Renfrew, Prof. Martin Goodman, Prof. Guy Stroumsa, Dr James Aitken, Dr Annalisa Marzano, Jeannine Pitas. I would be remiss if I were not to thank Maltese people: Dr. Nicole Lungaro-Mifsud, fr. Victor J. Camillieri, MSSP and people working for *Heritage of Malta*: Suzannah Depasquale and Charles Borg who made my research possible in the section of Jewish Catacombs in Malta. Needless to say, any errors of fact or interpretation that remain are entirely my own.

References

Albertz, R., 2001. *Die Exilszeit: 6. Jahrhundert v. Chr.* Stuttgart, W. Kohlhammer.

Albright, W. F. 1942. *Archaeology and the religion of Israel: the Ayer lectures of the Colgate Rochester Divinity School.* Baltimore, The Johns Hopkins Press.

Albright, W. F. 1957a. *From the stone age to Christianity: monotheism and the historical process,* 2nd edition, Garden City, N.Y., Doubleday, 1957.

Albright, W. F. 1957b. The High Place in Ancient Palestine. In: Valume du Congrès Strabourg, 1956. *Vetus Testamentum, Supplements* 4. 242–58.

André, L. 1985. *Le Culte des morts chez les Hébreux.* Paris.

Bickerman, E. 1951. Les Maccabées de Malalas. *Byzantion* 21.

Bickerman, E. 1958. The Altars of Gentiles: A Note on the Jewish 'ius Sacrum'. In *Revue Internationale des droits de l'antiquité* 5.

Bickerman, E. 1988. *The Jews in the Greek Age*. Cambridge, Cambridge University Press.

Brown, P. 1989. Redefining death. A halakhic perspective, In *L'Eylah. A Journal of Judaism Today*. London, vol. 28, 13–17.

Buhagiar, M. 1984. *The Maltese catacombs: characteristics and general considerations*, Malta, Historical Society.

Buhagiar, M. 1986. *Late Roman and Byzantine catacombs and related burial places in the Maltese Islands*, Oxford, B.A.R.

Camilleri, V. J. 2001. *Saint Agatha: An Archaeological Study of the Ancient Monuments at St Agatha's Building Complex: Crypt, Catacombs, Church and Museum*. Malta, MSSP.

Coulanges, F. de. 1877. *The Ancient City: A Study of the Religion, Laws and Institutions of Grece and Rome*. Boston, Lee and Shepard/New York, Dillingham.

Durkheim, E. 1915. *The Elementary Forms of the Religious Life: A Study in religious Sociology*. Trans. J. Swain. London, Allen and Unwin.

Ferrua, A. 1949. Antichita cristiane: le catacombe di Malta. In *La Civiltà Cattolica* N.2381, 505–15, Roma.

Fine, S. 2005. *Art and Judaism in the Greco-Roman World. Toward a New Jewish Archaeology*. Cambridge, Cambridge University Press.

Frazer, Sir J. 1919. *Folk-Lore in the Old Testament: Studies in Comparative Religion, Legend and Law*. London, Macmillan.

Gittlen, B. M. (ed.) 2002. *Sacred Times, sacred places. Archaeology and the religion of Israel*. Indiana, Winona Lake.

Goodenough, E. 1953–1968. *Jewish Symbols in the Greco-Roman Period*. N.Y., Pantheon Books.

Goodman, M. (ed.) 1998. *Jews in a Graeco-Roman World*. Oxford, Clarendon Press.

van Henten J. W. and P. W. van der Horst (eds). 1994. *Studies in Early Jewish Epigraphy*, Leiden, Brill.

Humphreys, S. C. 1981. Introduction: Comparative Perspective on Death. In S. C. Humphreys and H. King (eds). *Mortality and Immortality: The Anthropology and Archaeology of Death*. London, Academic Press, 1–13.

Johnston, P. S. 2002. *Shades of Sheol: death and afterlife in the Old Testament*. Leicester, Apollos; Downers Grove, Ill., InterVarsity Press.

Kaufmann, Y. 1953. *The Biblical account of the conquest of Palestine*. Jerusalem, Magnes Press, Hebrew University.

Kaufmann, Y. 1972. *The religion of Israel: from its beginnings to the Babylonian exile*. Translated and abridged by M. Greenberg. New York, Schocken.

King H. and Humphreys, S. C. (eds), *Mortality and Immortality: The Anthropology and Archaeology of Death*. London, Academic Press.

Lewis, H. A. 1977. *Ancient Malta. A study of its antiquities*. Gerrards Cross, Smythe.

Lightstone, J. N. 1984. *The commerce of the sacred: Mediation of the Divine among Jews in the Graeco-Roman Diaspora*. Chicago.

Lightstone, J. N. 1985. The dead in Late Antique Judaism: Homologies of Society, Cult and Cosmos. In R. Lemieux and R. Richard (eds). *Survivre ... la religion et la mort*, Cahiers de Recherches en Sciences de la Religion vol. 6, 51–79.

McCane, B. R. 1991. Bones of Contention? Ossuaries and Reliquaries in Early Judaism and Christianity. In *Second Century* 8, 235–246.

Nock, A. D. 1932. Cremation and Burial in the Roman Empire, *Harvard Theological Review* 25., repr. In *Essays on Religion and the Ancient World* (2 vols. Oxford, 1972), 321–59

Noy, D. 1998. Where were the Jews of the Diaspora buried? In: M. Goodman, (ed.). *Jews in a Graeco-Roman World*. Oxford, Clarendon Press, 74–88.

Noy, D. 1993–5. *Jewish Inscriptions of Western Europe*, 2 vols. Cambridge, Cambridge University Press.

Pedersen, J. 1926. *Israel: Its Life and Culture*. London, Oxford University Press.

Pearce, J., M. Millett and M. Struck (eds). 2000. *Burial, Society and Context in the Roman World*. Oxford, Oxbow Books.

Rajak, T. 1994. Reading the Jewish catacombs of Rome. In J. W. van Henten and P. W. van der Horst (eds). *Studies in Early Jewish Epigraphy*. Leiden, Brill, 226–241.

Quell, G. 1925. *Die Auffassung des Todes in Israel*. Leipzing, Deichert.

Roth, C. 1928–31. The Jews of Malta. In *Transactions of the Jewish Historical Society of England* 12, 187–251.

Schmidt, B. B. 1994. *Israel's beneficent dead: ancestor cult and necromancy in ancient Israelite religion and tradition*. Tübingen: Mohr (Forschungen zum Alten Testament II).

Ucko, P. J. 1969. Ethnography and Archaeological Interpretation of Funerary Remains. In *World Archaeology* Vol. 1, No. 2, 262–80.

de Vaux, R. 1958–60. *Les institutions de l'Ancien Testament*, Paris, Éditions du Cerf.

de Vaux, R. 1964. *Les sacrifices de l'Ancien Testament*. Paris, Gabalda.

Wright, G. E. 1946. *The challenge of Israel's faith*. London, SCM Press.

Wright, G. E. 1950. *The Old Testament against its environment*. London, SCM Press.

Wright, G. E. 1960. *Biblical Archaeology*. Philadelphia, Westminster Press.

Zammit, T. 1923. *St. Paul's catacombs and other rock-cut tombs in Malta*. La Valetta.

Computer Software and electronic sources:

Bible Works 5.0.020w 2001 *New Revised Standard Version. UBS4-NA27 Greek New Testament.*

Noy D. *The Jewish Catacombs of Rome: A Study of the Differences between the Monteverde and Vigna Randanini Catacombs*, http://www.lamp.ac.uk/noy/cataco~1.htm

ARCHITECTURAL ORDER AND THE ORDERING OF IMAGERY IN MALTA AND IRELAND: A COMPARATIVE PERSPECTIVE

Christopher Tilley

The purpose of this paper is to compare and contrast the visual imagery of Maltese and Irish temples in relation to the phenomenological experience of architectural form. The intention is to discuss the imagery as experienced in the flesh and interpret its significance in terms of its effects in relation to the sensory apparatus of an observer. The principal concern is not so much what these images might mean, but their agency, the work that they perform in relation to different architectural spaces. Specifically I intend to discuss the temples at Tarxien on Malta and Newgrange in Ireland. Tarxien is by far the most elaborately decorated of all the documented Maltese temples and one of the most architecturally complex. Newgrange has long been famous for its megalithic 'art' and the sophistication of its architecture. In brief, my argument will be that while very similar general principles are at work in both cases structuring the general relationship of imagery to architecture such as the importance of thresholds and doorways, nevertheless Tarxien and Newgrange may be understood as structural inversions of each other. Newgrange is, as it were, Tarxien stood on its head, or vice versa. Some of the major differences discussed are summarized in Table 17.1. In the conclusions an attempt is made to explain this difference in terms of very different forms of cult practices.

Imagery and architectural form

In the Tarxien temple complex decorated stones are found exclusively within the buildings. These are concentrated in the form of screens running across the front apses of the third or western temple and at the back of the forecourt. None are known from the first or eastern temple and only three stones are documented at the inner entrance to the second area of the middle temple. The only other carvings are found on two orthostats in room 13 adjoining both the western and the middle temples (see Figure 17.1). It is generally agreed that the eastern temple at Tarxien is earliest and the western temple latest and that at some point in the overall architectural development of the temple complex that the entrance to the western temple was the main or primary entrance way with others being blocked or closed down (Evans 1971; Trump 2000). The imagery is thus predominantly located in the most public and visible part of the temple space and most of it was clearly intended to be seen to dramatic effect.

By contrast, at Newgrange (see Figures 17.9 and 17.11) we find a completely different spatial organization of the imagery which also occurs at the nearby Dowth and Knowth temples (see Eogan 1986; O'Kelly and O'Kelly 1983). Decorated stones occur along the external kerbs of the mounds, above the Newgrange roofbox, throughout the passage at Newgrange and in the deepest and most inaccessible parts of the cruciform shaped terminal chamber.

Thresholds and their significance

The kerbs at Newgrange, Dowth and Knowth are continuous. This means that to enter into the temples one must clamber up and over the threshold stones to enter the passages, physically cross decorated stones. At Newgrange the entrance stone over which one must cross is profusely decorated with spirals. At Tarxien exactly the same thing happens but within the internal spaces of the temples. Entering into the terminal chamber of the third or western temple requires movement over the largest of the carved blocks in the Maltese islands decorated with two rows of elaborate C spirals. Similarly in the middle temple, entering into the middle transept requires movement over another stone with two spirals and passing between two further blocks flanking the passage each decorated with four spirals. This suggests that while at Newgrange entering into the temple itself from the outside was the most

TARXIEN	NEWGRANGE
Thresholds important	Thresholds important
Spirals dominant quantitatively & as perceived	Spirals dominant only as perceived
Graphic and iconic motifs	Graphic motifs only
Art On public display	Much hidden art
Art inside temple	Art inside & outside temple
Art ordered & framed	Art improvised, disordered & irregular
Vision dominant sense	Touch and sound dominant
Graphic and iconic motifs duplicated in ceramics	Absent or different on ceramics
Separation of the dead from temple space	Dead inside temple
Inhumation burial in Hypogeum	Destructive cremation burial
Dead buried below ground in rock cut tomb resembling temples above ground	Dead placed in temple above ground resembling underground cave
Human imagery (figurines)	Absent
Architectural space a shell	Architectural space a solid
Collective experience	Individual experience
Animal sacrifice in temple space	Absent
Imagery for the living that needs to be seen	Imagery for the dead that does not need to be seen
Releasing spiritual forces for benefit of living	Trapping and containing the souls of the dead
Subterfuge inside temple space	Subterfuge outside temple space
CULT FOR THE LIVING	CULT FOR THE DEAD

Table 17.1. Some similarities and contrasts between the art and architecture of Tarxien and Newgrange.

significant event, at Tarxien it was movement from one internal space to another *inside* the temple.

Aesthetics and organization of imagery

The carved blocks in the Tarxien temple have almost exclusively spiral and sweeping curvilinear designs. In many design fields the spiral is the basic component arranged in various ways: double opposed spirals arranged to resemble eyes, combinations of 'C' or returning 'S' shaped single spirals, volutes or semi-spirals all of which may be embellished with horns and tails (Ridley 1976, 21–2) There is an emphasis on the repetition, symmetry and lateral translation of the same designs within specific horizontal fields defined by carved relief borders. The dexterity and skill with which these motifs were executed and their aesthetic power all suggest the superimposition of a scheme or template in the mind on the blank medium of the soft globigerina limestone. Such patterns are 'good to think' with and the main effect is the emphasis on repetitions, rhythms, flows, continuity and order in terms of the arrangements of the elements. This, in Gell's (1998) terms is an enchanted technology. The carving of the designs is an act of technical virtuosity, one marvels at how it could be achieved, and the motifs act as mind traps. One

can become quite fascinated by the manner in which the carved lines flow across the stones and the directionality of this flow, to the right or to the left, from the end of one spiral into the beginning of another. The spirals all possess a double directionality according to whether you follow the lines from the inside to the outside or vice versa. Within the relief borders individual motifs typically flow into one another in single carved blocks in horizontal and vertical fields which have no definite beginning or end suggesting a sense of the infinite (Figures 17.2 and 17.3). The abstract character of the motifs encourage and permit multiple understandings. The flow of waves with their crests and troughs, tree like-forms, curving horn cores of rams or goats, the tails of fish, honeycombs and the presence of eyes have all been suggested in relation to the carvings at Tarxien and the contemporary paintings on the ceilings of the Hypogeum (Evans 1959; 1971; Ridley 1976; Grima 2001; Tilley 2004). Some iconic carvings also exist at Tarxien. Translating different types of motifs in terms of specific meanings or cultural connotations such as the movement of the waves or the shoots and branching growth of trees, or cosmological domains of land and sea is not strictly necessary to appreciate their significance since their power resides precisely in their indeterminate suggestivity or the multiple meanings that may be accrued. From a

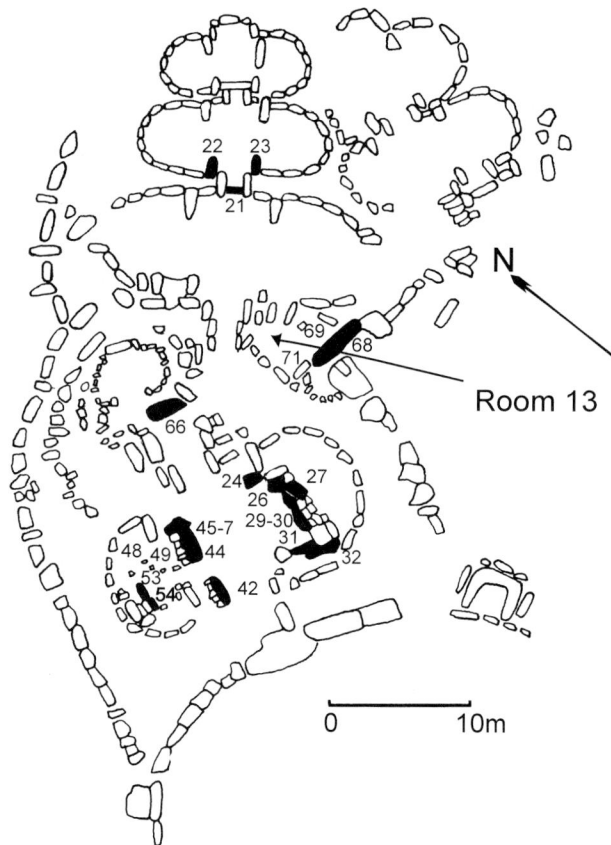

Figure 17.1. Plan of the Tarxien temples showing the positions of the decorated stones. After Ridley 1976.

phenomenological point of view what is really significant about these graphic designs is not so much what they might mean but their bodily effects in relation to an observer, what they do, how they ensnare and trap the eye, and visually or spatially contain within themselves the temporal and relational bodily movements required for their execution. In origin these carvings are all bodily performances. The indexical, rather than iconic, significance of these motifs is the manner in which time, and movement of the human body is incorporated into the material medium of the stone as a series of spatial flows of lines across the surface.

Two quite different visual effects of the Tarxien carvings, in relation to an observer, may be distinguished. The first occurs on panels with multiple and running conjoined motifs, which are by far the most common. In these cases the eye is encouraged to trace out the flow of the lines horizontally, or vertically, on the stone, or to try and do both at once. There is no 'correct' way to look at these motifs (see Figures 17.2 and 17.3). They are simultaneously one and many and the eye of an observer may 'enter into' the design field at any point, to the right, to the left or in the middle. The continuous flows of lines and their orderly but multiple directionalites produces a kind of cognitive dissonance insofar as that there is no obvious starting point as to where, or how, to look. The design field flows and moves but is simultaneously frozen and arrested. One is cognitively challenged to work out where the design is going and where it ends.

Figure 17.2. Running spirals and embellished volute decorations in the first apse to the left of the western or third temple at Tarxien. Source: Evans 1971.

Figure 17.3. Spiral compositions on replica of block 42 at Tarxien (for location see Figure 17.1). Source: Evans 1971.

Figure 17.4. Ocular spirals on threshold stone between the first and second rooms of the middle temple at Tarxien (Figure 17.1: No. 21). Source: Evans 1971.

The second visual effect occurs on stones where individual motifs are separated. At Tarxien these are almost exclusively the carved blocks with 'oculus spirals' (Figures 17.4 and 17.5). Such motifs do confront an observer much more in the manner of piercing eyes. One may trace the flow of the lines making up these spirals from the inside to the outside or vice versa. But there is a definite beginning or end and one may be drawn back and forth between the two. These motifs, because of their spatial separation and perfect symmetry 'look' at an observer in a manner in which the running spirals and volutes do not. The lines draw one's eye into and out of the individual motifs rather than between one motif and the next that has a very different cognitive effect, and at Tarxien this is strikingly varied in a quite deliberate fashion.

The ocular spirals all occur on three blocks in the middle temple. They mark the threshold and transition point between the first or outer, and second inner space of this three apse temple, unique in Malta (see Figure 17.1). One block, with two 'eyes' blocks the entrance to the inner temple space and one must walk up and over it. The lines on this stone (Figure 17.4) spiral inwards in an anti-clockwise movement to the right, and in a clockwise movement to the left. Having passed through the entrance corridor, one is confronted by a screen on either side, each decorated with four ocular horned spirals, a central disc and V wedges with a background of drilled holes (Figure 17.5). The spirals are significantly larger than found anywhere else at Tarxien. The remarkable thing about these screens is that the arrangement of the spirals suggests a perfect and identical symmetry in which one might expect the screen to the left to be a mirror image of that to the right. However, on closer inspection, the spirals on the screen to the left are arranged in a vertical plane and those on the screen to the right in a horizontal plane and the directionality of the lines making up the spirals is very different. On the left screen from the outside to the inside three spirals wind clockwise, one anti-clockwise. On the panel to the right clockwise and anti-clockwise spirals are paired on a horizontal plane. If we imagine the left hand screen placed upside down then we would get the same arrangement of paired clockwise and anticlockwise spirals

as on the right screen, a much more symmetrical arrangement, with clockwise and anti-clockwise spirals 'facing' each other across the space in between the two screens and the pairing of clockwise and anticlockwise spirals on each duplicating the arrangement of the spirals on the stone blocking access to the chamber. The important point here is that such an 'obvious' arrangement of the flow of these spirals was deliberately not intended. The visual experience of the blocking stone with a clockwise spiral to the left and an anticlockwise spiral to the right is only duplicated on the lower part of the right hand screen. It is reversed on the top of the same screen and occurs nowhere on the left screen.

Ridley suggests 'that the 'V' wedges on these blocks probably represent the nose and brow of the goddess...some effort seems to have been made to arrange the four eyes in a way that whichever way one approached, vertically, horizontally or even sideways, the eyes of the goddess would confront one' (Ridley 1976, 27). Irrespective of whether these spirals mean or signify eyes, the overall effect of the two screens is to create cognitive dissonance. The bodily experience of the two screens is to either see that to the left or the right. They cannot be seen at once. Similarity, but also difference, is recognized but to work out precisely what is happening requires an artificial paper analysis of the kind undertaken above, putting the blocks side by side and comparing and contrasting them, definitely not something that took place in the Maltese Neolithic. So what I am suggesting is the peculiar power and effect of these screens is to create a cognitive indecipherability or a sense of not being able to make sense of what one experiences, quite appropriate to their positioning in a significant transitional space between the outer and inner part of the temple.

The distinction drawn above between the bodily and cognitive effects of graphic designs that run and flow into each other and the panels with individual spirals is found also in relation to the iconic representations at Tarxien. These occur in the front left and right apses of the western or third temple and in room 13 (see Figure 17.1). In the left apse there are two carved blocks depicting processions of animals. One of these is opposite the entrance to this apse

Left

Right

clockwise   clockwise   anti-clockwise   anti-clockwise

anti-clockwise   clockwise   clockwise   anti-clockwise

clockwise   anti-clockwise   anti-clockwise   clockwise

anti-clockwise   clockwise   clockwise   anti-clockwise

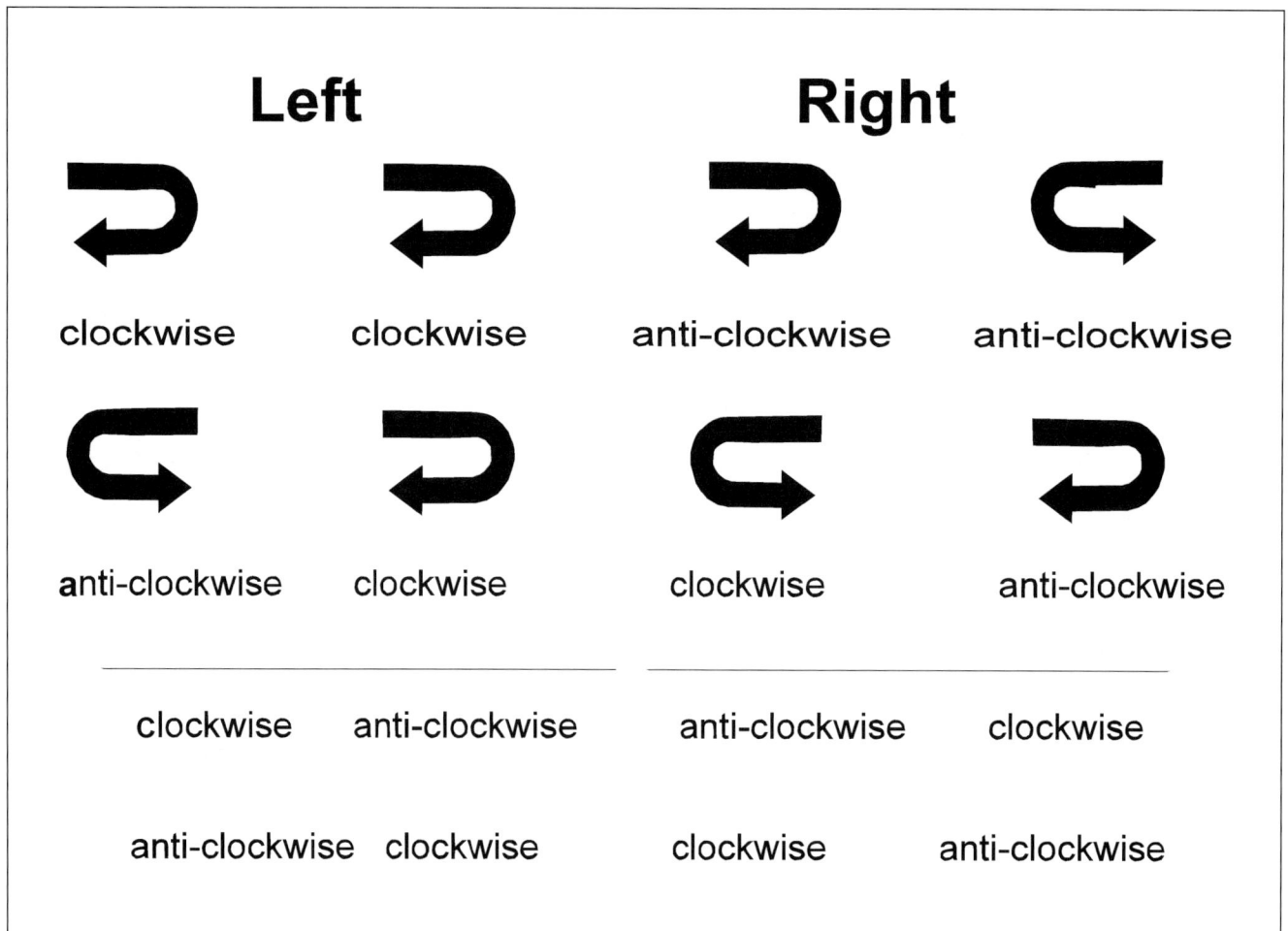

Figure 17.5. The decorated screens to the left and the right of the entrance passageway into the second room of the middle temple at Tarxien (See Figure 17.1: Nos 22 and 23). The directionality of the spirals is shown and below how these would appear if the left hand screen were placed upside down. Source: Evans 1971.

facing towards the central courtyard (Evans 1971, 119). It formed the threshold slab of an elaborate altar arrangement at the back of the apse. In the remaining part there is a procession, from left to right, of four sheep or goats, a pig and a ram with curling horns. These are seen in profile, facing to the right. Opposite and facing this slab is another frieze of animals this time arranged in two rows, and facing to the left, a procession of twenty two sheep or goats identical to those on the frieze opposite with the ram. The striking point about the ram is the manner in which the head is disengaged and turned to face towards and engage with the eyes of an observer, a striking iconographic detail and making it different from all the other animals (Figure 17.6). In the right hand apse at the front end there is a striking and huge sculpture of a large 'mother goddess'. Only the bottom part survives and it must originally have

been up to 2 m high. The position of the feet indicate that the face would be turned to make eye contact with the gaze of an observer (Figure 17.7). Looking into the eyes of this statue or at the face of the ram establishes a completely different connection between the observer and the observed. The latter looks back in a relation of intimacy totally different from seeing a person or an animal in profile which inevitably distances the relationship between observer and that observed. The other iconic representations are hidden away in room 13. These are huge compared with the small stone friezes in the front apse of the temple. Two humped-backed bulls over 3 m long face each other. Beneath one is another smaller animal described in the literature as being a sow with piglets (Figure 17.8). These are all seen in profile, like all the other animals apart from the ram.

The distinction drawn above between iconic repre-

Figure 17.6. The end of the decorated frieze in the front left apse of the western or third temple at Tarxien with ram with face turned towards an observer and pig and goat behind seen in profile.

Figure 17.7. The remaining part of the huge 'mother goddess' figure in the first right apse of the western or third temple at Tarxien. Photo: C. Tilley.

Figure 17.8 (left). Depictions of bulls and sow? with piglets in room 13 at Tarxien (Location: Figure 17.1: Nos 68–70). Source: Evans 1971.

sentations seen in profile, or those that face an observer, is similar to the relationship established between an observer and the 'ocular' spirals and the running graphic motifs on the friezes. In relation to the former the observer is visually drawn into the design, whereas in relation to the latter he or she remains 'outside' it. These are two quite different and striking experiential effects and spatially the relationship between these graphic and iconic designs alters. In the front apse and presumably the most public part of the temple an observer directly engages with some of the iconic designs but is visually perplexed by the running graphic designs on the screens running around the courtyard. Entry into the middle courtyard of the third temple is related to engaging with the ocular spirals while the animals in room 13 are disengaged from an observer. The visual effects of the graphic and iconic representations become effectively reversed as one moves towards the more inaccessible, hidden, back and dark areas of the temple complex.

The experience of the imagery at Newgrange is altogether different. A kerb of 97 slabs surrounds the cairn and of these 31 are decorated. They are concentrated in the southern part of the cairn to the left and right of the passage entrance with a few in the north-west and one in the north-east (Figure 17.9). We know that the imagery on some of the most elaborately decorated kerbstones was completely hidden (Figure 17.10). Of the kerbstones with visible decoration only three stand out, K1 the elaborately decorated entrance stone (Figure 17.11), K52 opposite it, (Figure 17.12) and K67 (Figure 17.13). These are all boldly carved in 'plastic' style to use O'Sullivan's (1986) term and all have prominent spirals. Standing any distance away from the Newgrange kerb it appears that these are the only decorated stones. The motifs on the other kerbstones are small, discrete, irregularly placed, and only cover a small surface area of the stones. Decorations on the two

kerbstones on either side of the entrance stone, K1, have been virtually obliterated by subsequent pick dressing. The reason for this must have been to better highlight and frame the motifs on the entrance stone itself and emphasize its significance. These three stones are in completely different areas of the cairn and are not intervisible. The passage to the chamber has a blocking stone that, when upright and in position, would fit perfectly. An outsider's impression might well be that Newgrange had three passages and chambers marked by these kerbstones, rather than one. The overwhelming effect of the continuous and unbroken kerb is to establish a fundamental distinction between the inside and the outside. It was on the outside of the tomb where the imagery was meant to be seen and was on public display, something much more dramatically

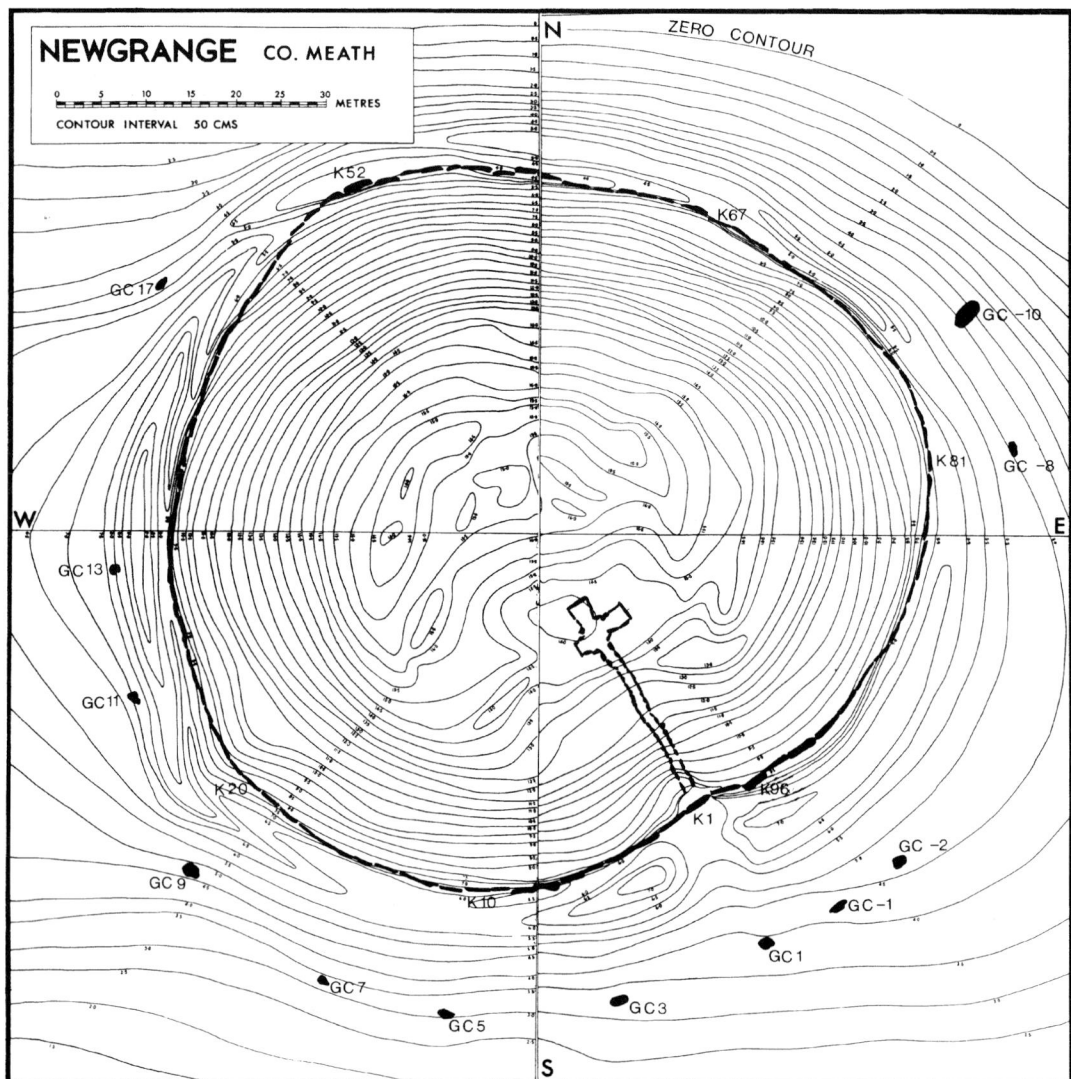

Figure 17.9. Plan of the Newgrange cairn showing kerbstones and the three kerbstones K1, K52 and K67, with bold 'plastic' decoration. Source: M. O'Kelly 1982.

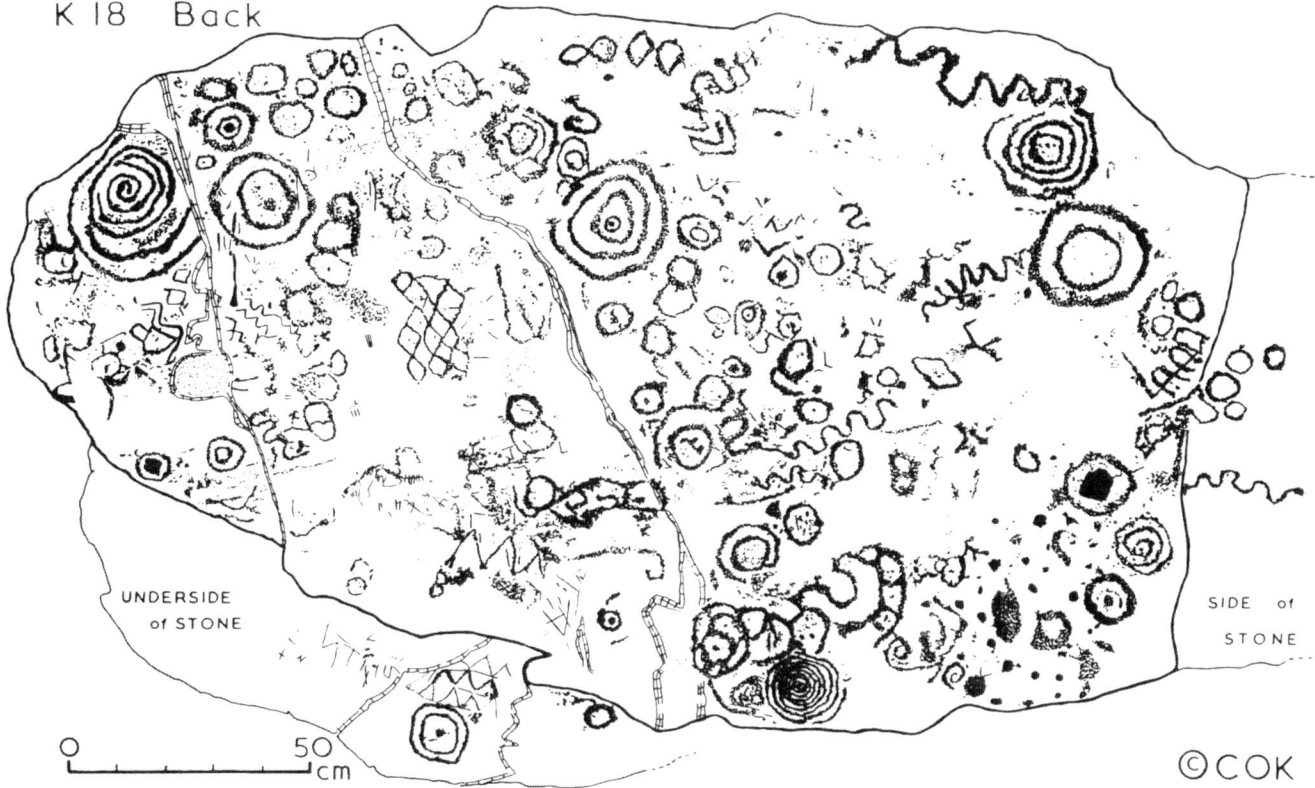

Figure 17.10. Hidden decoration on the back of Kerbstone 18 at Newgrange. Source: C. O'Kelly 1982.

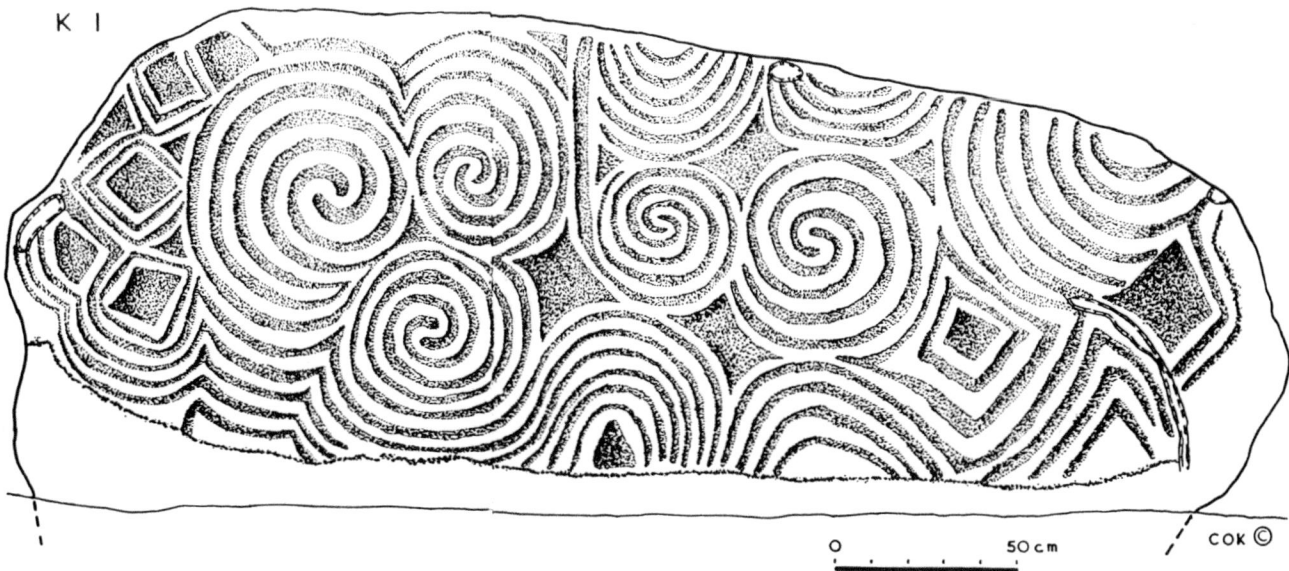

Figure 17.11. Newgrange: the elaborately decorated entrance stone. Source: C. O'Kelly 1982.

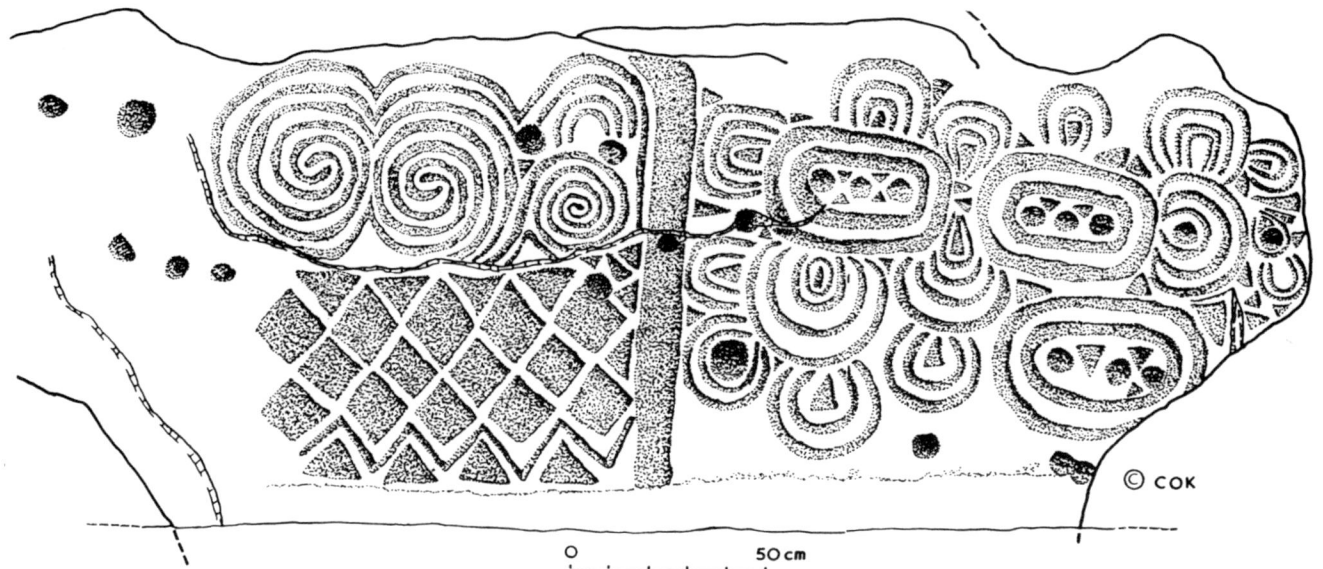

Figure 17.12. Newgrange: Kerbstone K52 situated opposite K1 on the circunference of the cairn. Source: C. O'Kelly 1982.

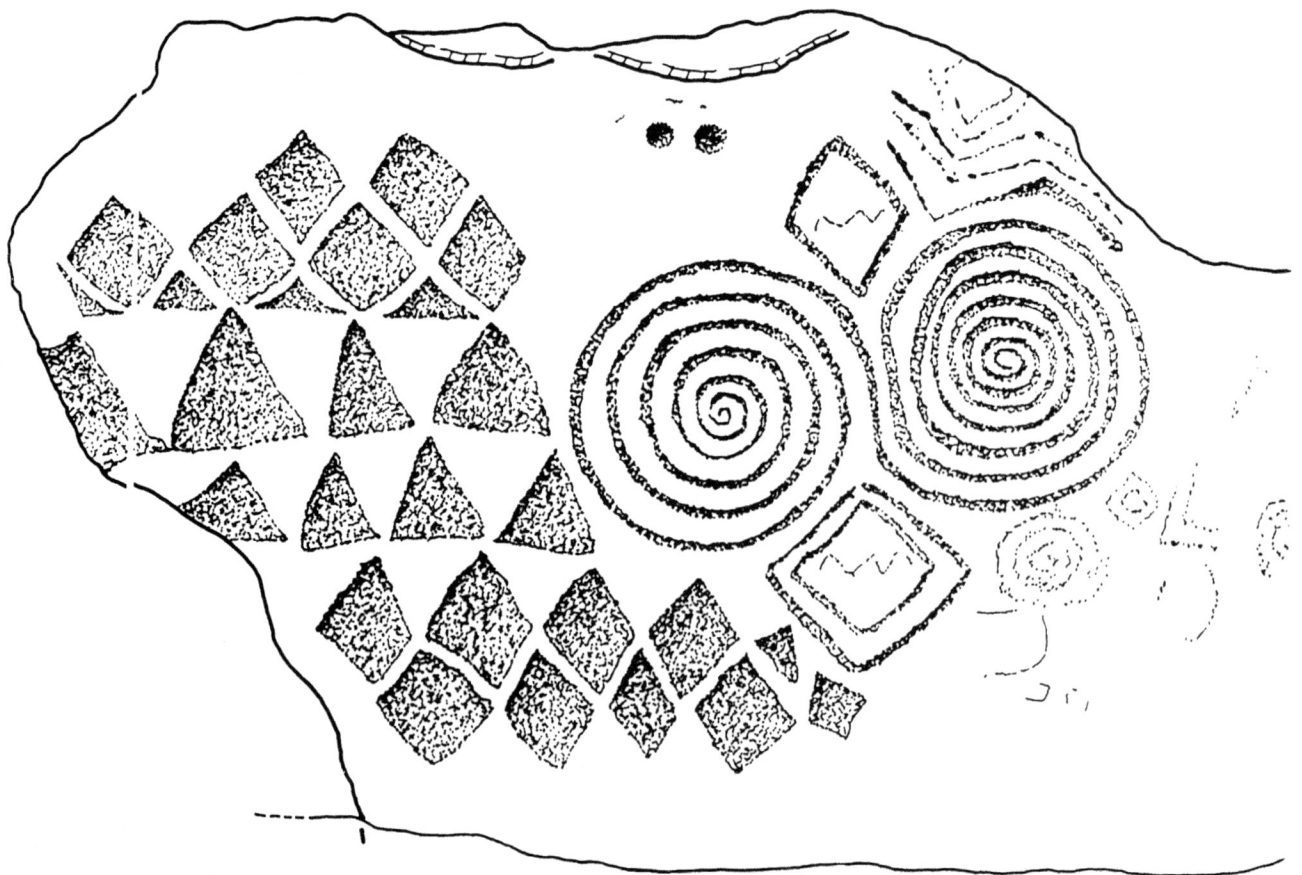

Figure 17.13. Newgrange: Kerbstone K67. Source: C. O'Kelly 1982.

evident at the neighbouring Knowth temple with large numbers of decorated kerbstones with bold and highly visual designs (Eogan 1986).

The motifs on the three highly visual stones in the Newgrange kerb constitute a very different style of imagery than that found at Tarxien. Firstly these are stones used as found, of markedly different shape and form. There are no relief borders to the motifs and the only border is effectively that of the stone itself. Prexisting hollows on the stones are incorporated into the design on K52 and the stone was deliberately chosen for this purpose. The adjacent stone, K51 has a much finer and smoother surface. In general the motifs make use and are integrated in relation to the preexisting surface features of the stone. This does not suggest some preexisting design template superimposed on the stone surface but that carving the stone surface drew out and incorporated organically that which was already there.

The visual enchantment of the Maltese decorated stones derives principally from their perfection and absolutely repetitive symmetries. The iconic images are supremely realist capturing the essences of animals and the human form. By comparison the graphic images of Newgrange are irregularly distributed over the stones because the medium, the stone itself, gives partial form to the motifs themselves and this, compared with Maltese limestone is an excessively hard and difficult medium to work with. The visual enchantment of the Newgrange images derives from the technological dexterity required to work this stone as much as the motif forms themselves. On K67 we see occular S or returning spirals which draw the eye inside them in a manner similar to the Maltese examples. On K1 and K52 the spirals interlock in a complex manner inviting one to trace and follow the maze of lines, in a similar manner to the decorated screen stones around the first court of the western temple at Tarxien. However the overall visual effect is disjointed by the presence of quite different graphic design elements on the same stone. It is most coherent on K1, the entrance stone. On K52 the spirals all occur above a crack forming a border between them and the lozenges below. It is interesting to note that there are very few visible spirals on the other decorated kerbstones. That on K97 adjacent to the entrance stone is virtually obliterated by pecking. Most of the spirals elsewhere on the kerb occur on the backs of the stones facing into the cairn, forever hidden.

Entering Newgrange requires climbing over the elaborately decorated entrance stone marking the threshold between the outer public space and the passage. Structurally this is equivalent to passing over the decorated stones in the middle temple at Tarxien. All the passage orthostats stones are picked dressed over all, or most of, their main faces making them appear uniform and undifferentiated in both a visual and a tactile sense as one moves down the passage. There is an absence of any other visually arresting

decoration except in a few cases. The only two orthostats with any visually striking or memorable designs are stones L19 and L22, which occur at or near the end of the passage on the left hand side (Figure 17.14). These both have pick dressing obliterating earlier motifs. For example the lower spirals on L19 are picked over, the upper spirals left to stand out on an undressed surface of the stone. The overall shape of L19 and the absence of any motifs at the top of the stone may suggest, as George Eogan (1998) has argued, that this stone is placed upside down and was brought from an earlier monument. As is the case for the kerb some stones with decorated surfaces in the passage are entirely hidden. Other stones possess a little decoration but this is either partially obscured through later surface picking, hidden beneath ground level, or only present on the partially exposed side rather than front and main faces of the stones. Some motifs are positioned towards the very top or bottom of the main faces of the stones. In the absence of detailed examination, with illumination, of the stones the impression of the passage is of orthostats picked all over but otherwise having only two decorated stones, a puritanical simplicity of form and design. Not only are motifs picked over to completely or partially obscure them but so also are surface hollows, depressions and previously picked grooves. 'Natural' or 'cultural' features marking or distinguishing individual stones are all treated in the same manner to create an overwhelming impression of uniformity.

From C. O'Kelly's excellent documentation of Newgrange the impression given is of a very elaborately decorated monument but this is false. Even in relation to the imagery that is not completely hidden, if her documentation was unavailable none of the decorations on the passage orthostats, apart from the panels of designs on the unpicked areas of L19 and L22 would be likely to be seen by a casual observer. None of these motifs are either highly visible as a result of both their position and/or the subsequent picking of the orthostat surfaces. To experience them at all requires very careful visual and tactile examination of the stone surface looking across and up or bending down. It also requires either being shown or knowing where to look. The final intention appears to have been to create a passage that was remarkably plain except for the presence of the surface picking enhancing every stone.

The visual impression of the chamber space continues the impression introduced in the passage of relatively little elaboration. There are only three stones, all decorated with spirals, which might be described as striking or dramatic. Only one of these is visible from the centre of the chamber space looking in any direction. To see the spirals in cell 1 would require looking into it, those in cell 2 are best seen looking out towards the passage (Shee Twohig 2000, 95). However, entering the right cell and looking upwards at

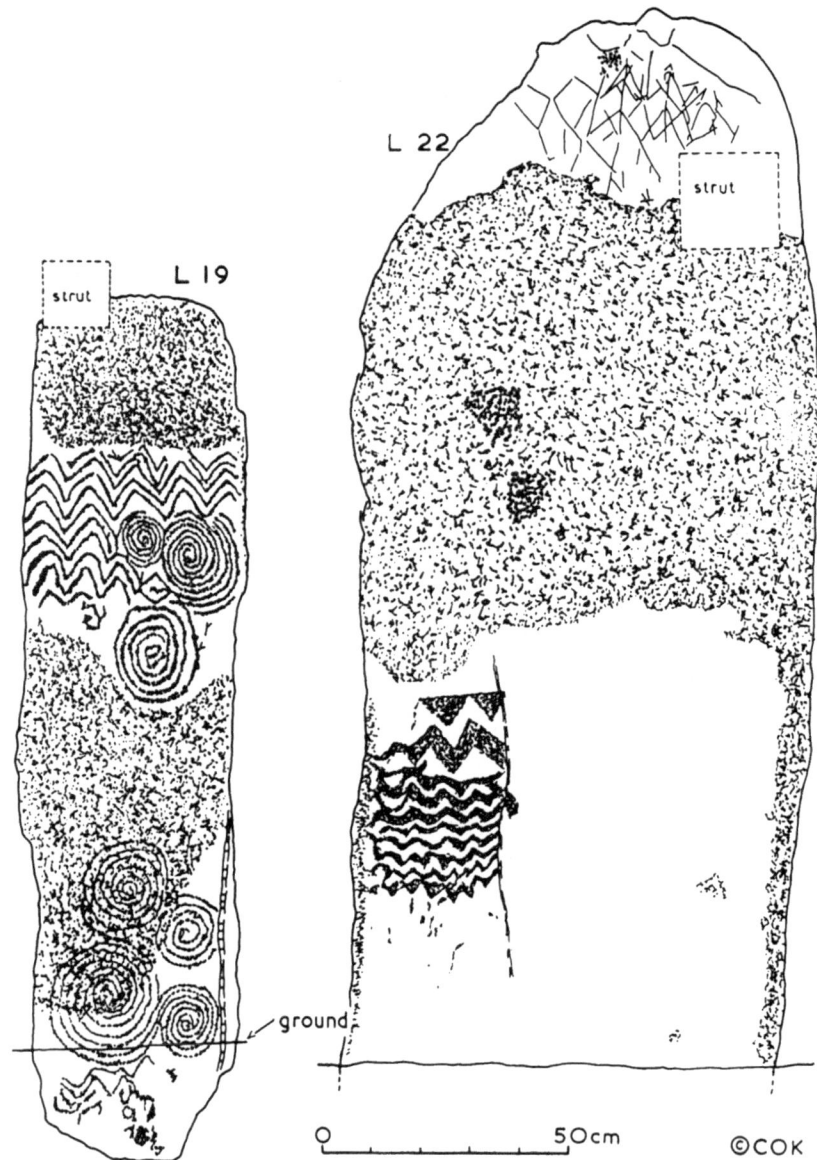

Figure 17.14. Decorated orthostats on the left (west) side of the passage at Newgrange. Source: C. O'Kelly 1982.

the underside of the capstone there is a revelation. The stone is covered with spirals and interlocking circular, lozenge and circular designs in baroque elaboration. The corbels on this cell immediately under the roofstone are similarly elaborately decorated. While these can be seen standing up the roofstone is best appreciated lying down and looking up. Even so some of the decoration is still not visible as it disappears under the roof corbels.

The effect of the light penetrating into the chamber on the mid winter solstice through the roof box is to dramatically illuminate a space that is normally very dark and various details of the motifs in the chamber and side cells become illuminated by the reflected light in a manner only possible through artificial illumination at any other

time. The beam from the roof box lasts for exactly 17 minutes (M. O'Kelly 1982, 124).

Besides the stones already mentioned certain other of the passage roofing stones and corbels in the chamber are decorated. Two corbels immediately behind the roof box have much decoration on their upper faces that was completely hidden during the Neolithic construction of the passage. Two other roof stones with hidden decoration were placed at the junction between the passage and chamber roofs, discovered during the excavation and restoration of the tomb (C. O'Kelly 1982, 99). The last roof slab over the opening from the passage to the chamber has picked lines of triangles visible from inside the chamber looking out. All this decoration, mostly hidden, emphasizes important transitional points from the inner to the outer part of the passage, and from the passage to the chamber.

In Newgrange the visually dominant visual images occur on the left passage orthostats L19 with three spirals, on the three stones in the left recess, each with one to three spirals, on orthostat C10 with its unique three-spiral motif and on the highly elaborate roof stone of the right or east cell. This again has a dominant central spiral motif together with circular motifs and ellipses. The emphasis on the spiral is the unique and memorable signature of this tomb. We can count the motifs inside Newgrange and find as C. O'Kelly (1973; 1982) and Shee Twohig (2000) do, that quantitatively lozenges and zig-zag motifs are the most common. However, the spirals are actually far more important and prominent in terms of the bodily experience of Newgrange. Newgrange might be described as a textbook example of the art of concealment employing the full range of possible techniques available:

- Completely hiding decorated stones during the building of the tomb either in the roof or in the floor making sure that these images could never be seen or experienced.
- Decorating stones in obscure areas where the images are easily likely to be missed- high up or low down or near to the corners and edges of stones.
- Placing parts of decorated stones over others so that the full extent of the image field remains invisible e.g. the roof slab in the right or left recess.
- Positioning images on the sides rather than the main faces of orthostats.
- Concealing images on the side faces rather than on the back stones of the cells.
- Picking over images so as to partially or completely obliterate them.
- Picking over and around hollows, depressions, grooves etc. on the stone in the same manner as images so as to create further ambiguity with regard to what is, or is not decorated and supposed to be there.

Using the relative lack and changing quality of natural light in the chamber and passage to enhance all these techniques and effects, the most striking visible images are in the deepest and darkest areas of the chamber which are never directly illuminated by the rays of the sun even on the winter solstice.

Subterfuge and visual deception appears to have been an important element in relation to the external kerb stones too and at Newgrange creating a false impression of the architectural form and nature of the monument appears to have primarily occurred in relation to the external kerb stones, as discussed above. At Tarxien this takes place within the temple interior with rooms hidden in between the walls such as room 13, which could also be secretly entered from the outside, and the provision of doorways

that could be blocked and the overall architecture of interconnecting temple spaces leading off to each other in unexpected directions. Again this points to the significance of the interior space of the Tarxien temples and the exterior space of the Irish passage graves.

Sensory experience

Both the entrance to the western temple at Tarxien and Newgrange face to the south-east in the direction of the midwinter sunrise. The construction of the Newgrange roofbox allows the sunlight to penetrate to the inner depths of the chamber. By contrast, the internal arrangements and alignments of the Tarxien temple complex are such that no sunlight could ever penetrate to the innermost areas of the temple complex. Direct light could be expected to penetrate from the main entrance to the back of the western temple which marks the limits of visibility from the entrance today and it is in this illuminated space where the majority of the visual imagery occurs. Elsewhere artificial illumination would be required. By contrast at Newgrange the provision of the passage roofbox allows the midwinter sun to penetrate right down to the innermost part of the temple lighting up a space and images that were normally hidden. So the innermost parts of Newgrange were seasonally illuminated whereas the internal areas of Tarxien were always dark. At Tarxien the light penetrating into the western temple would allow the images to be seen at any time of the year and those that would be most visible are in the front apses of the third temple. At Newgrange the images inside the temple that would be most easily seen would be those seasonally illuminated in the deepest recesses of the temple space. In both cases these are spirals.

Lewis-Williams and Pearce suggest that the overwhelming effect of being in the Irish temple interiors was one of sensory deprivation: 'if one stays still for long enough the silence and darkness envelope one; they seep deeper and deeper into one' (Lewis-Williams and Pearce 2005, 208). But such 'sensory deprivation' only relates to vision and the experience of the outside landscape. The reverse can be argued, rather than creating conditions for sensory deprivation, the experience of being inside the temple heightened sensory perception in relation to the burial and other rites that took place. Inside the temple a person was removed from everyday experience and transported into a world in which normal sensory faculties are altered. Touch and feel become essential and heightened because the spatial and visual orientation afforded by the outside world is lost. Temple air is still and silent but smell and sound are intensified within this confined space. The restricted character of the passage space inevitably brings one into contact with the stones on either side in a manner which does not occur in the Tarxien temples.

Lewis-Williams and Pearce however themselves make

the important point that the sound of the orthostats being picked, and the manner in which that sound would have been amplified within the tomb, would have been an important sensory dimension of its experience. Hammering a stone may have been a way of connecting with it, activating it, giving it potency, hence the presence of picking of some kind or another on virtually every orthostat within Newgrange. In this respect it is interesting to note O'Kelly's comment that the original shape of Newgrange, with its flat top, rounded sides and façade was that of a huge *drum* (M. O'Kelly 1982, 73). The presence of surface picking on virtually every orthostat in Newgrange and the obliteration of graphic motifs in the process is perhaps indicative of the increasing importance of tactile and auditory, as opposed to visual perception through time.

Mortuary practices

A very significant contrast between Tarxien and Newgrange concerns the relationship between the living and the dead. There is no indication whatsoever that the Maltese temples were places of burial unlike the Irish temples in which the remains of human cremations are deposited in the chambers. In Malta the ancestral dead did not rest in the Tarxien temples but in the underground chambers of the Hypogeum only 400 m away to the west. The inhumation of complete bodies appears to have been the preferred rite. Their remains were left in prepared beds of soil, subdivided by stone divisions and soaked red with the blood of imported ochre. The painted ceilings of the Hypogeum essentially replicate the running spiral and lunate forms of the Tarxien temple decoration. Zammit estimated that perhaps as many as 7,000 persons may have been buried there (Zammit 1930).

Pottery found in both the temples and the Hypogeum has the same curving arcs and spiral decoration as found on the carvings in the temples. A sacred thread is being drawn here between life and death. By contrast at Newgrange the bodies of the dead are consumed and destroyed by fire and their calcined bones, reduced to tiny fragments, are deposited on stone bowls in the chambers. Pottery is absent and we know that the decoration on so-called Carrowkeel ware that occurs sporadically elsewhere in Irish passage graves does not duplicate the geometric motifs and patterns engraved on the stones but is sparse consisting of straight or sagging dragged lines (Wadell 1998, 44; Eogan 1986, 141). So in Malta we find the same motifs occurring on different material media associated with both the living and the dead. In Ireland this translation of imagery in relation to different material forms does not take place. There is a distinction and separation between different domains, those related to the dead, and those related to the living.

In Malta the representation of the human form in small stone sculptures and figurines, in particular 'obese' representations of women is frequent and very similar figurines occur in both the Hypogeum and the Tarxien temples. These representations appear to indicate the significance of food transmission and feasting among and for the living. Such fleshy depictions of the human body are entirely absent in Ireland where mortuary practices reduce the body to dust. Feasting in the ceremonial context of the temple exteriors may well have been intimately linked with the propitiation of the dead rather than a celebration of the living.

Imagery and order

Evans describes the stone carvings from Tarxien in the following way: 'The most remarkable feature of the Maltese aesthetic is its evident dislike of straight lines and sharp angles, its translation of all form into soft, sweeping curves' (Evans 1959, 166). The imagery, and the sculptures, such as the 'sleeping lady' found in the Hypogeum, all suggested to him a 'massive calm, a stillness which marks a vigorous creative energy' (Evans 1959, 166). This 'calmness' that Evans refers to may be contrasted with the utterly different types of contrasting geometric motifs found at Newgrange spilling over the stones in different ways. There is an aesthetic 'wildness' to this imagery in the juxtaposition and arrangement of contrasting forms. Another way of putting this is that the Tarxien images are both repetitive and very orderly. In contrast the imagery at Newgrange is only repetitive in the sense that there are a limited number of geometric graphic motifs employed (far greater than at Tarxien) but they are dispersed across the stones in a very disorderly manner. There is no plan, here, no grand design. There is an improvised and contingent character to where and how the motifs appear on the stones. By comparison with Tarxien the Newgrange imagery appears disjointed and fragmented.

At Newgrange there are no images whatsoever that might be interpreted as iconic, although some scholars have seen the spirals in the interior as eyes (e.g. Crawford 1957). At the neighbouring temple of Knowth there are is at least one image that appears to be anthropomorphic. It occurs on an orthostat at a crucial transitional point between the inner and outer part of the Knowth West passage tomb (Figure 17.15). George Eogan (1986) has graphically described seeing this image for the first time on entering the tomb and its anthromorphic likeness has been discussed by others (O'Sullivan 1996). There is nothing calm about this image. Its visual effect is both wild and frightening.

Now if we envisage the architectural space of the Tarxien temple complex in the most basic way it is a shell internally subdivided by walls and divisions of various sizes and dimensions. Overall it is recessive space with the apses or rooms adjoining the forecourt areas becoming smaller as

Figure 17.15. The anthropomorphic imagery on orthostat 49 in the western passage grave at Knowth. Photo: C. Tilley.

one moves from the front to the back and innermost parts of the temple, areas that are not elaborated with imagery carved into the stones themselves. Any imagery that may have occurred here would have been portable in the form of sculptures and clay figurines and decorated vessels. The space of Newgrange and other Irish temples constitutes an almost exact inversion of this. These are all cairns or mounds in which most of the space enclosed and bounded off by the external kerb stones is a completely solid matrix of stones and turfs. The passages leading into the mound are extremely constricted and narrow. The terminal chamber, furthest away from the entrance always constitutes by far the largest and the highest space. Great uncertainty remains with regard to the roofs of the Maltese temples but it seems certain that these did not possess the narrowing and extremely high corbelled ceilings characteristic of many Irish temples. Such were the size of the major apses of the Tarxien temples and elsewhere that the walls could never have supported a stone vault. At a certain level the roof was

probably completed by a flat roof of timber beams, brushwood or clay (Trump 1990, 31).

Individual and collective experience

In the Irish temples only very small numbers of people could be physically accommodated within the terminal chambers the journey to which would have to be in single file because of the extremely constricted nature of the passage. By contrast the passage way areas into the temples at Tarxien and elsewhere are all short, a matter of a few metres and the internal court areas and side apses large enough to hold substantial numbers of people. Tourist groups of up to twenty can comfortably be accommodated today. The experience of moving down the long passageways of the Irish temples to the terminal chambers is of necessity highly individualized. Only one person at a time can undertake the journey and one remains in direct physical contact with the stones, which may be contrasted with the spacious trilithon doorways, courtyards and apses of Tarxien. The distinction is between an enforced individualized experience and a collective experience. We know, from the provision of numerous bar and rope holes that the various internal spaces of Tarxien could be closed and altered, at will be made mobile. By comparison the internal space of Newgrange was fixed and immobile. Since few could enter into it there was no necessity to seal off or hide its secrets.

Conclusions: spiritual release and spiritual containment

How might we understand these fundamental differences between the architecture and the imagery of Tarxien and Newgrange? My interpretation of this is that while in Malta the dead were regarded as essentially benign, in Ireland they were understood as potentially malicious. The whole point about the architecture of Irish passage graves seems to be about symbolically containing the spirits of the dead and preventing them from getting out.

In relation to the theme of this conference 'cult in context' in the Tarxien temples we have a cult for the living taking place both in the temple precincts and within at least more public areas within the temples themselves. At Tarxien there is strong evidence for animal sacrifice involving domesticated rams, male goats and oxen and that this took place within the temple precincts where their remains were deposited. At Newgrange there is no such evidence and animals and their remains were excluded from the temple spaces. This links well with the presence of carved depictions of animals at Tarxien, the occurrence of animal figurines and depictions of animals on pottery, and the complete absence of such iconic imagery in Ireland. In the Maltese case animals are a fundamental part of the temple rites, drawn into the human world. In the Irish case animal remains are completely absent and there is no evidence of animal sacrifice.

The practice of animal sacrifice was no doubt connected with the life-giving force of sacrificial blood. We have seen that the iconic imagery is located mostly in the most accessible part of the temple interior, a relatively light and airy space where it was meant to be seen and visually experienced. The aesthetic power of this imagery was primarily visual, exciting and teasing the mind. In various ways the iconic motifs represent sacrificial cults in action.

By contrast at Newgrange we witness imagery related primarily to a cult of the dead. The imagery inside Newgrange and indeed much of that on the external kernstones was never intended for public display and consumption. Much of it is hidden or not visually striking (Eogan 1997). The sensory experience inside Newgrange was primarily tactile and auditory, rather than visual. It simply did not matter whether or not the graphic imagery could be seen for this imagery belonged primarily to the dead who could 'see' and experience it from inside the tomb. Unlike the living the ancestral dead could still benefit from the experience of that which was hidden away. The important thing was that their remains be buried in the context of the magical power of decorated stones. These differences have to be understood in terms of relationships between the living and the dead.

Common links between Tarxien and Newgrange are the great significance of thresholds and transitional points and spiral motifs that link the living and the dead, but in very different ways. In Malta temples for the living and resting places for the dead were separated. The dead were buried under the ground in rock cut chambers of the Hypogeum themselves resembling temples. This architecture in the negative, decorated with spirals and running curvilinear motifs constitutes a perfect inversion of the temple spaces constructed on the ground. In Ireland, by contrast, the temples for the dead were also the focus for the ceremonies of the living. The dead were buried above the ground but in monuments that effectively resembled caves found below the ground. Thus in Malta we find temples under the earth and in Ireland caves above the earth, an upside down world. The architectural message about the relationship between the living and the dead appears to be the same in both cases: the world of the dead is a reversal of the world of the living. In Malta we witness an absolute spatial separation between the two domains. In Ireland this is only partial in terms of a distinction between the outside and the inside of the monuments.

We know that in Malta the spiral is directly associated with animal sacrifice. At Tarxien the front of an altar in the first courtyard of the western temple is decorated with a double row of branched spirals resembling the curling horns of a ram. In the middle of the lower row of spirals there is a carefully concealed cut hole with a lunate plug with the same spiral motif. Removing this plug, Zammit discovered that the altar had been hollowed out and contained a curved flint knife and numerous charred animal bones, principally of rams and or goats (Evans 1971, 121).

Inside Newgrange the spirals are concentrated in the chamber and associated with the dead. The Tarxien temples may thus be understood as architectural containers associated with tapping into the life forces associated with living beings that became released through sacrificial acts. By contrast Newgrange and other Irish temples may be understood as architectural snares for the spiritual forces associated with the ancestral dead. In the most general sense in the Maltese case the emphasis is on releasing spiritual forces and energies within the temple spaces, for the benefit of the living. In the Irish case the emphasis is on containing ancestral forces within the monument and preventing them from escaping outside into the world of the living. Symbolically then, the spiral in Malta is associated with the release of power, in Ireland and in an analogous way to the inside of the temple space, it acts as a trap and a container for the souls of the dead.

References

Crawford, O. 1957. *The Eye Goddess*. London.

Eogan, G. 1986. *Knowth*. London, Thames and Hudson.

Eogan, G. 1997. Overlays and underlays: aspects of megalithic art succession at Brugh na Boinne, Ireland. *Brigantium* 10, 217–34.

Eogan, G. 1998. Knowth before Knowth. *Antiquity* 72, 162–72.

Evans, J. 1959. *Malta*. London, Thames and Hudson.

Evans, J. 1971. *Prehistoric Antiquities of the Maltese Islands*. London, Athlone.

Gell, A. 1998. *Art and Agency*. Oxford, Clarendon Press.

Grima, R. 2001. An iconography of insularity: a cosmological interpretation of some images and spaces in the late Neolithic temples of Malta. *Papers from the Institute of Archaeology* 12, 48–65.

Lewis-Williams, D. and Pearce, D. 2005. *Inside the Neolithic Mind*. London, Thames and Hudson.

O'Kelly, C. 1973. *Passage-grave art in the Boyne valley*. *Proceedings of the Prehistoric Society* 39, 354–82.

O'Kelly, C. 1982. Corpus of Newgrange art. In M. O'Kelly *Newgrange*. London, Thames and Hudson,146–185.

O' Kelly, M. 1982. *Newgrange*. London, Thames and Hudson.

O'Kelly, M. and O'Kelly, C. 1983. The tumulus of Dowth, Co. Meath. *Proceedings of the Royal Irish Academy* 113, 136–90.

O'Sullivan, M. 1986. Approaches to passage tomb art. *Journal of the Royal Society of Antiquaries of Ireland* 116, 68–83.

O'Sullivan, M. 1996. Megalithic art in Ireland and Brittany: divergence or convergence? *Revue Archéologique de l'Ouest.* Supplément No. 8, 81–96.

Ridley, M. 1976. *The Megalithic Art of the Maltese Islands*. Poole: Dolphin Press.

Shee Twohig, E. 2000. Frameworks for the megalithic art of the Boyne valley. In A. Desmond, G. Johnson, M. McCarthy, J. Sheehan and E. Shee Twohig (eds). *New Agendas in Irish Prehistory*. Bray, Wordwell, 89–106.

Tilley, C. 2004. *The Materiality of Stone*. Oxford, Berg.

Trump, D. 2000. *Malta: An Archaeological Guide*. Malta, Progress Press.

Wadell, J. 1998. *The Prehistoric Archaeology of Ireland*. Galway, Galway University Press.

Zammit, T. 1930. *Prehistoric Malta: The Tarxien Temples*. Oxford, Clarendon Press.

Chapter 18

CULTURE AND CULT: SOME ASPECTS OF PASSAGE TOMB SOCIETY IN THE BOYNE REGION, IRELAND

George Eogan

The Boyne region has for long been recognised as a rich archaeological area, this fact is especially true of the passage tomb stage of the Neolithic with its spectacular monuments and the evidence that they provide for architecture, art and cult. The purpose of this contribution is, therefore, to review some of the developments that took place, to consider the background and to offer some interpretations. In Ireland passage tombs have a wide distribution from Cape Clear in the south to Fair Head in the north and from County Meath in the east to County Sligo in the west (Figure 18.1). It is in the latter area that the majority of tombs occur (Herity 1974, 233–55; 262–77), amongst them being great concentrations or cemeteries. In addition there is a scatter of tombs inland in Ulster, also in Leinster south of the Boyne and in west Munster (Figure 18.1). Some of these tombs have art but apart from Knockroe, Co. Kilkenny (O'Sullivan 1987), with its eighteen stones, the number of stones with art is limited to two or three per tomb.

The Boyne region (County Meath), in the east of the country, has a large number of passage tombs, about seventy examples (Figure 18.2) but it also has the largest number of stones with megalithic art from any area of Europe, about 550 examples. Elsewhere in Ireland, excluding Millin Bay, Co. Down (Collins and Waterman 1955) where, due to the fragmentary nature of the stones, about fifty pieces, the numbers of intact stones cannot be ascertained. From that evidence it is clear that the Boyne region is a leading area for such tombs, including the largest examples known. In order to offer some explanation as to why this may be so, and the factors that brought it about, a brief review of the Boyne region both from the geographical and archaeological points of view will be given.

In geographical terms the Boyne region embraces most of the area covered by the Ordnance Survey Map, Sheet 13, half-inch to a mile (1: 126, 720). This encompasses the County of Meath and part of the adjoining counties of Westmeath, Cavan, Louth and Dublin. (Figure 18.2). Predominantly this is outstanding agricultural land, it has

an outlet to the Irish Sea, into which the principal river of the area, the Boyne, with its main tributary the Blackwater, flow. Further south there are the Nanny and Delvin rivers; these also flow into the Irish Sea. Due to its location this was an area of easy settlement as defined by Fox (1952, 78) and accordingly would have been attractive to early farming communities. However, it is only within recent times that even a hint of settlement emerged. A programme of field walking a number of years ago by G. F. Mitchell yielded some diagnostic flint artefacts that could have dated from the Early Neolithic period. In some places the flints were in concentrations, these may suggest areas of activity, even possible domestic settlement. But it was only as a result of the Knowth excavations that positive evidence for Early ('Western') Neolithic occupation emerged, this consists of two phases, early and late. During the earlier phase, people lived in rectangular houses, four examples of which have been uncovered at Knowth (Eogan 1984, 211–44, Fig. 18.5; Eogan and Roche 1997, 5–50, also House A Figure 18.4) and the material culture consisted of round-bottomed vessels generally with simple rims and shoulders that are not well pronounced. Amongst the flint artefacts were leaf-shaped arrowheads and rounded scrapers (Eogan and Roche 1997, 5–50). This settlement was subsequently buried beneath the large mound. Due to the large size of that mound only small areas of it were excavated, these were inwards from the kerb so the extent of the settlement has not been determined but as it occurs underneath the large mound, on both west and east sides, it may have covered an extensive portion of that area, i.e. the hill-top. In the limited area uncovered there is no evidence for protection so it is possible that the area of habitation consisted of an open settlement with individual houses.

In contrast to the early stage, the later 'Western' Neolithic settlement is on flat ground just off the hill-top outside the later large mound on its north-western side. It predates Tombs 8, 10–13. Only a part has been excavated but that portion produced evidence for a sub-rectangular feature, a

IRELAND

- ◉ Large Cemeteries
- ⊙ Small Cemeteries
- ● Definite tomb
- ○ Possible tomb

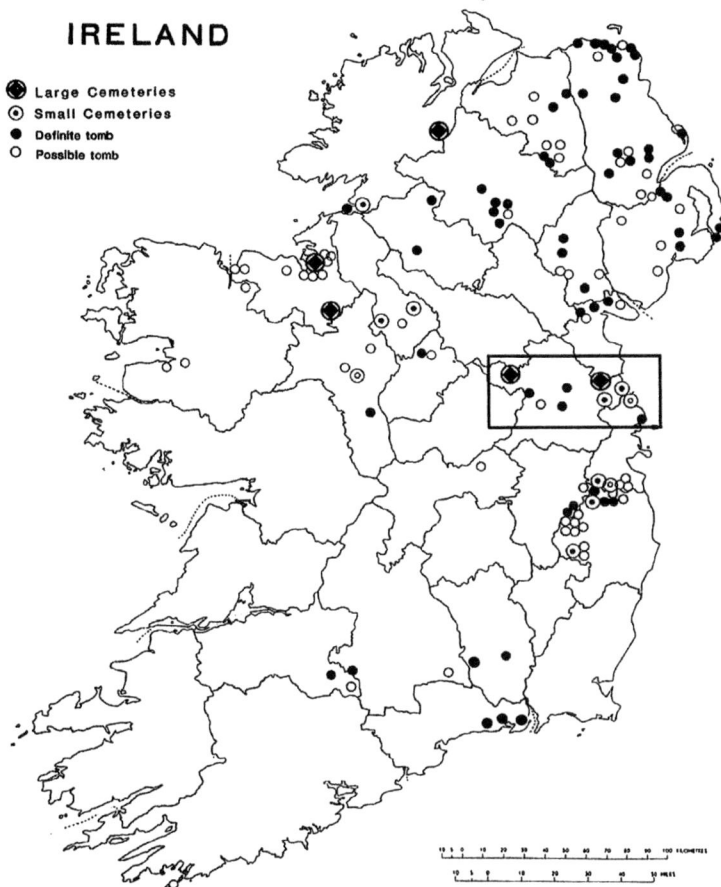

Figure 18.1. Distribution of passage tombs in Ireland (Boyne Region is boxed).

double-palisaded enclosure, areas of pebbling and other evidence for activity (Eogan 1984, 210–44, see also Figure 18.4). The sub-rectangular structure might be the remains of a house, 12.30 metres by 10.10 metres in external dimensions (Figure 18.4, House B). Otherwise there is no evidence for houses. This structure is early in the sequence as it is outside the inner palisade and is overlain by the outer palisade. The inner palisade, which was probably the earliest, appears to have enclosed a circular area about 100 m in diameter. Within it were areas of pebbling but no evidence for a structure. The outer palisade, which was concentric with the inner palisade, also seems to have enclosed a circular area that was about 120 m in diameter. Between both palisaded areas there were areas of pebbling, pits and flint-knapping but it has not been established if these were of contemporary date or consisted of external activity associated with the inner palisade. The precise function of these palisaded areas has not been conclusively established but despite the absence of house within the enclosures the nature of the finds suggest that the site was used for occupation rather than for cult purposes.

A contemporary site, mainly on pottery evidence, may be Newgrange, Site L (Lynch in O'Kelly *et al.* 1978, 263–65). This consisted of a discontinuous habitation layer but

no evidence for formal structures came to light. Despite this, it is likely that a house existed close-by.

Outside the Boyne region of County Meath there is also evidence for Early Neolithic settlement. A good example is the rectangular house at Newtown in the north of County Meath (Halpin 1995). It is also in that region that there is the only evidence for Early Neolithic megalithic tombs, a court tomb at Coraville and a portal tomb at Ervey (Eogan 1958) but geographically these tombs are part of the main northern group. Therefore, there was no tradition for the construction of megalithic tombs in the Boyne region before passage tomb times.

Taking the court and portal tomb distribution in the east of Ireland there is a gap between Mid Louth and south County Dublin (Figure 18.5). The relevant aspect of this distribution is that the gap is almost exclusively the area of passage tomb distribution. It might be speculated that the area was occupied by passage tomb builders and as a result was avoided by court and portal tomb builders. But current dating evidence shows that such tombs predate the passage tomb builders. For unknown reasons, court- and portal tomb people avoided that area but that does not mean that the area was uninhabited. As already shown Early Neolithic domestic occupation was a feature but unlike other parts

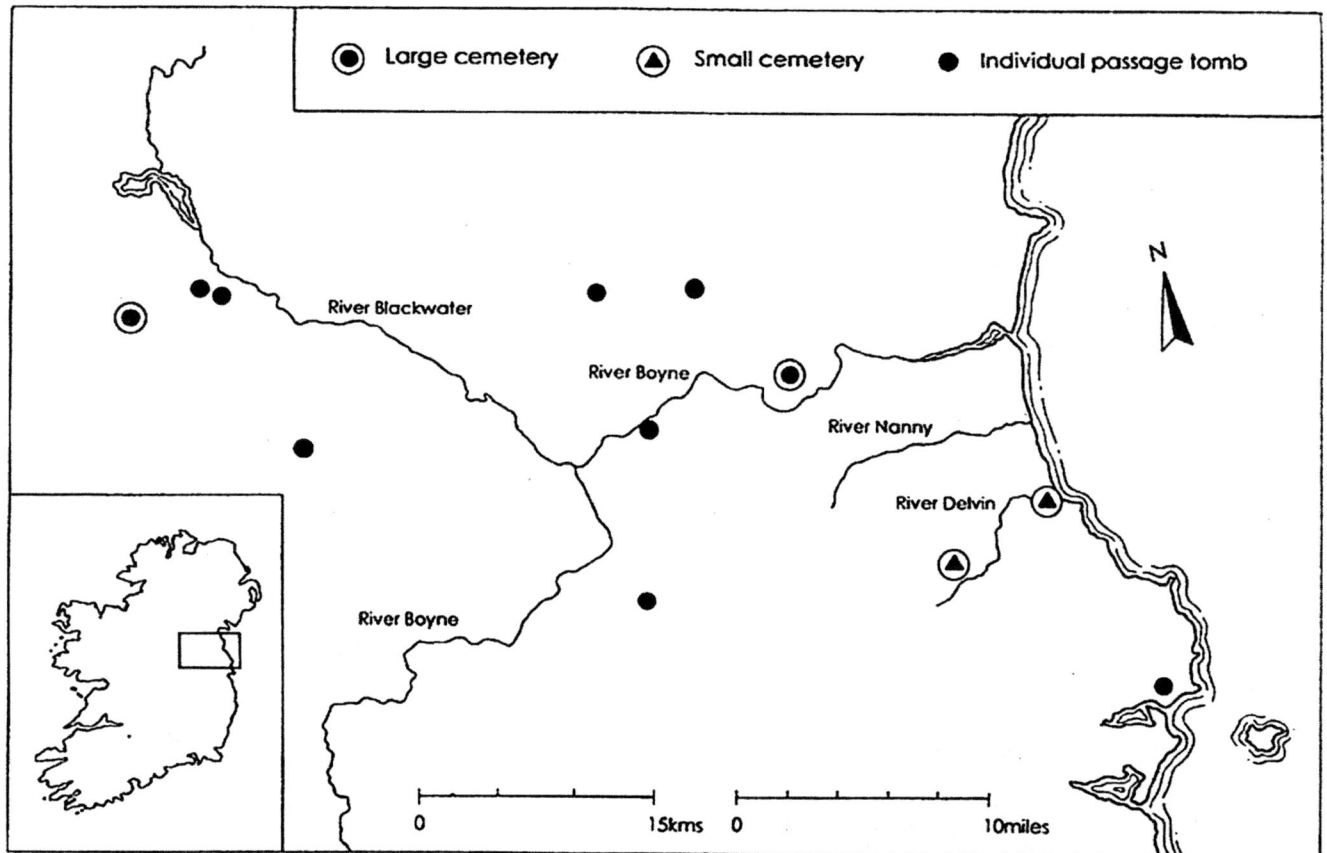

Figure 18.2. Distribution of passage tombs in the Boyne region (Co. Meath).

(Figure 18.5) there is only evidence for domestic settlement, definite evidence for cult and ritual does not exist. Anyway, the passage tomb builders seem to have occupied part of a cult void, which they filled by introducing a set of man material features which constituted religious activities. Tomb construction for burial and the associated megalithic art was a feature, this could have involved practices in which homage to the deceased must have been paramount, in other words a cult package emerged. In the Boyne area there is evidence for up to 70 tombs. Amongst these are some of the largest passage tombs known, Dowth, Knowth and Newgrange, the covering mound of each is over 80 m in maximum diameter. Another outstanding feature of the Meath tombs is the presence of megalithic art; there is evidence for about 550 individual stones. This is the largest number of such stones from any part of Europe. But the most remarkable thing about the Meath tombs is that their distribution is confined to a very restricted area, an area that is limited to the lower reaches of the River Boyne and the upper reaches of its tributary, the Blackwater. Geographically the area extends from the Irish Sea westwards to Slieve na Cailligh, a distance of close to 40 km and 20 km in maximum width from Tara to Rathkenny. On the east side the area is bounded by the Irish Sea, on the south

by flat lands, on the west by undulating countryside and lakes, on the north west there is the southern limits of the drumlin belt while on the north-east there is the hill country in the Collon area. Within this limited area are the great cemeteries of Brugh na Bóinne and Slieve na Cailligh, the lesser cemeteries of Clonsillagh-King's Mountain (Eogan 2000), Fourknocks (Hartnett 1957) and Bremore-Gormanstown (Herity 1974, 252, 255), there is no evidence for art at the latter sites. There are also a number of individual tombs with art; Mound of the Hostages, Tara, (O'Sullivan 2005), Rathkenny, (Shee-Twohig 1981, 236), Mullaghroy (Eogan and O'Broin 1998) and Broadboyne Bridge (Eogan 1974).

As already noted, for any part of Europe it is this region that has the greatest collection of art, and extraordinarily, outside that area in Ireland there are only about 50 stones, from 16 tombs (the number of complete stones with art from Millin Bay, County Down cannot be determined). In addition to the large number of stones with art, amongst them are some of the most outstanding works of art, such as the entrance stone to Newgrange, large, and what is also remarkable is the size of the three great Brugh na Bóinne tombs, Knowth, Dowth and Newgrange. It is clear that this very limited Boyne area was a particular and special place

Figure 18.3. Ground plan of Early Neolithic house A, Knowth, Co. Meath (after Eogan and Roche 1998, figure 1).

in Europe during the time of the passage tomb complex.

Various views have been put forward regarding the role of megalithic art Coffey (1892, 22) considered it as decoration, Claire O'Kelly has also inclined to that interpretation (in M. J. O'Kelly 1982, 148) but also involving symbolism. Breuil (1934) considered that an anthropological element was present, a view that to some extent was also held by Herity (1974, 91–115). In Shee-Twohig's view (1981, 140) the art acted as a magico-religious symbolism guarding the tombs. A view that has been gaining some currency within recent years is that megalithic art could be explained in the same way that Southern African Palaeolithic art has been interpreted, largely that it emerged when people were in altered states of consciousness, a state that could have been induced by drug-taking (Lewis-Williams and Pearce 2005; Helvenston and Bahn 2002). On both chronological and geographical grounds it is most unlikely that such explanations could explain the use of Neolithic/Chalcolithic megalithic art in

western European lands. It is much more likely that it was in those regions and in those times that megalithic art emerged as part of the ritual practices of the passage tomb builders. During the later part of the Neolithic and Chalcolithic periods, Western Europe witnessed a cultural effervescence. This expressed itself architecturally and also artistically. The passage tombs of the Boyne region represent an outstanding demonstration of such achievements. Boyne art is an aspect of passage tombs and therefore, a cult feature. Virtually every passage tomb that has been excavated produced evidence for burial, almost exclusively cremation, often this took place successively (Eogan 1986, figure 20). The art was applied both internally and externally but it seems to have had a different role in the different areas yet it was part of a complex of connected parts. At Knowth the internal art may have had a dual function; that at ground level could have been a form of grave goods (Eogan 1986, figure 76). For the large mound it is interesting to note that grave goods are rare, so art may

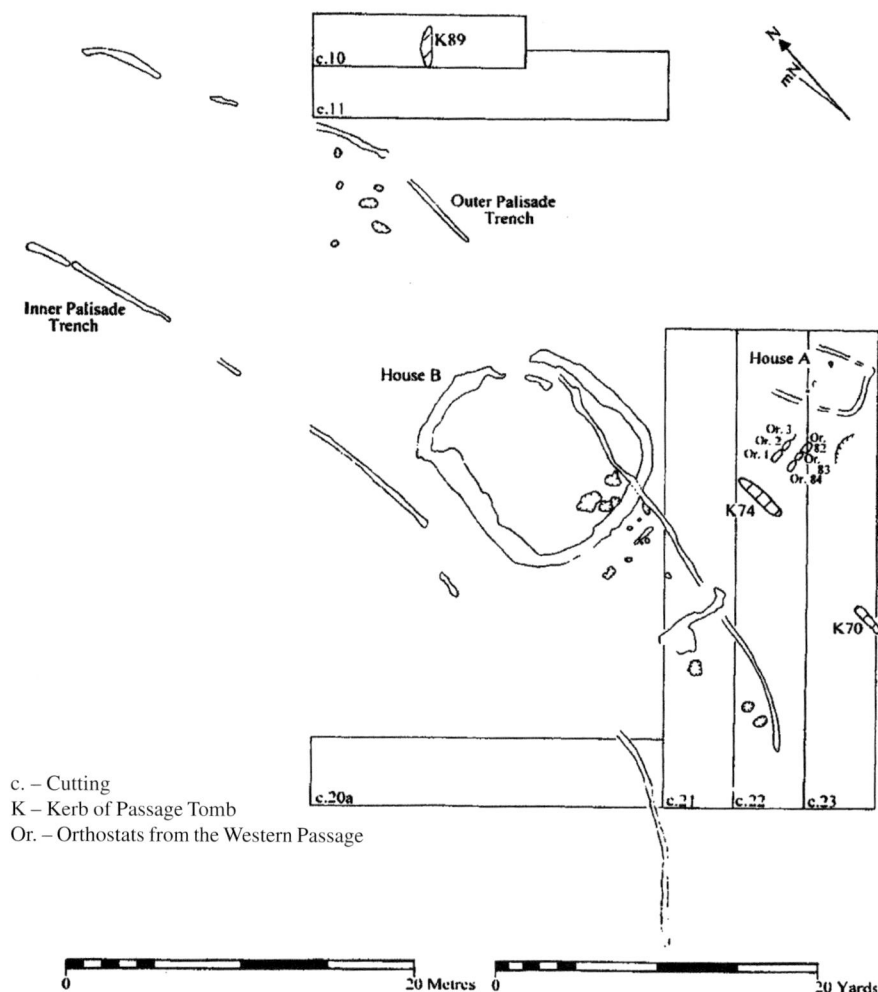

Figure 18.4. Ground plan of excavated portion of later Neolithic settlement, Knowth (after Eogan and Roche 1984, figure 74).

have been an alternative. The other form of internal art is at a higher level and it might have functioned as a form of communication between the deceased and the living (Eogan 1986, figure 73). The external art on the kerb of the large mound had a different function. It may be considered that cult practices now took place outdoors and that the kerb art was part of a processional way, each stone may have conveyed a special message or represented a particular aspect of religious or cult practices. These may have been special events that took place at a particular period of the year such as at the time of the winter solstice at Newgrange (O'Kelly 1982, 124).

Discussion

Already in pre-passage tomb times the Boyne region was opened up for farming but there is no evidence for cult or ritual practices at that time. Neither does it appear that those Early Neolithic inhabitants contributed directly to the emergence of passage tomb society. On the contrary it seems that passage tombs were the product of a new cult and cultural element. On the evidence provided by the distribution of the tombs the area of activity was quite small but at least from the points of view of cult and culture it was a favoured area. It contains the largest number of stones with art for any one Irish county or for any one European region but also the largest and most spectacular tombs. These people farmed the rich lands of the area but they had access to other natural resources, not only the local geology that provided suitable buildings stones but also stones that provided convenient surfaces for applying art. As a result a materially wealthy society emerged, a society that was also artistically competent in which cult and ritual constituted a significant element. These elements were not solely of native origin but were part of a wider West European ritual zone, the needs of which involved the creation of Europe's greatest architectural and engineering structures of their time, such as those of the Boyne region.

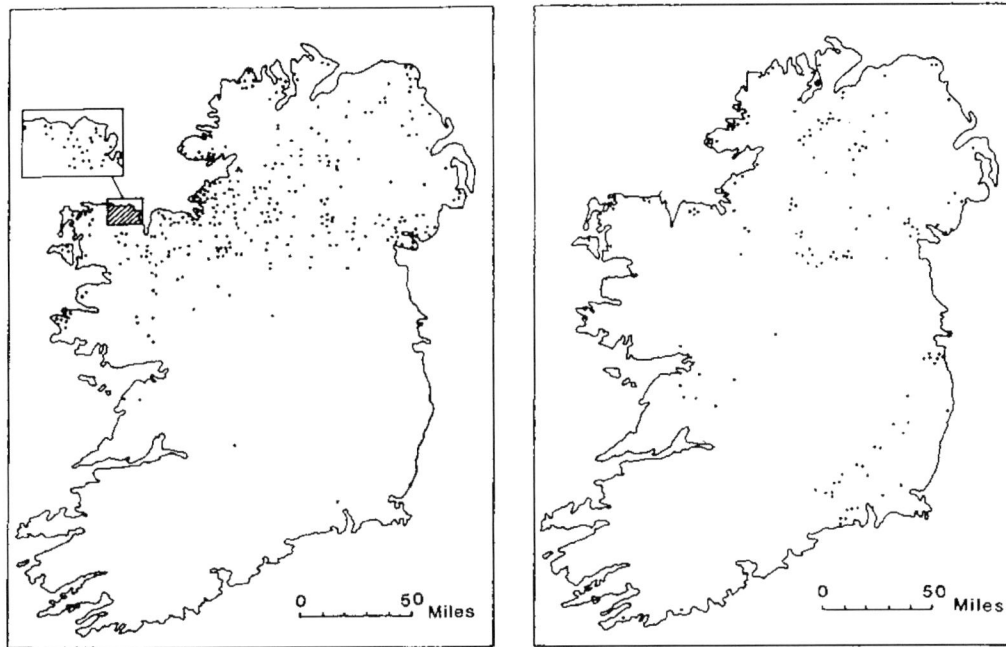

Figure 18.5. Distribution of long-barrow tombs (court left and portal right) in Ireland (after Ó Nualláin 1979).

In turn the Boyne region influenced external areas such as North Wales and the Orkneys. It was this combination of cult and ritual that produced within a limited geographical area one of the most outstanding archaeological complexes of Neolithic Europe.

References

Breuil, H. 1934. Presidential Address for 1934. *Proceedings of the Prehistoric Society of East Anglia.* 7, 289–322.

Coffey, G. 1892. On the tumuli and inscribed stones at Newgrange, Dowth and Knowth. *T. R. I. A.* 30, 1–96.

Collins, A. E. P. and Waterman, D. M., 1955. *Millin Bay, Co. Down.* Belfast, Stationery Office.

Eogan, G. 1958. The Gallery Graves of Meath. *J. R. S. A. I.* 88, 179–84.

Eogan, G. 1974. A Probable Passage Grave Site near Broadboyne Bridge, Co. Meath, *J. R. S. A. I.* 104, 146–50.

Eogan, G. 1984. *Excavations at Knowth 1: Smaller Passage Tombs, Neolithic Occupation and Beaker Activity.* Dublin, Royal Irish Academy.

Eogan, G. 2000. A group of megalithic monuments at Kingsmountain-Clonsillagh, Co. Meath, *Ríocht na Midhe* 11, 1–6.

Eogan, G. and Ó'Broin, N. 1998. A decorated stone at Mullaghroy, Co. Meath, *Ríocht na Midhe* 9, No. 4, 10–15.

Eogan, G. and Roche, H. 1997. *Excavations at Knowth. 2: Settlement and ritual sites of the fourth and third millennia*

B.C. Dublin, Royal Irish Academy/Department of Arts.

Eogan, G. and Roche, H. 1998. Neolithic Habitation at Knowth, Co. Meath. *Ríocht na Midhe*, 9, 1–9.

Fox, C. 1952. *The Personality of Britain.* Cardiff, National Museum of Wales.

Halpin, E. 1995. Excavations at Newtown, Co. Meath, in Eoin Grogan and Charles Mount. *Annus Archalogiae.* Dublin: Organistion of Irish Archaeologists.

Hartnett, P. J. 1957. Excavation of a passage grave at Fourknocks, Co. Meath, *P. R. I. A.* 58C. 197–277.

Helvenston, P. A. and Bahn, P. G., 2002. *Desperately Seeking Transplants.* New York, R. J. Communications LLC.

Herity, M. 1974. *Irish Passage Graves.* Dublin, Irish University Press.

Lewis-Williams, D. and Pearce, D. 2005. *Inside the Neolithic Mind.* London, Thames and Hudson.

O'Kelly, M. J. 1982. *Newgrange Archaeology, Art and Legend.* London and New York, Thames and Hudson.

O'Kelly, M. J., Lynch, F. and O'Kelly, C., 1978. Three Passage Graves at Newgrange, Co. Meath. *P. R. I. A.* 78C, 249–352.

Ó'Nualláin, S. 1979. The megalithic tombs of Ireland. *Expedition* 21, No. 3, 6–15.

O'Sullivan, M. 1987. The Art of the Passage Tomb at Knockroe, County Kilkenny. *J. R. S. A. I.* 117, 84–95.

O'Sullivan, M. 2005. *Duma na nGiall, Tara: The Mound of the Hostages.* Dublin, Wordwell-UCD School of Archaeology.

Shee-Twohig, E. 1981. *The Megalithic Art of Western Europe.* Oxford, The Clarendon Press.

Chapter 19

WORKING STONE: MAKING MONUMENTS IN THE IRISH NEOLITHIC

Gabriel Cooney

Introduction

The focus of this paper is the use of stone in the construction of megalithic mouments in the Neolithic, with particular reference to Ireland. This forms part of a wider concern with how people both lived with and engaged with stone during this period which has been influenced closely by a long interest in Neolithic monuments (e.g. Cooney 1979; 2006), a more recent focus on Irish stone axes (e.g. Cooney and Mandal 1998) and on understanding the archaeological record at the stone axe quarry site of Eagle's Nest, Lambay. The complexity of the latter, the interplay between extraction and deposition, the use of the source and a range of lithics brought to the site (Cooney 2005) indicates a complexity and subtlety in the use of and meanings ascribed to stone. More broadly tacking between different kinds of material manifestations in stone of human activity; monuments and objects and different scales of activity; literally monumental and 'handeable', has led me to the view that despite the central role that the study of stone has in our narratives of the Neolithic our categorisation of its uses in terms of scale and purpose has often obscured what is after all the essential character of stone, that it is both enduring – 'rock of ages' (Craig 1996, 259) – and capable of cultural transformation. It is those two properties that make it such a richly metaphoric and symbolic medium (e.g. Tilley 2004; DeMarrais 2004; Scarre 2004) for people technologically familiar with the working of stone. It is also both relevant and crucial to remember Lemonnier's (1993, 3) answer to the question of why technology requires a sociological approach; because techniques are above all social productions. The processes that channel material actions in working stone are always embedded in a broader symbolic system (Renfrew 2004, 30).

We recognise the validity of such an approach in relation to specific raw materials, such as quartz (e.g. Darvill 2002; Cooney 2000) but much more frequently we tend to compartmentalise the use of stone (even where the same lithic sources are being used, such as sandstone) as suggested above and to distinguish between monumental: small-scale, ceremonial: domestic, utilised: unutilised, products:debitage modes of use. How does this approach sit with our understanding that for stone-using prehistoric societies the landscape would have been viewed as alive, redolent with inherent potency? That understanding resonates with the notion of rock as vivid and active, and to quote Ingold (1993, 162) that the landscape, including stone, is not a mere backdrop to human history but is forever being actively constituted, understood and interpreted through the activities of people who live in it. Now this is not to deny that the working of stone can be for the most mundane purpose, as captured in the concept of the 'rock breaker', but to understand that this has to be set along side the potential of an unworked stone or boulder to be redolent with cultural meaning and memory and the reminder that the mundane can also easily echo and relate to other places and other contexts – the link is human experience and belief. As Casey (2001, 415) has argued the presence of a place can be compressed into a single sensation which can evoke that place instanteously. Feeling the texture of stone in one place and context can transport us to somewhere else.

I want to take this perspective in looking at the use of stone in Irish megalithic tombs, arguing that the working of stone was not just the background for the construction of monuments but formed part and parcel of the form and meaning of these new places, where human experience was used to create links and resonances between the materials, meaning and memory of other places. To provide a focus for the argument there will be a discussion of three different megalithic monuments in Ireland. But in the context of the theme of cult in context on Malta I wanted to begin by referring to the senses of islandness that we can see in Malta and Ireland, both in terms of similarity and difference, and also to comment on the term 'cult'.

Living in and making island worlds

Rather than focusing on potential links in the Neolithic archaeology of Ireland and Malta which has been an occasional theme in the past (e.g Ó Ríordáin and Daniel 1964, 128–30), it seems to be much more useful to begin with the recognition that while the monuments are very different, in both cases we are dealing with island worlds. Robb's (2001, 192) observation in relation to Malta that islands are key to the process by which islanders construct their own worlds is relevant to Ireland also. Islands are not just a passive background context in this regard but they form a symbolic as well as physical resource; a rich source of ideas and distinctiveness. This does not imply isolation, there is evidence in both Ireland (e.g. Cooney 2000) and Malta (Trump 2004, 66–7) for wider, regional networks of contact and exchange in which island sources and coastal travel played an important role. As Malta is a small island world consisting of three main islands; Malta, Gozo and Comino, Ireland at a much larger scale is an island with many offshore islands, at least 300 of some size (Walsh 2004). This diversity of island size, the presence of many offshore islands, both close to the shore and at some distance from it, weather and sailing conditions that frequently make uplands look like islands (Cooney 2004) must have increased the potential power of the island as a metaphor when monuments were constructed. Through their construction the meanings of place could be bounded, intensified and condensed, as on an island. Tilley (2004) set out to establish how Maltese cultural distinctiveness was established through temple use and construction. He argued that the temples were embodiments of ideas and were material metaphors through which the island world become known. The key point here to understand is the central significance of the local landscape, particularly on an island. For example, the colour, shape and tactile differences between the globigerina and coralline limestone are as central to interpreting the Maltese monuments as they are to knowing the intricate topography of the islands. Certainly on Gozo it is hard to resist the suggestion that the temples were designed and placed to mimic the typical flat-topped hills (Trump 2000, 164), an analogy strengthened by examples such as the ring of natural coralline boulders sitting on a small hill near Heqqa Point on the north coast of Gozo. This sense of landscape continuity and transformation through the active use of rock is returned to below in discussing Irish megalithic monuments.

It is now widely agreed that religious and cosmological beliefs underpinned the creation of megalithic monuments (e.g. see discussion in Scarre 2004) and I would concur with Insoll that we should start from the premise that religion 'is the framework into which all other aspects of archaeology, of past life, can be placed (Insoll 2004, 22). In this context when preparing the paper I started to think about the word cult, which I had been using un-problematically, and to ask whether in fact it was relevant to to my concern with the materiality of stone in monuments. A short, concise definition provided by Luhrmann (1997, 92) is that cults are groups that follow an unorthodox religion or are centred on a single person or principle, often associated with curing or salvation. Luhrmann (1997, 93) also observed that anthropologists are habitually nonchalant in their use of terms and that they rarely use the term in respect of religious groups they have actually studied. Anthropological studies tend to focus on the symbolic creativity and the healing aspects of cults and in this regard have paid particular attention to cargo cults; religious movements focused on material goods where deprivation is cured by means of acquiring Western goods through ritual, bringing about social revitalisation and the return of the ancestors. Insoll (2004, 5, 96–7) suggests that cult is in fact a weak term carrying connotations of something marginal, unusual and infrequent but which archaeologists (e.g. Renfrew 1985) have used on the basis that it is a way of recognising religion because it is seen as involving the use of special artefacts and/or special places and therefore might be discerned archaeologically. So, implied in these definitions are two broad approaches to cult; firstly practices that suggest a reaction against a dominant religious or cultural system within which people feel deprived and secondly a limited view of the role of religion in everyday life which perhaps tells us more about contemporary archaeological attitudes to religion (Insoll 2004, Chapter 3) than prehistoric religious practices. Neither of these approaches seem particularly appropriate or useful in the context of the discussion of Irish megalithic monuments. What may be of relevance is the notion of the symbolic creativity and the healing aspect of cults with their connections to wider, shared religious practice. More broadly the Oxford English Dictionary (2003) defines the origin of the word as deriving from the notion of 'worship' or homage paid to a divinity and it is in this wider sense that the term is used and understood here. The focus in Irish megalithic tombs on the deposition of selected human remains suggests that here a primary concern was the creation of the community of ancestors and the relationship of this ancestral world with the living.

Stones in action

Megalithic tombs are one of the characteristic features of the Irish Neolithic period (4000–2500 BC). There are over 1500 of monuments known which have been classified into four major types (e.g. Cody 2002). Not surprisingly there have been a diversity of interpretation and archaeological approaches to the study and understanding of these monuments. This is exemplified in work at what is internationally the best known complex of sites, namely the passage tomb complex at Brú na Bóinne.

But running through this work has been a focus on monumentality, on the construction of the megalithic structures and their covering mounds. The working and placement of the stone that makes up these monuments has often been viewed as a background; providing the necessary physical components for the architectural forms that are perceived as constituting the monument. In a related way when art occurs in the passage tomb complex the stone is often viewed as a neutral, static background, even where orthostatic or roof-slab form may influence the placement and style of art (but see O'Sullivan 1997). Following on the general argument presented above I would like to suggest that it is the active working of stone, and the incorporation of that stone in a variety of forms, not just those formally regarded as structural elements, that actually created and constitute the monument. Recognising that this was done in combination with materials placed *in* these structures I want to develop this argument using three relatively simple monuments, each an example of one of the three types of megalithic tomb that were current during the fourth millennium BC in Ireland. The three case studies are; Altdrumman portal tomb, Co. Tyrone (Ó Nualláin 1983, 102); Site 16 in the passage tomb complex at Knowth, Co. Meath (Eogan 1984, 109–32) and the Corracloona court tomb, Co. Leitrim (Kilbride Jones 1974).

Altdrumman portal tomb

Altdrumman, Co. Tyrone is a portal tomb situated on an undulating ridge about 300 m north of and overlooking a lake called Lough Macrory. The monument consists of a pair of matched portal stones 1.3 m in height and a backstone, all supporting a large capstone. Taken in isolation the monument resembles many other Irish portal tombs (see Ó Nualláin 1983), but what makes it striking and provides a different perspective is that it faces into a rock outcrop located only 3 m to the east. It is very clear that this outcrop was quarried to provide the structural elements of the stones of the monument. The orthostats and roof have literally been hewn from the outcrop. Viewed from the north and south the outcrop and monument form an integrated monumental feature (Figure 19.1). There was no need to add a cairn as the effect of monument and outcrop combined looks like a long cairn. Here an existing prominent landscape feature was transformed and this transformation provided a social arena, literally a place carved in and out of rock, for further activity. In this case the monument was added to the place.

Corracloona court tomb

This site which was excavated in 1953 (Kilbride Jones 1974) has had some prominence in the literature since its first discovery because of the so-called kennel-hole in the base of the door slab which closes the front of the chamber (de Valera and Ó Nualláin 1972, 58–59). The court is funnel-shaped and the chamber has an irregular rectangular shape. It is interesting that a quarried face of sandstone bedrock was used as a substitute orthostat on the inner northern side of the chamber and that the bedrock formed part of the floor of the chamber. Slabs of sandstone were also used to pave the court and a wall built across the front of the court, apparently to constrict access (Figure 19.2). Ronayne (1994, 71–3) has drawn attention to the interplay between architecture and landscape in the form and setting of Corracloona and it seems very likely that we are seeing a drawing in of the outcrop here into a narrative of ancestry and origins (e.g. Fowler 2004, 97). The different spaces provide arenas for different kinds of experience and contact with the past and the sacred, the hillslope immediately to the west from where you can look down on the monument, the court with its paving and deposits of flint artifacts and designed restriction of access with the wall across the front. The kennel-hole would also have restricted access but also allowed people to see and touch what was beyond, in the sacred space as defined by rock and built by people.

Figure 19.1. View of Altdrumman, Co. Tyrone portal tomb from the south.

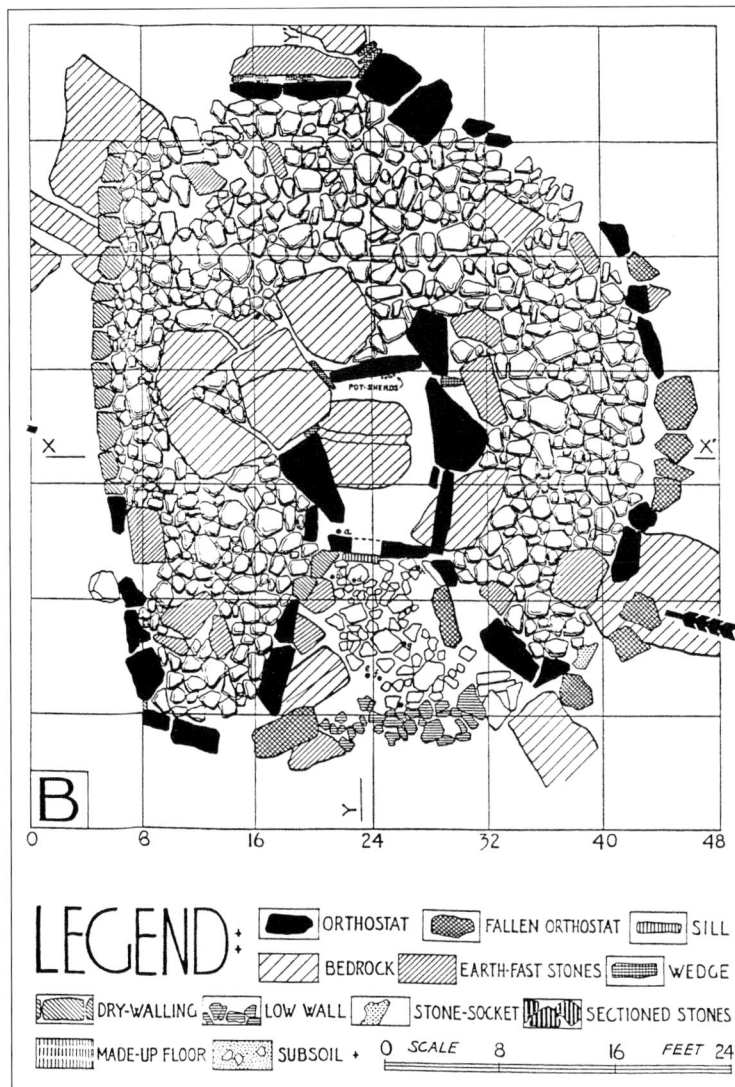

Figure 19.2. Plan of Corracloona, Co. Leitrim (after Kilbride Jones 1974).

De Valera and Ó Nualláin (1972, 59) expressed some skepticism about the site both on account of the unusual nature of the chamber and in particular the kennel-hole. However, looking more widely the concept of portholes or small gaps between orthostats to both facilitate and restrict access has been noted in Neolithic chambered tombs in Ireland and Britain (Fowler 2004, 99). Indeed bearing in mind artistic licence the destroyed façade of the court tomb at Annaghcloghmullin, Co. Armagh (Figure 19.3) seems to provide a striking example of a porthole effect (Borlase 1897). Darvill (2004, 51–2) has drawn attention to the juxtaposition and pairing of flat-topped and pointed stones in the entrances to long barrow chambers as having a sexual symbolism, but in relation to the particular focus of his discussion, the long barrows of the northeast of the Isle of Man, the pairing also creates the effect of a port-hole or funnel-hole, for example at Cashtal yn Ard (Darvill 2004, figure 6.4).

Knowth Site 16 passage tomb

This tomb forms part of the complex of small passage tombs clustered around the very large mound covering two passage tombs, Site 1, at Knowth (Eogan 1984; 1986; Eogan and Roche 1997). It is located immediately north of Site 1, predates Site 1 and was partially removed to facilitate the construction of the large mound. In turn there was then a deliberate re-adjustment of both monuments; a gap was left in the kerb of Site 1 on the western side of the mound of Site 16, the outer part of the passage of Site 16 was re-constructed to provide continued access to the chamber and the southern side of this outer passage was formed by one of the kerbstones of Site 1 (Figure 19.4).The structure consisted of a passage divided by sills leading to an end chamber which is trapezoidal in form. There was a cairn core outside and surrounding the chamber and beyond this mound material formed of local glacial till (redeposited

Figure 19.3. Annaghcloghmullin, Co. Armagh, view of the façade (after Borlase 1897).

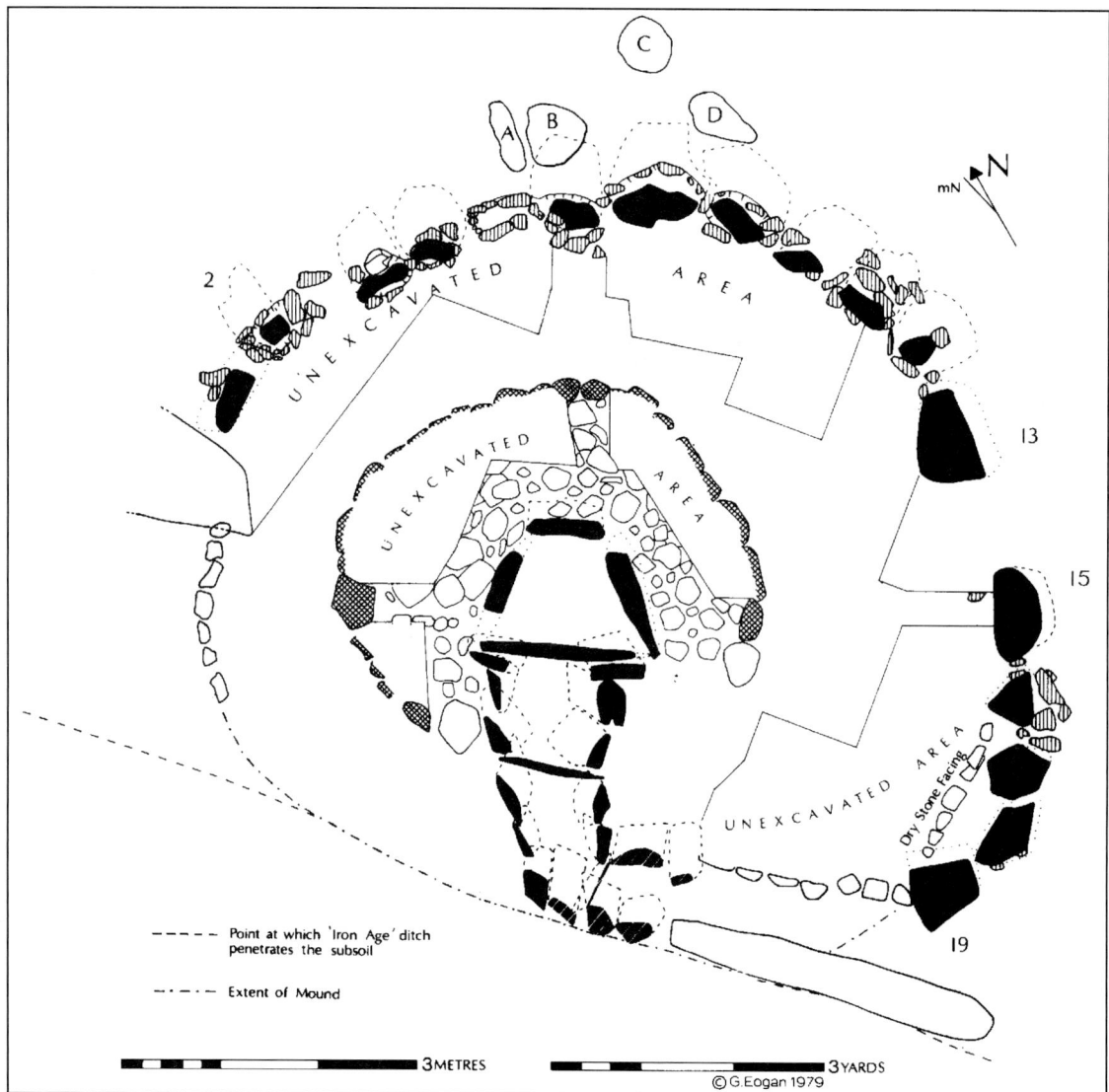

- - - - Point at which 'Iron Age' ditch penetrates the subsoil

- · - · - Extent of Mound

© G.Eogan 1979

Figure 19.4. Plan of Knowth Site 16, Co. Meath (after Eogan 1984).

boulder clay) out to the kerb that defined the edge of the monument. Deposits of cremated bone and objects occurred both in the chamber and the inner segment of the passage. There were five separate deposits, each consisting of a small number of adults and children, and at least sixteen individuals were identified.

All the stones of the passage and chamber are of greywhacke, a fine-grained sandstone while the kerbstones are of more varied composition and small rounded boulders are prominent in the stone settings within the mound and in the cairn core. Sourcing the greywhacke, which was the most important single stone used in the construction of the passage tombs in the Boyne Valley, is a current focus of research (Phillips *et al.* 2001; 2002). Here what is important is that the detail of the excavation stratigraphy and recording allows us to say is that the working of the stone and what we might dismiss as the working debitage was integral both to making the monument and to the actions that took place within it. For example, spalls from the working of the greywhacke provide support in the sockets of the orthostats. But the most significant interplay between structural stone and debitage is in the placement of the burial deposits (Figure 19.5). In the chamber there were

three cremation deposits. The primary deposit was placed on the old ground surface, spalls of greywhacke were placed around the edge of this to act as support for a slab which was placed on top. Eogan (1984, 115) argues that this primary deposition and the placing of the flag happened before the roof of the chamber was put in place. A second cremation deposit was placed on this flag and was covered by a paving of greywhacke spalls. This sequence is matched in the inner segment of the passage and the stratigraphic sequence suggested that a period of time elapsed between the placement of the first and second deposit. The excavator argues (Eogan 1984, 123) that the paving placed over the second deposit and forming the floor of the passage was only put in place after the the passage was remodelled, ie after the construction of Site 1. What is important here is that spalls of greywhacke are used to define this re-dedication and re-alignment of the monument. There was subseqently a third deposit placed in the chamber. Here then material that would be usually written off as mundane, a by-product of the working of the important stones is in fact integral to the central human actions within, and to the history of, the monument.

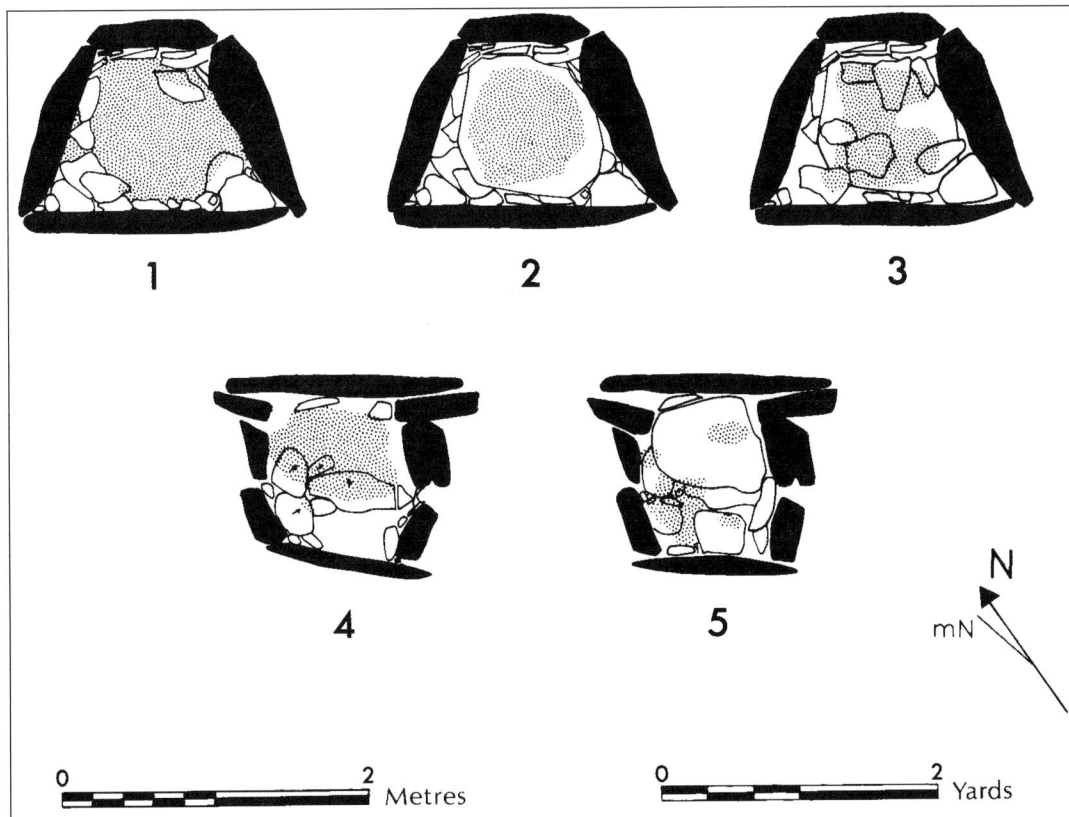

Figure 19.5. Detailed plan of phases of deposition in chamber area, Knowth Site 16 (after Eogan 1984).

Conclusion

In discussing the Maltese temples Tilley (2004, 89) observed that they mediated the landscape through architecture so that people could re-think themselves and their place in the world. Here I have argued that to understand how that mediation was effected and effective we could usefully combine approaches from the study of monuments, objects and practices and change our focus. It was the working and re-working of stone viewed as being imbued with symbolic power that made such places as megalithic monuments special. In Irish megalithic tombs as in the Maltese temples we see an interplay between respect for the materials that were being used and the places they came from with the deliberate shaping of stone to create monuments. We can also discern a similar concern with the distillation of ideas of access and remoteness, the human and the sacred, past and present, light and dark in both Irish tombs and Maltese temples, even if they had different religious foci; tombs for the dead, temples for the living. They also both capture the notion of what the transformation of stone in monuments is about; breaking it open by human action and in doing so creating new materialized arenas for human experience. The presence of port-holes in the Maltese temples (see discussion in Tilley 2004) and the analogous features in monuments in the Irish Sea area pointed to above exemplify the perceptual complexity of these arenas. It is increasingly recognised that the selection of stone was an important form of engagement with the natural and spiritual world (e.g. Bradley 2000; Cummings 2002) but we also need to focus now on issues such as the location of sources, quarrying and the way stone was worked, the linkages between what we term and differentiate as worked and unworked, structural and artifactual stone, the placement and deposition of stone. All contributed to the active creation and maintenance of relationships between individuals, the material world which they made and lived in and the ancestral past.

Acknowledgements

My thanks to Blaze O'Connor, Finola O'Carroll and Muiris O'Sullivan for their comments on an earlier draft of the paper, to Stephen Clarke and Margaret Ronoyne for information on Corracloona and to George Eogan for discussion of Knowth Site 16 and to the editors for their patience.

References

Borlase, W. C. 1897. *The Dolmens of Ireland*. 3 vols. London, Chapman and Hall.
Bradley, R. 2000. *An Archaeology of Natural Places*. London, Routledge.
Casey, E. S. 2001. Body, self and landscape: a geophilosophical inquiry into the place-world. In P. C. Adams, S. Hoelscher and K. E. Till (eds). *Textures of Place: exploring humanist geographies*. Minneapolis University of Minnesota, 403–25.
Cody, E. 2002. *Survey of the Megalithic Tombs of Ireland. Vol. VI. Co. Donegal*. Dublin, The Stationery Office.
Cooney, G. 1979. Some aspects of the siting of megalithic tombs in County Leitrim. *Journal of the Royal Society of Antiquaries of Ireland* 109, 74–91.
Cooney, G. 2000. *Landscapes of Neolithic Ireland*. London, Routledge.
Cooney, G. 2004. Neolithic worlds: islands in the Irish Sea. In V. Cummings and C. Fowler (eds). *The Neolithic of the Irish Sea: materiality and traditions of practice*. Oxford, Oxbow Books, 145–59.
Cooney, G. 2005. Stereo porphyry: quarrying and deposition on Lambay, Ireland. In P. Topping and M. Lynott (eds). *The Cultural Landscape of Prehistoric Mines*. Oxford, Oxbow Books, 14–29.
Cooney, G. 2006. Newgrange – a view from the platform. *Antiquity* 80, 697–710.
Cooney. G. and Mandal. S 1998. *The Irish Stone Axe Project. Monograph 1*. Dublin, Wordwell.
Craig, D. 1996. *Landmarks: an exploration of great rocks*. London, Pimlico.
Cummings, V. 2002. Between mountains and sea: a reconsideration of the monuments of south-west Scotland. *Proceedings of the Prehistoric Society* 68, 125–46.
Darvill, T. 2002. White on Blonde: quarts pebbles and the use of quartz at Neolithic monuments in the Isle of Man and beyond. In A. Jones and G. MacGregor (eds). *Colouring the Past*. Oxford: Berg, 73–91.
Darvill, T. 2004. Tales of the land, tales of the sea: people and presence in the Neolithic of Man and beyond. In V. Cummings and C. Fowler (eds). *The Neolithic of the Irish Sea: materiality and traditions of practice*. Oxford, Oxbow Books, 46–54.
DeMarrais, E. 2004. The Materialization of Culture. In DeMarrais, E, Gosden, C. and Renfrew, C. (eds). *Rethinking Materiality: the engagement of mind with the material world*. Cambridge, McDonald Institute Monographs, 11–22.
de Valera, R. and Ó Nualláin, S 1972. *Survey of the Megalithic Tombs of Ireland. Vol III. Cos Galway, Roscommon, Leitrim, Longford, Westmeath, Laoighis, Offaly, Kildare, Cavan*. Dublin, The Stationery Office.
Eogan, G. 1984. *Excavations at Knowth 1*. Dublin, The Royal Irish Academy.
Eogan, G. 1986. *Knowth and the Passage Tombs of Ireland*. London, Thames and Hudson.
Eogan, G. and Roche, H. 1997 *Excavations at Knowth 2*. Dublin, The Royal Irish Academy.
Fowler 2004. In touch with the past? Monuments, bodies and the sacred in the Manx Neolithic and beyond. In V. Cummings and C. Fowler (eds). *The Neolithic of the Irish Sea: materiality and traditions of practice*. Oxford, Oxbow Books, 91–102.
Ingold, T. 1993. The temporality of the landscape. *World Archaeology* 25, 152–74.
Insoll, T. 2004. *Archaeology, Ritual and Religion*. London, Routledge.
Kilbride Jones, H. E. 1974. The excavation of a cairn with kennel-

hole entrance at Corracloona, Co. Leitrim. *Proceedings of the Royal Irish Academy* 74 C, 171–82.

Lemonnier, P. 1993. Introduction. In P. Lemonnier (ed.). *Technological Choices: transformation in material cultures since the Neolithic*. London, Routledge, 1–35.

Luhrmann, T. 1997. Cults. In T. Barfield (ed.). *The Dictionary of Anthropology*. Oxford, Blackwell, 92–4.

OED 2003. *Oxford Dictionary of English*. 2nd edition. Oxford, Oxford University Press.

Ó Nualláin, S. 1983. Irish portal tombs: topography, siting and distribution. *Journal of the Royal Society of Antuquaries of Ireland* 113, 75–105.

Ó Ríordáin, S. P. and Daniel, G. 1964. *Newgrange and the Bend of the Boyne*. London, Thames and Hudson.

O'Sullivan, M. 1997. On the meaning of megalithic art. *Brigantium* 10, 23–35.

Phillips, A., Corcoran, M. and Eogan, G. 2001. Derivation of the Source Localities for the Kerb, Orthostat and Standing Stones of the Neolithic Passage Graves of the Boyne Valley, Co. Meath. Unpublished report for the Heritage Council.

Phillips, A., Corcoran, M. and Eogan, G. 2002. *Identification of the Source Area for Megaliths Used in the Construction of the Neolithic Passage Graves of the Boyne Valley, Co. Meath*. Unpublished report for The Heritage Council.

Phillips, A, Corcoran, M. and Eogan, G. 2002. *Derivation of the Source Localities for the Kerb, Orthostat and Standing Stones of the Neolithic Passage Graves of the Boyne Valley, Co. Meath*.

Unpublished report for The Heritage Council.

Renfrew, C. 1985. *The Archaeology of Cult*. London, Thames and Hudson.

Renfrew, C. 2004. Towards a Theory of Material Engagement. In DeMarrais, E, Gosden, C. and Renfrew, C. (eds). *Rethinking Materiality: the engagement of mind with the material world*. Cambridge, McDonald Institute Monographs, 23–31.

Robb, J. 2001. Island identies: ritual, travel and the creation of difference in Neolithic Malta. *European Journal of Archaeology* 4, 175–202.

Ronayne, M. 1994. *Located Practices: deposition, architecture and landscape: Irish court tombs*. Unpublished MA thesis. University College Cork.

Scarre, C. 2004. Displaying the Stones: the Materiality of 'Megalithic' monuments. In DeMarrais, E, Gosden, C. and Renfrew, C. (eds). *Rethinking Materiality: the engagement of mind with the material world*. Cambridge, McDonald Institute Monographs, 141–52.

Tilley, C. 2004. *The Materiality of Stone: explorations in landscape phenomenology*. Oxford, Berg.

Trump, D. H. 2000. *Malta: an archaeological guide*. 3rd edition. Valletta, Progress Press

Trump, D. H. 2004. *Malta: prehistory and temples*. 2nd edition. Valletta, Midsea Books/Heritage Malta.

Walsh, D. 2004. *Oileáin: a Guide to the Irish Islands*. Bangor, Pesda Press.

Chapter 20

TOWARDS THE WITHIN:
STONEHENGE AND ITS PURPOSE

Timothy Darvill

Stonehenge on the southern side of Salisbury Plain in central-southern England has been admired, described, and puzzled over many times. It stands as an icon for prehistoric times and a challenge for archaeological interpretation as it has never satisfactorily been explained or understood. Much attention has been directed to when, how, and by whom it was built, and with modest success, but rarely are the questions of why it was built and continually refurbished addressed. Richard Atkinson, rather despairingly once commented that 'to all these questions beginning 'Why?' there is one short, simple and perfectly correct answer: we do not know, and we shall probably never know' (1979, 168), but that should not be cause to give up trying. Mike Parker Pearson's proposal, based on a formal analogy developed through dialogue with his Malagasy colleague Ramilisonina, posits that the stones were monuments to the ancestral dead (Parker Pearson and Ramilisonina 1998a). In its stripped-back form it is a view that resonates with ideas of stone as an eternal material explored at around the same time by Barbara Bender (1998, 76), Alasdair Whittle (1997, 152), and others (Pollard and Gillings 1998, 158–9). Nor is so different from Aubrey Burl's portrayal of a 'mortuary-house for the mighty dead' (1987, 172) or indeed Geoffrey of Monmouth's view back in the fourteenth century AD that Stonehenge was a memorial to British kings lost in battle against the Saxons (Monmouth 1966, 195; Parker Pearson and Ramilisonina 1998a, 324). At a deeper level, Parker Pearson's model involves accepting a set of complex metaphorical associations in which life and death, wood and stone, summer and winter, and the rising and setting of the sun stand in opposition to each other. Stonehenge was a ceremonial circle built for the exclusive use of the ancestors with ceremonies of the living population focused around Durrington Walls. The Avon and the Stonehenge Avenue both physically and metaphorically served to link the domain of the living with the domain of the ancestors (Parker Pearson and Ramilisonina 1998a, figure 7).

There is much in this model to commend it, despite reservations over the use of ethnographic analogy (Barrett and Fewster 1998; Whittle 1998; and see Parker Pearson and Ramilisonina 1998b) and some obvious difficulties with matching up elements of the archaeological record which in part at least will be resolved through the work of the Stonehenge Riverside Project currently unfolding through the combined research power of staff from five university departments working together (Parker Pearson *et al.* 2006). In this paper, however, I would like to suggest a different approach. Instead of simply taking the monument as it is visible today in its decayed state (Figure 20.1), as others have done, I would like to follow the advice of the aptly named Australian house-trance band Dead Can Dance, and go '*Towards the Within*' by looking deeper into Stonehenge taking more account of its construction sequence, materials, arrangement, structure, associations, and related folklore in a way that relates architecture and form to ritual and meaning.

The early years

Prior to about 2600 BC, Stonehenge was a bog-standard henge, one of about 60 or so scattered at intervals across the British Isles. Its initial construction about 2950 BC places it towards the beginning of the tradition of building such things; an example of what Jan Harding (2003, 13) has usefully termed Formative Henges with the ditch set around the outside a modest bank. The causewayed construction of the ditch and its overall size invites comparisons with Flagstones, Dorset (Woodward 1988) and other formative henges such as Llandegai A, Gwynedd (Lynch and Musson 2001, 36–48) and Castell Bryn-Gwyn, Anglesey (Wainwright 1962). The ditch fills that include structured deposits near segment terminals, the presence of material already old when deposited, and episodes of back-filling and re-digging serves to support Isobel Smith's suggestion that henges developed out of the traditions

Figure 20.1. Stonehenge from the northeast looking southwestwards. (Photograph by Timothy Darvill)

formerly represented by causewayed enclosures (Smith 1966, 474). Associations with Grooved Ware pottery, postholes suggesting timber settings in the interior, the ring of 56 Aubrey Holes that once supported timber uprights along the inner edge of the bank, the deposition of human burials as disarticulated remains or cremations (Cleal *et al.* 1995, 451–61), and perhaps even the presence of a few stone pillars (e.g. the Station Stones forming a rectangular four-poster and Stone 95 (Slaughter Stone) and Stone D near the NE entrance forming a portal setting), are all entirely consistent with the construction and use of henge monuments across Britain, and have been well-documented by Aubrey Burl (1969, 4–10).

The first big break

What first distinguishes Stonehenge from other henges is the construction of the so-called 'Double Bluestone Circle' sometime in the 27th or 26th centuries BC, Phase 3i in conventional construction sequence for the site (Cleal *et al.* 1995, 169–88). Other henges had their stone circles, as for example at Avebury, Wiltshire, Arbor Low, Derbyshire, and Ring of Brodgar on Mainland Orkney, and of course many perfectly good stone circles were built in places where no henge had been established. But whereas most of these sites used stones quarried from within 10 km or so, at Stonehenge the pillars comprised blocks of dolerite, rhyolite, and volcanic ash (collectively referred to as

'bluestones') brought from the Preseli Hills some 250 km away to the west. Beaker pottery is closely associated with these works at Stonehenge, and as elsewhere in Europe the mid third millennium BC also sees a growing interest in solar alignments, especially the rising and setting positions at the summer and winter solstices, which are often embedded in the very structure of monuments. By this time the earlier ditch was substantially filled and would have been visible as a shallow depression flanking a fairly denuded bank. Changes may have been made to the alignment of the northeast-facing entrance and an embanked Avenue added to join the earthwork enclosure with Stonehenge Bottom which in this period may have contained a springhead or small stream. There is ambiguity as to whether the Avenue continued eastwards and then southwards to join the Avon at this stage (see Darvill 2006, 158–61). There is no doubt, however, that the orientation of the Avenue in is western part fixes into the landscape an alignment northeastwards with the rising mid-summer sun over Sidbury Hill beyond Larkhill and an alignment southwestwards with the setting mid-winter sun over Wilsford Down very near to the position of the Wilsford Shaft.

Roughly in the centre of the earlier earthwork monument was the Double Bluestone Circle, about 26 m in external diameter with an elaborated entrance opening to the northeast (Figure 20.2). This important structure is rather poorly known through excavated pairs of stone sockets (the

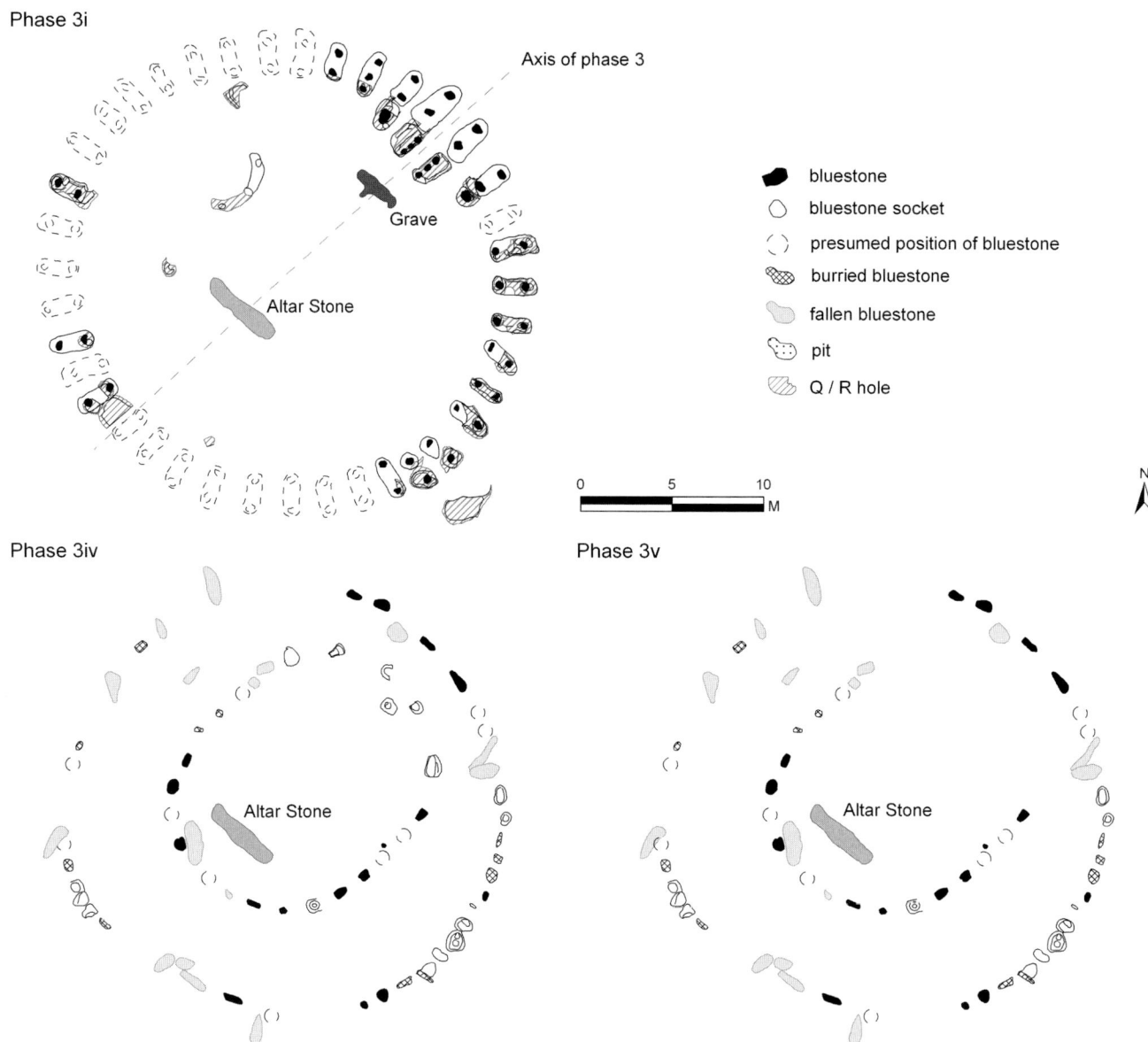

Figure 20.2. Phase plans showing the arrangement if bluestones during successive re-modellings between c.2600 and 2200 BC (Drawing created by Vanessa Constant after Cleal et al. 1995, figures 80, 81,116, and 117)

Q and R holes) and is sometimes reconstructed as a partial ring, semi-circle, oval, or horseshoe open to the west. Certainly it is well represented in its eastern sector where its form is convincing, although the western half is more problematic as excavations here have been less extensive and later disturbances of greater impact. The paired sockets in cutting C52 made by Richard Atkinson and others in 1958 lie in an undisturbed area and support fully the circular form of the Double Bluestone Circle predicted some years before (Atkinson 1956, 46–50). Assuming pairs for stones around the full circumference and a doubling of the circuit at the entrance then about 80 pillars are involved.

They are known to be 'bluestones' on the basis of fragments and stumps left in some of the sockets in which they stood before being dismantled around 2400 BC when the site was extensively remodelled. It is assumed that these same stones were re-used during the remodelling and reappear again in Phase 3.iv–v; certainly the number is about right.

Apart from aspects of its basic plan, very little is known about the Phase 3.i Double Bluestone circle. The pillars may or may not have been graded in height around the circumference, and there may have been some patterning to the way different lithologies were used. There are hints of architectural sophistication as mortise holes are present in at least two blocks used in the Phase 3.iv structure (Stones 36 and 150) suggesting the presence of trilithons as part of the Double Bluestone Circle (perhaps flanking the entrance?) or free-standing within it. A further five bluestones in the Phase 3.iv structure display traces of working that that relates to some earlier arrangement which may plausibly be considered the Phase 3.i Double Bluestone Circle.

Ever increasing circles

Never still for long, the central stone setting at Stonehenge was remodelled in what might be best seen as a continuous project involving refurbishments and rearrangements over the centuries following 2300 BC. Local sarsen stones (at least two types) were widely used for the larger components while stones from more distant sources included sandstone (at least two types, one perhaps originally part of the Phase 3.i structure), limestone, and of course the 80 or so 'bluestone' pillars comprising spotted dolerites, unspotted dolerites, rhyolites, and tuffs. Most significant is the fact the bluestones were retained and again set up in Phases 3.iv-v as two concentric rings, albeit more widely spaced than in Phase 3.i, with the five great trilithons set between the two circuits. The central axis on the summer and winter solstice was retained (Figure 20.2).

Geological studies of the extant bluestones (c. 40 out of the original 80 or so) serve to emphasis the heterogeneity of the group. H. H. Thomas recognized this in his seminal account of the stones which securely linked them to outcrops in the Preseli Hills (1923). And further work by a team based in the Open University using chemical analysis has tightened the identifications and provided links to a series of specific outcrops over an area of several square kilometres centred on Carn Menyn which is considered the most likely source for one of the most distinctive kind of bluestone, the spotted dolerite that was also used for making axes and shafthole implements found scattered widely across southern Britain (Petrological Group XXIII; Thorpe et al. 1991; Williams-Thorpe et al. 2004; 2006). The OU work was intended to substantiate the view that glacial action was responsible for the movement of the stones from southwest Wales to Salisbury Plain (Williams-Thorpe et al. 1997), a view that has been widely discredited by geologists, geomorphologists, and glaciologists (Green 1997; Scourse 1997; Castleden 2001). In fact when the results from the meticulous studies by the OU are re-examined within a more distinctively archaeological analysis a wholly different interpretation emerges.

The outer ring of c. 40 bluestones, referred to as the Bluestone Circle, comprises mainly unfashioned blocks (Figure 20.3a) of stone from a wide range of sources around the main Preseli ridge: rhyolites, tuffs and ashy slates from the Fishguard Volcanic Group from the north side, rhyolites and tuffs from the Sealyham Volcanic Group on the south, and various spotted and unspotted dolerites from intrusive dykes forming the main ridge (see Evans 1945 and Bevins et al. 1989 for details of the outcrops). The inner setting started 95 an oval setting of c. 25 stones but is later modified to form a horseshoe through the removal of 6 stones in the northeast sector perhaps to allow easier access to the central area (Figure 20.2). In contrast to the Bluestone Circle, all the stones of the Bluestone Oval / Bluestone Horseshoe are spotted dolerite whose most likely source lies on the central Preseli ridge at Carn Menyn and/or Carn Goedog (Thorpe et al. 1991). The blocks themselves are shaped (Figure 20.3b), graded in height with the tallest in the southwest sector, and in some cases have the slightly trapezoidal outline seen also in stone axes made of the same material. Indeed the axe may be a significant element in the understanding of this monument as miniature axes and soft chalk axes are known from the area (Annable and Simpson 1964, items 18 and 20) and what appear to be copper or bronze axes of forms circulating in the later third millennium BC form the dominant motif of the rock art visible on stones 3, 4, 5, and 53 (Cleal et al. 1990, 30–4).

Comparing the disposition of the stones in Phases 3.iv-v at Stonehenge with the distribution of source outcrops in the eastern Preselis there is a remarkable correspondence between the actual landscape and the constructed monument that in a way forms a microcosm of the wider world (Figure 20.4). Carn Menyn lies in the centre with its outcrops of columnar spotted dolerite, around about are the outcrops of other dolerites, rhyolites, and tuffs. Below Carn Menyn are the headwaters of the Western Cleddau flowing south to join the Bristol Channel at Milford Haven to form the first leg of a waterbourne journey that many see as the route by which the bluestones were transported to Stonehenge, the final part of which involves being rafted along the Avon and portage across the downs (perhaps even along the Avenue) to the site (Atkinson 1979, 105–16).

Many authors have noted that the scientific evidence linking the Stonehenge Bluestones with a source outcrop in the Preseli Hills of west Wales resonates well with the oral traditions and folklore still circulating in the early fourteenth century AD that must have inspired Geoffrey of Monmouth's account of Stonehenge told through the words and deeds of King Auralius and the wizard / prophet Merlin (Piggott 1941; but see Burl 1985 for contrary view). However, the link between the landscape of the bluestone source (considered to be in Ireland by Geoffrey of Monmouth) and the form of the monument is another peculiarity of the story that now appears to find archaeological support. When first discussing the proposed monument Merlin informs Aurelius that if the stones 'are placed in position around the site, in the way in which they are erected over there, they will stand for ever' (Monmouth

Figure 20.3. Bluestones at Stonehenge (Phase 3.v).
A. (above) Stone 46 in the outer Bluestone Circle.
B. (right) Stone 61 in the inner Bluestone Horseshoe.
(Photographs by Timothy Darvill)

1966, 196). And later, when Merlin is actually building the monument, we read that he [Merlin] 'obeyed the King's orders and put the stones up in a circle round the sepulchre, in exactly the same way as they had been arranged on Mount Killaraus' (Monmouth 1966, 198).

Looked at in this way the Bluestones take on a new significance as the central theme of the Stonehenge story and one might argue that they are central to the monument's meaning and use over several centuries. Ethnography helps here. Tim Insoll's idea, based on fieldwork amongst Tallensi communities in northern Ghana, of shrines being 'franchised' through the introduction of stones from a distant source is especially relevant (Insoll 2006). Elaborating shrines in this way gave them power and meaning, meeting local demands, and also setting up a centre whose fame and reputation spread out to provide a draw to pilgrims and little economic benefit to the host population. In this case the reason for moving rocks probably lay in the importance ascribed to rock as a direct product of the Earth within Tallensi cosmologies. What might be the reason for the third millennium BC franchising of Stonehenge?

One line of thinking that has perhaps been overlooked again takes as its cue the writings of Geoffrey of Monmouth. When Aurelius bursts out laughing at the idea of bringing stones from a far-distant land Merlin is quite plain in his retort: 'try not to laugh in a foolish way, your Majesty'. 'What I am suggesting has nothing ludicrous about it. These stones are connected with certain secret religious rites and they have various properties which are medicinally important. Many years ago the Giants transported them from the remotest confines of Africa and set them up in Ireland at a time when they inhabited the country. Their plan was that, whenever they felt ill, baths should be prepared at the foot of the stones; for they used to pour water over them and to run this water into baths in which their sick were cured. What is more, they mixed the water with herbal concoctions and so healed their wounds. There is not a single stone amongst them which hasn't some medicinal virtue' (Monmouth 1966, 196).

A strong belief in the curative powers of the stones continued into post-medieval times (Grinsell 1975, 7–8). William Stukeley writing in the mid eighteenth century laments the destruction of the stones by 'the unaccountable

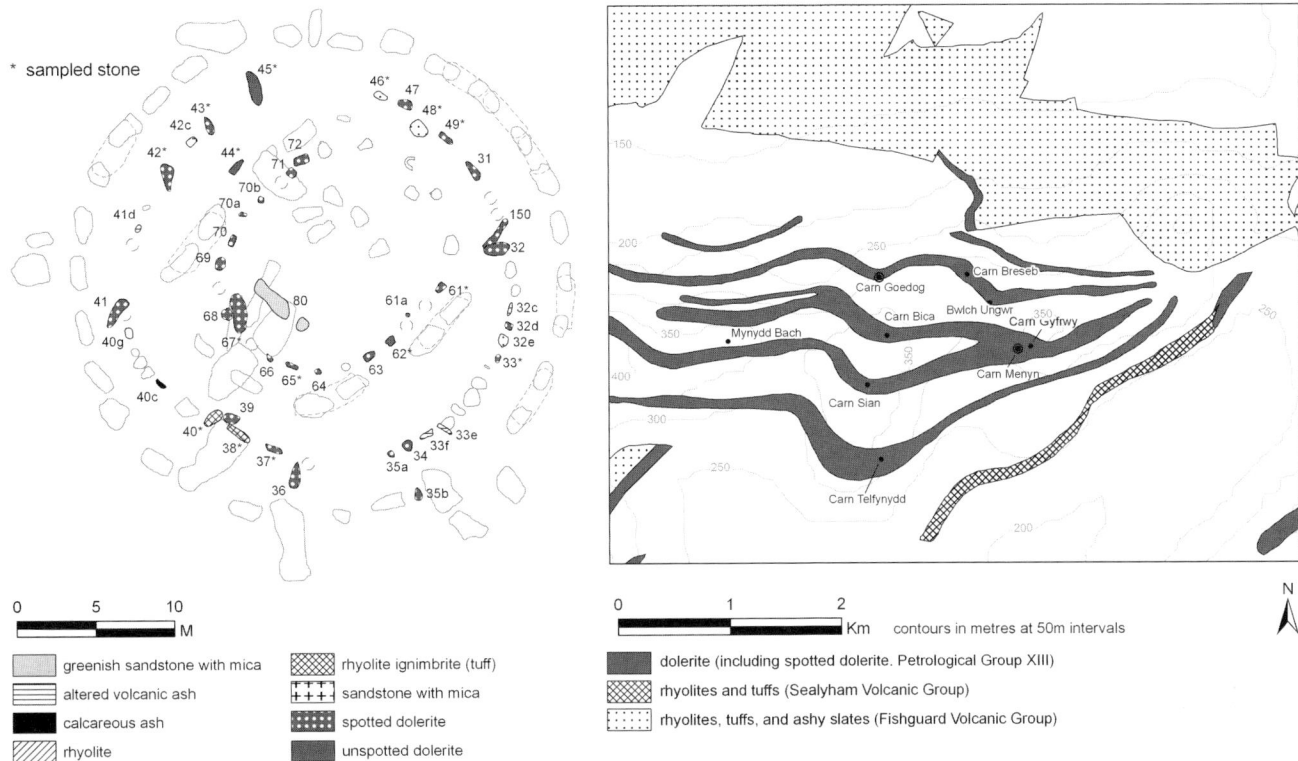

Figure 20.4. Arrangement of the bluestones in Phase 3.v at Stonehenge (left) and principal rock outcrops in the eastern Preselis (right). (Drawing created by Vanessa Constant after Darvill 2006, figure 50)

folly of mankind, in breaking pieces off with great hammers. This detestable practice arose from the silly notion of the stones being factitious' (1740, 5). There are late eighteenth century pictures of people hammering bits off a fallen Bluestone (Chippindale 2004, figure 47) and it is a powerful tradition and one that is an odd thing to invent. So do other strands of evidence support a similar position?

To the Preselis and back

One possibility is to consider the archaeological record of the area from which the stones originally came: north Pembrokeshire. Work here by Geoff Wainwright and I to provide a secure archaeological context for the source of the Bluestones in the eastern Preselis has revealed a wealth of evidence in an area where surprisingly little archaeological work had previously taken place (Drewett 1983; 1984; 1985; Darvill and Wainwright 2002a). What appears to be a causewayed enclosure at Banc Du 8.5 km west of Carn Menyn was built in the mid fourth millennium but was seemingly reoccupied in the later third millennium BC at just the time that the Bluestone trail was at its most active (Darvill *et al.* 2005, 22–3). Along the south side of the Preselis there are four stone circles (Darvill and

Wainwright 2003a; Darvill *et al.* 2003) and an extensive ceremonial complex at Glandy Cross (Kirk and Williams 2000; Darvill and Wainwright 2002b, 23–6). Pairs of standing stones seem to lie adjacent to routes leading onto the uplands as if they were symbolic gateways between adjacent worlds (Darvill *et al.* 2003, 3–4), and rock art panels occur in broadly similar locations as if signing the land (Darvill and Wainwright 2003b). An oval setting of spotted dolerite pillars within sight of Carn Menyn provides a near perfect match in its plan and orientation for the central oval setting in Phase 3.iv at Stonehenge (Darvill 2006, figure 51). Broken and abandoned pillar-stones lie scattered around the Carn Meini outcrops (Darvill *et al.* 2005, 20) while a stone wall about 1m thick links natural rock outcrops across the neck of a promontory forming the highest part of Carn Menyn enclosing a space from which stones have certainly been removed for use elsewhere (Darvill *et al.* 2004, 18). Most unusual, however, are what have been called 'enhanced springheads' where natural springs issuing from the living rock have been elaborated with the construction of pools. Two adjacent to Carn Meini have round cairns built on the up-slope side and are associated with panels of rock art. One of them, Ffynnon Beswch (Figure 20.5) on the east side of Carn Siân still runs and is recognized as a healing spring (Darvill *et al.*

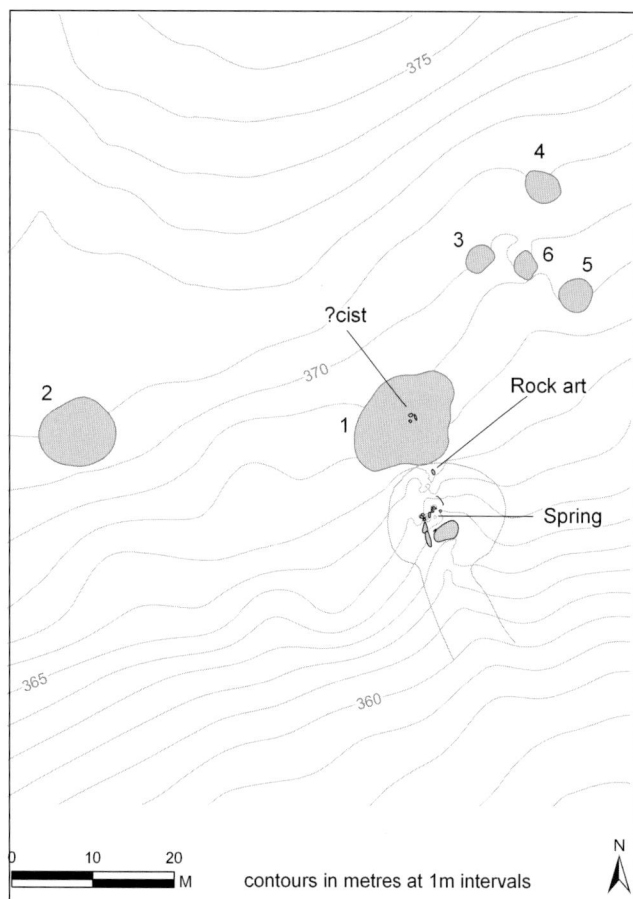

Figure 20.5. Plan of the enhanced springhead near Ffynnon Beswch. Cairns numbered 1 to 6. (Drawing created by Vanessa Constant after Darvill et al. 2004, figure 4)

2004, 106–7). Indeed, Frances Jones has shown that Pembrokeshire has the greatest concentration of sacred wells/springs in Wales, that many are associated with megalithic monuments, and that many are considered to have curative powers (Jones 1992). From the perspective of the source area, rocks franchised with curative powers is a strong possibility. Is there anything from the third and second millennia BC in the Stonehenge landscape that might support such an idea?

Chips of what appears to be bluestone have been found at other sites in the vicinity of Stonehenge, mainly small pieces fist-sized or less. Some may be debris from shaping the dolerites, rhyolites and tuffs during construction works, some might be fragments broken off the monument in prehistoric or later times. J. F. S. Stone records the existence of a scatter of what he calls Bluestone fragments near the western end of the Stonehenge Cursus (1948, figure 4), but fieldwalking during the Stonehenge Environs Survey in 1982–4 revealed remarkably little additional evidence here or elsewhere (Richards 1990, 25) and there is always the

possibility that some of Stone's finds derived from ballast or construction material associated with the military railway line that ran from Ratfyn Junction through Fargo Plantation to Druids Lodge in the period 1914–28 (RCHM 1979, xxiii–iv; Darvill 2006, 271).

Some bluestone fragments have a more secure context. Three round barrows excavated by William Cunnington and Richard Colt Hoare in the early nineteenth century (Winterbourne Stoke 28; Amesbury 4; and Amesbury 45) certainly contained pieces of bluestone which Engleheart (1932) has suggested may derive from the primary burials (but cf. Stone 1948, 16). More recently, Paul Ashbee's excavation at Amesbury 51 south of the Cursus adds a more secure case. Here under a round barrow with a causewayed ditch was an unusual central grave in the form of a 1.5 m deep rectangular shaft into which a timber-framed structure had been built. The primary burial was that of an adult male who had undergone surgery through trephination. Beaker pottery was associated with this burial and two or three others later added to the wooden chamber. In the fill of the grave was a piece of rhyolite, with six further pieces in secondary contexts (Ashbee 1978, 24). Three pieces of worked bluestone, two of spotted dolerite and one of rhyolite, were also present in the fill of the mid third millennium BC beaker grave dug into the ditch at Stonehenge. Here excavations by John Evans revealed that the adult male interment had been shot in the chest by three arrows, one of which proved fatal (Evans 1984). While often regarded as a sacrificial killing or execution, it is equally possible that this badly wounded individual was brought to Stonehenge in the hope aiding recovery.

East of the Avon finds of bluestone associated with burials are less common, but excavations at Amesbury 71 by Patricia Christie in 1961 revealed a secondary burial cut into the ditch and covered by a low flint cairn that comprised the remains of an adult male aged 20–30 years who had not only had surgery through trephination but had survived long enough for the bone to re-grow around the opening (Christie 1967). And at Boscombe Down the well-publicised find known as the Amesbury Archer was the richly furnished burial of an adult male aged about 35–45 years who had seemingly travelled to Wessex from Alpine Europe but who had suffered a traumatic injury to his left knee with the result that his left leg became wasted as he walked with pronounced limp carrying his weight on his right leg (Fitzpatrick 2003, 148). Could this man, perhaps with what appears to be his son who was buried in an adjacent grave, have come to Wessex as pilgrims hoping for a miraculous cure and for some reason spent the rest of their days on Salisbury Plain?

Further research is needed on the burials from the Stonehenge landscape to access their overall state of health and the incidence of debilitating disease in as much as such ailments leave skeletal traces. However, it is important to note here that the concentration of barrows around Stonehenge is probably one of the greatest in Europe. More than a 1000 examples are known, mainly of the later third and early second millennium. Typically each contains between five and ten burials so that a dead population of between 5000 and 10,000 men, women, and children might be expected. Insufficient settlements of the period are known in the vicinity to account for such a host, and thus a steady influx of visitors from beyond the region might be suspected. Alternatively, it might have become traditional for people to be brought back to this sacred area for burial. Rather important here is the fact that apart from the beaker burial already noted there are no known burials at Stonehenge in the period between *c.* 2600 and 1700 BC when barrow-building was at its height. Moreover, as several authorities have noted, the distribution of the main barrow groups seems to form two or three roughly concentric rings around Stonehenge with very few barrows in the immediate vicinity of the site. The majority occupy the ridges encircling the bowl-shaped landscape in which Stonehenge sits as if the intention was that those buried in the barrows could spend eternity overlooking the central sacred site.

Of Bluestone and sarsen

If, as I have proposed here, the Bluestones provided the main focus for the development of Stonehenge what about the Sarsen elements: the five central trilithons and the outer sarsen circle? Elsewhere (Darvill 2006, 144–5) I have suggested that the five trilithons could usefully be seen as deities presiding over the central area and the events that took place there. Taking the proposals set out by Kristian Kristiansen and Thomas Larsson (2005) for the prevalence during the third millennium BC of deities who were twins – often portrayed as the 'divine twins' – I have suggested that perhaps the central trilithon is a representation of twin gods later known in the Greco-Roman pantheon as Apollo and Artemis, god and goddess of the sun and moon respectively with Apollo also the god of healing and prophecy. Mainly resident in his traditional home at Delphi in Greece he is often believed to have spent the three months of the year either side of the winter solstice in his homeland, the land of the Hyperborians which is usually considered to be the British Isles (Salt and Boutsikas 2005, 570). Oversight of the shrine at Stonehenge by such a powerful deity for perhaps a quarter of the year has interesting resonance with the proposed winter-time use of Durrington Walls (Albarella and Serjeantson 2002; Albarella and Payne 2005) and the idea that perhaps pilgrims to Stonehenge travelled by way of the Avon and the Avenue on auspicious occasions.

No-one would wish to miss an appointment with the almighty and so some kind of time-indicating device might be expected in the structure of Stonehenge itself. The solstical alignments may be a component of such a system, but also notable is the outer sarsen circle. Although there were 30 uprights, Stone 11 in the southeast sector is actually half-size, shorter and slightly narrower than the rest. How it supported the adjoining lintels above is uncertain, if it ever did, but the number 29.5 is interesting because, as Gerald Hawkins has noted, the average length in solar days of a lunar month measured between full moons is 29.53 (1973, 183). The stones of the outer circle could quiet simply have been the physical representation of a calendar, one for each day of the month, that allowed quick and easy reckoning of when the gods were in residence and for how long.

Conclusions

Investigating the working and use of prehistoric cult sites is of course fraught with difficulties as by definition the work is mainly concerned with the intangible. By focusing on context, sequence, and association some progress can be made especially, I would suggest, by working at several scales at the same time. If there is such a thing as a 'secret' of Stonehenge, as so many writers insist, then revealing it involves patterns not just in the things that can be seen at the site itself but in the meanings and roles that all the various components might have in a working scheme. I do not believe that Stonehenge was a place for the dead in its later stages, rather I think it was a place where worlds collided and that what we see is a technology to mediate the desires of the mortals with the perceived powers of the gods.

Acknowledgements

Thanks to Geoff Wainwright for so many fruitful discussions about Stonehenge and its purpose, to Yvette Staelens for help preparing this paper, and to Vanessa Constant for preparing the illustrations.

References

Albarella, U. and Payne, S. 2005. Neolithic pigs from Durrington Walls, Wiltshire, England: a biometrical database. *Journal of Archaeological Science* 32, 589–99.

Albarella, U. and Serjeantson, D. 2002. A passion for pork: meat consumption at the British late Neolithic site of Durrington Walls. In P. Miracle and N. Milner (eds). *Consuming passions and patterns of consumption.* Cambridge, McDonald Institute for Archaeological Research, 33–49.

Annable, F. K. and Simpson, D. D. A. 1964. *Guide catalogue of the Neolithic and Bronze Age collections in Devizes Museum.* Devizes, Wiltshire Archaeological and Natural History Society.

Ashbee, P. 1978. Amesbury Barrow 51: Excavations 1960. *Wiltshire Archaeological and Natural History Magazine* 70/71 (1975/76), 1–60.

Atkinson, R. J. C. 1956. *Stonehenge*. London, Hamish Hamilton.

Atkinson, R. J. C. 1979. *Stonehenge* (Revised edition). Harmondsworth, Penguin.

Barrett, J. and Fewster, K. 1998. Stonehenge: *is* the medium the message. *Antiquity* 72, 847–2.

Bender, B. 1998. *Stonehenge: Making spaces*. Oxford, Berg.

Bevins, R. E., Lees, G. J. and Roach, R. A. 1989. Ordovician intrusions of the Strumble Head – Mynydd Preseli region, Wales: lateral extensions of the Fishguard volcanic complex. *Journal of the Geological Society of London* 146, 113–23.

Burl, H. A. W. 1969. Henges: internal features and regional groups. *Archaeological Journal* 126, 1–28.

Burl, A. 1985. Geoffrey of Monmouth and the Stonehenge bluestones. *Wiltshire Archaeological and Natural History Magazine* 79, 178–83.

Burl, H. A. W. 1987. *The Stonehenge People*. London, Dent.

Castleden, R. 2001. The epic of the Stonehenge bluestones: were they moved by ice, or by people? *3rd Stone* 39, 12–25.

Chippindale, C. 2004. *Stonehenge Complete* (new and expanded edition). London, Thames and Hudson.

Christie, P. M. 1967. A barrow cemetery of the second millennium BC in Wiltshire, England. *Proceedings of the Prehistoric Society* 33, 336–66.

Cleal, R., Walker, K. E. and Montague, R. 1995. *Stonehenge in its landscape. Twentieth-century excavations*. London, English Heritage Archaeological Report 10.

Darvill, T. 2006. *Stonehenge: the biography of a landscape*. Stroud, Tempus.

Darvill, T., Morgan Evans, D. and Wainwright, G. 2003. Strumble-Preseli Ancient Communities and Environment Study (SPACES): Second report 2003. *Archaeology in Wales* 43, 3–12.

Darvill, T., Morgan Evans, D. and Wainwright, G. 2004. Strumble-Preseli Ancient Communities and Environment Study (SPACES): Third report 2004. *Archaeology in Wales* 44, 104–8.

Darvill, T., Morgan Evans, D., Fyfe, R. and Wainwright, G. 2005. Strumble-Preseli Ancient Communities and Environment Study (SPACES): Fourth report 2005. *Archaeology in Wales* 45, 17–24.

Darvill, T. and Wainwright, G. 2002a. SPACES – exploring Neolithic landscapes in the Strumble-Preseli area of southwest Wales. *Antiquity* 76, 623–4.

Darvill, T. and Wainwright, G. 2002b. Strumble-Preseli Ancient Communities and Environment Study (SPACES): First Report 2002. *Archaeology in Wales* 42, 17–28.

Darvill, T. and Wainwright, G. 2003a. Stone circles, oval settings and henges in southwest Wales and beyond. *Antiquaries Journal* 83, 9–45.

Darvill, T. and Wainwright, G. 2003b. A cup-marked stone from Dan-y-Garn, Mynachlog Ddu, Pembrokeshire, and the prehistoric rock art from Wales. *Proceedings of the Prehistoric Society* 69, 253–64.

Drewett, P. 1983. *Mynydd Preseli 1983. First interim report*. London (Institute of Archaeology, University of London, limited circulation typescript report).

Drewett, P. 1984. *Mynydd Preseli 1984. Second interim report*. London (Institute of Archaeology, University of London, limited circulation typescript report).

Drewett, P. 1985. *Mynydd Preseli 1985. Third interim report*. London (Institute of Archaeology, University of London, limited circulation typescript report).

Engleheart, G. 1932. The age of Stonehenge: a criterion. *Antiquaries Journal* 12, 17–23.

Evans, J. G. 1984. Stonehenge – The environment in the Late Neolithic and Early Bronze Age and a Beaker-age burial. *Wiltshire Archaeological and Natural History Magazine* 78 (1983), 7–30.

Evans, W. D. 1945. The geology of the Prescelly Hills, North Pembrokeshire. *Quarterly Journal of the Geological Society of London* 64, 273–96.

Fitzpatrick, A. P. 2003. The Amesbury Archer. *Current Archaeology* 16.4 (no. 184), 146–52.

Green, C. P. 1997. The provenance of rocks used in the construction of Stonehenge. In B. Cunliffe and C. Renfrew (eds). *Science and Stonehenge* (Proceedings of the British Academy 92). Oxford, The British Academy, 257–70.

Grinsell, L. V. 1975. *Legendary history and folklore of Stonehenge*. St Peter Port: Toucan Press.

Harding, J. 2003. *Henge Monuments of the British Isles*. Stroud, Tempus.

Hawkins, G. S. 1966. *Stonehenge decoded*. London, Souvenir Press.

Insoll, T. 2006. Shrine franchising and the Neolithic in the British Isles: some observations based upon the Tallensi, Northern Ghana. *Cambridge Archaeological Journal* 16.2, 223–238.

Jones, F. 1992. *The Holy Wells of Wales*. Cardiff, University of Wales Press.

Kirk, T. and Williams, G. 2000. Glandy Cross: a later prehistoric monument complex in Carmarthenshire, Wales. *Proceedings of the Prehistoric Society* 66, 257–96.

Kristiansen, K. and Larsson, T. 2005. *The rise of Bronze Age society*. Cambridge, Cambridge University Press.

Lynch, F. and Musson, C. 2001. A prehistoric and early medieval complex at Llandegai, near Bangor, North Wales. *Archaeologia Cambrensis* 130, 17–142.

Monmouth, G. (Trans. L Thorpe). 1966. *Geoffrey of Monmouth. The history of the Kings of Britain*. Harmondsworth, Penguin.

Parker Pearson, M., Pollard, J., Richards, C., Thomas, J., Tilley., Welham, K. and Albarella, U. 2006. Materializing Stonehenge. The Stonehenge Riverside Project and new discoveries. *Journal of Material Culture* 11(1/2), 227–61.

Parker Pearson, M. and Ramilisonina. 1998a. Stonehenge for the ancestors: the stones pass on the message. *Antiquity* 72, 308–26.

Parker Pearson, M. and Ramilisonina. 1998b. Stonehenge for the ancestors: part two. *Antiquity* 72, 355–6.

Piggott, S. 1941. The sources of Geoffrey of Monmouth. II. The Stonehenge story. *Antiquity* 15, 305–19.

Pollard, J. and Gillings, M. 1998. Romancing the stones: towards a virtual and elemental Avebury. *Archaeological Dialogues* 5, 143–64.

RCHM [Royal Commission on Historical Monuments (England)]. 1979. *Stonehenge and its environs*. Edinburgh, Edinburgh University Press.

Richards, J. 1990. *The Stonehenge Environs Project*. London,

English Heritage, HBMCE Archaeological Report 16.

Salt, A. and Boutsikas, E. 2005. Knowing when to consult the Oracle at Delphi. *Antiquity* 79, 573–85.

Scourse, J. D. 1997. Transport of the Stonehenge bluestones: testing the glacial hypothesis. In B. Cunliffe and C. Renfrew (eds). *Science and Stonehenge* (Proceedings of the British Academy 92). Oxford, The British Academy, 271–314.

Smith, I. F. 1966. Windmill Hill and its implications. *Palaeohistoria* 12, 469–81.

Stone, J. F. S. 1948. The Stonehenge Cursus and its affinities. *Archaeological Journal* 104, 7–19.

Stukeley, W. 1740. *Stonehenge, a Temple Restor'd to the British Druids*. London, W Innys and R Manby.

Thomas, H. H. 1923. The source of the stones of Stonehenge. *Antiquaries Journal* 3, 239–60.

Thorpe, R. S., Williams-Thorpe, O., Jenkins, D. G. and Watson, J. 1991. The geological sources and transport of the bluestones of Stonehenge, Wiltshire, UK. *Proceedings of the Prehistoric Society* 57, 103–57.

Wainwright, G. J. 1962. The excavation of an earthwork at Castell Bryn-Gwyn, Llanidan parish, Anglesey. *Archaeologia Cambrensis* 111, 25–58.

Whittle, A. 1997. Remembered and imagined belongings: Stonehenge in its traditions and structures of meaning. In B. Cunliffe and C. Renfrew (eds). *Science and Stonehenge* (Proceedings of the British Academy 92). Oxford, The British Academy. 145–66.

Whittle, A. 1998. People and the diverse past: two comments on 'Stonehenge for the ancestors'. *Antiquity* 72, 852–4.

Williams-Thorpe, O., Green, C. P. and Scourse, J. D. 1997. The Stonehenge bluestones: a discussion. In B. Cunliffe and C. Renfrew (eds), *Science and Stonehenge* (Proceedings of the British Academy 92). Oxford, The British Academy. 315–34.

Williams-Thorpe, O., Potts, P. J. and Jones, M. C. 2004. Non-destructive provenancing of bluestone axe-heads in Britain. *Antiquity* 78, 359–79.

Williams-Thorpe, O., Jones, M. C., Potts, P. J. and Webb, P. C. 2006. Preseli dolerite bluestones: axe-heads, Stonehenge monoliths, and outcrop sources. *Oxford Journal of Archaeology* 25.1, 29–46.

Woodward, P. 1988. Pictures of the Neolithic: discoveries from the Flagstones House excavations, Dorchester, Dorset. *Antiquity* 62, 266–74.

Chapter 21

WALKING THE TRACK AND BELIEVING: THE SWEET TRACK AS A MEANS OF ACCESSING EARLIER NEOLITHIC SPIRITUALITY

Clive Jonathon Bond

Introduction

This paper concerns the continued debate on the meaning of the Sweet Track (Coles 1999) excavated in the peat moors of central Somerset in 1971 (Figure 21.1). The focus is what this structure meant to those who constructed it. Four aspects are discussed:

- *Artefact and assemblage:* the Sweet Track as a Neolithic 'package'
- *Site:* the wood, layout and structure
- *Landscape:* walking the track and believing
- *Interpretation:* memorable places and Neolithic spirituality.

Social meaning for those who constructed the Sweet Tack would have operated at several levels: being there, day, month, journeying to this setting (perhaps seasonal and operating over generations). Meaning would be lodged in the social construction of this humanised place (Tilley 1994).

Artefact and assemblage: the Sweet Track as a Neolithic 'package'

Two structures were excavated; the substantial plank-roundwood Sweet Track and the Post Track, a slight, timber-post alignment (Coles and Orme 1976). Three types of artefact dominate: wooden objects/implements, lithics (flint tools or waste) and pottery. The Sweet Track as a Neolithic 'package' can be summarised in three themes:

Wooden objects/implements

At many trench locations wooden artefacts have been recorded, within or beside the track (for example, see Coles and Orme 1976). Different types of wood were used: yew, ash, oak, pine; many wooden objects are recorded (Coles *et al.* 1973, 284, figure 12). Previously few comments have been made on the motivation for artefact discard or deposition. Most of these objects were termed 'equipment' (Coles *et al.* 1973, 288).

Pottery

The excavated pottery is of the plain bowl tradition; the upright and more numerous carinated bowls (Bond 2003, figure 1.8). Cleal has drawn attention to the forms present (2004, 178). Diversity in forms is observed, the assemblage is assigned to the 'earliest or contact Neolithic' (Cleal 2004, 181). Lipid analysis has also demonstrated some pots were used to carry milk inferring 'dairying' (Evershed pers. comm. in Coles 2004, 1.0.1). The pottery context is attributed to prehistoric accidents (Figure 21.2); people slipped, breaking the vessel they carried (Coles and Orme 1976, 65). This hypothesis has been recently questioned (cf. Bond 2003, 2004a).

Lithics and stone

Excavated was a total of 45 lithics, all of quality green-black-grey Downland flint (Bond 2004b, 46). This included one polished/ground flake, a chipped flint axe in pristine condition (Coles *et al.* 1973, 289, Plate XXVI, left) and 4 leaf-shaped arrowheads, three with organic residue attached (bindings). All flint was imported/exchanged Downland nodule flint (Bond 2004b, 131). The polished/ground axe flake may be interpreted as a by-product of a fragmentation rite. Aveling and Heron were able to identify an adhesive by chromatography on one leaf-shaped arrowhead as a birch bark 'tar' (1998, 6). This 'hafting agent' was employed during the Mesolithic and Neolithic. A polished/ground jadeite axe was also recorded from the Railway Site, excavated beside the track. Most lithics were waste, 27/45 (60%). The flaking technology was characteristically earlier Neolithic (Bond 2004a, 46, figure 5): narrow flake or flake-blade, parallel-sided blanks with soft-hammer or punch mode of percussion (Brown 1986, 16). All lithics were

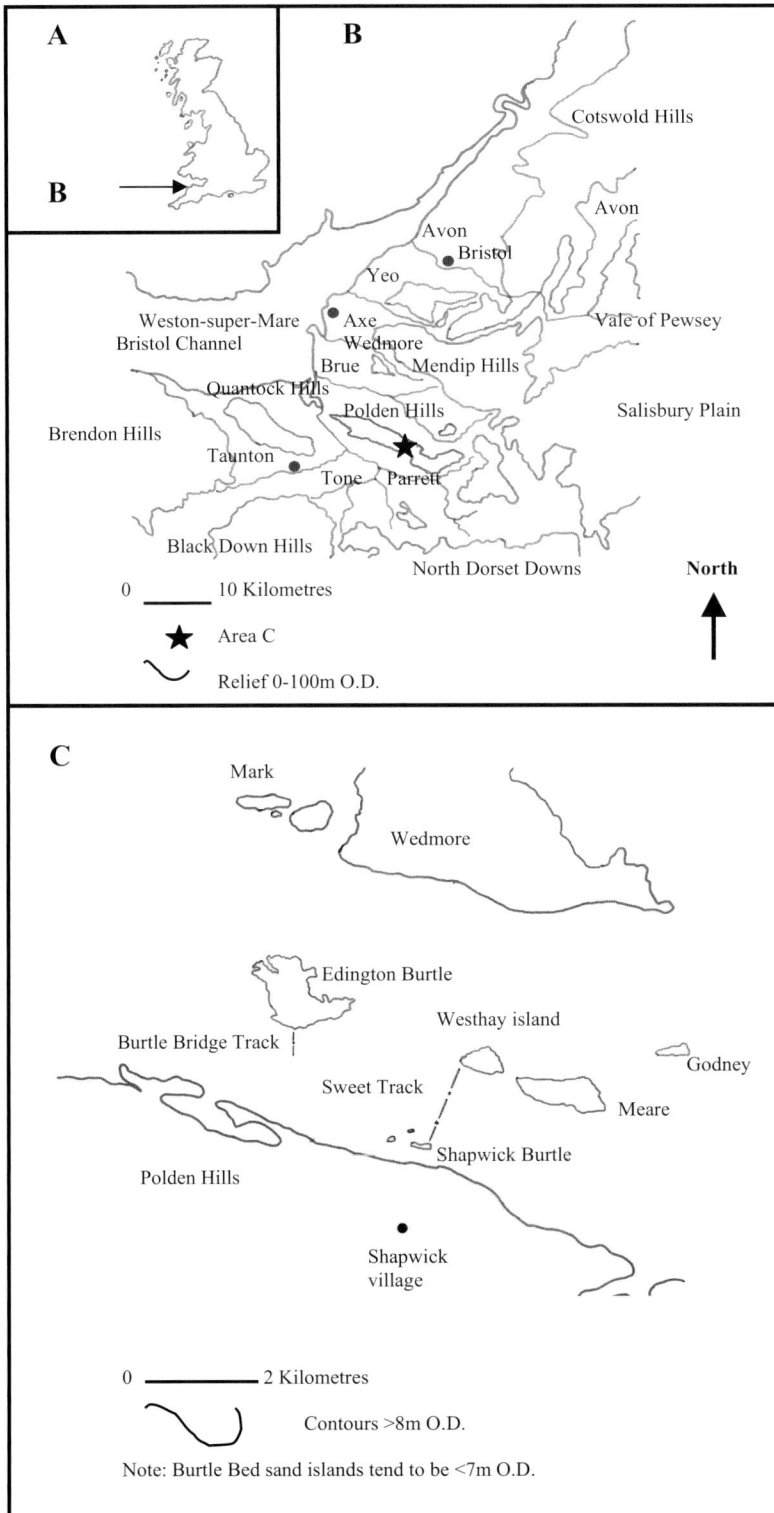

Figure 21.1. Location: UK, Somerset, the Brue Valley and the Sweet Track.

viewed as contemporary with both the Sweet and Post tracks. All three artefact types support a highly mobile community, but importantly mixing Mesolithic and Neolithic crafts/practices.

The materials evident may have been symbolically imbued: a juxtaposition of wood (living, dry) or earth/stone/clay (dead, dry and relatively permanent) may have been transformed by intentional deposition into, or onto, a swamp surface (living, wet, ever changing). Such perceptions of objects/materials may have been part of a set world view, part of an elemental cosmology (cf. Richards 1996). At this track location on the interface of wet-/dry-land, this perception may have been explicitly grounded in a Mesolithic sense of place. This humanised place was commonly in seasonal flux, between nature and the inhabited world: flora, fauna, water and peat (viewed as an in-between substance, sometimes wet/dry, liquid/solid).

Site: the wood, layout and structure

The position of wood excavated beside the track; the size, orientation, whether it would provide a suitable path has not been addressed. All wood, even if excavated away from the track, was argued to be either a result of flooding or part of the track (Coles and Orme 1984, 18, 24–28, figure 20). Flooding or intentional removal of wood by past peoples certainly happened (see Coles and Orme 1984, 15–17), but is only a minor factor.

Commonly oak planks were used. Bog oak was used at the Burtle terminal, linking wood pieces, with charcoal-spread, to the sand island (Coles et al. 1973, 278–280, figure 11). Bog oaks and other tree stumps have been utilised locally at this time: the Burtle Bridge Track (Bond 2003, 21) and the Chilton Track 5 (Coles et al. 1970, 132, plate XXI). Noteworthy is the inclusion of mature timbers; a 70 year old ash tree excavated at the Drove Site, the Post track (Coles and Orme 1979, figure 25). Knowledge of, and visits to, wood sources is implied. Indeed, the material link – bridging the wet 'lag' between sand island and *phragmites* peat – by a bog oak may have been symbolic. The people who built these structures were forest dwelling peoples drawing their identity and beliefs from their environs (Evans et al. 1999). The bog oaks may suggest procurement of fallen oaks, from a distant tree fall, the rotten trunk being dug out from the peat. Did this wood retain a notion of other worldliness? Bog oaks may have been perceived to bridge a supernatural portal.

Much wood, as mapped in excavation trenches appears disorientated (examples of this can be seen in excavated Section SWTC Site, 31–37m in Coles and Orme 1984, fig. 42; Section Factory (F) Site, 0–4m in Coles et al. 1973, fig. 2; Section Drove (D) Site, 25–30m in Coles and Orme 1979, fig. 42). Quantities of wood are not laid along the track north-south axis. Most wood is slanted away from the track axis. This patterning would not be the result of 'abandonment' or flooding (Coles and Orme 1979, figure 27, no. 6). Instead, a succession of events may be evidenced; dumping, maintenance and/or offerings.

Cut wood of all sorts appears to be distributed in an uneven pattern across the trench (see Coles et al. 1974, plate XXVI, where chipped flint was excavated in-situ). Whilst some areas are sparse in timbers, others are dense (for example Coles and Orme 1984, figures 25–28). This is interpreted as denoting intentional manipulation and

placement of wood during use or abandonment. Recorded are quantities of cut-wood showing signs of previous use (bore holes and gouges). Some wood may have been part of other structures as previously observed (Coles et al. 1973, figure 2). This phenomenon has been seen in other prehistoric tracks locally and is here considered intentional (cf. Bond 2006). Parts of known or ancient tracks were perhaps dismantled, collected, not as a raw material but a symbolic capital! It appears this symbolic practice commenced with the Sweet Track and Post track. Coppice woodland (for poles of oak, ash or hazel), or the use of timbers, may have been obtained from other structures. Wood sources also indicate knowledge of the surrounding area (Rackham 1979, 59, 61) perhaps where others frequented.

A pertinent aspect is whether the wood was of the size that could support a walkway (Table 21.1). From the larger trenches excavated, totalling 14 some 1159 measurements have been extracted from published plans. Included is a representative sample of all roundwood, planks, boards and timbers excavated in 367.75 m of the track. Wood was often not lengthy or wide enough to carry the feet of a person (mean width: 0.26–0.50 m). This confirms comments on only being able to walk single-file or pass with close body-contact (Coles and Coles in Hillam et al. 1990, 217). Most wood was less than 1 m length. This size may equate to an easy 'carry' length or cut length from coppiced woodland. Logically wood length would have been a premium in order to construct and link timbers in the linear structure. It seems then, rather than a 'single structure', constructed over the short term (Morgan 1984, 62), the track can be perceived as a series of on going works active over 10–15 years. Even with a slight sample-fraction excavated of the total length, 1.8 km, this is valid. These calculations suggest it may not have been a simple walkway. The track would be a difficult journey; slippery under foot at times; flooding dislodging timbers; often an un-passable path.

A quantity of wood is recorded in this 367.75 m of trenches (Table 21.1). All of it, if laid end-to-end gives 1233.52 m. This quantity of wood could cover the track route distance 3 times over. Over use of wood is demonstrated. Repair and maintenance would not employ this quantity.

The Sweet Track tracing depositional events

The clustering of wood at certain locations along the north-south track alignment signalling activity away from the track fits well with activity at short distance away from this axis with artefact discard/depositional events. Most artefacts were recorded between 0.10 m – 0.70 m either side the track line (Bond 2003, 8, 12, Tables 1.12 and 1.13). Also noted was emphasis on recovery of artefacts on the western side into or within the peat (Figure 21.2). More

West   **North ↑**   **East**

Westhay, Limestone island

% total of artefact find spots: 63.7%   % total of artefact find spots: 36.2%

Lithics:	*Pottery:*	*Site:*	*Pottery:*	*Lithics:*
–	17	WA	1	–
4 (including the core/nodule)	–	TG	–	2
–	5	SA	2	–
–	4	R	4	1 (the Jadeite Axe)
1	–	KD	–	1
7 (including the Flint Chipped Axe and Arrowheads)	–	F	–	8 (including an Arrowhead)
2	1	D	1	2
1	8	C	6	1
–	–	B	–	–

Shapwick Burtle, sand island

| 15 (29.4%) | 36 (70.5%) | | 14 (48.2%) | 15 (51.7%) |

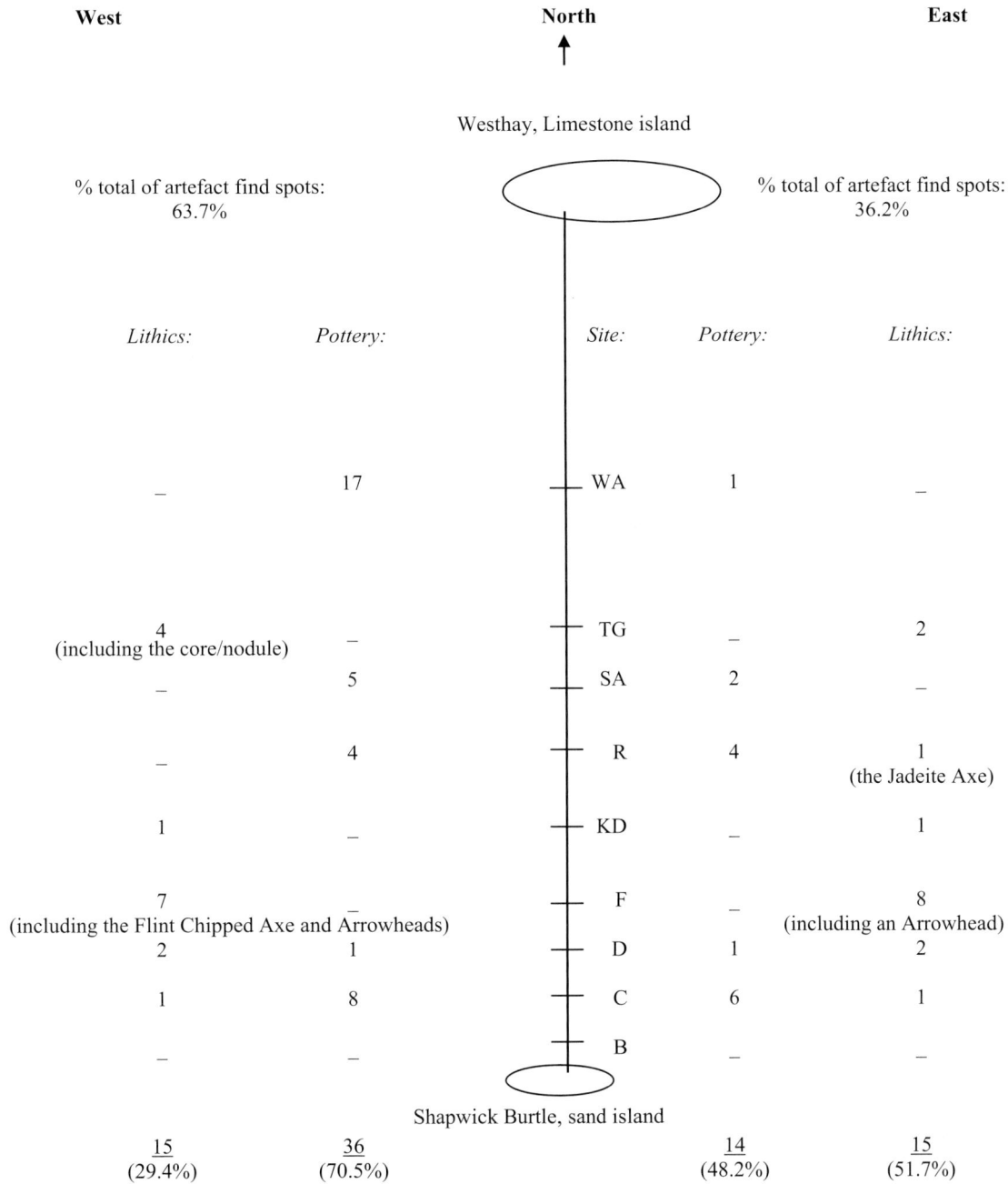

(Artefact-based data collated from the publication in Coles and Orme, 1976, 1979, 1984; Coles *et al.* 1973).

Notes:

(i) Included under the values for lithics are some wooden artifacts, all taken to have functioned as implements; 1 knife, 2 arrow shafts (Coles *et al.* 1973, fig. 2)

(ii) No data was plotted or discussed in detail in the publication of the Sweet Track terminal excavation at Site B (Coles *et al.* 1973, 276–292, fig. 11). Therefore, a quantitative assessment was not possible.

Figure 21.2. A schematic diagram showing the distribution, number and type of findspots excavated along the Sweet Track (after Bond 2003, fig. 1.6).

Site (north-south)	Trench length (m)	Wood measurements (m/cm)		Length:			Width:			Reference
		Number of measurements (extracted)	Total measured length	Mean	Median	Mode	Mean	Median	Mode	
WA	0–9.90	59	50.37	0.85	0.57	0.41	0.37	0.3	0.3	Coles and Orme 1984, figs. 48–49
TG	0–59	266	297.88	1.11	0.75	0.42	0.42	0.31	0.8	Coles and Orme 1984, figs. 37–45
SA	0–8	41	26.88	0.65	0.43	0.39	0.45	0.4	0.7	Coles and Orme 1984, figs. 35–36
R	0–131.25	274	371.27	1.36	1.10	0.80	0.26	0.20	0.20	Coles and Orme 1976, figs. 24a–24d
QZ	0–10.70	62	43.98	0.70	0.53	0.78	0.49	0.4	0.8	Coles and Orme 1984, fig. 32
QV	0–3.60	27	26.55	0.98	0.79	0.41	0.43	0.29	0.1	Coles and Orme 1984, fig. 30
QD	0–2.80	31	15.01	0.48	0.42	0.55	0.47	0.5	0.6	Coles and Orme 1984, fig. 28
KD	0–1.60	9	5.12	0.56	0.47	NA	0.44	0.4	0.8	Coles and Orme 1984, fig. 27
GZ	0–1.90	18	8.04	0.42	0.36	0.42	0.50	0.6	0.8	Coles and Orme 1984, fig. 26
GB	0–2	15	8.84	0.58	0.41	0.21	0.37	0.3	0.3	Coles and Orme 1984, fig. 25
F	0–55	131	142.36	1.09	0.72	0.6	0.41	0.4	0.5	Coles et al. 1973, fig. 2
D	0–51	108	135.73	1.25	0.81	0.81	0.47	0.45	0.8	Coles and Orme 1979, fig. 42
C	0–19	100	82.40	0.82	0.62	0.22	0.45	0.5	0.5	Coles and Orme 1984, figs. 20–21
B	0–12	18	19.09	1.06	0.57	0.48	0.15	0.1	0.1	Coles et al. 1973, fig. 11
Totals	367.75	1159	1233.52							

Table 21.1. Measurements on wood timbers, planks, boards and roundwood extracted from published plans of the excavated Sweet Track and Post Track.

rarely, as with the polished/ground jadeite axe finds were excavated beneath wood as if hidden (Bond 2003, Table 1.3). Pottery or lithics were also excavated in clusters or single finds. These patterns are interpreted as 'discard' or 'depositional' events (Bond 2003, 24).

Landscape: walking the track and believing

The sensory experience of walking or pausing, along or beside, the track would change from the time of year, season and hour. What you saw, touched, smelt and heard would vary depending on timing and who accompanied you (in single-file). Questions are raised: who used it, how often and why? Perhaps it formed part of a vision quest? This may have been a means of communing with the supernatural world.

An alternative interpretation of the track is argued: it was a means of experiencing/accessing the wetland.

Flooding in the winter with the loss of the track layout to water would render the path traceable but un-passable. The surrounding landscape would be open, allowing ranging vistas. Vegetation would be low, the Burtles giving a slight rise, perhaps with a thicket of oaks. With the eye's north view attention would be drawn to the forested Wedmore Ridge and looming Mendip plateau. In the summer the track would be overgrown, a hidden place, yet open to the sky. At night the sky would be open aloft with stars, the passage on foot pitch-black; a path feared imbued with supernatural resonance.

The track may equally have been a corridor into a natural world that few would have been aware of. Even when maintained, reeds cut, planks and pegs repaired or replaced this would have been a secret place, hidden, with solitude. Different views from the track would be available: moving or standing still; entering or emerging from the wetland; going to fish, gather, or hunt; going to meet others or to

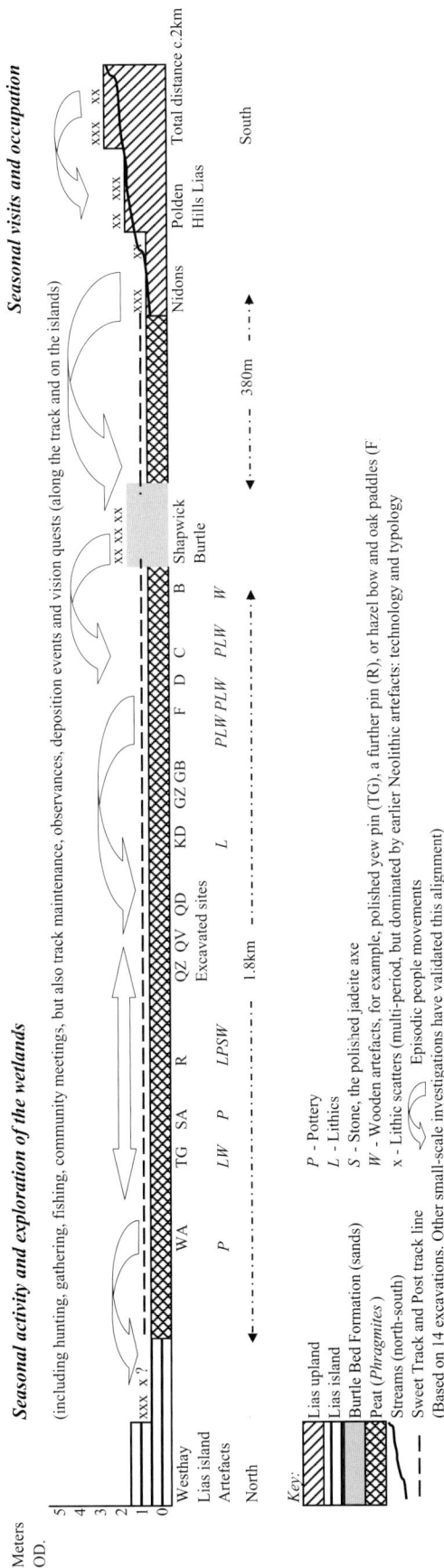

Figure 21.3. A model for the use and perception of the wet and dry Sweet Track landscape.

contemplate. The implication is that this track was not only used to traverse the wetland but as a means of entering it/becoming part of it. In walking the track the individual would learn to understand the natural elemental forces: water, earth, placated by wood, clay and stone. Artefacts may have attested observances (Figures 21.2 and 21.3).

Interpretation: memorable places and Neolithic spirituality

The systematic field survey of the Shapwick Project has produced *c.* 2600 lithics. The largest component for one period, 41% was ascribed to be earlier Neolithic (Bond forthcoming), as is the case across this landscape (Bond 2006). These multi-period lithic scatters represent palimpsest activity over generations, with repeated and seasonal visits of groups (cf. Bond 2004a, 46–48). The spatial focus is on the north-south stream lines, from the upper Polden Hill slopes, to the lower slopes. Springs also form a locus of concentrations, but overall the pattern is linear.

The linear direction of these scatters must reflect an interest in the wetland and the trackway/Shapwick Burtle axis. Would it be unreasonable to argue that this cumulative patterning in habitation reflected something of the cosmology of those dwelling in this land? Hodder's 'linear order' (1990, 245) may be materialised here. The linear, stream-based choreography may also relate to 'sight-lines' (Evans *et al.* 1999, 250–251) enabling movement in thicketed woodland. This spatial relationship between upland/wetland may also be seen as symbiotic, particularly when returning to the composition and ordering, perhaps placement of wood at the Sweet Track. Wood procurement would bind communities together, between stream-based locales, or more distant settings along the upper reaches of the Polden Hills or out in the islands. The meaning of the wood (different species, their locations may have been differently understood). The combination of people involved in track construction/maintenance, or depositional observances, would facilitate group integration, political cohesion, perhaps with peoples who were only present over a few weeks in a year.

The mapped lithics isolated memorable places on the adjacent dryland. A proportion would be contemporary with the Sweet Track or the Post track. This gives a framework for local cosmology. An important underlying theme is water. Water, settlement by, guidance along or passage to and across appears central. These practices and beliefs may have originated in a cult.

Conclusions

The Sweet Track is a product of a specific engagement with place; a localised element of regional earlier Neolithic beliefs (Bond 2003; 2004a; 2006). This is argued to

Landscape knowledge	cal BC (including dendro-chronology)	Events	Description	Ref.
Shapwick Heath: loss of traditional hunting grounds (Mesolithic presence reduced)	5195–4850	Estuarine silts deposited, Shapwick Heath	OxA-11232, 6075±45 BP, charcoal wood bark: marine inundation lasted between 30 to 750 years	1
Meare, wetlands: later Mesolithic and/or earlier Neolithic mobile groups?	4710–4440	Microscopic fragments of charcoal deposited at Ham Walls, Meare	Wk-5293, 5730±60 BP, charcoal in base of peat/clay interface (human presence)	2
Meare, wetlands: later Mesolithic and/or earlier Neolithic mobile groups?	4570–4290	Microscopic fragments of charcoal deposited at Ham Walls, Meare	Wk-5294, 5580±70 BP, charcoal recorded in base of peat infilled channel (erosion and human presence)	2
Failand Ridge: later Mesolithic mobile groups	4370–4050	Excavated pit, with microlith – scalene triangles, Birdcombe, Wraxall	Beta-147106, 5420±60 BP, charcoal oak (Trench D), associated with later Mesolithic 'narrow blade' industry	3
Mendip Hills	3960–3650	Excavated hearth, Lower Pitts Farm, Priddy	GrN-7800, 5000±80 BP, charred heather, 'brown occupation level' (interpreted as a hut foundation)	4
Shapwick Heath	3950	Clearance	Dendrochronology: clearance episode, implicated in the inclusion of timbers from small oak trees (dating to 100–150 years before felling)	5
Shapwick Heath	3838	Excavated oak timbers, felled and incorporated in the Post Track	Dendrochronology: clearance episode, implicated in the inclusion of 3 timbers from small oak trees (dating to 100–150 years before felling)	5
Shapwick Heath	3806–07	Sweet Track: wood felled and structure constructed	Dendrochronology: wood felled, split and prepared in the winter, with a spring build date(s)	5
Shapwick Heath	3804–3800	Sweet Track: planks cut and repaired	Dendrochronology: Planks cut, particularly from the southern part (Drove Site), impling repeated maintenance episodes	5
Failand Ridge: later Mesolithic mobile groups	3640–3360	Excavated pit, with microliths, Birdcombe, Wraxall	Beta-147105, 4700±50 BP, charcoal oak (Trench D), associated with later Mesolithic 'narrow blade' industry	3

Notes: Re-calibration achieved by using atmospheric data from Reimier *et al.* (2004), OxCal version 3.10 (Bronk Ramsey 2005) and the INTERCAL04.14c calibration curve.

Determinations are presented at 2σ, 95.4% probability.

References: Gardiner in Hosfield 2005 [3], Hillam *et al.* 1990 [5], Jones *et al.* 1988 [2], Taylor 2001 [4], Tinsley 2002 [1].

Probable 'contact' or 'pioneer' phase, (cf. Cleal 2004, 181; Thorpe 1999, 94–99).

Table 21.2. Summary of events in the regional and local landscape, c.5200 to 3300 cal. BC.

represent a unique cosmology: a spiritual component (Flannery and Marcus 1998, 47)

Water appears central and the term 'cult' may be applied. Cult equates to 'religious worship expressed in customs, ritual and ceremonies' (Garmonsway 1991, 184). All are implied with the Sweet Track. The attributes of water were central to this earliest of Neolithic cosmologies; a force to be negotiated, mediated or placated. Cult signifies the presence of 'beliefs and practices associated' with a deity (Goring 1992, 127).

Why a water cult?

The significance of water may be found in the Mesolithic landscape evidence (Figure 21.3 and Table 21.2). Here it is acknowledged that the Sweet Track was set within an historical landscape. People already knew places frequented over millennia by successive generations. Places were named and understood.

On the adjacent hill slopes to the Sweet Track, an important feature of the settlement pattern is now established: 17.8% of lithics are assigned to the early Mesolithic whereas 1.8% assigned to the later Mesolithic. A substantial reduction is observed (Bond forthcoming). This split in occupation intensity is understood in environmental terms. On the cusp between the early and later Mesolithic, Shapwick Heath was impacted by the localised Postglacial Marine Transgression, at 5195–4850 BC (Figure 21.3 and Table 21.2). This deposition of estuarine clay/silt is contemporary with, or at least in part, the major reduction in presence of later Mesolithic lithics. Later Mesolithic groups appeared to move onto upland locales in the Mendip Hills (Bond forthcoming, 2006). It is now possible to suggest this event lasted between 30 to 750 years, but altered the landscape use and perception of the last hunter-gatherers providing a taboo or even myth that the builders of the Sweet Track manipulated. This may well be the origin of a water cult, embedded in tradition, memory and myth (Table 21.2).

Creating prehistoric myths

The experience of walking the Sweet Track may have been grounded in these distant events, some 1245–900 years prior to the felling of trees on the Polden Hills in 3950 BC. A conservative, traditional small-scale society may have understood this event, retained it in story telling, over c. 50 – c. 36 generations later. Oral traditions have been able to demonstrate this longevity, for example, aboriginal landscape and the reverence for the Dream Time and the remembering of paths (Taçon 1999). Stone artefacts key to the transfer of cultural memory can also play a role (Taçon 1999). Other long term cycles for wetland deposition have been noted operating over millennia (Pryor 2005, 215–217). Knowledge of the past, the supernatural and places may have been framed by cultural memory and belief. A similar framework of remembering could have been established with pottery, lithic/stone or wood objects, over generations, both on islands in this wetland. Cultural memory can have a long currency particularly when fixed by belief originating from a witnessed environmental change; the Shapwick Heath marine inundation. The Sweet Track may have later monumentalised these events experienced by the last hunter-gatherers.

Walking the track was explicitly keyed into belief, perhaps for two coexistent communities inhabiting one river valley (Table 21.2). The Sweet Track, it can be argued, offers a unique means of accessing the earliest Neolithic spirituality. This elemental-spirituality originated from, and fixed to, a setting with a Mesolithic 'inheritance'. Here,

beliefs, perception and experience of these wetlands, their islands and spiritual agents were mediated for both hunter and herder peoples. This engagement may be what typified this earliest 'contact' or 'pioneer' phase of the Neolithic (Thorpe 1999, 94–96). The pottery was just one category of artefact, a transformed element (clay/earth), that can be identified as critical to this new way of being, realised at first 'contact' (Cleal 2004, 181). Each element, meshed with water, drawing herder and hunter, their different cultural traditions and beliefs together in one place.

Acknowledgements

The following peoples are to be thanked: Mr. Steve Minnitt (Somerset County Museum, Taunton) and Dr. Christopher Chippendale (Museum of Archaeology and Anthropology, the University of Cambridge) both provided access to archives; Professor John Coles was helpful in clarifying project details.

References

Aveling, E. M. and Heron, C. 1998. Neolithic glue from the Sweet Track, Somerset, England. NewsWARP. The Newsletter of the Wetland Archaeology Research Project 23, 5–8.

Bond, C. J. Forthcoming. The lithic assemblage. In M. A. Aston and C. M. Gerrard (eds). The Shapwick Project. English Heritage Archaeological Reports. London, English Heritage.

Bond, C. J. 2003. The coming of the earlier Neolithic, pottery and people in the Somerset Levels. In A. M. Gibson (ed.). Prehistoric Pottery. People, pattern and purpose. Oxford: Archaeopress/British Archaeological Reports, International Series 1156/Prehistoric Ceramic Research Group Occasional Publication No. 4, 1–27.

Bond, C. J. 2004a. The Sweet Track, Somerset: a place mediating culture and spirituality? In T. Insoll (ed.). Belief in the Past. The Proceedings of the 2002 Manchester Conference on Archaeology and Religion. Oxford, Archaeopress/British Archaeological Reports, International Series 1212, 37–50.

Bond, C. J. 2004b. The supply of raw materials for later prehistoric stone tool assemblages and the maintenance of memorable places in central Somerset. In E. A. Walker, F. Wenban-Smith and Healy, F. (eds). Lithics in Action. Papers from the Conference Lithic Studies in the Year 2000. Oxford, Oxbow Books/Lithic Studies Society Occasional Paper No. 8, 124–139.

Bond, C. J. 2006. Prehistoric settlement in Somerset. Landscapes, material culture and communities, 4300 to 700 cal BC. Vols. I and II and DVD. Unpublished Ph.D. thesis. Winchester, The Department of Archaeology, Faculty of Social Sciences, The University of Winchester (an accredited college of the University of Southampton).

Bronk Ramsey, C. 2005, OxCal. 3.10. Oxford, Research Laboratory for Archaeology and the History of Art, University of Oxford.

Brown, A. G. 1986. Flint and chert small finds from the Somerset

Levels, Part 1: The Brue Valley. *Somerset Levels Papers* 12, 12–27.

Cleal, R. M. J. 2004. The dating and diversity of the earliest ceramics of Wessex and South-west England. In R. M. J. Cleal and J. Pollard (eds). *Monuments and Material Culture. Papers in honour of an Avebury archaeologist: Isobel Smith*. Salisbury, Hobnob Press, 164–192.

Coles, B. J. 1999. *Somerset and the Sweet conundrum*. In Harding, A. F. (ed.). Experiment and Design: Archaeological Studies in honour of John Coles. Oxford, Oxbow Books, 163–169.

Coles, B. J. 2004. *Sweet Track Draft Archaeological Management Plan*. Exeter, GT/July 2004.

Coles, J. M. and Orme, B. J. 1976. The Sweet Track, Railway Site. *Somerset Levels Papers* 2, 34–65.

Coles, J. M. and Orme, B. J. 1979. The Sweet Track, Drove Site. *Somerset Levels Papers* 5, 43–64.

Coles, J. M. and Orme, B. J. 1984. Ten excavations along the Sweet Track (3200 bc). *Somerset Levels Papers* 10, 5–45.

Coles, J. M., Hibbert, F. A. and Clement, C. F. 1970. Prehistoric roads and tracks in Somerset, England: 2. Neolithic. *Proceedings of the Prehistoric Society* 36, 125–151.

Coles, J. M., Hibbert, F. A., and Clements, C. F. 1973. Prehistoric roads and tracks in Somerset, England: 3. The Sweet Track. *Proceedings of the Prehistoric Society* 38, 256–293.

Evans, C., Pollard, J. and Knight, M. 1999 Life in Woods: tree-throws, 'settlement' and forest cognition. *Oxford Journal of Archaeology,* 18(3), 141–254.

Flannery, K. V. and Marcus, J. 1996. Cognitive Archaeology. In R. W. Preucel and I. Hodder, (eds). *Contemporary Archaeology in Theory: a Reader*. London, Blackwell, 350–363.

Garmonsway, G. N. 1991. *The Penguin Concise English Dictionary*. Revised. London, Bloomsbury Books.

Gardiner, P. 2003. Caught in the act – where is this transition? In L. Bevan and J. Moore (eds). *Peopling the Mesolithic in a Northern Environment*. Oxford, British Archaeological Reports, International Series 1157, 103–112.

Goring, R. 1992. *The Wordsworth Dictionary of Beliefs and Religions*. Edinburgh, W. and R. Chambers Ltd.

Hillam, J., Groves, C. M., Brown, D. M., Baille, M. G. L., Coles, J. M., and Coles, B. J., 1990, Dendrochronology of the English Neolithic. *Antiquity* 64, 210–220.

Hodder, I. 1990. *The Domestication of Europe*. Oxford: Blackwell.

Hosfield, R. 2005. Part 2. Palaeolithic and Mesolithic. In C. J. Webster (ed.). *South West Archaeological Research Framework: Draft Resource Assessment*. Taunton, Environment Department, Somerset County Council, 22–61.

Jones, J., Cameron, N., Haslett, S., Smith, D., and Tinsley, H. 1998. *Palaeoenvironmental analyses from Ham Walls, Meare, Somerset*. Unpublished manuscript transcript, dated March 1998. Bristol, School of Geological Sciences, University of Bristol.

Morgan, R. A. 1984. Tree-ring studies in the Somerset Levels: the Sweet Track 1979–1982. *Somerset Levels Papers* 10, 46–64.

Pryor, F. 2005. *Britain AD: a quest for Arthur, England and the Anglo-Saxons*. London, Harper Perennial.

Rackham, O. 1979. Neolithic woodland management in the Somerset Levels: Sweet Track I. *Somerset Levels Papers* 5, 59–61.

Reimier, P. J., Baille, M. G. L., Bard, E., Bayliss, A. J. W., Beck, C. J. H., Bertrand, Blackwell, P. G., Buck, C. E., Burr, G. S., Cutler, K. B., Damon, P. E., Edwards, R. L., Fairbanks, R. G., Friedrich, M., Guilderson, T. P., Hogg, A. G., Hughen, K. A., Kromer, B., McCormac, G., Manning, S., Ramsey, C. Bronk, R. W., Remmele, S., Southon, J. R., Stuiver, M., Talamo, S., Taylor, F. W., van der Plicht, J. and Weyhenmeyer, C. E. 2004. IntCal04 terrestrial radiocarbon age calibration, 0–26 cal kyr BP. *Radiocarbon*, 46(3), 1029–1058.

Richards, C. 1996. Henges and Water. Towards and elemental understanding of monumentality and landscape in late Neolithic Britain. *Journal of Material Culture*, 1(3), 313–336.

Taylor, J. J. 2001. A burnt Mesolithic hunting camp in the Mendips: a preliminary report on structural traces excavated on Lower Pitts Farm, Priddy, Somerset. In S. Milliken and J. Cook (eds). *A Very Remote Period Indeed. Papers on the Palaeolithic Presented to Derek Roe*. Oxford, Oxbow Books, 260–270.

Thomas, J. S. 1999. *Understanding the Neolithic*. London, Routledge.

Thorpe, I. J. N. 1999. *The Origins of Agriculture in Europe*. Paperback edition. London, Routledge.

Tinsley, H. M. 2002. *Pollen analysis of peat sampled from borehole A Shapwick Heath, Somerset*. Unpublished manuscript dated 30/07/2002. Bristol, School of Geographical Sciences, University of Bristol.

Taçon, P. S. C. 1999. Identifying Ancient Sacred Landscapes in Australia: from physical to social. In W. Ashmore and A. B. Knapp (eds). *Archaeologies of Landscape. Contemporary Perspectives*. Oxford, Basil Blackwell, 33–57.

Tilley, C. 1994. *A Phenomenology of Landscape. Places, Paths and Monuments*. London, Berg.

Chapter 22

RESTING IN PIECES: DEPOSITION PRACTICES AT THE MOUND OF THE HOSTAGES, TARA, IRELAND

Muiris O'Sullivan

The Mound of the Hostages is a passage-tomb constructed on the Hill of Tara, county Meath (Figure 22.1) in the centuries before 3000 cal. BC (O'Sullivan 2005). A variety of depositional arrangements were associated with its foundation, involving the remains of an unknown number of individuals. Within the tomb, large numbers of individuals were represented in the primary cremation masses and this rite appears to have continued from the Middle Neolithic into the Late Neolithic, post-3000 BC. In all, an absolute minimum of 237 adults are represented amongst the cremated bone from the tomb and its margins, while a minimum of ten children and twenty infants are also attested. Some unburned Neolithic skulls were inserted during the Late Neolithic and further burials occurred during the Early Bronze Age, attention switching from the tomb to the overlying mound *c.* 2000 cal. BC. By the time the last burial was inserted in the north-west quadrant of the mound *c.*1700 cal. BC, the site had been a focus of human bone deposition for some fifteen hundred years. The evidence suggests that many of the deposits were inserted as part of the construction ritual, the individual playing a subordinate role to the monuments.

Pre-cairn deposit

Pre-cairn activity in the form of pits, fires and a ditch was uncovered during the excavations and there is some evidence that an intervening surface between at least some of these and the cairn may have been specifically prepared in advance of the construction. Embedded in this surface, a few metres south-east of the centre of the cairn, the excavation team in 1959 unearthed unburned human bone, including the lower end of an adult femur (**X** in Figure 22.2). The care with which passage-tomb features are organised precludes any notions that this may have been an accidental or casual deposit, but the fact that the bone is not cremated is also significant because the early deposits at the site habitually involve cremation. The unburned bone,

a token as distinct from a full skeleton, must therefore be interpreted as a foundation deposit.

Perimeter deposits

A number of small but deliberate deposits of human bone, invariably cremated, were also encountered on the old ground surface beyond the edge of the cairn. The original number of these is unknown and the discovery of an isolated example (Burial 16) about 9 m west of the cairn in a single extended cutting (O'Sullivan 2005, figures 10 and 189) suggests that additional examples may still lie undisturbed west of the Mound of the Hostages. The cremated bone from these deposits was normally crushed beyond recognition but, where identification was possible, it was consistently human. In only one case (Burial 3) was there sufficient cremated material (860 cc) to justify considering it the remains of an individual, an interpretation supported by the presence of two matching specimens of internal *acoustic meatus* in this particular deposit. Radiocarbon determinations were secured from eleven of the seventeen deposits and the results are remarkably consistent, all dating to the span from 3400–3100 cal. BC, inseparable from the early deposits in the megalithic tomb and concurrent with the building of the great Boyne Valley sites. There was a bead in Burial 10 and a bone pin in Burial 13 but otherwise no grave goods. Twelve of the seventeen deposits were associated with neat stone settings to be described below the remainder were small scatters or concentrations of bone without stone settings. The most common form of stone setting consisted of a flat floor stone, no more than 20–30 cm in length, with tiny slabs set on edge to form a low rim around the verge. In some cases, there was a capstone. These settings were like tiny individual chambers and they might be envisaged as miniscule satellites in the manner of those at Knowth.

Apart from Burial 3, the skull fragments from which are taken to represent an adult, the individuality of the deceased

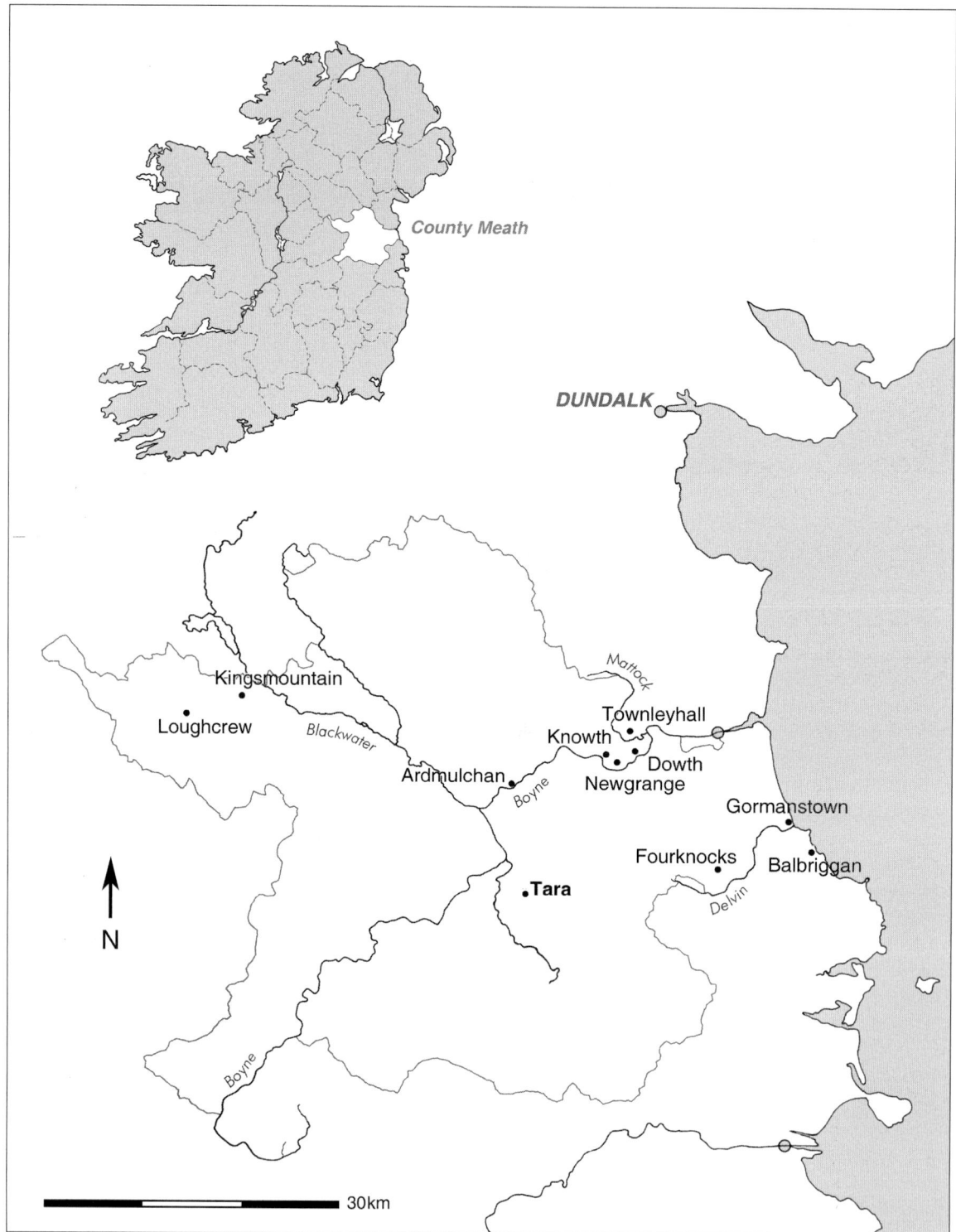

Figure 22.1. Tara in its regional setting around 3000 BC, showing the location of other passage tombs along the Boyne/ Blackwater artery.

Figure 22.2. Plan of Neolithic features at the Mound of the Hostages, including pre-cairn traces and human bone deposits at the perimeter. The edge of the cairn and mound respectively are indicated.

appears to have been deliberately obliterated in death. In the absence of a megalithic kerb, the small collections of bone fragments may have served as votive deposits surrounding the sacred area rather than burials in the traditional sense. If this is the case, the individual is playing a subordinate role to the place itself, thus inverting the assumed set of priorities. The vast majority of the deposits occurred along the southern half of the perimeter. This preference for the sunny southern side of the cairn, reflecting similar inclinations in the distribution of megalithic art along the kerbs at Knowth and Knockroe (O'Sullivan 2004, 47), might be linked with the well established interest of the passage tomb builders in the daily passage of the sun across the sky.

Pre-cairn annexes

Three compartments, each containing a mass of cremation, were located outside the tomb but against the tomb orthostats. They were carefully constructed, with paved floors, and insulated from the fill of the tomb by small slabs placed in the gaps between the relevant tomb orthostats, with twenty-five of these slabs occurring in Cist I alone. Two of the three annexes were neatly defined by small

orthostatic walls covered with roofing slabs and it is possible that the third was also covered originally. The annexes, although unique in construction and the magnitude of the their contents, are in keeping with the occurrence of pre-cairn burial cists at other sites, such as Carrowmore 4 (Burenhult 1980, 70–81).

In total, the annexes contained cremated bone representing an absolute minimum of fifty-five adults. Although only a fraction of the numbers represented in the main tomb, the figures for each annexe stand comparison with the totals in many megalithic tombs. Child bone was present in all three annexes while unburned bone representing a total of four infants was recorded, with at least one in each annexe. The infant and child bones were isolated specimens, insufficient to suggest that even a partial skeleton was involved, which suggests that their presence was more about token representation than formal burial. In the case of infants, the lone specimens were invariably the long bones from limbs. A pair of fused unburned adult vertebrae, located amongst the cremated material in Cist II, might be taken to indicate an awareness of arthritis and an isolation of its effects for symbolic purposes. The range of grave goods associated with the deposits was reasonably typical of the normal Irish passage-tomb assemblage: pins of bone and antler, beads and pendants, balls, bone tubes, flint flakes and Carrowkeel ware. However, when the assemblages are examined individually and compared in detail, the impression of homogeneity proves to be misleading, for all the balls occur in Cist II while all the pendants occur in Cist III. Intact Carrowkeel bowls were retrieved from Cists I and III, which is in marked contrast to the main tomb where a considerably greater number of individuals were represented but only one Carrowkeel pot occurred (and it was in fragments). The bowl in Cist III, a large vessel, lay at the top of the cremation mass and was itself filled with cremated bone while the comparatively tiny bowl in Cist I lay on its side amongst the bone. The fact that the bowls survived intact in these sealed compartments suggests that the fragmentation of Carrowkeel pottery within the more accessible chamber area of passage tombs is a product of secondary disturbance rather than deliberate annihilation.

The combination of homogeneity and differentiation amongst the three cists is striking. Only beads and bone pins occur in all three cases, while adults, children and infants are also universal. There is one striking anomaly amongst the cremated bone. Although virtually all major collections at the site produced an approximately equivalent number of left-side specimens and right-side specimens of *internal acoustic meatus*, there was an unusual over-representation of left-side specimens in both Cist II and Cist III. In total, these two cists produced forty-seven left-side specimens and only thirty right-side specimens, with six indeterminates. This might suggest a peculiarity of the cremation process or possibly a differential collection of remains post-cremation.

Margins of the tomb

Cremated bone was encountered not only within the tomb but also in the orthostat trench around the tomb. Some of this material could arguably and convincingly be attributed to natural spill between the orthostats; more of it is demonstrably not due to such processes. In particular, a substantial collection lay in the fill of the trench behind the back stone of the chamber. This was clearly in place before the cairn was erected and was incorporated as part of the backfill around the stone. Including this material, at least nineteen adults and four children are represented amongst the material from the margins. At Knockroe, county Kilkenny, a similarly substantial collection of cremated bone with associated passage tomb artefacts was found on the pre-cairn surface immediately beside the eastern tomb (O'Sullivan 1995, 22). This adds strength to the suggestion that human bone was being incorporated not as an act of reverence for the individuals concerned but as part of the construction ritual.

Tomb interior

Although the mass of cremated bone within the tomb is the largest collection at any megalithic tomb in Ireland or perhaps even Europe, its value as an indicator of cult activity in the Neolithic is diminished by considerable disturbance during the early Bronze Age, in the centuries leading up to 2000 BC. Of the three successive compartments in the tomb, it was only in the middle compartment that Neolithic deposits were left relatively undisturbed; elsewhere they were scooped aside or trodden on, so that the excavators in the 1950s were reduced to categorising the multiplicity of layers and pockets of bone as variously *clean cremation*, *dirty cremation* and *very dirty cremation* in order to indicate the level of disturbance in each case. Retrospective interpretation is also hindered by the different excavation and recording techniques used by Ó Ríordáin, who examined a considerably part of the fill in 1956, and his successor de Valera who completed the task in 1959.

In spite of these difficulties, the evidence from the tomb provides important insights into Neolithic depositional practices. As in the case of the annexes, virtually every significant collection of cremated bone from the tomb included sporadic infant long bones, always unburned, and some evidence of children, often in the form of deciduous teeth. The infants were generally about term. Besides the individuals represented in the annexes and along the margins of the tomb, an absolute minimum of 155 adults, twelve infants and about seven children are indicated within the megalithic tomb. In addition, a cluster of unburned adult skulls was located on the right-hand side of the middle compartment. As outlined in O'Sullivan (2005, 114–6), the precise number of skulls is difficult to establish in hindsight but there may have been *c.* 8–10 present. During the excavation of Cist II, for example, a group of four skulls were revealed within the tomb when the sealing stones in the gap between orthostats R1 and R2 were removed. Further skulls in the middle compartment were revealed when the tomb interior was being excavated. The remaining skeletal parts of the individuals were not found. At one point in the excavation, a collection of mandibles was encountered in this area, confirming that the skulls were introduced collectively and not necessarily intact. Radiocarbon samples were derived from two of the skulls in the second compartment. GrA-18353 developed as 4060±50 BP and GrA-18374 came out as 4230±50 BP, indicating a date range of *c.* 3100–2500 cal. BC, suggesting that the skulls were inserted in the Late Neolithic , a few centuries after the initial wave of deposition in the Middle Neolithic.

Many discoveries of unburned bone specimens were made amongst the cremated bone, but such was the disturbance at the site that it is difficult to be definitive about its overall significance because many of the specimens were smaller bones that might conceivably have filtered into the cremations from the overlying Early Bronze Age skeletons. On the other hand, specific instances in sealed environments are more convincing, such as the fused arthritic vertebrae described earlier. In life, there would presumably have been considerable pain and immobility associated with this condition and, perhaps, the offending skeletal parts have been singled out for special attention in death. In the light of the manipulation of infant bones and adult skulls described above, not to mention the crushed cremated bone represented amongst the perimeter deposit, the notion that isolated specimens might have been accorded special attention is not far-fetched, but it would take a detailed forensic examination of the skeletal material from the tomb and a review of the fill stratigraphy to pursue the suggestion properly.

Symbolic objects

In addition to the treatment of human bone, the grave goods incorporated with the cremation deposits are an important indicator of ritual choice. As in other primary contexts at the site, a large collection of typical Irish passage tomb artefacts were found amongst the cremation bone, including antler and bone pins, pendants, beads, tubes, balls and flint flakes. In his analysis of the stone artefacts from the excavations, excluding flint and chert, Dr Steve Mandal found that the overwhelming majority of Neolithic objects were made from locally available material. The collection of pendants was a notably exception to this general pattern (Table 22.1):

	Decorated	Undecorated	Total
Serpentine	2	7	9
Jasper		4	4
Gabbro		2	2
Sedimentary		6	6
Quartz		1	1
Bone	4	1	5
TOTAL	6	21	27

Table 22.1. Classification of Neolithic pendants from the Mound of the Hostages, indicating a strong preference for non-local stones.

Of the twenty-two examples fashioned from stone, nine were made from serpentine, a green greasy-looking stone, and four from jasper, a red iron-rich mineral, neither of which is represented amongst the other Neolithic artefacts. Although jasper would have been available in the general locality, serpentine sources are located much further away, in the Killary Bay area of Galway and Mayo. The implication, that pendants carried a special significant in the funerary ritual, is supported by the evidence from Cist

III, the only annexe to contain these objects. The pendants in this case were fashioned from bone, an unusual choice of material for pendants as noted earlier, and all three were decorated. Only three further decorated pendants occurred amongst the twenty-five pendants located within the tomb. Significantly, two of the three were serpentine and the third was bone, this being one of only two bone pendants in the tomb, the other an undecorated example of unusually flattened profile and exceptionally straight-sided shape. Perhaps pendants denoted status, acted as heirlooms or were cult objects. The twin significance of their materiality and decoration mirrors the interaction of special stones and megalithic art in the architecture of many passage tombs (O'Sullivan 1997, figure 2).

The communicative value of the pendants encourages a closer look at the iconography of the other artefacts, notably bone and antler pins for example. Although mushroom-headed antler pins have become synonymous with passage tombs, an overall count of pinheads from the site produces interesting results (Table 22.2):

Heads of mushroom-head antler pin	10
Heads of (sheep) metatarsal bone pins	27
Heads of other types of bone pins	9
TOTAL	46

Table 22.2. Pinheads from burial contexts at the Mound of the Hostages.

This suggests that bone pins may be more common than antler pins at passage tomb sites and that the much-overlooked metatarsal pin may have played a more prominent role than the mushroom-headed pin. What is perhaps even more interesting is that the antler pins appear to derive consistently from red deer, while the metatarsal pins are invariably fashioned from sheep bone. This situation is not unique to the Mound of the Hostages, because the same pattern has been recognised at Knockroe, for example. Both metatarsal pins and mushroom-headed pins, seemingly from the sheep and red deer respectively, are a consistent feature of passage-tomb cremation deposits. In this context, the occurrence of other animal bone discoveries from the Mound of the Hostages may be on interest (Table 22.3):

Context	Deer	Sheep	Cattle	Pig
Beneath the cairn			1	1
Cairn mass			11	1
Mound			5	2
Tomb		2	3	3

Table 22.3. Occurrence of unworked bone from selected animals at the Mound of the Hostages, showing the non-representation of sheep and deer remains in various contexts.

Although the numbers are possibly too low to be over-emphasised, it is nevertheless interesting that neither sheep nor deer, the two animals represented amongst the pins, are represented amongst the general animal bone from the site, apart from the two specimens of sheep bone discovered in the inner compartment of the tomb, which can almost certainly be regarded as later additions attributable to the foxes whose bones are also represented in the same context. We might reasonably infer that animals had ritual meaning in the passage-tomb cult and that the various types of animal played different roles in the ceremonies.

Conclusion

The Mound of the Hostages was a focus of human bone deposition over the course of approximately fifteen centuries beginning in the Middle Neolithic. During that time, the role and status of the human remains evolved through various phases. At the beginning, the individual was suppressed through the inclusion of only part of the skeleton, the crushing of cremated bone beyond recognition or the massing of cremated bone from large numbers into a homogenous deposit. The role of human remains as an element of the construction ritual rather than its *raison d'être* is underlined by the peculiar treatment of infant bone as described above. The impression is of meaning being constructed, negotiated and transmitted through the human remains. Viewed from this perspective, the nest of Late Neolithic skulls in the middle compartment of the tomb is best explained in terms of cult rather than disposal of the dead. Although, at first sight, the subsequent Early Bronze Age burials in the tomb and mound look like standard interments of individuals, this impression is again not sustained when the burials are examined in detail, which is outside the scope of this paper. The peculiar treatment of the individual highlights the fundamental status of the Mound of the Hostages as the foundation monument of the Hill of Tara, the nucleus around which a major ceremonial landscape evolved during the later prehistoric period.

References

Burenhult, G. 1980. *The Archaeological Excavation at Carrowmore, Co. Sligo, Ireland.* Theses and Papers in North-European Archaeology 9, Institute of Archaeology, University of Stockholm.

O'Sullivan, M. 1995. The eastern tomb at Knockroe. *Old Kilkenny Review*, 11–30.

O'Sullivan, M. 1997. On the meaning of megalithic art. *Brigantium* 10, 23–35.

O'Sullivan, M. 2004. Little and large: Comparing Knockroe with Knowth. In Helen Roche et al. *From Megaliths to Metals: Essays in Honour of George Eogan.* Oxford, Oxbow Books, 44–50.

O'Sullivan, M. 2005. *The Mound of the Hostages, Tara.* Dublin, Wordwell.

Chapter 23

ENCLOSING PLACES: A CONTEXTUAL APPROACH TO CULT AND RELIGION IN NEOLITHIC CENTRAL EUROPE

Peter F. Biehl

In this article, I will discuss a contextual approach to the archaeology of cult, ritual and religion stressing the symbolic entanglement of material culture, place and landscape. In a case study – the Neolithic enclosures of the first half of the fifth millennium BC in Central Europe, particularly the Middle Neolithic circular enclosure in Goseck in Germany – I will elaborate how ritual practices function at both a community and at an individual level, and as social and communicative acts. I will also demonstrate why ritual practice needs to be contextualized with the material culture and the place associated with it in order to understand and theorize its meaning and its multi-scalar nature.

Introduction – the archaeology of cult, ritual and religion

One of the main problems with the archaeology of cult, ritual or religion is definition (Insoll 2005, 45). In an excellent introduction to the archaeology of cult, ritual and religion Timothy Ingold discusses these shortcomings (Ingold 2004) and concludes that 'what is required in considering the archaeology of cult and religion is a rethink of the method and theory involved in this key area of archaeology' (Insoll 2005, 48; see also Garwood *et al.* 1991, vii). In this article I will not try to resolve this problem in developing just another vague definition of these related yet differing terms (Bertemes and Biehl 2001, 12–16). Rather, I will focus on the methodological issues involved with the underlying concepts. In particular, I will focus on the concept of 'cult places' and their complex role regarding religious beliefs as prescribed ways of understanding and ritual practices as prescribed ways of behaving. Following Insoll, I will use 'cult' and 'cult place' as a term referring to religious ceremonies (Insoll 2004, 45).

Anthropologists, sociologists, historians and philo-sophers have often turned to religion and ritual as a 'window' on the cultural dynamics by which people make and remake their world (Bell 1992, 3). It is owing to these disciplines that we have a clearer understanding of the essential distinction between belief and ritual, between faith and practice, and between myth and religion. These disciplines complement our work – and we need to take advantage of any help they can offer. In particular, the use of ethnographic analogy to bridge sometimes immense gaps of time and location is a great temptation in archaeology, but we need to use analogies with a deliberate concern for the distinctions between ethnographic data and archaeological sources (Biehl 1996; 1999). But, even with analogical support, we still face the dilemma that ritual actions are not always clearly separated from the acts of everyday life (Bradley 2005, 3; Garwood *et al.* 1991, viii). We have also to take into consideration that the extent to which certain patterns related to religion and ritual are restricted to particular social groups. Elites are generally more visible in the archaeological records than other social groups because they control the material manifestations of religion and power in life as well as in death. More importantly, religion and ritual can be enmeshed with everyday functional activity, and thus are difficult to distinguish archaeologically. This is also true for locations. We can try to identify places where religious or ritual actions took place or where practices were systematically repeated.

We also have thorny questions about spirituality. These cannot be answered archaeologically, as spirituality does not materialize directly in the archaeological record. What we have are the acts – or more precisely, the traces of artefacts used for the acts or the place where the acts occurred and also physical results of the acts (deposits, ditches, etc.). We can analyse religious and ritual acts through time and space and try to understand the role they played in specific societies. A good starting point for our analysis is to think of religion and myth as prescribed ways of understanding, while cult and ritual offer prescribed ways of behaving. As archaeologists, we possess a realm of monuments, images and material remains that exposes us to a wide range of paths that, if followed methodically and with some degree of imagination, can bring us closer to the understanding of cult, ritual and religion in preliterate societies.

The method of contextual attribute analysis

The key element on which my thesis is based is the concept of 'context'. The importance of 'rigorous contextual approaches to the study of ritual (in terms of its social role, and in the reconstruction of particular practices), and to the interpretation of belief systems to which ritual practices referred and from which they took meaning' has repeatedly been stressed (Garwood *et al.* 1991, vii). Moreover, Garwood et al. aptly stress that 'while "contextual" archaeology should perhaps simply be equated with "good" archaeology, the critical recognition that social action and the social constitution of material culture can only be properly understood in context, both cultural and material, is as significant for the interpretation of ritual as for every kind of archaeological study' (Garwood *et al.* 1991, vii). However, 'we are all aware of the difficult issues surrounding contexts and that easy-to-read contexts are more of a rarity than a norm' (Conkey and Tringham 1998, 28). This is especially true for the Neolithic circular enclosures with their multi-phased ditches and wooden palisades which cannot be conceived as so-called 'closed finds' such as burials, depositions or burnt down buildings etc. (Montelius 1903; see also Eggers 1986, 91, 91–105; Trigger 1989, 157). The 'rediscovery' and appraisal of context is due to Ian Hodder's seminal work on so-called 'contextual archaeology' (Hodder 1987; see also Papaconstantinou 2006). But my conception of context differs in a couple of points from Hodder's definition. I agree with his definition of the context of an archaeological attribute as 'the totality of the relevant environment, where "relevant" refers to a significant relationship to the object - that is, a relationship necessary for discerning the object's meaning' (Hodder 1991, 143; see also Hodder 1982a, 23, 27, 211; 1985, 14; 1987, 4; 1991, 121–155; 1999); and also that a context is always 'situation specific'. But I disagree with his somehow relativistic statement that context also depends on and varies with the dimensions of variation in similarities and differences being considered, and with the questions being asked. This consequently leads him to the conclusion that 'in many areas contextual archaeology can hardly begin until more data have been collected' (Hodder 1991, 146). Elsewhere (Biehl 1999, 2003, 2006) I have argued against Hodder's assertions that, firstly, 'an object out of context is not readable', and secondly, that 'in prehistoric archaeology, the further one goes back in time, so that the survival rates

diminish, the more difficult it becomes to ground hypotheses in data' (Hodder 1991, 146), and have suggested the concept of a 'structural context' of an artefact, which gives us the tools to include 'artefacts out of context' – which overwhelmingly form the archaeological record – in our analyses.

Does this mean that we cannot study these Neolithic monuments contextually because we have only artefacts, which to use Hodder's definition are 'out of context?'. I believe we can. Elsewhere, I have demonstrated that we can use artefacts without any secure context and include them in our analyses (Biehl 2003, 2006). I have named the method I use 'contextual attribute analysis' and have suggested that we conceive of an artefact as a 'closed find' unto itself, that is, that we consider each object a contextual structure replete with meaningful attributes. When we look at the artefact, we must see it as the result of a system of making. That is, we must assume that it did not come about by random, but that somehow it was thought about and considered useful within a set structure (Biehl 2003, 2006). When all of the attributes have been analysed and compared, we can begin to understand the significance of an artefact and eventually gain insight into its hidden symbolism and the communication system embedded in it.

I believe that we can use contextual attribute analysis in the same way for places and monuments such as Neolithic circular enclosures. We should begin to view each enclosure as a context in itself. In other words, an enclosure should be analysed as a contextual structure of meaningful attributes, or a 'structural context' of both the artefact and of the place. I see the two as entangled and that through ritual practice/action, an artefact/material culture was 'transferred' into a religious/ritual object used in or in relation to a cult place. In regard to the latter, we can differentiate five interactive zones, which can be interrelated with other attributes (Figure 23.1). This diagram is a simplified and modified version of a diagram created by François Bertemes (in press). The original diagram has been translated into English and was published in the introductory chapter of the book *The Archaeology of Cult and Religion* (Bertemes and Biehl 2001, 20, figure 4):

1. Cult Place: the physical location where the ritual/ ceremony was practiced.
2. Imagery: the images connected to the ritual practice.
3. Devices and Support: everything (also paraphernalia) used in or to support a ritual/religious act.
4. Participants: the people actively and passively involved in a ritual practice/action.
5. Ritual Practices/Actions: the actual act/gesture that holds a ritual/religious meaning/function.

All zones are interrelated and cannot be analysed separately. The identification of a cult place can only be studied in combination with the religious ceremony or ritual

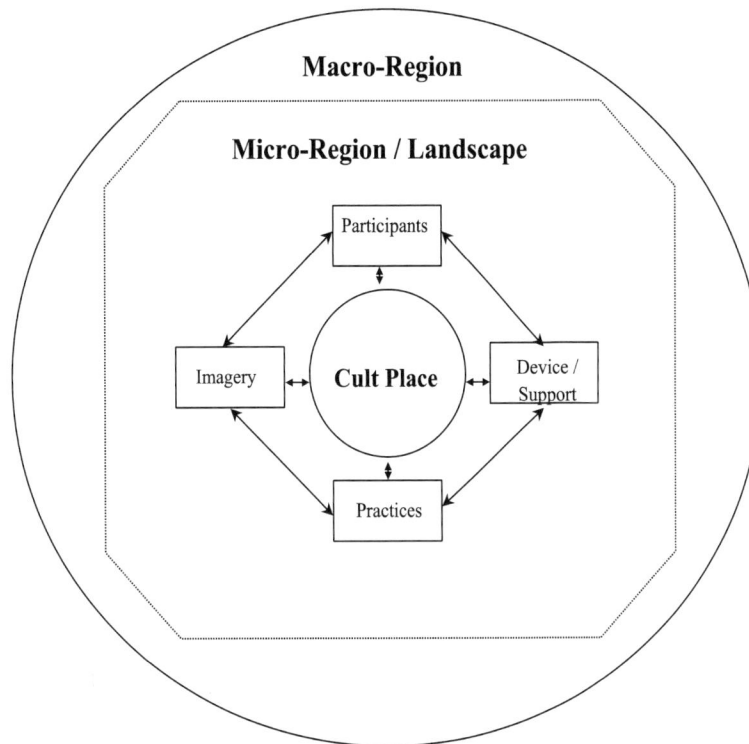

Figure 23.1. Diagram of the structural context of a cult place.

practiced in or at it and with the material culture and individuals involved (Bertemes and Biehl 2001, 18).

With this as our theoretical and methodological framework, we can begin to recognize the system under which such a monument was created by conceptualising all discernible and chronological contemporaneous attributes of its structure. Though this procedure does not allow us to view the monument as a physical end-product but we can study it as the material reflection – or the 'coming into form/being' – of a vast variety of individual and collective decisions that were both practical and symbolic. These decisions underscore and may help us read and reconstruct the cultural rules to which the builders of the enclosure had to conform. In order to study these attributes and begin to see patterns in them, we must first separate all discernible attributes into the smallest of categories. That means chronological and geographical, material and symbolic and even functional.

Once we accept the idea that such a system may have existed within a prehistoric community, we must then decipher what roles the individual and the group played, how the system was transmitted and what meanings such enclosed spaces embedded in the system carry. Before I discuss the various meanings and ritual practices often associated with them, I will discuss my case study and show how I have applied a contextual attribute analysis to the Goseck circular enclosure.

Neolithic enclosures in Europe

Neolithic enclosures have been known in Europe for over hundred years and have fascinated archaeologists and the public alike. The first Neolithic enclosure was discovered in Krpy in Bohemia towards the end of the 19th century (Woldřich 1886; Petrasch in press). The image of monumental architecture made of stone, wood or earth constructed some seven thousand years ago was so powerful that it has long incited archaeologists to search for the origin of this European phenomenon and to investigate its spread and function.

There has been extensive research over the last 20 years on Neolithic enclosures (Petrasch 1990, Trnka 1991, Andersen 1997, Darvill and Thomas 2001, Schier 2005, Bertemes, Biehl and Meller in press) and the overall spread of enclosed sites can now be seen 'as ranging across most of the lower-lying plains and river systems from the Black Sea in the east to Portugal in the west, and from Sicily in the south to Scotland in the north' (Darvill and Thomas 2001, 7). Niels Andersen has catalogued some 800 enclosed Neolithic sites within this area, all dating from the sixth to the third millennium BC and points out that they are just a fraction of known Neolithic enclosures (Andersen 1997, 11). This is due to the fact that large swaths of Europe sat behind the Iron Curtain for decades, and we still do not have a proper idea of how Neolithic enclosures were distributed in many nations from the former Eastern Bloc. That is because until 1989, political and military conditions made it virtually impossible to do sustained aerial surveys in these regions. But more importantly, if we have a closer look at Andersen's catalogue and distribution map (Andersen 1997, 134–135, figure 178) we realize that only a few of the enclosed sites dotting this landscape have been uncovered or excavated fully. This fragmented state of research might be one reason why the functions of the sites have been debated for decades. Clearly, knowing only little about each site provides dangerously wide berth for interpretation.

Today, wading through all the possible theories, we can see three major trends in the way Neolithic enclosures are perceived in the archaeological record: First, it is clear now that Neolithic enclosures were an extremely widespread phenomenon across Europe. Second, their variation in form and context is so evident that one can agree with Timothy Darvill and Julian Thomas that 'the idea that all Neolithic enclosures had a similar role or function within the societies that created and used them is as laughable as the idea that some kind of universal classification can be applied to all sites' (Darvill and Thomas 2002, 13). And finally, the map of Neolithic enclosures remains a map of the distribution of the application of techniques such as aerial and geophysical survey techniques. The total number remains unknown, but clearly these enclosures were abundant. But how should we go about understanding them? I believe it's too difficult to approach such a large class of archaeological monuments in sweeping spatial and chronological frameworks. Instead, I argue that it's much more promising to start working at a more basic, individual level. That is, to look at one site first and analyse and contextualise it within the landscape in which its meaning and function was embedded and the region to which it belonged culture-historically (Andersen 1997).

The best way for me to explain my contextual approach to cult places is to discuss it with a specific case study. I will, therefore, focus on the so-called *Kreisgrabenanlagen* – circular ditched enclosures – of the Central European Middle Neolithic of the first half of the fifth millennium BC – specifically on the site of Goseck. The enclosure in Goseck (Saxony-Anhalt, Germany) has been fully excavated between 2002–2005. The excavation has been co-directed by François Bertemes and myself and carried out within the framework of an apprentice field school by students mainly from the Institute of Prehistoric Archaeology at the Martin-Luther-University Halle-Wittenberg, funded by the State of Saxony-Anhalt, the Heritage Management Service and several sponsors. A publication of the Goseck enclosure is forthcoming as a monograph in 2007 (Biehl in press (a); for preliminary excavation reports, see Bertemes, Biehl, Northe and Schröder 2004; Bertemes and Biehl 2005, Becker,

Bertemes, Biehl and Schier 2005; Biehl in press (b)).

The C-14 dates and the analysis of its material culture show that the site can be dated to the so-called Middle Neolithic *Stichbandkeramik* or culture with *Stroke-Ornamented Pottery* (*c.* 4900–4600 BC). Up to now we know of approximately 120 circular enclosures (Neubauer and Trnka 2005a, 4) belonging to a culture complex of Theiß–Herály–Csöszhalom, Lengyel, Stichbandkeramik, Oberlauterbach, Rössen and Großgartach in a circum-scribed area reaching from Slovakia and Hungary in the East to Bavaria in the South and Hesse and Brandenburg in the West and North.

Goseck serves well to introduce the Middle Neolithic variant of enclosed sites in Central Europe since it was built and used during the few centuries in which this type of enclosures suddenly emerges and then abruptly disappeared again. Like most enclosures of this time period, it is situated on a slightly sloped loess-covered terrace in an open un-wooded landscape and close to a spring and a river.

From 2002 to 2005 we fully excavated the enclosure, and in 2006 it was reconstructed on its original location (Figure 23.2). Like so many discoveries in countries of the former Eastern Bloc, the site was first discovered in 1991 as intensive aerial photography that prohibited until 1989 was done. After its discovery it was analysed and docu-mented with a geophysical survey, which took place in 1995 (Bertemes *et al.* 2004, 137–139).

The enclosure consisted of a circular ditch over 70 m in diameter, furnished with three entrances with out-turned terminals and with traces of two wooden palisade rings inside it, each with a narrow in-turned entrance which exactly lined up with the ditch entrances (Figures 23.2 and 23.4). The ditch in Goseck was some 3 m wide, and its V-shaped section reached most likely over 3 m and narrows at its bottom to 30 cm. It had an earth bank in front of the ditch, which we could document in the profile and the filling of the ditch. The V-shaped ditch silted up quickly by natural erosion of the loess and was cleaned out and re-cut several times. The upper part of the profiles of the ditch shows a darker and more homogeneous layer and the building of humus indicates that the ditch was open and unused over a longer period of time. We still don't know just how long this period was, but it may have been as long as the construction – that is the wooden parts endured. There is no evidence that they were renewed. It is important to note that we have found no evidence of structures inside the enclosure. Some contemporary pits close to the eastern and western entrances of the enclosure (both inside and outside) may have been connected with ritual practices and depositions, which I will discuss later. Two larger pits at the western entrance to the enclosure have calcined walls and floors, which indicate that fires burnt here. These pits had a thick layer of ashes with pieces of charcoal and shards of stroke-ornamented pottery. We can assume that

Figure 23.2. Reconstructed enclosure in Goseck at its original location (photo by Ingo Hoffmann and Ralf Schwarz, Landesamt für Denkmalpflege Sachsen-Anhalt, Halle/Saale).

these pits were also used for some sort of action, possibly some sort of ritual actions (Figure 23.3). Interestingly, finds such as pottery and stone tools were deposited only in the entrance area in the South. The same is true for animal bones, most of which come from cattle.

There was something else very interesting – a special type of a burial found in the inner southeast area of the enclosure (Figure 23.3). Here, parts of an adult skeleton were deposited together with two flint arrow-heads and clots of ochre. This discovery is not only fascinating in terms of the question of ritual actions that might have taken place inside the enclosure, but also because it can help date the enclosure and clarify its relative chronology: The burial has been cut by the outer palisade and it looks very much like the skeleton was knowingly deposited there before or in the course of the construction of the wooden palisades (The results of an extensive set of C-14 dates – not known to the date of publication of this article – will provide a better understanding of the relative chronology of the monument). Similar deposition of human bodies or

body parts are known from Friebritz in Lower Austria and Ippesheim in Hesse (Neubauer and Trnka 2005b; Neugebauer-Maresch 2005; Schier 2005b).

In addition to the Middle Neolithic features there are four other interesting discoveries which I would like to briefly mention because they are important for the overall argument in this article: Outside of the enclosure, we found a grave of a 1–2 year old child with two pots of the Linear Pottery Culture (*c.* 5200 BC). Some pits – chronologically about 2000 years younger than the enclosure – close to but outside the eastern entrance of the enclosure had calcined walls and floors indicating fires. Interestingly, they seem to have been thoroughly cleaned out after usage so that there were no remains of the fire nor any artefacts. Even more interestingly is to note that the pits contained human bones. Furthermore, there are two small ditches leading towards the enclosure. Both ditches have been excavated and were *c.* 30–50 cm wide and 20–40 cm deep and belong to a later time period. And finally, outside the enclosure, we also surveyed and partly excavated a longhouse most likely from

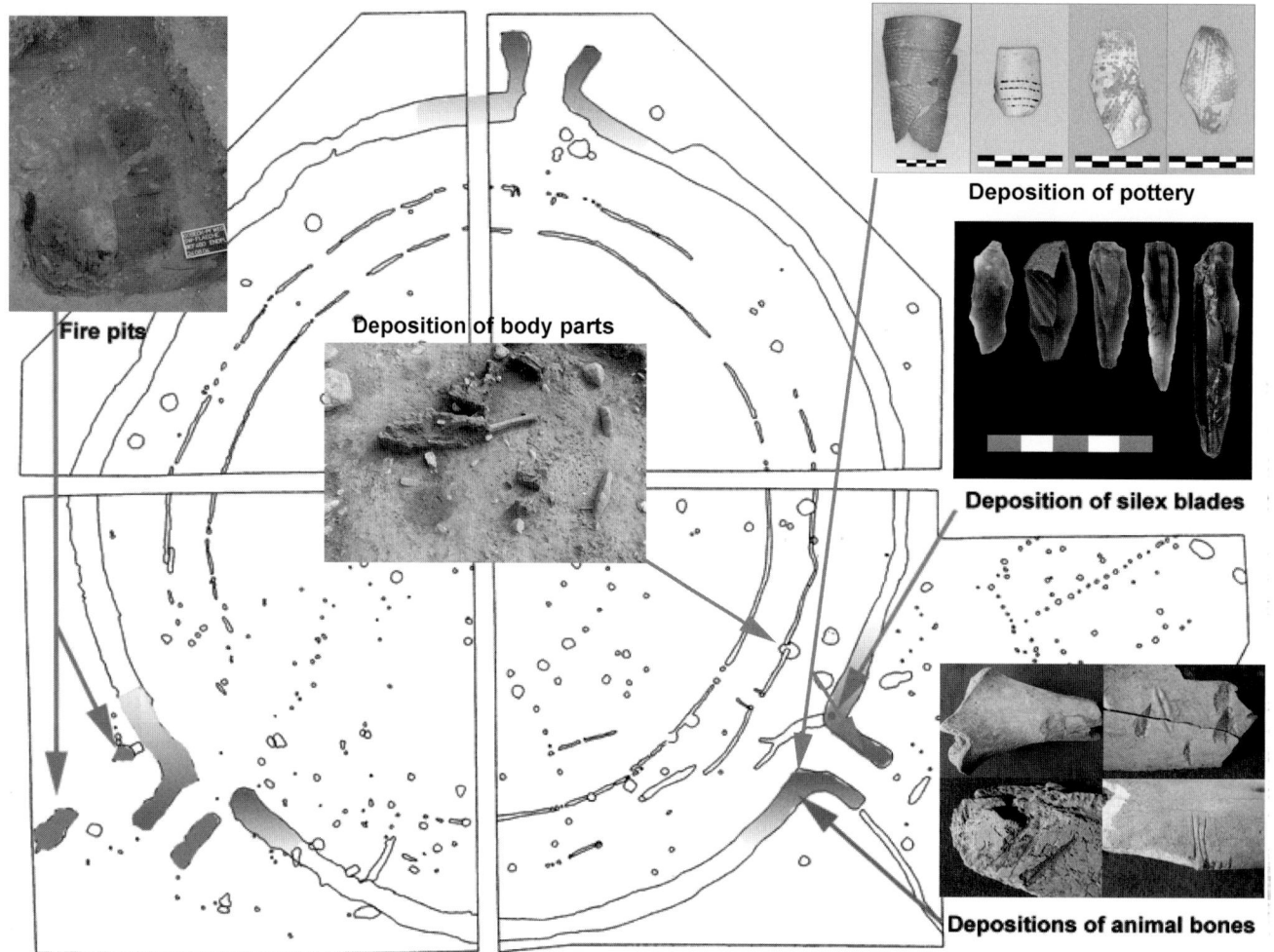

Figure 23.3. Goseck excavation plan with disposition patterns.

the Early Bronze Age (*c.* 1600 BC). All these features show that this place was occupied long before and long after the enclosure was built and used.

Now that I have introduced the site, I want to discuss what sort of meaning and function this type of enclosed place might have had and why were those places built and enclosed the way they were?

Enclosing space – meanings and functions of enclosed cult places

I will again focus on the concept of 'cult places' and their complex role regarding religious beliefs – as prescribed ways of understanding – and ritual practices – as prescribed ways of behaving. But I will also discuss the agency of such places regarding identity, memory, and experience. The embodiment of enclosed spaces represents the intersection of temporality, spatiality and materiality. Central to this concept of cult places and ritual practices is the recognition

that it is through the human body that the world is perceived and experienced, and places are the focal points of our embodied ritual practices and religious experience. In this way, cult places can be understood as the contexts of practice, experience, and materiality. They shape the meanings of experience and provide the resources that enable human action. A cult place is first and foremost a mutually constitutive relationship between embodied human subjectivities and the phenomenal world around them, whereby both are simultaneously and continuously brought into being and as such the foundation for human experience and being-in-the-world, extending far beyond the physical world. It is important to stress that cult places can be understood as always to be in the process of becoming or to be more like events rather than static end products. They not only exist as material entities, they also happen. They are continuously being made and remade, and are always changing. In this way then, the becoming of a cult place is inseparable from the occurrence of the structuration

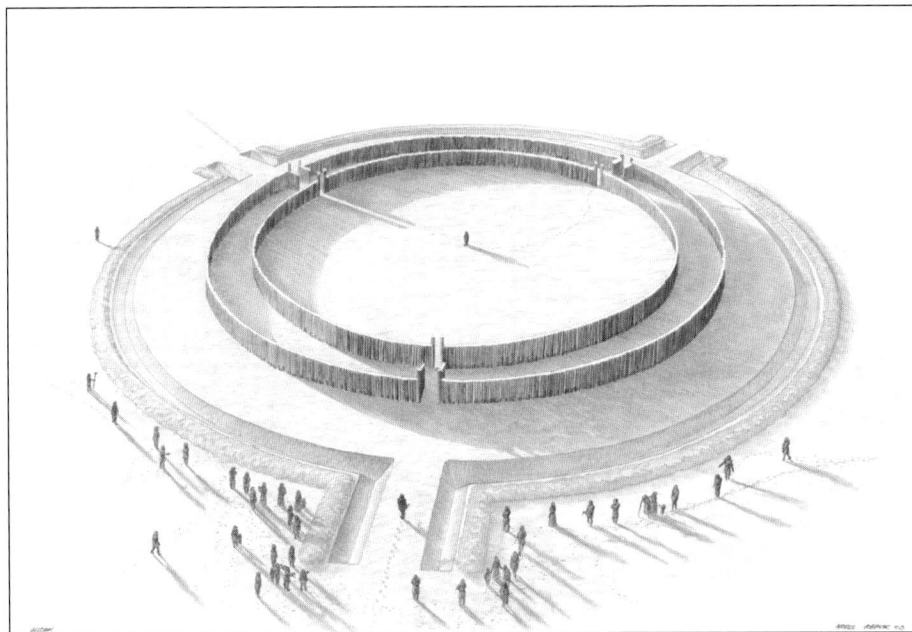

Figure 23.4. Drawing with a reconstruction of the Goseck enclosure (drawing by Karul Schauer, Landesamt für Denkmalpflege Sachsen-Anhalt, Halle/Saale).

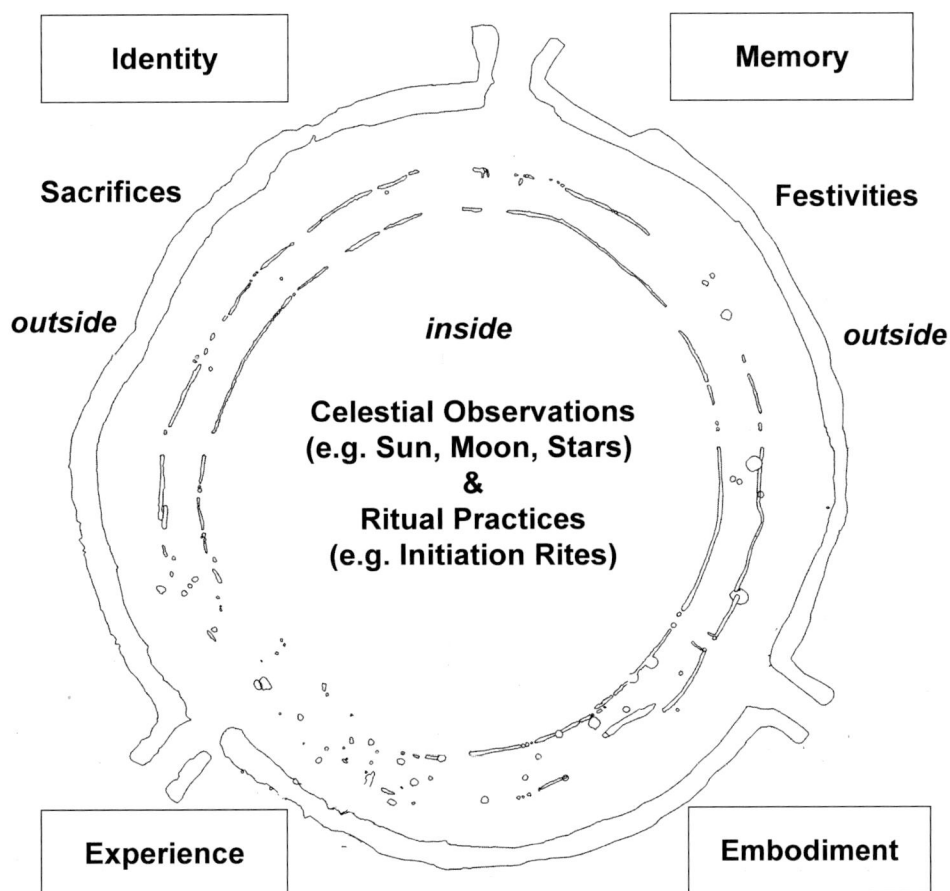

Figure 23.5. Diagram of the multi-scalar approach to cult places.

process in place. A cult place, therefore, is the continuous process through which human agency, experiences, culture, power relations, social structure, and the transformation of the material world become integrated and reproduced.

The contextual approach applied to the Goseck enclosure not only moves us away from thinking about a cult place as a static end product, it also emphasizes the *multiscalar nature* of place and illuminates the broader context of power relations and social structures within which place is both product and producer (Figure 23.5). The contextual approach helps us to recognize that the enclosed place is constructed and reconstructed continuously through reiterative practices. It is not only the product of human practice and experience, it also is the arena through which they emerge.

The question still is, what sort of practices occurred inside and outside those mysterious places and how can we grasp them archaeologically? And why were those places built and enclosed the way they were?

To begin with, I discount defence and fortification. Had these been major factors, one could expect more of these kinds of sites in Europe and throughout the Neolithic. One would also expect traces of violence and destruction along with corresponding artifacts. In Goseck, the earth bank *in front* of the ditch also clearly speaks against such an interpretation. Use as a corral or kraal can also be excluded: it took too much human labour to build and maintain these enclosures for the construction for such a mundane task to have been worthwhile. Also the fact that there was no phosphate in the ground clearly speaks against such a function. Moreover, in Goseck the entrances through the palisades are way too narrow to have been designed for cattle or other animals to pass through.

Some scholars interpret these places as centers or 'central places' of socio-political pre-eminence (Bertemes *et al.* in press), where labour could be mobilized for impressive collective undertakings, but the most intriguing interpretation – and the one I most closely adhere to – is that these enclosures functioned as cult places. This kind of interpretation has vast and endlessly exciting possibilities and seems to me the most logical and all-encompassing explanation, the sites not only be linked with ritual actions but also with means of consecrating place, of marking time, of honouring ancestors and as the symbolic representation of communal cohesion. The defined ways in which people must have approached, entered and experienced such monuments could be seen as a metaphor for the regularities of the comings and goings of their own lives, both from year to year and from generation to generation; this could have been done through reinforced attachment to specific places, chosen times for communal gathering and ritual, predetermined ways of seeing and experiencing ordered space.

One important part of these ceremonies and rituals was most likely feasting. This can be seen at Goseck in the structured depositions of animal bones (with cut marks and signs of extracting the marrow), of stone tools (for slaughtering the animals), pottery (for food and drink) and fire pits (for cooking the meat and food) (Figure 23.3). Another important part of the rituals was human sacrifices and the deposition of the body or parts of the body at meaningful places inside the enclosure. The fact that we only find single bodies or maximal two bodies like in Friebritz highlights the importance of the people deposited and/or the ritual involved. And finally, we have to take other rituals such as rites of passage/initiation rites into account. This becomes clear when we think of the enclosed places as frontiers between inside:outside, culture:nature, domesticated:wild, sacred:profane etc (Stäuble, in press). The architecture of the ditched circular enclosures supports such an interpretation: The entrances, for example, are often constricted and people would have been forced to enter in single file or double file causing them to enter the enclosed place in procession. Alex Gibson highlights that this was 'perhaps an essential part of the ritual, by severely restricting access to the enclosures and necessitating controlled and ordered entry' (Gibson in press). For him this suggests that 'at least some were closed monuments. If such is the case, they must have been closed, both physically and visually, to certain members of the community at certain times. Perhaps the ceremonies were even based on cults with several degrees of initiation'. In Goseck the entrances through the ditch are exactly aligned with the narrow entrances through the palisades (Figure 23.3). This construction restricts the physical as well as the visual access to the enclosure, which is especially important regarding the practices inside and outside the Goseck enclosure. And we should also think about the visual and acoustic effects created by wooden palisades of *c.* 2.5 m height. Even when we are standing in the enclosure today our experience of light, colour and sound as well as the general feeling of insular and important as well as being protected from views from outside.

External views may have been very focused, for example on specific solar, lunar or stellar events. Archaeo-astronomers have insisted on the astonishingly precise stellar orientations of numerous megalithic sites (Ruggles and Whittle 1981, Schlosser and Cierny 1996, Ruggles 1998). They have also managed to formulate (or re-formulate) complex calendrical functions for these stone circles or circular enclosures (Becker and Fassbinder 2005; Schier 2005b; Schmidt and Kaler 2005; Zotti 2005a and b; see also Biehl in press). Indeed, although they seem simple on the outside, these monuments may have served complex and highly advanced cyclical purposes. This is, naturally, a subject of great debate. Nevertheless, there is a growing body of evidence to suggest that solar observation was practised at these sites. The number of cardinal orientations encountered is too many to be coincidental. For instance, at Goseck, Wolfhard Schlosser was able to demonstrate the circular enclosure might have served as a solar observatory (Bertemes *et al.* 2004, 141; Biehl in press (c); Schlosser in press): The orientations of the southern entrances of the ditch and the palisades form an exact bearing to observe the winter solstice. Holes in the northern part of the palisades are also exactly aligned with the summer solstice. These measurements are too exact to be merely random.

Summary

To conclude, I firmly believe that these enclosures were used as places for ritual practice. To me, the evidence is overwhelming both in terms of material culture and in interpretive possibility. In order to develop a theoretical framework for archaeologists seeking to identify cult places and to recognize the equipment for ritual practices, we need to rely on some sort of method to analyze and interpret sites and their material culture. For me, the most important criteria here is the context. By this I mean both the structural context of the artifact and of the place. I see the two as interconnected and that through ritual practice/action, an artifact/material the place and the material culture used in or in relation with it was 'transferred' into a cult place and the material culture into a religious/ritual object. I want to stress the multi-scalar nature of enclosed places and the broader context of social structures and religious belief systems within which place is not only the product of ritual practices and experience, but also the arena through which they emerge.

As I see it, mono-causal interpretations need to be replaced by a more complex concept of religion and ritual including multi-causal and multi-scalar interpretations as I have demonstrated with the Goseck case study. I would also argue that the people who built and used the Goseck enclosure might have conceived it as a 'sacred place'. 'To say that a specific place is a sacred place is not simply to describe a piece of land, or just locate it in a certain position in the landscape. What is known as a sacred site carries with it a whole range of rules and regulations regarding people's behaviour in relation to it, and implies a set of beliefs relating to the non-empirical world, often in relation to the spirits of the ancestors, as well as more remote or powerful gods and spirits' (Carmichael *et al.* 1994, 3).

References

Andersen, N. H. 1997. The Sarup Enclosures. The Funnel Beaker Culture of the Sarup site including two causewayed camps compared to the contemporary settlements in the area and other European countries. Moesgaard, Aarhus University Press (Jutland Archaeological Society Publications XXXIII: 1).

Becker, H., Bertemes, F., Biehl, P. F. and Schier, W. 2005. Zwischen Himmel und Erde. *Archäologie in Deutschland*. Heft 6, 2005, 40–43.

Bell, C. 1992. *Ritual Theory, Ritual Practice.* Oxford/New York, Oxford University Press.

Bertemes, F. In press. *Der mittelbronzezeitliche Kultgraben von Drama und seine kulturhistorische Stellung in Südosteuropa.* Bonn, Habelt (Saarbrücker Beiträge zur Altertumskunde).

Bertemes, F. and Biehl, P. F. 2005. Goseck: Archäologie geht online. *Archäologie in Deutschland*. Heft 6, 2005, 36–38.

Bertemes, F., Biehl, P. F., Northe, A. and Schröder, O. 2004. Die neolithische Kreisgrabenanlage von Goseck, Ldkr. Weißenfels. *Archäologie in Sachsen-Anhalt* 2, 2004, 137–145.

Bertemes, F., Meller, H. and Biehl, P. F. (eds). In press. *Neolithische Kreisgrabenanlagen in Europa / Neolithic Circular Enclosures in Europe.* Halle/Saale: Veröffentlichungen des Landesamtes für Denkmalpflege und Archäologie Sachsen-Anhalt – Landesmuseum für Vorgeschichte.

Biehl, P. F. 1996. Symbolic Communication Systems. Symbols on Anthropomorphic Figurines in Neolithic and Chalcolithic Southeast Europe. *Journal of European Archaeology* Vol. 4, 153–176.

Biehl, P. F. 1999. Analogy and Context: A Re-Construction of the Missing Link. In L. Owen and M. Porr (eds) *Ethno-Analogy and the Reconstruction of Prehistoric Artefact Use and Production.* Tübingen: MoVince Verlag (Urgeschichtliche Materialhefte 14), 13–26.

Biehl, P. F. 2003. *Studien zum Symbolgut der Kupferzeit und des Neolithikums in Südosteuropa.* Bonn, Habelt Verlag (Saarbrücker Beiträge zur Altertumskunde, Bd. 64).

Biehl, P. F. 2006. Figurines in Action: Methods and Theories in Figurine Research. In R. Layton, S. Shennan and P. Stone (eds). *A Future for Archaeology – the Past as the Present.* London, UCL Press, 199–215.

Biehl, P. F. In press (a). *Die Neolithische Kreisgrabenanlage von Goseck. Untersuchungen zur Chronologie, Funktion und Bedeutung Neolithischer Kreisgrabenanlagen in Mitteleuropa.* Halle: Veröffentlichungen des Landesmuseum für Vorgeschichte Halle.

Biehl, P. F. In press (b). Multifunktionalität und soziale Praxis. Überlegungen zur Bedeutung der Stichbandkeramischen Kreisgrabenanlage von Goseck. In F. Bertemes, P. F. Biehl and H. Meller (eds). In press. *Neolithische Kreisgrabenanlagen in Europa / Neolithic Circular Enclosures in Europe.* Halle/Saale, Veröffentlichungen des Landesamtes für Denkmalpflege und Archäologie Sachsen-Anhalt – Landesmuseum für Vorgeschichte.

Biehl, P. F. In press. Measuring Time in the European Neolithic via Circular Enclosures. In C. Renfrew and I. Morley (eds). *Measuring the World and Beyond. The Archaeology of Early Quantification and Cosmology.* McDonald Institute Monographs. Oxford, Oxbow Books.

Bradley, R. 2005. Ritual and Domestic Life in Prehistoric Europe. London, Routledge.

Carmichael, D. L., Hubert, J. and Reeves, B. 1994. Introduction. In D. L. Carmichael, Hubert, J., Reeves, B. and Schanche, A. (eds). *Sacred Sites, Sacred Places.* London, Routledge (One World Archaeology), 1–8.

Conkey, M. W. and Tringham R. E. 1998. Rethinking Figurines:

A Critical View from Archaeology of Gimbutas, the 'Goddess' and Popular Culture. In L. Goodison and C. Morris (eds). *Ancient Goddesses. The Myths and the Evidence.* London, British Museum Press 1998, 22–45.

Darvill, T. and Thomas, J. (eds). 2001. *Neolithic Enclosures in Atlantic Northwest Europe.* Neolithic Studies Group Seminar Papers 6. Oxford, Oxbow Books.

Garwood, P., Jennings, P., Skeates, R. and Toms, J. (eds). 1991. *Sacred and Profane.* Proceedings of a Conference on Archaeology, Ritual and Religion Oxford, 1989. Oxford Committee for Archaeology Monograph No. 32, Oxford, Oxbow.

Garwood, P., Jennings, P., Skeates, R. and Toms, J. 1991. Preface. In P. Garwood, P. Jennings, R. Skeates and J. Toms (eds). 1991. *Sacred and Profane.* Proceedings of a Conference on Archaeology, Ritual and Religion Oxford, 1989. Oxford Committee for Archaeology Monograph No. 32. Oxford, Oxbow Books, v–x.

Gibson, A. In press. Palisade enclosures and timber circles in Britain and Ireland. In F. Bertemes, P. F. Biehl and H. Meller (eds). *Neolithische Kreisgrabenanlagen in Europa / Neolithic Circular Enclosures in Europe.* Halle/Saale: Veröffentlichungen des Landesamtes für Denkmalpflege und Archäologie Sachsen-Anhalt – Landesmuseum für Vorgeschichte.

Hodder, I. 1982a. *The present Past: An Introduction to Anthropology for Archaeologists.* London, Batsford.

Hodder, I. 1982b. *Symbols in Action. Ethnoarchaeological studies of material culture.* Cambridge, Cambridge University Press.

Hodder, I. 1985. Postprocessual Archaeology. In M. B. Schiffer (ed.) *Advances in Archaeological Method and Theory*, Vol. 8, 1–26. New York, Academic Press.

Hodder, I. 1987. The Contextual Analysis of Symbolic Meanings. In I. Hodder (ed.) *The Archaeology of Contextual Meanings*, 1–10. Cambridge, Cambridge University Press (New Directions in Archaeology).

Hodder, I. 1991. *Reading the Past. Current Approaches to Interpretation in Archaeology* (Second Edition). Cambridge, Cambridge University Press.

Hodder, I. 1999. *The Archaeological Process. An Introduction.* Oxford/Malden, Blackwell.

Insoll, T. 2004. Archaeology, Ritual, Religion. London, Routledge (Themes in Archaeology).

Insoll, T. 2005. Archaeology of Cult and Religion. In C. Renfrew and P. Bahn (eds). *Archaeology: The Key Concepts.* London, Routledge, 45–49.

Montelius, O. 1903. Die Methode. In *Die älteren Kulturperioden im Orient und in Europa* I. Stockholm.

Neubauer, W. and Trnka, G. 2005a. Rätselhafte Monumente der Steinzeit. In F. Daim and W. Neubauer (eds). *Zeitreise Heldenberg. Geheimnisvolle Kreisgräben* (Katalog zur Niederösterreichischen Landesausstellung 2005). Horn-Wien: Verlag Berger, 3–9.

Neubauer, W. and Trnka, G. 2005b. Totenbrauchtum. In F. Daim and W. Neubauer (eds). *Zeitreise Heldenberg. Geheimnisvolle Kreisgräben* (Katalog zur Niederösterreichischen Landesausstellung 2005). Horn-Wien, Verlag Berger, 223–224.

Neugebauer-Maresch, C. 2005. Tod im Kreisgraben. In F. Daim and W. Neubauer (eds). *Zeitreise Heldenberg. Geheimnisvolle Kreisgräben* (Katalog zur Niederösterreichischen Landesausstellung 2005). Horn-Wien, Verlag Berger, 224–227.

Papaconstantinou, D. (ed.) 2006. *Deconstructing Context. A Critical Approach to Archaeological Practice.* Oxford, Oxbow.

Petrasch, J. 1990. Mittelneolithische Kreisgrabenanlagen in Mitteleuropa. *Bericht Römisch Germanische Kommission 71*, 407–564.

Ruggles, C. 1998. Ritual astronomy in the Neolithic and Bronze Age British Isles: patterns of continuity and change. In A. Gibson and D. Simpson (eds). *Prehistoric Ritual and Religion: Essays in Honour of Aubrey Burl.* Stroud, Alan Sutton, 203–208.

Ruggles, C. and Whittle, A. (eds) 1981. *Astronomy and Society in Britain During the Period 4000–1500 BC.* Oxford, British Archaeological Reports 88.

Schier, W. 2005a. Kalenderbau und Ritualkomplex. *Archäologie in Deutschland*, Heft 6, 2005, 32–35.

Schier, W. 2005b. Kopfüber ins Jenseits. Ein Menschenopfer in der Kreisgrabenanlage von Ippesheim? In F. Daim and W. Neubauer (eds). *Zeitreise Heldenberg. Geheimnisvolle Kreisgräben* (Katalog zur Niederösterreichischen Landesausstellung 2005). Horn-Wien, Verlag Berger, 234–238.

Schlosser, W. and Cierny, J. 1996. *Sterne und Steine: eine praktische Astronomie der Vorzeit.* Darmstadt: Wissschaftliche Buchgesellschaft.

Schlosser, W. In press. Astronomische Untersuchungen der Kreisgrabenanlage von Goseck. In F. Bertemes, P. F. Biehl and H. Meller (eds). *Neolithische Kreisgrabenanlagen in Europa / Neolithic Circular Enclosures in Europe.* Halle/Saale, Veröffentlichungen des Landesamtes für Denkmalpflege und Archäologie Sachsen-Anhalt – Landesmuseum für Vorgeschichte.

Schmidt-Kaler, T. 2005. Die Neolithische Kalender-Revolution. *Archäologie in Deutschland*, Heft 6, 2005, 31.

Stäuble, H. In press. Stichband Keramische Kreisgrabenanlagen aus Sachsen. Neues zueimem altem Therma? In F. Bertemes, P. F. Biehl and H. Meller (eds). *Neolithische Kreisgrabenanlagen in Europa / Neolithic Circular Enclosures in Europe.* Halle/Saale: Veröffentlichungen des Landesamtes für Denkmalpflege und Archäologie Sachsen-Anhalt – Landesmuseum für Vorgeschichte.

Trigger, B. G. 1989. *A history of archaeological thought.* Cambridge, Cambridge University Press.

Trnka, G. 1991. *Studien zu mittelneolithischen Kreisgrabenanlagen.* Wien, Mitteilungen der Prähistorischen Kommission der Österreichischen Akademie der Wissenschaften 26.

Woldřich, J. N. 1886. Beiträge zur Urgeschichte Böhmens (III. Teil), Reste der neolitischen Ansiedlung bei Řepín, MAGW 16, 1886, 72–96.

Zotti, G. 2005a. Kalenderbauten? Zur astronomischen Ausrichtung der Kreisgrabenanlagen in Niederösterreich. In F. Daim and W. Neubauer (eds). *Zeitreise Heldenberg. Geheimnisvolle Kreisgräben* (Katalog zur Niederösterreichischen Landesausstellung 2005). Horn-Wien, Verlag Berger, 75–80.

Zotti, G. 2005b Kalender der Steinzeit. *Archäologie in Deutschland*, Heft 6, 2005, 27.

Chapter 24

CARVING IDENTITY: THE SOCIAL CONTEXT OF NEOLITHIC ROCK ART AND MEGALITHIC ART

Blaze O'Connor

Introduction

Material culture, some of which might be termed 'art', is understood as playing a key role in actualising religion and cult. Particular modes of visual culture have come to form a focus for archaeologists seeking to investigate the belief systems of past communities. Traditionally, these art forms have been envisaged as ones produced during, and playing a role in, ritual events that were controlled by select and dominant social groups. As a result, these types of interpretations confine our narratives to a rather narrow cross section of past communities. However, more recently, research across the humanities has increasingly acknowledged the embedded nature of ritual, belief and visual culture, recognising that they can be enacted and produced in multiple contexts (e.g. Insoll 2004; Alexander 2003). This has led research to take a fresh look at practices that exist beyond the traditional 'centres of the sacred', and beyond orthodox iconography. Within the context of Neolithic and Bronze Age research, archaeologists have begun to explore material practices that operated outside the realms of the monuments that supposedly reflected or shaped the 'dominant discourse' of the time, and formed the focus of 'ritual landscapes'. This work has also questioned the supposedly restricted, even exclusive, nature of the social groups that were able to access and manipulate these ritual landscapes (e.g. Brück 2001).

This paper investigates stone carving traditions of the later Neolithic to Early Bronze Age (EBA) in Britain and Ireland. During this period a number of carving practices developed, which, although operating within quite different contexts over a considerable period of time, explicitly referenced one another in material and formal terms. These include megalithic art, of which passage tomb art represents a specialised form, rock art on natural stone surfaces, carved stone balls, mobiliary art, decorated cist slabs, votive cup stones, and the broader and remarkably long-lived practice of cup marking. There are recurring links between these carving practices and monuments or sites that played a role

in funerary rituals and dedicatory or commemorative traditions. For the purposes of this paper, the social contexts of two practices in particular, rock art and passage tomb art, will be explored, and the Meath-Louth-Monaghan region on Ireland's eastern seaboard will form the geographic focus.

Art and identity

In assessing our current understandings of the social context of these two traditions, it seems that our interpretations have been coloured by our modern understandings of contemporary European art and particular forms of high-status ritual art in non-western societies. Typically these worlds are perceived (though not always correctly) as removed from the everyday, and out of reach of the 'ordinary' person and his or her daily life. This association with remote locations, accessible only to restricted audiences, fits in with ideas as to how Neolithic people interacted with the tradition of passage tomb art, where access to the confined tomb interiors is thought to have been restricted to elite groups (e.g. Richards 1993, 151; Cooney and Grogan 1994, 55–8; Barrett 1994, 15). It is telling that recent literature has frequently positioned rock art, or particular types of rock art such as complex or abstract forms, at the limits of the everyday, lived landscape (e.g. Bradley 1997; 2000, 71; Waddington 1996). Without attempting to resolve the definition of art and its problematic relationship to ancient practices here (see Layton 1991, 4–41; Gell 1998, 5–7 and 12–27; Dutton 1998), it must be remembered that this notion of seclusion, potentially carrying with it exclusivity, is not necessarily inherent in the production of all visual culture. It is therefore not a 'given' for carving practices during prehistory, but a question yet to be answered.

As Gell (1998, 73) has noted, 'high-status ritual art' has traditionally received more attention than 'decorative art' applied to objects, due to the tendency to view the former as roughly equivalent to Western notions of fine art. Both ritual art and fine art have conventionally been stereotyped as, to borrow Gell's term, 'gender-exclusive male cult rituals' (*ibid*). Prehistoric rock art provides an interesting arena in this regard. It does not fall into the decorative arts category, yet a broad range of ethnographic studies suggest that we cannot *assume* that the practice was linked to a specific age, gender or class group. In fact, various ritual art practices (including rock art), have been shown to involve widely varying social groups *within* individual communities as direct or associated participants, or to be accessible to varied groups and whole communities (e.g. Taçon 1992; 1994, 120; Watson 2003; Martin 2003; Smith and Blundell 2004). In some communities, particular types of art production are not the domain of the specialist, but skills learned and practiced by many (Dutton 1998; Layton 1991, 229–30). Particular sites may be gender-exclusive to males or females, whilst others relate to life events for groups of very different ages, including children (e.g. True and Griset 1988 on girls' puberty ritual paintings in California). It is also worth remembering that prehistoric children's footprints have been discovered at several Palaeolithic rock art caves in France (Bahn and Vertut 1997, 10–11). These examples are clearly distant in geographical and/or chronological terms from the assemblages forming the subject of this paper. Nevertheless they demonstrate that rock art sites were, and are, accessible to people of varied ages, genders, and social classes (see Conkey 1997). What this discussion offers is the possibility that both restricted *and* open forms of carving practices can be identified during the Neolithic (see also Purcell 2001). Although particular sites point to the likely existence of specialist carvers, the general prevalence of stone working skills during the Neolithic and EBA raises the possibility that wider groups of people were involved in various ways in quarrying, transporting, shaping, dressing and in some cases perhaps even carving stone. The restricted nature of access to passage tombs can also be overstated. It should be remembered that much of the visible art lies on the exterior surfaces of these monuments, and at entranceways that may have been viewed by larger groups of people.

Passage tomb art consists of carvings incorporated into monuments in both visible and non-visible architectural contexts, whilst rock art is characterised by motifs pecked into the surfaces of *in situ* outcrops and boulders. In Britain and Ireland, these two traditions are now recognised as being broadly contemporaneous, as opposed to strictly chronological developments in visual culture, with both practices originating during the Neolithic (O'Connor forthcoming). Although each exhibits its own idiosyncrasies with regard to technique, medium, motif range, composition, and landscape contexts, there are also significant similarities between the two practices. Both employ a pecking technique, probably using a stone implement and mallet, and both utilise a restricted range of abstract motifs incorporating cups and curvilinear elements that frequently interact with the natural features of the stone. The connections between these two traditions are reinforced by particular cases where we see motifs that epitomise one tradition (such as horned spirals or cup-and-ring motifs) occasionally turning up in the other.

It is true that the two traditions do not overlap fully in terms of their spatial distribution, but in particular regions they co-occur in close proximity, notably in Ireland. Such is the case in the Meath-Louth-Monaghan region where, in addition to the well-known concentrations of passage tomb art in the Boyne Valley (Eogan 1986; O'Kelly 1982) and at Loughcrew (Shee Twohig 1981), there are two notable concentrations of rock art. The first is in Ballinvally, below the summits of Loughcrew (Shee Twohig 2001), and the second, the area of focus here, runs inland from the foot of the Cooley Peninsula and just over the Monaghan border where the lowland terrain shifts to an undulating drumlin landscape. A dense cluster of rock art panels lies in the townland of Drumirril, nestled to the west of a bend in the River Fane. Similar regional clusters are evident across the British Isles, and it seems likely that these places formed a focus for carving activity by communities from the surrounding region. The Louth-Monaghan rock art is also associated with several carved stones that seem to represent a former complex of decorated megalithic monuments centred on the confluence of the Kilcurry and Castletown Rivers (O'Connor forthcoming).

Natural monuments

In the Louth-Monaghan region, rock art occurs on outcropping ridges of Inniskeen formation turbidite, better known as greywacke. The natural characteristics of this dense, durable and fine-grained stone make it an ideal carving medium, a fact that appears to have been well appreciated by the carvers of both rock art and passage tomb art. The Louth-Monaghan outcrops form part of the wider Longford/Down Lower Palaeozoic Silurian zone, which was an important source of quarry stone for the Boyne Valley passage tombs (Eogan 1986, 113). The characteristic graded bedding patterns of this stone renders it easily quarried, and means that the exposed and weathered outcrop faces tend to be the finer-grained ones, offering readymade carving surfaces. The core distribution of rock art panels lies along a linear spread of outcropping rock and the cluster of panels at Drumirril coincides with a closely packed series of small outcrop 'islands'. It is tempting to propose that this linear distribution of outcrops and ridges formed an important means of navigating through the undulating lowland landscape, and that the convergence of these landforms at Drumirril lent this locale a distinctive character, to which the carvers responded.

The panels located at the edges of the known distribution mark the juncture between the Inniskeen turbidite, and the related formations to the west and north, suggesting that the carvers actively differentiated between particular types of stone when selecting carving sites.

The outcrops in this region frequently take on a mound- or cairn-like appearance, due to their highly localised and pronounced convex form (Figure 24.1). At the centre of the Drumirril cluster is a distinctive outcrop formation comprised of angular segments that rise diagonally out of the ground, lending it the appearance of having been artificially constructed from stones piled on top of one another (Figure 24.2). At some of the carved hilltops of Drumirril, their resemblance to built monuments has been enhanced by the creation of ditched and banked enclosures, though the date of these features is yet to be established (Figure 24.3). Often, the outcrops are lent a more topographically and visually distinctive appearance by certain approaches to the site from positions in the surrounding landscape, whilst they are hardly discernable from others. Frequently, the most densely decorated faces are those readily visible from the approaches which lend the outcrops this distinctiveness, while other faces remain uncarved. The carvings repeatedly occur on the sloping to vertical surfaces at the periphery of these formations, echoing the placement of some of the most visually dominant passage tomb ornament on the vertical faces of outer kerbstones. The apparently intentional selection of natural features that resemble built monuments as carving locales is particularly interesting given the presence of passage tomb art in the immediate region (O'Connor *ibid*). This may explain why these natural features made such effective locales for carving practices. By visually referencing the related tradition of passage tomb art, the carvers would have tapped in to and expressed a whole range of ideological and social connotations. With their higher proportion of sloping and vertical decorated surfaces, the motifs on these distinctive outcrops could also have been viewed by larger groups of people.

Why did Neolithic communities engage simultaneously in two stone carving traditions exhibiting such strong formal and material similarities? What were the social contexts of these practices? In addition to the regional clusters featuring large concentrations of carved panels, as at Drumirril, we also see rock art dispersed widely across the regional landscape. This general pattern contrasts with the distribution of passage tomb art, which tends to occur in large complexes of passage tombs or in single isolated monuments. If Drumirril represents a regional centre for carving how should we interpret the dispersed rock art panels in this region?

Archaeological context

Recent road developments in the Louth-Monaghan area have revealed several new Neolithic to EBA sites ranging from the remains of Neolithic timber buildings to other forms of occupation activity such as temporary stake structures, pits, and hearths (e.g. Bennett 2003, 255–7; 2004, 357; see also O'Connor forthcoming). Their distribution is likely to be considerably more widespread than the road intakes imply, and current evidence suggests that a dispersed mosaic of occupation sites may have existed across the lowlands of this region. Despite the limitations of the current distribution map, these sites are closing in on the rock art, with some located just a few hundred metres away from the dispersed carved panels (e.g. at Tankardsrock). This is quite a different picture from the widely held view of rock art being situated on the periphery of the lived landscape. The positioning of rock art has been demonstrated to be highly sensitive to subtle features of the local topography. This implies that people made detailed 'readings' of the landscape when selecting locations for the creation of new panels, and possessed intimate knowledge of these places when locating an existing site. With people conducting their daily lives close by, it is tempting to see the dispersed panels as local points of ritual focus within the everyday lived landscape. This is not surprising given the evidence for ritual activity within settlements, for instance in the form of votive deposits and pits exhibiting carefully structured fills (e.g. Logue 2003; see also Brück 1999). The presence of a range of single or paired panels dispersed across the wider region may indicate that rock art sites were visited on a more regular basis by wider ranges of social groups than passage tomb art.

In order to investigate the archaeological context of rock art in further detail, a large-scale geophysical survey was conducted at Drumirril, followed by targeted excavation (O'Connor 2003; forthcoming). This revealed a range of material dating from Early Neolithic, Middle Neolithic, Late Neolithic to EBA, and Early Christian periods, within metres of the carved panels. Features included areas of burning directly on the carved outcrop surfaces, small deposits of burnt flint at the base of panels, and a pit containing carinated pottery characteristic of the Early Neolithic, quartz cobbles, charcoal, and worked flint. A co-axial fieldsystem and six enclosures, five of which encompass key clusters of rock art panels, were also identified. Within one of these enclosures was an unusual timber post structure surrounding a stone setting and pit with an internal posthole. The structure appears to have burnt to the ground, after which the area was sealed with a layer of quarried greywacke slabs and cobbles. Inevitably these initial findings raise many questions, particularly with regard to the date of different activities, and their relationship to the rock art. However, this work does suggest

Figures 24.1 and 24.2. The rock art outcrops at Drumsinnot, Louth (left), and Drumirril, Monaghan (right).

Figure 24.3. One of the carved rocky hilltops at Drumirril defined by an enclosing ditch and bank.

that, far from being remote locales visited exclusively for carving rituals, the rock art at Drumirril represents a ritual component embedded in a complex living landscape where a much wider range of activities occurred over a considerable period of time.

Carving contexts

Can the carvings themselves also tell us about the contexts in which these traditions operated? O'Sullivan (1986) has identified two contrasting passage tomb art styles, 'plastic' and 'depictive', though individual carvings are not always easily classified (Figure 24.4). While the depictive style is present in both focal and satellite tombs, the plastic style is predominantly limited to the former (O'Sullivan 1986, 78–9). Depictive motifs are characterised by their two-dimensionality, and somewhat haphazard compositions where varied motifs compete with one another for space. These motifs were generally carved before the panels were placed in the tombs, and are frequently located in hidden positions, apparently operating independently of visibility (e.g. see Eogan 1984, 80–9 and 172–77). At Newgrange, it is in the hidden depictive compositions that we see the cup-and-ring motifs typical of rock art occur most frequently (see O'Kelly 1982). In contrast, the later plastic style art was carved *in situ* on accessible surfaces after tomb construction. Plastic art took into account the form of the stone surface, producing a sculptural quality approaching the three-dimensional. These panels were more carefully finished with even, regular forms and balanced symmetrical arrangements flooding their stone canvases. The motifs overlie, and sometimes obscure or outsize, the earlier depictive style designs, and appear to be intended for prominent visual display (O'Sullivan 1986, 75–6). At Newgrange, Knowth and Fourknocks, the dominant plastic style designs on display are characterised by their stylistic unity as panel groups (Shee Twohig 1981; O'Kelly 1982; Eogan 1986). This unified quality might be said to lend them a sense of authoritative credibility, since it implies a structured and predefined approach to carving. It remains unclear whether these might have actually been masterminded or influenced by particular individuals, or the 'unifying force or personality' described by O'Sullivan (1981 Vol.1, 175; 1986, 74), or carried out by numerous hands.

Despite their limited motif range, rock art compositions tend to be idiosyncratic, irregular, and informal, lending them a multi-authored character. Unlike passage tomb art, unified *oeuvres* can rarely be identified. The motifs and compositions are cumulative, with design elements combined and recombined in innovative ways, elaborating on existing features, establishing new connections and responding to the stone 'canvas'. The endless novelty in the compositions brings to mind Brück's discussion of

relational identity (2001; 2004; see also Fowler 2004) and the considerable variability exhibited in Neolithic depositional practices. Brück has observed that 'it is hard to imagine that each of so many [idiosyncratic] depositional events was orchestrated by some dominant power; are we not hearing "a cacophony of voices"?' (2001, 660 citing Bender 1993, 275).

Yet, even *within* these more idiosyncratic rock art compositions, contrasts in technique and composition have been described between two styles of rock art that are somewhat reminiscent of the distinctions between plastic and depictive passage tomb art (Waddington *et al.* 2005; Connolly 1991, 37–8). The first has been described as highly responsive to the natural topography of the stone, where motifs are well defined and carefully composed with a concern for symmetry and even forms. The second is more roughly, superficially or haphazardly pecked and irregular in form. Examples of these contrasts are shown in Figures 24.5 and 24.6, where two panels from Magheranaul, Donegal, display quite different approaches to carving despite their location within just a few metres of one another. In rare cases, such as at Hunterheugh Crags, Northumberland (Waddington *et al.* 2005), and Kilmartin, Argyll, chronological relationships between these two styles are evident, with the 'crude' (depictive) style seemingly postdating the 'sensitive' (plastic) style (O'Connor forthcoming).

However, the distinction may not be a strictly chronological one, but one indicative of divergent roles or contextual origins. It seems possible that in both passage tomb art and rock art, the depictive style may represent 'votive motif deposition' practices, whilst in the plastic style the emphasis is on display and the creation of a 'visually arresting' aesthetic (Bradley 1997, 74; Gell 1992). In the former it seems that the act of creation, and involvement in the carving process, took precedence over the production of a predefined symbolic composition, with individual moments in time and individual agency playing a key role in the development of the compositions. The production of depictive art, with its emphasis on the performative aspects of carving, may have formed an important stage in the preparation and transformation of the megalithic blocks for their new monumental contexts. This process, associated with the laborious procurement and transport of the stones before they were set into place within built monuments, might well have involved wider groups and audiences than those that eventually controlled the access to the tomb interiors. If these stylistic distinctions indeed reflect contrasts in carving contexts during the construction and use of passage tombs, then the tentative identification of depictive and plastic styles within the rock art tradition suggests that these sites may also have been visited and recarved under quite varied social contexts.

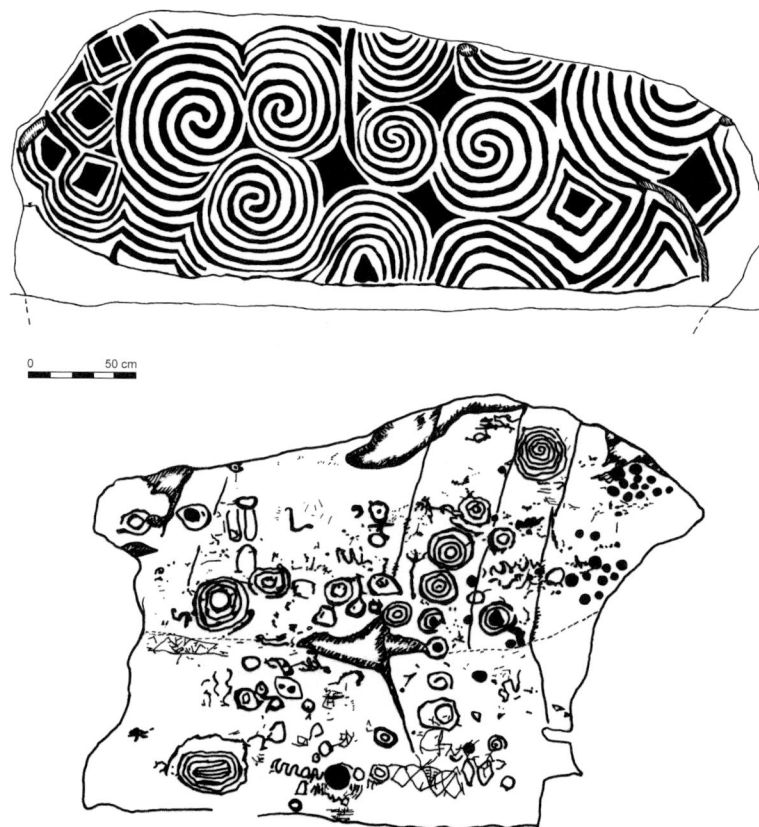

Figure 24.4. Examples of plastic (above) and depictive (below) style panels at Newgrange (drawings by Aaron Watson after O'Kelly 1982).

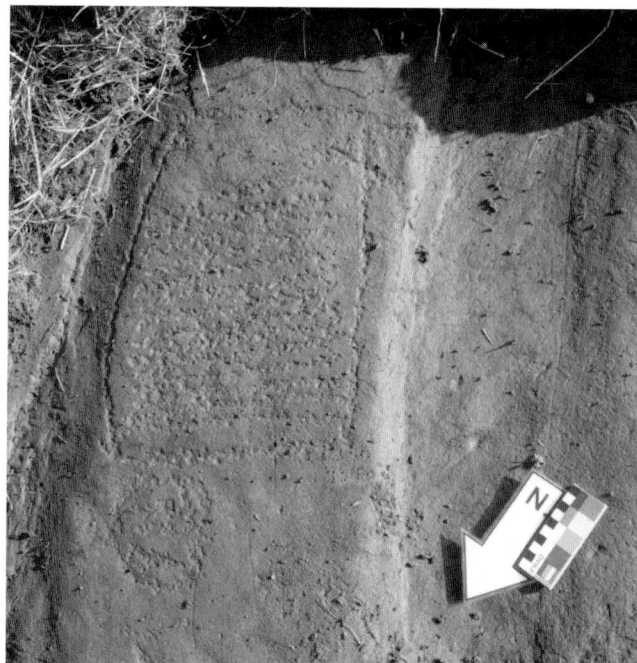

Figures 24.5 and 24.6. Outcrop rock art panels exhibiting two contrasting carving styles at Magheranaul, Isle of Doagh, Donegal.

Conclusion

By opening rock art sites to more varied audiences from communities living nearby, a new light is cast on the ways that carving practices may have served to express and create social and individual identity. Rather than assuming that all Neolithic carving traditions were the realm of select social groups, it might be more useful to look at the broad range of 'art practices' that perhaps engaged different social groups within given communities, and to explore their distinctions and interrelationships. Whilst there were domains within which particular art forms were perhaps confined to restricted audiences, alongside these there were other practices that operated within their own systems of knowledge and power. These contrasts emphasise the key role that art forms play in maintaining, challenging and renegotiating different forms of social identity. Although the distinct nature of passage tomb art and rock art suggests they may have played quite different roles in the formation of social identity, this does not necessarily rule out an overlap between the social groups and individuals involved in creating and viewing both the traditions. The types of formal and material overlaps and references between the two practices reinforce this potential ambiguity. As Brück (2001; see also Thomas 1996; Bender 1998) has suggested, different aspects of people's relative identity are played out in different contexts of action. By opening up our understandings of the social context of prehistoric carving practices, we need not negate the potential power of material practices in the creation of interpersonal difference, but it does question the manner in which these differences might have been achieved.

Acknowledgements

This research was supported by the UCD Humanities Institute of Ireland Post Doctoral Fellowship, the Government of Ireland Scholarship from the Irish Research Council for Humanities and Social Sciences, the UCD Open Postgraduate Scholarship and Dublin City Council Higher Education Grants. My thanks to Gabriel Cooney for his helpful comments.

References

Alexander, V. 2003. *Sociology of the Arts*. Oxford, Blackwell.

Bahn, P. and Vertut, J. 1997. *Journey Through the Ice Age*. London, Seven Dials.

Barrett, J. 1994. *Fragments from Antiquity. An Archaeology of Social Life in Britain 2900–1200BC*. Oxford, Blackwell.

Bender, B. 1993. 'Introduction: Landscape – meaning and action'. In B. Bender, (ed.). *Landscape: Politics and Perspectives*. Oxford, Berg, 1–17.

Bender, B. 1998. *Stonehenge: Making Space*. Oxford, Berg.

Bennett, I. (ed.), 2003. *Excavations 2001. Summary Accounts of Archaeological Excavations in Ireland*. Bray, Wordwell.

Bennett, I. (ed.), 2004. *Excavations 2002. Summary Accounts of Archaeological Excavations in Ireland*. Bray, Wordwell.

Bradley, R. 1997. *Rock Art and the Prehistory of Atlantic Europe: Signing the Land*. London, Routledge.

Bradley, R. 2000. *An Archaeology of Natural Places*. London, Routledge.

Brück, J. 1999. 'Ritual and rationality: Some problems of interpretation in European archaeology', *European Journal of Archaeology* 2(3), 313–44.

Brück, J. 2001. 'Monuments, power and personhood in the British Neolithic', *Journal of the Royal Anthropological Institute* 7(4), 649–667.

Brück, J. 2004. 'Material metaphors. The relational construction of identity in Early Bronze Age burials in Ireland and Britain', *Journal of Social Archaeology* 4(3), 307–333

Cooney, G. and Grogan, E. 1994. *Irish Prehistory: A Social Perspective*. Dublin, Wordwell.

Conkey, M. 1997. 'Beyond art and between the caves: Thinking about context in the interpretive process'. In M. Conkey, O. Soffer, D. Stratmann and N. Jablonski (eds). *Beyond Art. Pleistocene Image and Symbol*. San Francisco: California Academy of Sciences, 343–367.

Connolly, M., 1991. 'A prehistoric decorated pillar-stone from Teeromoyle, Co. Kerry', *Journal of the Kerry Archaeological and Historical Society* 24, 32–39.

Dutton, D.1998. 'Tribal art'. In M. Kelly (ed.). *The Encyclopedia of Aesthetics*. New York, Oxford University Press, 404–406.

Eogan, G. 1984. *Excavations at Knowth I: Smaller Passage Tombs, Neolithic Occupation and Beaker Activity*. Royal Irish Academy Monographs in Archaeology 1. Dublin, Royal Irish Academy.

Eogan, G. 1986. *Knowth and the Passage Tombs of Ireland*. London, Thames and Hudson.

Fowler, C. 2004. *The Archaeology of Personhood: An Anthropological Approach*. London, Routledge.

Gell, A. 1992. 'The technology of enchantment and the enchantment of technology'. In J. Coote and A. Shelton (eds). *Anthropology, Art and Aesthetics*. Oxford, Clarendon Press, 40–67.

Gell, A. 1998. *Art and Agency. An Anthropological Theory*. Oxford, Clarendon Press.

Insoll, T. 2004. *Archaeology, Ritual, Religion*. London, Routledge.

Layton, R. 1991. *The Anthropology of Art*. Second Edition. Cambridge, Cambridge University Press.

Logue, P. 2003. 'Excavations at Thornhill, Co. Londonderry'. In I. Armit, E. Murphy, E. Nelis and D. Simpson, *Neolithic Settlement in Ireland and Western Britain*. Oxford, Oxbow Books, 149–55.

Martin, C. 2003. 'Marks of contemplation: Cup-and-ring rock-art from Ireland', *Before Farming* 2003/3 (5), 1–11.

O'Connor, B. 2003. 'Recent excavations in a rock art landscape', *Archaeology Ireland* 17(4): 14–16.

O'Connor, B. forthcoming. *Inscribed Landscapes. Contextualising Atlantic Rock Art*. Oxford, Oxbow.

O'Kelly, M. 1982. *Newgrange. Archaeology, Art and Legend*. London, Thames and Hudson.

O'Sullivan, M. 1981. 'The Megalithic Art of Site 1 at Knowth and its Context in Ireland'. Unpublished M.A. Thesis, University College Dublin.

O'Sullivan, M. 1986. 'Approaches to passage tomb art', *Journal of the Royal Society of Antiquaries* 116, 68–83.

Purcell, A. 2001. 'The rock-art landscape of the Iveragh Peninsula, County Kerry, south-west Ireland'. In G. Nash, and C. Chippindale (eds), *European Landscapes of Rock-Art*. London, Routledge, 71–92.

Richards, C. 1993. 'Monumental choreography: Architecture and spatial representation in late Neolithic Orkney'. In C. Tilley (ed.), *Interpretative Archaeology*. Oxford, Berg, 143–178.

Shee Twohig, E. 1981. *The Megalithic Art of Western Europe*. Oxford, Clarendon Press.

Shee Twohig, E. 2001. 'Change and continuity: Post passage tomb ceremonial complex near Loughcrew, Co. Meath', *Revue Archaeologique de l'Ouest*, Supplement 9, 113–124.

Smith, B. and Blundell, G. 2004. 'Dangerous ground: A critique of landscape in rock-art studies'. In C. Chippindale and G. Nash (eds). *The Figured Landscapes of Rock-Art. Looking at Pictures in Place*. Cambridge, Cambridge University Press, 239–62.

Taçon, P. 1992. 'Somewhere over the rainbow: An ethnographic and archaeological analysis of recent rock paintings of Western Arnhem Land, Australia'. In J. McDonald and I. Haskovec (eds). *State of the Art: Regional Rock Art Studies in Australia and Melanesia*. Occasional Aura Publication 6. Melbourne, Archaeological Publications, 205–15.

Taçon, P. 1994. 'Socialising landscapes: the long-term implication of signs, symbols and marks on the land', *Archaeology in Oceania* 29, 117–29.

Thomas, J. 1996. *Time, Culture and Identity. An Interpretive Archaeology*. London, Routledge.

True, D. L. and Griset, S. 1988. *Exwanyawish*: A Luiseño sacred rock, *Journal of California and Great Basin Anthropology* 10(2), 270–4.

Waddington, C. 1996. Putting rock art to use. A model of early Neolithic transhumance in north Northumberland. In P. Frodsham (ed.). *Neolithic Studies in No-Man's Land* (Northern Archaeology 13/14). Newcastle, The Northern Archaeological Group, 147–177.

Waddington, C. with Johnson, B. and Mazel, A. 2005. Excavation of a rock art site at Hunterheugh Crag, Northumberland, *Archaeologia Aeliana* 34, 29–54.

Watson, C. 2003. *Piercing the Ground*. Fremantle, Fremantle Arts Centre Press.

Chapter 25

ANIMISM IN THE ROCK ART AND MATERIAL CULTURE OF PREHISTORIC SIBERIA

Liliana Janik

This paper presents a preliminary study of rock art and material culture from Lake Baikal in Siberia, and argues that this art can be interpreted as a manifestation of ritual beliefs and practices based on shamanism and animism through ritual practices based on the notion of embodied realism.

Embodied realism and the archaeology of cult

Religious events are explained or illustrated with the use of metaphors containing stories from life – expressed in Embodied Realism – experience to which believers can relate (Lakoff and Johnson 1999). An 'Embodied realism' approach starts with the understanding that we conceptualise the world around us (implicitly and explicitly) in two ways: firstly by our bodily experiences, using the capacities of our bodies, including all our senses; and secondly the body and mind are inseparable in creating and shaping the world around us. These experiences allow us to create metaphors and concepts to which we can relate while making sense of the world around us. Because we live in different natural, social and cultural environments, despite our common biological make up, we create different metaphors and concepts, both as individuals and collectively as communities. This, as I elaborate below, is vital in communicating and sharing concepts and set of beliefs.

The role of visual narrative and material culture in the constitution of religious beliefs

The use of visual narrative is important in many religious practices, and in communicating metaphorical stories the use of visual stimuli that can be instantly recognised by the believers of a particular religion is essential. These experiences can be categorised very generally into two main kinds: one reflects the mythological reality conveyed in the religious stories; and the second reflects the experience of a particular believer or community of believers in participating in this mythological reality, for instance by taking part in ritual events where particular items of material culture are used to signify particular elements of this mythological reality, or through being exposed to particular visual stimuli that enable the believer to move again into a mythological reality. Material culture and depictions are the vehicles that help us move between worlds, the world of everyday life and the world of mythological reality. It is essential that mythological reality is recognised by us through our bodily experience (participation in rituals) as well as through the stories we can relate to that describe mythological events (Christmas or Easter), because through such engagement we build physical and spiritual affinity to the beliefs that in turn creates deep brain neural connections that can be called on by our memory, instantly bringing spiritual and religious experience to our lives. Material culture and depictions continue despite changes within religions or even the collapse of some religious beliefs. They are the embodiment of concepts that allow human beings to move between worlds, and therefore they are very important in understanding past and contemporary societies. I would suggest that they are concepts that transcend time and space. One such concept is animism.

Animism

Animism is a spiritual and anthropological concept originally formulated by Tylor in his work concerning early religion (Bird-David 1999). Animism, it has been argued, represents the most primitive and first stage of the evolution of religious belief. It is based on the premise that that all animate and non-animate things were considered to have souls. Later it was thought that when they were outside those entities, souls become spirits. In recent years Bird-David took up the idea of animism within anthropology. She argues that not all inanimate objects have qualities and powers of anime, but only those that stay in a tangible relationship between inanimate and anime.

Animism is concept that has not been used by archaeologists in interpreting prehistoric beliefs, in contrast to shamanism, which has become the most popular explanation for the religion of prehistoric fisher-gatherer-hunters and early farming communities in Europe. If we start to think about animism as a concept rather than the most primitive form of religious belief, as part of other religions, and if we stop categorising communities on the basis of food procurement or production, we can see that animism is still a widespread phenomenon within different religious beliefs and practices. Giving sacred/divine qualities to features in the natural world constitutes the beliefs and practices of Shamanism, classical Greek religion, Norse religion and even modern Christianity, while cross-cutting different modes of production, natural environments and a time-span of thousands of years. I suggest that animism was probably part of prehistoric spiritual life since it expresses itself in a variety of different beliefs and religious practices up to the present.

Turning to archaeological data, I suggest the that concept of animism can be well employed in interpreting different rock art locations, where visual narrative indicates a place of strong spiritual power. While looking for forms of animism in the past I propose to look at a particular quality of geomorphological forms in the landscape where individual features have been signified by placing carvings on them. Carvings might reflect the spiritual power of the rock, or give meaning to the rock on which they appear, or both at once. The carving of a rock surface is a good indicator of the relationship between inanimate geomorphological features and prehistoric communities. The visibility of carvings allows us to posit such a relationship, which would otherwise be almost impossible to detect by contemporary archaeologists. The relationship between the mountain and the community can be further traced by the images carved into the rock and the material culture represented, as will be seen below when we consider the relationship between anthropomorphic carvings and the shape of pendants placed in graves. The intricacy of possible relationships and interactions where geomorphological features become animate entities as indicated by archaeological data, point to utility of the understanding of animism as a set of relationships between humans, animate and inanimate parts of natural world, where the life of one part is always related to the life of the other (Bird-David 1999).

Archaeological data itself becomes primary in this approach as we try to find the most suitable interpretative modes to infer about the past. This is not a positivist approach in which data on its own can provide us with the answers to archaeological questions. It is not also the approach that prioritises theory, as often seen in works of post-processual archaeology (cf. Janik 1999; 2007). It is rather an interwoven process where archaeological data is a closed set of knowledge for a particular time and space. We can learn more about that data by employing new analytical techniques, or acquire more archaeological material, still as we interpret it all the information we have are there. At the same time the theory we use to interpret this data can be modified, altered or changed. We can therefore interpret archaeological data from different perspectives and view points, but the data is still the same, which is why I would like to propose the fundamental importance of archaeological data over any theoretical approach. I would further suggest that it is archaeological data that sets archaeology apart from other disciplines such as anthropology, ethnography or history.

Animism by itself has not in recent years been an important part of archaeological interpretation of past religion, although it has been implicitly present as an element within shamanism. Within certain shamanistic traditions, some geomorphological features are considered to have spirits living in them. This belief in the presence of spirits in the natural landscape is not restricted to shamanism being found in many religions. What is important here is the animistic notion that spirits inhabit inanimate items, in this case elements in the natural landscape. They are found in the religious belief systems of a wide range of large scale, complex societies, for example classical Greece, contemporary Japan and contemporary France. I suggest that the phenomenon of geomorphological features possessing spiritual powers, either by themselves or by being inhabited by particular spirits, is generally and cross-culturally spread through time and space. Animism, from the view point of embodied realism, is thus a concept that provides inanimate objects and features of natural environment as a metaphor that allow us to relate to them. Such places can be archaeologically detected, according to Bradley, by carving rocks and by placing offerings in particular places in the landscape (Bradley 2000).

The reasons for defining those particular places, according to Bradley, may lie in the relationship between the place and various sets of beliefs. A particular location is signified by particular images and is related to the communities who carved them and who see them. I suggest that even when beliefs have altered, the importance of the location as part of real/symbolic landscape, as a place of spiritual power, can be long term. This can be illustrated by the example of the healing waters of Lourdes. It is believed that the spiritual power of the Virgin Mary was transformed into the grotto and the spring, and expressed itself in the healing properties captured in the water from this particular cave. The cave itself was used in the more distant past as a shrine to Persephone, the Greek Goddess of Spring Growth and Queen of the Underworld.

Mythological reality captured in rock art location and narrative

I suggest that, for heuristic reasons, we can usefully divide rock art depictions into three categories. The first category of rock art carvings comprise abstract forms and images that have no visual narrative, understood here as the intentional manner in which the artist or artists have constructed any particular composition by linking depictions into a visual story we can 'make sense of' by looking at, or where depictions are executed in such way that we do not see a coherent visual story, but simply a juxtaposition of images. These images define the mythological or secret/symbolic landscape where particular divinities or spirits live. I suggest that these can be seen in cases of so-called Atlantic rock art, with their distinctive abstract spiral forms (Bradley 1997). It can also be argued that single realistic carvings on rocks can be part of the same type. These carvings are thought to embody the spiritual powers that are believed to inhabit particular geomorphological features. Examples include the reindeer at Josarsakubben and the bear from Valle, Norway (Gjerde 2006), rock art sites that have no implicitly recognisable visual narrative.

The second category of rock art comprises depictions with a well-constructed visual narrative. These images depict what is believed to have happened in the landscape, often a mythological landscape. The third category is a combination of the first and second. The location of the second category is not restricted to the spiritual or mythological landscape it portrayed, and therefore it may not be restricted to particular geomorphological forms or places in the landscape. The location of rock art in this category is governed instead by the need to show the events captured in the carvings. Examples include the rock art complexes of Zalavruga in Northern Russia (Janik et al. 2007) and Alta in Norway (Helskog 1999.). Those locations are both full of visual compositions that depict multifaceted stories, and the visual narratives they display evoke the viewers' bodily everyday experiences, for example skiing or walking through snow using snow shoes. These are experiences that almost all the people living in the far north of Europe, where these carvings are located, have had in the past and present, therefore one can with ease relate to those images. Other depictions relating to terrestrial and aquatic hunting are slightly different. While in the past taking part in such activities was common, today first hand experience is rarer. We build our understanding in different ways in the contemporary world, not by participating in it *per se*, but through experiencing it in a 'second hand' way; for example, written stories, films, and the general aversion to whale hunting in many countries, make us aware about the topics carved. Through these common experiences of past people mythological stories have been shown/illustrated: the visualisation of the

Universe, composed of three worlds as in some mythologies of Northern peoples, is carved in Alta according to Helskog (Helskog 1999). As I have suggested above, the real – mythological worlds are interwoven, because only through the use of embodied realism can believers relate to mythological stories. What we see here is the duality of visual narrative in the forms of those two realities.

Long term visual stimuli of religious narrative: a case study from Lake Baikal

The case study presented in this paper has two major qualities lacked by some archaeological data; it has survived for thousands of years, and it has been exposed to past and present communities without obstruction, for example being covered by sediments or by changes in water level.

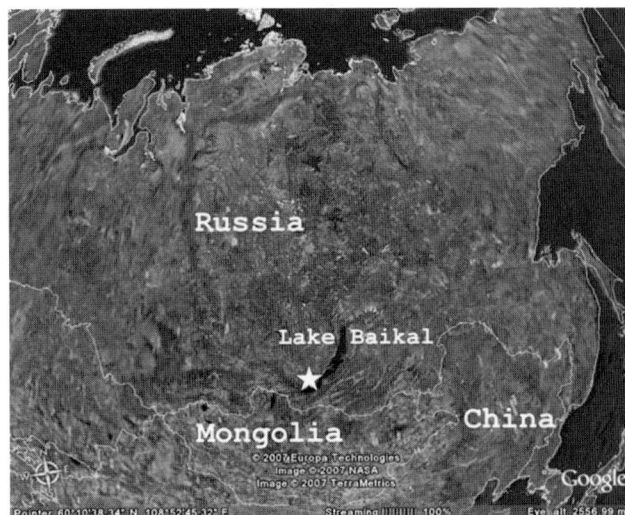

Figure 25.1. Map of part of Eurasia. The Sagan Zaba rock art site is marked by a star.

The rock carvings of Sagan Zaba (Figure 25.1), located in a small cove by the shore of Lake Baikal, Siberia, were first recorded in the summer of 1881 by N. N. Agapitov. Later archaeological research was carried out in the cove by A. P. Okladnikov in the late 1960s and early 1970s (Okladnikov 1974). The carvings of Sagan Zaba did not have to be 'discovered' as such by archaeology, because as a result of their location on the cliff flanking the cove they were not covered by sediments and were always visible, from the time of their creation until the present day (Figure 25.2).

The name Sagan Zaba means White Cove (Figure 25.3), taken from the colour of the rock from which the cliffs enclosing the cove are formed, and the boulders and pebbles on and by the beach, which is in stark contrast to the surrounding vegetation-covered hill tops and the darker

Figure 25.2. Panoramic view towards the cove from the Lake Baikal (photo L. Janik).

Figure 25.3. View of the carved cliff with the various colour characteristics (photo L. Janik).

rock of other cliffs nearby. The natural qualities of place create a special ambience to the cove. This special feeling is enhanced by the white cliffs and stones, the sheltering properties offered by the cove, offering protection from the strong winds that sweep across Lake Baikal, and the relatively easy access to adjoining parts of the landscape provided by the small stream which occupies an old river bed leading up to a small glacier in the hills. The rock art can be only partially appreciated as part of the white colour scheme in some parts of the cliff since some of it has disappeared since A. P. Okladnikov's original publication due to weathering. In addition, the colour of the rock surface has been darkened as a result of an attempt at conservation carried out by Russian conservators and archaeologists in the 1980's, trying to stop the process whereby thin layers of the cliffs surface were flaking off leading to the loss of rock carvings. The extent of the loss can be assessed through comparing the results of the author's own survey undertaken in 2006 with the records made in 1925 by T. I. Cavenkov, and by A. P. Okladnikov in the early 1970s.

The cove is known to have been occupied from Mesolithic, but the rock art is dated on the basis of stylistic characteristics to the Bronze Age and Iron Age (Okladnikov 1974, 74–77) (Figure 25.4). This is based on the presence of elk in the earlier period, and deer with a mounted hunting scene in the later. Aseyev dates the horned depictions after Okladnikov to the 'late or middle Glazkovo period, i.e. about 1500–1300 BC' of the Bronze Age (Aseyev 2006, 57).

Interpretation of the carvings

The interpretation of the carvings is linked to the shamanic practices that have taken place in the region, and representations of accompanying material culture. Two major elements in the carvings indicate that the rock art captured within it shamanic powers. These are the depictions of shamans or shamanic spirits, namely the images of anthropomorphic figures with horns. The group composed of free standing figures are either wearing head

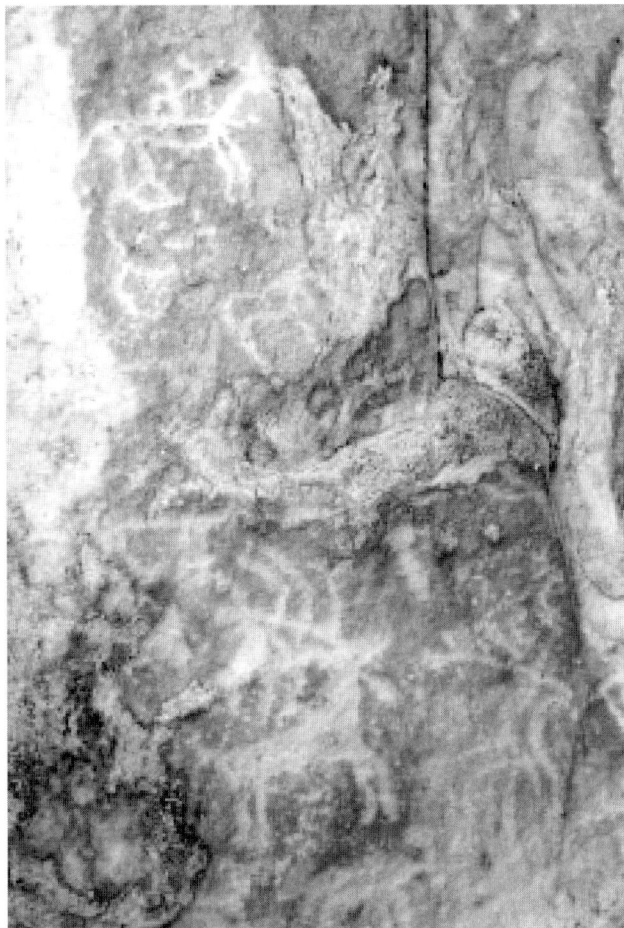

Figure 25.4. Iron Age carvings of deer and hunters riding horses (photo L. Janik).

Figure 25.5. Bronze Age carvings of figures with head dresses or horns (Photo. L. Janik).

dresses or their heads have horns (although some of these horns appear more like hare or rabbit ears) (Figure 25.5).

The figures either stand alone or hold hands (the hands have four fingers and sometimes one of the fingers is finished with a circle). On one depiction two figures are joined together (Figure 25.6). The phenomena of being joined together or twinning was used by Aseyev to argue that the metaphor represented in the carvings of Sagan Zaba is old and can be found in other archaeological finds such as anthropomorphic figurines, citing examples from Bazaikha and Torgashino on the Yenisei river (Aseyev 2006, 57). These depictions are composed of two figures joined together. These are interpreted by Okladnikov, and subsequently by Aseyev, directly from ethnographic records as 'paired spirits symbolising the Universe … known to occupy a central place in Evenk sacrifical areas and tribal sanctuaries. Family spirit guardians, *dzuolins*, venerated by the Nanay shamans, serve as an example of married couple. Orochon Evenks have amulets for men and women representing idols which are commonly called *savakichan*.

According to Nanay belief, one helps in hunting and keeping the reindeer herd, while the other aids women in keeping the home…. In Altai, the Kumandins and Shore considered the *orokenne*r (spirit helping in child-birth) to be married couples. Paired images of Fire Master called *Sakhalae Khatun* and *Sakhjadai Ubugun* among the western Buryats probably perform the same function…' (Aseyev 2006, 58). I emphasise the need for some caution in using ethnographic analogies in the interpretation of these images (Janik 1999), since the spectrum of possible correlations is vast, from child bearing to Fire Masters. What remains significant, is that the form of the double figure is present in archaeological remains and ethnographic records spanning many millennia.

Relationship between grave goods and rock art

The shape of the human figure with horns, similar to carvings on the cliff of Sagan Zaba, have been found in the context of burials in the Kurma XI cemetery, Grave 1, in

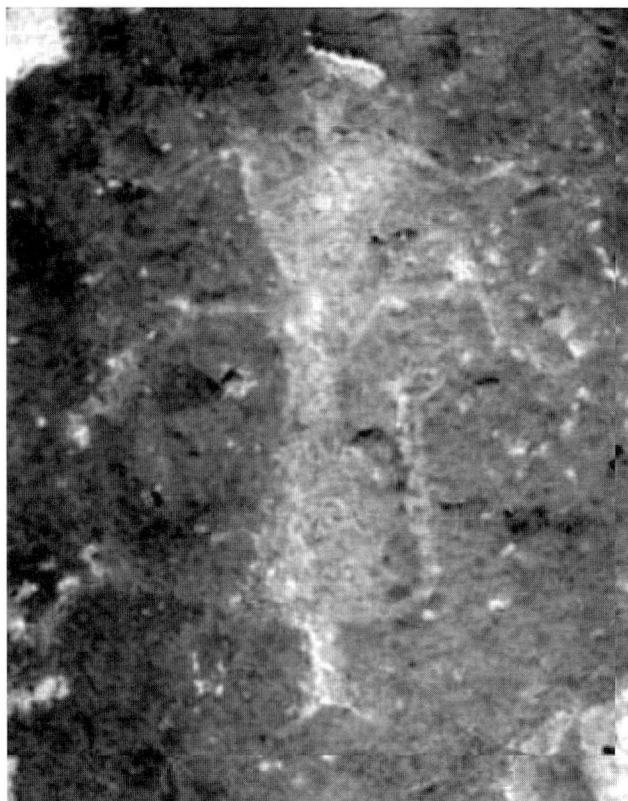

Figure 25.6. Carving of two figures joined together.

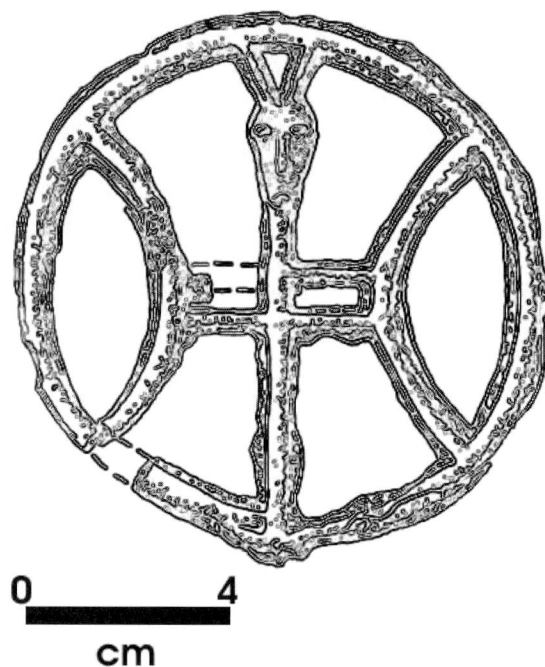

Figure 25.7. Circular medallion with horned head human figure (modified after Goriunova and Webber 2003, 111).

the region of Maloe More (Small Sea) by Lake Baikal, dated to the Bronze Age. The other thirty-four graves in this cemetery are considered to be burials of shamans and elite members of the community. None of the graves are those of children (Goriunova and Webber 2003). The anthropomorphic image from the grave which resembles images from the cliff of Sagan Zaba is part of an openwork copper/bronze medallion placed in a birch-bark container found on the chest of the deceased. The individual buried was a male, twenty-five to thirty years old, lying on his back fully stretched, his head turned sideways, facing north. A number of pendants were deposited in the grave: 'it appears that pendant ornaments of red deer teeth had been fastened to the headdress and clothing of the deceased. A large number of ornaments (thirty-three items) were found on, under, and around the skull. In the right eye socket was a disc of white nephrite and another red deer-tooth pendant. The pendant were also found in the area of the chest (three items) and at the left wrist (six items)' (Goriunova and Webber 2003, 111). Other items were found within and above the burial, within the mound of the grave which was packed with five layers of stone slabs.

The pendant on the chest of the deceased which has visual analogies with the carvings of Sagan Zaba is 10 cm in diameter and has a clearly visible anthropomorphic face

(Figure 25.7). The authors argue that the medallion, with its depiction of a horned head, suggests that its owner, the occupant of this particular grave, was a shaman (Goriunova and Webber 2003). They put forward three arguments to support this contention. The first is based on the observation that although the grave goods had been disturbed, they had not been stolen. The second argument is based on Okladnikov's proposition that horned heads represent shamans. The third argument is the setting of the horned head within the circular medallion rather than a simple plaque, indicative of the mythical properties of the Heaven-Universe captured by the double circle of the medallion as well as shaman round drum. Summarising these three arguments, Goriunova and Webber argue that the horned shaped head enclosed in a double-circle medallion reflected the mythological properties of the Heaven-Universe and belong to shaman. This in turn has been used by Aseyev to argue that rock carvings of Sagan Zaba had shamanic properties where the shamanic rituals 'were practiced by the people of Baikal' (Aseyev 2006, 59).

The depiction of two joined figures is understood as representing sexual intercourse (Aseyev 2006, 57; Okladnikov 1974, 87). The act itself is performed in a shamanic context in the presence of free standing horned figures and the act itself is performed by the horned figures therefore it is argued that such association indicates multitude of spirits. The rock itself therefore holds all the powers of spirits carved on it with all their individual powers and all their multiple powers united together.

Using archaeological interpretations as proposed by Russian and Canadian archaeologists based on the understanding of religious beliefs, rituals and mythological stories of Northern Peoples, and the archaeological data of carvings, pendants and grave goods provides us with a multiple relational picture of interactions between them. The cliff at Sagan Zaba has a recursive relationship with the spirit world. The spirits derive power from the special nature of the location itself. This spiritual power is expressed through the rock art on the cliff face, images which in turn enhance the sense of spirituality of the place. An association is made between the cove and the shaman, who is in contact with the spirit world, through the shared designs in the rock art and on the pendant with which the shaman was buried. The bearer of the medallion quite likely took part in rituals at the cove, by the cliff which bore the rock art images linking the medallion to the representations of the spirits, and hence, through the power of the visual narrative of the rock art, to the spirits themselves.

Conclusion

This paper has presented a case study from prehistoric rock art at Lake Baikal in which it was argued that animism needs to be incorporated more fully into archaeological interpretations of religious belief and rituals. It was argued that, in the case of rock art, an approach which draws on embodied realism offers an effective and innovative framework for understanding these forms of belief which transcends the limitations imposed by the use of cross-cultural ethnographic analogy. Building on the pioneering work of Richard Bradley, which has demonstrated the significance of the relationships between geomorphological forms in the natural landscape and the communities which lived around them and for whom they acquired ritual or religious importance, this study has suggested that this relationship is reflexive, and provides further evidence for the ways in which the religious significance of particular places can be continued over very long periods of time.

Acknowledgements

Firstly, I would like to thank C. Malone and D. A. Barrowclough for inviting me to take a part in the conference as well as for their patience. I thank also S. Howlett, A. W. Webber, O. I. Goriunova, O. I. and M. K. Jones. I owe particular gratitude to S. Kaner for his critical reading and improvement of this paper.

References

Aseyev, I. V. 2006. Ritual objects from Neolithic site at the Elgen River mouth and their relevance in prehistoric, eastern Siberian shamanism. *Archaeology, Ethnography and Anthropology of Eurasia*, vol. 26, no. 2, 53–60.

Bird-David, N. 1999. 'Animism' revisited. *Current Anthropology*, vol 40, Supplement, February, 67–91.

Bradley, R. 2000. *An Archaeology of Natural Places*. London, Routledge.

Bradley, R. 1997. *Rock Art and the Prehistory of Atlantic Europe: Signing the Land*. London, Routledge.

Gjerde, J. M. 2006. The *location* of rock pictures *is* an interpretive element. In R. Barndon, S. M. Innselset, K. K. Kristofferson and T. K. Lødøen (eds). *Samfunn, Symboler og Identitet*. Bergen, Universitet i Bergen Arkeologiske Shifter.

Goriunova, O. I., Webber, A. W. 2003. Gravesite with an openwork medallion from Bronze-Age Kurma XI cemetery (Lake Baikal). *Archaeology, Ethnography and Anthropology of Eurasia*, vol. 16, no. 4, 110–115.

Helskog, K. 1999. The shore connection. Cognitive Landscape and Communication with Rock Carvings in Northernmost Europe. *Norwegian Archaeological Review*, vol. 32, no. 2, 73–94.

Janik, L 1999. Rock art as a visual representation or how to travel to Sweden without Christopher Tilley. In J. Goldhahn (ed.). *Anthology of Rock Art*, British Archaeological Report, International Series 794.

Janik, L. 2007. In press. Why does Difference Matter? The creation of personhood and the categorisation of food among prehistoric fisher-gatherer-hunters of Northern Europe. In A. Cannon (ed.). Structured Worlds. *The Archaeology of Hunter-Gatherer Thought and Action*. London, Equinox.

Janik, L. with C. Roughley, K. Szczesna. 2007. In press. Skiing on the rocks: experiencional art of prehistoric fisher-gathers-hunters from Northern Russia. *Cambridge Archaeological Journal*.

Lakoff, G. and M. Johnson, 1999. *Philosophy in the Flesh*. New York, Basic Books.

Okladnikov, A. P. 1966. *Petroglify Angary*. Novosibirsk, Nauka.

Okladnikov, A. P. 1974. *Petroglify Baykala- pamatniki drevney kultury narodov Sibiri*. Novosibirsk, Nauka.

Chapter 26

THE SACRED ENGAGEMENT: OUTLINE OF A HYPOTHESIS ABOUT THE ORIGIN OF HUMAN 'RELIGIOUS INTELLIGENCE'

Lambros Malafouris

Introduction: why religion needs material culture?

The question that motivates the central hypothesis advanced in this paper regarding the emergence of early religious thinking is the following: 'why does religion need material culture?' What basic functional or symbolic need renders material culture an indispensable and universal component of religion and ritual activity? A common temptation, obvious in a number of recent archaeological and anthropological studies, is to seek an answer in the field of memory (Boyer 1993; 1996; 1998; 2001; McCauley and Lawson 2002; Whitehouse 2000; 2004; Mithen 1998a). This paper argues that material culture does much more than simply offer a symbolic channel for the externalization, communication, and thus successful cultural transmission, of religious ideas. Although the mnemonic significance of the ritual object is not denied, it is proposed that the argument from memory, as traditionally premised, fails to provide a cognitively adequate account of the complex affective ties and multimodal interactions that characterise the distinctive phenomenology of religious experience. Moreover, and from a long-term evolutionary perspective, it is argued that the commonly implied ontological priority of the religious idea, over its material expression, leaves us with no explanation about why, and how, religious concepts emerge in the context of human cognitive evolution. Drawing on the theoretical lines of the Material Engagement approach (Malafouris 2004; Renfrew 2004) I want to advance a different hypothesis that places material culture at the heart of the human capacity for religious thinking (cf. Day 2004).

The human 'religious sense': basic ingredients of 'religious intelligence'

I want to start by clarifying how I conceptualise religious

thinking or intelligence. Drawing on a number of recent studies at the interface between religious studies and cognitive sciences (Boyer 1993; 1996; 1998; 2001; McCauley and Lawson 2002; Whitehouse 2000; 2004; Guthrie 1993) I propose that there are three principal elements that characterize and constitute this type of thinking (Figure 26.1): (a) Animism: the attribution of life or spirit to inanimate things and events, (b) Anthropomorphism: the attribution of human characteristics to nonhuman things or events, and finally (c) The transcendental stance: beliefs about the supernatural (spirits, deities, soul, life after death, eschatology, imperceptibles, and Autoscopic phenomena (AP).

For my purposes in this paper I suggest that the above three features taken together constitute what I call the basic human 'religious sense', and the aim of the hypothesis advanced in this paper is to point a possible direction of research for answering how did this basic religious sense evolve and originate? Answering that, I suggest, we need to consider each of the three features independently in order to explore their cognitive and neurological foundation. This will enable us to overcome the problem of the folk-psychological status of these notions, and thus, to reveal some possible links and connections of interest at the intersection between cognition and material culture. But first two important clarifications are in order:

a) The first point pertains to the issue of ritual. The absence of ritual from the above triadic nexus of religious intelligence can raise a number of questions: Is not ritual a constitutive part of our basic religious intelligence? Is not ritual the principal means for the enactment and re-enactment of religious thinking through embodied action and mediated performances? Since I shall not be dealing with the issue of ritual in this paper it is necessary to summarize my position on this crucial issue. My claim, very briefly is, that

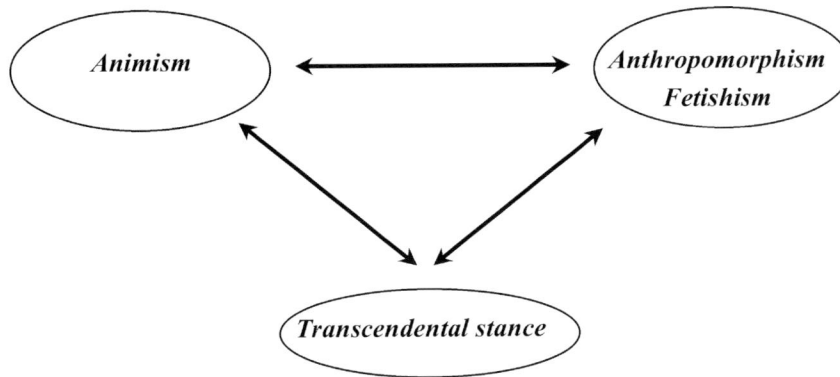

Figure 26.1. The basic cognitive nexus of Religious Intelligence.

although ritual is undoubtedly a constitutive element of religious behaviour it does not constitute a principal causal factor in the emergence of religious intelligence. More specifically, although ritual behaviour temporally precedes the origin of religious thinking, it should not be understood as the cause of it. Ritual may well be the performative, individual or collective, mnemonic device *par excellence,* but there is nothing inherently religious about it. Outside the nexus of religious intelligence ritual is simply a manifestation of the social character of the human mind. More simply, human religious intelligence did not emerge because of ritual, although it did made use of ritual (symbolism was another domain that religious thinking did capitalize) in order to solve the problem of its cultural transmission.

b)   The second point concerns the cognitive and neurological processes that, as I will discuss below, can be associated with the identified anthropological phenomena that constitute the hypothesized nexus of human religious sense. It is important to clarify at the outset that the proposed associations do not mean to imply anything more than a mere *correlation* between processes manifest at radically different time scales and levels of experience. Thus, these processes should be conceived as the continuous and interactive aspects of an unfolding extended and distributed cognitive system. The (neuro-) archaeological perspective adopted in this paper is firmly grounded and emanates from the general theoretical framework of the Material Engagement approach (Malafouris 2004). Consequently, I have no intention of reducing the complicated, mediated and variable aspects of religious intelligence to the neuronal level. I simply believe that a naturalized account of religious thinking needs to start from some concrete and well identified elements of religious thought and building upon that to explore the complicated and irreducible phenomenology of

religious experience. The cognitive science of religious behaviour offers such a starting point.

Animism as Theory of Mind (ToM)

I start with animism, and I suggest, following Guthrie (1993), that far from a strange, primitive, or irrational way of engaging and making sense of the world, animism, from an evolutionary perspective should be understood as an intelligent perceptual strategy. Animism is universal because seeing as a form of active visual exploration and interpretation constantly embodies the element of choice and thus a gamble (cf. also Johnson 2003; Scholl and Tremoulet 2000). From such an angle, animism as a perceptual strategy that 'aim highest (by attributing the most organization and hence significance to things and events) have the greatest potential payoffs and lowest risks' (Guthrie 1993, 6). Indeed as Guthrie characteristically observe 'it is better for a hiker to be mistake a boulder for a bear than to mistake a bear for a boulder' (Guthrie 1993, 6). If one wants to take this argument a step further the question to ask is what cognitive mechanism can account or explain animism. Attempting to offer a possible direction for answering that I suggest that animism, as a cognitive process, should be seen as a part of that aspect of human social intelligence that goes under the name Theory of Mind (ToM). Theory of Mind (ToM) or mentalizing (thinking about the contents of other people's minds) refers to the process(es) by which humans attribute unobservable mental states to others (Gallagher and Frith 2002; Frith and Frith 2003; Vogeley *et al.* 2001; Leslie 1987). ToM comprise the mental processes which allow us to apprehend the psychological properties and beliefs of another and thus what enables social relations as well as agency attribution.

For many years the crucial question for cognitive neurosciences has been whether ToM, and by extension human social cognition, draws on a unique and specialized set of cognitive processes and networks, evolved to deal with the human social domain, or whether ToM and social cognition simply represent a special instance of more general-purpose cognitive processes, like those involved in perception, language, memory etc. A number of recent imaging studies support the view of a distinct social-cognition network, the neural correlates of which can be found primarily in the medial prefrontal cortex (mPFC) (e.g. Mitchell *et al.* 2005). But even if we accept that this distinct pattern of neural activation support inferences about the psychological aspects of other people, how does it relate, or, can help us understand the phenomenon of animism?

Putting it very briefly my suggestion is the following: What it means in neurological terms to apply ToM to the non-animate, is to process and interact with things using those mechanisms and neural networks that we customarily use for interacting with people. More simply it means that you expand the boundaries of social mind by incorporating into the field of social cognition inanimate elements and things. This 'hypertrophy of social cognition' (Boyer 2001), which may initially appear as a misapplication of ToM capacities or a false attribution of agency, can be used in the context of a religious experience as a powerful strategy of selective attention, memory and body-schema expansion.

What is also important to mention in relation to our present discussion is that ToM in addition to its traditional frontal lobe activations has been recently associated with a different area, known as the temporo-parietal junction (TPJ) (Saxe and Kanwisher 2003; Saxe and Wexler 2005). This area, traditionally associated with a number of tasks within the spectrum of human social cognition, such as human face identification tasks and identification of biological motion, has also been very recently identified as a key brain area behind various autoscopic phenomena that may also have played a crucial role in the development of religious thinking (Blanke *et al.* 2004; Blanke and Arzy 2005).

Autoscopic phenomena (AP) constitute a well defined-group of primarily visual experiences during which the subject has the impression of seeing a second own body in extrapersonal space. Three distinct forms of autoscopic phenomena have been defined (Figure 26.2): (a) Autoscopy (AS), (b) Out-of-body experience (OBE), and (c) Heautoscopy (HAS). Autoscopic phenomena (AP) are important for our current discussion because they challenge the spatial unity of the isolated self as the subject of experience. In particular, in autoscopic situations the self experiences itself 'beyond the corporeal boundaries' (Blanke *et al.* 2004; Blanke and Arzy 2005). Given the importance of the relation between self and the body in the context of religious experience many neuroscientists and philosophers have argued for a possible connection between AP and the origin of the proto soul-concept and of other religious experiences characterized by feelings of expanding one's body beyond its physical limits or by a sense of splitting the self (Metzinger 2005).

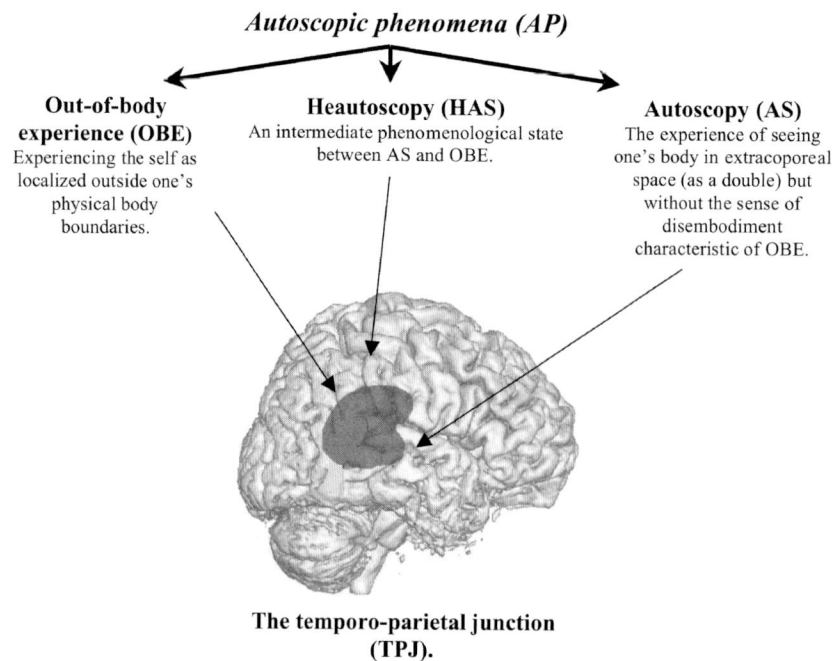

Autoscopic phenomena (AP)

Out-of-body experience (OBE)
Experiencing the self as localized outside one's physical body boundaries.

Heautoscopy (HAS)
An intermediate phenomenological state between AS and OBE.

Autoscopy (AS)
The experience of seeing one's body in extracoporeal space (as a double) but without the sense of disembodiment characteristic of OBE.

The temporo-parietal junction (TPJ).

Figure 26.2. Types of autoscopic phenomena associated with the brain area known as the temporo-pariteal junction (redrawn from Arzy et al. 2005, figure 1 and 3).

Anthropomorphism as metaphor

Anthropomorphism can be broadly defined as the attribution of human characteristics to nonhuman things, and according to Guthrie, similarly with the case of animism previously discussed, 'we anthropomorphize because guessing that the world in humanlike is a good bet' (2003, 3; cf. also Barrett and Keil 1996). For our purposes here however, I want to explore anthropomorphism from a different angle. Specifically, drawing on the general principles of Embodied Cognition and Metaphor Theory (e.g. Lakoff 1987; Lakoff and Johnson 1980) I suggest that anthropomorphism should be understood as a metaphoric projection. A metaphoric projection is essentially the conceptual mapping between a familiar or concrete and an unfamiliar or abstract, phenomenal domain. Obviously the crucial function of metaphoric mappings is to project – and not represent – the structure (spatial, perceptual or other) of a concrete and directly meaningful domain of experience (e.g. the embodied experience of weight) upon a meaningless abstract conceptual one (e.g. the concept of weight). Given that the human bodily experience offers the most intimate source of pre-conceptual structure, it follows that the human body will serve as the most basic source domain for such metaphoric conceptual mappings:

> Our brains are structured so as to project activation patterns from sensorimotor areas to higher cortical areas.... Projection of this kind allow us to conceptualize abstract concepts on the basis of inferential patterns used in sensorimotor processes that are directly tied to the body (Lakoff and Johnson 1999, 77).

Until very recently little was known about the possible neurological foundation of the above processes and about how imagining and doing might use a shared neural substarte. It was primarily in the last decade that new exciting discoveries like the so-called 'mirror neurons' and the development of 'simulation' and 'neural exploitation' theories that provided for the first time a mechanism with a clear neurological foundation for grounding the general premises of embodied cognition (Gallese and Lakoff 2005; Gallese 2005). Moreover a recent neuroimaging study led by V. S. Ramachandran showed the brain area known as the angular gyrus is most probably the 'metaphor centre' of the human mind (Ramachandran et al. 2005). Lesions in the angular gyrus have been consistently associated with a deficit in methaphoric thinking, a fact which may explain the strategic location of this region at the crossroads of the temporo-parietal areas associated with touch, hearing and vision (occipital). This finding is important not only because of the close anatomical proximity between the temporo-parietal junction TPJ and the angular gyrus AG but also because the latter is disproportionately larger in hominids than other primates.

The sacred engagement: anchoring the transcendental stance

So far we have exposed a possible neuromatrix between the identified core aspects of religious thinking placing our emphasis on a possible link between the TPJ and the angular gyrus. What remains to be sown is why the construction of such a link is important and what possible role material culture may have to play in this respect. To this end and within the limits of this paper two important things need to be emphasised: The first is the immediate connection that TPJ offers between embodiment, body schema and the complex experiences of OBE and AS. The second is the possible role of the angular gyrus AG in integrating these powerful experiences with more abstract aspects and autonoetic conceptualisations, such as that of a proto-soul concept. These ideas fit nicely with many contemporary arguments that see early shamanic experiences having an important role in early religious thinking and the development of human cognition (Clottes and Lewis-Williams 1998; Lewis-Williams 2002; Rossano 2007). However, one crucial difference of the hypothesis advanced here needs to be underlined: The identified nexus of religious intelligence claims no particular association with shamanism. Although, the processes of animism, fetishism, anthropomorphism and the transcendental stance (especially second order intentionality associated with autoscopic phenomena) may be familiar features of shamanic ritual; these dimensions are before, and above all, basic features of the human social mind and of the complex ways this mind engages and interacts with the material world. In other words, I may suggest, critically rephrasing the title of a recent article on the topic by M. Rossano (2007), that if there was a single special element in the process of human becoming then it has to be 'mediation' rather than 'meditation', it was because of mediation that humans came to meditate after all. Having clarified that let me now return to answer the question we posed at the beginning of this paper and which motivates the hypothesis advance here: *Why does religious thinking need material culture?*

Obviously, no single answer can do justice to the complex affective and multifaceted operations that define the phenomenology of the sacred engagement in its many cross cultural and historical manifestations – a simple look to the variety of ritual and religious experiences described by the papers of this volume would suffice to confirm that. However, if we approach the above question from the specific view point that concerns the possible cognitive origin of early religious intelligence, a possible answer may start to be sketched – or so I claim in this paper. To focus the possible parameters of our discussion I will take issue with a recent argument by Steven Mithen (1998) and use the famous 30,000-year-old Höhenstein-Stadel lion-man statuette from Germany (Marshack 1990; Mithen 1996) as a concrete example of such an early (Upper Palaeolithic) 'sacred engagement'. The question to ask is what can this specimen of therianthropic art tell us about early religious intelligence and its relationship with material culture? Why 'turning something that is eternal and supernatural into something that is transient and material' (Mithen 1998a, 100) like this small (28 cm) ivory figurine?

The answer that Mithen proposes to this question can be summarised as follows: First, following his well-known 'cognitive fluidity hypothesis' (1996) he suggests that the emergence of religious ideas 'is most likely no more than an epi-phenomenal consequence' (Mithen 1998a, 101) of this cognitive transition. Then he proposes that the critical feature and common characteristic of these ideas is that they contradict our intuitive understanding of the world. Drawing primarily on the work of Pascal Boyer (1993; 1996) he argues that the cognitive function of those violations to our intuitive understanding of the world is to make them attention-grabbing and thus enhance their cultural saliency and significance. This process according to Mithen is not itself sufficient to secure their cultural transmission because while religious ideas 'need to violate some aspects of our intuitive knowledge of the world to have salience, they also need to conform to some aspects of this to have survival value' (1998a, 102). This becomes possible by projecting onto them features that conform to our intuitive understanding of the world, and this is the reason behind the human-like, anthropomorphic or animistic elements that often characterize supernatural creatures. It is through such projections that religious ideas are 'anchored in the human mind' and it is only those ideas that most easily find such an 'anchor' that are likely to survive (1998a, 102).

Up to this point all the processes described above are 'mental' or 'internal', that is, firmly situated within the boundaries of skin and skull. Religious concepts and ideas emerge inside the mind and are subsequently anchored through various internal 'intuitive strategies' in order to gain survival value. Let me call that 'first order anchoring argument'; evidently in itself it does not answer our initial question about the fundamental role that material symbols and images play in the context of religion and ritual. Yet it is this argument that formulates the conceptual basis from which Mithen's answer derives. For indeed there is a 'second, and perhaps far more significant, way in which religious ideas are anchored' and through which they gain extra survival value: 'they are represented in material form' (1998a, 103). I call this 'second order anchoring argument'.

Obviously for Mithen the reason why religion needs material culture is essentially to overcome the limits that biological memory imposes on the process of religious transmission. Religious concepts and ideologies needed to be externalised in material form so that they can be effectively remembered. This is a part of the process that Mithen describes elsewhere as the 'disembodiment of mind into material culture' (1998b). Naturally, the mnemonic significance of the image is not to be disputed. I believe however, that the general argument from memory (see also McCauley and Lawson, 2002), although powerful, suffers from a very important shortcoming: it fails to provide an adequate explanation for how religious ideas emerge in the first place.

Take for instance our example of the 30,000-year-old Höhenstein-Stadel lion-man statuette. The first question that this object, of what we might term 'hybrid-type' imagery, raises is how such a strange creature – half lion and half man – could have originated in the image-maker's imagination? According to Mithen's argument our question, as stated above, poses no real problems. The cognitively fluid mind has no problem imagining and inventing concepts and creatures that violate our intuitive knowledge of the world. The problem is rather how to remember and transmit such counterintuitive ideas (Mithen 1998a, 104). It is only at this point that material culture enters into the picture. In other words, religious ideas appear as the natural epiphenomena of cognitive fluidity. Religious concepts and ideologies are natural because they relate to the intuitive knowledge regarding psychology, biology and physics, which are genetically encoded in the human mind (Boyer 1993; 1996; Mithen 1998a). This is precisely the point where my disagreement with Mithen's argument lies. Whereas Mithen perceives material anchors in the conventional sense of external representations, I propose they should be instead perceived as enactive signs, that is, as signs that *bring forth* rather than simply represent a pre-existent concept (Malafouris, in press).

From such an enactive perspective, the capacity of cross-domain conceptual mapping that characterize the counter-intuitive projections, of the type we discussed in the above example, could not have been possible to realise in the absence of some 'external scaffolding' such as the one provided by the figuration itself. Thus, the cognitive significance of the Hohenstein-Stadel figurine is much more than a simple mnemonic trick. More specifically, my argument is that although the cognitive efficacy of the figurine may well be seen as that of a material anchor, this would be a material anchor that enacts and objectifies, rather than represents, the conceptual blending between intuitive and counterintuitive domains of experience (Hutchins 2005; Fauconnier and Turner 2002). From this point of view, cognitive projections like those we see realised in and through material culture are neither substitutes nor translations of pre-existing concepts into matter. The iconicity of the image does not simply reflect visual resemblances but rather establishes ontological ones; it is significant for what it *does* rather than what it *refers*

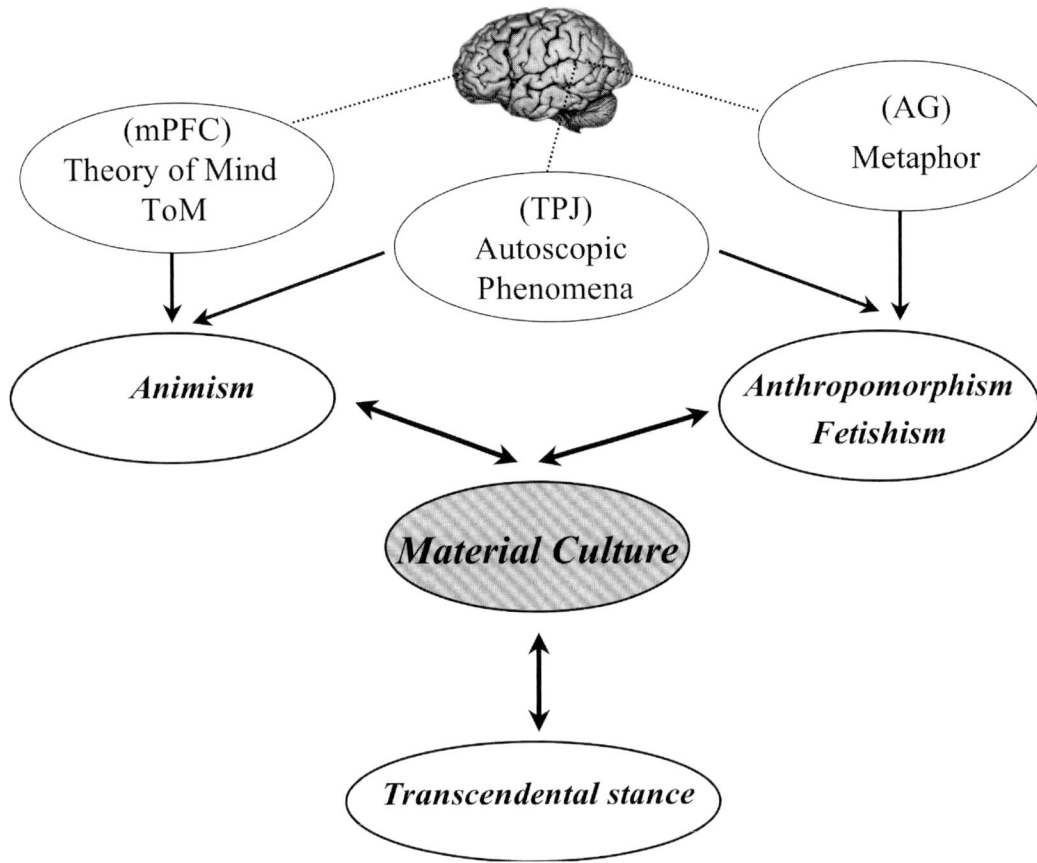

Figure 26.3. The neuro-cultural matrix active at the origin of 'religious intelligence'.

to as a message or metaphor. In our previous example, the figurine serves as the tangible medium of integration between the domain 'human' and the domain 'animal' so that the domain 'supernatural creature' can emerge. In other words, 'first' and 'second' ordering anchoring are not the separate and discrete stages of a 'mentally' driven sequential process. They are instead the continuous and interactive parts of an extended cognitive system (Figure 26.3) that incorporates materiality in order to solve the problem of the absent 'representational stability' (see also Hutchins 2005) enabling thus the emergence of the transcendental stance.

Acknowledgements

I would like to thank Caroline Malone, David Barrowclough and Simon Stoddart for their kind invitation to contribute to this volume and their editorial comments. The research presented is sponsored by the Balzan Foundation.

References

Arzy, S., Moshe I., Landis T. and Blanke, O. 2005. Speaking with one's self. *Journal of Consciousness Studies*, 12, 11, 4–29.

Barrett, J. L. and Keil, F. C. 1996. Conceptualizing a non-natural entity: anthropomorphism in God concepts. *Cognitive Psychology* 31, 219–247.

Boyer, P. 1993. *The Naturalness of Religious Ideas, a Cognitive Theory of Religion*. Berkeley, University of California Press.

Boyer, P. 1996. What makes anthropomorphism natural: intuitive ontology and cultural representation. *Journal of the Anthropological Institute* 2, 83–97.

Boyer, P. 1998. Cognitive Tracks of Cultural Inheritance: How Evolved Intuitive Ontology Governs Cultural Transmission. *American Anthropologist* 100(4), 876–889.

Boyer, P. 2001. *Religion Explained: Evolutionary Origins of Religious Thought*. New York, Basic Books.

Blanke, O. and Arzy, S. 2005. The out-of-body experience: disturbed self-processing at the temporo-parietal junction. *Neuroscientist 11*, 16–24.

Blanke O., Landis T., Spinelli L. and Seeck M. 2004. Out-of-body experience and autoscopy of neurological origin. *Brain* 127, 243–58.

Clottes, J. and Lewis-Williams J. D. 1998. *The Shamans of prehistory: trance and magic in the painted caves.* Harry Abrams, New York.

Day, M. 2004. Religion, off-line cognition, and the extended mind *Journal of Cognition and Culture* 4 (1), 101–121.

Fauconnier, G. and Turner, M. 2002. *The Way We Think: Conceptual Blending and the Mind's Hidden Complexities.* New York, Basic Books.

Frith, U. and Frith, C. D. 2003. Development and neurophysiology of mentalizing. *Philosophical Transactions of the Royal Society of London. Series B, Biological Sciences,* 358, 459–473.

Gallagher, H. L. and Frith C. D. 2002. Functional imaging of theory of mind. *Trends in Cognitive Sciences* 7, 77–83.

Gallese V. and Goldman A. 1998. Mirror neurons and the simulation theory of mind reading. *Trends in Cognitive Sciences* 2, 493–501.

Gallese, V. 2005. Embodied simulation: From neurons to phenomenal experience. *Phenomenology and the Cognitive Sciences* 4, 23–48.

Guthrie, S. E. 1993. *Faces in the Clouds. A New Theory of Religion.* Oxford, University Press.

Hutchins, E. 2005. Material anchors for conceptual blends. *Journal of Pragmatics* 37, 1555–1577.

Johnson, S. C. 2003. Detecting agents. *Philosophical Transactions of the Royal Society of London. Series B, Biological Scien*ces, 358, 549–559.

Lakoff, G. and Johnson, M. 1980. *Metaphors We Live By.* Chicago, University of Chicago Press.

Lakoff, G. 1987. *Women, Fire, and Dangerous Things: What Categories Reveal about the Mind.* Chicago, University of Chicago Press.

Lakoff, G. and Johnson, M. 1999. *Philosophy In the Flesh, The Embodied Mind and Its Challenge to Western Thought.* New York, Basic Books.

Leslie, A. 1987. Pretense and Representation: The origins of 'Theory of Mind'. *Psychological Review* 94, 412–426.

Lewis-Williams, D. 2002. *The Mind in the Cave.* London, Thames and Hudson.

Lewis-Williams, D. 2003. Overview. In Review Feature, The Mind in the Cave: Consciousness and the Origins of Art. *Cambridge Archaeological Journal* 13, 2, 263–79.

Malafouris, L. 2004. The Cognitive Basis of Material Engagement: Where Brain, Body and Culture Conflate. In E. DeMarrais, C. Gosden and C. Renfrew (eds). *Rethinking Materiality: The Engagement of Mind with the Material World,.* Cambridge, The McDonald Institute for Archaeological Research, 53–62.

Malafouris, L. in press. Before and Beyond Representation: Towards an enactive conception of the Palaeolithic image. In C. Renfrew and I. Morley (eds) *Material Beginnings: A global prehistory of figurative representation.* Cambridge, The

McDonald Institute for Archaeological Research.

McCauley, R. N. and Lawson, T. E. 2002. *Bringing Ritual to Mind.* Cambridge, Cambridge University Press.

Metzinger, T. 2005. 'The pre-scientific concept of a 'soul'. A neurophenomenological hypothesis about its origin'. In M. Peschl (ed.). Auf der Suche nach dem Konzept/Substrat der Seele. Ein Versuch aus der Perspektive der Cognitive (Neuro-) Science. Wurzburg, Konigshausen und Neumann.

Mithen, S. J. 1996. *The Prehistory of Mind.* London, Thames and Hudson.

Mithen, S. J. 1998a. The Supernatural Beings of Prehistory and The External Storage of Religious Ideas. In C. Renfrew and C. Scarre (eds). *Cognition and Material Culture: the Archaeology of Symbolic Storage.* Cambridge, The McDonald Institute Monographs, 97–106.

Mithen, S. J. 1998b. Introduction. In S. Mithen (ed.). *Creativity in Human Evolution and Prehistory.* London and New York, Routledge, 1–15.

Ramachandran, V. S., Azoulai S., Stone L., Srivasan, A. V. and Bijoy N. 2005. Grasping with metaphors and thinking with pictures. Presented at the American Psychological Society annual convention in Loss Angeles (May 26–29).

Renfrew, C., 2004. Towards a Theory of Material Engagement, in E. DeMarrais, C. Gosden, and C. Renfrew (eds) *Rethinking Materiality: The Engagement of Mind with the Material World.* Cambridge, The McDonald Institute for Archaeological Research, 23–31.

Rilling, J. K., Sanfey, A. G., Aronson, J. A., Nystrom, L. E. and Cohen, J. D. 2004. The neural correlates of theory of mind within interpersonal interactions. *NeuroImage,* 22, 1694–1703.

Rossano, M. J. 2007. Did meditating make us human? *Cambridge Archaeological Journal* 17, 1, 47–58.

Saxe, R. and Kanwisher, N. 2003. People thinking about thinking people. The role of the temporo-parietal junction in 'theory of mind'. *Neuroimage,* 19, 1835–1842.

Saxe, R., Carey, S., and Kanwiser, N. 2004. Understanding other minds: Linking developmental psychology and functional neuroimaging. *Annual Psychological Reviews,* 55, 87–124.

Saxe, R. and Wexler, A. 2005. Making sense of another mind: the role of the right temporo-parietal junction. *Neuropsychologia* 43, 1391–1399.

Scholl, B. J., and Tremoulet, P. D. 2000. Perceptual causality and animacy. *Trends in Cognitive Sciences,* 4, 299–309.

Vogeley, K., Bussfeld, P., Newen, A., Hermann, S., Happe, F., Falkai, P., Maier, W., Shah, N. J., Fink, G. R., and Zilles, K. 2001. Mind reading: Neural mechanisms of theory of mind and self-perspective. *Neuroimage,* 14, 181.

Whitehouse, H. 2000. *Arguments and Icons: Divergent Modes of Religiosity.* Oxford, Oxford University Press.

Whitehouse, H. 2004. *Modes of Religiosity.* Walnut Creek, CA, AltaMira Press.

Chapter 27

TIME, CYCLES AND RITUAL BEHAVIOUR

Iain Morley

Introduction: practical ritual

This paper attempts to touch upon a number of issues attendant upon considering the nature, purposes and motivations for ritual activity; there is not the space to do more than scratch the surface of either the relevant literature or the implications of the considerations here, but it is hoped that there is enough to form a starting point for further thought and investigation.

It is a truism that within archaeology there has, at times, been a tendency for apparently purposeless activities identified in the archaeological record to be interpreted as being 'ritual' activities. In other words, activities that we see in the archaeological record that do not appear to have an immediate survival value or explanation, or seem to be basically beyond our interpretation, have often been labelled 'ritual'. This does not allow us to say much about either the particular activity, ritual in general, or about the people involved, if this is where the interpretation ends. The trend in the discipline, as evidenced by this volume, has more recently been away from basic categorisations towards attempts to understand the complexity of the activities and the motivations and experience of the people creating the record.

Nevertheless, a perennial problem associated with consideration of 'ritual' and 'religion' (and, similarly, 'cult'), whether in the present or past, has been in delineating the meaning of those terms. Thinking of activities which fall under their rubric is not difficult; thinking of activities which *do not* do so is more problematic. Any activity, individual or collective, which corresponds to some prescribed guidelines or procedure could be termed 'ritualised'. Where does the dividing line, if any, between 'ritualised' and 'standardised' lie? What is the difference, if any, between 'ritual' and 'ceremony'? In their common usage they cannot be differentiated on the basis of the former being 'religious' and the latter being 'secular', because with our current vocabulary we can easily speak of religious ceremony and secular ritual. Should we

want to make this distinction between religious and secular anyway, when in many contemporary and probably most past societies such a distinction could be argued not to exist?

We are in a position whereby if we agree tight definitions for these terms we may simply be creating a vocabulary which consists of a series of classifications which might not, in fact, represent legitimate categories into which to place the behaviours that we are seeking to understand. Indeed, in considering the nature of 'ritual', 'cult' and 'religious' activities in the past, it is important to remember that, on the basis of what we know of other societies from around the world, and ours until very recent years, for the vast majority of people for the vast majority of the past there would be no separation between 'religion' and other daily activities – a religious belief system provides ethics, moral guidelines, laws, explanations and understandings of the world in the broadest sense, and of people, illness and death. It is philosophy, science, law and medicine, and insuperably part of daily life.

So the distinction that we have typically imposed on the archaeological record between 'ritual' and practical' may be considerably at odds with the beliefs and motivations of the individuals who carried out these activities, whom we are seeking to understand. 'Ritual' and belief might be as much a part of a daily practical activity such as making a tool out of stone or metal, or cooking a meal, as they were part of some activity like making a votive offering in the corner of a room. By the same token, making a votive offering in a corner of a room might have been seen as just as 'practical' as making a tool or a meal. Each of these is an activity which an individual may believe that they have to carry out in their daily life in order to make the world the way they need it to be in order to survive.

From the perspective of ritual practitioners we might safely say that every ritual activity has a *practical* purpose, whether or not that purpose is evident to us. Of course, rituals can fulfil many roles within a society for the different people observing or participating in them, including providing a forum for understanding and perpetuating values and beliefs (Rappaport 1999; Hinde 1999; Broom 2003). However, whilst this might be a desired role of rituals in general it is unlikely to be the only justification for an individual ritual, or the major motivation for all of the participants, who may well be concerned with more tangible, material consequences (even if such tangible, material consequences are perceived to occur via an intangible, immaterial intermediary).

Archaeologically, we are left with traces of consequences of activities – direct and indirect, planned and unplanned consequences. The difference between what we are likely to interpret as 'practical' and what we might call 'religious' activity is the extent to which the causal relationship between the activity and the desired – or perceived – outcome is interpretable from the record, and thus the extent to which a particular outcome can be reliably tied to a particular action. For any activity there are potentially numerous simultaneous outcomes, and thus numerous causal relationships with consequences, some of which may be directly evident to the archaeological interpreter, and others which may not preserve at all. A particular difficulty is in identifying relationships between actions and consequences which are not directly causal but which may have been perceived as such by the practitioners of the activities.

Ritual and time

Whatever the precise nature of the relationships were that were attributed by past peoples as existing between certain events, there is clearly an underlying belief that carrying out a particular activity will lead to a particular consequence, which is predicated on a comprehension of cause-and-effect relationships between events. Indeed, there appear to be two major, related, motivating concerns underlying ritual activity – one is concerned with the aforementioned cause-and-effect relationships between events, including human actions; the other with the passage of time, in the sense that particular events which occur periodically have a differential significance and have a sequential relationship with each other. These concerns are absolutely inter-related in that there can be no awareness of cause-and-effect without a recognition of the sequential nature of events – time – whether this is understood in a linear or cyclical way.

The following outline ways in which such concerns may be manifest:

– *Ritual activity as a marker of events* – in which sense the ritual itself is motivated by the passage of time, occurrence or recurrence of a stage in the life of the community or of an individual. The execution of the

ritual must thus also be contingent on the recognition of certain cues.

– *Ritual activity as a means of recreating a past event* – in which case the ritual activity may be seen as a literal recreation of a past event in the present, on the basis of a cyclical notion of time, and motivated by a desire to ensure that the events which followed the event in the past follow it again (e.g. amongst the Navajo; Griffin-Pierce, 1992). As well as being reliant on a cyclical notion of time it is also reliant on a notion of cause-and-effect and a sequential nature of events (a cyclical conception of time obviously does not deny linearity of time in the sense of causes and consequences, it simply relies on a belief that a linear sequence is limited and repeated).

– *Ritual activity as a means of influencing events* – in which case the ritual activity is a way of taking an active role in cause-and-effect relationships, creating a 'cause' with an anticipated effect, anticipated on the basis of past experience. This may be perceived as a direct causal relationship, or an indirect one, through appeal to a super-natural intermediary, for example.

It seems that there are rather blurry boundaries between our (human) comprehension of sequences of events, and of cause-and-effect relations of events. As Barber and Barber (2004, 249) put it, we have a tendency to rationalise events on the basis of *post hoc ergo propter hoc – after* this, therefore *because* of this; i.e., retrospective attribution of a cause-and-effect relationship to two events that are temporally close. By extension, under some circumstances, if one carries out a certain action and observes a certain event, one is inclined to believe firstly that the event is a consequence of that action, and secondly that the same consequence will be attendant on repeating that action. A desire to influence cause-and-effect sequences, especially those which relate to events important for individual and group survival, underlies much of ritual activity, but may be (mis)applied to sequences of events with no cause-and-effect chain linking them.

Ritual, time and cosmology in foraging societies

For many societies, some of the most striking apparently causal relationships are those between terrestrial events, especially seasonal events, and cosmological events. Once there is an awareness of sequences of events, coupled with a recognition of recurrence of events (together constituting an awareness of cyclicality) recurrent cues can act as signals of the imminence of events. An awareness of sequence of events, and of recurrence of sequences of events, thus allows for expectations about the future to be held. Because certain terrestrial events occur at certain times of the year, and certain cosmological events occur at certain times of the year, it is a small step to believe that there is a causal relationship between the two. Because the movement of the celestial bodies, and the progress of the seasons (and all else that entails – such as leaves turning brown in autumn, animal migrations, the appearance of buds in spring etc.) both have the same underlying cause, namely the earth's movements in space (rotation on its axis and orbit around the sun), there can easily appear to be causal relationships between these phenomena – when in fact their relationship comes from a shared cause, rather than a causal relationship between them. In spite of this the precursor can be used as a predictor for the subsequent other change.

The astronomical knowledge of traditional societies is not something that has always been investigated (or reported, at least), but Fowler and Turner (1999) review a selection from around the world, and Williamson and Farrer (1992) and their contributors discuss a number of Native American examples. Observation of the cyclical movements of astronomical bodies (sun, moon stars, including planets) occurs in many traditional foraging societies, and that knowledge is integrated into other cyclical activities and phenomena that are experienced – ecological, subsistence, ritual/ceremonial and social. This integration of the celestial cycles with terrestrial cycles and activities can be through interpretation of them as having a powerful causational relationship, or as markers for recognised events. Indeed, our view that there are two spheres of existence (celestial and terrestrial) which need to be integrated may well be at odds with traditional views, in which the astronomical bodies and their movements could be seen as being as much part of the world as clouds, birds, rain, or other phenomena.

The appearance and disappearance of particular con-stellations is used by different groups to mark the passage of time, or to mark the appropriate moment at which to carry out a particular activity (Farrer 1992; Young 1992; Fowler and Turner 1999). According to Fowler and Turner hunter-gatherers appear not to have used planetary movements as a cue for the orientation of any buildings, only for calendrical purposes, although they point out the possibility that much rock-art was orientated towards celestial events. Amongst more sedentary foraging societies the entrances of structures may be orientated with particular reference to sunrise, for example (Navajo, Griffin-Pierce 1992), or particular 'seats' or locations may be constructed as markers and points of observation (Miller 1992). The progress of the cycles of celestial bodies are often followed with reference to particular terrestrial features, which, naturally leads to the sense of movement of the heavenly bodies in relation to a fixed earth.

As Farrer (1992) illustrates, the relationship between the cosmological bodies and events on the earth can have both literal and metaphorical content. Amongst the Mescalaro Apaches, for example, the stars can guide people in space (aiding in navigation) and in time (their move-ments and positions being used to time particular events – for example, girls' puberty rites), but they also provide metaphorical guidance as to how life should be lived and a reminder of the order of the universe, via the narratives associated with them, and their ordered progression in the sky. The fact that their orderly progress is observable nightly, and that particular constellations appear and disappear at particular times of the year in predictable fashion, allows the cosmological bodies' movements to form a regular reminder, and lynchpin for these beliefs (Farrer 1992).

Similarly, amongst the Navajo (Griffin-Pierce 1992), the narratives associated with the movements of the constellations provide strong moral guidance on the way to live life and maintain 'harmony in their lives and in the universe' (1992, 111), and the constellations themselves provide powerful and universally visible reminders of those stories and values. The ritual action of representing a constellation in a sand painting on earth is seen to bring order and harmony, both through allegory in the story associated with the constellation, and through the action of its representation. Similar relationships exist amongst many other groups too, including the Cahuila (Bean 1992) and Zuni Pueblo (Young 1992).

Ecological conditions do have a bearing upon how significant such observations are likely to be – largely because they can determine the extent to which such phenomena can be observed. For example, living in deep forest, in which views of the sky are rarely unobstructed, it is much more difficult to make observations of long-term movements of the stars – as is evidenced by the Malaysian Batek who live in deep forest (Endicott 1979, cited in Fowler and Turner 1999). Of course, a group living in an environment that experiences heavy cloud cover frequently during a particular season will experience a perhaps strikingly punctuated progress of the stars on the occasions when they are clearly visible. The same would be true of a population that spent certain periods of the year under dense forest cover and other periods in open ground. Whilst populations in these ecological situations may have less detail to their cosmological systems, some have nevertheless maintained precise temporal markers throughout the year, provided by astronomical bodies. For example, the Quinault of the Pacific north-east coast of America used a pole or designated tree, viewed from a particular 'seat', as a terrestrial marker for the sunrise or sunset on the solstices (Miller 1992). They also used a 'sundial' technique of laying a pole along the shadow cast by a designated tree and noting when the pole pointed to a marked point on the ground, indicating how many days remained before a particular event (Miller 1992).

Most hunter-gatherer societies use the cycle of the moon

as a marker for durations of fixed length (the 29.5 day cycle being extremely regular) (Fowler and Turner 1999). In addition to providing a fixed duration period for reckoning the passage of time, lunar cycles are also tied in with terrestrial events such as women's menstrual cycles. This thus links a cosmological phenomenon to a terrestrial/biological one which is of great significance, relating as it does to fertility and reproduction, as well as the various social and ritual activities attendant upon female fertility. In the case of the Cahuilla of California, extensive series of stories are concerned directly with the Moon (*Menil*) and her role in prescribing the correct actions to be carried out by women during puberty, menstruation and pregnancy, as well as social values, games, play, music and dance.

In each of these cases in the preceding paragraphs the reckoning of the passage of time via the recurrence of celestial and terrestrial events forms a fundamental part of marking and managing social, ceremonial and subsistence activities on earth. The point where the reckoning of time and its relationship with ritual really meets with the spiritual are in the narratives that seek to *explain* these relationships between the cosmological and terrestrial – in other words, where the natural and super-natural meet in explanations of the world. Typically, and possibly universally, these explanatory narratives involve anthropomorphic entities as 'spiritual' aspects of the celestial bodies themselves, or as agents behind them. Indeed, there is an explicit association between celestial bodies and spiritual beings amongst most hunter-gatherer societies, with at least the sun and the moon both being considered as spiritual beings (Fowler and Turner 1999), and in many cases, the morning star, evening star and constellations too (e.g. Farrer 1992; Young 1992; Griffin-Pierce 1992; Bean 1992; and others in Williamson and Farrer 1992).

This common thread of an attribution of human-like agency to phenomena is derived from a tendency to explain events in terms which are familiar, namely in terms of human action, motivation and relationships. Humans possess a powerful ability to comprehend and anticipate the motivations and emotions of others, namely a profound awareness of theory of mind and individual intentionality (see, for example, Guthrie 1992; Hinde 1999), and this seems to lead to a tendency to explain events and phenomena in human terms, as narratives of intentional action. The explanation of the movements of celestial bodies in terms of familiar models (see, for example, Fowler and Turner, 1999; Gibbon 1964; 1972; Farrer, 1992; Young 1992; Griffin-Pierce 1992; Bean 1992), lends such explanations a narrative structure, and also makes them readily comprehensible and memorable. However, there are inevitably aspects of the phenomena being explained that are clearly at odds with the terrestrial, natural behaviour which provides the models for the explanation;

thus these aspects are considered to be supernatural, and the agents behind the phenomena are thus themselves supernatural/spiritual. In short, the explanation of the movements of celestial bodies in a narrative form (i.e. in anthropomorphic or, at least, natural and familiar, terms) lends itself towards a conception of such beings as 'spiritual' or super-natural. As Fowler and Turner (1999) put it 'The strong spiritual essence attributed to celestial beings has provided both charter and explanation for seasonal recurrences' (1999, 422–23) and, one might suggest, for daily, monthly, life-cycle, social and ritual activities that are related to these cycles. In turn, rituals provide systems and actions which are concrete and rooted in reality, and thus give a justification, and concrete and real forum for thinking about concepts and beings which are intangible and super-natural, or as Rappaport (1979) puts it, ritual realises the structure embodied in the Holy, and 'the unfalsifiable [the Holy] supported by the undeniable [ritual] yields the unquestionable, which transforms the dubious, the arbitrary and the conventional into the correct, the necessary and the natural' (217).

Certainly ritual activities can have an important role in reiterating those narratives and information contained within them. However, it can be argued that when rituals are principally concerned with time, causal relationships between events and the agents believed to underlie them, these foci would be seen by the participants as being far from dubious or arbitrary. Indeed, in the cases described above the beliefs underlying the rituals being enacted are at the outset *motivated by* a concern with the correct, necessary and natural – the correct, necessary and natural sequences and timings of events in the world, in its widest sense, and human actions. Certainly these may be validated by the ritual activities, but often the motivation for the activities is the explanation of these apparently causal relationships, and having positive influence over them.

Summary

Precisely delineated definitions of ritual activity are problematic, but one common feature is the belief in their practical efficacy through cause and effect relationships. An understanding of cause and effect relationships is predicated on conceptions of time – indeed, the marking of time, the influencing of perceived causal relationships, and the recreation of past sequences of events are principal concerns of ritual activities. The passage of time is marked effectively by many traditional hunting, gathering and foraging societies by observations of celestial phenomena, and these also provide strong examples of apparent causal relationships between the natural (terrestrial) and super-natural (cosmological) elements of the world, as well as cyclical notions of time and the prediction of events. Such temporal cues and perceived relationships form major foci

for ritual activity and explanatory narratives concerning
the workings of the cosmos and humans' place in it, and
influence upon it.

We have a strong inclination to believe that events that
are close in time are causally related (*post hoc ergo propter
hoc*) (Barber and Barber 2004), which leads both to the
belief that celestial and terrestrial events are directly related,
and that if a particular event or action has been followed by
a particular consequence before, it will be so again – and
thus that there is the potential to influence events with
particular actions.

Often such sequences of events and causal relationships
are explained, understood and remembered in human
terms; we most readily understand and explain things in
terms of human appearance and action, so tend to attribute
human-like agency to objects, events and sequences of
events (Guthrie 1992; Hinde 1999). However, in the case of
time and celestial events, aspects of the phenomena being
explained are clearly at odds with the terrestrial, natural
behaviour which provides the models for the explanation,
so these agents are often seen as powerful and 'supernatural', and are also memorable and long-lived (Boyer
1993; 1996; 2001). Consequently, rituals dealing with such
phenomena usually attempt to mark or influence them
through interaction with a super-natural intermediary.

References

Barber, E. W. and Barber, P. T. 2004. *When They Severed Earth from Sky: how the human mind shapes myth*. Princeton, Princeton University Press.
Bean, L. 1992. Menil (Moon): symbolic representation of Cahuilla woman. In R. A. Williamson and C. R. Farrer (ed.). *Earth and Sky: visions of the cosmos in Native American folklore*. Albuquerque, University of New Mexico Press, 162–83.
Boyer, P. 1993. *The Naturalness of Religious Ideas: a cognitive theory of religion*. Berkeley, University of California Press.
Boyer, P. 1996. What makes anthropomorphism natural: intuitive ontology and cultural representation. *Journal of the Anthropological Institute* 2, 83–97.
Boyer, P. 2001. *Religion Explained: the human instincts that fashion gods, spirits and ancestors*. London, William Heinemann.
Broom, D. M. 2003. *The Evolution of Morality and Religion*. Cambridge, Cambridge University Press.
Endicott, K. 1979. Batak Negrito religion: the world-view and rituals of a hunting and gathering people of Peninsula Malaysia. Oxford, Clarendon Press.
Farrer, C. 1992. '…by you they will know the directions to guide them': stars and Mescalero Apaches. In R. A. Williamson and C. R. Farrer (ed.). *Earth and Sky: visions of the cosmos in Native American folklore*. Albuquerque, University of New Mexico Press, 67–74.
Fowler, C. S. and Turner, N. J. 1999. Ecological/cosmological knowledge and land management among hunter-gatherers. In R. B. Lee and R. Daly (ed.). *The Cambridge Encyclopedia of Hunters and Gatherers*. Cambridge, Cambridge University Press, 419–425.
Gibbon, W. B. 1964. Asiatic parallels in North American star lore: Ursa Major. *Journal of American folklore* 77, 236–50.
Gibbon, W. B. 1972. Asiatic parallels in North American star lore: Milky Way, Pleiades, Orion. *Journal of American folklore* 85, 236–47.
Griffin-Pierce, T. 1992. The *Hooghan* and the stars. In R. A. Williamson and C. R. Farrer (ed.). *Earth and Sky: visions of the cosmos in Native American folklore*. Albuquerque, University of New Mexico Press, 110–130.
Guthrie, S. E. 1992. *Faces in the Clouds: a new theory of religion*. Oxford, Oxford University Press.
Hinde, R. A. 1999. *Why Gods Persist: a scientific approach to religion*. London, Routledge.
Miller, J. 1992. North Pacific Ethnoastronomy: Tsimshian and others. In R. A. Williamson and C. R. Farrer (ed.). *Earth and Sky: visions of the cosmos in Native American folklore*: 193–206. Albuquerque, University of New Mexico Press.
Rappaprt, R. 1979. *Ecology, Meaning and Religion*. Richmond, North Atlantic Books.
Rappaport, R. 1999. *Ritual and Religion in the Making of Humanity*. Cambridge, Cambridge University Press.
Williamson, R. A. and Farrer, C. R. 1992. *Earth and Sky: visions of the cosmos in Native American folklore*. Albuquerque, University of New Mexico Press.
Young, M. J. 1992. Morning Star, Evening Star: Zuni traditional stories. In R. A. Williamson and C. R. Farrer (ed.). *Earth and Sky: visions of the cosmos in Native American folklore*: 75–100. Albuquerque, University of New Mexico Press.

Chapter 28

THE SHIPPING NEWS: LAND AND WATER IN BRONZE AGE SCANDINAVIA

Richard Bradley

The passage of the sun

Pascal Boyer (2001) has argued that religious belief is a natural consequence of the workings of the human mind. It depends on what he calls 'spontaneous intuition'. For Boyer, religious interpretations of the world do not arise from exceptional experiences but from the problems of accounting for everyday phenomena. That idea provides the starting point for my paper.

I am concerned with the period between about 1600 and 500 BC in Denmark, southern Sweden and the south of Norway. This was a time when some striking features could be observed in the natural environment. Some are long lived and characterise those areas today, whilst others would have had a particular impact during the second and first millennia BC. They operated on different time scales from one another but each would have posed problems that required an answer. It is the answers suggested by Bronze Age archaeology that I wish to consider here.

My starting point is a simple one. South Scandinavia has a lengthy coastline, broken by rivers, inlets and lakes. It also possesses many offshore islands. These features are important for such areas provide abundant evidence of settlement and frequently include high densities of Bronze Age monuments. Whether we consider the lakes or the open sea, water would have provided the background to peoples' lives.

One problem confronted them on a daily basis. For those living close to the seashore it was from the water that the sun rose in the morning. It moved across the sky until it disappeared. For many observers it would have set in the sea. That raised a difficult question. How did the sun return to its original position whilst it was hidden from view? Was it carried beneath the water until it reappeared at dawn? During the day it had moved from left to right. During the hours of darkness did it pass beneath the surface, travelling from right to left? That distinctive cycle was repeated every twenty four hours.

A second cycle extended over the course of the year. The days became shorter in winter and were longer in summer. The balance of darkness and light obviously changed with the seasons, but there were also contrasts between the southernmost parts of my study area and regions further to the north where the sun was absent for longer periods during the winter; during the summer there were many hours of daylight. These striking contrasts between different regions of Scandinavia would have been apparent to people travelling any distance.

Those features are obvious today, but now they are explained in scientific terms. Another development would have been especially troubling during prehistory. This was the changing relationship between land and sea which was caused by isostatic uplift. Again it varied from one region to another, but there are places in which the shoreline rose considerably during the Bronze Age (Ling 2004; Ling and Bengtsson 2006). The water's edge retreated at a rate that would have been apparent at the time and, as submerged rocks broke the surface, offshore islands appeared. Monuments were built there, and some of the islands themselves would have looked like cairns which had freshly emerged from the sea.

All these developments must have been obvious to people who travelled by boat, so it is hardly surprising that the ship became important in the visual culture of prehistory. Seagoing vessels were also necessary for bringing bronze to Northern Europe. Depictions of ships played a major role in Bronze Age Scandinavia. There were many carvings of these vessels on or close to the shoreline. There are also cairns in the form of a boat which prefigure the well known burials of the Iron Age. It is entirely logical that the ship should have played a part in an ancient system of belief (Ballard *et al.* 2004).

An important starting point is the work of Flemming Kaul (1998) who has studied the decorated metalwork of Bronze Age Denmark. His research has placed a special emphasis on the relationship between boats and the sun. He considers the drawings which show ships carrying the sun. Some travel from left to right and should depict its movement during the day; these are often accompanied by a horse. The vessels that travel from right to left Kaul interprets as 'night ships'. They seem to depict the sun when it is carried beneath the sea accompanied by a snake or by a fish. In Kaul's interpretation these artefacts depict the daily cycle and distinguish between the movement of the sun across the sky and its invisible passage beneath the ocean. It follows that his scheme is primarily concerned with the relationship between land and water (Figure 28.1A).

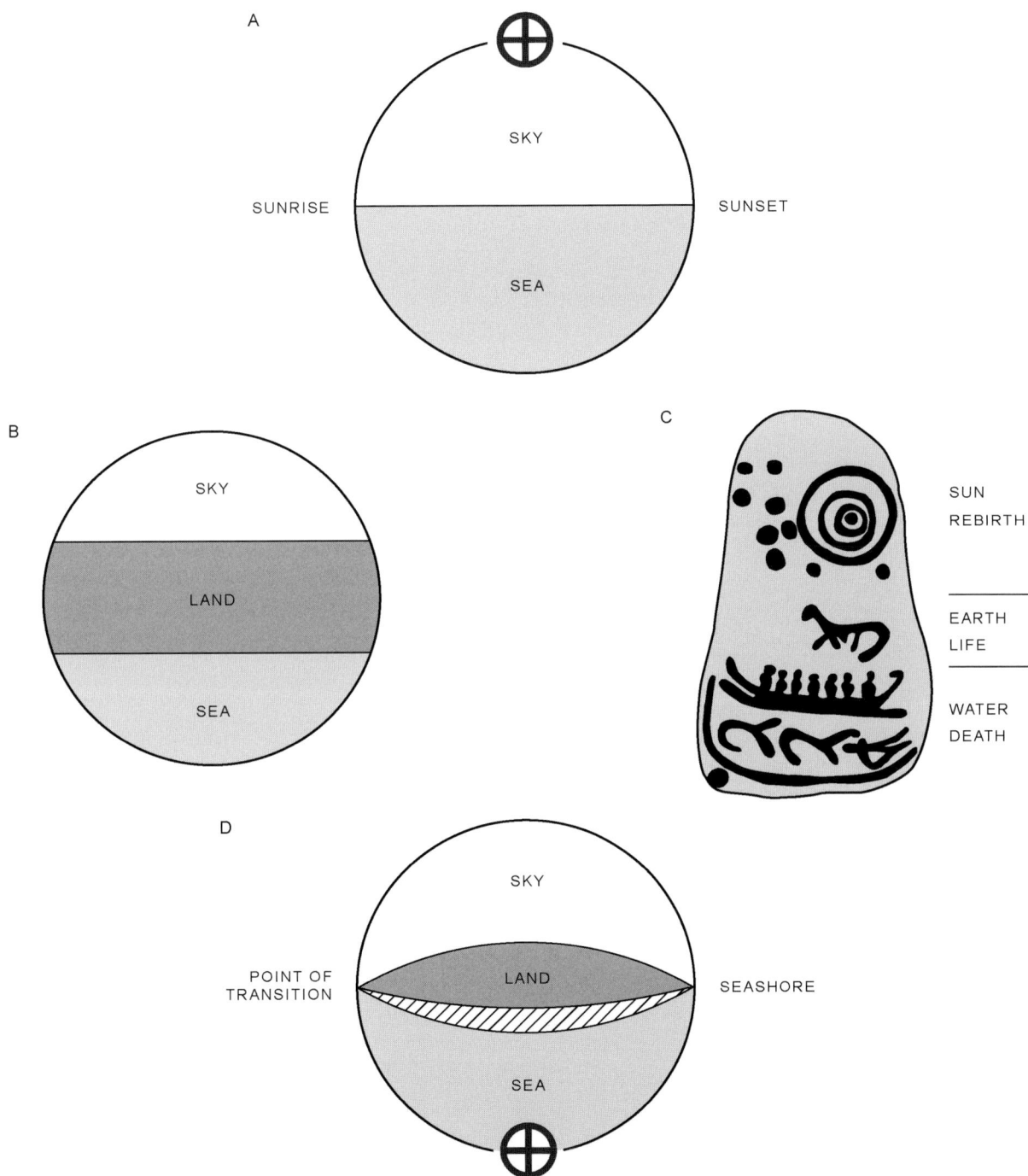

Figure 28.1. A. The relationship between the sea, the sky and the sun according to Kaul (1998); B. The three layers in South Scandinavian rock art postulated by Bradley (2006); C. The three layers depicted on the decorated stone from Klinta, Öland, together with Goldhahn's interpretation of the imagery (after Goldhahn 2005); D. The siting of rock carvings by the seashore where the sun rises and sets and where the sky meets the land and the sea (after Bradley 2006).

Kaul compares these visual images with those found in rock art. Their distributions overlap, but these carvings include a wider range of images. Two features stand out. As well as the sea and sky, there are scenes that have no counterparts on the decorated metalwork. Animals play a prominent role and so do humans, carts and footprints. Although some of the images resemble the sun symbols found in Denmark, the repertoire of South Scandinavian rock art is much more varied. At the same time a number of the decorated panels seem to be organised in relation to three horizontal layers, with a vertical axis communicating between them. As well as an emphasis on the sea and sky, there is a concern with the land (Figure 28.1B; Bradley 2006). That is particularly interesting as the drawings of ships are most frequent close to the water's edge, which is the only place where all these layers converge (Figure 28.1D).

Kaul's interpretation can be extended into other spheres. Decorated razors provide an important clue. Most of them come from burials, but an important feature is that these artefacts are unburnt and had not been present on the pyre. Perhaps they had been used to prepare the body for the funeral. Some of the drawings of ships in South Scandinavian rock art are also associated with the dead. They may be found inside burial cists and were surely employed in mortuary ritual (Randsborg 1993). That may be why the cairns associated with Late Bronze Age cremations sometimes assume the form of a boat (Artelius 1996).

Kaul's scheme extends into yet another domain, for it is thought that the rock carvings were associated with the fertility of the human and animal populations. That could account for the phallic imagery found in Bohuslän and for scenes of cultivation in areas without much arable land. The long winters in the north of the study area might have posed a special challenge. Fertility would have been a particular concern as land emerged from the sea.

Perhaps these explanations can be combined. The daily movement of the sun provides an image of death and regeneration and so does the passage of the seasons so apparent in Northern Europe. The hours of sunlight diminish and then increase again, so that the contrast between winter and summer becomes all important. Just as the vegetation dies and comes back to life, the passing of the seasons might provide a metaphor for human extinction and resurrection.

That has been proposed by Joakim Goldhahn in a study of the imagery associated with Bronze Age burials in Sweden (2005 Chapter 2). He has identified three layers in the carvings found on these sites. Here they are illustrated by a decorated stone associated with a cairn on Öland (Figure 28.1 C). The bottom layer represents water and is illustrated by two boats. True to Kaul's interpretation, the lower vessel travels from left to right and is associated with

horses. The second level Goldhahn interprets as the land, and here it is represented by a solitary horse, whilst the uppermost layer includes a set of concentric circles thought to depict the sun. These carvings show the sea, the land and the sky, but for Goldhahn they also stand for death, life and rebirth. Perhaps the ships were carrying the dead just as they carried the sun (Randsborg 1993).

Is it possible to explore this scheme on a larger scale: to trace its development beyond the individual rock carving to the landscape as a whole? I shall consider two Swedish sites: the rock carvings at Högsbyn and the ship settings at Snäckedal.

Högsbyn (Figure 28.2)

The Late Bronze Age rock carvings at Högsbyn are well known from a study by Christopher Tilley which makes many of the observations that I shall draw on here (Tilley 1999, Chapter 5). The aim of this account is to suggest how they might be related to the broader themes of my paper.

Högsbyn is unusual because the rock carvings are far inland, although the connection with water remains as they are associated with a lake. They occur on a series of rocks located on a hillside running down to the shore. On the higher ground there are Bronze Age cairns, one of them of exceptional size. In the opposite direction the carvings extend to the water's edge where they have been submerged from time to time. They are also directed towards an offshore island which resembles another cairn. Tilley argues that the carved rocks were viewed in sequence following a path leading upslope from the shore. In that case people would have been moving towards the largest monument in the area.

He makes the important point that the rock carvings would not have been visible between November and the end of March because they were buried by snow. It follows that they were probably visited in summer. Then the sun would have risen in the north east. It travelled south so that it could have been seen above the lake, and once it had passed over the water it came back to the land where it set. Thus it would have moved around the zone of carvings from dawn to dusk. The sun set behind the high ground north west of the lake and reappeared the next morning close to the main group of cairns.

That connection is surely illustrated by the distributions of some of the images. Two concentrations of circular motifs of the kind interpreted as sun symbols occur towards the extremes of the zone of carved rocks. This is also where the main concentrations of ship carvings are found. The largest of these are close to the shore and most of them are travelling towards the water. They are associated with elaborate circular designs as if they are carrying the sun.

There are other cases in which the carvings define a direction of movement. The most obvious examples are the

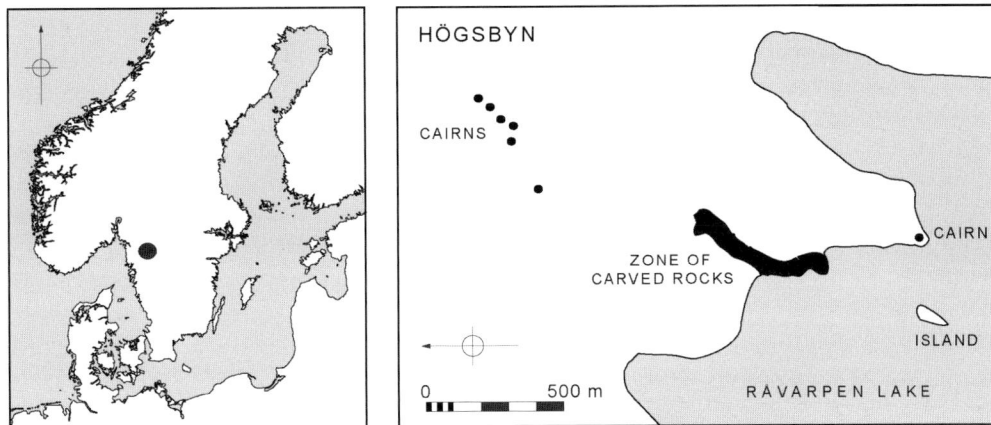

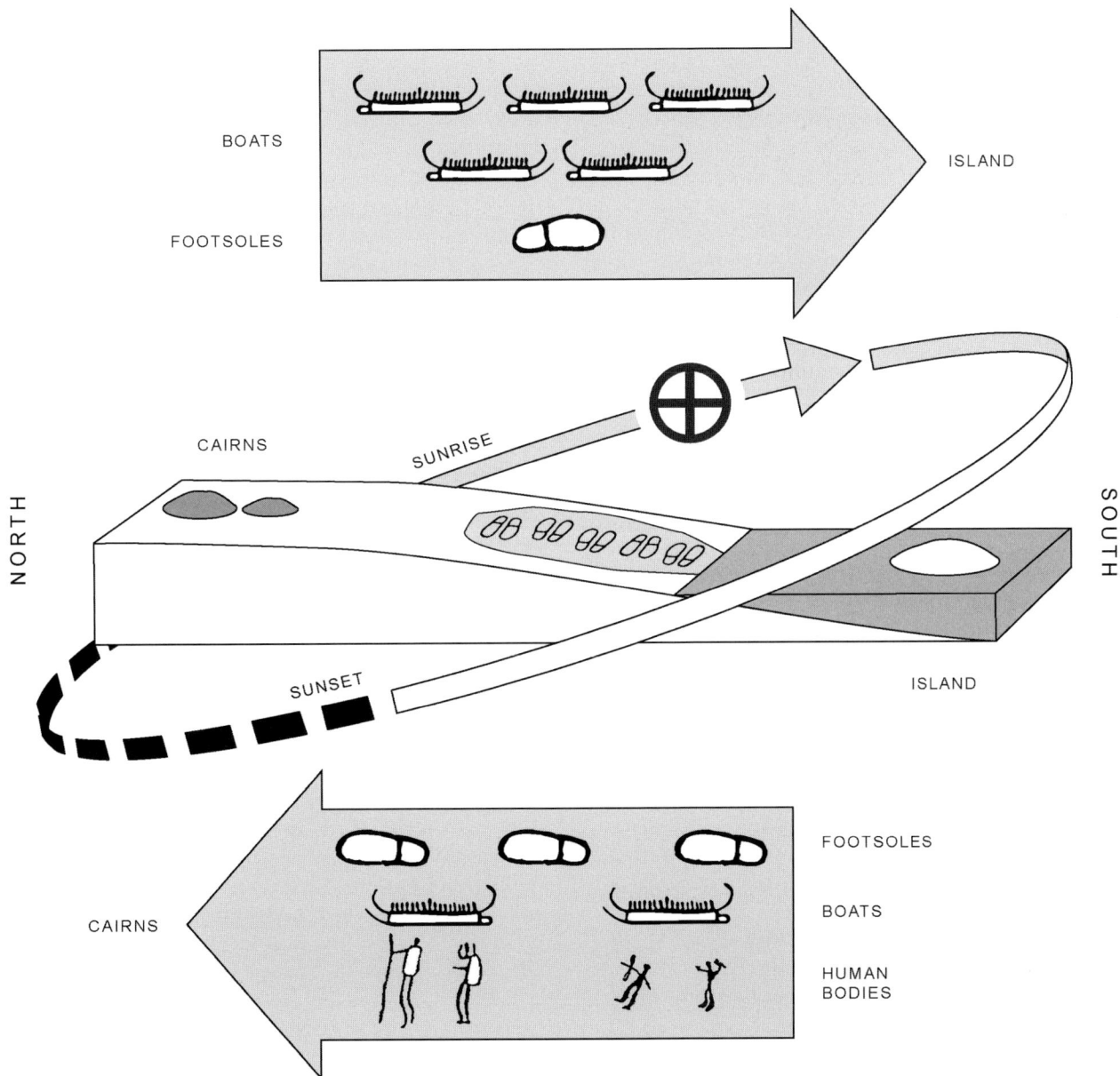

Figure 28.2. (Upper): The location of the rock carvings, the cairns and the offshore island at Högsbyn (after Tilley 1999). (Lower): Major trends in the carved imagery in relation to the passage of the summer sun.

drawings of ships, the majority of which travel down to the lake. A few footprints also follow a course from north to south, but the main emphasis seems to be on the movement of the sun between the high ground and the water's edge. That is reflected by pairs of carved footprints which could mark the positions of observers looking towards the eastern horizon.

Fewer ships are sailing away from the lake in the direction of the cemetery, and this axis is emphasised by a larger number of isolated footprints. At either limit of the zone of carved rocks there are pairs of footprints facing west towards the setting sun. Still more important is a pattern first identified by Tilley: the human figures depicted in this medium also change their character from one end of the complex to the other. Those near the lake are diminutive and lack any obvious characteristics. Further upslope they increase in scale, so that the figures found towards the northern limit of the site are armed with weapons and are clearly male. He describes this process as 'a narrative about becoming human' (1999, 171). I agree with this, but perhaps this interpretation makes most sense when it is considered in relation to the passage of the sun. During the summer it followed a course leading from land to water and then back again. It also formed a link between the sunrise and a major cemetery, the lake and an offshore island. Some of the carvings describe the same passage between land and water, whilst others follow a course leading upslope towards the cairns. That cycle is not unlike the scheme proposed by Kaul, and Tilley is surely correct to interpret the carvings at Högsbyn in relation to 'life, death and the regeneration of life' (1999, 171).

Snäckedal (Figure 28.3)

Snäckedal is a low hill which overlooks a bog a kilometre inland from a former inlet of the Baltic. There are over thirty monuments on the site. They include mounds of burnt stone along the edge of the wetland, but pollen analysis suggests that no one was living in the vicinity.

The cemetery contains four groups of monuments. The largest cairns extend in a row across the highest ground. The example in the centre of the complex is accompanied by an enormous ship setting which divides the cemetery in half. A field study that I carried out with Dag Widholm suggests that the site developed in two stages (Bradley and Widholm 2007). The oldest monuments were four large cairns, which were supplemented by groups of smaller monuments in a subsequent phase. The largest cairns were possibly built during the Early Bronze Age. The smaller structures are of Late Bronze Age type.

A remarkable feature of Snäckedal is the juxtaposition of ship settings and rectilinear cairns, whose proportions resemble those of domestic buildings. They can also be compared with the small 'cult houses' found at cemeteries

of this period (Victor 2002). These kinds of monuments occur together on other sites, but the only ship settings in the locality are two examples a short distance north of the cemetery.

The longest ship setting divides the clusters of monuments into two groups. Those in the northern part of the cemetery contain all the remaining ship settings. All but one of the rectilinear stone settings are in the opposite half of the cemetery. Although there are small circular cairns in all four groups of monuments, it seems as if the site had been organised around the contrast between structures which referred to the land, and those related to the sea. The major cairns were along the boundary where those elements met. This was marked by an enormous monument in the form of a boat.

In two cases the ship settings were so well preserved that it was possible to tell the direction in which they were travelling. The largest was sailing inland towards the biggest cairn. It was probably paired with a newly discovered example which was also orientated on one of the older monuments, but in this case it was going in the opposite direction. Where one ship follows a course extending westwards from an inlet of the Baltic, the other was moving back towards the head of the same channel. The remaining ship settings in the cemetery are aligned on individual round cairns, but it is impossible to distinguish the prow from the stern. On the other hand, the ships found outside the cemetery are clearly travelling away from Snäckedal towards another arm of the Baltic.

The cemetery at Snäckedal emphasises two important relationships – the connection between ships and the dead, and the contrast between land and water – but neither is directly related to the movement of the sun. Here the alignment of the ship settings may be significant. The largest examples in the cemetery connect the monument at Snäckedal with the Baltic Sea. One travels towards the largest cairn in the direction of the setting sun. The other returns from the cemetery but approaches the risen sun. They seem to be paired with one another, but the fact that they travel in opposite directions recalls Kaul's interpretation of the decorated metalwork. The isolated ship settings outside the cemetery at Snäckedal are directed to a different point on the coast. They face the only part of the sky where the sun would never appear. Within the site itself the ship settings emphasised the distinction between land and water. In the wider landscape perhaps they expressed the difference between day and night. Thus monuments that were dedicated to the dead were also related to the sun.

Summary

I have suggested that some of the religious concepts evidenced in Bronze Age Scandinavia developed out of the experience of living in landscapes that were constantly

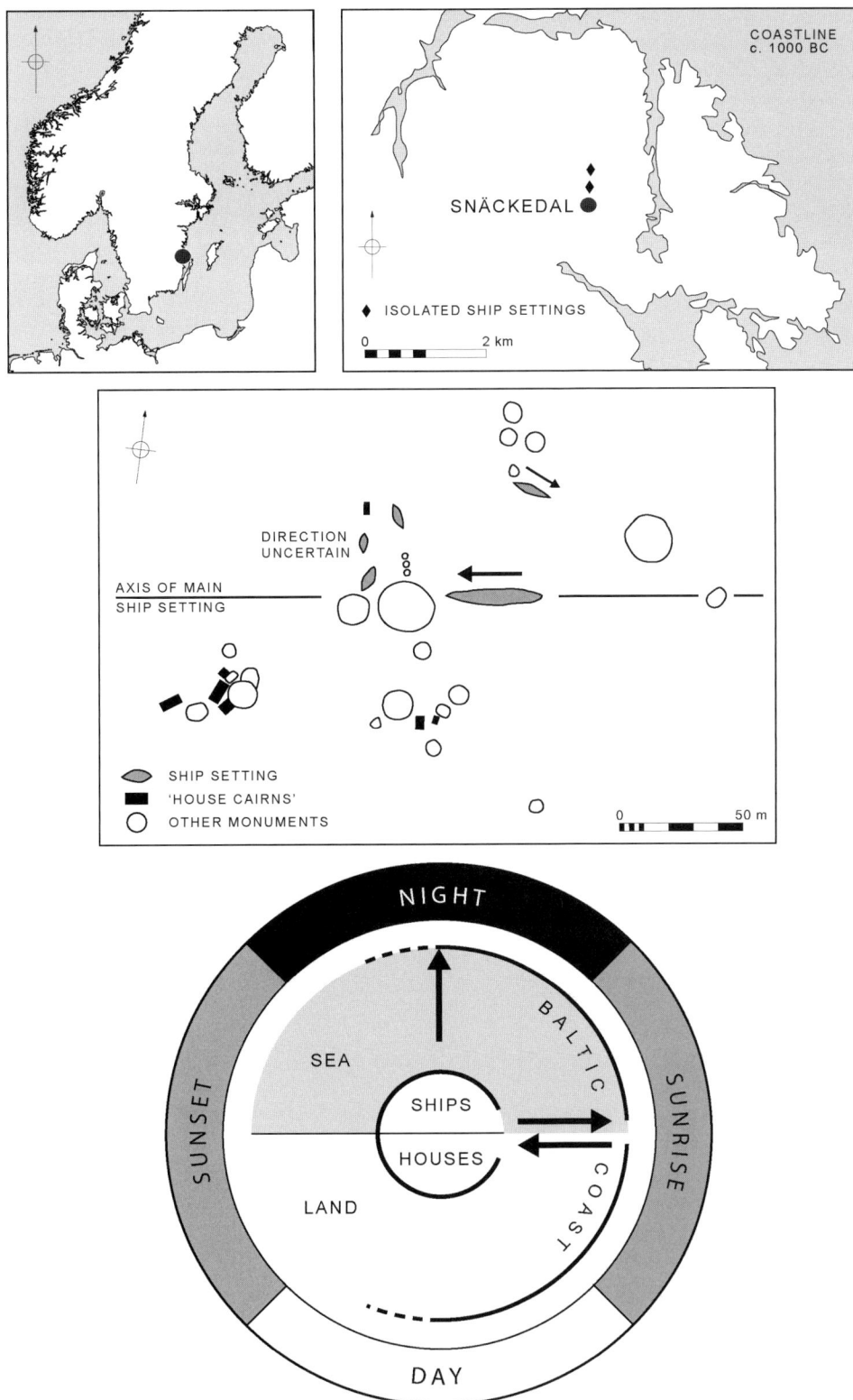

Figure 28.3. (Upper): The siting of the cemetery at Snäckedal in relation to the Bronze Age shoreline and the positions of two isolated ship settings (after Bradley and Widholm 2007). (Centre): Outline plan of the cemetery at Snäckedal emphasising the contrasting distributions of 'house cairns' and ship settings (after Bradley and Widholm in prep.). (Lower): Divisions within the cemetery at Snäckedal in relation to the orientations of the ship settings and the position of the sun.

changing: landscapes in which the movements of the sun were all important and the relationship between land and water assumed a special significance. In particular, I have discussed the cosmology postulated by Flemming Kaul. I have also attempted to develop his analysis in two case studies, one of a group of rock carvings and cairns, and the other of a cemetery with ship settings. There is considerable diversity, and yet it seems as if there are common elements at all these different scales. It remains to establish their limits and that will not be easy, but it is a good reason to take this analysis further in the future.

Acknowledgements

I am most grateful to Dag Widholm who worked with me at Snäckedal and to Tim Phillips who accompanied me on my visit to Högsbyn. The illustrations are by Aaron Watson.

References

Artelius, T. 1996. *Långfard och återkomst - skeppet i bronsålderns gravar.* Kungsbacka, Riksantikvarieämbetet.

Ballard, C., Bradley, R. Nordenborg Myhre, L. and Wilson, M. 2004. The ship as symbol in the prehistory of Scandinavia and South-east Asia. *World Archaeology* 35, 385–403.

Boyer, P. 2001. *Religion Explained.* London, Heinemann

Bradley, R. 2006. Danish razors and Swedish rocks. Cosmology and the Bronze Age landscape. *Antiquity* 80, 372–89.

Bradley, R. and Widholm, D. 2007. *The mountain of ships. The organisation of the Bronze Age cemetery at Snäckedal, Misterhult, Småland.* In B. Hårdh, K. Jennebert and D. Olausson (eds) *On the Road. Studies in Honour of Lars Larsson.* Stockholm, Almqvist & Wiksell International, 246–52.

Goldhahn, J. 2005. *Från Sagaholm till Bredarör.* Göteborg: Göteborgs Universitet. Gotarc Serie C Arkeologiska Skrifter 62.

Kaul, F. 1998. *Ships on Bronzes. A Study in Bronze Age Religion and Iconography.* Copenhagen, National Museum.

Ling, J. 2004. Beyond transgressive lands and forgotten seas: towards a maritime understanding of rock art in Bohuslän. *Current Swedish Archaeology* 12, 121–40.

Ling, J. and Bengtsson, L. 2006. Maritime representations in vertical space. In R. Barndon, S. Innselset, K. Kristoffersen and T. Lødøen (eds). *Samfunn, symboler og identitet – Festkrift til Gro Mandt på 70-årsdrsdagen.* Bergen, Universitetet i Bergen Arkeologiske Skrifter, 525–38.

Randsborg, K. 1993. Kivik. Archaeology and iconography. *Acta Archaeologica* 64.1, 1–147.

Tilley, C. 1999. *Metaphor and Material Culture.* Oxford, Blackwell.

Victor, H. 2002. *Med graven som granne. Om bronsålderns kulthus.* Uppsala, Uppsala University Department of Archaeology and Ancient History. Aun 30.

Chapter 29

THE LATE CLASSIC DROUGHT CULT: RITUAL ACTIVITY AS A RESPONSE TO ENVIRONMENTAL STRESS AMONG THE ANCIENT MAYA

Holley Moyes

Introduction

Beginning in the 1970's there has been a steadily increasing number of archaeological, iconographic, and epigraphic studies regarding ancient Mesoamerican caves (Brady and Prufer 2005). The most important collective finding of these studies is the establishment of caves as sacred space and their almost exclusive use as ritual venues by Pre-Columbian people (Brady 1989; Stone 1995). While studies have been important in the establishment of caves as ritual space there has been little or no research that identifies temporal changes in ritual cave usage. Practice theory provides a broad framework in which to conduct such a study. Sherry Ortner characterizes the study of practice not just as a methodology to locate the point of view of agents but one that seeks to understand 'the configuration of cultural forms, social relations, and historical processes that move people to act in ways that produce the effects in question' (1989, 12). It is not surprising that Ortner advocates an historical overview and considers a long temporal perspective to be vital to the study of changes in practice. This suggests that despite limitations of their data, archaeologists are in a unique position to evaluate ritual transformations over considerable time scales. Changes in practice may be studied in the archaeological record by taking a behavioural approach. The approach shifts research efforts away from the interpretation of the meaning of artefacts to those aimed at understanding the behaviours that created the site's depositional patterns (Reid *et al.* 1975; Schiffer 1995; 1996; 1999; Walker 1995). Once changes in ritual behaviours are defined, it is possible to correlate them with social, political, and environmental factors and thereby reconnect religious rites with the contexts in which they took place and had meaning.

In this chapter I use this approach to define changes in ritual practice between the Early Classic (AD 250–600) and Late Classic (AD 700–900) periods at Chechem Ha Cave, an ancient Maya ritual site in western Belize. Ritual transformations are identified through evaluating changes in the use of space and differences in the condition and placement of artefacts, and variation in the use-intensity of the site. A Geographic Information System (GIS) was created for the site to facilitate the spatial analyses and organize the data. A rigorous assessment of the site's chronology was undertaken using radiocarbon dates and ceramic chronology.

What I refer to as *use-intensity* is a study that is closely related to what is known in anthropological contexts as 'ritual density'. This examines why some societies or historical periods have more ritual than others (Bell 1997, 173). In the archaeological record, *use-intensity* can be studied by identifying a material signature that correlates with ritual activity. This measure must be distinguished from estimates of frequency of use because, depending on the signature that is used, it is impossible to distinguish whether the deposits are a result of more or fewer discrete rituals, the participation of more or fewer individuals in a fixed number of rituals, the result of rituals of a longer or shorter duration, or the effects of a change in ritual practice. Two methods can help to resolve this issue. One is to use multiple proxies and the other is to employ an *indirect* signature that is a consequence of ritual activity but not part of the ritual itself.

I begin with a short discussion of the cognitive associations and general meaning of Mesoamerican caves. This is followed by a description of Chechem Ha Cave and a brief report of the work conducted at the site. Results of the analyses are discussed and ritual transformations occurring between the Early and Late Classic periods are identified. Having identified these transformations, I situate ritual changes within broader socio/political and environmental contexts and discuss their implications.

218 HOLLEY MOYES

Cave rites

In Mesoamerica caves are integrally connected with water and fertility. This phenomenon is demonstrated in iconography from the early Olmec civilization dating from 1200–200 BC on the El Rey monument from Chalcatzingo (Figure 29.1). Although it has been variously interpreted, scholars agree that the image represents a man who is a king or ancestor sitting on a cloud scroll within a cave (Angulo 1987, 133–158; Grove and Gillespie 1984, 110–111; Reilly 1994, 78–79). Mist or smoke emanates from the entrance and clouds rain on the scene. Corn and other vegetation is depicted on the surface on top of the cave.

The same cave/fertility theme is pervasive throughout Mesoamerica and is found much later in the Preclassic Maya murals from San Bartolo, Guatemala that date to the first century BC (Saturno et al. 2005). The mural on the north wall illustrates a creation event in which maize tamales and gourds of water are being handed out of entrance of a cave, probably the cave of origin. The association suggests that both the first maize and primordial

water originated in caves. The ancient Maya Maize God is depicted at the mouth of the cave accepting the offerings. The seventeenth century Popol Vuh story of the Maya creation tells us that the Maize God is intimately connected with caves as he is an Underworld denizen.

The archaeological record also suggests that among the Classic period Maya many of the cave rites were related to rain control. This is not surprising when we consider that a number of deities thought to reside in caves were associated with agricultural success. For instance, in Classic period iconography, Chac the Maya Rain god, is depicted sitting in a cave house (Coe 1978, 78, no.11). A reified example of this was found at the Classic period cave of La Pailita in Guatemala where a life size sculpture of Chac sits on a throne in the cave's interior (Graham 1997). Water rites are also suggested at the Late Classic site of Balankanche in Yucatan where large anthropomorphic censors modeled with images of the central Mexican rain god Tlaloc were discovered surrounding a large stalagmitic column (Andrews 1970, 69).

Activity areas in caves that appear to be focused on

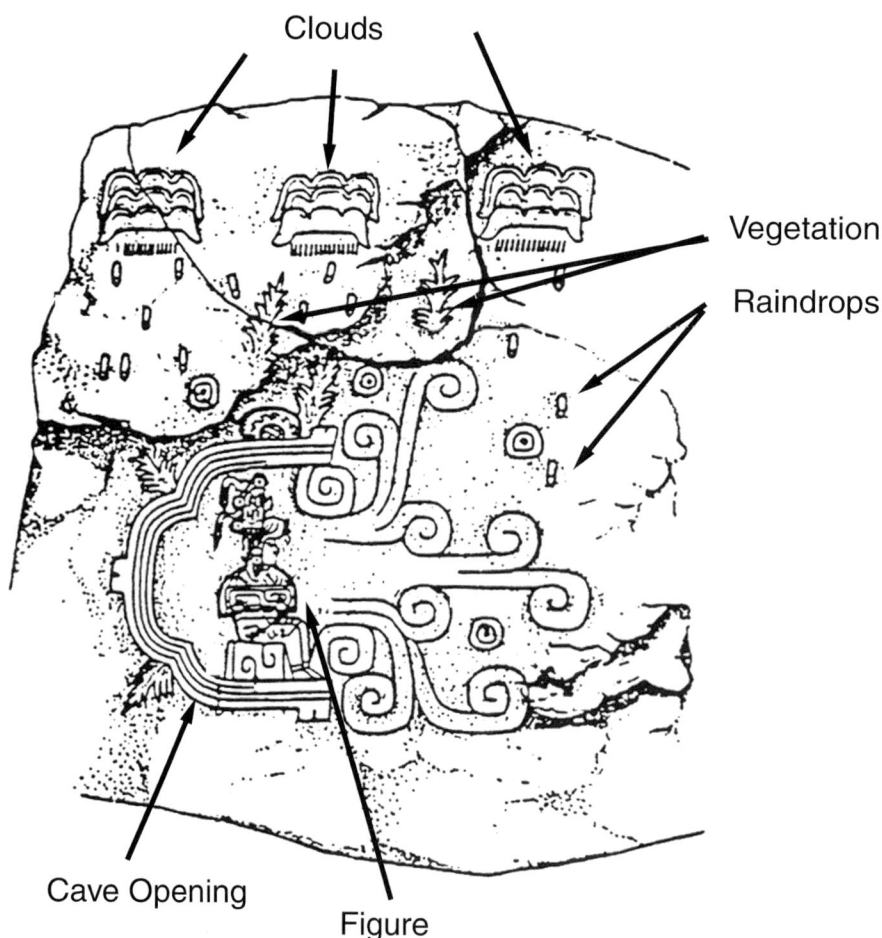

Figure 29.1. El Rey monument is a bas relief illustrating an important person sitting within a cave. Clouds rain on top of the cave and plants are shown growing on the surface (after Reilly 1994, 85).

water features also suggest that water was an important element in cave rites. In his survey of 48 caves in the Yalahau area of Quintana Roo, Dominique Rissolo (2001; 2005) noted that many of the caves in his survey contained interior water features such as intermittent pools. Both rock art and architectural modifications tended to be associated with these features and art from the cave of Pak Che'n contained rain-god motifs. Similarly, a spatial analyses conducted in the Main Chamber of Actun Tunichil Muknal demonstrated that 51% of the artefact assemblage was placed in intermittent pools (Moyes 2001; 2002; Moyes and Awe 1998; 2000).

Given that cave rites were strongly associated with agricultural success entailing the control of rainfall, we might expect cave ritual to be influenced by climatic factors. The use of ritual as a technology to anticipate and minimize agricultural risk, has been demonstrated among the modern Maya by David Freidel and Justine Shaw (2000). Based on the 43 ethnographic and ethnohistoric cases studied, they reported that where agriculture was risky it was primarily due to water availability. What this implies is that ethnographically, water availability is one of the primary concerns of modern Maya agriculturists and that ritual investment is somewhat linked to agricultural risk based on environmental factors.

The cave

Chechem Ha Cave has been under investigation by the Western Belize Regional Cave Project (WBRCP) under the direction of Dr Jaime Awe since 1998. It is located on the western bank of the Macal River near the Guatemalan border (Awe *et al.* 2005). The cave is a complex system that contains over 300 m of tunnels consisting of two primary conduits, Tunnel 1 and Tunnel 2 (Figure 29.2). There are four side passages and elevated eleven shelves located from 3–7 m above the Tunnel 1 floor. Artefacts are found throughout the entire cave system in niches and alcoves along the tunnel floors, in the elevated passages, and on all eleven shelves (Moyes 2004; 2005; 2006).

Based on calibrated radiocarbon dates reported at the 2–sigma range, the site dates from the Early Middle Preclassic period (1100–820 BC), possibly as early as 1300 BC, to the end of Late Classic period as late as AD 960. The entrance of the cave was blocked with medium to large sized boulders sometime prior to AD 960. This correlates roughly with the Classic Maya Collapse and agrees with termination events from the two nearest surface sites Las Ruinas de Arenal (Taschek and Ball 1999) and Minanhá (Iannone 2001; 2005) occurring approximately AD 850.

Chechem Ha contains the earliest radiocarbon dates for ritual cave use in the Maya lowlands and is contemporaneous with the earliest settlements in the Belize

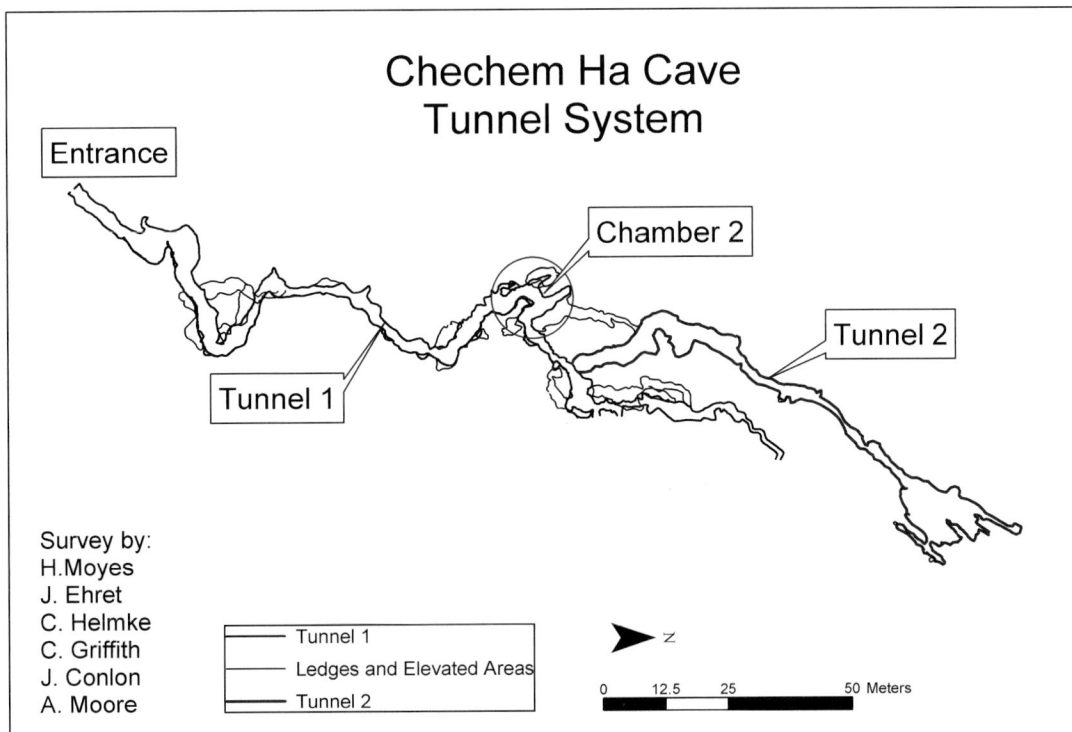

Figure 29.2. Map of Chechem Ha tunnel system.

Valley. This is important because the cave's use spanned the 2,000-year development of Maya kingship to its ninth century collapse thus providing a broad temporal perspective on ritual cave use within a single site.

Methods

Two field seasons were spent mapping the cave's surface artefacts (Moyes 2004; 2005; 2006). A test-pitting program conducted in the third season revealed that the site contained deep subsurface deposits. In the forth season a broad horizontal excavation (2 m × 8 m) was conducted in Chamber 2, an area located 134 m from the cave entrance. The excavation consisted of 17 natural and cultural layers that were excavated to bedrock. This area was crucial in understanding the cave's use because of its geographic location in the center of the tunnel system. To enter the deeper parts of the tunnel system one must traverse this chamber. Therefore the sediments in the chamber were expected to contain a comprehensive record of the cave's overall use.

To establish the site's chronology there were 44 AMS dates collected from multiple surface and sub-surface contexts that were processed at the University of Arizona Accelerator Mass Spectrometry (AMS) Laboratory. Dates were calibrated using Oxcal 3.9 and are reported at the 2 sigma probability range unless otherwise specified. The ceramic chronology used James Gifford's (1976) type-variety-mode system for the Belize Valley. Ceramics were the most numerous artefacts within the cave. There were a total of 1901 ceramic sherds, whole, or partial vessels of which 470 were typed for chronology (Jaime Awe personal communication 1999; James Aimers pers. comm. 2003; Joseph Ball pers. comm. 1999; Joseph Ball and Jennifer Taschek pers. comm. 2005, Ishihara 2000; Kay Sunahara pers. comm. 2001).

Two proxies provided quantitative measures for the site's use-intensity – ceramics (sherds and reconstructable vessels) and the number of charcoal flecks present in the excavated deposits. Evidence that the Maya used wood torches to light their way in caves is abundant (Morehart 2005; Morehart et al. 2005) and charcoal flecks from torches are found in virtually every utilized cave dark zone in Mesoamerica. Chamber 2, the area of the most intensive excavations, was located far into the dark zone of the cave and was necessarily lit by torches. Flecks from the torch fires were deposited on every excavated level and there is no evidence to suggest that there were changes in fuel use over time. These data provide a good indirect proxy for use-intensity because torchbearing is not directly linked to the ritual itself. Ceramics are a direct proxy because they are likely to be used within rituals or as votive offerings.

Recording of charcoal flecks was accomplished using a GIS technology called *Photomapping*, developed by Mark

Aldenderfer and Nathan Craig (Aldenderfer and Craig 2002; Craig 2000; Craig and Aldenderfer in press; Moyes et al. in press). The technique uses digital photographs to record each level of the excavation units and was perfect for rapidly piece-plotting large numbers of charcoal flecks in the field. The excavation was blocked off into 1 m grid squares. Each square of each level was photographed and the photos were imported into ArcMap 8.1 where they were rubber sheeted (or stretched) onto a grid. They could then be brought up onto the computer screen and artefacts were digitized onto the photos while viewing them in the field, which insured the accuracy of the data. By stitching together the 1 m units each level could be viewed in a single screen. An example of a finished photomap is illustrated in Figure 29.3.

Results

AMS dates from the Chamber 2 excavations determined that Levels 1–13 dated to the Maya era. The number of charcoal flecks per level ranged from 265 to 8,244. A correction to the raw data was made because the excavated surface areas were not of identical size on each level. As the excavations progressed the cave walls curved inward and spatial areas narrowed toward the bottom. The number of flecks from each level was divided by the area of excavation to create a use-intensity index (Figure 29.4). The number of flecks per level fluctuates considerably and the cave's heaviest use dates from the Terminal Preclassic to the beginning of the Early Classic period 210–420 AD (reported at the 92.6% probability). After this time, use-intensity wanes and by the Late Classic period there is very little charcoal found in the chamber. This is curious because Late Classic ceramics were found on the chamber's surface and on Ledge 9 above the chamber floor indicating that the chamber was in fact used during this time.

The ceramic analysis tells a very different story. Counts from both surface and subsurface contexts indicate that over 50% of the assemblage dates to the Late Classic Spanish Lookout complex (700–900 AD). Based on these data alone one might expect that the cave underwent it's most intensive usage in Late Classic period, but the charcoal proxy measure suggests that this is not the case (Figure 29.5). What these data do suggest is that in the Late Classic period deposition of ceramic vessels or sherds in the cave became the focus of ritual activity to the exclusion of more prolonged rites or ritual performances. Ritual participants could not have spent long periods of time in the cave because long rites would have produced greater amounts of charcoal rain from torches. This is supported by the fact that many Late Classic period activities occurred on high ledges or in other restricted spaces that limited the number of participants. The condition of the ceramic assemblage changed somewhat between the Early and Late Classic periods as well. In the Early Classic period whole or

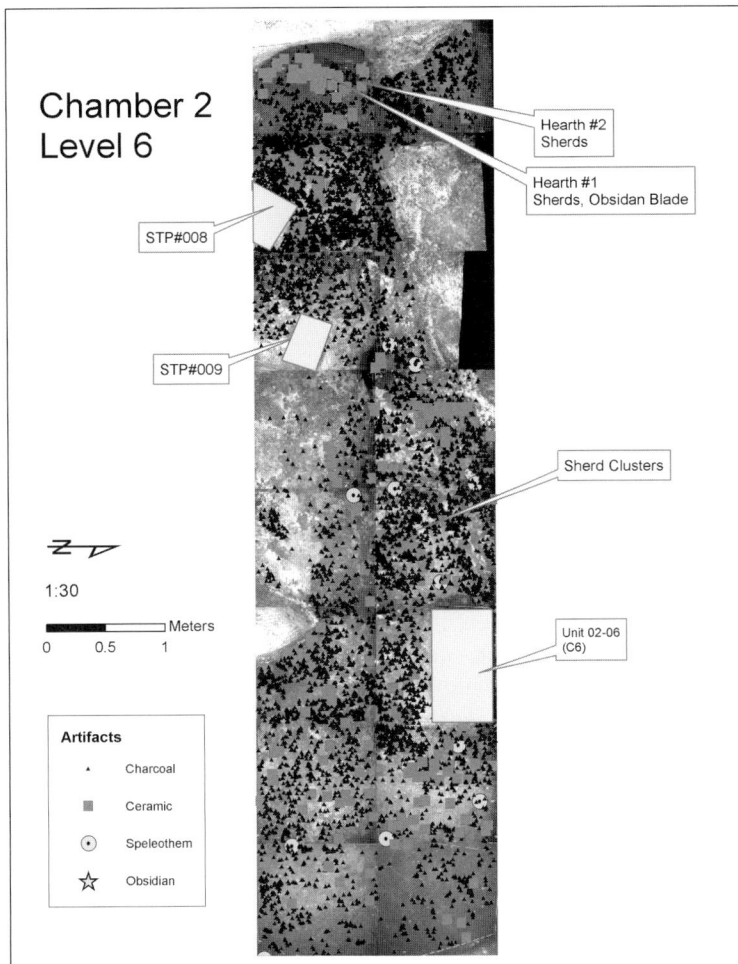

Figure 29.3. Photomap of Level 6.

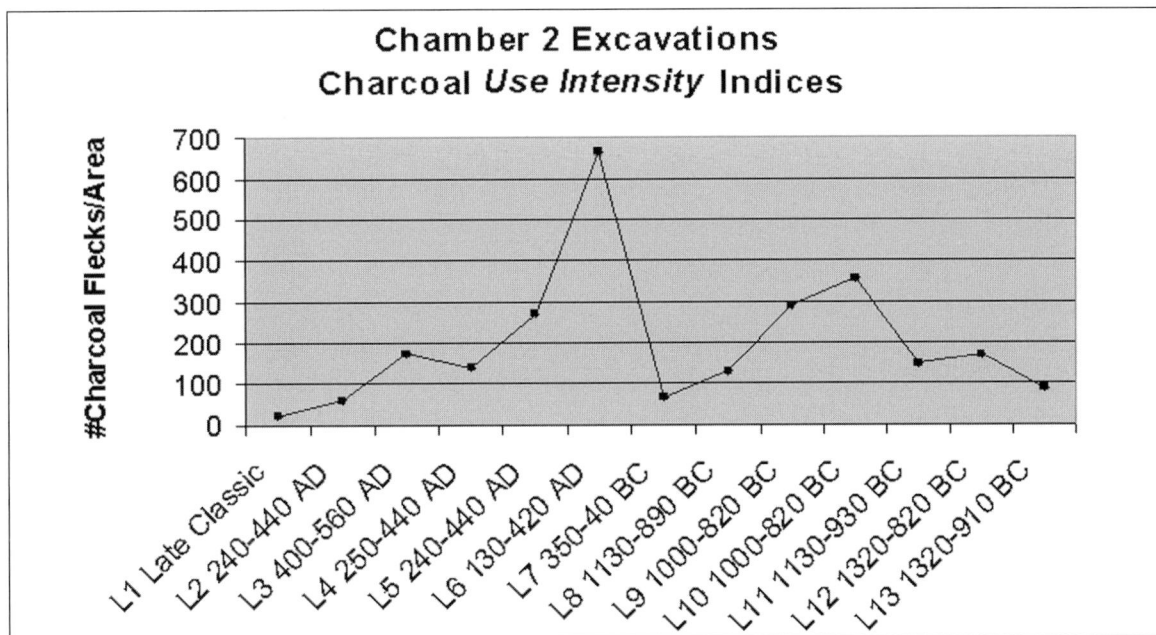

Figure 29.4. Graph of use-intensity index shows numbers of charcoal flecks by excavated level divided by surface area of excavated space. Chart moves from youngest to oldest deposits.

222   HOLLEY MOYES

partially intact vessels are rare. The only intact jar dating to this period is located on Ledge 10. In the Late Classic there are 51 fully intact vessels and numerous others that are partially intact. Most of these intact or partially intact vessels are jar forms though large bowls are present as well (Figure 29.6).

Throughout the cave system there was a change in the use of space between the Early and Late Classic periods (Figure 29.7). Early classic distributions fell into three major areas: the passage leading to Chamber 2, Ledge 10 located in Chamber 2 and in the deepest passages of Tunnel 1. During the Late Classic period ceramics were more widely distributed throughout the site. At this time Ledge 10 fell out of use but the other ten ledges were used for the first time in the cave's history. In addition to the ledges, artefacts were also placed in the elevated passages and crawl spaces. While some of these spaces were used in earlier periods they clearly became the activity areas of choice in the Late Classic. Radiocarbon dates based on five samples collected from the ledges and from Elevated Passage 3 agree with the ceramic chronology indicating that these changes in practice occurred after AD 680 and before AD 960 (Table 29.1).

The change in practice is not limited to Chechem Ha but is a widespread phenomena throughout Belizean cave sites. Some sites were only used in the Late Classic period but all

known Maya cave sites in Belize show evidence of Late Classic usage. Whole or partial vessels including medium to large jars, large bowls, or dishes dating to this period are found in many sites in similar contexts such as hard to reach or remote areas. These vessels are reported by the Western Belize Regional Cave Project in the Entrance Chambers and Main Chamber at Actun Tunichil Muknal (Griffith 1998; Moyes 2001; Moyes and Awe 1998; 2000), Barton Creek Cave (Mirro and Mirro 2001), Laberinto de las Tarantulas (Helmke et al. 1999), and Yaxteel Ahau (Mirro and Halperin 2000; Owen and Gibbs 1999). In his survey of 48 caves in southern Belize, Keith Prufer (2002) also found numerous sites containing partial or whole Late Classic vessels placed in difficult-to-access or remote areas. The pattern was also noted at Edward Quiroz Cave in the Chiquibul region of southern Cayo District (Pendergast 1971) and at Rio Frio Cave E in the Mountain Pine Ridge (Pendergast 1970). In the Caves Branch area Elizabeth Graham and her colleagues (1980) illustrated a number of Late Classic jars and bowls from the high ledge at Footprint Cave and numerous intact Late Classic jars and dishes were found in Alcoves I and II at Actun Polbiche in the Sibun Hills (Pendergast 1974). Patricia McAnany and her colleagues (2003) also working in the Sibun area reported large Late to Terminal Classic vessels found in inaccessible areas at Pottery Cave.

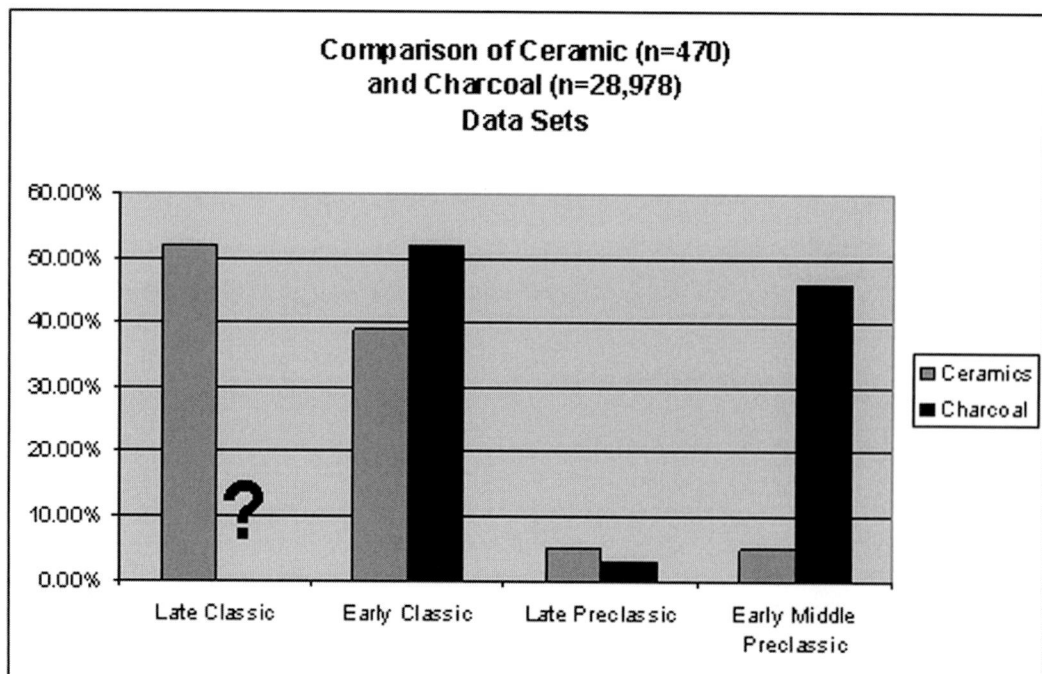

Figure 29.5. Chart shows the percentages of ceramic and charcoal data sets for each major temporal period. There is less than 1% of the total number of charcoal flecks on the surface of Chamber 2 which is curios considering that over 50% of the ceramics in the cave dated to the Late Classic period.

Figure 29.6. Photo illustrating differences between typical Early and Late Classic cave ceramic assemblages. a) Early Classic assemblage is highly fragmented whereas b) Late Classic assemblage contains larger number of whole or partial vessels.

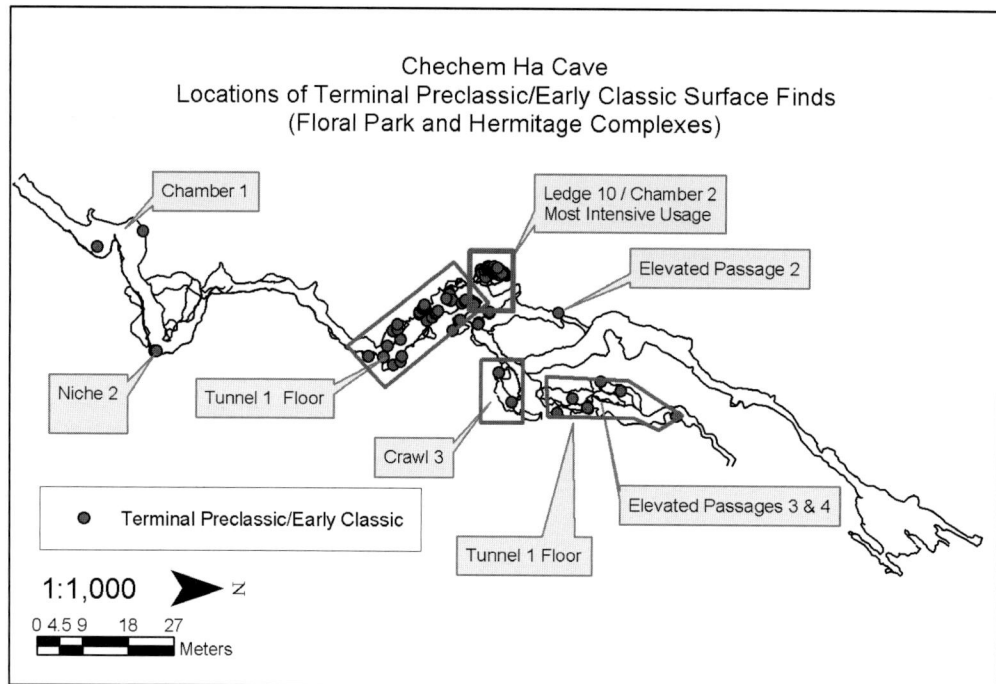

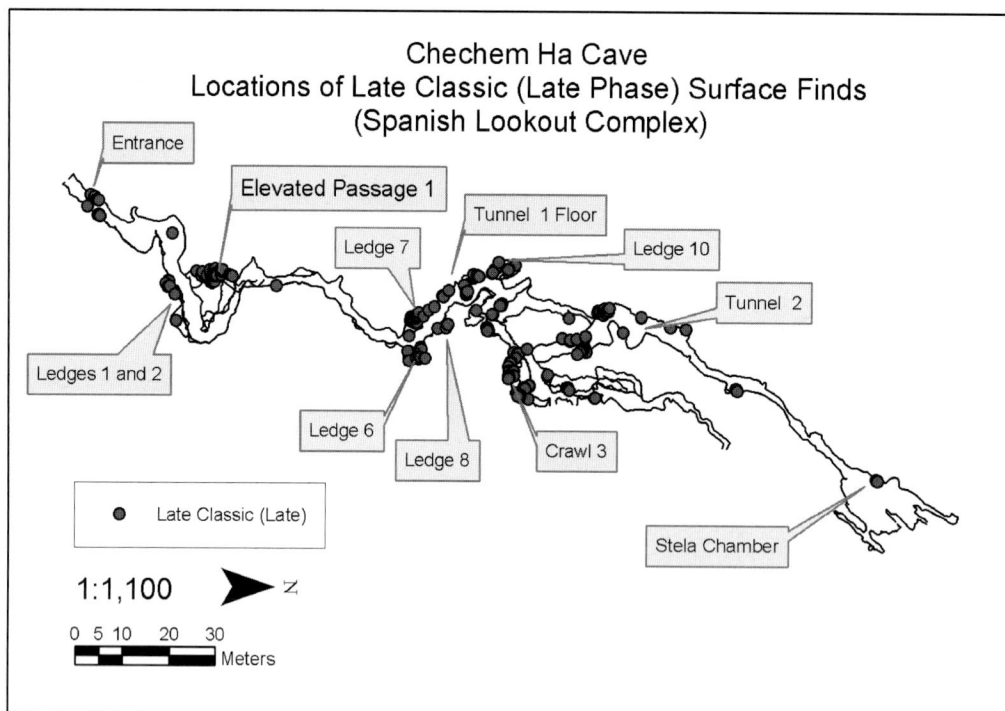

Figure 29.7. *Maps of cave illustrating differences in the distributions of ceramics between the Early (top) and Late (bottom) Classic periods. In the Late Classic ceramics are more widely distributed throughout the site. Ledges and high level passages become the preferred activity areas at this time.*

AZ Lab #	Period	Area	Radiocarbon Age	Calibrated Date 2 Sigma	Alternative Probabilities
AA57293	Late Classic	Ledge 6	1187±33	AD 720–960	
AA57288	Late Classic	Ledge 4	1210±31	AD 690–900	AD760–900(85.4%)
AA59754	Late Classic	Ledge 6	1224±38	AD 680–900	
AA59753	Late Classic	EP3	1239±36	AD 680–890	
AA57291	Late Classic	Ledge 7	1244±31	AD 680–890	

Table 29.1. Late Classic AMS dates calibrated using OxCal 3.9.

Caves and climate

Because of the cognitive association between caves and agricultural or water-related rites, one might expect a relationship between caves and the environment; particularly fluctuations in rainfall. Speleothems from caves provide one of the best local rainfall reconstructions in paleoclimate research. Speleothems include both stalactites and stalagmites, usually formed by calcite deposition that accumulated as bands or rings (Ford and Williams 1989; Hill and Forti 1997). In areas with annual wet and dry seasons the bands suggest yearly events much like tree rings (Baker *et al.* 1993; Genty and Quintif 1996; Holmgren *et al.* 1999; Railsbeck *et al.* 1994; Webster 2000, 63–65). Bands can be dated using radiocarbon or Uranium-series (U-series) dating (Broecker and Olson 1965; Schwarcz and Rink 2001).

James Webster (2000) conducted a paleoclimate study of relative rainfall availability using a speleothem collected from the Macal Chasm in western Belize, a cave located approximately 5 km from Chechem Ha. Webster evaluated the thickness and frequency of bands, their colour, luminescence, and isotopic ratios ($\delta^{18}O$). He found that between AD 700 and AD 1225 there was a long dry period with spikes one standard deviation below average occurring approximately AD 809, 928, 1126, and 1206. The first two spikes in dryness roughly correlated with the Classic Maya Collapse in the ninth century. The severity and length of this dry period is not paralleled at any other time in Maya history. Webster's data is in general agreement with the results from Lake Chichancanab in the nearby Petén (Hodell *et al.* 2001) although the speleothem is a better proxy for this study as it is locally obtained and is derived by a more fine-grained approach. Webster's data suggests a temporal correlation between the onset of this dry period and the change in practice noted at Chechem Ha Cave and elsewhere.

Iconography of jars

Not only is there a strong temporal correlation that suggests a ritual response to this period of increasing dryness, but the presence of large jars is suggestive as well. In both modern Maya ethnography and ancient iconography large jars are associated with water deities. Ethnographic evidence from Lake Atitlan in Guatemala illustrates that Maria Castellana, a female creatrix is associated with the moon (Tarn and Prechtel 1986, 176). The moon itself is envisioned as a large water jar that turns on its side during rainy season until the water spills out. Images in the Dresden codex suggest that this is an ancient belief. On page 74 an old woman named in the codex as *Chac Chel* or Goddess O, the Moon Goddess, hangs in the sky (Taube 1992, 100; 1995, 71) (Figure 29.8). In her hands is an inverted jar from which she pours water onto the earth. She is depicted similarly on page 43b. In the Madrid Codex flood pages she is seen in a similar position on pages 10b and 29b. On page 30a of the Madrid both she and Chac the rain god are in similar poses pouring water from inverted jars. Because she is pictured in the cave paintings at Naj Tunich, James Brady (1989, 47–49) has long argued that the association with caves extends not only to Chac the rain god but to this female deity as well.

The Late Classic drought cult

Data from ancient Maya caves in Belize suggests that the changes in ritual practice in the Late Classic period represent a drought cult pervasive at a regional scale. At Chechem Ha Cave the phenomena can be temporally circumscribed beginning after AD 680 and ending by AD 960. The correlation between the changes in practice and the onset of a prolonged dry period can hardly be accidental. The deposition of large jars in hard to reach areas and restricted spaces also suggests that rituals at this time became more costly and esoteric. We may conclude that in the Late Classic period the environmental change was drastic enough to have affected the everyday lives of Maya people. The study not only defines the behaviors that produced the artifact record but implies a cognitive aspect as well. No matter the severity of the dry period as it relates to the Classic Maya Collapse, the data from the ritual sites suggest that we are witness to the collective response of a *perceived* stress.

Figure 29.8. Page 74 of the Dresden Codex illustrates the Moon Goddess hanging in the sky. In her hands is a large jar from which she pours water. Taube (1988a, 146; 1995, 71) has interpreted this scene as the primordial flood event. Chac the rain deity is positioned below.

Acknowledgments

I would like to thank Dr Jaime Awe, the Director of the Institute of Archaeology and principal investigator for the Western Belize Regional Cave Project (WBRCP) as well s members of the Belize Institute of Archaeology, John Morris, George Thompson, and Brian Woodeye. Appreciation is extended to the Morales and Plytez families, to the 2003 the crew: Jim Aimers, Mark Aldenderfer, Nathan Craig, Anthony Beardsall, Grant Polley and Connie Price. Mark Aldenderfer provided computer equipment for the project and Nathan Craig was instrumental in implementing the *photomapping* technique. Various aspects of the project were funded by an NSF dissertation improvement grant to Dr Ezra Zubrow, the Foundation for the Advancement of Mesoamerican Studies, the Cave and Karst Conservancy, the Cave Research Foundation, and the Mark Diamond fund at the University at Buffalo.

References

Aldenderfer, M. and Craig, N. 2002. A GIS-based in-field data recording system for archaeological excavation. Paper presented at the 13th Annual Workshops in Archaeometry, University at Buffalo.

Andrews, E. W. 1970. *Balankanche, Throne of the Tiger Priest.* New Orleans, Middle American Research Institute Publication 32.

Angulo, J. V. 1987. The Chalcatzingo Reliefs: an Iconographic Analysis. In *Ancient Chalcatzingo*, edited by David C. Grove. Austin, University of Texas Press, 133–158.

Awe, J. J., Gibbs, S. and Griffith, C. 2005. Stelae and Megalithic Monuments in the Caves of Western Belize. In J. E. Brady and K. M. Prufer (eds). *In the Maw of the Earth Monster: Mesoamerican Ritual Cave Use.* Austin, University of Texas Press, 223–248

Baker, A., Smart, P. L., Edwards, R. L. and Richards, D. A. 1993. Annual Growth Banding in a Cave Stalagmite. *Nature* (364), 518–520.

Bell, C. 1997. *Ritual Perspectives and Dimensions.* Oxford, Oxford University Press.

Brady, J. E. 1989. *Investigation of Maya Ritual Cave Use with Special Reference to Naj Tunich, Peten, Guatemala.* Ph.D. University of California.

Brady, J. E. and Prufer, K. 2005. Maya Cave Archaeology: A New Look at Religion and Cosmology. In K. M. Prufer and J. E. Brady (eds). *Stone Houses and Earth Lords: Maya Religion in the Cave Context.* Boulder, University Press of Colorado, 365–380.

Broecker, W. S. and Olson, E. A. 1960. Radiocarbon Measurements and Annual Rings in Cave Formations. *Nature* (185), 93–94.

Coe, M. 1978. *Lords of the Underworld.* Princeton: Princeton University Press.

Craig, N. 2000. Real-Time GIS Construction and Digital Data Recording of the Jiskairumoko Excavation, Peru. *The Society for American Archaeology Bulletin* 18(1), 24–28.

Craig, N. and Aldenderfer, M. In press. Future directions in the recording of archaeological excavations using GIS. In S. Branting (ed.) *Future Directions in GIS*. Oxford, Archaeopress.

Moyes, H., Craig, N. and Aldenderfer, M. In press. A GIS-based Approach to Identifying Ritual Activity. In Cave Dark Zones, *Journal of Cave and Karst Studies*.

Ford, D. C. and Williams, P. W. 1989. *Karst Geomorphology and Hydrology*. Boston: Unwin Hyman.

Freidel, D. and Shaw, J. 2000. The Lowland Maya Civilization: Historical Consciousness and Environment. In R. J. McIntosh, J. A. Tainter, and S. K. McIntosh (eds). *The Way the Wind Blows: Climate, History, and Human Action*. New York: Columbia University Press, 271–300.

Genty, D. and Quintif, Y. 1996. Annually Laminated Sequences in the Internal Structure of Some Belgian Stalagmites: Importance for Paleoclimatology. *Journal of Sedimentary Petrology* 66 (1), 275–288.

Gifford, J. C. 1976. *Prehistoric Pottery Analysis and the Ceramics of Barton Ramie in the Belize Valley*. Memoirs of the Peabody Museum of Archaeology and Ethnology 18, Cambridge, MA, Harvard University.

Graham, E., McNatt, L. and Gutchen, M. A. 1980. Excavations in Footprint Cave, Belize. *Journal of Field Archaeology* (7),153–172.

Graham, I. 1997. Discovery of a Maya Ritual Cave in Peten, Guatemala. *Symbols* (Spring), 28–31.

Griffith, C. 1998. Excavations and Salvage Operations in Actun Tunichil and Actun Uayazba Kab, Roaring Creek Valley, Belize. In J. J. Awe (ed.) *The Western Belize Regional Cave Project: A Report of the 1997 Field Season*. Durham, Dept. of Anthropology. Occasional Paper No. 1, University of New Hampshire, 37–70.

Grove, D. C.and Gillespie, S. 1984. Chalcatzingo's Portrait Figurines and the Cult of the Ruler. *Archaeology* 37(4), 27–33.

Helmke, C. G. B., Griffith, C. S., Mirro, M. J. 1999. The 1996 and 1998 Investigations at Laberinto De Las Tarantuals, Cayo District, Belize. In J. J. Awe (ed.) *The Western Belize Regional Cave Project: A Report of the 1998 Field Season*. Durham, Department of Anthropology, Occasional Paper No. 2, University of New Hampshire, 205–221.

Hill, C. A., and Forti, P. 1986. *Cave Minerals of the World*. Huntsville, AL, National Speleological Society.

Holmgren, K., Karlén, W., Lauritzen, S. E., Lee-Thorp, J. A., Partridge, T. C., Piketh, S., Repinski, P., Stevenson, C., Svanered, O. and Tyson, P. D. 1999. A 3,000-Year High-Resolution Stalagmite-Based Record of Paleoclimate for Northeastern South Africa. *The Holocene* 9(3), 295–309.

Hodell, D. A., Curtis, J. H., Brenner, M. and Guilderson, T. P. 2001. Solar Forcing of Drought Frequency in the Maya Lowlands. *Science* (292), 1367–1370.

Hodell, D. A. 2001. Fall of the House of Minanhá: A Case of Late Classic Political Disruption in West Central Belize. In G. Iannone, R. Primrose, A. Menzies, and L. McParland (eds) *Archaeological Investigations in the North Vaca Plateau, Belize: Progress Report of the Third (2001) Field Season*. Peterborough, Dept. of Anthropology, Trent University, 127–133.

Iannone, G. 2005. The rise and fall of the house of an ancient Maya petty royal court. *Latin American Antiquity* 16(1), 26–44.

Ishihara, R. 2000. *An Investigation of the Ancient Maya Ritual Cave Activity at Actun Chechem Ha, Cayo District, Belize*. B.A. Japan, University of Tsukuba.

McAnany, P. A., Berry, K. A. and Thomas, B. S. 2003. Wetlands, Rivers, and Caves: Agricultural and Ritual Practice in Two Lowland Maya Landscapes. In G. Iannone and S. V. Connell (eds) *Perspectives on Ancient Maya Rural Complexity, Monograph 49*. University of California, Los Angeles, The Cotsen Institute of Archaeology, 71–82.

Mirro, M. and Halperin, C. 2000. Archaeological Investigations on Ledge 1 of Actun Yaxteel Ahau, Roaring Creek Valley, Cayo District, Belize. In *The Western Belize Regional Cave Project: A Report of the 2000 Field Season*. Durham, Department of Anthropology, Occasional Paper No. 4, University of New Hampshire, 263–280.

Mirro, M. and Mirro, V. 2001. A Report of the 2000 Field Season at the Barton Creek Cave, Cayo District, Belize. In *The Western Belize Regional Cave Project: A Report of the 2000 Field Season*. Durham, Department of Anthropology, Occasional Paper No. 4, University of New Hampshire, 97–126.

Morehart, C. T. 2005. Plants and Caves in Ancient Maya Society. In K. M. Prufer and J. E. Brady (eds) *Stone Houses and Earth Lords: Maya Religion in the Cave Context*. Boulder, University Press of Colorado, 167–186.

Morehart, C. T., Lentz, D. L. and Prufer, K. M. 2005. Wood of the Gods: The Ritual Use of Pine (Pinus spp.) by the Ancient Lowland Maya. *Latin American Antiquity* 16(3), 255–274.

Moyes, H. 2001. *The Cave as a Cosmogram: The Use of GIS in an Intrasite Spatial Analysis of The Main Chamber of Actun Tunichil Muknal, A Maya Ceremonial Cave in Western Belize*. M.A., Florida Atlantic University.

Moyes, H. 2002. The Use of GIS in the Spatial Analysis of an Archaeological Cave Site. *Journal of Cave and Karst Studies* 64(1), 9–16.

Moyes, H. 2004. *Changes and Continuities in Ritual Practice at Chechem Ha Cave, Belize:Report on Excavations Conducted in the 2003 Field Season*. Report submitted to the Foundation for the Advancement of Mesoamerican Studies, Inc., Available from: http://www.famsi.org/reports (cited 15 December 2006).

Moyes, H. 2005. The Sweatbath in the Cave: A Modified Passage in Chechem Ha Cave, Belize. In K. M. Prufer and J. E. Brady (eds). *Stone Houses and Earth Lords: Maya Religion in the Cave Context*. Boulder, University Press of Colorado, 187–212.

Moyes, H. 2006. *The Sacred Landscape as a Political Resource: A Case Study of Ancient Maya Cave Use At Chechem Ha Cave, Belize, Central America*. Ph.D. State University of New York at Buffalo.

Moyes, H. and Awe, J. J. 1998. Spatial Analysis of Artifacts in the Main Chamber of Actun Tunichil Muknal, Belize: Preliminary Results. In J. J. Awe (ed.). *The Western Belize Regional Cave Project: A Report of the 1997 Field Season*. Durham, Dept. of Anthropology. Occasional Paper No. 1, University of New Hampshire, 23–36.

Moyes, H. and Awe, J. J. 2000. Spatial Analysis of an Ancient Cave Site. *ArcUser* 3(4), 64–68.

Ortner, S. B. 1989. *High Religion: A Cultural and Political History of Sherpa Buddhism*. Princeton, Princeton University Press.

Owen, V. A. and Gibbs, S. 1999. Report of Investigations on Ledge 2 at Actun Yaxteel Ahau, Roaring Creek Valley, Belize. In J. J. Awe (ed.). *The Western Belize Regional Cave Project: A Report of the 1998 Field Season*. Durham, Department of Anthropology, Occasional Paper No. 2, University of New Hampshire, 186–204.

Pendergast, D. M. 1970. A. H. *Anderson's Excavations at Rio Frio Cave E, British Honduras*. Toronto, Art and Archaeology Occasional Papers 20, Royal Ontario Museum.

Pendergast, D. M. 1971. Excavations at Euduardo Quiroz Cave, British Honduras (Belize). Toronto, Art and Archaeology Occasional Paper 21, Royal Ontario Museum.

Pendergast, D. M. 1974. Excavations at Actun Polbiche, Belize. Toronto, Archaeology Monograph 1, Royal Ontario Museum.

Prufer, K. M. 2002. *Communities, Caves, and Ritual Specialists: A Study of Sacred Space in the Maya Mountains of Southern Belize*. Ph.D. Southern Illinois University.

Railsback, L. B., Brook, G. A., Chen, J., Kalin, R. and Fleisher, C. J. 1994. Environmental Controls on the Petrology of a Late Holocene Speleothem from Botswana with Annual Layers of Aragonite and Calite. *Journal of Sedimentary Research* A64 (1), 147–155.

Reid, J. J., Schiffer, M. B. and Rathje, W. J. 1975. Behavioral Archaeology, Four Strategies. *American Anthropologist* 77, 864–869.

Reilly III, F. K. 1994. *Visions to Another World: Art, Shamanism, and Political Power in Middle Formative Mesoamerica*. Ph. D. University of Texas.

Rissolo, D. A. 2001. *Ancient Maya Cave Use in the Yalahau Region, Northern Quintana Roo, Mexico*. Ph. D. University of California, Riverside.

2005. Beneath the Yalahau: Emerging Patterns of Ancient May Ritual Cave Use from Northern Quintana Roo, Mexico. In J. E. Brady and K. M. Prufer (eds). *In the Maw of the Earth Monster: Mesoamerican Ritual Cave Use*. Austin, University of Texas Press, 342–372.

Saturno, W. A., Taube, K. A., Stuart, D. and Hurst, H. 2005. The Murals of San Bartolo, El Petén, Guatemala, Part 1: The North Wall. *Ancient America* No. 7.

Schiffer, M. B. 1995. *Behavioral Archaeology First Principles*. Salt Lake City: University of Utah Press.

Schiffer, M. B. 1996. Some Relationships Between Behavioral and Evolutionary Archaeologies. *American Antiquity* 61, 643–662.

Schiffer, M. B. 1999. Behavioral Archaeology: Some Clarifications. *American Antiquity* 64 (1), 166–168.

Schwarcz, H. P. and Rink, W. J. 2001. Dating Methods for Sediments of Caves and Rockshelters with Examples from the Mediterranean Region. *Geoarchaeology* 16(4), 355–371.

Stone, A. J. 1995. *Images of the Underworld: Naj Tunich and the Tradition of Maya Cave Painting*. Austin, University of Texas Press.

Tarn, N. and Prechtel, M. 1986. Constant Inconstancy: The Feminine Principle in Atiteco Mythology. In G. Gossen (ed.) *Symbol and Meaning Beyond the Closed Community: Essays In Mesoamerican Ideas*. Albany, The Institute for Mesoamerican Studies, The University at Albany, State University of New York, 173–184.

Taschek, J. T., and Ball, J. W. 1999. Las Ruinas de Arenal: Preliminary Report on a Subregional Major Center in the Western Belize Valley (1991–1992 Excavations). *Ancient Mesoamerica* 10, 215–235.

Taube, K. 1992 *The Major Gods of Ancient Yucatan*. Washington, D.C., Dumbarton Oaks.

Taube, K. 1995 *The Legendary Past: Aztec and Maya Myths*. Austin, University of Texas Press.

Walker, W. H. 1995. Ceremonial Trash? In J. M. Skibo, W. H. Walker, and A. E. Nielsen (eds) *Expanding Archaeology*. Salt Lake City, University of Utah Press, 67–79.

Webster, J. W. 2000. *Speleothem Evidence of Late Holocene Climate Variation in the Maya Lowlands of Belize Central America and Archaeological Implications*. Ph.D. University of Georgia.

Chapter 30

CULT IN COMETARY CONTEXT

Patrick McCafferty

Introduction

In prehistory, people seem to have devoted much more effort to building structures for ritual, cult and religion than for domestic use. Stonehenge, Newgrange, the Egyptian pyramids, and Maltese temples are all significantly more impressive than contemporary houses. Why was cult so important?

To date, many attempts to answer this question have been unconvincing. For example, the suggestion that the pyramids were built primarily as an elaborate calendar to aid farming can be dismissed since a simple arrangement of posts would have achieved the same objective.

One might hope that mythology, with stories that echo prehistoric society, would help us understand the nature of ancient gods. Sometimes it is easy to connect these gods with particular attributes (e.g. Neptune is the god of the sea) but all too often, they defy such simple associations, and their actions in myth are impossible to relate to the physical world: for example, how did Zeus, apparently the god of thunder, become father of all other gods?

Astronomy may hold the key to all of these issues – and by explaining the actions of the gods in the myths, may even help to increase our understanding of ancient structures and enigmatic rituals. So, let's raise our heads from our trenches and take a brief look at the stars.

Tails of Taurid comets

On most clear nights of the year, one may see shooting stars or meteors. These are caused when tiny particles of space-dust strike the earth's atmosphere at a tremendous speed of 10 to 70 kilometres per second and are vaporized to become trails of burning gas. Occasionally, many meteors are seen to radiate from a single point in the sky: each year, there are roughly twenty such events, known as meteor showers. An even more spectacular event – a meteor storm – occurred in November 1799, when millions of shooting stars radiated from a single point in the constellation Leo

(Von Humboldt 1805, Chapter 1, 10). At the time, nobody knew what caused this event, or a similar one in November 1833. But when the same thing happened in November 1866, it was realised that the meteors were caused by dust from the tail of Comet Tempel-Tuttle, on its 33-year orbit (Bailey, Clube and Napier1990, 110–112).

Of the twenty meteor showers experienced by earth each year, most are short-lived, lasting for just a few hours, as the earth passes through the narrow trail of dust left by a comet. Some showers take longer, lasting for days or even weeks, suggesting that the system is more dispersed, and therefore older. The longest duration shower is the Taurid system, which lasts for a month each November and June, and coincides with Comet Encke, on its 3.3 year orbit.

In addition to dust particles, the Taurid system also contains large material, as demonstrated in June 1975, when seismometers installed by the Apollo astronauts on the Moon detected a swarm of large Taurid boulders striking the Moon (Dorman *et al.* 1978, 3621). It is even thought that the Tunguska Event, in which an object, roughly 50 m in diameter, exploded five miles high in the atmosphere on 30 June 1908, and flattened 2,000 km^2 of forest, was caused by part of the Taurid system (Kresák, L. 1978, 130). In short, some astronomers have concluded that a large comet broke up in the inner solar system thousands of years ago (Clube and Napier 1982).

Let's take a look at comets: typically, these consist of a relatively small nucleus, *c.* 10 km diameter, composed of ices, dusts and organic material. When heated by the sun, a large cloud of gas called the coma is formed. The material ejected from the comet is pushed away from the comet by the solar wind to form two tails: a yellow dust tail that reflects sunlight, and a blue gas tail that glows like a fluorescent bulb. These tails always point away from the sun, and can be hundreds of millions of kilometres long, forming a spectacular sight in the night sky.

If a large comet really was seen in the sky in prehistory, it would have appeared particularly bright. Each year, there would have been two meteor showers – one during daylight and one at night. Most of the time, the orbits of the earth and comet would not intersect, but in some epochs, lasting roughly a century, when the earth and comet debris passed through the same point in the sky (Steel and Asher 1996, 128), the meteor showers could have become fireball storms, with whole swathes of land blasted by heaven. One would expect to find a record of such events in history or myth.

Tales of torrid comets

Comets can appear in many unusual shapes (Sagan and Druyan 1997, 172–194). Occasionally, jets of gas erupt from the nucleus; there can be multiple tails, with disconnection events, in which the tail flickers and is disrupted; there can even be a sunward spike; or shrouds of comas; and of course, the shape seen from earth is influenced by the angle at which the comet is seen.

When one examines the historical record, this variety of shapes is apparent. Comets are recorded as hairy stars, as beards, darts, swords, discs, barrels, horns, torches, horses, fleece, a crown and a spear – and that's just by Pliny, writing in ancient Rome (Pliny, Book II, Chapter 22). The comet of AD 1602 was described as 'a soldier wearing chain-mail' (Johnson 2004, 416). The Chinese knew them as 'broom stars' and on the Mawangdui silk, depicted 29 different comets, with descriptions of the effects of each. A sample, shown in Figure 30.1, shows comets that look like a Christmas tree or a stag with antlers. The comet shown on the right is particularly interesting: we recognize it as the swastika.

Today, because of the murderous legacy of the Nazi party, the swastika induces us with a sense of horror. It wasn't always so. The swastika was once used widely as a good-luck symbol. It is a symbol almost as deeply ingrained in eastern religions as the cross in Christianity, adorning statues of the Buddha and the entrances to Hindu temples. It is found in the art of geometric Greece c. 600 BC, and earlier in time at Hisarlik, thought to be the site of Troy (Wilson 1894, 809–833). One can even find the symbol in Ireland, as St. Bridget's cross.

Its geographical distribution throughout Europe and Asia could be attributed to cultural contact, but this cannot explain the use of the symbol in North America. The astronomer Carl Sagan proposed that a rotating comet with four jets of gas, facing earth, could have been the inspiration for the swastika (Sagan and Druyan 1997, 190).

Comets do indeed rotate. For example, Pliny classified one comet as Hippias: 'like a horse's mane; it has a very rapid motion, like a circle revolving on itself' (Pliny, Book II, Chapter 22). Interestingly, the Irish god Manannan mac Lir, with his three legs, could travel faster than any chariot over land and sea (Mullens 1940, 99–100). Manannan gave his name to the Isle of Man, whose flag (Figure 30.2) depicts three rotating legs. Here we see a clear correspondence between comets and myths, and can begin to imagine that a rotating comet with three jets of gas became known as Manannan in Britain and Ireland.

It can be difficult for us to imagine just what prehistoric viewing people would have thought of a comet in the sky. In 1976, Comet West (Figure 30.3) graced the sky, with its impressive yellow dust tail and fluorescent blue gas tails. Nobody described this comet as a fish! Yet, with just a little imagination, one can see a head, a split tail, and even fins. With this in mind, perhaps a comet inspired the mythical salmon of knowledge, caught after seven years and cooked by Finn, the bright superhero, on a spit (rotation again).

One of Pliny's descriptions of a comet is even more intriguing: 'a white comet with silver hair so brilliant that it could not be looked at, and having the face of a deity in human form' (Pliny, Book II, Chapter 22). When we reflect that the word comet comes from the Greek word for hair, and that comets such as Comet Donati (Figure 30.4) look almost like humans, or at least like wigs, we can easily imagine that a prehistoric civilization might have thought they saw a god in the sky.

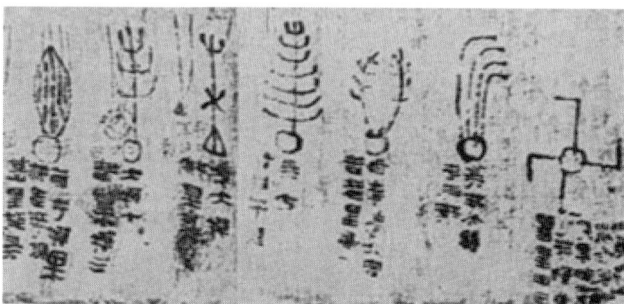

Figure 30.1. Mawangdui Silk.

Figure 30.2. Isle of Man triskele.

Figure 30.3. Comet West, 1976.

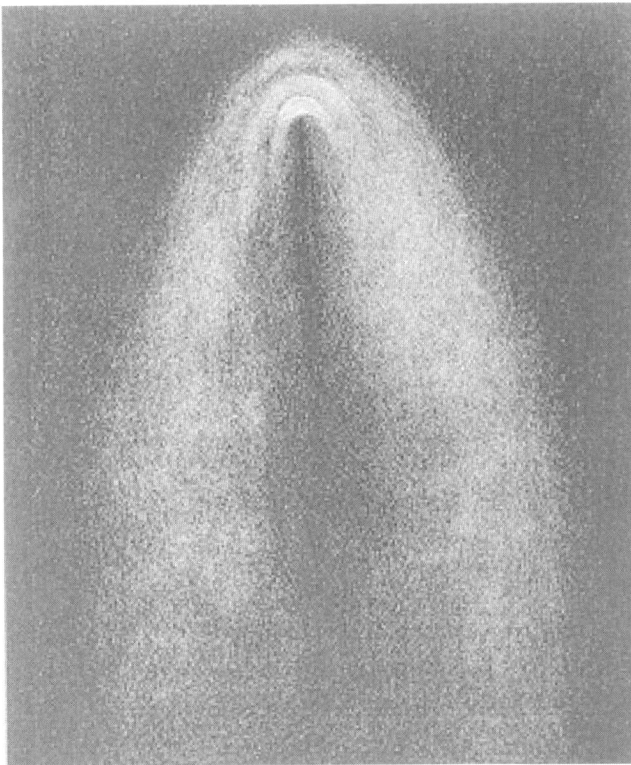

Figure 30.4. Comet Donati, 1858.

It is most interesting to compare Pliny's comet, and Comet Donati, with the description of the Irish superhero Cúchulainn: 'he had three distinct heads of hair... he wore at his white clear breast... a brooch of light-gold and silver – a shining source of light too bright in its blinding brilliance for men to look at' (Kinsella 1969, 156). Was Cúchulainn a comet? His ability to change shape, and to destroy huge areas with his Tunguska-like thunder-feat,

strongly suggests that he was. Furthermore, the main events in his life, occurring when he was 4, 7, 14, and 17, coincide with the return times of Comet Encke (McCafferty and Baillie 2005, 129).

Comets – the misidentified gods

If at least two Irish gods, Cúchulainn and Manannan, were probably comets, and if the swastika, which adorns the temples and statues of the gods was also a comet, what can that tell us about cult and religion in prehistory? What role did comets play in ancient cult?

One can imagine that people might once have worshipped the earth, the sea, the air or wind, volcanoes, the moon and tides, and of course the sun. All of these can affect their lives. They may have also worshipped abstract qualities such as love and fertility, knowledge, masculinity and femininity, light and darkness, or the embodiment of good and evil. Gods and icons have been identified for many of the above qualities, but curiously, no god has ever been identified as a comet god. I would argue most firmly that comets, and comet gods, have been wrongly identified and mistakenly classified as gods of the sea, sun or planets. We've already met Manannan, who with his three legs travelled faster than any chariot over land and sea. Although he is clearly a comet god, he is labelled the Irish god of the sea.

In ancient Greece, Apollo, the bright-faced son of Zeus, shot silver arrows that brought plague and rode a winged tripod across the sea. His birth on Delos caused an earthquake and tsunami. Such characteristics suggest he is also a comet god, but because of his shining face, he is interpreted as the Greek Sun God, despite the existence of Helios, the Sun God. The same happens in Ireland with Lugh of the Long Hand. He is the grandson of Balor, whose eye can burn all of Ireland in a flash. One day, Lugh rose in the west with his face shining as bright as the sun (Squire 1998, 111). Because of this, he is interpreted as the Irish sun god (Cook 1906, 141), even though the sun never rises in the west and does not have a long hand. A comet can. This sun-induced blindness extends even to art, where objects that clearly resemble comets have been interpreted as the sun. In Egypt, the Aten is depicted as a large disc with rays extending in only one direction. It is commonly referred to as a sun-disc, when its shape, and the little hands at the end of the long arms, suggest that the Aten was a comet.

Sometimes, when the comet god is not as bright as the sun or moon, Sirius, the brightest star in the sky, is invoked to replace the comet in our interpretations. The Egyptian goddess Hathor can appear as a cow with a bright disc between her horns. She looks red. One night, she took up a cudgel and wiped out half of the Egyptians (Spence 1915, 167). Despite the obvious comet imagery, Hathor is widely thought to be Sirius, rising with the Nile floods (Spence 1915, 168). The possibility that just four thousand years ago, Sirius was red, poses huge problems for stellar astronomers, because they have to explain how it transformed from a red giant to the white star seen today. Luckily for them, an examination of Chinese astronomical records has shown that Sirius was always white (Jiang 1993, 226). *Ergo* Hathor is not Sirius but was most probably a bright red comet.

Labelling comet gods as solar, planetary or stellar gods may explain their brightness, but fails to explain all those other things that comets do. Like Comet Shoemaker Levy IX in 1992, comets can split into many smaller comets, thus multiplying and forming offspring, just like the pantheon of gods, and unlike the sun and planets. Comets can have numerous arms and even multiple heads, just like the gods in Indian temples. The attributes of many gods more closely match those of comets than of any other body in space and the conclusion that many gods were comets is inescapable.

Comets and archaeology

If comet gods have been misidentified to such an extent, has their potential effect on humanity also been ignored? Like Thor and Jupiter, comets can throw 'bolts from the blue', thunderbolts that appear from a clear blue sky, causing tremendous damage. No other astronomical body can do this. They can shroud the earth in a dust-veil, proving that they are stronger than the sun, and even affecting the fertility of the earth. By blocking the sunlight that grows the crops that feed the people who stay healthy when nourished, they can even cause plagues.

Mythology is full of stories of sky gods destroying humans. In the Iliad, Homer recounts how the gods appeared on a ten-year cycle and intervened to bring about the destruction of Troy. If we take the story seriously, we are forced to conclude that cometary debris helped cause the destruction of the Anatolian and Mycenaean cities of the Middle Bronze Age and ushered in the Greek Dark Age. Similarly, the clusters of myths around other times of profound change in the archaeological record (3100 BC, 2350 BC, and AD 540) further suggest that comets and their debris have impacted humanity.

The possibility that a comet helped to destroy civilisations in the past five thousand years is shocking, as revolutionary for archaeology as the discovery of the Iridium layer at the K/T boundary for palaeontology (Alvarez *et al.* 1980, 1095). More evidence is required before such a revolutionary idea becomes accepted as fact, but right now, few archaeologists seek such evidence and the idea is rarely discussed, even as a theory. If one examines any textbook on archaeology and looks up the word 'comet' in the index: one will see that there, between 'comb' and

'copper', it is glaringly absent. In fairness to archaeologists, the word is also absent from any books on mythology or anthropology, but the result of this is that archaeologists do not even consider the cometary paradigm when excavating sites and therefore discard that crucial layer of dust lying just above the habitation layers. This is completely understandable, but by digging for the equivalent of dinosaur bones, rather than the Iridium layer, archaeologists have probably been discarding key pieces of evidence for decades.

Conclusion

If our ancestors really inhabited a world where comets periodically appeared in the heavens and caused all hell to break loose from the sky, and people felt the displeasure of comet gods as meteoritic thunderbolts and crop failures, we can understand why they told myths about sky gods and cometary superheroes. We may even appreciate why they devoted such energy to build monuments to placate angry gods who deserved to be feared, and worshipped. Prehistoric people did not ignore the comet gods. Why, then, have archaeologists ignored comets?

Acknowledgments

I wish to thank my supervisors Prof. Donall O'Baoill (School of Irish and Celtic Studies, Queens University Belfast) and Prof. Mark Bailey (Armagh Observatory) for their continued support and encouragement. Many of the ideas in this paper have been developed with Prof. Mike Baillie (School of Geography, Archaeology and Palaeoecology, Queens University Belfast), to whom I owe an immense gratitude.

References

Alvarez, L. W., Alvarez, W., Asaro, F. and Michel, H. V. 1980. Extraterrestrial Cause for the Cretaceous-Tertiary Extinction. *Science* 208, 4448, 1095–1108.

Bailey, M. E., Clube, S. V. M., Napier, W. M. 1990. *The Origin of Comets*. London, Pergamon Press.

Clube, S. V. M. and Napier, W. M. 1982. *The Cosmic Serpent: A Catastrophist View of Earth History*. London, Faber and Faber.

Cook, A. B. 1906. The European Sky-God. V. The Celts. *Folklore* 17, 2, 141–173.

Dorman, J., Evans, S., Nakamura, Y. and Latham, G. 1978. On the time-varying properties of the lunar seismic meteoroid population. *Proceedings Lunar Planetary Science Conf*erence 9, 3615–3626.

Jiang, X. 1993. The colour of Sirius as recorded in ancient Chinese texts. *Chinese Astronomy and Astrophysics* 17, 2, 223–228.

Johnson, C. 2004. 'Periwigged Heralds': Epistemology and Intertextuality in Early American Cometography. *Journal of the History of Ideas* 65, 3, 399–419.

Kinsella, T. 1969. *The Tain. Translated from the Irish Epic Tain*

Bo Cuailnge. Oxford, Oxford University Press.

Kresák, L. 1978. The Tunguska object: a fragment of Comet Encke? *Bulletin Astronomical Institute Czechoslavakia* 29, 129–134.

McCafferty, P. and Baillie, M. 2005. *The Celtic Gods – Comets in Irish Mythology*. Stroud, Tempus.

Mullens, H. G. 1940. Illustrations of the Classics from Mann. *Greece and Rome* 9, 26, 96–101.

Pliny. *Historia Naturales*, Book II.

Sagan, C and Druyan, A. 1997. *Comet*. London, Headline.

Spence, L. 1994 [1915]. *Egypt Myths and Legends*. London, George G. Harrap. Republished as *Egpyt*. Middlesex, Senate Press.

Squire, C. 1998 [1912]. *Celtic Myth and Legend: Poetry and Romance*. London, The Gresham Publishing Company. Republished as *Mythology of the Celtic People*. Middlesex, Senate Press.

Steel, D. I. and Asher, D. A. 1996. When might 2P/Encke have produced meteor storms? In B. A. S. Gustafson and M. S. Hanner (eds). *IAU Colloq. No. 150: Physics, Chemistry and Dynamics of Interplanetary Dust*. Astronomical Society Pacific Conference Series 104, 125–128.

Von Humboldt, A. and Bonpland, A. 1805. *Voyage aux Régions Équinoctiales du Nouveau Continent, fait dans les Années 1799–1804*. Paris, I. Schoell.

Wilson, T. 1894. *The Swastika, The Earliest Known Symbol, and its Migrations*. Report of the U. S. National Museum, 757–1030.

Chapter 31

CULT IN CONTEXT IN JOMON JAPAN

Simon Kaner

Some three thousand years ago, at a place later to become known as Chikamori, a circular arrangement of split wooden posts was set up in the damp coastal plain overlooking the Sea of Japan. The wooden posts were made of chestnut. Only their bases were preserved in the rich dark soils of the plain. Reconstructed at least six times, a circle of eight massive split trunks, are thought to have reached towards the sky (Habu 2004, 193–5). The posts were set up by people who derived most of their subsistence needs from the natural world around them, unlike the agriculturalists across the ocean, and yet they perceived the bounty of the forests, rivers and seas through a cultural filter, a filter which comprised a system, or systems of beliefs, beliefs which were expressed through sets of practices which they believed put them in touch with spirits including ancestors. These practices included the setting up of large wooden posts and arrangements of such posts. Away from the wetlands of the coastal plains, in mountain plateaus and basins, people built monuments in the landscape out of stone. Stone pavements, standing stones, and circles of stone piles were to be encountered throughout the landscapes of the prehistoric Japanese archipelago. Constructed by people who inhabited small village communities usually comprising a handful of pit dwellings, these monuments may have been aligned with particularly significant features in the landscape, including mountain peaks, and may have held some calendrical significance, their spatial arrangements associated with the movements of celestial bodies. These people were the inheritors of a tradition of pottery production which made extensive and imaginative use of systems of decoration using cords made from twisted plant fibres, known to modern archaeologists as Jomon.

Wooden posts comparable to Chikamori were set up in a number of locations in the Jomon landscapes. Heading east from Chikamori, on the eastern side of the Noto Peninsula, at Mawaki, where dolphins were being extensively exploited several thousand years prior to the construction of the Chikamori wooden circle, a wooden

post carved with spiral designs was discovered amid the archaeological debris of the settlement. Further east again, beyond the wild coasts later known as Oyashirazu, where black cliffs loom down to the shore, a shore which produced highly prized greenstone nodules which offered a resource that was one of the most valued commodities, exchanged along networks that stretched from one coast of Honshu to the other, another great wooden post was set up at Teraji,

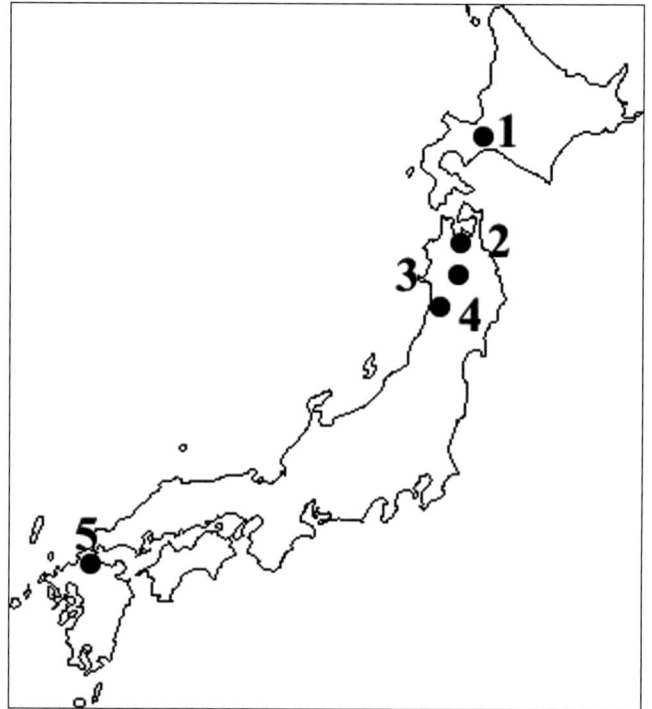

Figure 31.1 Map of Japan showing sites mentioned in the text and close-up of central Honshu region.1. Kakinoshima; 2. Ishidotai; 3. Oyu; 4. Sannai Maruyama; 5. Yamaga; 6. Chikamori; 7. Chojagahara; 8. Fujihashi; 9. Kinsei; 10. Mawaki; 11. Motoyashiki; 12. Murajiri; 13. Sakai A; 14. Teraji; 15. Toya; 16. Yokomine.

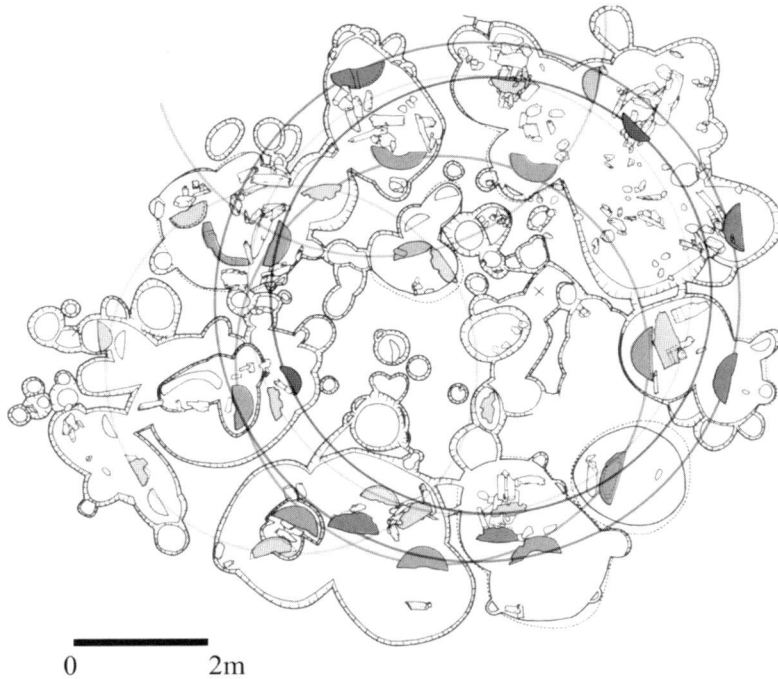

Figure 31.2 Plan of Chikamori (after Asahi Shimbun 1986)

0   2m

surrounded by a carefully constructed stone platform. At the northern tip of Honshu, at Sannai Maruyama, the largest-known pillared construction was set up at the edge of the greatest settlement of the Jomon period, where over 500 people are thought to have lived at any one time, in a community of pit houses, large public buildings. Linear cemeteries, where the earthly remains of ancestors were set to rest were removed from the more ephemeral graves of young children, and are thought to have been restricted to the areas immediately adjacent to the dwellings of the living.

The establishment of these great pillars by Jomon foragers has been interpreted by archaeologists as evidence for ritual occasions in prehistoric Japan, comparable to a set of spectacular ritualised activities in central Japan centred on the great Shinto shrines at Lake Suwa in Nagano Prefecture (Ashai 1986). These interpretations draw on additional evidence from the Jomon for the existence of ritual specialists, often referred to as shamans. One such individual is considered to have lain beneath the sand dunes at Yamaga in Kyushu at the western extremity of the archipelago. Another may have been buried wrapped in lacquered cloths at Kakinoshima B in Hokkaido in the northern part of the archipelago. A further example is brought to life in the pages of a modern archaeological text book, wearing a clay mask, brandishing an animal-shaped figurine, and sporting a salmon-skin coat, coordinating communal ceremonies, public rituals which offered the opportunity to reaffirm, reproduce and transform relations with each other and with the other world, the world occupied by spirits and ancestors (Habu 2004, 218; Suzuki 1988, 121).

As communicators or mediators with the spirits, these ritual specialists found themselves in, or perhaps rather, worked toward being in, a position from which they could manipulate and control that relationship. This would be the argument put forward by Brian Hayden and those who consider that evidence for an increase or intensification of ritual activity is a corollary of an increase in social complexity (Hayden 2003). To what extent were these ritual specialists operating in a discursive fashion? Could they have explained their actions in a rational fashion, described to an outside observer how they schemed and plotted to benefit themselves to the maximum by taking advantage of their position, perhaps dressing their account up in terms of altruistic motives, of making their special powers available for the greater good of the community. Or were they operating on an entirely practical level, just doing what they perceived as coming 'naturally' to them. These questions lead to some fresh perspectives on the archaeology of cult. Can we address how prehistoric ritual practitioners perceived the nature of their beliefs? Was there a coherence to the various practices which archaeologists reconstruct as 'ritual'? Or was there rather a ramshackle collection of half-remembered 'ways of doing things', a bundle of behaviours that varied through time and space, reinvented at periodic gatherings and events at specific locations, bundles of beliefs that included as many contradictory and dissonant elements that had to be taken into account, as there were coherent and complementary aspects?

If the latter, then we can perhaps better understand why ritual activities are often dangerous interruptions of a more mundane set of actions. It would have been difficult to initiate, control and contain the gatherings that may have taken place at the sites now interpreted as 'ritual' by archaeologists. It can be argued that the ritual practitioners were working hard to maintain some form of egalitarian ideology, and that various rituals operated as levelling mechanisms, smoothing out the inevitable hierarchical kinks and crinkles that threatened the underlying ethos of sharing and reciprocity that structured most Jomon social interactions. On the other hand, it could be argued, as would Hayden and others, that aggrandizing individual shamans used rituals to control and influence their contemporaries. It will be argued here that the diversity of monument forms in the later Jomon and the complex developmental histories attests to the reproduction and transformation over time of a series of subtraditions of ritual practice, and that the reconstruction of these developmental histories provides the context for the understanding of cults in the Jomon.

Generative schemes

Subtle and not-so-subtle differences in ritual practices from one community to another may have operated to define those communities, and quite possibly acted to shock and upset neighbours, close and distant. And yet these webs of difference may well have been produced through the operation over time of comparable generative schemes, in which key individuals drew on their knowledge of how to do things, in attempts to achieve the maximum efficacy for the rites and practices being undertaken. There is considerable evidence for well-developed social networks in the Jomon, along which travelled individuals, commodities such as obsidian and salt, information and knowledge, so that the members of the foraging communities across the archipelago knew something of other ways of doing things, with which to distinguish there own ways of acting. This information flow doubtless influenced the historical development of cult practices and the belief systems they materialised. Understanding how these bundles of cult beliefs were generated and altered over time and space requires an appreciation of the generative schemes that underlay them. This consideration of generative schemes also encourages us to consider the variability within the archaeological evidence we have for these practices, rather than trying to 'lump' it all together as evidence for shared ritual packages. Of course prehistoric archaeologists are at a major disadvantage compared to the ethnographer who is able to observe the rituals first hand, interview those taking part, and even participate in the practices themselves. The majority of the material objects used in rituals have long since disappeared, along with access to the 'participants' conceptions of the significance given to these items. And yet we can begin our analyses with the appreciation of the temporality of the ritual process, and accept that ritual traditions do need to be proactively reproduced over time. In this way, we can begin to consider how to move away from overly general explanations of Jomon ritual objects, notably figurines and stone bars, to interpretations which look for slight changes and developmental sequences over time, set in the context of developmental histories of the cult places which have been identified throughout the archipelago. Each of these locations has an 'occupational history', as do the settlements themselves (Kaner 2004). The stone circles, for example, of Oyu or Komakino, have complex developmental sequences which, even if not as dramatic as that at Stonehenge, are evidence for the temporality of the ritual bundles we envisage taking place there (Kodama 2003). It is likely that the construction, alteration and repair of these monuments played an important part in the rituals themselves.

We can probably never get as close to these generative scheme as does, for instance, Fredrik Barth who, writing of the Mountain Ok peoples of Papua New Guinea, was able to propose and expound the hypothesis that 'it has been through the operation of repeated oscillations of cosmological lore between its private keeping and its public manifestation by responsible cosmologists in sequestered temples, that such modifications over time of Ok cosmological traditions have in fact taken place' (Barth 1987, 31). And yet we need to build the existence of such schemes into our understandings of prehistoric ritual.

Transformation and transcendence

Two concepts which are of use in considering Jomon cult activities are transformation and transcendence. The ability of an agent to transform itself into a different form is a trope that has considerable resonance through Japanese religion, and indeed religion across the globe. The shaman goes through a transformation en route to communicating with the spirits. Individuals go through a series of transformations in the course of their lives – birth, childhood, puberty, initiation, marriage, bereavement, death – many of which may have been marked by rites of passage, from one state to another. In the Jomon, such rites of passage may have included the extraction or filing of certain teeth, the donning of shell bracelets, the wearing of clay masks, the piercing of ears to facilitate the wearing of elaborate ear ornaments, or the smashing of large quantities of ceramics. Indeed, the complex designs on the surface of the Jomon pots may themselves have been materialisations of this transformation and the transcendance it afforded.

Beyond reaction and resistance

The last two millennia of the Jomon period in the Japanese archipelago, the time at which the wooden posts at Chikamori and Teraji were established, are considered to be a time of increased ritualism. Indeed, in one interpretation of the long term history of Jomon culture, this ritualism is understood as the inevitable outcome of the material constraints on the development of Jomon economics and society, resulting from the inability of Jomon people to overcome the restrictions of the hunting and gathering mode of production (Wajima 1962). Other scenarios have the Jomon people engaged in increasingly elaborate (and desperate) ritual practices as they attempted to adjust to environmental deterioration towards the end of the period – slightly lower temperatures, hunting pressures reducing the amount of game available, possible pandemics reducing the population and so forth (Kobayashi and Hara 1993). A third model has Jomon 'natives' performing increasingly elaborate rituals in an (ultimately fruitless) attempt to resist the impact of foreign cultures bringing with them rice farming and a whole new way of life (Kobayashi 2004). I will argue that rather than being a direct expression of such concerns, the apparent development of ritualistic material culture in the last stages of the Jomon period are part of a longer-term tradition of ritualised activities, the constraints upon whose development may have been altering, as were the contexts in which their trajectories were played out. But these existing models do not allow for the agency of the ritual practitioners, which was of great significance in the development of the ritual subtraditions of the last millennium BC.

Cult traditions in the later Jomon

The rest of this paper considers aspects of the archaeological record from central Honshu, which demonstrate the potential for addressing the reproduction and transformation of traditions of cult practice in the later Jomon period, in the context of the developmental histories of ritual ocations. The official history of Nagano Prefecture begins its section on Jomon society and its demise with a discussion of the development of Jomon culture and ritual life. The various components of the Jomon ritual repertoire have suggested that Jomon lives were strongly suffused with a sense of magic. In addition, rather than deeply held personal beliefs, this magic world was about social rituals and group-oriented ceremonial occasions, which helped bind the social individuals together into a strong sense of community. The first development of a more ritualised lifestyle is the appearance of the stone paved building, often with elaborate entrance ways, at the end of the Middle Jomon about 3000 BC. At this time, settlements appear to have become much smaller, with only one or two buildings being occupied at any one time, in which are discovered a variety of stone objects, including large stone grinders and broken stone bars. Very often, there are burial urns placed beneath the entrance corridors. Great cemeteries also built up around some of these houses, for example at Kitamura. While at Kitamura most of the graves are earthen pit graves, one of the distinctive developments of the Late Jomon period is the appearance of stone built graves and stone cist graves. In many examples of large cemeteries of stone built graves, such graves are often found in association with stone paved buildings. From the Late Jomon on there are very few settlements as such in Nagano Prefecture. Instead, most sites comprise of cultural layers with very few buildings, perhaps one or two buildings. This change in settlement pattern is considered to represent something of a cultural stagnation, and yet the number of ceremonial features and tools undergoes a considerable expansion. These features are echoed elsewhere in the eastern part of the archipelago: bank-enclosed cemeteries, the kanjo-dori of Hokkaido and the stone circles of northern Honshu (Ikawa-Smith 1992; Kodama 2003). These sort of sites appear to have operated as regional ritual centres.

The early part of the Final Jomon in Nagano is characterised by very large numbers of ceremonial objects, including a range of polished stone objects, some exquisitely decorated, including stone bars of various sizes, along with ceramic and stone plaques, a variety of pottery ear ornaments, and lacquered combs and pins, jade beads and other ritual 'accessories'. There is also a florescence in the use of ceramic figurines. The most famous are the burnished 'goggle-eyed' figurines which originated in northern Honshu (Figure 31.3), a late manifestation and transformation of a tradition of figurine manufacture which has its origins much earlier in the Jomon (Naumann 2000).

As mentioned above, the prevailing interpretation for the changes in Jomon occupation is the climatic change which affected the archipelago after the Middle Jomon, the period of the warmest conditions in the Holocene. Average annual temperatures dropped by one or two degrees centigrade, ushering in what is called a little Ice Age. The warm temperate (and very productive in terms of biomass) deciduous forests were replaced by cool temperate (and less productive) forests (Yasuda and Miyoshi 1998).

Further changes occurred in settlement and ritual practice at the beginning of the first millennium BC, as a single pottery style, represented by the Obora or Kamegaoka series, spread across the whole of eastern Honshu, subsuming the marked regionalism that preceded it. The numbers of sites, in common with the rest of eastern Japan, declined dramatically, and site location also changed, with an apparent shift from the well-drained river terraces to the alluvial lowlands. Settlement shifted to natural levees in lowlying river plains and the margins of coastal sand dunes. People were choosing to live at around 10 m above sea level. The decrease in average temperatures at this time was associated with a drop in water levels and the spread of alluvial areas, allowing an increase in the exploitation territories of the Jomon communities. Indeed, part of the

Figure 31.3 Final Jomon 'goggle-eyed' figurine (after Munro 1908).

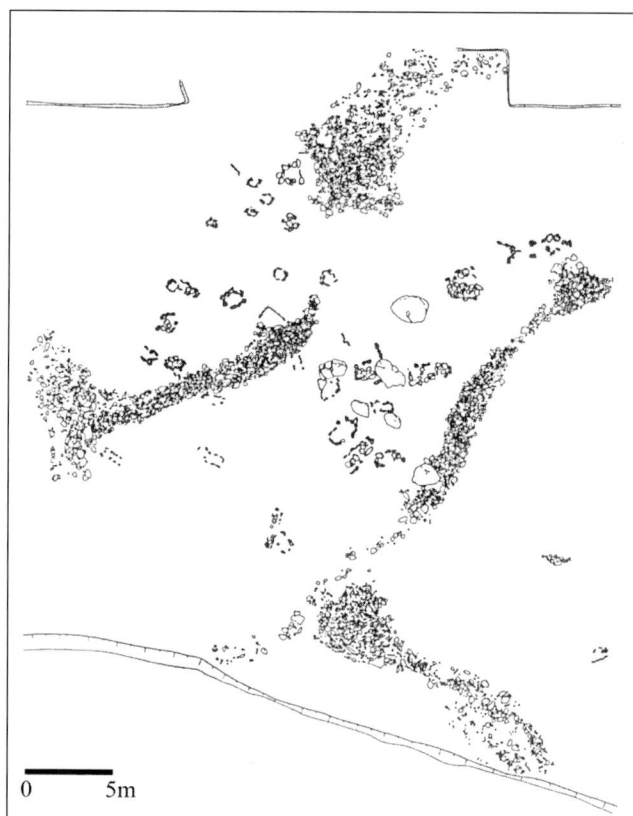

0   5m

Figure 31.4 Plan of stone arranged features at Kagomine (after Niigata-ken 1986).

apparent decline in site numbers might be explained by the fact that many sites could be deeply buried in the alluvium. For example at the Omaruyama site in Kashiwazaki city, artefacts were recovered from a depth of over 10 m. The construction of a new motorway has resulted in the discovery of some exceptionally well-preserved Final Jomon sites in the Niigata Plain, such as Aota (Kobayashi 2004).

The rich diversity of ritual artefacts is known from a series of Final Jomon sites. The manufacture of jadeite beads had reached a peak in the middle of the Middle Jomon, but in the Final Jomon production once again became important, although by this time it was raw materials that were being exported rather than finished items. Materials other than jadeite were used, and the types of beads increased to include small round beads, cylindrical beads and comma-shaped beads. These small beads appear to have been strung together and are often found in pits, suggesting that they were now personal ornaments. This period also witnesses a change in the ways in which animal bones came to be associated with humans. For example, Shotatsu site has produced bones with evidence for tooth ablation and associated with monkey bones. Figurines continue to be an important artefact type. Most of the figurines were found broken up and it is hard to say much

about context, although there are a few sites across the archipelago which have produced large numbers of figurines.

Overlooking the Takada Plain, surrounded by a series of impressive peaks, is a plateau some 350 m above sea level, which today is the home of the Matsugatoge hot spring resort, in whose grounds were discovered the Kagomine site, excavated in 1985. This large site, extending over at least two hectares, comprises a settlement and ritual location. The 1985 excavations uncovered a series of stone constructions, mainly built out of river cobbles. One of these arrangements extended about 40 m NE–SW, with a width of 3 m, with a big boulder at one side, with a stone alignment to the south side. This latter features included some 80 circular and rectangular stone arrangements, the circular ones being about 60 cms in diameter, the rectangular ones being 150 × 60 cms. Around these features a series of buried pottery urns were recovered, containing fragments of bone and ear ornaments. The artefacts span from the later part of the Late Jomon to the Yayoi period, with a clear concentration in the later Late to the early Final Jomon. The artefacts have marked similarities with those from Tohuku, Shinshu and Hokuriku. The spherical pottery objects and stone stamps are very typical of the

Figure 31.5 Plan of Fujihashi (after Nagaoka-shi 1992).

Chubu and Hokuriku regions, while the arrowheads and beads are of stone from the Katakai River, Itoigawa and Shinshu regions, all attesting to the existence of widespread social networks at this time.

The arranged stone features are located on the relatively high point, and the artefacts were clustered around the paved areas. It therefore seems that there was a distinction between ordinary, everyday dwelling space, and ceremonial space. There are many other examples from elsewhere in central Honshu.

Fujihashi is a Late to Final Jomon site located on the Higashi Kubiki Hills near the Shinano River, at a height some 30 m above sea level. Again, it produced a combination of ritual artefacts and apparently everyday features and tools. First investigated by the Nagaoka Municipal Science Museum in 1951, when many artefacts were received from the later stages of the Final Jomon period, following further investigations in 1975-1976 it was designated a site of National Historic Importance in 1978, and subsequently a historical park, complete with reconstructed Jomon buildings, was established. Four artefact clusters and a number of hexagonal plan buildings were discovered. A continuity of pottery styles was recovered, with the main occupation focusing on the Toya 1 and Toya 2 phases. Many subsistence related stone tools were found, including arrowheads, polishing stones and querns, polished stone axes, awls, along with various ritual objects, including stone bars and stone rods. Just to the south, occupation continued into the Yayoi period at the Otate site. The architecture at Fujihashi is important as it seems that pillared buildings were the norm, rather than the pit houses which are well known from the rest of the Jomon.

At Teraji, a location where jadeite objects and serpentinite axes were bring produced in large numbers in the Middle Jomon, a setting of wooden posts and a stonelaid pavement were dated to the Final Jomon. This site was located on a relatively lowlying terrace and alluvium, some 400 m from the current shore of the Japan Sea. It formed part of a cluster of sites which were important semi-precious stone manufacturing sites, with Chojagahara about 5 kms to the east, and Sakai A about 16 kms west. The site was discovered with the construction of the Hokuriku mainline railway tracks at the end of the Meiji period, and was investigated between 1968 and 1973 by the Omi Town Board of Education. At Location A, a 14 m long stone pavement was found, a circular setting of wooden posts, stone cist graves, and part of a wooden pillar associated with a hearth-shaped stone feature, some 2 m across. Charred human bone fragments representing the remains of at least eleven individuals were found with this latter feature, some of which had evidence for tooth filing. Associated artefacts included serpentinite axe roughouts and raw materials, jadeite beads, hammer stones, whetstones, stone rods, stone stamps, fragments of goggle-eyed figurines, spherical clay objects, and lacquered combs.

There are a series of other sites in Niigata which demonstrate the continuity of occupation over much of the later Jomon period. For example, Murajiri is a late Middle to Final Jomon settlement in Shibata City located at a height of 36–39 m above sea level, 2–5 m above the adjacent Sakai River. During rescue excavations in 1980 and 1981, 14 house pits and hearths and 136 pits were discovered. In the northern part of the prefecture, in the mountains close to the border with neighbouring Yamagata Prefecture, Motoyashiki is part of a cluster of sites discovered and

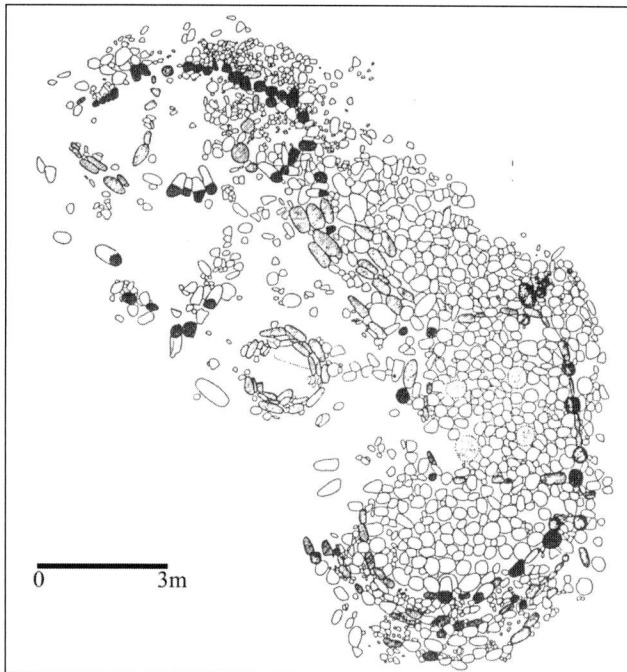

Figure 31.6 Plan of Teraji (after Niigata-ken 1986).

excavated in advance of the Miomote Dam project which provided further evidence for the complex developmental histories of ritual locations at this time (Niigata Prefectural Museum of History 2002).

Each of these sites and locations has a complicated occupational history which developed within the context of extensive social networks, which appear to have become particularly marked in the Late and Final Jomon. The similarities in material culture along with the increasing differentiation between high status and ordinary items has been used to argue the presence of increasing vertical hierarchies, legitimating themselves over the longer term through ritual practices which attempted to allay the effects of environmental deterioration (Habu 2004). While this model may have some validity, it does not help us understand the nature of the history of ritual subtraditions across the later Jomon period. In order to do this, we need to consider the specificity of the developmental histories of ritual or cult locations, whether in settlement contexts or in situations removed from the everyday sphere of activity. The variety of forms of feature recognised as ritual, especially in terms of the stone arranged features, platforms, pavements, and stone alignments, suggests that difference was an important component on these local ritual sub-traditions.

Conclusion

In this paper I have explored manifestations of ritual activity in the later part of the Jomon period in central Honshu in the Japanese archipelago. Beginning at the circular arrangement of timber posts at Chikamori, I have suggested that we need to develop frameworks for addressing the motivations of those involved in cultic activities. Most histories of Japanese religion begin well after the Jomon period, perhaps appropriate given the normal dependence of history on written sources, but unfortunate in that it has not encouraged Japanese archaeologists to engage with broader understandings of how religious traditions and cult practices change through time. One possible defining characteristics of cult is the presence within a community of 'a group having an exclusive ideology and ritual practices centred on sacred symbols, especially one characterised by lack of organisational structure' (Hanks 1986, 379). It is the potential that this absence of rigid organisational structure that we need to explore in order to further understand the history of Jomon cult practice, a history which is an essential component in reassessing the creativity and innovation that underpinned this successful adaptation that lasted over ten millennia.

This essay has not attempted to provide a comprehensive overview of the nature of the archaeological record for ritual and religious practices in the Jomon period. Relatively recent accounts have already done this for western-language readers (Habu 2004; Kobayashi 2004; Naumann 2000). Instead, I have attempted to question some of the taken-for-granted's which structure, and to an extent have constrained, the development of a fuller archaeology of cult in the Jomon period. The data is there if, to adapt a suitably cultic aphorism, the spirit is willing.

Our models need to incorporate the specific context provided by the developmental histories of Jomon ritual sites in order to appreciate the complexity of processes, motivations and actions comprising the reproduction and transformations of ritual traditions. In this way we can begin to transcend generalising statements about possible correlations between environmental deterioration, increasing social complexity and intensification of ritual activity, moving instead towards an understanding of how the perceptions of those involved in ritual practices shaped the reproduction of those practices, and an appreciation of the nature of underlying generative schemes and the significance of the transformation of traditions of ritual practice.

Figure 31.7 Ritual artefacts from the later Jomon (after Nagaoka-shi 1992).

Acknowledgements

This paper draws in part on an assessment of the archaeology of the Shinano and Chikuma Rivers, part of the Shinano Project funded by the British Academy. Thanks are due to the other members of the project, Toru Miyao of the Niigata Prefectural Museum of History, Liliana Janik, Oki Nakamura and Helen Lewis, and to the many Japanese archaeologists who made the results of their research available to me. This project would not be possible without the support of Professor Tatsuo Kobayashi at Kokugakuin University, Tokyo, and colleagues at the Sainsbury Institute for the Study of Japanese Arts and Cultures.

References

Asahi Shimbun 1986. Jomonjin no kazoku seikatsu [The family lifestyles of Jomon people]. Shukan Asahi Nihon no rekishi [Weekly Asahi Encyclopedia: History of Japan] 37.

Barth, F. 1987. *Cosmologies in the making: a generative approach to cultural variation in inner New Guinea.* Cambridge, University Press.

Habu, J. 2004. *Ancient Jomon of Japan.* Cambridge, University Press.

Hanks, P. (ed.) 1986. *Collins Dictionary of the English Language.* London and Glasgow, Collins.

Hayden, B. 2003. *Shamans, sorcerers and saints.* Washington DC, Smithsonian Books.

Ikawa-Smith, F. 1992. Kanjo-dori: communal cemeteries of the Late Jomon in Hokkaido. In Aikens, C. M. and S. N. Rhee (eds) *Pacific Northeast Asia in Prehistory: Hunter-fisher-gatherers, farmers and socio-polotical elites.* Pullman, Washington State University Press, 83–89.

Kaner, S. 2004. Occupational histories of Jomon settlements. *Bulletin of the International Jomon Culture Conference* 1: 41–43.

Kobayashi, T. 2004 (translated and adapted by Simon Kaner and Oki Nakamura). *Jomon Reflections.* Oxford, Oxbow Books.

Kobayashi, T. and Hara H. (eds) 1993. Kodai no Nihon 7: Chubu [*Ancient Japan Volume 7:* Chubu]. Tokyo, Kadokawa Shoken.

Kodama, D. 2003. Komakino stone circle and its significance for the study of Jomon social structure. In Habu, J., J. S. Savelle, S. Koyama and H. Hongo (eds) *Hunter-Gatherers of the North Pacific Rim.* Osaka, Senri Ethnological Series No. 63, 235–262.

Munro, N. G. 1908. *Prehistoric Japan.* Yokohama.

Nagaoka-shi 1992. *Nagaoka-shi shi [History of Nagaoka].* Shiryo ron 1 koko [Data volume 1: Archaeology]. Nagaoka, Nagaoka City.

Nagaoka City Fujihashi Site Excavation Committee 1977. *Fujihashi iseki.*

Nakazato Village Board of Education. 1987. *Kagomine Iseki Hakkutsu Chosa Hohoku.*

Naumann, N. 2000. *Japanese prehistory: the material and spiritual culture of the Jomon period.* Wiesbaden, Harrassowitz Verlag.

Niigata-ken 1986. Niigata ken shi [History of Niigata Prefecture]. *Tsushi ron 1. Genshi kodai [Narrative Volume 1: Prehistory and Ancient periods].* Niigata, Niigata Prefecture.

Suzuki, K. (ed.) 1988. *Jomonjin no seikatsu to bunka [Lifestyle and culture of Jomon people].* Tokyo, Kodansha.

Teramura Kiyoaki, A. and S. 1987. *Shiseki Teraji Iseki.* Omi Town Board of Education.

Wajima, E. 1962. Josetsu: nook-bokuchiku hassei izen no genshi kyodotai [Introduction: primitive communities before agriculture and animal husbandry]. In :*Kodaishi Koza [Lectures in Ancient History].* Tokyo, Gakuseisha: 1–16.

Yasuda, Y. and Miyoshi, N. 1998. Zusetsu Nihon retto shokusei shi [*An illustrated history of flora in Japan].* Tokyo, Asakura Shoten.

Chapter 32

BRINGING DOWN THE MOUNTAIN: STANDING STONES ON THE NORTHERN AND CENTRAL TIBETAN PLATEAU, 500 BCE – 500 CE

Mark Aldenderfer

Standing stones – *rdo-ring* (glossed in English as 'long stones') – are a common yet poorly understood aspect of the archaeology of the Tibetan plateau (Figure 32.1). Appearing in complex geometric arrays, small groups, or singly, these stones were described by many of the early explorers of the plateau and its surrounding regions. Standing stones first became known to the west at the beginning of the twentieth century, when the Tibetologist M. J. Bacot in 1907 described what he called a 'megalith' observed in eastern Tibet (Macdonald 1953, 64). Standing stones were subsequently reported by Franke (1907; 1914) in both western Tibet and Poo in the Sutlej valley near a village called Dralang. He described them simply as 'perpendicular stones', with one further labelled as a 'lingam', making reference to the sacred standing stones of Shaivism. Perhaps the most important of these early descriptions of standing stones was made by George Roerich (1930). During his Central Asiatic Expedition from 1925–28 which explored what was then called Chinese Turkestan, the Altai, western Mongolia, and parts of northern and western Tibet, he discovered a number of archaeological sites with standing stones called by the locals as *rdo ring*, but which Roerich (1930, 33) labelled menhirs, cromlechs, and alignments. One of these sites, known as Doring, had the remains of an impressive alignment that combined eighteen rows of smaller standing stones, a circle of larger ones, and an arrow-shaped alignment pointing due west (Roerich 1930, 16). Among the speculations he offered as an interpretation of this set of alignments were broad similarities of the Tibetan alignments with the megalithic cultures of western Europe, and the presence of the arrow as a reflection of the indigenous 'nature cult', which he said included sun and fire worship, among other things.

More recently, John Bellezza (2001; 2002; in press) has described dozens of sites with various combinations of standing stones discovered during his expeditions to the Changtang (the northern portion of the Tibetan plateau)

over the past 15 years. Unable to excavate or collect materials from the sites due to permit restrictions, he used oral tradition, Buddhist and Bön textual references, and simple observation to both classify and interpret these stones. In his latest analysis, he places standing stones (named variously by him as pillars, stelae, and menirs) into the following categories: isolated pillars and arrays of pillars without associated structural remains, pillars enclosed by quadrilateral structures, rectangular arrays with associated structures, and domestic pillars. His interpretations of these combinations include monuments for clans and chieftains, cultic sites for the worship of indigenous, pre-Buddhist deities (often appropriated by Buddhists later in time for their own worship), memorials and ritual structures for the deceased, and territorial or boundary markers. Bellezza, while acknowledging the role of indigenous development and elaboration of pillar complexes, traces their origin in northern Tibet to extensive contact with the Iron Age societies of Eurasia, particularly southern Siberia and Mongolia.

There is the long-standing belief, then, that these stones served some role in the religious life of the peoples who erected them, and each of their original interpretations emphasized their role in 'cultic' activities. While these arguments are plausible, what does it mean to call these stones 'cultic' or anything else that pertains to religion? What do these interpretations really say about the stones and their place, in the sense of Tilley (1994), in both the cognitive and physical worlds of their creators?

Aside from the difficulties of knowing in any meaningful way the ancient mind, the determination of the place of these standing stones has been hampered by a number of factors. First, very little systematic archaeological research has been conducted on the Tibetan plateau. As I have shown elsewhere (Aldenderfer and Zhang 2004), an appreciation of a deep Tibetan past is a comparatively recent phenomenon and can be traced to the advent of Chinese-sponsored

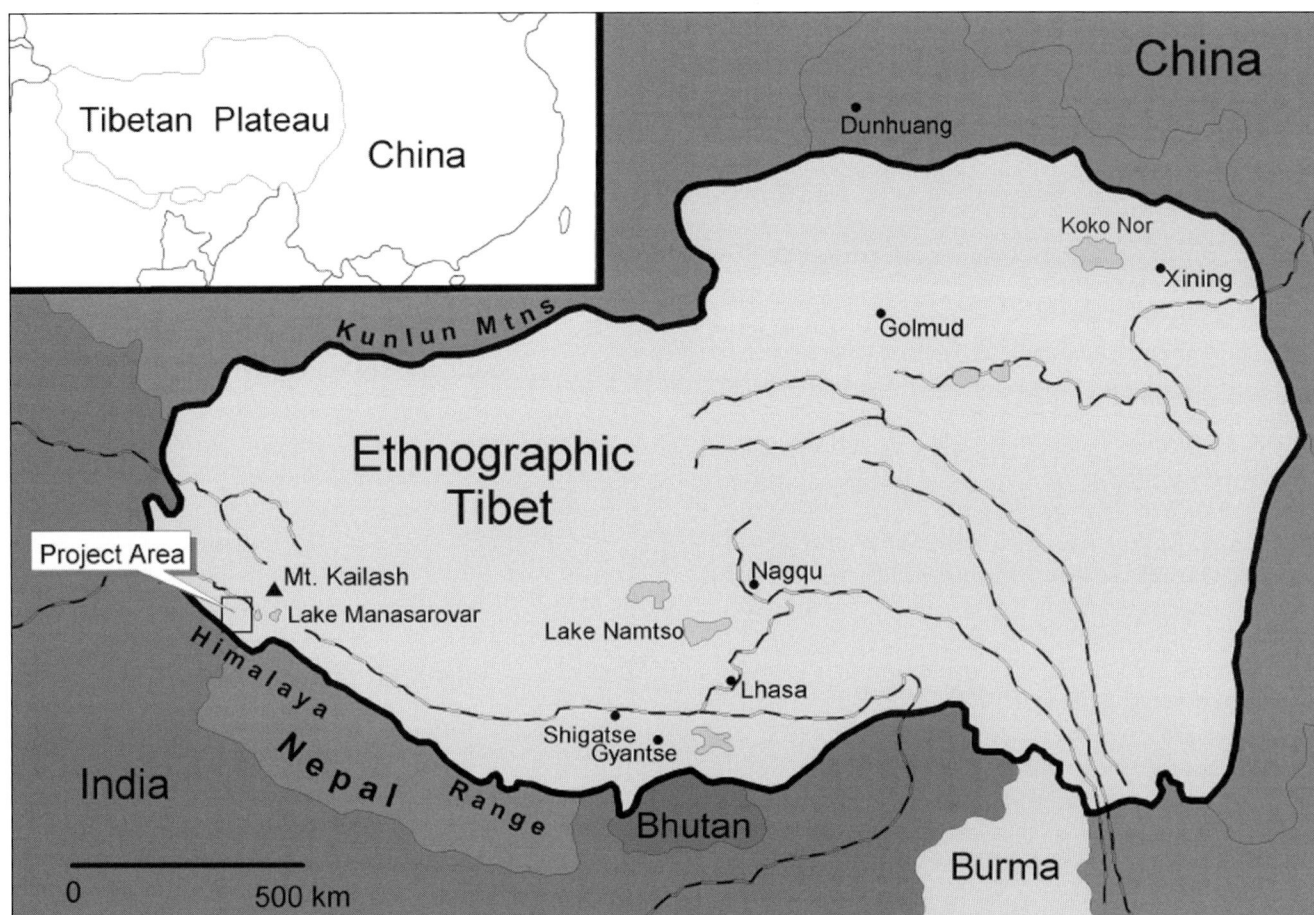

Figure 32.1. General location of research in far western Tibet.

research on the plateau in the late 1970s and early 1980s. Further, few sites with standing stones been recorded, let alone excavated, and thus chronological control either by radiometric dating or assemblage comparisons is almost non-existent. Thus, what may be visually similar may well be temporally distant. Second, most explanations of observed variability in artefact patterning in space and time are strongly diffusionist in tone. Ideas, religions, and subsistence technologies are believed to have originated elsewhere, primarily Central Asia or the lowlands of China to the east, and the indigenous inhabitants of the plateau were simply their passive recipients. Demic diffusion is the primary alternative explanation, and while there is no question that peoples from elsewhere moved onto and across the plateau, none of these models envision the interactions the migrants might have had with indigenous inhabitants (Aldenderfer 2006). Third, diffusionist explanations establish the origins of cultural phenomena, but once present, the interpretation of their meaning then derives from the extensive use of oral tradition, local history and myth, ethnographic research, and Tibetan Buddhist religious doctrine. As Bellezza's work has shown, these

can be remarkably useful and important if used judiciously. But it is also clear that most of these histories, and certainly Tibetan Buddhist religious concepts, arrive substantially later in time than the emplacement and use of these stones. Archaeology thus takes on its "handmaiden" role, its familiar position in the Chinese scheme of historiographic research into the literate past (von Falkenhausen 1993).

But there is one class of *rdo ring* – the standing stones found in domestic contexts – that have a sufficiently secure archaeological and temporal context that permits a nuanced examination of their possible social, religious, and ritual roles in early Tibetan society. First discovered in 2001 in far western Tibet in Ngari Prefecture at the Din dun site (Aldenderfer 2003; Aldenderfer and Moyes 2004, figure 1), the stones are in a village context that has been radiocarbon dated and falls within an age range of 550 BCE – CE 100 thus making the site pre-Buddhist but with an as-yet unknown cultural affiliation. I have argued that these stones had a role in the worship of mountain deities (*yul lha*) which is thought to have considerable antiquity. While I stand by that interpretation, I believe that it is incomplete, and in this paper, I seek to expand upon it through a deeper consideration the context of the stones as well as a more theoretically informed approach to the analysis of ritual and religious expression.

Space to place: ritual, religion, and cult in theoretical context

Little or no consensus exists as to the definition of ritual, religion, and cult, nor is there much agreement on appropriate theoretical constructs useful in their study no matter how they are defined (Insoll 2004). And because religion sits at the nexus of social, cognitive, and behavioural domains, no single theoretical perspective can nor should hope to capture what religion and its material representation 'mean'. In this sense, following Tilley (1994), I seek to take the 'spaces' of *rdo ring* in these village contexts and attempt to interpret, insofar as that is possible, their 'place'. I turn to a pragmatic approach to the study of religion, ritual and cult in general, and the role of these stones in specific. Here, I mean pragmatism in the philosophical sense, and ask the question of cultural phenomena 'What difference would it make to us in our interpretation of the past if some statement about it were true?' Here, outcomes, not origins are what matter (Kaplan 1964, 42). Does our use of some theoretical construct or combination of them advance our understanding, interpretation, or knowledge of the past, and in what way? I thus borrow from phenomenology, cognitive processualism, structuralism, and other theoretical perspectives if they help me interpret and understand the past a bit more clearly. But any interpretation must be constrained by rigorous observation, description, and analysis – or in other words, the data.

One broad category of theoretical thinking in anthropology – practice theory – has some importance in this discussion. Practice seeks to understand experience in the lived environment – spaces at multiple scales – and attempts to show how reflection on experience leads to a deeper understanding how people and their actions both condition and are conditioned by those spaces. As Fogelin (2006, 65) notes, '...practice theory elevates material remains from mere reflections of past culture, to former participants in a complex dialectical relationship between material human action, and the complex ideological concepts of human experience'. In effect, practice is one component of learning about place in the past. Practice is especially effective at approaching past ritual activity, in that it is defined by Bell (1999) and others as regularized, habituated performance.

But practice can become particularistic, and it must be leavened by concepts that speak to greater generality. One domain of interest is the relationship between religion and power. Numerous authors from distinct theoretical traditions have observed that religion can be a powerful engine not only of social control but also of social transformation. Consistent with a practice approach, agents can and do modify and manipulate religious constructs but to what ends depends on context and historical trajectory (Aldenderfer 1993). Thus religion may support existing social relations or serve to subvert them. It follows that material expressions of religious practice may reflect power relationships as well via their treatment, placement, or modification.

Finally, I turn studies of the perception of landscape features and the emerging field of ethnoecology with specific regard to mountains. As I noted above, I have already made a claim that domestic *rdo ring* are representations of mountain deities known to be of great importance on the Tibetan plateau. But the dangers of over-reliance on analogy are well-known, and thus it becomes important to seek other lines of evidence that may be used to corroborate the importance of mountains in ancient belief systems. Experimental studies have demonstrated that there are broad cross-cultural regularities in the semantic categories humans use to organize visual information (Mojsilović and Rogowitz 2004). Among them are the high-level categories 'human' vs. 'non-human' and 'natural' vs. 'human-made'. Of more significance for this study is that other cues, including 'sky', 'water', and 'mountains' are salient aspects of human visual perception and classification. Note that this does not claim these cues have the same meanings, but simply that people use these cues to organize experience. Further, these should not be seen as static binary oppositions commonly postulated by structuralists. These findings are bolstered by studies from ethnoecology that show that mountains and 'high places' have visual salience, and are used for orientation and landscape classification (Smith and Mark in press; Johnson 2000). Mountains are seen by many ethnographers as 'focalizing' symbols that condense the importance of activities conducted upon then, near them, or within sight of them (Hanson 1994; Turner 1967). These observations place into context discussions by Bradley (2000) on the relationships of monuments and topography, and at least in part, help to understand how some monuments, like mounds, for example, may represent mountains and why monuments on them or near them may well be in some sense 'sacred' or special significance.

The spaces of domestic rdo ring

Enough archaeological research has been done in far western Tibet to define patterns in the spaces, or patterns of placement, of domestic *rdo ring*. In addition to Din dun, where they were first identified, Bellezza (2001, 237–243) has identified domestic rdo ring at rDo Dril bu, and over the course of field work in the summer of 2006, I discovered two more villages with them in the upper Sutlej drainage in a portion of it called Kyunglung (the Valley of the Eagle).

Domestic *rdo ring* are found in three distinct spaces: within complex, high status, residential structures, at the edges and boundaries of villages, and finally, 'above' villages but within apparently non-residential constructions.

There are three *rdo ring* at Din dun – one in a complex residential structure (Structure 4) interpreted, based on architectural details and assemblage content, to be the dwelling of a high status family (Figures 32.2a and 32.2c), and two others found at the eastern and western limits of the village (Figure 32.2d). Excavations in two of these contexts – Structure 4 and the stone on the eastern side of the village – did not recover artefacts or other evidence of activity performance. Bellezza (2001, 237–43; 411) reports the discovery of a site called, rDo Dril bu, which is located northwest of Lhasa, and in this village of more than 13 residential structures, one (the 'Founder's House' as labelled by Bellezza) contains a standing stone very similar to that found at Din dun (Figure 32.2b). The structure is essentially identical to Structure 4 at Din dun in terms of architectural detail, complexity, and form. Although systematic work was not possible at the Kyunglung villages, inspection showed that each had *rdo ring* at their eastern and western boundaries, and at one of these, BKY2, a standing stone was found in a large, complex residential structure similar to those at Din dun and rDo Dril bu. Yet another stone at this site was found within a large rectangular structure found at the northern edge of the village, which is pushed up against a long ridge (Figure 32.3a). Atop this ridge was found a large, toppled *rdo ring* as well as a series of bench-like constructions built along its entire length (Figure 32.3b). These constructions are small, not residential in nature, and have not been defined elsewhere in the region. They are also dissimilar to the rectangular enclosures of the *rdo ring* at the edges of the villages.

Spaces to places: visibility of, access to, and representation of rdo ring

What do these contexts suggest about practice, and can the combined theoretical perspectives be used to interpret the potential places of the domestic *rdo ring*? To interpret the place of *rdo ring*, I will use three concepts: visibility, access, and representation. Visibility, derived from practice, questions how the stones and associated architecture can be seen and from where; access, also derived from practice, is concerned how easy it is to approach *rdo ring*; finally, representation refers to the stones themselves, and asks if they possess features that serve to connect them to other features in both the natural and built environment. Note that each of these concepts is likewise concerned with perception and the salience (or lack thereof) of space.

rDo ring within the high status residences have restricted visibility, and can only be observed from inside the house. But their consistent spatial placement within the structure – always in a small chamber at the west end of the house, implies that although passers-by would not be able to see the stone itself, they would be aware of the presence of the stone in a specific space within the house. We know somewhat less of the full range of visibility of the stones at the edges or boundaries of villages. Assuming that the rectangular structures were roofed, the stones could have been seen only through open entrances. However, the structures housing the stones would be known to all passers-by as well as people approaching the villages. The *rdo-ring* atop the ridgeline above BKY2 would have been difficult for most inhabitants of the village to see on a daily basis, but it would have been visible from across the valley as well from up-and-down river. The stone was not housed in a structure, is at the highest point of the ridge, and would have been in plain sight from considerable distances.

Access to the stones within the high status residences is quite restricted, and would have involved entering the house and moving through narrow corridors. Further, the chambers with which these stones reside are quite small as well, suggesting only a very small number of people could observe them at a time. The *rdo ring* at the boundaries of the villages are found in simple buildings and with easy access. However, the spaces within the structures are small, and would not have permitted large numbers of people to be in them at any one time. Access to the stone atop the ridge could only be accomplished by walking through the village and ascending its steep slopes. The stone could only be approached along the narrow axis of the ridge that was crowded with small constructions, thus limiting movement as well as the number of people who could gain direct access to it.

As for the stones themselves, while they are of different sizes, with one exception, they are nevertheless quite similar. They are triangular in form, with massive bases, and each has a single modification to the tip. Aside from shaping, none show other decorations or modifications. Although only one stands erect today (that at BKY2), each was meant to do so.

These patterns of space mediated by visibility, access, and representation combine to offer insights into the consistent, but also varied, places of the domestic *rdo ring*. Limited visibility and access to the stones within the high status houses and the site boundaries speaks to control, but also to identification. That is, within the houses, it appears that residents there have a close relationship to the meaning of the stone and to display it within the residence. No others within the village have this right or privilege. But the placement of the stones at the village boundaries likewise suggests identification of the inhabitants of the village with the meaning of the stones as well as to the people within the high status houses. Here, I believe the stones signal inclusion. The stone atop the ridge, however, appears to be sending a different message. Not seen from below, but

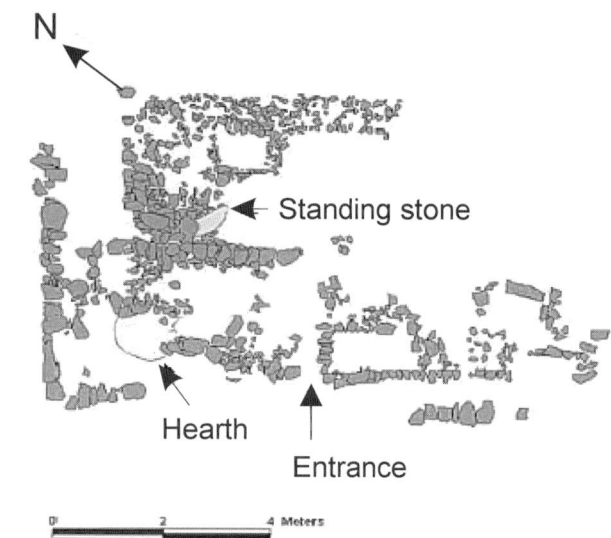

2a

2c

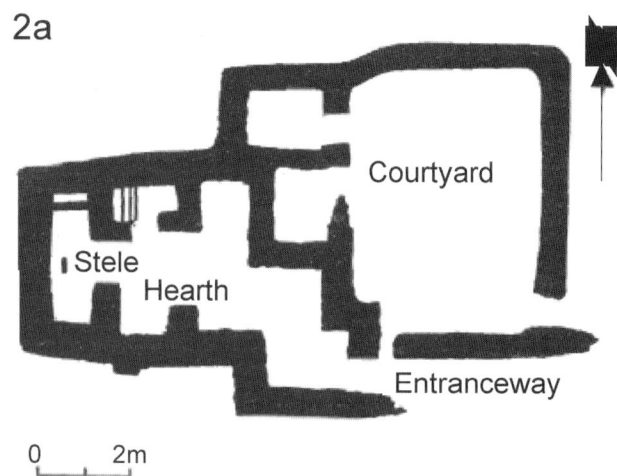

2b   2d

Figure 32.2a. Plan view of Structure 4 at Din dun; b. Plan view of the 'Founder's House' at rDo Dril bu (after Bellezza 2001: 237–43; 411); c. The rdo ring *within Structure 4 at Din dun (photograph by the author); d. The* rdo ring *at the western side of Din dun. Note the remains of the rectangular structure toward the upper right of the image. (Photograph by the author).*

instead from without, it appears to identify the village below and its included inhabitants, as belonging to this place or this location on the landscape. Thus this stone creates a larger relationship with the village and the surrounding landscape. But recursively, the stones can also be seen as have been brought into both the household and the village, thus becoming part of the human community of this place.

I further see the stones as a mimesis of mountains and high places. Although not directly representative of any specific mountain, their wide bases taper into triangular forms reminiscent of surrounding high places. The ridgeline above the village is a locus of ritual action, and the large *rdo ring* signifies the physical relationship of that ritual to that high place. The stones in the village thus focalize the power of the ritual conducted above it, and bring it into the community. This tentative and speculative scenario is not far from the ethnographically recorded observation that mountains in the Himalayas are seen as protector deities, and that the protection of this deity both sits above and is brought within the village.

Figure 32.3a (above). The rdo ring *within the rectangular structure at BKY2. (Photograph by the author).*
Figure 32.3b (below). The rdo ring *found atop the ridgeline above BKY2. (Photograph by the author).*

Conclusions

In this paper I have sought to interpret the place of domestic *rdo ring* in far western Tibet using a combination of theoretical perspectives melded together via a pragmatic approach to understanding the past. While we may be no closer to understanding the meaning of these stones to the people who used them, I believe I have outlined a plausible scenario whereby an ethnographic pattern seen in their use in ritual today may have been created. Both the spaces and places of these stones are complex, yet the patterns of their use are interpretable as the identification of entire village in general and one household in particular with the *rdo ring* and the inclusion of the power of the stone within the domestic sphere. The village itself is identified within the landscape by the stone above it. Finally, the stone itself is identified with the mountain. As the focalizing symbol of the mountain it both sits above the village but has also been brought down to it.

Acknowledgements

This research has been made possible by the early generosity of Thomas J. Pritzker. My colleagues at Sichuan University in Chengdu, PRC, Huo Wei and Li Yongxian, have taught me much of what I know of Tibetan prehistory, and for that I am deeply grateful. Aspects of field research have been funded by the National Geographic Society in 2004 and by a grant from the National Science Foundation (ATM/HSD-0527620) awarded to me in 2005. The views in this paper are my own, and do not reflect those of NSF.

References

Aldenderfer, M. 1993. Ritual, hierarchy, and change in foraging societies. *Journal of Anthropological Archaeology* 12, 1–40.

Aldenderfer, M. 2003. Domestic *rdo-ring*? A new class of standing stone from the Tibetan plateau. *Tibet Journal* 28 (1 and 2), 3–20.

Aldenderfer, M. 2006 [2003]. Ethnogenesis, migration, diffusion, or all of the above? The pre-Buddhist archaeology of northern Tibet. Review of *Antiquities of Northern Tibet: Pre-Buddhist Archaeological Discoveries on the High Plateau*, by John Vincent Bellezza, 2001; and *Antiquities of Upper Tibet: Pre-Buddhist Archaeological Sites on the High Plateau*, by John Vincent Bellezza, 2002. *Journal of East Asian Archaeology* 5(1–4), 471–478.

Aldenderfer, M. and Moyes, H. 2004. Excavations at Dindun, a pre-Buddhist village site in far western Tibet. In Huo Wei and Li Yongxian (eds) *Proceedings of the First International Conference on Tibetan Archaeology and Art*. Chengdu, China, Center for Tibetan Studies, Sichuan University, 47–69.

Aldenderfer, M. and Zhang, Y. 2004. The Prehistory of the Tibetan Plateau to the 7th C. AD: Perspectives and Research from China and the West since 1950. *Journal of World Prehistory* 18(1), 1–55.

Bell, C. 1999. *Ritual Perspectives and Dimensions*. Oxford, Oxford University Press.

Bellezza, J. 2001. *Antiquties of Northern Tibet, Pre-Buddhist Archeological discoveries on the High Plateau, Findings of the Changthang Circuit Expedition, 1999*. Delhi, Adroit Publishers.

Bellezza, J. 2002. *Antiquities of Upper Tibet: Pre-Buddhist Archaeological Sites on the High Plateau. Findings of the Upper Tibet Circumnavigation Expedition, 2000*. Delhi, Adroit Publishers.

Bellezza, J. In press. *Antiquities of High Tibet*. Delhi, Adroit Publishers.

Bradley, R. 2000. *An Archaeology of Natural Places*. London, Routledge.

Fogelin, L. 2006. *Archaeology of Early Buddhism*. Lanham, MD, Altamira Press.

Francke, A. 1907. *A History of Western Tibet, One of the Unknown Empires*. London, Patridge.

Francke, A. 1914. *Antiquities of Indian Tibet*. Archaeological Survey of Indian 38, Part 1: Personal Narrative. Calcutta.

Hanson, K. 1994. Transformed on the Mountain: Ritual Analysis and the Gospel of Matthew. *Semia* 67, 147–170.

Insoll, T. 2004. *Archaeology, Ritual, Religion*. Routledge, London.

Johnson, L. 2000. A Place That's Good: Gitksan Landscape Perception and Ethnoecology. *Human Ecology* 28, 301–325.

Kaplan, A. 1964. *The Conduct of Inquiry*. Chandler, San Francisco.

Macdonald, A. W. 1953. Une note sur les mégaliths Tibétains. *Journal Asiatique* 241, 63–76.

Mojsilović, A. and Rogowitz, B. 2004. Semantic Metric for Image Library Exploration. *IEEE Transactions on Multimedia* 6, 828–838.

Roerich, G. 1930. *The Animal Style among the Nomad Tribes of Northern Tibet*. Prague, Seminarium Kondakovianum.

Smith, B. and Mark, D. In press. Do Mountains Exist? Toward an Ontology of Landforms. *Environment and Planning B (Planning and Design)*.

Tilley, C. 1994. *A Phenomenology of Landscape*. Oxford, Berg.

Turner, V. 1967. *The Forest of Symbols. Aspects of Ndembu Ritual*. Ithaca, Cornell University Press.

Von Falkenhausen, L. 1993. On the Historiographical Orientation of Chinese Archaeology. *Antiquity* 87, 839–849.

Chapter 33

THE MEANING OF RITUAL DIVERSITY IN THE CHALCOLITHIC OF THE SOUTHERN LEVANT

Yorke M. Rowan and David Ilan

This paper explores ritual behaviour, religious belief and their nexus to power during the Chalcolithic period (*c.* 4500–3600 BC) of the southern Levant. Recurring symbolically charged artefacts and their contexts suggest an overarching, region-wide cosmology or religious framework. At the same time, we argue for diverse, coexisting modes of ritual behaviour practiced by different sorts of ritual specialist. The Chalcolithic seems to exhibit the earliest evidence for the incorporation and control of ritual and ideology by the elite as a power strategy.

Chalcolithic social organization

Coming on the heels of the Neolithic, the Chalcolithic period (*c.* 4500–3600 BC) of the southern Levant is thought by some (Levy 1986; 1998) to have had ranked, hierarchical societies. Diverse, elaborate mortuary practices, prestige items and evocative imagery complement social phenomena such as population growth, localized settlement hierarchy and limited craft specialization. Yet the typical trappings of chiefdoms – monumental architecture, elaborate mortuary displays, elite-controlled craft production and large storage areas with limited access – are largely absent (Bourke 2001, 151; Joffe 2003, 53). These ambiguities have led to debate over whether southern Levantine Chalcolithic society was in fact 'chiefdom'-like or relatively egalitarian (Gilead 1988). Despite such reservations, the Chalcolithic's sophisticated metallurgy, craft specialization relying on exogenous resources (copper, basalt, ivory), and rich cave tomb deposits, have induced a number of scholars to adopt the chiefdom model of organization (Gopher and Tsuk 1996; Gal *et al.* 1996; Schick 1998).

It is more likely, however, that different organizational models are applicable to different parts of the southern Levant. Rich caches of copper, ivory and other exotic items would appear to preclude small-scale corporate group organization ('egalitarian societies') in the northern Negev, Jordan Valley and coastal plain, for example (Figure 33.1). Most suggestive in this regard is the Nahal Mishmar Hoard,

where over 400 copper objects were cached with human burials (Bar Adon 1980). By the same token, the restricted evidence for metallurgy suggests control over ore sources, technical knowledge or both (Golden forthcoming). On the other hand, the dearth of metals, metallurgy and recognizable prestige items, together with homogeneous, small-scale architectural organization in the Golan suggest little in the way of social or political hierarchy (Epstein 1998, figure 1).

Levy argues that chiefdoms in the Beersheva Valley arose from a need to insure stability and control over arable land and pasture for an expanding population (Levy 1998). Essentially, this model suggests that asymmetrical power relations developed from risk management. Building on Gosden's (1989) work, Levy (1998, 240–241) posits that the Beersheba valley Chalcolithic was a debt-based society, in which gifting was used to create indebtedness and social inequality.

Emergence of more permanent leadership positions, however, may be rooted in social factors rather than resource constraints. Clark and Blake (1994), for example, argue that in Early Formative Chiapas persistent inequality arose at a time of low population density and little environmental pressure. The Chalcolithic of the southern Levant was also a period of agro-pastoral intensification and increased abundance of goods exchanged between sub-regions. Rather than view emerging elites as a consequence of resource scarcity and resultant conflict, we posit that the opportunity for individuals to wield influence and gain power arose from conditions of *resource abundance*. There are many paths to persistent inequality, but resource abundance is a frequent precondition (Aldenderfer 1996, 17). Ritual practices provided a fundamental avenue for gaining, maintaining and perhaps reifying new positions of more permanent leadership during the Chalcolithic. Earle (1997, 154) feels that public ceremonial events are not an ideal basis for power because of their transitory nature; the absence of capital investment means that ritual performances are soon no more than a memory. This can be true

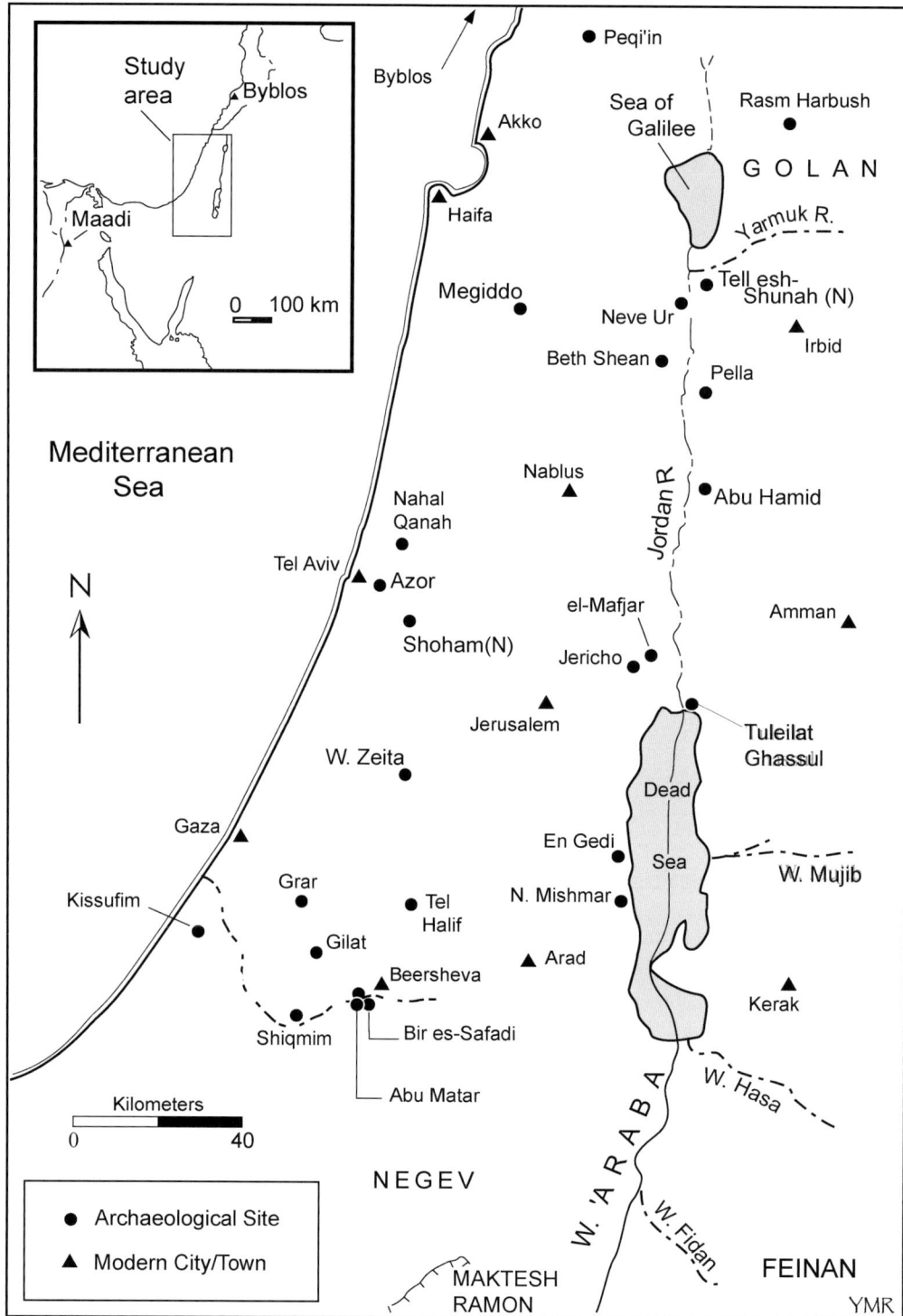

Figure 33.1 Selected Chalcolithic sites in the study area.

for non-capital intensive ritual, but when ritual does entail such investment, ritual becomes a valuable power gathering strategy. This will be demonstrated below.

Religious practice and specialists

Another dichotomous debate concerns 'shamanistic' versus 'priestly' forms of religion in the southern Levantine Chalcolithic. Those who advocate egalitarian social organization argue for shamans and adherents of chiefdom models propose that priests controlled venues of ritual practice. Many scholars have pointed out problems with the loose application of the term 'shaman' (e.g. Kehoe 2000; Bahn 2001; Insoll 2004). Price (2001, 6) points out that shamanism is, and always has been, an externally imposed construction of academics. Nevertheless, it serves as a useful concept which, if defined clearly and applied judiciously, recognizes a pattern of ritual behaviour and religious belief. A shaman may be described as a religious specialist whose powers focus on curing, prophecy and sorcery. Shamans are often held to exert control over weather, animals and enemies. They often act as intermediaries between their community, clan or an individual and the supernatural, particularly during times of crisis such as sickness or death. To do so, they may engage in soul flight, undergo trances or transform to spirit helpers. Shamans typically gain their power through a sudden 'divine' strike or inspiration.

Priests, in contrast, more commonly inherit their power or derive it from the codified, ritual knowledge necessary to conduct public rites for the benefit of a community or village. These rites may be calendrical or performed at critical junctures in ecological cycles (e.g. Lessa and Vogt 1979, 301).

Ritual specialists without formal office (such as shamans) are found in many societies other than hunter-gatherers, ranging from agrarian societies (e.g. Toro diviners and spirit mediums of east Africa [Childs 1998]) to industrial nation-states (e.g. Korea, Kendall 1996). Shamans can exist in sedentary, complexly organized societies. Priests and shamans coexisted among some Native American Plains groups and among the Navaho (Lessa and Vogt 1979, 301). Their practices may operate within a larger religious system (Walter 2001; Winkelman 1992).

Ritual was practiced in a variety of contexts in the Levantine Chalcolithic: within households, in special places within villages and in formalized, extramural spaces. This variety suggests a diversity of coexisting ritual specialists, shamans and priests, operating within the framework of a common religious worldview. Two examples, from very different structured environments of the Levantine Chalcolithic, illustrate a common material culture and

iconography on the one hand, and different forms of ritual practice on the other. These are both sites with a largely ceremonial nature. Many further parallels and an even greater diversity could be drawn from large domestic sites, such as Shiqmim, and from mortuary contacts, but these will be discussed elsewhere (Ilan and Rowan in prep.; Rowan and Ilan in prep.).

Sacred places, sacred rites
Ein Gedi

The small complex at Ein-Gedi contains four primary components: a courtyard, two broad rooms and a gatehouse situated on a remote promontory overlooking the Dead Sea, between two springs, Ein Gedi and Ein Shulamit (Ussishkin 1980, figure 1). In the center of the courtyard a shallow circular stone feature was possibly a pit, although Mazar (2000) has proposed that it demarcated a sacred tree, a phenomenon known from later temples. In the main rectilinear (c. 19.70 m × 5.2/5.50 m) broad room a stone bench or ledge abutted each of the long walls. Directly opposite the entrance, a semi-circular, single course, stone feature abutting the northern long wall encompassed a white non-local crystalline limestone drum (altar?). A ceramic bull, or ram, carrying two churns was recovered nearby (Ussishkin 1980, figure 11). The broad room floor was perforated with a series of small shallow pits (c. 50–70 cm) containing ash, charcoal and one of the few complete vessels: a fenestrated pedestal bowl, upside down atop two ibex or gazelle horns. Many other such horns were recovered in this room.

In addition to mollusca, animal bones and horns (ibex?), excavations recovered two pendants, two beads, and a predynastic Egyptian alabaster jar fragment; the last item, found near the central courtyard basin, is a unique import for the period. The majority of the assemblage consisted of fenestrated, pedestal bowls and the pointed bases of 'cornets'. A total of at least nine fenestrated pedestal bowls were recovered at Ein Gedi, most in the broad room. This is a substantial number in contrast to other, much larger excavations at domestic sites, and it underscores the ritual centrality of this form.

The large number of cornets is also significant. Cornets are infrequent at most sites, particularly those in the Beersheba Basin, such as Shiqmim, Abu Matar, and Bir es-Safadi (Levy and Menahem 1987; Commenge-Pellerin 1987, 1990). The uneven distribution of cornets at different sites may reflect chronological, regional or cultural factors, but the high frequency of cornets at Ein Gedi is probably indicative of ritual performance.

The Ein Gedi complex is isolated and lacks the debris of domestic production (pottery, cooking, flint knapping, etc.). This small assemblage highlights three repeated elements:

ceramic fenestrated stands, ceramic cornets, and ruminant horns. Virtually all researchers agree that Ein Gedi functioned as a specialized ritual complex (most recently for example Levy 2006, Mazar 2000, Ussishkin 1980), or even a 'temple' (Gilead 2002, Ottoson 1980), but does this necessarily imply formal roles of religious authority? Given the rather formalized nature of its construction, the focusing devices and the lack of evidence for continuous activity, this compound probably included ritual specialists who cared for the structure, performed rituals, and provided instruction to visitors.

Gilat

Gilat is a 12 hectare site located at the interface between the northern Negev and more humid coastal plain. Architecture and stratigraphy are rather disturbed through multiple Chalcolithic reoccupations, but the assemblage from Gilat is remarkably rich (Levy *et al.* 2006; Commenge *et al.* 2006a; 2006b). Amongst the highlights are zoo- and anthro-pomorphic figurines, the remarkable Gilat Lady and the Ram with Cornets in particular, (e.g. Alon and Levy 1989; Commenge *et al.* 2006b Figures 15.1–6).

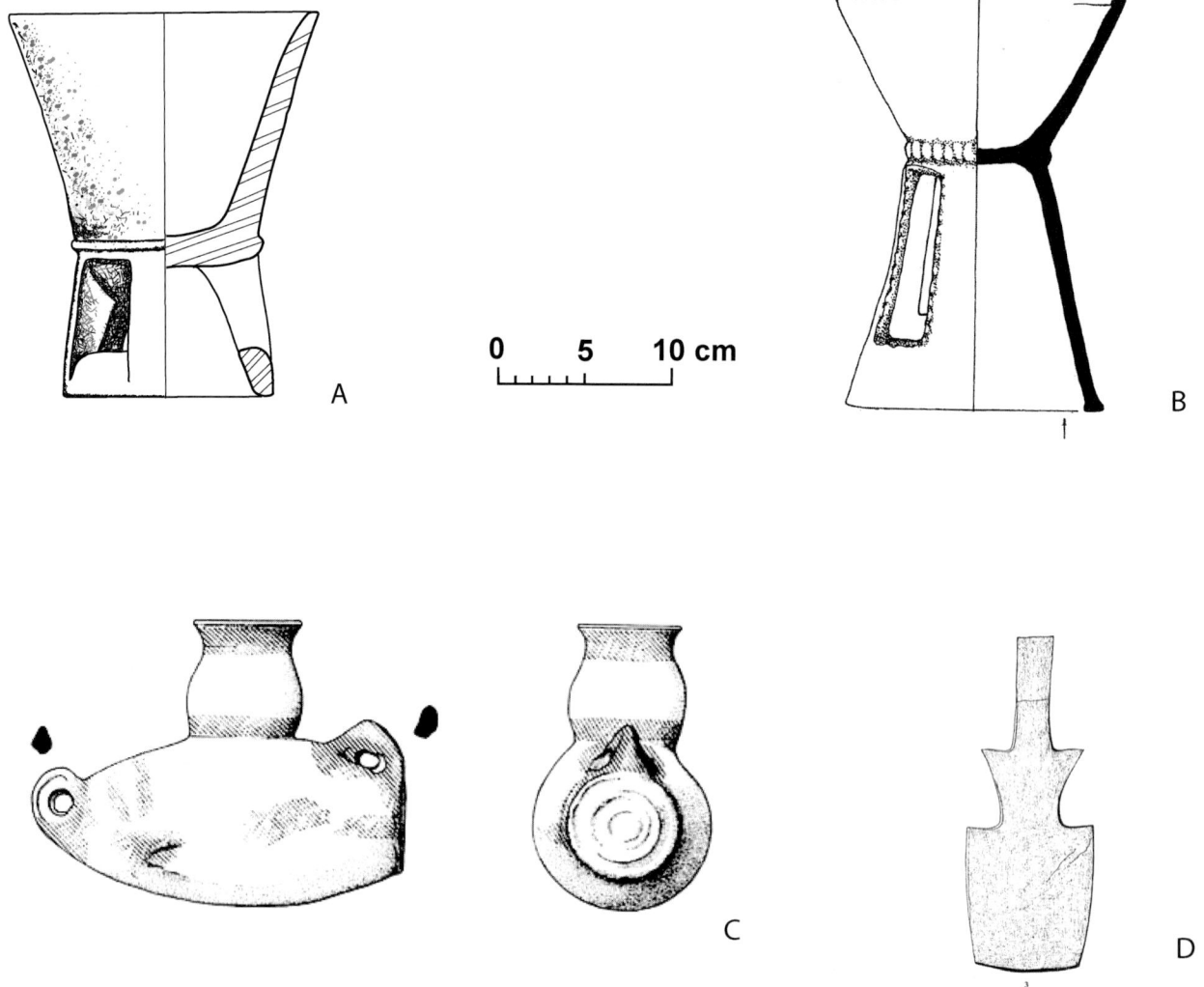

Figure 33.2. Chalcolithic artifacts. A: basalt pedestalled, fenestrated stand from (after Rowan 1998: Fig. 30A); B: ceramic pedestalled, fenestrated stand (from Epstein 1998:22.1); C: miniature churn from Kissufim (from Goren 2002: Fig. 4.5.3); D: sandstone violin-shaped figurine from Gilat (from Commenge et al. 2006, Fig. 15.16.3).

Levy, the primary excavator, argues convincingly that the site was a regional pilgrimage center (Alon and Levy 1989; Levy *et al.* 2006). One indicator is the so-called 'torpedo jars' (large, thick–walled, cylindrical, amphora-like vessels) found only at Gilat and made of non-local clays. Gas chromatography analysis of torpedo jars samples by Burton identified lipids consistent with olive oil transport (Burton and Levy 2006). Probably cultivated for the first time during the Chalcolithic (Neef 1990; Zohary and Hopf 1993), olive oil was almost certainly a valuable commodity. Pottery from Gilat shows more diversity of form than is typical at Chalcolithic sites, including miniature versions of standard vessels as well as forms unknown or absent at other sites. These include vessels such as cylindrical basins, tubular beakers, pointed bases, chalices on stems, as well as closed forms, such as miniature churns (Figure 33.2c) and the 'torpedo jars' (see Commenge *et al.* 2006a). Like most Chalcolithic sites, the majority of ceramic vessels (*c.* 70%, Goren 2006, 371) recovered from Gilat were made of locally available clays, but petrographic study indicates that relatively high percentages of a few forms were imported, quite unlike other Chalcolithic sites (Goren 1995, 295; Goren 2006, 371).

The rich assemblage from Gilat, derived primarily from pits and fills, incorporates many stone maceheads, including a few early predynastic Egyptian examples, and a large corpus of palettes and spindle whorls, some of non-local minerals (Rowan *et al.* 2006). Six pieces of obsidian were traced to Anatolia and are unique for the period, save for one piece from Ghassul (Yellin *et al.* 1996). The mollusc shell sample, much larger than at most other sites, includes Nile, Red Sea and Mediterranean species (Bar Yosef Mayer 2006). Hundreds of ostrich egg shell fragments were found and one cache included the intentional burial of four whole ostrich eggs grouped together in a shallow pit (Levy *et al.* 2006, plate 5.35). A burial of an aged dog, accompanied by a complete, atypical, double-handled tubular beaker, represents one of the earliest of a canine with mortuary goods (Levy *et al.* 2006, plate 5.58; Grigson 2006, plate 6.3b). In stark contrast to typical settlement sites, hundreds of ceramic and basalt fenestrated stand fragments (Figure 33.2a, b) occur (the nearest basalt source is 2–3 days journey away [Amiran and Porat 1984; Rowan *et al.* 2006]). One of the most distinctive artefact categories is the 'violin shaped figurine' (Figure 33.2d). Seventy-six were recovered from Gilat, more than all other Levantine sites combined (Commenge *et al.* 2006b). These are probably schematic renditions of the female form, as testified by two examples with breasts (one each from Peqi'in and Shiqmim), usually rendered in stone. The contours resemble the frontons on a number of ossuaries (secondary burial containers), a theme we will explore in greater detail elsewhere (Rowan and Ilan forthcoming).

Except for one stone example, there are no ossuaries at Gilat. But burials abound in all strata – a minimum of 91 individuals found in pits, silos, mortuary structures and fills. Burials were primary, though scattered bones and incomplete skeletons were common (Smith *et al.* 2006). A collective burial in a large, shallow, mudbrick-lined pit – perhaps initially intended to be a silo – contained the complete skeletal remains of nine individuals (Smith *et al.* 2006, figures 8.3–4b). Below was a layer of animal bones and sherds just above the paved floor of the structure (Levy *et al.* 2006, figure 5.20). About one meter away and stratigraphically linked to the burial structure was a mud-plastered pit containing a complete basalt fenestrated stand (similar to Figure 2a) and burned gazelle horn cores (Levy *et al.* 2006, figure 5.21), a combination of elements reminiscent of the Ein-Gedi deposits. To this we should remember that cornets are a significant component in both assemblages. The similarity of cornets to horns has been noted (Cameron 1981, 24–25); they may have an overlapping or related function.

Relative to area excavated, burial density at Gilat is much higher than at any other settlement site of the period. The burials do not seem to cluster spatially (though many were concentrated in open, plaza areas in the southeast of the site), nor were patterns in age, sex or other criteria detected (Smith *et al.* 2006). The combination of horns and fenestrated vessels next to burial features suggest that mortuary rites were a central function of the site and perhaps part of the pilgrimage process. At the same time, these and other components have parallels in the Ein Gedi deposits, which, though not directly associated with burials, are ritual (and perhaps mortuary) in nature.

Despite the intriguing and exotic nature of the assemblage excavated at Gilat, there is little evidence for formal roles of authority; no monumental construction, no concentrated storage area, no evidence for restricted access and no burials with prestige goods. Palaeopathological examination reveals some of the poorest health for a southern Levantine Chalcolithic population (Smith *et al.* 2006). Gilead (2002) argues that Gilat was more domestic in nature and inhabited by either shamans or a religious society. Although he doesn't define these terms, his point is important: this site is vastly different from the Ein Gedi sanctuary. Gilat includes a large quantity of prosaic material culture, with an assemblage of standard flint waste typical of most Chalcolithic villages (Rowan 2006). If Gilat was indeed a pilgrimage center, and we agree with Levy's interpretation, mortuary rites were part of the package. This suggests two centers of ritual practice, quite different in nature. Are they contemporaneous sites serving different populations, different purposes, or controlled by different types of practitioner?

Concluding remarks

The Chalcolithic is a period of transition when the egalitarianism apparent in the Neolithic was being supplanted by a more ranked society, at least in some regions. At the same time, the formal elements of ritual architecture (i.e. 'temples'), rather clearly defined by the Early Bronze Age (EBA), were not yet codified. The Ein Gedi complex may represent a prototype (cf. Kempinski 1972). Unlike the subsequent EBA however, the Chalcolithic displays a range of ritual structures and practices, from sites of singular ritual function to complex sites with domestic, mortuary and internal ritual practices, demonstrated by Ein Gedi and Gilat respectively. This diversity in ritual practice makes it unlikely that permanent, formalized ritual authorities dominated the religious and social landscape.

The formalized space of the Ein Gedi structure, which functioned as a 'temple/sanctuary/ritual space', lacks those elements that we might associate with chiefly attempts to legitimise authority. Ritual equipment abounds, but the valuable, prestige 'cultic' items such as basalt vessels, copper maceheads and standards, ivory, and palettes are all missing, save the single imported Egyptian fragment. Given this context, we would suggest that an effort to legitimise authority needs to be demonstrated, not assumed. Not all religious phenomena serve to legitimise elite authority.

By the same token, the existence of some centralized, formalized ritual activity is likely. Chiefly power and rule is often legitimised through access to the sacred and the divine; some chiefdoms are described as theocratic societies. Such elites may have existed during this period, perhaps in restricted regions such as the Beersheba drainage system, or perhaps they characterize a later phase of the Chalcolithic as it merged into the EBA in the mid fourth millennium BCE. Our internal chronology lacks the resolution to warrant firm conclusions.

For the time being, rather than view the Chalcolithic as a period of either chiefdoms with priests, or one of corporate group societies with limited, context-specific religious practitioners – shamans – we posit multiple forms of religious practice. Ritual was not the exclusive tool of elites, nor was it solely *ad hoc* and shamanistic. The rituals of priests were probably different in expression from those of shamans, though overlap is certainly likely. Both operated within an overarching religious belief system with a common iconography.

This system was oriented around otherworldly concerns that incorporated, in addition to recurrent iconography, ritual items such as cornets, fenestrated stands and horns, all of which occupied diverse spaces for ritual practice in variable modes. We have moved beyond the simplistic equation of the 'odd' with ritual, but we have some ways to go before we successfully re-connect ritual practice with

context. We are reminded of the Hopewell Complex of the Ohio River Valley: both are rich in iconography and exotic goods manufactured by specialists, frequently deposited in mortuary contexts. Yet both lack the clear evidence for chiefdoms. What is really interesting about the Levantine Chalcolithic is that we may be observing the actual genesis of more locale-specific, occasion-specific categories of religious leadership and ritual practice – priests. In any event, it is time to move beyond the opposed extremes of shamans vs. priests, a dichotomy that reflects implicit neo-evolutionary models and simplistically conflates the diverse practices of different communities into caricatures of religious reality.

Acknowledgements

The authors would like to thank Caroline Malone and David A. Barrowclough for organizing the conference in which this paper was presented. In addition, we would like to thank Morag Kersel for commenting on earlier versions of this paper. We would also like to extend our thanks to the Fulbright Scholar Program (Jordanian-American Commission for Educational Exchange) for the funding support (to YMR) which allowed participation in this conference.

References

Aldenderfer, M. 1996. Preludes to power in the highland Late Preceramic Period. In K. Vaughn, D. Ogburn and C. A. Conlee (eds). *Foundations of Power in the Prehispanic Andes*, Archaeological Papers of the American Anthropological Association, Vol. 14. 13–35.

Alon, D. and Levy, T. E. 1989. The archeology of cult and Chalcolithic sanctuary at Gilat. *Journal of Mediterranean Archaeology* 2, 163–221.

Amiran, R. and Porat, N. 1984. The basalt bowls of the Chalcolithic Period and the Early Bronze Age I. *Tel Aviv* 11, 11–19.

Bahn, P. 2001. Save the last trance for me: An assessment of the misuse of shamanism in rock art studies. In H. P. Francfort and R. N. Hamayon (eds). *The Concept of Shamanism: Uses and Abuses*. Bibliotheca Shamanistica, vol. 10: 51–93. Budapest, Akademiai Kiad.

Bar-Adon, P. 1980. *The Cave of the Treasure: the Finds from the Caves in Nahal Mishmar*. Jerusalem, The Israel Exploration Society.

Bar-Yosef Mayer, D. E. 2006. Marine and riverine shells from Gilat. In T. E. Levy (ed.). *Archaeology, Anthropology and Cult: The Sanctuary at Gilat, Israel*. London, Equinox, 320–326.

Bourke, S. J. 2001. The Chalcolithic Period. In B. Macdonald, R. Adams, and P. Bienkowski (eds). *The Archaeology of Jordan*. Sheffield, Sheffield Academic Press, 107–163.

Burton, M. and Levy, T. E. 2006. Appendix I. Organic residue analysis of selected vessels from Gilat – Gilat torpedo jars. In T. E. Levy (ed.). *Archaeology, Anthropology, and Cult: The Sanctuary at Gilat, Israel*. London, Equinox, 849–62.

Cameron, D. O. 1981. *The Ghassulian Wall Paintings.* London, Kenyon-Dean Ltd.

Childs, S. T. 1998. Social identity and craft specialization among Toro iron workers in western Uganda. In C. Costin (ed.). *Craft and Social Identity.* Archaeological Papers of the American Anthropological Association, Vol. 8, 109–121.

Clark, J. D. and Blake, M. 1994. The power of prestige: competitive generosity and the emergence of ranked societies in lowland Mesoamerica. In E. M. Brumfiel and J. Fox (eds). *Factional Competition and Political Development in the New World.* Cambridge: Cambridge University Press, 17–30.

Commenge-Pellerin, C. 1987. *La Poterie d'Abou Matar et de l'Ouadi Zoumeili Beershéva) au IVe millénaire avant l Ère Chretienne.* Paris, Association Paléorient.

Commenge-Pellerin, C. 1990. *La Poterie de Safadi (Beersheva) au IVe millenaire avant l'ere chretienne.* Paris, Association Paléorient.

Commenge, C., Alon, D., Levy, T. E. and Kansa, E. 2006a. Gilat ceramics: Cognitive dimensions of pottery production. In T. E. Levy (ed.). *Archaeology, Anthropology and Cult: The Sanctuary at Gilat (Israel).* London, Equinox, 394–506.

Commenge, C., Levy, T. E., Alon, D. and Kansa, E. 2006b. Gilat's figurines: Exploring the social and symbolic dimensions of representation. In T. E. Levy (ed.) *Archaeology, Anthropology and Cult: The Sanctuary at Gilat (Israel).* London, Equinox, 739–830.

Earle, T. E. 1997. *How Chiefs Come to Power: The Political Economy in Prehistory.* Palo Alto, Stanford University Press.

Epstein, C. 1998. *The Chalcolithic Culture of Golan.* IAA Reports, No. 4. Jerusalem: Israel Antiquities Authority.

Gal, Z., Smithline, H. and Shalem, D. 1996. A Chalcolithic burial cave in Peqi'in. *Qadmoniot* 111, 19–24.

Gilead, I. 1988. The Chalcolithic period in the Levant. *Journal of World Prehistory* 2, 397–443.

Gilead, I. 2002. Religio-magic behaviour in the Chalcolithic period of Palestine. In S. Ahituv and E. D. Oren (eds). *Aharon Kempinski Memorial Volume: Studies in Archaeology and Related Disciplines.* Beer-Sheva, Ben-Gurion University of the Negev, 103–128.

Golden, J. Forthcoming. *Dawn of the Metal Age: The Origins of Social Complexity in the Southern Levant.* London, Equinox.

Gopher, A. and T. Tsuk 1996. The Chalcolithic assemblages. In A. Gopher (ed.). *The Nahal Qanah Cave: Earliest Gold in the Southern Levant.* Monograph Series of the Institute of Archaeology. Tel Aviv, Tel Aviv University, 91–138.

Goren, Y. 1995. Shrines and ceramics in Chalcolithic Israel: The view through the petrographic microscope. *Archaeometry* 37, 287–305.

Goren, Y. 2006. The technology of the Gilat pottery assemblage: A reassessment. In T. E. Levy (ed.). *Archaeology, Anthropology and Cult. The Sanctuary at Gilat, Israel.* London, Equinox, 369–93.

Gosden, C. 1989. Debt, production and prehistory. *Journal of Anthropological Archaeology* 8, 355–387.

Grigson, C. 2006. Farming? Feasting? Herding? Large mammals from the Chalcolithic of Gilat. In T. E. Levy (ed.). *Archaeology, Anthropology and Cult: The Sanctuary at Gilat, Israel.* London, Equinox, 215–319.

Ilan, D. and Rowan, Y. M. In prep. *Poor man, rich man, shaman, priest? Religious specialists during the Chalcolithic of the southern Levant.*

Insoll, T. 2004. *Archaeology, Ritual, Religion.* New York, Routledge.

Joffe, A. H. 2003. Slouching toward Beersheva: Chalcolithic mortuary practices in local and regional context. In B. A. Nakhai (ed.). *The Near East in the Southwest: Essays in Honor of William G. Dever.* AASOR Vol. 58. Boston, ASOR, 45–67.

Kehoe, A. B. 2000. *Shamans and Religion. An Anthropological Exploration in Critical Thinking.* Long Grove, IL, Waveland Press.

Kempinski, A. 1972. The Sin Temple of Khafaje and the Temple at Ein Gedi. *Israel Exploration Journal* 22, 10–15.

Kendall, L. 1996. Korean shamans and the spirits of capitalism. *American Anthropologist* 98(2), 512–527.

Lessa, W. A. and Vogt, E. Z. 1979. *Reader in Comparative Religion* (4th ed.). New York, Harper and Row.

Levy, T. E. 1986. Social archaeology and the Chalcolithic period: Explaining social organizational change during the 4th millennium in Israel. *Michmanim* 3, 5–20.

Levy, T. E. 1998. Cult, metallurgy and rank societies – Chalcolithic period (*c.* 4500–3500 BCE). In T. E. Levy (ed.). *The Archaeology of Society in the Holy Land.* London, Leicester University Press, 226–244.

Levy, T. E. 2006. Archaeology, anthropology and cult: Exploring religion in formative middle range societies. In T. E. Levy (ed.). *Archaeology, Anthropology and Cult: The Sanctuary at Gilat, Israel.* London, Equinox, 3–33.

Levy, T. E. and Menachem, N. 1987. The ceramic industry at Shiqmim: Typological and spatial consideration. In T. E. Levy (ed.). *Shiqmim I,* BAR International Series 356. Oxford, BAR, 313–331.

Levy, T. E., Alon, D., Rowan, Y. M., and Kersel, M. 2006. The sanctuary sequence: Excavations at Gilat: 1975–77, 1989, 1990–92. In T. E. Levy (ed.). *Archaeology, Anthropology and Cult: The Sanctuary at Gilat, Israel.* London, Equinox, 95–212.

Mazar, A. 2000. A sacred tree in the Chalcolithic shrine at En Gedi: A suggestion. *Bulletin of the Anglo-Israel Archaeological Society* 18, 31–36.

Neef, R. 1990. Introduction, development and environmental implications of olive culture: The evidence from Jordan, in S. Bottema, G. Entjes-Nieborg, and W. Van Zeist (eds). *Man's Role in the Shaping of the Eastern Mediterranean Landscape.* Rotterdam: Brookfield, 132–264.

Ottoson, M. 1980. *Temples and Cult Places in Palestine.* Uppsala.

Price, N. 2001. An archaeology of altered states: Shamanism and material culture studies. In N. Price (ed.). *The Archaeology of Shamanism.* New York, Routledge, 3–16.

Rowan, Y. M. 2006. The chipped stone assemblage at Gilat. In T. E. Levy (ed.). *Archaeology, Anthropology and Cult: The Sanctuary at Gilat.* London, Equinox Press, 507–574.

Rowan, Y. M. and Ilan, D. In prep. *Cult, Cache and the Subterranean: Death's Dominion during the Chalcolithic Period of the Southern Levant.*

Rowan, Y. M., Levy, T. E., Alon, D. and Goren, Y. 2006. The ground stone industry: Stone bowls, grinding slabs, palettes, spindle whorls, maceheads and related finds. In T. E. Levy (ed.). *Archaeology, Anthropology and Cult: The Sanctuary at*

Gilat. London, Equinox Press, 575–684.

Schick, T. 1998. *The Cave of the Warrior. A Fourth Millennium Burial in the Judean Desert*. Jerusalem, Israel Antiquities Authority.

Smith, P., Zagerson, T., Sabari, P., Golden, J., Levy, T. E., and Dawson, L. 2006. Death and the sanctuary: The human remains from Gilat. In T. E. Levy (ed.). *Archaeology, Anthropology and Cult: The Sanctuary at Gilat, Israel*. London, Equinox, 327–366.

Ussishkin, D. 1980. The Ghassulian shrine at En-Gedi. *Tel Aviv* 7, 1–44.

Walter, D. 2001. The medium of the message: Shamanism as localized practice in the Nepal Himalayas. In N. Price (ed.). *The Archaeology of Shamanism*. New York, Routledge, 105–119.

Winkelman, M. 1992. *Shamans, Priest and Witches: A Cross Cultural Study of Magico-Religious Practitioners*. Anthropological Research Papers No. 44, Arizona State University, Tempe.

Yellin, J., Levy, T. E. and Rowan, Y. 1996. New evidence on prehistoric trade routes: the obsidian evidence from Gilat, Israel. *Journal of Field Archaeology* 23(3), 361–368.

Zohary, D. and Hopf, M. 1993. *Domestication of Plants in the Old World*. Oxford, Clarendon Press.

Chapter 34

HOUSING THE DEAD: BURIALS INSIDE HOUSES AND VESSELS IN THE NEOLITHIC BALKANS

Goce Naumov

The majority of researched Neolithic sites in the Balkans contain burials that provide a general picture for both the anthropological character of their Neolithic populations, and also of their relationship with death. The majority of the burials occur within settlements rather than on or outside their periphery. The number of burials in the settlement do not correspond to the likely number of inhabitants within the settlement, and it must be assumed that most of the deceased were buried outside their settlement. It remains uncertain why only a few individuals from each generation and period were buried beneath the settlement, but whilst there are several possible answers to this question, it should be emphasized that this kind of ritual was typical in the Early Neolithic. The answer therefore lies in the socio-religious structure of the newly arrived inhabitants and their relation with the creation of new communities, settlements and dwellings. Interestingly, the largest number of burials found within the settlements, between or even inside the houses, belong to infants and children, follow next by women, and then males. From the total of 38 burials found in Neolithic sites from the Republic of Macedonia, aproximately 20 are neonates, infants, and juveniles, 11 are female, 8 are male and 2 are anthropologically undefined individuals (Garašanin and Garašanin 1961, 15, 16; Garašanin 1969, 18; Gimbutas 1976, 375–410; Veljanovska 2000, 45; Veljanovska 2006, 341). In Bulgaria from around 100 intramurial burials, 46 skeletons belong to neonates, infants, and juveniles, 17 to females, 8 to males and around 20 to anthropologically undefined individuals (Bačvarov 2003, 23–98). In the Starčevo group, which spreads over Serbia, Croatia and Bosnia, of 84 anthropologically defined skeletons, those of 39 children dominate, females represent 25 and males 20 skeletons (Stanković 1992, 58–73; Bailey 2000, 123). *Of about* 190 individuals found at Lepenski Vir, the number of the neonates (without that of infants and juveniles) is more than half the total, compared to that of buried adults (Borić and Stefanović 2004, 532, figure 8). In Greece, the number of inhumed individuals within the settlement is

smaller. From around 40 burials, 22 belong to children, 3 to women, while 2 skeletons and 11 craniums are of uncertain sex, the rest are anthropologically unidentified bones and skeletons (Perlès 2001, 274–280; Bačvarov 2003, 171, 172, 183–189). From this data we can assume that mortality among the neonates, infants, juveniles and women was much higher than that of males. On the other hand, this statistic indicates the probability of possible age and sex selection made during the burial rite within the settlements. For example, in the Early Neolithic phases of Amzabegovo (Republic of Macedonia), 14 of the 23 skeletons belong to neonates, infants and juveniles, 8 are female skeletons and only one is male (Gimbutas 1976, 375–398). Considering that in this phase the settlement had about 300 houses possibly with 1000–1500 inhabitants (Gimbutas 1976, 34, 37), the number of burials (in the present sample) is far below the middle level of mortality in the settlement. This points toward selection of 'privileged' individuals, especially children and women for burial within the settlement. Their number dominates even in the most specific form of Neolithic funerary rite, those practiced inside the house (Figure 34.1).

1. Burials inside the houses

In the Neolithic, the house was a space where part of the family was created, raised, but also ended its life. Although it was not practical, some of the deceased were buried beneath the floor, placed in specific peripheral areas, i.e. next to the walls, close to ovens or hearth and rarely in the pits used for grain storage. The most usual funerary form was inhumation, which was practiced inside burial pits, vessels and ovens. Infant and adult burials placed next to house walls are found in Madjari (Macedonia), Kazanlak and Rakitovo (Bulgaria), Lepenski Vir, Grivac (Serbia), Vinkovci (Croatia) and Çatal Höyük. Preventing possible damage to the corpse, they were placed in the non-frequented area of the house (Figure 34.2). One example from Çatal Höyük indicates that neonates were buried high

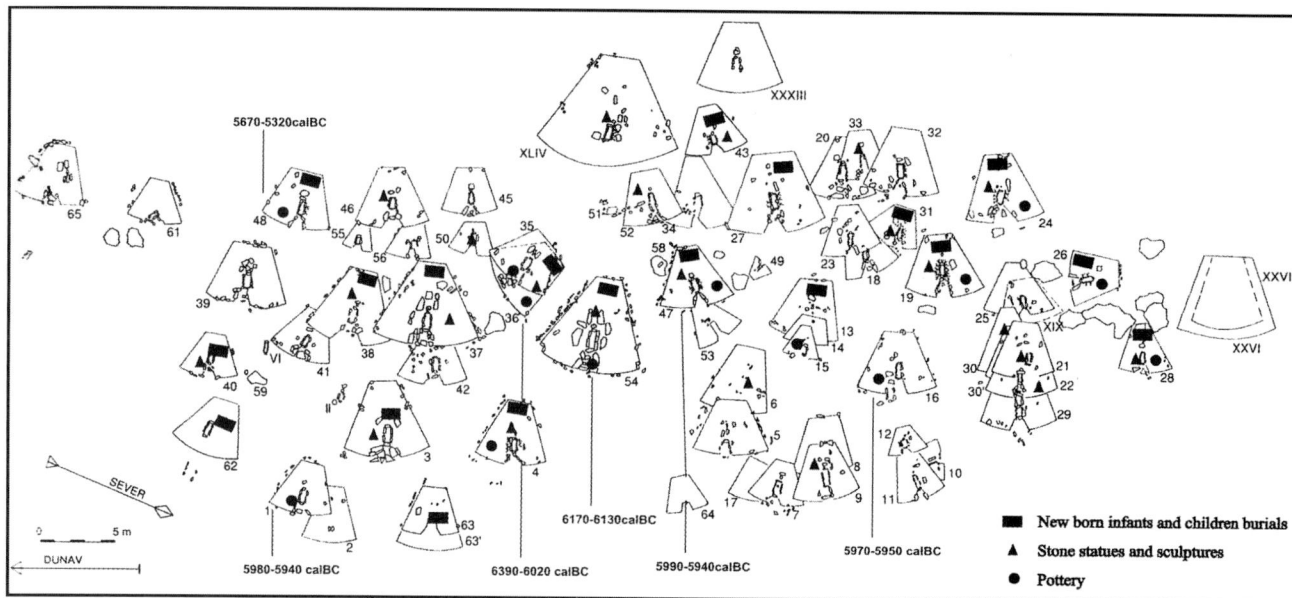

Figure 34.1. Intramurial burials, Lepenski Vir (Serbia) (Budja 2004, fig. 20).

Figure 34.2. Infant burial next to the south wall of the house, Madjari (Macedonia) (photo: D. Karasarlidis, courtesy of Museum of Macedonia).

within the walls (Bačvarov 2003, 179). One hypothesis suggests that during the building of a new house, infants were intentionally killed as offerings. However, new analysis of the Lepenski Vir burials shows that all neonate burial pits were cut through existing floors (Figure 34.3), so that, at least on this site, the possibility of infanticide is rejected by the researchers (Borić and Stefanović 2004, 541). Examples from Haçilar, Kazanlak, Tell Azmak (Bulgaria), Prodromos (Greece), Lepenski Vir and Višesava (Serbia) show, crania was sometimes buried within the house (Bačvarov 2003, 70, 175; Bačvarov 2004, 153; Borić 2002, figure 7; Borić and Stefanović 2004, 541; Garašanin

Figure 34.3. Neonate burials in the house 24, Lepenski Vir, Serbia (Borić & Stefanović 2004, fig. 10).

1979, 123). A large house at Prodromos, contained 11 skulls (Figure 34.4), which points to a funerary rite that includes exhumation and reburial (Perlès 2001, 279). Similar rites of extraction, washing or removal of the deceased's bones are still practiced among some populations in the Balkans.

The Neolithic burial rites confirm the practice of the separate burial of the mandible, especially those of young individuals. Examples of this rite were excavated in Govrlevo (Macedonia), where a mandible was found next to a pot. This practice is also confirmed in Slatina, Kremikovci (Bulgaria), Agios Petros (Greece) and Bukovačka Česma (Serbia) (Bačvarov 2003, 84, 85, 184; Stanković 1994, 60). One hypothesis suggests that body parts buried below the dwelling came from high status or esteemed ancestors. In addition, there are a large number of Slavic rites in the Balkans where it was/is believed that the ancestors dwell exactly below the threshold and hearth of the house (Truhelka 1930; Niderle 1956, 86, 88; Blagojević 1984, 237, 238; Čajkanović 1985, 194–202; Mikov and Lozanova 1996, 44). The threshold was seen as a place where, directly or indirectly, communication with the ancestors was made through sacrifice or stepping over the threshold (Chausidis 1996, 43; Bocev 2001, 207–211).

2. Matrilineal features of the house

As noted above, most skeletons found inside Balkan Neolithic dwellings belong to babies, children and women. Excepting the early phases of Amzabegovo (already mentioned), a similar relation between ages and sexes can be found in Karanovo and Lepenski Vir. Thus, in the second phase of Karanovo, most of the burials are those of infants, whilst at Lepenski Vir in only 19 dwellings, 41 neonates are found (Bačvarov 2003; Borić and Stefanović 2004). According to these data we can infer that the frequency of intramural burials of children and women was symbolically related to the house. Noting the level of mortality between the ages and sexes in the community, it seems there was selection of deceased individuals for house burials. The mortality of males within the settlement cannot have been as small as the statistical data suggests, and it can be supposed that most of them were buried outside the settlement, whilst children and female had 'priority' in the intramural burials. The children were important in the preservation of communal continuity, and had an essential part even in the funerary rituals.

Some burial features reflected the woman's part in the reproduction of society, especially as a mother, since she produced those who would ensure the existence of the community. Frequent pregnancy and birth took place in the house, with the mother manifested as a character, symbolically related to its semantic features. The house is the space where the community is created, and is therefore analogous to the female body where similar functions were performed: impregnation, growth and birth. This analogy between the female reproductive organs and the house continues more subtly with the children. As the children are created and formed in the mother's womb, after their birth, they also grow and mature in the house. The earliest years of their childhood are spent in and around the house under the care of their mothers. It was believed that, if a child dies at an early age, its rebirth will be ensured with it's burial inside the womb of his mother-house, but also in the vicinity of his real birth-giving mother. The relationship between children, mother and house are confirmed by the numerous domestic objects in the burial context, and also by the many ethnographic parallels that contribute to an understanding of Neolithic funerary rites (Chausidis 1994, 200–213; Chausidis 1996, 37–52). The relationships between Neolithic artefacts, the burials and their memory in the nineteenth and twentieth century rites, allows a potential interpretation of some of the Neolithic cults.

a) Models of the figurine – house

During the excavation of Neolithic settlements in the Republic of Macedonia, a specific kind of ceramic object is found, so far limited to this territory (Sanev 1988, 15–18; Chausidis 2004; Kolištrkovska-Nasteva 2005, 54–70). These represent sculptures which unite two kinds of artefacts, figurines and models of houses, they are therefore known as models of figurine-house (Figure 34.5). They are divided into two parts: the upper part, where the figurine is represented and the lower part, where instead of thighs and legs, the house is shown. Some models emphasise stylized anthropomorphic features, whilst others have detailed architectonic characteristics.

These semantically conceived models emphasize the feminine character of the house, which is represented as part of the female body i.e. the part where the reproductive process is active. On one of the example, the belly is

represented in the state of pregnancy, suggesting the figurine symbolically bears the embryo where the house is placed (Figure 34.5: 4). It can be concluded that in the Neolithic, the house was conceived as a space with exclusively feminine features and symbolic functions – conception, incubation, birth and growth. Consequently, we can interpret the burial of the deceased (in fetal position) inside the house as a metaphor for the fetus in the womb.

b) Burials inside and around the oven

If we accept that a house in the Neolithic was conceived of as a female body, then it is probable that part of the inventory of finds found within it's interior were related to funerary rites. In that context, the hearth and oven had symbolic meaning with the same metaphoric function as those organs of a women's abdomen which stimulate the conception and development of the embryo. Food was prepared near these structures. created, and afterwards through the cooking, baking or roasting process, was transformed into sustenance in a changed form and characterister. The shape of the Neolithic ovens, their power to modify and also their radiant heat, can also suggest a semantic relationship to the key features of the women's abdomen. Some anthropomorphic models of ovens indicate that during the rites, they were perceived as human body or as mythic figures with human features (Figure 34.8: 2–6). Examples from Progar, Vinča, Medvednjak (Serbia) include models with incised hands, stylized breasts and broken heads (Petrović 2001, 12–14). In contrast to them, the gynekomorphic shape of the Màrtély (Hungary) model shows similarities between oven and female abdomen during pregnancy (Gimbutas 1989, 148, figure 228). The

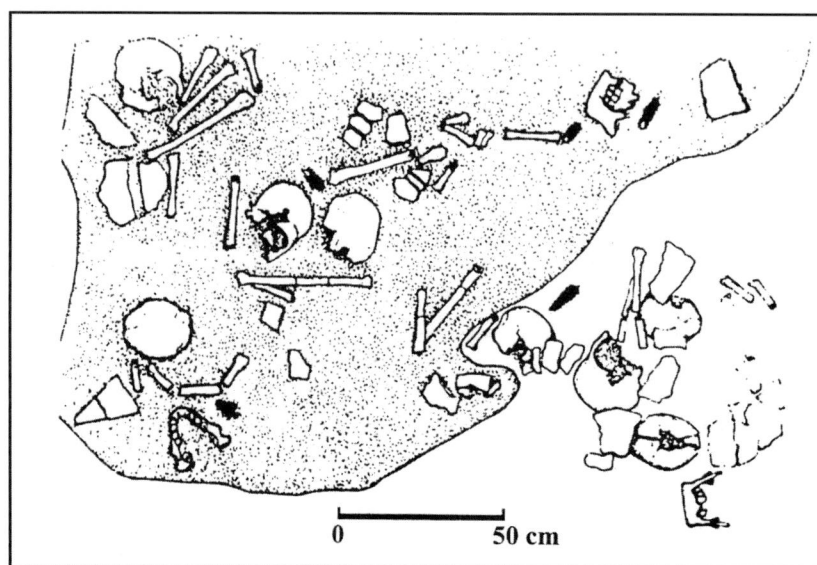

Figure 34.4. Exhumated burials inside the dwelling, Prodromos (Greece) (Bačvarov 2003, fig. 6.19).

frequent burial of infants near to hearths and ovens, or inside ovens, was not coincidental (Figure 34.6). Examples from Karanovo, Azmak, Kazanlak, Samovodene (Bulgaria), Agios Petros (Greece), Parta (Romania), Curmatura (Hungary Plate 34.2: 1) and even from Çatal Höyük prove this hypothesis (Bačvarov 2003, 28, 60, 69, 88, 184; Garašanin 1979, 160; Gimbutas 1989, 151; Moses 2006, 182).

This burial tradition of placing, or 'throwing', neonates and infants near to or inside the oven continued into later prehistory and Antiquity, in the rites related to the construction of furnaces for metallurgy, and also in Christian legends and Macedonian folk stories (Truhelka 1930, 5; Durman 2004, 28; Gabelić 1991, 87; Naumov 2006a, 76–78). Among the Acheva tribe, the fetus was burnt and then buried in a pit below the oven strcuture (Durman 2004, 28). In many Macedonian folk stories children were thrown into ovens, so that later they can become wiser or 'gildted' (Stojanović 1999, 186, 187). This

suggests that children were a precondition for the operation of the oven in order to realize its role as modifier. Children were also conceived of as an 'alchemic' substance which can regenerate and transform. Thus, even in the Neolithic, infants buried below the oven, were perhaps placed there 'to stimulate' the oven, so it would function more effectively. Conversely, it may have been believed that deceased children placed below an object with vital functions for the community, were reborn in the same house.

c) Burials in the bag

Although rare, on a small number of sites some of the deceased were buried in a bag or wrapped with cattail or linen. In Kovaćevo (Bulgaria) there are two neonates and an infant found buried with cattail (Bačvarov 2003, 33). According to the position of the legs, it is considered that one neonate from Lepenski Vir was buried in a bag (Borić and Stefanović 2004) (Figure 34.7). This practice has it's own parallels in the rites of the Saracatsans. Until the

Figure 34.5. Macedonian figurine-house models.
1: Porodin, Kolištrkovska – Nasteva 2005, 59, fig. 43.
2: Dobromiri, Vasileva 2005, 27.
3: Madjari, Kolištrkovska – Nasteva 2005, 59, fig. 42.
4: Govrlevo, Chausidis 1995, 32, fig. 6.
5: Stenće, Zdravkovski 2005, 27, fig. 10.
6: Madjari, Kolištrkovska – Nasteva 2005, 60, fig. 44.
7: Suvodol, Kolištrkovska – Nasteva 2005, 61, fig. 45.
8: Mrševci, Kolištrkovska – Nasteva 2005, 64, fig. 48.

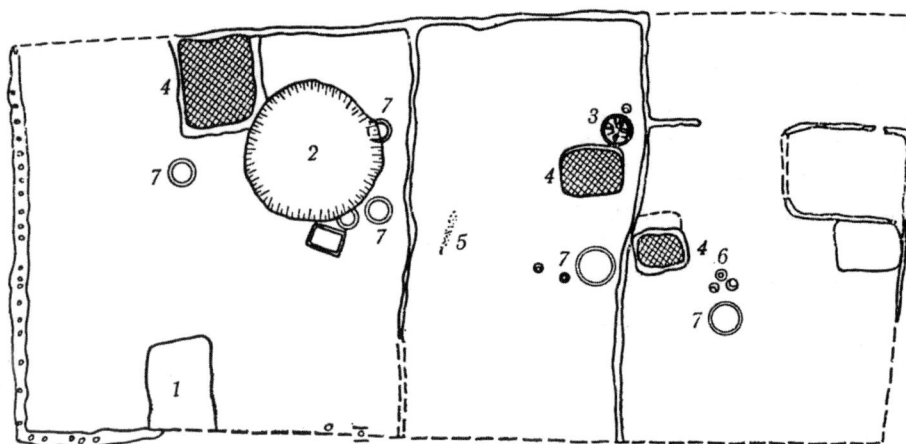

Figure 34.6. Burial in the vessel next to oven, Azmak (Bačvarov 2004, fig. 2).

Figure 34.7. Neonate burial inside the bag, Lepenski Vir (Serbia) (Borić & Stefanović 2004, fig. 13).

3. Burials inside the vessels

Placing dead infants in symbolic 'wombs' occurred not only in the case of houses, ovens and bags, but also in vessels. Vessels, like wombs, can store substances. They serve as containers that can incubate or modify at a higher temperature. For that reason, vessels were often utilised in the expression of some semantic aspects of Neolithic beliefs (Naumov 2005), especially those related to burial (Naumov 2006a, 72–74). Neolithic vessels had smaller dimensions, so only infant burials were placed inside (Figure 34.9). This tradition continues in later periods of prehistory when it is manifest in adult burials inside *pithoi* (Neuman 1963, 162; Mitrevski 1997, 288–290, 300; Mitrevski 2001, 21, 25) (Figure 34.10). Infant burials inside vessels have been found at Amzabegovo, Azmak, Rakitovo and Kovaćevo, and burnt skull fragments along with cereals were found inside an anthropomorphic vessel from Gorza, Hungary (Gimbutas 1976, 396; Bačvarov 2003, 33, 60; Radunčeva *et al.* 2002, 35, 150; Hodder 1990, 52; Grifoni Cremonesi 1994, 185). At Ezero (Bulgaria) and Obre (Bosnia), buried infants were covered by a vessel, in Tečič a painted vessel was found below the face of a skeleton, whilst in Kazanlk, the vessel was placed upside down, next to the skeleton (Bačvarov 2003, 45, 61; Stanković 1992, 68; Garašanin 1979, 122), similar to a burial from Amzabegovo, where one 4–6 months old infant, was buried inside a vessel with intentionally broken handles and base (Gimbutas 1976, 396) (Figure 34.9: 1, 2). The vessel was inverted, with the broken bottom upward and the rim face down, suggesting in the context of the funerary rite, that the vessel had the function of the womb. We can assume that the infant's rebirth was expected, after symbolically 'passing through' the uteral channel symbolized by the rim. The relationship between a vessel, a woman and her reproductive organs is represented in anthropomorphic vessels (Figure 34.11 and Figure 34.12: 1–3). Since the earliest Neolithic phases, there were vessels with elements of the human body, especially those with emphasized feminine traits. Although

middle of the twentieth century they buried their dead neonates in a bag, which was hung over the bed of the parents for 40 days before the funeral (Antonijević 1982, 134). The bag symbolically represented the womb i.e. the space where the child was during the development process from embryo to fetus and baby. Alternatively, the bag could represent the neonate's placenta. This is possible considering the important role of the placenta in the post-birth rites of some Slavic populations (Blagojević 1984, 220). Washing bones with wine before placing them inside a white bag, a few years after the funeral, is still often practice in the Balkans.

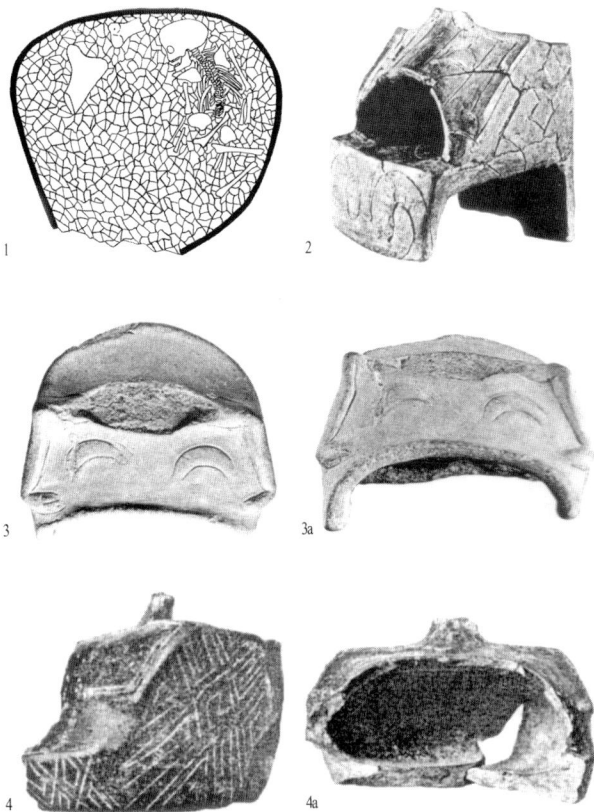

Figure 34.8. Burial inside the oven and models of anthropomorphic ovens.
1: Curmatura (Hungary), Gimbutas 1989, 151, fig. 233.
2: Medvednjak (Serbia), Petrović 2001, 13, fig. 3.
3: Progar (Serbia), Petrović 2001, 12, fig. 1a.
3a: Progar (Serbia), Petrović 2001, 12, fig. 1b.
4: Vinča (Serbia), Petrović 2001, 13, fig. 2c.
4a: Vinča (Serbia), Petrović 2001, 13, fig. 2a.

Figure 34.9. Burial vessels.
1: Amzabegovo (Macedonia), Sanev et al. 1976, fig. 42.
2: Amzabegovo (same one in different position), Gimbutas 1976, 397, fig. 242.
3: Rakitovo (Bulgaria), Bačvarov 2004, 158, fig. 1.1.
4: Kovačevo (Bulgaria), Bačvarov 2004, 158, fig. 1.2.
5: Tell Hazna (Near East), Bačvarov 2003, 141, fig. 4.7.
6: Tell Soto/Tell Hazna? (Near East), Bačvarov 2004, 159, fig. 3.

these vessels were not directly involved in the funerary rituals, except the one from Gorza, still they were active in performing the role of female. In addition to this function, there are also anthropomorphic urns (Figure 34.13), vessels which in later periods of prehistory were used for placing the cremated remains of the deceased (Naumov 2006b). Interestingly, the 'feminity' of anthropomorphic vessels remained even at the iconographical level (Naumov 2006a, 66–68), with facial traits modelled almost identically on the faces on the figurine-house models, mentioned above (Figure 34.14; Figure 34.12: 4–6; Figure 34.5). This iconographic similarity indicates that these objects, although different in their use, had the same semantic concept that suggests that, even in funerary contexts, the relation between the vessel, house and woman was equally present.

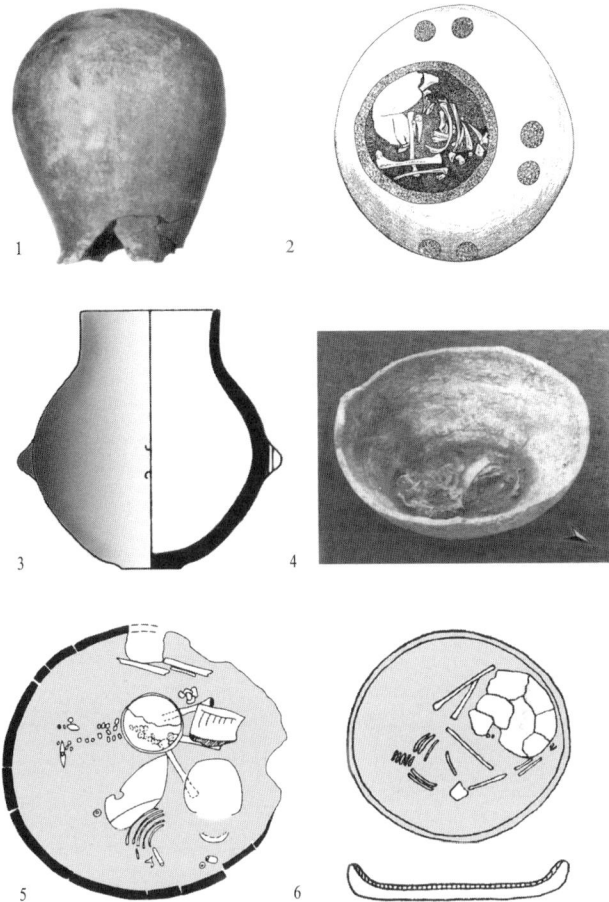

This relationship is present throughout the Slavic lingual area. Certain types of vessels, some even used in the Neolithic for burials (Naumov 2006a, 73), were named as 'lonec, karlice, bochvi, zdjelica' i.e. with terms which identify some parts of the female genital area (Chausidis and Nikolov 2006, 104–107). The relationship between a woman, her house and her symbolic involvement in domestic and funerary rites, has almost uninterrupted continuity from the Neolithic, through Antiquity and the Middle Ages, until archaic forms of contemporary folklore (Chausidis, in press).

Figure 34.10. Burial inside pithos, Vardatski Rid, Macedonia (Papazovska 2006, fig. 3).

Figure 34.11. Anthropomorphic vessels.
1: Amzabegovo (Macedonia), Gimbutas 1976, 241, fig. 209.
2: Vinča (Serbia), Gimbutas 1989,52, fig. 88.
3: Bekasmegyer (Hungary), Gimbutas 1989, 22, fig. 35.
4: Gradešnica (Bulgaria), Todorova & Vaisov 1993, pl. 446.
5: Vinča (Serbia), Garašanin 1982, 16, fig 21.
6: Szombately (Hungary), Gimbutas 1989, 37, fig.61.
7: Vinča (Serbia), Stalio 1977, fig. 69.
8: Svodina (Chech Republic), Pavuk1981, 39, fig. 24.
9: Orlavat (Serbia), Gimbutas 1989, 48, fig. 83.

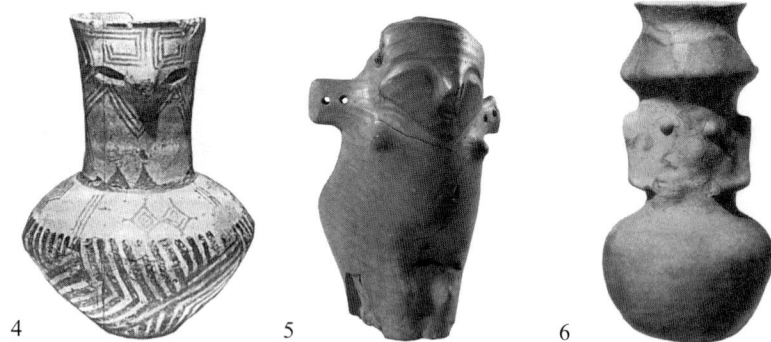

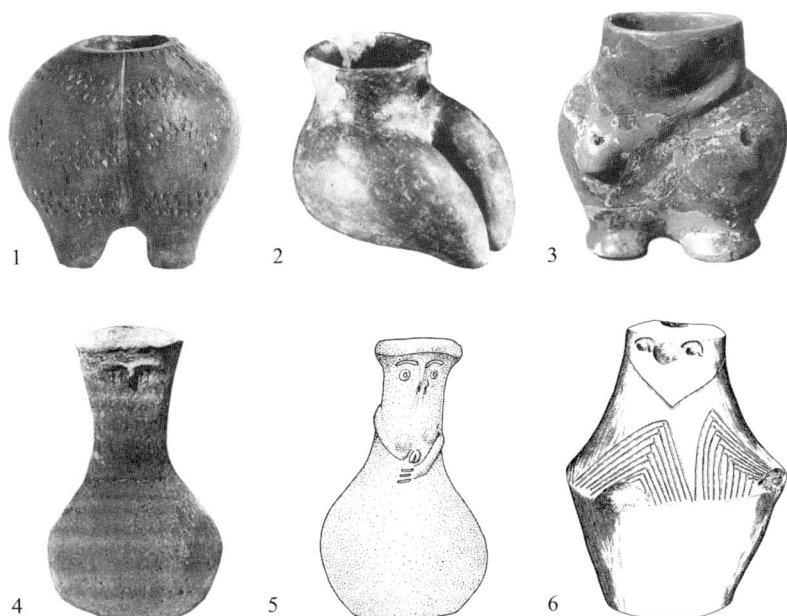

Figure 34.12. Anthropomorphic vessels
1: Vršnik (Macedonia), Kolištrkovska – Nasteva 2005, 58, fig. 42.
2: Drenovac (Serbia), Stalio 1977, fig. 203.
3: Rakitovo (Bulgaria), Radunćeva et al. 2002, 54, pl. 41: 3.
4: Ćavdar (Bulgaria), Todorova & Vaisov 1993, pl. 29.
5: Kazanlak (Bulgaria), Todorova & Vaisov 1993, 215, fig. 204.
6: Radajce (Serbia), Gimbutas 1989, 38, fig. 62.

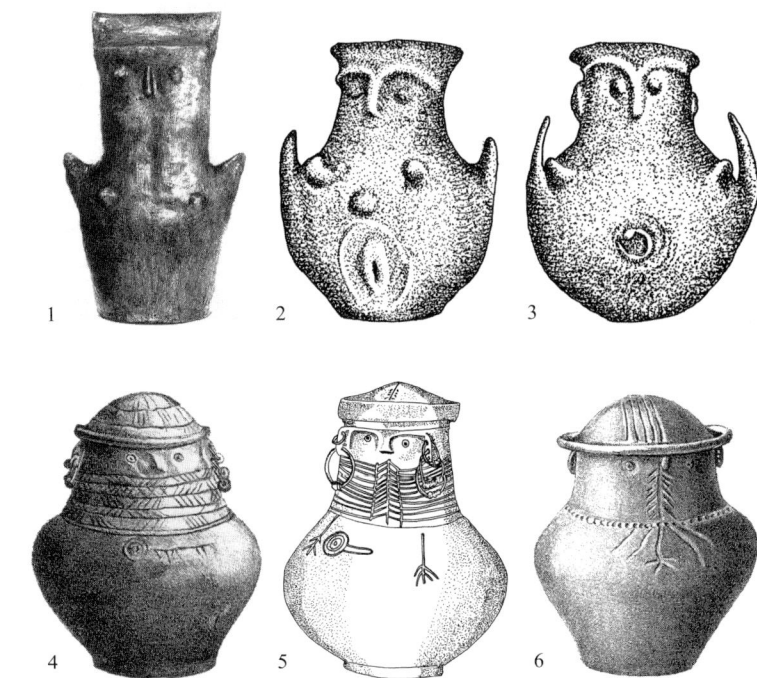

Figure 34.13. Burial urns.
1: Center (Hungary), Gimbutas 1989, 191, fig. 291.
2: Lemnos (Greece), Gimbutas 1989, 191, fig. 292: 1.
3: Troy (Turkey), Gimbutas 1989, 191, fig. 292: 2.
4: Friedensau (Germany), Hoernes 1925, 531, fig. 8.
5: Pomerania (Poland), Gimbutas 1989, 245, fig. 383: 2.
6: Sampohl (Germany), Hoernes 925, 531, fig. 7.
7: Hoch – Redlau (Germany), Hoernes 1925, 531, fig. 3.
8: Hoch – Redlau (Germany), Hoernes 1925, 531, fig. 6.
9: Chiuisi (Etruria/Italia), Janson 1975, 123, fig. 189.

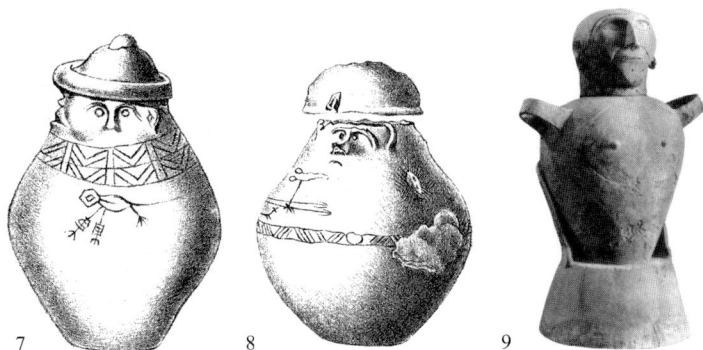

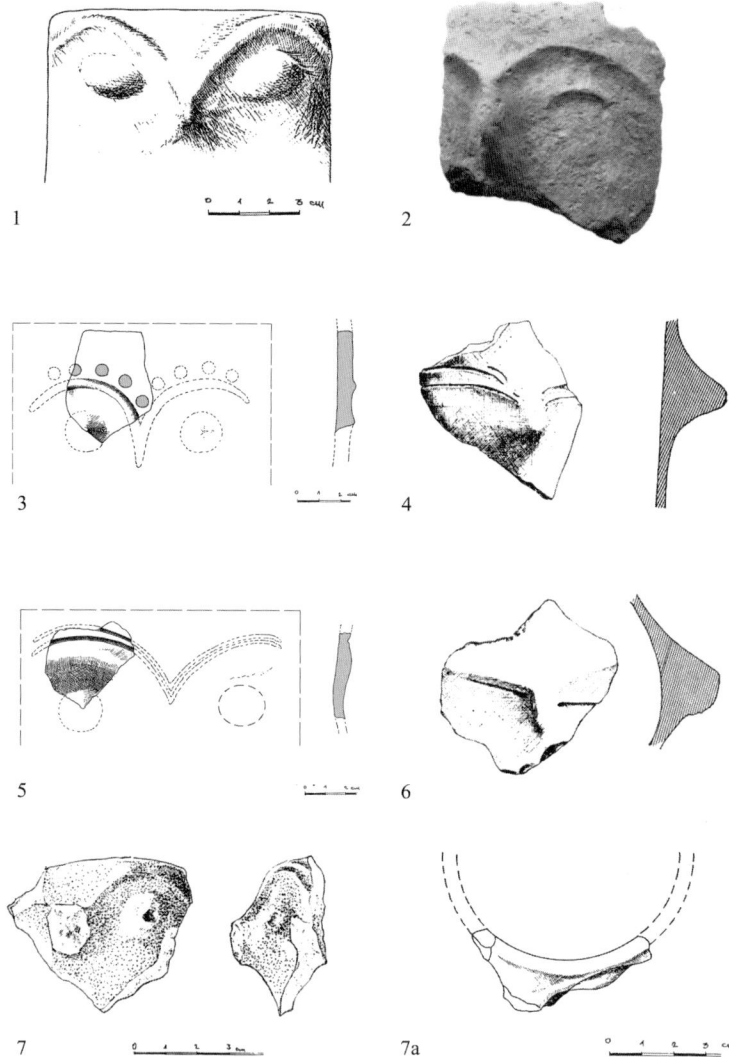

Figure 34.14. Fragments of anthropomorphic vessels from Macedonia.
1: Amzabegovo (Macedonia), Gimbutas 1976, 230, fig. 191.
2: Zelenikovo (Macedonia), Galović 1964, pl. 17: 3.
3: Amzabegovo (Macedonia), Gimbutas 1976, 217, fig. 160.
4: Angelci (Macedonia), Sanev & Stamenova 1989, pl. VI: 7.
5: Amzabegovo (Macedonia), Gimbutas 1976, 231, fig. 194.
6: Angelci (Macedonia), Sanev & Stamenova 1989, pl. VI: 5.
7–7a: Amzabegovo (Macedonia), Gimbutas 1976, 230, fig. 189, 190.

4. Rebirth in the burial womb

The house as a funeral space unites infant burials in vessels, bags and ovens. The debate over the predominance of child burials in dwellings rejected hypothesis of infanticide (Borić and Stefanović 2004, 541), although contemporary substitutes for this ritual act were present among recent Balkan populations (Čajkanović 1985, 196–202). The large number of these burials could be a result of possible birth-control within a settlement, where infants were intentionally killed so that the community would not damage its socio-economic structure. In that case, one question remains open, why should a child be buried, if it does not have an important role for the family or community?

It now seems that this burial practice was the result of biological factors. The ecological conditions combined with low immunity among neonates and infants resulted in their high mortality. In Amzabegovo of 34 skeletons, almost 50 % were infants and around 15 % juveniles (Gimbutas 1976, 410). The community was forced into performing measures in order to maintain its own continuity. Probably as a reaction to this frequent, and tragic situation, the burials inside the house were placed inside a space which was conceived of as 'capable of regeneration', so that children would be symbolically reborn there. There are several ethnographic examples of Slavic populations that practiced child burial in the house for similar reasons. In the periods of high child mortality, the family buried the last deceased child in the house. It was believed that, if buried in the sacred corner, below the window or below the parent's bed, the child would be protected by the house and its relatives (Mikov and Lozanova 1996, 37–48). Among the Mazurs in Poland, it was believed that if a dead child is buried below the threshold, it will become 'klobuk', creature-dwarf which will bring wealth to the family (Niderle 1956, 86, 88). It is assumed that this practice caused the appearance of domestic dwarfs, living next to the hearth or below the threshold and floor (Naumov 2006a, 78).

The place chosen for performing this ritual act was significant. First, because of its practical function, the house was a center where the most essential activities of the community were practiced. Provisions were stored there, food was cooked, children were born and raised, and generally, there the family was created and preserved. All of these domestic activities were a woman's duty and responsibility, so that she was a character, not by accident equated with the house. Among the people of the Balkan area there was an old saying that: 'the house does not lie on the ground, but on the woman' (Malešević 1995, 178–182).

In conclusion, I propose that models of the figurine-house directly indicate the symbolic conception of the Neolithic house. This is expressed in the intramural burials that were related to the cognitive perception of the architectonic space. The female character of the house corresponds with the patterning of internal burials symbolising the dead body, under the auspices of the 'house–mother', which will be reborn and returned to the family with the woman's next pregnancy. This ritual practice would thus provide and maintain the birthrate during critical periods, so the communities existence would continue, although respect for certain family members and the need to keep their presence in the home caused the burial of adults inside the house. Finally, intramural burials were initiated or caused by cultic behaviour, guided in two ways. First directed toward the house and its sanctity as woman-birth giver, which was manifested figuratively with the production of models of figurine-houses or models of ovens and houses with feminine features. The second cult was directed towards the deceased, and it can be only assumed that it was part of a rich and complex system of rites for communication with the world of dead. In such ways, by expressing respect of the ancestors and giving offerings in their name (food and liquids as substitutes for body and blood), it was expected that the ancestors as representatives of the imaginary, and yet for the Neolithic people, still present world of spirits, would engage in the protection and prosperity of the house where they once lived. These two cultic forms operated in the context of preserving the life and wellbeing of the family, and through them, the whole community. The matrilineal character of these forms of cults, manifested by the burials within the settlements, inside houses, ovens and vessels, developed a religious structure which related the individual and community with the numinous features of their surrounding.

Acknowledgements

I would like to thank Caroline Malone and David Barrowclough for their dedicated assistance during the editing of this paper and to Nikos Chausidis for profound discussions and indications on the useful references. I'm also grateful to Orhideja Zorova for helpful comments and corrections on an earlier draft of this paper, to Miloš Bilbija for sharing the specifications of his research in Govrlevo, to Darko Karasarlidis for making the photo of infant burial from Madjari and to Museum of Macedonia for allowing me to publish the photo of Madjari burial.

References

Antonijević, D. 1982. *Obredi i običaji balkanskih stočara.* Beograd: Srpska akademija nauka i umetnosti.

Bačvarov, K. 2003. *Neolitni pogrebalni obredi.* Sofia: Bard.

Bačvarov, K. 2004. The Birth-giving Pot: Neolithic jar burials in Southeast Europe. In Nikolov et al. (eds) *Prehistoric Thrace*: 151–160. Sofia – Stara Zagora: Institute of archaeology with museum – BAS, Regional Museum of History – Stara Zagora.

Bailey, D. 2000. *Balkan Prehistory. Exclusion, incorporation and identity.* London and New York: Routlege.

Blagojević, N. 1984. Običaji u vezi sa rodjenjem, ženidbom i smrću u titovoužičkom, požeškom i kosjeričkom kraju. *Glasnik etnografskog muzeja,* 48: 209–310.

Bocev, V. 2001. Ulogata na pragot vo običaite na Makedoncite. *Makedonski folklor,* 58/59: 207–211.

Borić, D. 2002. The Lepenski Vir conundrum: reinterpretation of the Mesolithic and Neolithic sequences in the Danube Georges. *Antiquity* 76: 1026–1039.

Borić, D. and Stefanović, S. 2004. Birth and Death: infant burials from Vlasac and Lepenski Vir. *Antiquity* 78: 526–546.

Budja, M. 2004. The transition to farming and the 'revolution' of symbols in the Balkans. From ornament to entoptic and external symbolic storage. *Documenta Praehistorica* XXXI: 59–81.

Chausidis, N. 1994. *Mitski sliki.* Skopje: Misla

Chausidis, N. 1995. Predistorija, in *Makedonija kulturno nasledstvo,* 17–45. Skopje: Misla.

Chausidis, N. 1996. The House and it's Symbolic Meanings. *Macedonian Heritage,* 2: 37–52.

Chausidis, N. 2004. *Majka – Kukja – Atena – Sofia, tipologija i semiotika na eden tip neolitski žrtvenici od R. Makedonija.* Paper presented at the XVIII simposium of Macedonian archaeological science association, Gevgelija.

Chausidis, N. and Nikolov, G. 2006. Crepna i vršnik. Mitološko – semiotićka analiza. *Studia Mythologica Slavica,* 9: 97–160.

Chausidis, N. In press. Ženata kako personifikacija na prostorot za živeenje (od neolitot do sovremeniot folklor). In *Makedonskiot teatar vo kontekst na Balkanskata teatarska sfera.*

Čajkanović, V. 1985. *O magiji i religiji.* Beograd: Prosveta.

Durman, A. 2004. *The Lame God of Vučedol. Why do all gods of metallurgy limps?* Vukovar: Gradski muzej Vukovar.

Gabelić, S. 1991. *Ciklus arhandjela u vizantiskoj umetnosti.* Beograd: Srpska akademija nauka i umetnosti.

Galović, R. 1964. Zelenikovo – neolitsko naselje. *Zbornik Narodnog Muzeja* V: 127–167.

Garašanin, M. and Garašanin, D. 1961. Neolitska naselba "Vršnik" kaj selo Tarinci. *Zbornik na štipskiot naroden muzej* II: 7–40. Štip.

Garašanin, M. 1969. Barutnica, Amzabegovo – višeslojno neolitsko naselje, *Arheološki Pregled* 11: 15–19.

Garašanin, M. 1979. Centralno – balkanska zona. In A. Benac (ed.) *Praistorija jugoslavenskih zemalja II – neolit*: 79–212. Sarajevo, Academy of Science and Art of Bosnia and Hercegovina.

Garašanin, M. 1982. *Umetnost na tlu Jugoslavije – Praistorija*. Beograd: Izdavački zavod Jugoslavija.

Gimbutas, M. 1976. *Neolithic Macedonia*. Los Angeles: University of California.

Gimbutas, M. 1989. *The Language of the Goddess*. London: Thames and Hudson.

Grifoni Cremonesi R. 1994. Observations on the problems related to certain cult phenomena during the Neolithic in the Italian Peninsula. *Journal of European Archaeology vol. 2.2*: 179–197.

Hodder, I. 1990. *The Domestication of Europe – Structure and Cognistency in Neolithic Societes*. Oxford: Blackwell.

Hoernes, M. 1925. *Urgeschichte der Bildenden Kunst in Europa*. Wien: Kunstverlag Anton Schroll and Co.

Janson, H. W. 1975. Istorija umetnosti. Beograd: Izdavački zavod Jugoslavija.

Kolištrkovska – Nasteva, I. 2005. *Praistoriskite dami od Makedonija*. Skopje: Muzej na Makedonija.

Mikov, L. and Lozanova, G. 1996. Burial in one's own land. *Glasnik etnografskog instituta SANU* XLV: 37–48.

Mitrevski, D. 1997. *Protoistoriskite zaednici vo Makedonija*. Skopje: Republički zavod za zaštita na spomenicite na kulturata.

Mitrevski, D. 2001. *Staromakedonskiot grad na Vardarski Rid*. Skopje: Fondacija Vardarski Rid.

Moses, S. 2006. Children and Childhood in Tradition and Ritual at Çatalhöyük. In *Çatalhöyük From Earth to Eternity*. Istanbul: Yapi ve Kredi Bankasi, 170–184.

Naumov, G. 2005. Neolitski slikani ornamenti, *Kulturen Život* 3: 66–77.

Naumov, G. 2006a. Sadot, pećkata i kukjata vo simbolićka relacija so matkata i ženata (neolitski predloški i etnografski implikacii). *Studia Mythologica Slavica* 9: 59–95.

Naumov, G. 2006b. *The Vessel as a Human Body: Neolithic anthropomorphic vessels and their reflection in later periods*, paper presented at international conference for Prehistoric pottery "Breaking the Mould: challenging the past through pottery". Manchester.

Neumann, E. 1963. *The Great Mother*. New York: Bollingen Foundation.

Niderle, L. 1956. *Slavjanskie drevnosti*. Moskva.

Papazovska, A. 2006. Pogrebuvanja na Vardarski Rid, in Mitrevski, D. (ed.). Vardarski Rid. Skopje: Fondacija Vardarski Rid, 385–397.

Pavuk, J. 1981. *Umenie a život kamennej*. Tatran.

Perles, C. 2001. *The Early Neolithic in Greece. The first farming communities in Europe*. Cambridge: Cambridge University Press.

Petrović, B. 2001. Model neolitske peći iz Progara. *Godišnjak grada Beograda* XLVII – XLVIII: 11–21.

Radunćeva, A. *et al.* 2002. *Neolitnoto selište do grad Rakitovo*. Razkopki i proućvanija XXIX, Sofia.

Sanev, V. 1988. Neolitskoto svetilište od "Tumba" vo Madjari. *Macedoniae Acta Archaeologica* 9, 9–30.

Sanev, V. and Stamenova, M. 1989. Neolitska naselba "Stranata" vo selo Angelci. *Zbornik na trudovi*: 9–63. Strumica.

Sanev, V. et al. 1976. *Praistorija vo Makedonija*. Skopje: Arheološko društvo na SR Makedonija.

Stalio, B. 1977. *Neolit na tlu Srbije*. Beograd: Narodni Muzej.

Stanković, S. 1992. *Sakralna mesta i predmeti u starijeneolitskim kulturama Centralno – balkanskog područja*. PhD. Dissertation, Beograd.

Stojanović, L. 1999. Sparagmosot i antropofagijata kako inicijacisko doživuvanje. *Makedonski folklor* 53, 183–193.

Todorova, H. and Vaisov, I. 1993. *Novo – kamennata epoha v Blgarija*. Sofia: Nauka i Izkustvo.

Truhelka, Č.1930. Larizam i krsna slava. *Glasnik skopskog naučnog društva* VII – VIII: 1–33.

Vasileva, M. 2005. *Kade e našeto minato. Voved kon praistorijata na Pelagonija*. Bitola: Visoi.

Veljanovska, F. 2000. *Antropološki karakteristiki na naselenieto na Makedonija od neolit do Sreden Vek*. Skopje: Republički zavod za zaštita na spomenicite na kulturata.

Veljanovska, F. 2006. Neolitski skeletni naodi od Pista – Novo Selo, *Macedoniae Acta Archaeologica* 17: 341–350.

Chapter 35

A FIRE CULT IN SOUTH EUROPEAN CHALCOLITHIC TRADITIONS? ON THE RELATIONSHIP BETWEEN RITUAL CONTEXTS AND THE INSTRUMENTALITY OF FIRE

Dragos Gheorghiu

Introduction

Discussion of cult(s) in the Chalcolithic societies of South East Europe meet with general agreement on limiting the subject to anthropomorphic figurines (see Bailey 2000, 102), small ceramic objects described as 'altars', or to 'temples', 'cult buildings', or 'shrines' (Dumitrescu 1968; Radunćeva 1989; Chapman 1991; Lazarovici *et al.* 2001), which differ little from houses in settlement (see Ursulescu 2001). The complex religious experience of the tell builders of the fifth millennium BC is reduced to these few components disregarding the fact that all the Chalcolithic cultures of South East Europe resulted from a combination of natural elements like clay, water, and fire, whose significant presence have been the subject of a cult in different societies around the world. Of these elements fire is the main absentee from the study of the cult and religion of South East European Chalcolithic societies (cf. Biehl *et al.* 2001), although it is very common in the archaeological record, through the various pyro-objects, and through the remains of fired objects, houses or settlements.

How can the complexity of a cult of fire be approached?

Extensive information about a fire cult in a traditional society is offered by the *Rig Veda*, (Eliade 1977a, 282) which presents a large spectrum of cultic elements for Agni – the god of fire, worshipped *'day by day with prayer* as *lord and master of the home* and *sovereign lord of men (Rg.V.II, 1, 1–2, 9, 14), domestic priest, divine minister of sacrifice, invoker, greatest bestower of wealth, dispeller of the night, ruler of sacrifices, guard of the Law (Rg.V I, 1, 1–2, 7–9), lord and master in our home,* and last, but not least the way by which *mortal men give sweetness to their drink' (Rg.V II, 1, 1–2, 9, 14).*

These attributes present the cult of Agni as the result of the addition and intertwining of various rituals (performed in different contexts) which can be used as a model for the identification of cult in prehistoric traditions. From our archaeological perspective, the main value of the text is that it identifies pyro-rituals in diverse contexts and reveals connections of meaning between them. These may infer the presence of a fire cult in the Chalcolithic traditions of South Eastern Europe, a subject neglected until now by archaeologists. Thus a second basic question is: how can a prehistoric fire ritual be approached? According to Lewis (1980, 6), there are two kinds of theories on ritual: those which insist on the individuality of ritual ('contrasting ritual/magical activity with technical/utilitarian activity', Bell 1992, 70), and those which stress the identity of ritual with other human activities (Althabe 1987). According to some anthropologists ritual is a non-instrumental action with symbolic or expressive value (Douglas 1973), while for others it is an instrumental act (Bell 1992, 70).

I consider that the aspects of ritual complexity that can be reconstructed from the archaeological record of prehistoric households and settlements are those derived from the technology of that society (i.e. the making and utilization of objects and the use of various instruments, including fire, or in other words, the instrumental aspect of rituals). A technological process of making objects (i.e. a *chaîne-opératoire*) can be identified within a ritual process, since this is the result of repetitive (Goody 1977), formalized procedures (Rappaport 1979), whose stages cannot be changed, and can be perceived as a 'technological ritual' of making. This relationship between technology and ritual was not exploited by archaeologists because technology was, and still is, positioned in the profane zone of human activity (see, for example, Dobres 2000, 70 ff.), the ritual characteristics being identified with the secular ritualization (Moore and Myerhoff 1977) or the mundane *habitus* (Bourdieu 1977; Gosden 1994, 119; Dobres 2000, 137 ff.) because 'technical activity is described as pragmatic... and instrumentally effective' (Bell 1992, 70). One example of ritual may result from the direct relationship between the Pyroinstruments (see Gheorghiu in press) that support combustion and control air-draught. The present paper will describe and interpret these specific technological rituals.

Given that a ritual is contextual (Bell 1992, 220; Gosden 1999, 129), my approach will begin with the presentation and analysis of different kinds of pyro-contexts, from the macro-scale of geography to the micro-scale of household pyro-technologies. I will discuss the *state of interaction* between rituals (in the interactionist perspective set by Goffman 1973, or of the anthropology of communication, (Winkin 1996) and will describe the experimentation of some of the contexts analysed.

The natural context

The geographical context of this study is the left bank of the cyclically flooded wetlands of the Lower Danube river area in southern Romania (Figure 35.1). Palynological evidence indicates cycles of burning of the rich local vegetation (Carciumaru *et al.* 2004) (Pyne 2001, 66 ff.), which served to both fertilize the fields and to clear the wetland environment of settlements. At the base of the Harsova Tell (Boian tradition, second half of the sixth millennium to first half of the fifth millennium BC (Bem 2000–2001, 49, figure 7)) sections created by river erosion outside the perimeter of the protective palisade, show numerous overlapped layers of burnt vegetal material resulting from cyclical flooding events. In this case the repetitive natural process is reflected culturally by the pyrotechnology which was part of a recurrent ritual.

The architectural context

Intra-settlement spatial organization forms a second theme. The Lower Danube Chalcolithic was characterized by the emergence of tell-settlements, which after a period of dynamic settlement (Neagu 2000, 27; Bailey *et al.* 2002) were burnt and abandoned. The overlapping tell-settlements formed a cultural and natural alluvium or as defined by Andrew Sherratt (1997, 22) 'habitation monuments'. They were built according to an organized plan (Comsa 1997; Todorova 1982), and surrounded by ditches and a palisade (Comsa 1963; Comsa 1997; Pandrea *et al.* 1999). It is generally agreed that the dimensions of these structures of separation indicate that their role was more symbolic than defensive (Hasotti 1997, 77; Marinescu-Bilcu 1974, 20); and for the wetland tells I ascribe, an additional protective function against flooding (Gheorghiu 2006a).

Compared with the nearby open, flat settlements, such as Cascioarele-Ostrovel (Dumitrescu 1965), Radovanu (Comsa 1997, 150), Uzunu, or Tangaru (Gheorghiu 2006a, 7), tells surrounded by ditches and palisades seem to have

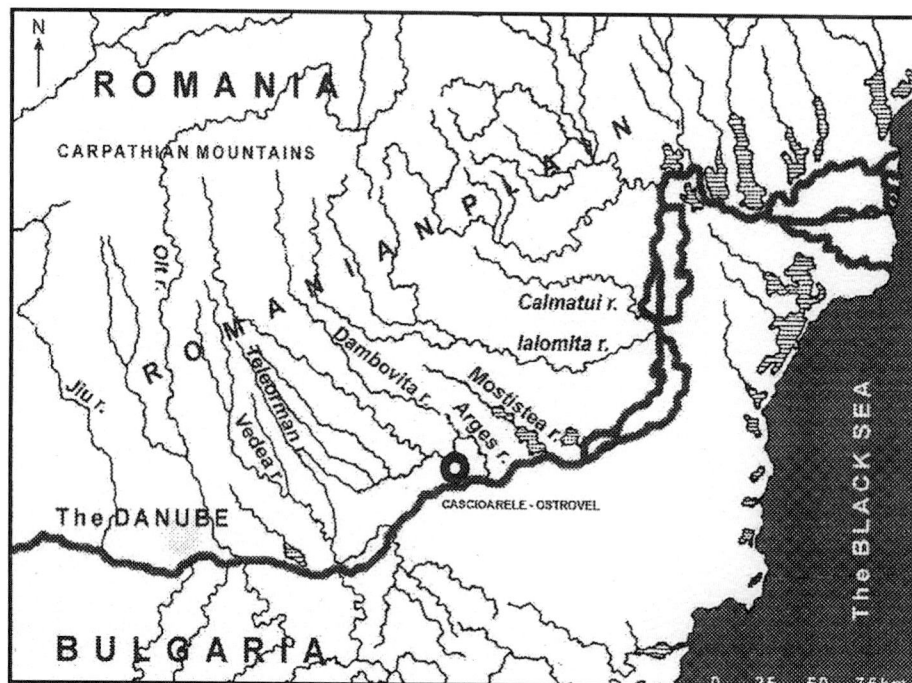

Figure 35.1. Map of the Lower Danube region showing the position of the Cascioarele-Ostrovel tell-settlement.

been strongly ritualized spaces. They underlined rites of separation with a standardized geometrical spatial organization which generated particular proxemics.

The cyclical dynamic occupation of the land and the uses of fire

The Late Chalcolithic *tells* of the Lower Danube were located in particular places, but their development was not the result of continuous growth (Bailey 1997; Gheorghiu 2006a), but of temporary settlement. This was characterized by cyclical firing and abandonment which seems to have been specific to the Balkan area (Erdoğu 2005, 31; van Andel *et al.* 1995). Douglas Bailey (1997), for instance, identified thirteen overlapping levels of settling at the Ovčarovo tell, separated by levels of abandonment. An unequivocal example of cyclical burning and abandonment in the Lower Danube area is the Cascioarele-Ostrovel tell, situated on a lake island near the Danube River (Dumitrescu 1965; 1986). Here, at the first fired occupation level a house was excavated with two plastered wooden posts covered with coloured patterns. Because of its rich interior design, it was interpreted by the excavator as a cultic building. The fired level was separated from the second fired level by a layer of alluvium resulting from the flooding of the Danube River.

The second fired level of occupation produced an architectural model and was interpreted as a 'sanctuary' or a 'temple' (Dumitrescu 1968). The second level was also covered with a layer of alluvium. Excavation of the third level revealed an architectural complex of sixteen fired houses (Dumitrescu 1986, 74). Cascioarele-Ostrovel tell's sequence of fired and alluvial layers, is a good example of the ritual (i.e. an intentional repeated action) of setting fire to the settlement and the palisade which protected it against flooding (Gheorghiu 2006a).

The house

Tell houses are an ideal subject for the study of ritual contexts because they are the result and focus of several rituals of construction and deconstruction (Gheorghiu 2001) and the location for many others. From the perspective of the relationship between the tell and its environment, each house seems to have been the consequence of the first stage of de-contextualization from the landscape of the building materials (an operation equivalent to a sort of annihilation of the natural order). Clay, wood, straw and reed were brought inside the settlement (Figure 35.2) and there re-contextualized within the cultural order of the tell-settlement (Figure 35.3). Therefore to deconstruct (to fire) a house was an action equivalent to the deconstruction (firing) of the landscape (for similarities between the firing regimes of villages and landscapes (Pyne 2001, 113).

Figure 35.2. A wattle and daub house in the process of building, Vadastra village 2005.

Figure 35.3 A finished wattle and daub house, Vadastra village 2003.

The technological context

A further ritual context to be analysed is that of the pyrotechnologies of the household using the principle of air-draught. These represent technological rituals which function on similar physical principles and human actions. The design of Chalcolithic houses was shaped by a composite assemblage of air-draught pyro-objects. The perforated walls look very similar to those used in structures designed for the dairy production process (Todorova 1982, 84, figure 50; 120, figures 73–74; Voinea 2005, plate 81, figures 12–13; plate 88, figure 14; plate 89, figures 4–5), whose function is to dry, to heat food and drink, to boil, to bake, to keep embers burning, to smoke, to start fire, and to draw out smoke.

From the spatial organization of the interior of the houses, as well as from the numerous miniature clay models (like the Ovǧarovo model of the interior of a house; (Todorova 1982, 40, figure 24)) it seems that the most important pyro-object was the oven, which was modelled in the shape of a small house. The air-draught of the oven was controlled by means of ceramic devices. The large aperture of the oven mouth, with its associated large covers, was used to control air flow (this type of object being frequent in the Cucuteni-Tripolye tradition). The dome aperture, with its small flues or ceramic plugs (Merkyte 2005, 52/53, figure III, 13), sometimes has anthropomorphic traits (see *Civilizatia Boian* 1999: 43, figure

82). Some Balkan anthropomorphic clay models have perforations and openings for air-draught, (Naumov, *this volume*), and stress the similarities between the female body and the house-shaped oven, an analogy that can be found within the *Homeric Hymns* which ascribes to this pyro-object a cultic role under the female symbolism of Hestia, the goddess of the oven, and implicitly the goddess of fire (*Homeric Hymns,* To Hestia, I, 5, in Humbert 1936). Traces of fire inside one of these pyro-instruments (Naumov, *personal communication*), may suggest a connection between the symbolism of fire and that of the female body (for ethnographic examples of a relationship between female sexuality and fire see Eliade 1977b). It is tempting to associate this interpretation in the Chalcolithic Balkans to the existence of a gendered deity of fire, with and without an iconic representation.

Another pyro-instrument with perforations which emerged at the beginning of the Neolithic, and spread in diverse Chalcolithic traditions, from the Levant (see Rowan, this volume) to the Balkans, and was ascribed to the cult arena but whose function has not yet been identified, is represented by cups with perforated pedestals. One function for these objects, if they were positioned on embers, was to warm a liquid content. An additional use was as a censer, as experiments seem to confirm. In the north-east of the Lower Danube area, the Cucuteni-Tripolye tradition used this type of vase, some of which have traces of soot deposits and an alteration in the painting on the lower part of the pedestal, which infers that they were positioned in embers. One remarkable Cucuteni vase (labelled by archaeologists as 'The Dance from Frumusica') has a preserved pedestal with several slits, which represents a group of anthropomorphic figurines positioned in the round. I interpret this as being the evocation of an enchained human group surrounding the fire, in a collective trance-like attitude. Last but not least, the most important pyroinstrument of the Chalcolithic was the up-draught kiln with a perforated platform. This structure helped to create a high quality and diverse ceramic production. Its presence is attested archaeologically from the sixth millennium BC in Mesopotamia (Simson 1997, 39) and in South Eastern Europe around the fifth to fourth millennia BC (Markevic 1981 and Comsa 1976, 25). Although not yet identified by archaeologists in the Lower Danube area, probably because of their eccentric position in relation to settlements, the up-draught kilns with perforated platforms are known in the Gumelnita tradition. This is inferred by the high quality of the ceramics and the technique of three-phase firing with yellow patterns on a black background (a technique rediscovered by the Greeks in the sixth century BC, Gheorghiu 2006b, 31). Experiments with kilns reveal a special relationship between the operator and the pyro-instrument, a phenomenological experience with mystical significance (Gheorghiu 2007). This is the reason why I believe that household pyro-technology, using the same physical principle, could have had a spiritual quality beside its profane use.

Ceramic models: house, fire and rituality

Among the objects from the technological context which demonstrate the control of fire through the use of air-draught, were the so-called 'cheese-strainers' (Figure 35.4) modelled in the form of small corbel-shaped ceramic vases with perforated walls. Their presence in the archaeological record continues into the Bronze Age. Jacqui Wood ascribes to them the function of 'Bunsen lamps' for metal working (Wood 2007; Wood cited in Gibson 2002), as 'portable kilns' (Harding 2007; and as 'fire vessels' (Merkyte 2005, 52). My experiments have showed that an additional function for the Chalcolithic objects could have been as ember-protectors and fire-starters. This function is shared with another category of ceramic objects with larger perforations, identified in the present paper as 'censer', some of them exhibiting an architectural shape. I believe that the particular iconic form, function and provenience of this second object category could present new data on the ritual relationship between Chalcolithic pyrotechnology and the house. This idea is inspired by the experimental work I carried out building replicas of prehistoric wattle and daub houses defended by palisades (Gheorghiu 2005). There seems to be a very high degree of similarity between the image of a row of ordered houses (Figure 35.5) surrounded by a palisade, seen from a certain distance from the settlement, and the 'incensors' from the tells of Cascioarele-Ostrovel (Figure 35.6) and Gumelnita (Figure 35.7), which can be decoded as the image of a group of houses behind a palisade (Gheorghiu 2002, 103; Gheorghiu

Figure 35.4 Replicas and original (down right) corbelled-shaped pyro-objects, Vadastra village 2002.

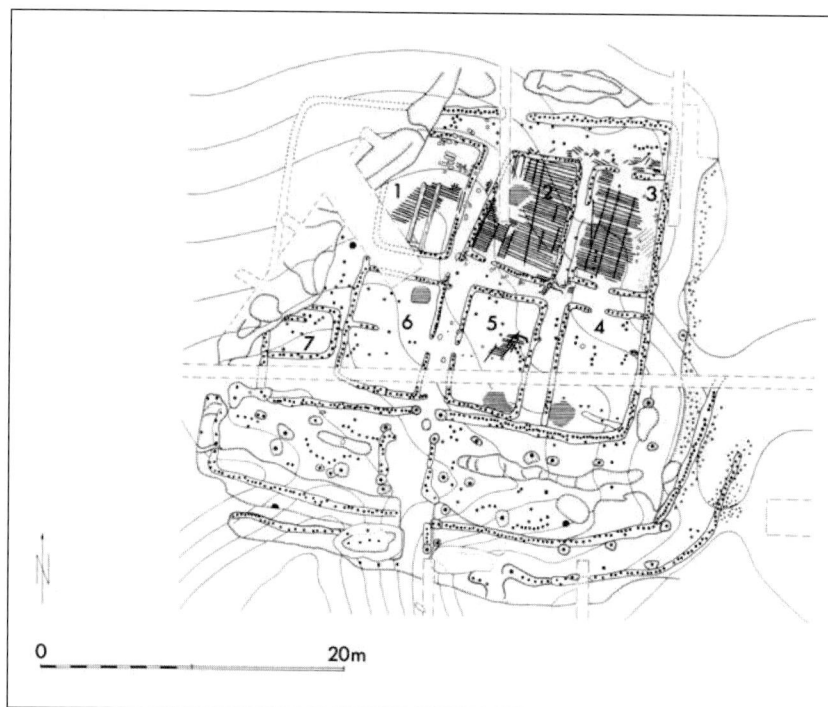

Figure 35.5 Plan of Ovcarovo tell (Bulgaria) with a double palisade (after Todorova 1982) and a tentative reconstruction of a house, Vadastra village 2005).

Figure 35.6. Ceramic model from Cascioarele-Ostrvel tell. Gumelnita tradition (National Museum of History, Bucharest).

2003, 41; Gheorghiu 2005). Other air-draught objects of this kind, like the houses with perforated walls and roofs from Sultana (Figure 35.8), Kodzadermen (Gaul 1948) and Drama tells (Lichardus *et al.* 1996, 30, figure 12) could be interpreted as representing the whole settlement. The number of perforations of the objects mentioned generally corresponds with the number of houses in a level of the settlement. They can therefore be interpreted as the number of 'smokes' or 'fires', which are an index for the hearths and, consequently, houses in the settlement. The last pyro-object to be discussed within this context is the interior of the house. Its intended function was to create a powerful up-draught during occupation as well as during its final destruction. All of the house's openings would generate a strong air-draught that could control the combustion of the walls and ceiling. The wattle and daub construction of the walls would permit a good circulation of air and flames during their combustion.

In conclusion to this discussion of the technological context, all the pyro-objects found within the Chalcolithic household, or in relation to it, and which contain perforations, were used to control air draught, demonstrating a structured and ordered, even instrumental (i.e. ritualistic) utilization of fire.

The firing of the house as a macro context and the ceramic models as a micro constructed context

From the many examples dating from the prehistoric Anatolian-Balkan technocomplex, it seems likely that a fire cult existed which is invisible in the material culture 'package', except for the fired houses. In Anatolia, at PPNB Čayönü and at the early Neolithic site of Yumuktepe (Caneva 1999, 109), alongside the ritual of burying buildings (Özdoğan 1999, 50–51), there is an indication of funerary rituals in relation with the firing of houses. However, the examples from the mid phase of the Skull building and the house from the cell phase from Čayönü are not yet convincing enough to demonstrate an intentional act of combustion (Özdoğan, pers. comm.).

The first mention in the archaeological literature of burnt houses and settlements in the Lower Danube-East Carpathian Chalcolithic (Figure 35.9) dates from as early as the mid 1950s (Berciu 1959; Petrescu-Dambovita and Florescu 1959; Dumitrescu and Dumitrescu 1959), but the notion of intentional firing of the Balkan-Lower Danube houses and settlements only came at the end of the last century (Stevanović 1997; 2002; Chapman 1999;

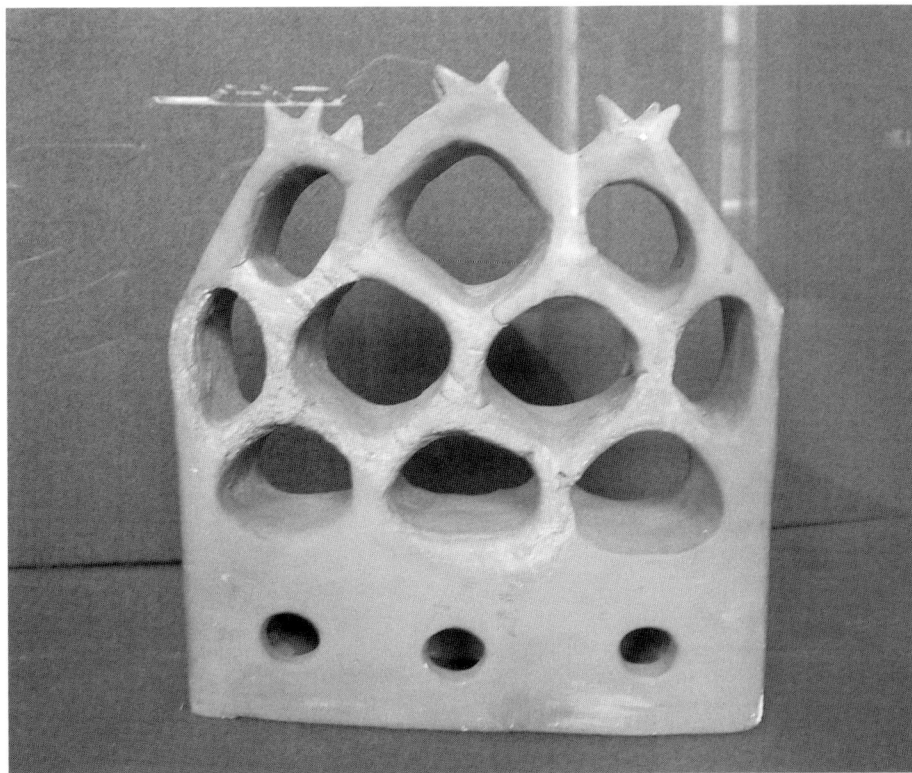

Figure 35.7. Ceramic model from Gumelnita eponymous tell. Gumelnita tradition. (Oltenita Museum of History).

Figure 35.8. Ceramic model from Sultana tell. Gumelnita tradition (Oltenita Museum of History).

Gheorghiu 2005) inspired by the work of Professor Ruth Tringham (Tringham 1992; 1994; Tringham and Krstič 1990), although recent approaches do not credibly explain the intentionality of the firing process (like that of Bankoff and Winter 1979), which was not tested in actual experiments. For this reason, I believe that direct experimentation with the air-draught process of firing on full-scale replicas of prehistoric houses can help us understand the possible intentionality and instrumentality of the combustion process and allow us to analyse it within the cultic context.

Experiment: an artificial context for archaeological inspiration

An experiment with the combustion of a full-scale wattle and daub house could help us to understand better the behaviour of the materials (Tringham 1978, 182), the technological and ritual processes of building (cf. Mathieu 2002), and also enable us to imagine the theatrical context of the ritual itself. There are innumerable details of the processes studied that cannot be imagined, and which can only be observed in the experimental built context (Figure 35.10). All the experiments of combustion that I have coordinated (Gheorghiu 2005) have revealed the difficulty of firing a wattle and daub *megaron* house or palisade, up to the moment when one exploited the air-draught created by the architectural openings (Figures 35.11 and 35.12)

Figure 35.9. Layers of fired houses at the base of the Harsova tell on the Danube river banks. Boian tradition.

Figure 35.10. Experiment of firing a wattle and daub house, Vadastra village 2006.

Figure 35.11. A strong air-draught produced by the combustion of the interior of the house. Vadastra village 2006.

Figure 35.12. A ceramic tube created after the combustion of a structural post. Vadastra village 2006.

and employed an unusual amount of combustive material inside the structure. Only then did one reach the high temperatures identified in the fired daub found in the archaeological record. The air-draught is another invisible detail that needs experimentation in order to be made visible. During the process of combustion, the house transforms itself into a gigantic brazier. The lateral windows and the attic openings generate an air-draught sufficient to initiate the combustion of the inner wooden structure, which in time creates ceramic tubes and discontinuities within the walls that function like the perforated surface of household pyro-instruments. When seen at night-time, the process of combustion of the internal wooden structure of the walls appears like a series of bright light spots where the clay protection of the wood structure has fallen off (Figure 35.13).

One of the revelations of the experiments came from the work with the air-draught of the architectural models of the 'censer'. A similar visual experience to the combustion of a wattle and daub house can be obtained when putting embers inside these ceramic objects, (Figure 35.14) because the air-draught created through the lateral perforations generates smoke and flames which burst through other perforations in the palisade or the roof of the models (Figure 35.15). While not yet recognised as representing a form of experimental archaeology (Mathieu 2002, 4), the phenomenological experience of the reconstructed contexts

offers the archaeologist the chance of a more nuanced interpretation, particularly when trying to identify the ritual actions of the intentional firing of houses. The personal emotional experience of reconstructing mentally the real event and the real context generated by these small clay models allowed me to view them as 'object-context evokers', like a sort of ritual instrument used by individuals (perceived in Turner's [1974] perspective of the 'performative' approach to the social drama) to evoke at a micro-scale the macro-scale process of firing the real houses (Figures 35.16–17).

Concluding remarks

There are two cultic aspects which can be identified from the experiments of firing the house: the influence of the physical process on the *sight* and *memory* of the participants and the *energy expenditure* (Renfrew and Bahn 1991, 360; Renfrew 1997, 31) needed to achieve the process of combustion. The firing of a house or settlement can be imagined as significant community rituals. The collective, monumental effort to cut, bring and position the building materials, and later the fuel, would involve most, if not all, the community. The spectacular images generated by the process of combustion would be impressed upon the individual's and the community's visual memory.

If a monument means an oversized 'construction to

Figure 35.13. Image of the combustion of the house at night, Vadastra village 2006.

Figure 35.14. Experiment with the replica of the Cascioarele-Ostrovel clay model positioned on embers. Vadastra village 2003.

Figure 35.15. Experiment with the replica of the Cascioarele-Ostrovel clay model positioned on embers. Vadastra village 2003. One can see the direction of air-flow which goes in at the base of the object.

Figure 35.16. Experiments with the combustion of a wattle and daub house and the use of Cascioarele-Ostrovel model as incensor, Vadastra village 2006.

Figure 35.17. Experiments with the combustion of a wattle and daub house and the Sultana model, Vadastra village 2006.

remind the later generations of what had gone before' (Bradley 2002, 110), these tells seem to have been a special kind of monument, with a different type of visibility, which insists on the rite of separation. To fire a house is a process of irreversible transformation into ceramics of a part of the building material which symbolizes the landscape. The firing could represents an act of setting the memory of the place (and of the landscape) into a durable material (Regenye, in press), and of transforming *in time* a segregated place in the landscape into a visible monument. If the separation of habitation by means of ditches and palisades from the rest of the environment is interpreted as a technique to create a ritual context (as the result of rites of passage/separation), then the tell should be approached as a ritual arena and a cultic place.

One can conclude that the contextual character of rituals allows a multi-scalar analysis which, moving from macro to micro perspectives, could be an efficient instrument for identifying unnoticed associations of significance in the archaeological record.

A comparative approach between different levels of ritual offers the possibility of discovering relationships of meaning between different levels of ritual activity. For example, the analogies of shape between oven and house, or the functional analogy between the fire starters, up-draught kilns and house-like 'censers' on one hand, and

the interior space of the house on the other, or the symbolic analogy between the firing of the landscape and the firing of the house.

The distinctive individuality of the Chalcolithic in the Lower Danube area can be found in the explicit visualization of the relations between the levels of ritual contexts expressed within the material culture. The interaction between the macro rituals of the community and the micro rituals of the household, are manifested most eloquently through 'object-context evokers'. These objects represent the visualization of the symbolic relationship between household rituals and the cyclical firing of houses, which demonstrate a direct relationship between several ritual contexts at different dimensional scales. The coherence of cult appears to be based on the instrumentality of fire. All the analogies between forms and between technologies, could have worked more efficiently under an altered perception of the ritual contexts. The corbelled 'fire-starters', the perforated pedestalled cups, and the house models, 'censors', probably also served this purpose.

Finally, the phenomenological sensorial experience of the Chalcolithic pyroinstruments (which used the air-draught to animate the fire inside them), could be sensed as being the material support for an *animated* presence, which could have been perceived by prehistoric people as representing a *being*, a deity of fire.

Acknowledgements

The author would like to thank the following. Dr Caroline Malone (University of Cambridge), for the invitation to participate to the conference, her proof reading of this paper and for her constant kind support; Dr David A. Barrowclough (University of Cambridge) for the kind help in organizing my travel to the UK and for correcting my English in the final paper; Dr Simon Stoddart (University of Cambridge) for his kind care and scholarly dialogue during the conference; Mr Robin Hardie (University of Cambridge) for improving the English of the paper presented at the conference; Professor Mehmet Özdoğan (University of Istanbul, Turkey) for sharing the information about the fired houses from Anatolia; Dr Goce Naumov (Republic of Macedonia) for the information on house-figurines; Dr Romeo Dumitrescu (Cucuteni Foundation, Romania) for financing the building of the house for experiment and for allowing the study of the Cucuteni pedestalled vases from the Foundation's collection; Dr Fabio Cavulli (University of Trento, Italy) for the methodological support in preparing the experiment of combustion of the house; Dr Alex Gibson (Bradford University) for initiating the use of prehistoric 'Bunsen lamps' and for collaboration on up-draught kilns experiments; Dr Dorin Teodorescu (Romanian Ministry of Culture, Department of Olt County, Slatina, Romania) for his continuous support of the experiments; Catalin Oancea, Marius Stroe, Dragos Manea, and Stefan Ungureanu, (artists and students of the National University of Arts, Bucharest) for building the wattle and daub prehistoric house; Andreea Oprita (student, National University of Arts, Bucharest) for building the replica of the Cascioarele ceramic model; Marin Batranca and Adrian Penescu (Vadastra village, Romania) for the help in organizing the experiments, and, last but not least, Cornelia Catuna for the editorial help. All the experiments were possible due to two CNCSIS grants (Nos. 1612 and 945), one grant from the Romanian Ministry of Culture (2005) and the financial support of the Cucuteni Foundation (2005 and 2006).

Photographs by Dragos Gheorghiu (1–9, 12, 14–17) and Gelu Serseniuc (10,11,13).

References

Althabe, G. 1987. Les rites contemporains. *Terrain* 8. Paris, Mission du Patrimoine.

Bailey, D. W. 2000. *Balkan Prehistory. Exclusion, Incorporation and Identity*. London and New York, Routledge.

Bailey, D. W. 1997. Impermanence and flux in the landscape of early agricultural in South Eastern Europe. In J. Chapman and P. Dolukhanov (eds). *Landscapes in flux. Central and Eastern Europe in Antiquity*. Oxford, Oxbow Books, 41–58.

Bailey D. W., Andreescu, R., Howard. A.J., Macklin, M.G. and Mills, S. 2002. Alluvial landscapes in the temperate Balkan Neolithic: transition to tells. *Antiquity* 76, 349–355.

Bankoff, F., and Winter, F. 1979. A House-burning in Serbia. *Archaeology* 32, 8–14.

Bell, C. 1992. *Ritual Theory, Ritual Practice*. Oxford, Oxford University Press.

Bem, C. 2000–2001. Noi propuneri pentru o schita cronologica a eneoliticului romanesc. *Pontica* XXXIII–XXXIV, 25–120.

Berciu, D. 1959. Sapaturile de la Tangaru si Petru Rares. *Materiale si Cercetari Arheologice*. Bucharest, Editura Academiei, 137–146.

Biehl, P. F., Bertemes, F., and Meller, H. (eds) 2001. *The Archaeology of Cult and Religion*. Budapest, Archaeolingua.

Bourdieu, P. 1977. *Outline of a Theory of Practice*. Cambridge, Cambridge University Press.

Bradley, R. 2002. *The Past in Prehistoric Societies*. London, Routledge.

Caneva, I. 1999. Early farmers on the Cylician coast: Yumuktepe in the Seventh Millennium BC. In M. Özdoğan and N. Bašgelen (eds). *Neolithic in Turkey. The Cradle of Civilization*. Istanbul, Ancient Anatolian Civilization Series 3, 105–114.

Carciumaru, M., Plesa, M., and Margarit, M. 2004. *Omul si plantele. Manual de Analiza Carpological*. Targoviste, Cetatea de Scaun.

Chapman, J. 1999, Deliberate house-burning in the prehistory of Central and Eastern Europe. In A. Gustafsson and H. Karlsson (eds). *Glyfer och arkeologiska rum–en vanbok till Jarl Nordbladh*. Gotarc Series A, Vol.3. 113–126.

Chapman, J. 1991. The creation of social arenas in the Neolithic and Copper Age of South east Europe: the case of Varna. In P. Garwood, P. Jennings, R. Skeates and J. Tomas (eds). *Sacred and Profane*. Oxford, Oxbow Books, 152–171.

Civilizatia Boian pe teritoriul Romaniei, [cat.] 1999. Calarasi, The Lower Danube Museum.

Comsa, E. 1997. Tipurile de asezari din epoca neolitica din Muntenia, *Cultura si Civilizatie la Dunarea de Jos* XV, 144–164.

Comsa, E. 1976. Caracteristicile si insemnatatea cuptoarelor de ars din aria culturii Cucuteni-Ariusd. *SCIVA* 27, 1, 23–33.

Comsa, E. 1963. Unele probleme ale aspectului cultural Aldeni II. *SCIV*, 14, I, 10–11.

Dobres, M-A. 2000. *Technology and Social Agency. Outlining a practice framework for archaeology*. Oxford, Blackwell.

Douglas, M. 1973. *Natural Symbols*. New York, Random House.

Dumitrescu, H. 1968. Un modèle de sanctuaire découvert dans la station énéolithique de Cascioarele. *Dacia* NS XII, 381–394.

Dumitrescu, H. and Dumitrescu, V.1959. Sapaturile de la Traian-Dalul Fantanilor. *Materiale si Cercetari Arheologice*. Bucharest, Editura Academiei,157–178.

Dumitrescu, V. 1986. Stratigrafia asezatii-tell de pe ostrovelul de la Cascioarele. *Cultura si Civilizatie la Dunarea de Jos* 2, 73–81.

Dumitrescu, V. 1965. Principalele rezultate ale primelor doua campanii de sapaturi din asezarea neolitica tarzie de la Cascioarele. *SCIV*, 16, 2, 215–237.

Eliade, M. 1977a. *From Primitives to Zen. A Thematic Sourcebook of the History of Religions*. San Francisco, Harper and Row.

Eliade, M. 1977b. *Forgerons et Alchimistes*. Paris, Flammarion.

Erdoğu, B. 2005. *Prehistoric Settlements of Eastern Thrace*. BAR International Series 1424. Oxford, Archaeopress.

Gaul, J. H. 1948. *The Neolithic Period in Bulgaria*. Cambridge, MA, Peabody Museum of Harvard University.

Gheorghiu, D. In press. Chalcolithic pyroinstruments with air-draught: an outline. In D. Gheorghiu (ed.). *Fire As An Instrument: The Archaeology of Pyrotechnologies*. BAR International Series. Oxford, Archaeopress.

Gheorghiu, D. 2007. Between material culture and phenomenology: the archaeology of a Chalcolithic fire-powered machine. In D. Gheorghiu and G. Nash. *The Archaeology of Fire. Understanding Fire as Material Culture*. Budapest, Archaeolingua.

Gheorghiu, D. (ed.). In press. *The Archaeology of Pyrotechnologies. Fire as an Instrument*. BAR International Series. Oxford, Archaeopress.

Gheorghiu, D. 2006a. The formation of tells in the Lower Danube wetland Late Neolithic. *Journal of Wetland Archaeology* 6, 3–18.

Gheorghiu, D. 2006b. On Chalcolithic ceramic technology: A study case from the Lower Danube traditions, 29–42. In D. Gheorghiu (ed.) *Ceramic Studies. Papers on the Social and Cultural Significance of Ceramics in Europe and Eurasia from Prehistoric to Historic Times*. BAR International Series 1553. Oxford, Archaeopress.

Gheorghiu, D. 2005. *The Archaeology of Dwellings. Theory and Experiments*. Bucharest, Editura Universitatii Bucuresti.

Gheorghiu, D. 2003. Water, tells and textures: a multiscalar approach to Gumelnita hydrostrategies. In D. Gheorghiu (ed.). *Chalcolithic and Early Bronze Age Hydrostrategies*, British Archaeological Reports1123. Archaeopress, Oxford, 39–56.

Gheorghiu, D. 2002. On palisades, houses, vases and miniatures: The formative processes and metaphors of Chalcolithic tells. In A. Gibson (ed.). *Behind Wooden Walls: Neolithic Palisaded Enclosures in Europe*. British Archaeological Reports 1013, Archaeopress, Oxford, 93–117.

Gheorghiu, D. 2001. Tropes in material culture, In D. Gheorghiu (ed.). *Material, Virtual and Temporal Compositions: On the Relationship between Objects*. British Archaeological Reports 953. Oxford, Archaeopress, 17–26.

Gibson, A. 2002. *Prehistoric Pottery in Britain and Ireland*. Stroud, Tempus.

Goffman, E. 1973. La *Mise en Scène de la Vie Quotidienne. Les Rites d'Interaction*. Paris, Éditions de Minuit.

Goody, J. 1977. 'Against ritual': loosely structured thoughts in a loosely defined topic. In S. F. Moore and B. G. Myerhoff (eds). *Secular Ritual*. Amsterdam, Van Gorcum.

Gosden, C. 1999. *Anthropology and Archaeology. A Changing relationship*. London, Routledge.

Gosden, C. 1994. *Social Being and Time*. Oxford, Blackwell.

Harding, A. 2007. Hearth and oven in Early Iron Age Sobiejuchy, Central Poland. In D. Gheorghiu and G. Nash (eds). *The Archaeology of Fire. Understanding Fire as Material Culture*. Budapest, Archaeolingua.

Hasotti, P. 1997. *Epoca neolitica in Dobrogea*. Constanta, Muzeul de Istorie Nationala si Archeologica.

Homère, *Hymnes*. 1936. Humbert, J. (ed.). Paris, Collection des Universités de France, Les Belles Lettres.

The Hymns of the Rigveda, I–III. 1889–9. Trans Ralph T.H. Griffith, adapted by M. Eliade. Benares.

Lazarovici, G., Drasovean, Fl. and Maxim, Z. 2001. *Parta*. Timisoara.

Lewis, G. 1980. *Day of Shining Red: an Essay on Understanding Ritual*. Cambridge, Cambridge University Press.

Lichardus, J., A. Fol, Getov, L., Berthemes, F., Echt R., Katincarov, R. and Krastec Iliev, I. (eds.) 1996. *Bericht über die bulgarish-deutschen Ausgrabungen in Drama (1989–1995)*. Mainz am Rhein, Philipp von Zabern.

Marinescu Bilcu, S. 1974. *Cultura Precucuteni pe teritoriul Romaniei*. Bucharest, Editura Academiei.

Markevic, V. I. 1981. *Pozne-Tripolskie plemena severnog moldovii*. Khishinev.

Mathieu, J. R. 2002. Introduction: Experimental archaeology. Replicating past objects, behaviors and processes. In J. R. Mathieu (ed.). *Experimental Archaeology. Replicating Past Objects, Behaviours and Processes*. BAR International Series 1035. Oxford, Archaeopress, 1–12.

Merkyte, I. 2005. Lîga. Copper Age strategies in Bulgaria. *Acta Archaeologica* Vol. 76, 1.

Moore, S. F. and Myerhoff, B. G., (eds.), 1977. *Secular Ritual*. Amsterdam, Van Gorcum.

Neagu, M. 2000. Comunitatile Boian-Giulesti din Valea Dunarii. *Istros* X, 25–34.

Özdoğan, M., 1999. Čayönü. In M. Özdoğan and N. Başgelen (eds.). *Neolithic in Turkey. The Cradle of Civilization. Istanbul. Ancient Anatolian Civilization Series* 3, 35–63.

Pandrea, S., Sarbu, V., Neagu, M. 1999. Cercetari arheologice in asezarea gumelniteana de la Insuratei-Popina I, Jud.Braila. Campaniile 1995–1999. *Istros*, 9.

Petrescu-Dambovita, M. and Florescu, A. C. 1959. Sapaturile arheologice de la Trusesti (Raportul de sapaturi din 1954–1957). *Materiale si Cercetari Arheologice*. Bucharest, Editura Academiei, 147–155.

Pyne, S. J. 2001. *Fire. A Brief History*. London, The British Museum Press.

Raduncǐeva, C. 1989. La societé dans les Balkans à l'âge du cuivre. *Dossiers Historie et Archéologie* 137, 46–55.

Rappaport, R., 1979. *Ecology, Meaning and Religion*. Richmond, Calif, North Atlantic Books.

Regenye, J. In press. Preserved in fire. Late Neolithic settlement structures in Western Hungary. In D. Gheorghiu (ed.). *Fire as an Instrument. The archaeology of Pyrotechnologies*. BAR International Series. Archaeopress, Oxford.

Renfrew, C. and Bahn, P. 1991. *Archaeology, Theories, Methods and Practice*. London, Thames and Hudson.

Renfrew, C. 1997. The Archaeology of religion. In C. Renfrew and E. Zubrow (eds). *The Ancient Mind. Elements of Cognitive Archaeology*. Cambridge, Cambridge University Press.

Sherratt, A. 1997. The significance of Neolithic houses in the archaeological record of southeast Europe. In M. Garasanin, N. Tasic, A. Cermanovic-Kuzmanovic, P. Petrovic, Z. Milic and M. Ruzic (eds). *Antidoron Dragoslav Srejovic*. Belgrade, Centre for Archaeological Research, 195–207.

Simson, J. 1997. Prehistoric ceramics in Mesopotamia. In I. Freestone and D. Gaimster (eds). *Pottery in The Making. World Ceramic Traditions*. London, British Museum Press.

Stevanović, M. 2002. Burned Houses in the Neolithic of Southeastern Europe. In D. Gheorghiu (ed.). *Fire in*

Archaeology. BAR International Series 1098. Oxford, Archaeopress, 55–62.

Stevanović, M. 1997. The Age of clay. The Social dynamics of house construction. *Journal of Anthropological Archaeology* 16, 334–395.

Todorova, H. 1982. *Kupferzeitliche Siedlungen in Nordosbulgarien*. Műnchen, C. H. Beck.

Tringham, R.1994. Engendered places in prehistory. *Gender, Place and Culture* 1, 169–203.

Tringham, R. 1992. Households with faces: The Challenge of Gender in Prehistoric Architectural remains, In J. Gero and M. Conkey (eds). *Engendering Archaeology. Women in Prehistory*. Oxford and Cambridge, Blackwell, 93–131.

Tringham, R. 1978. Experimentation, ethnoarchaeology, and the leapfrogs in archaeological methodology. In R.A. Gould (ed.). *Explorations in Ethnoarchaeology*. University of New Mexico, 169–199.

Tringham, R., and Krstić, D. 1990. Conclusion. Selevac in the wider context of European prehistory. In R. Tringham and D. Krstić (eds). *Selevac. A Neolithic village in Yugoslavia*.

Monumenta Archaeologica 15. Los Angeles, University of California Press, 567–617.

Turner, V. 1974, *The Drums of Affliction*. Oxford, Oxford University Press.

Ursulescu, N. 2001. Position des constructions-sanctuaires dans les habitats de l'Énéolithique ancien de la Roumanie. *Cultura si civilizatie la Dunarea de Jos* XVI–XVII, 42–47.

van Andel, T. H., K.Gallis and G. Toufexis, 1995. Early Neolithic farming in Thessalian river landscape. In L. Lewin, M. G. Macklin, and J. C. Woodward (eds). *Mediterranean Quaternary River Environements*. Rotterdam, Balkema, 131–144.

Voinea, V. M. 2005. *Ceramica complexului cultural Gumelnita – Karanovo VI. Fazele A1 si A2*. Constanta : Ex-Ponto.

Winkin, Y. 1996. *Anthropologie de la communication*. Bruxelles, De Boeck.

Wood, J. In press. A re-interpretation of a Bronze Age ceramic was it a cheese mould or a Bunsen burner? In D. Gheorghiu (ed.). *Fire as an Instrument. The Archaeology of Pyrotechnologies*. BAR International Series. Oxford, Archaeopress.

Chapter 36

A CONTEXTUAL APPROACH TO ANCIENT EGYPTIAN DOMESTIC CULT: THE CASE OF THE 'LUSTRATION SLABS' AT EL-AMARNA

Kate Spence

The royal city of Akhetaten (el-Amarna) was founded soon after 1350 BC by king Akhenaten as a royal residence city and centre for the worship of the visible sun disk (Aten) whom he had promoted to the position of state god to the exclusion of most of the traditional Egyptian pantheon. Two major temples dedicated to the Aten are found in the central city but, as was common in Egypt, access to the inner parts of these state temples is likely to have been restricted to the royal family and those holding priestly offices. The broader impact of Akhenaten's religious changes on the beliefs of the city's inhabitants is difficult to assess, but the nature and scope of non-royal cult activity are of considerable interest in their own right.

Significant evidence for non-royal cult activity is found at the site. Only a few communal shrines have been identified within the main city at Amarna (Kemp 1989, 283–5, 293) although more have been found at the outlying Walled Village (Bomann 1991). Within the grounds of some of the largest houses in the city, freestanding shrines were constructed, sometimes within gardens walled off from the house and approached through pyloned entrances (Ikram 1989). Stevens (2003) provides a good overview of evidence for cult within the houses. Altars, usually small and constructed of mud brick, are found in some dwellings and these are considered the most significant permanent installations for cult activity (Stevens 2003, 145–9). This paper presents the preliminary results of a study of a group of stone installations found in some of the houses, usually referred to in English-language publications as 'lustration slabs'. A few comparable structures are found in non-domestic contexts but these will not be discussed here as a result of space restrictions. There are no known textual references to these features and none is decorated or inscribed so interpretation must be archaeological and context based.

Form and context

The 'lustration slabs' are rectangular platforms constructed of stone: the majority are of limestone although a few are sandstone. No examples have been excavated since the 1930s so the present study is based on published records and archive materials. Exact dimensions have rarely been recorded but, measuring from published plans, they seem to vary in size from approximately 2.7 × 1.5 m (Figure 36.1: house P47.2; Borchardt and Ricke 1980, plate 27) to around 0.6 × 0.6 m (house N48.18 west; Borchardt and Ricke 1980, plate 56). The larger examples tend to be constructed from shallow stone slabs set in lime mortar (Figures 36.1–36.3) whilst some of the smaller ones are carved from a single slab of stone and are often squarer than the larger examples. Each has a raised rim around the perimeter (or the front three sides where the installation is set against a wall) and there is usually a smaller block placed in front of the centre at a slightly lower level than the floor of the feature. Where the platform is placed adjacent to a wall, the wall behind is often lined with a row of additional stone slabs or plaster (Figure 36.3). In well-recorded examples it is clear that the surface of the platform slopes slightly (e.g. Borchardt and Ricke 1980, 158, Abb. 24) towards either a depression (often circular e.g. Figure 36.2), or a spout through which liquid could run off to be collected in a basin or pot adjacent to one of the sides (Figure 36.3). The majority of these features are found in the central halls of houses (Figure 36.1). Evidence for over 80 can be identified: more than half are well preserved and the rest are represented by traces of stone or plaster. Given that other stone features such as lintels, basins and column bases have frequently been removed from the houses for reuse, and that traces were frequently not carefully recorded at the time of excavation, it is likely that the original number of platforms was much higher.

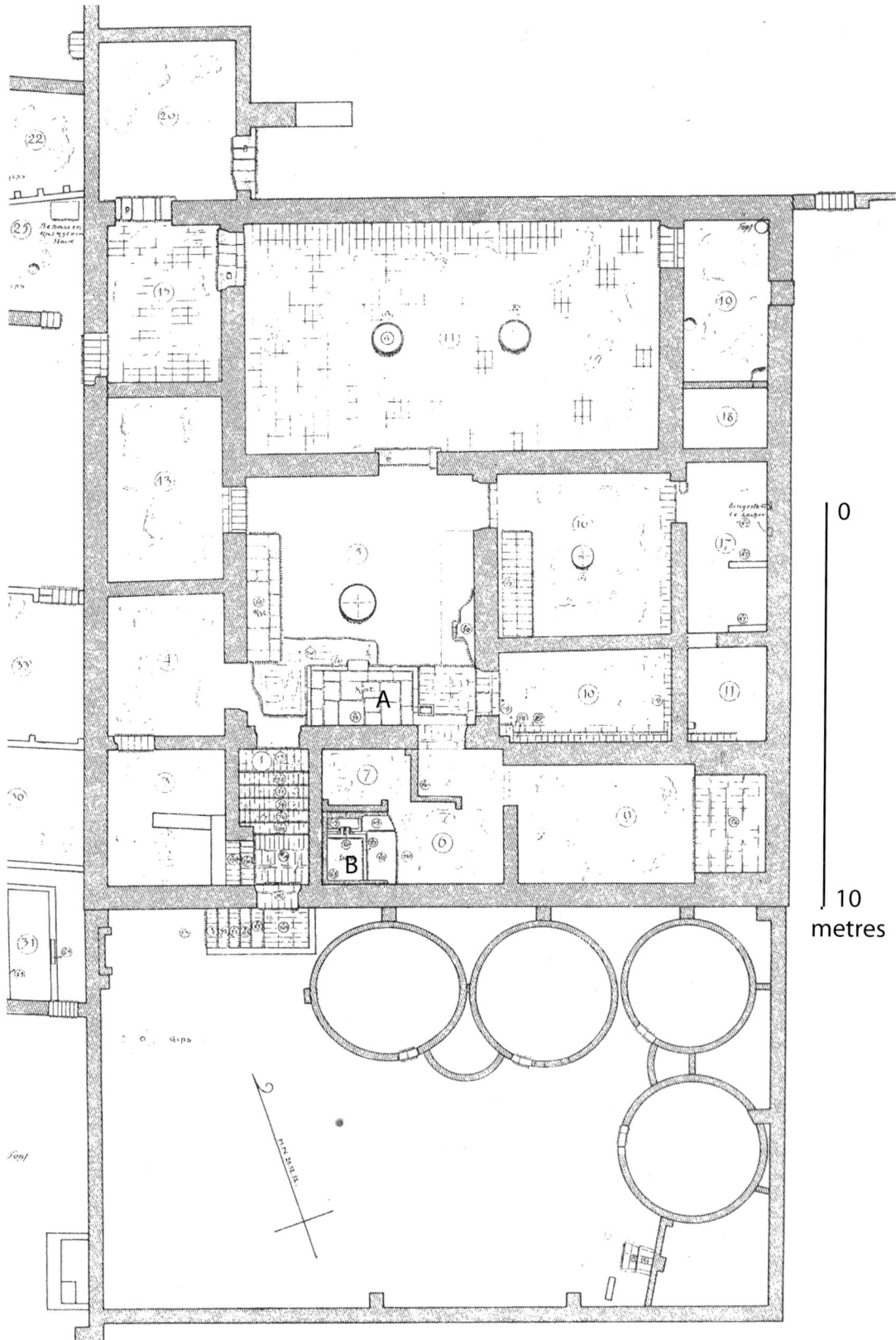

Figure 36.1. The house of the sculptor Thutmose (P47.2). The 'lustration slab' (labelled A) is situated in the central hall, approximately opposite the entrance. The stone bathroom tray is labelled B; it is situated in the private apartments and is further screened. Borchardt and Ricke (1980, plan 27) reproduced with kind permission of Gebr. Mann Verlag.

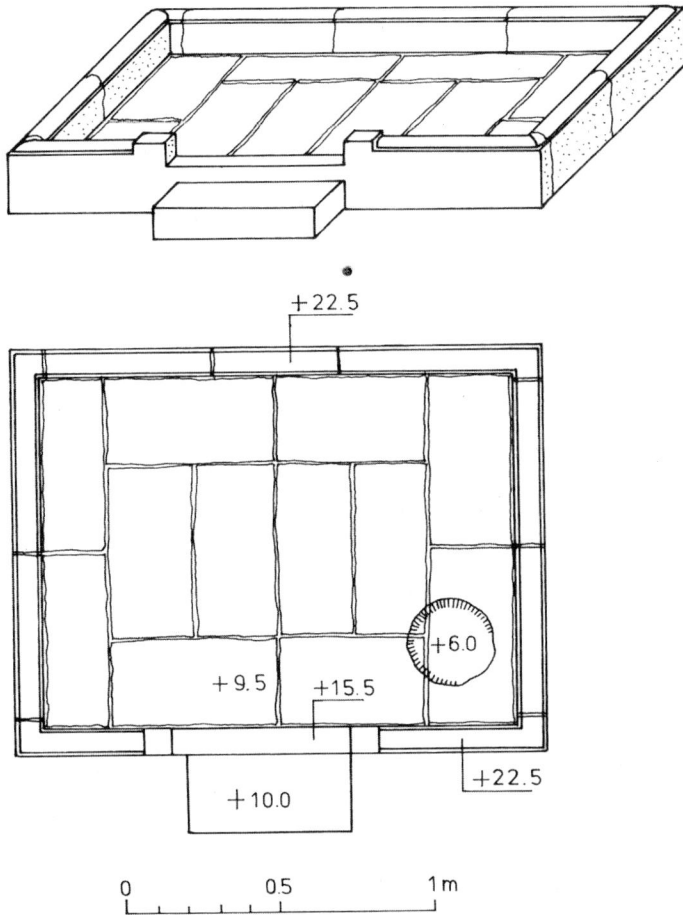

Figure 36.2. 'Lustration slab' in the house of the general Ramose (P47.19). This feature was located in front of a double false door and was not attached directly to the wall. Borchardt and Ricke (1980, Abb. 13) reproduced with the kind permission of Gebr. Mann Verlag.

These features have been variously interpreted. Petrie labels them as 'stone tray' or 'trough' on his plates (Petrie 1894, plate 38–39). In the publications of the Deutsche Orient-Gesellschaft, which excavated the majority of the houses, they are interpreted as stands for water-jars, presumably intended to protect the mud floor of the house from water damage (Ricke 1932, 31; Borchardt and Ricke 1980, 17) although the latter publication also accepts the possibility that they may have been for washing. In the publications of the Egypt Exploration Society they are described as 'lustration slabs' suggested to be for pouring water, perhaps containing natron, over the hands and feet (Peet and Woolley 1923, 40, 44–5). Barry Kemp describes them as washing places (Kemp 1989, 295–6) whilst Anna Stevens (2003, 155 and 160) suggests that they could have been used for washing preliminary to another ritual within domestic cult although she argues that they may also have served other cultic and mundane uses. Here they will usually be referred to as 'stone platforms'.

The apparent closest parallel for the form of the stone platforms is found in the bathroom installations constructed in many of the larger houses (Peet and Woolley 1923, 45). These usually comprised a shallow monolithic stone basin,

approximately square, with a spout positioned over a basin or pot sunken into the floor. (These objects are, in isolation, impossible to distinguish from some of the smaller monolithic 'lustration slabs' which were probably originally cut for use in bathrooms.) The parallels with bathrooms give credibility to the various interpretations associating the slabs with washing, but there are differences between the form of the majority of stone platforms and the bathroom features, and there are significant differences in architectural context (Figure 36.1).

The majority of 'lustration slabs' are considerably bigger than the shallow bathroom basins. The bathroom basins have no special arrangement for access whereas in the stone platforms access is carefully treated. There is usually a centrally placed step and the rim of the slab is usually lowered adjacent to this step. In some cases the ends of the rim are carefully carved into 'posts' (Figure 36.2). In a few cases the access step is angled, creating a miniature ramp, sometimes also with balustrades (Figure 36.3). It should be noted that, as the platforms are rarely more than 15 cm high and the balustrades are low, features such as steps, ramps and balustrades are unnecessary in pragmatic terms.

The locations of the two sets of features within houses

Figure 36.3. 'Lustration slab' in house O46.6. This example has an angled 'ramp' with balustrades and a basin for run-off to the left. The wall behind was originally lined with upright slabs now missing or broken. Borchardt and Ricke (1980, Taf. 22B) reproduced with the kind permission of Gebr. Mann Verlag.

are strikingly different (Figure 36.1). The bathroom is found amongst the innermost rooms of the house, usually adjacent to the bedroom that forms the culmination of the sequence of spaces leading from the entrance through the ground floor to the bedroom. Within the bathroom, the washing area is almost always further secluded by the provision of screen walls. In contrast, the vast majority of stone platforms (*c.* 92%) are found in central halls. This seems to have been the most important and formal room in the house: it is the location of the dais on which the householder sat to receive visitors and the room giving access to the upper storey (Spence 2004) and all inner rooms of the house. The seven probable examples of stone platforms not found in the central hall are found in prominent locations at the front of the house (two examples), in the west hall (one example) or in the inner square hall, a formal room found in the largest houses which replicates many of the features of the central hall (four examples).

Although similarities in form are less immediately striking, there are interesting parallels between the stone platforms and house altars, particularly in terms of context. The majority of house altars are found in central halls although some examples are found in other rooms, particularly the inner square hall, as is also the case with the stone platforms. House altars and stone platforms can be located against any wall, but in both cases there is a preference for the east wall with just under half of examples located to the east in each group (for the altars see Borchardt 1923, 21–3; Stevens 2003, 148–9 (some of those classified

by Stevens as 'north wall' are oriented north-east)). In the case of the house altars, Borchardt (1923, 22–3) suggested that this orientation was toward the rising sun. Construction materials differ: the house altars are constructed of mud brick with the exception of the altar found in the house of Panehesy which was of stone (Pendlebury 1951, 26–7, plates XXX.1, XXXI). The altars also tend to be smaller, higher and without arrangements for fluid run-off. However, many altars show a similar concern with spatial definition through the use of a parapet or rim, and many also show elaborate and presumably symbolic access arrangements in the form of mud-brick stairs or ramps centrally placed on the front sides of the structures (Stevens 2003, 146–8). Many of the altars were painted white giving them a superficial similarity with the material of the platforms.

Two other aspects of the context of stone platforms are particularly striking. Firstly, there appears to be a negative correlation with features of known cultic significance such as house altars and garden shrines. I am aware of only one house in the whole city (P48.2; Borchardt and Ricke 1980, 217–21, plate 63) that has a stone platform, a house altar and a garden shrine (but note that Kemp (1989, 293) considers this a communal shrine – if this is correct, no excavated house at the site has all three features); this is a medium-sized house and contained objects associated with royal and household cult. While it is relatively common for garden shrines and house altars to occur in the same dwelling, the overlap between stone platforms and garden shrines, or stone platforms and house altars is surprisingly small given a general tendency towards redundancy in matters of cult, and a tendency amongst the Egyptian elite to amass multiple indicators of status within the same dwelling (Crocker 1985; Shaw 1992). Around 36% of garden shrines occur in houses that also have a house altar. However, although there are considerably more stone platforms than either garden or house shrines, only about 5% of stone platforms occur in houses with garden shrines and less than 9% in houses with altars (figures are provisional as a result of difficulty defining some features). This suggests that the slabs may have a specific cultic significance but it also strongly indicates that they are not secondary features such as ritual purification areas reliant on a further cultic focus in the near vicinity.

Secondly, stone platforms occur in houses of very different scales. They are most common in large elite houses but they are also found in some of the smallest houses at the site (e.g. Figure 36.4: O49.19 north, Borchardt and Ricke 1980, plate 83) which do not contain many other stone elements or status indicators suggesting that they are features of considerable significance to the household, and that this significance occurs across the social spectrum. Crocker's study of status symbols at el-Amarna ranked 'lustration slabs' low as indicators of status (Crocker 1985, 63).

The role of the 'lustration slabs'

The stone platform occurs in the most important and formal room of the house and is the most prominent feature within it on account of its size, material and colour. This was the room in which the house owner sat raised on a dais to receive visitors, but the dais on which he sat was often smaller than the stone platform and was constructed of mud brick in contrast to the shining white stone of the platform (Figure 36.1). In houses where there was a 'lustration slab' it therefore formed a focal point within the principal room, reducing the formal setting of the house owner to the position of a secondary feature. This alone suggests that the slab had a cultic role as it seems inconceivable that a mundane feature would be permitted to rival the setting of the head of household, given the attention paid by the Egyptians to hierarchy and its materialization in architecture.

The spouts, basins or depressions for collecting run-off, rims, sloping surfaces and back-panels to protect the mud-brick walls from splashing all suggest that the stone platforms were intended for activities involving the use of liquids. However, washing seems an unlikely interpretation. If the slabs had served important social rituals such as hand and foot washing, it seems unlikely that they would have been so big or so visually prominent, and they would have been more common in elite houses and very uncommon in small houses without bathrooms. Amongst a number of possible interpretations of the platforms mentioned briefly by Stevens (2003, 155, 160) is a suggestion that they could have served as settings for purification or libation rituals. Ritual purification seems an unlikely interpretation in the domestic context as there is little correlation between the stone platforms and garden and house shrines (see above). The context suggests that the platform was the focus of cult activity and not an adjunct

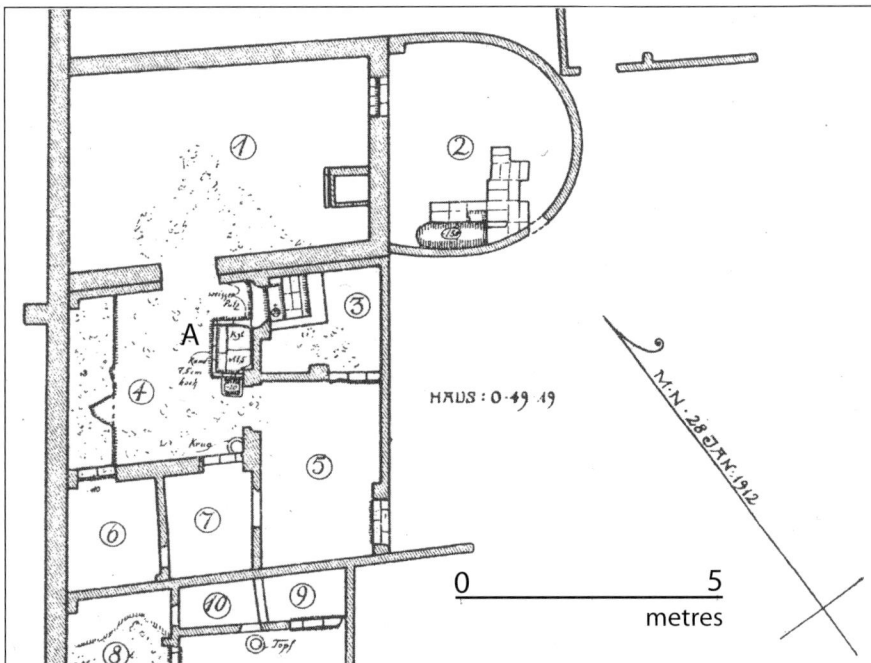

Figure 36.4. 'Lustration slab' (A) in small house O49.19. The house originally comprised rooms 3–7 and was later been enlarged with the addition of spaces 1 and 2, both of which were probably unroofed. The 'lustration slab' dominates the principal room (4) and is situated opposite a mud dais. The house has no bathroom. Borchardt and Ricke (1980, plan 83) reproduced with the kind permission of Gebr. Mann Verlag.

to it and an association with the pouring of libations, a primary cult activity attested in depictions at Amarna (e.g. Davies 1905, plate V; Pendlebury 1951, plate XXXI) and throughout the pharaonic period in Egypt, seems its most likely role. Pouring libations, particularly of water, was a standard part of the offering cult in Egypt and often occurred alongside the presentation of food offerings and/or incense. It can have purificatory or alimentary significance although both may be present in a single action; where libations are poured over an offering table the alimentary aspect is thought to be particularly prominent (Borghouts 1980).

The stone platforms form a separated place within the space of the central hall, distinguished from their surroundings through material (stone), colour (white) and the use of a balustrade forming a low boundary. The provision of a step or miniature ramp in the majority of cases suggests that the cult participant may have been intended to step onto the platform in all but the smallest examples, although note that steps are provided for some small mud altars, perhaps serving to suggest the accessibility of this liminal space rather than to encourage physical access. With the exception of hypaethral cult settings for the Aten where the focus was on the visible sun disk, cult activity in Egypt required a tangible focus and this may have taken the form of a two- or three-dimensional image set on a podium or

table at the rear of the platform or painted on the wall behind; several of the platforms stand in front of vertical niches, at least some of which were decorated with scenes of religious significance (Stevens 2003, 149–52). Tables or portable altars for offerings may have been placed in front of the images on the platform.

A small house (U35.25) from the North suburb at Amarna has an unusual feature of mud brick set into a doorway off the central hall (Figure 36.5; Frankfort and Pendlebury 1933, plates VI, XXI.1). Painted white, this has been interpreted as a house altar. It has a low raised platform of a layer of bricks painted white and has low walls of bricks set on edge to the rear and on the side that does not abut a structural wall. Behind the platform, centrally placed, is a rectangular block of white painted mud-brick forming some sort of podium and in front of it, in the centre of the platform, is the white-painted shaped foot of a mud object, probably an offering stand. I would suggest that this feature, representing a podium and stand on a low platform may replicate the arrangement of wooden altars or podia and the stone, ceramic or metal offering stands perhaps found on the stone platforms.

Outside house U37.1b is a mud-brick altar on a platform with a setting for an offering table in front of it; this is the only structure of its kind found outside a house but it provides another instance of an altar on a platform

Figure 36.5. Offering place in small house U35.25. The feature is constructed from whitewashed mud brick. In the centre at the rear is a solid rectangular podium and the raised platform in front of it is enclosed with bricks laid on edge. In the centre of the platform is the curved foot of a further feature of mud: this is very similar to the shape of an offering stand. This feature may replicate the arrangement on cult furniture on a stone platform. Frankfort and Pendlebury (1933, XXI.1) reproduced with the kind permission of the Egypt Exploration Society.

(Frankfort and Pendlebury 1933, 13, plate III, XIX.2; Ikram 1989, 94). In a larger house from the North Suburb, U37.1 (Frankfort and Pendlebury 1933, 12, plates III, XVIII.4) a whitewashed mud 'trough' with a wooden cover was constructed on a stone slab in a corner of the room with what appears to be a low mud enclosure in front of it: perhaps a larger version of a podium at the rear of a stone slab. Small stone offering tables and basins with spouts were found in the Walled Village at Amarna (Peet and Woolley 1923, plates XIV.5).

Discussion and conclusions

There is thus good reason to argue that the stone platforms were settings for domestic cult. Their form is more consistent than that of the group of features collectively described as 'house altars' and there are more stone platforms than either house altars or garden shrines, rendering them the most common type of installation for domestic cult in the city. The fact that they are found in houses of all scales shows that the practices they represent were of relevance to all social groups but they were by no means universally materialised in permanent form: the majority of houses have no preserved permanent feature that can be associated with domestic cult, although this does not rule out the presence of portable altars and offering tables (Stevens 2003, 161–2) or cult installations on the roof as is shown in images from Karnak (Traunecker 1988, figures 1–3).

One of the most significant problems encountered in dealing with the platforms and other installations for domestic cult lies in establishing the identity of those toward whom the cult was directed. The cult focus could be a divinity, either the Aten or a traditional god, several of whom are attested in images from Amarna despite prohibition. Two- and three-dimensional representations of the king and royal family were found in many houses and seem to have been cult images, and other images and objects associated with cult are also found (Stevens 2003, 158–9). There is only limited evidence for ancestral cult in the Amarna houses (Stevens 2003, 164–5) but, given that pouring libations for ancestors is explicitly stated in New Kingdom instruction texts to be important ('Libate for your father and mother who are resting in the valley...' (Lichtheim 1976: 137)), an association of the stone platforms with ancestor worship should be carefully considered as the city's inhabitants were far from family tombs where such cult activity would usually have taken place. However pouring libations, usually in association with the offering of food and sometimes also incense, was

a prominent part of both divine and ancestral cult and provides no unambiguous pointers. It is clear from textual sources that, in both divine and ancestral cult, the intention was to honour and provide for the deities or ancestors involved, with the expectation that they would act for the benefit of the cult participant. A clear distinction between 'cult of' and 'cult for' ancestors (or deities) as suggested by Renfrew (this volume) is thus difficult to establish in the Egyptian context. It should also be noted on the basis of textual sources that while the distinction between divine, royal and ancestral cult may seem self-evident to us, the boundaries between them are in practice very blurred in Egypt and cult activity may have been directed simultaneously or sequentially toward a number of different foci.

The stone platforms are also interesting in that they bring aspects of formal cult practice more usually associated with temples and tomb chapels into the dwelling. They are clearly designed for actual use with liquids (rather than token offerings) and are large suggesting a significant level of ritual activity and thus the potential manifestation of transcendent beings in cult objects within the house. This provides a link for the household with the intangible and, perhaps, with the past through ancestor cult, legitimating the head of household (the chief participant in images of cult found within houses at sites such as Deir el-Medina (e.g. Demarée 1983, plate VI, A21; plate VII, A26)) within the formal setting of the central hall. It is also worth considering what happened to the offerings presented in domestic cult. Within temples, offerings were presented to a number of gods (usually ordered hierarchically) and then divided up between priests and staff (Altenmüller 1982), a practice usually interpreted from an economic perspective as payment. In the Amarna houses, if food and drink similarly offered to ancestors or gods was then consumed by the household, as seems likely, this would feed divinities and/or the dead as part of the provisioning of the household and bind the household to the transcendent through shared meals, adding ritual significance to every day activities within the house.

Acknowledgements

This research was aided by a grant from the Thomas Mulvey Fund. I am most grateful to the Managers for their support. I am also grateful to Barry Kemp and the Egypt Exploration Society for permission to consult unpublished excavation records, and to Gebr. Mann Verlag and the Egypt Exploration Society for permission to reproduce Figures 36.1–4.

References

Altenmüller, H. 1982. Opferlauf. In W. Helck, and W. Westendorf (eds). *Lexikon der Ägyptologie*, Band IV. Wiesbaden, Harrassowitz, 596–7.

Borchardt, L. 1923. *Porträts der Königin Nofret-ete aus den Grabungen 1912/13*. In *Tell el-Amarna*. Leipzig, Hinrichs.

Borchardt, L. and Ricke, H. 1980. Die *Wohnhäuser in Tell El-Amarna*. Berlin, Gebr. Mann Verlag.

Bomann, A. 1991. *The Private Chapel in Ancient Egypt. A study of the chapels in the Workmen's Village at El Amarna with special reference to Deir el Medina and other sites*. London and New York, Kegan Paul International.

Borghouts, J. F. 1980. Libation. In W. Helck and W. Westendorf (eds). *Lexikon der Ägyptologie*, Band III. Wiesbaden, Harrassowitz, 1014–5.

Crocker, P. T. 1985. Status Symbols in the Architecture of el-'Amarna. *Journal of Egyptian Archaeology* 71, 52–65.

Davies, N. de G. 1905. *The Rock Tombs of El Amarna. Part II. The Tombs of Panehesy and Meryra II*. Egypt Exploration Fund Memoir 14. London, Egypt Exploration Fund.

Demarée, R. J. 1983. *The 3h ikr n R^c-stelae: On ancestor worship in ancient Egypt*. Leiden, Nederlands Instituut voor het Nabije Oosten.

Frankfort, H. and Pendlebury, J. D. S. 1933. *The City of Akhenaten. Part II. The North Suburb and the Desert Altars*. Egypt Exploration Society Memoir 40. London, Egypt Exploration Society.

Ikram, S. 1989. Domestic Shrines and the Cult of the Royal Family at el-'Amarna. *Journal of Egyptian Archaeology* 75, 89–101.

Kemp, B. J. 1989. *Ancient Egypt. Anatomy of a Civilization*. First edn. London, Routledge.

Lichtheim, M. 1976. *Ancient Egyptian Literature*. Volume II: *The New Kingdom*. Berkeley, University of California Press.

Peet, T. E. and Woolley, C. L. 1923. *The City of Akhenaten*, Part I. *Excavations of 1921 and 1922 at el-'Amarneh*. Egypt Exploration Society Memoir 38. London, Egypt Exploration Society.

Pendlebury, J. D. S. 1951. *The City of Akhenaten*. Part III: *The Central City and the Official Quarters*. Egypt Exploration Society Memoir 44. London, Egypt Exploration Society.

Petrie, W. M. F. 1894. *Tell el Amarna*. London, Methuen.

Ricke, H. 1932. *Der Grundriss des Amarna-Wohnhauses*. Liepzig, Hinrichs.

Shaw, I. 1992. Ideal Homes in Ancient Egypt: the Archaeology of Social Aspiration. *Cambridge Archaeological Journal* 2/2, 147–66.

Spence, K. 2004. The Three-dimensional Form of the Amarna House. *Journal of Egyptian Archaeology* 90, 123–52.

Stevens, A. 2003. The material evidence for domestic religion at Amarna and preliminary remarks on its interpretation. *Journal of Egyptian Archaeology* 89, 143–68.

Traunecker, C. 1988. Les Maisons du domaine d'Aton à Karnak, *Cahiers de Recherches de l'Institut de Papyrologie et d'Egyptologie de Lille* 10, 73–93.

Chapter 37

THE ULTIMATE REDUNDANCY PACKAGE: ROUTINE, STRUCTURE, AND THE ARCHAEOLOGY OF RITUAL TRANSMISSION

Camilla Briault

More than twenty-five years ago, Rappaport (1979, 174) argued that any anthropological account of ritual ought to be able to explain the universal as well as the particular, and suggested that it is only through studying those features common to all ritual systems that we may be able to discern, as he put it, 'whatever may be peculiar to ritual'. Although the symbolic content of ritual had long been seen and therefore focussed on by anthropologists as its defining characteristic, Rappaport (1979, 175) claimed, rather controversially, that ritual's capacity to symbolise is in fact its *least* distinctive feature, as it is shared with a whole nexus of other symbolic forms, such as myth, poetry, graphic art and architecture. Rappaport argued instead that a focus on the 'obvious' but often overlooked aspects of ritual should lead to a better understanding of what distinguishes ritual from other types of social practice. It is therefore only in the explicit combination of a series of formal characteristics that ritual emerges as a specific behavioural category.

One of these formal characteristics often observed in ritual systems but rarely investigated in functional terms is redundancy: formal, stereotyped, repetitive action (Rappaport 1979, 175; Tambiah 1979, 119). This neglect is perhaps due to the pervasiveness of redundancy in many forms of ritualised behaviour that lie outside the sphere of religion. Indeed, Goody (1977, 28) has noted that 'routinisation, regularisation, repetition, lie at the basis of social life itself'. Further, the term 'redundancy' or 'redundant' often has negative connotations, implying something superfluous or unnecessary. In many contexts, however, 'redundancy' is used to denote a failsafe, or back-up. In engineering, for example, redundancy is the duplication of critical components of a system for the purpose of increasing the overall reliability of that system. Similarly, in electronics, redundancy refers to the repetition of electronic elements in order to provide alternative functional channels in case of error or failure. In the

terminology of computer storage, 'data redundancy' and 'data reliability' are interchangeable. But it is in communications theory that redundancy is most important, serving to reduce equivocation (Leach 1966). Redundancy is thus a vital part of language, with the repetition of parts or all of a message acting to circumvent transmission errors.

In ritual, an act of *symbolic* communication, redundancy performs a very similar function. Any performative activity is inherently a contingent process, interactive and therefore risky (Turner 1967). There is always something aesthetically or practically at stake, and the success of the performance depends on whether the performers can 'bring it off' (Schieffelin 1998, 199). The prescribed, highly repetitive nature of ritual behaviour is thus deliberate, and serves to limit the potential for deviation in ritual practice. Circumventing transmission errors in ritual is crucial. Not only does getting it wrong risk a loss or distortion of meaning (Schechner 1988, xiv), but failure to perform a ritual properly can often incur moral reprimand or social exclusion (Liénard and Boyer 2006, 823), with the ever-present threat that the ritual will not have the desired result – perform a rain dance incorrectly and it won't rain. The stakes are therefore very high, and rules and contracts govern the performance of ritualised activities, working to make the performance, the participants, the place, safe, framing the action and protecting the players (Schechner 1988, xiv).

Social anthropologists have argued that bodily and semantic memories created through repeated experience of ritual performances can act as mechanisms through which the structure and sequence of those performances are transmitted (e.g. Connerton 1989, 102; Rowlands 1993, 141; Whitehouse 1996, 109–14). However, routinised behaviour in itself is not sufficient to ensure the accurate reproduction of rituals over long periods of time. Ritual performance therefore conventionally employs a host of additional strategies to limit the potential for deviation in cult practice and to guide the participants as they act, watch and perform. These include not only the prescription of specific material objects to be used in the performance itself, but also spatial settings and iconographic devices which may frame or cue behaviour (Giddens 1984, 118–122; Rapoport 1990, 9–10), and sensory experiences such as smells, tastes, sounds and movement (Connerton 1989, 4–5; Whitehouse 1996, 112; Pearson 1998, 35).

While this profusion of cueing devices may appear excessive or superfluous, each one acts as a corrective mechanism, serving to reduce slippage in the transmission of religious ideas and practices, and each therefore essential to the successful reproduction of ritual systems over long periods of time. As Leach (1966, 404) has said in reference to communications theory, 'if a sender seeks to transmit a message to a distant receiver against a background of noise, ambiguity is reduced if the same message is repeated over and over again by different channels and in different forms'. Rituals and their material attributes are therefore 'information-bearing procedures' (cf. Hodge and Kress 1988, 4), message systems characterised by high redundancy in order to limit the potential for imperfect transmission.

Nevertheless, while ritual is a powerful traditionalising tool (Moore and Myerhoff 1977, 5), and therefore often changes slowly, emphasising continuity at the expense of innovation (Bradley 1991, 212), changes in ritual practice do still occur. These can either be the result of deliberate modification, perhaps for political reasons (e.g. Bloch 1986); unconscious memory failure on the part of ritual practitioners (e.g. Barth 1987); the merging together of separate religious traditions (Shaw and Stewart 1994); or perhaps simply imperfect transmission, particularly in the case of rituals performed infrequently with long periods of latency in between (e.g. Whitehouse 2000). This is where an archaeological perspective, with its traditional emphasis on tracking diachronic change over long time periods, can be of particular advantage. Indeed, as Goody (1977, 34) has argued, 'the function of ritual can be better elucidated under changing rather than static conditions'. Archaeology in fact has much to offer the study of stability and flux in ritual systems. Archaeologists are in a good position to demonstrate the social nature of material practices (Gardner 2004, 4) and ritual, as a type of materialised social practice, should be susceptible to the same kinds of rigorous contextual approaches used in all archaeological inference (*contra* Hawkes 1954, 162). Moreover, archaeology is multi-scalar, concerned with the short and the long term, with the micro and the macro, with individuals and with populations, and an archaeology of ritual transmission can take advantage of this multiscalarity by looking at the transmission process on several different levels, from changes at individual ritual sites and in types of objects and symbols used, to larger historical narratives describing the process of ritual transmission in specific regions and periods.

Changes in the media employed to fashion ritual symbols and objects may be a reflection of broader economic trends, and crucial in this respect is an examination of the periods and places in which specific representations are 'switched on', or selected out for special treatment. For example, we might expect to see greater elaboration of rituals and their equipment during periods of political instability, such as state formation or collapse (Rappaport 1971, 61–2). A contextual approach should also help to identify and elucidate smaller scale cultural processes such as competition between local groups, which may well be manifested at least in part in an intensification of ritual activity and upgrading of its trappings (Douglas and Isherwood 1996, 43).

While micro-scale analysis can spotlight local trajectories and look at diachronic change in cult practice at the level of the site or the region, looking at the bigger picture facilitates an analysis of the active role of material culture in structuring ritual practice and in organising its transmission. Not only can assemblages of specific objects be used to identify a ritual context (Renfrew 1985, 24), but they can also be used to investigate the transmission of ritual practices through time, by examining whether the kits are added to or scaled down, which objects within the kit are elaborated and which remain the same, and what is the significance of the periods and places at which these changes take place. Moreover, changes in the medium and frequency of particular types of ritual object or symbol over time and space can also be explored in order to assess the extent to which variability in materials might signify imperfect transmission rather than deliberate modifications in ritual practice.

One strategy often employed to circumvent transmission errors in ritual is the architectural specification of ritual spaces. In terms of archaeology, the built environment is perhaps one of the most unambiguous clues we can use to interpret past ritual events. Spatial framing devices such as paths and corridors can act as a permanent, materialised record of the choreography of a ritual event. Indeed, choreography is one of the key variables around which performance organises its resources (Pearson 1998, 35). Materially, frames can take the form of architecturally specified routes and spaces, in which case they might act as a 'physical base for knowledge storage' (Renfrew 2005, 23), or a mnemonic device: a reminder of how to act in a particular place. Settings thus shape social practices through cueing behaviour (Rapoport 1990, 9–10). By defining settings, architecture makes particular actions possible, and, crucially, encourages more explicit forms of interaction and communication, such as speech-acts or ritual performances (DeMarrais 2005, 18). Bourdieu's (1977, 90–1) analysis of the Kabyle house reveals the complex set of oppositions that structure both the house itself and the activities that take place inside it. Materialisation is therefore an active, reflexive process, and has much in common with Bourdieu's (1977) and Giddens' (1979; 1984) models of the perpetual reproduction of culture (or *habitus*/structure) though practice. This repeated practice not only results in the transmission of knowledge and values, but it also allows them to be shared broadly amongst the members of a society. The use of this concept for archaeology is that the materialisation of culture provides scope for analysing the ways in which knowledge, practices and materials articulate to establish contexts for interaction (DeMarrais 2005, 11).

While settings of interaction are essential to specifying the contextuality of an occasion (Giddens 1984, 86–8), the use of strategic patterns of movement in time and space marks out an activity as something removed from the everyday. Choreography thus serves as an 'attention-focussing device' (cf. Renfrew 1985, 18), distinguishing performers from spectators, permitting and restricting access and creating boundaries, frames, and spaces within spaces. The materialisation of choreography – its realisation in architectural form – is perhaps the most extreme method of 'fixing' a performance by limiting the potential for deviation. Physically choreographing a space will create a stable performance setting (cf. Rapoport 1990, 9–10), determining bodily movements, flow and directionality and dictating the numbers of people involved and the relative positioning of watchers and watched. Built spaces for ritual will therefore frequently employ fairly unambiguous cues, such as pathways, crossings and backdrops. While this is equally true of many other types of space – a supermarket, for example, will deliberately guide shoppers in a predetermined circulatory pattern, past displays of special offers and expensive but unnecessary trimmings – ritual, particularly when it has no written texts to back it up, is different because getting it wrong carries a greater risk. The vast redundancy seen in some spatial cueing devices, such as frescoes painted up the side of staircases depicting people walking up the staircases, or evoking a perpetual procession, certainly seems reasonable in this context. But choreographed spaces also memorialise ritual events. Permanently inscribing the physical trajectories of ritual performance on the ground not only serves to evoke memories of past performances, but also indicates a desire publicly to commemorate those performances by bringing ritual into daily life, thereby both establishing and ensuring continuity with the past.

Although ritual performance will always be most visible, and therefore most archaeologically recoverable, in the spaces set aside for its sole usage, locales and settings can also be constituted without architecture. From the structured deposition of particular artefact types at ritual sites, we can infer differential activity areas (Richards and Thomas 1984). Moveable props can be used as framing and staging devices to focus attention and bracket out visual irrelevance (Miller 1985, 127–35; Pearson 1998, 34–5). Various foregrounding devices act to present the spectacle as a spectacle, removed from the everyday. Performance thus resembles a 'scene of crime' in which everything is potentially important and present on purpose: 'whatever passes the boundary and enters the theatrical space is declared significant' (Pearson 1998, 34). Ideas of on- and off-stage, the organisation of lines of sight, scale and perspective, and the composition of bodies and objects in space all work to define the ritual arena and the number of people involved, and these are all aspects of ritual practice than be attested archaeologically and studied through time.

Giddens' (1984, 119) conception of 'locales' in addition emphasises how roles show up more clearly in highly structured situations, and this may be evident in the archaeological record in areas for the relative positioning of watcher and watched. Proxemic codes, the set of meanings carried by physical relationships in space, are often articulated through forms of speech that express social meanings in spatial terms, for example 'pecking order', 'high status', 'grovelling' (Hodge and Kress 1988, 52). These forms of speech are materialised in performance, often through the placing of people and objects in particular relation to each other (for example, on thrones). The ordering of bodies in physical space therefore determines the nature of their relationships in social space. However, as Schieffelin (1998, 207) has said, the nature of these relationships is not specified prior to the performance, but rather is constituted within it. Indeed, one of the characteristics of performance is that, as a forum for challenging the everyday, and thus for negotiating as well as reproducing asymmetrical power relationships, performance may be dangerous and subversive (cf. Turner 1967). Nevertheless, mindful of the ways in which the material record can mask social reality (cf. Ucko 1969; Shanks and Tilley 1982), an archaeological analysis of the settings designed for ritual performances (e.g. Rappaport 1990, 9–10; DeMarrais 2005, 15–20) can attempt to uncover some of these relationships.

The redundancy inherent in ritual can thus be turned to the archaeologist's advantage. If each of the cueing devices used in ritual is seen as a separate mechanism through which the structure and sequence of ritual practice can be transmitted, then the long-term history of entire ritual systems can be examined using traditional archaeological techniques. Moreover, archaeology is particularly well placed for looking at the relationship between changes in ritual and social change. Fifty years after Hawkes' (1954) deliberate sidelining of religion from archaeological discourse, it is clear that the material trappings of ritual practice can often provide archaeologists with a dataset comparable in terms of contextual information to that derived from other social and material practices that have long been regarded as less difficult to quantify and examine. Indeed, ritual practice can often be studied at a high enough resolution to take a diachronic and multi-scalar perspective. By doing this, we should be able to understand the particular contribution made by the different components of ritual practice to the reproduction and transformation ritual systems over time, and thus focus on those aspects of ritual that may be obvious, but have been neglected for too long.

References

Barth, F. 1987. *Cosmologies in the Making: A Generative Approach to Cultural Variation in Inner New Guinea.* Cambridge, Cambridge University Press.

Bloch, M. 1986. *From Blessing to Violence: History and Ideology in the Circumcision Ritual of the Merina of Madagascar.* Cambridge, Cambridge University Press.

Bourdieu, P. 1977. *Outline of a Theory of Practice.* Cambridge, Cambridge University Press.

Bradley, R. 1991. Ritual, time and history. *World Archaeology* 23 (2), 209–17.

Connerton, P. 1989. *How Societies Remember.* Cambridge, Cambridge University Press.

DeMarrais, E. 2005, The materialization of culture, in E. DeMarrais, C. Gosden, and C. Renfrew (eds). *Rethinking Materiality: The Engagement of Mind with the Material World,* 11–22. Cambridge, McDonald Institute of Archaeological Research.

Douglas, M. and Isherwood, B. 1996. *The World of Goods.* New York, Basic Books.

Gardner, A. 2004. Introduction: social agency, power, and being human. In A. Gardner (ed.). *Agency Uncovered: Archaeological Perspectives on Social Agency, Power and Being Human*: 1–15. London, UCL Press.

Giddens, A. 1979. *Central Problems in Social Theory.* London, Macmillan.

Giddens, A. 1984. *The Constitution of Society: Outline of the Theory of Structuration.* Cambridge, Polity Press.

Goody, J. 1977. Against 'ritual': loosely structured thoughts on a loosely defined topic. In S. F. Moore and B. G. Myerhoff (eds). *Secular Ritual*: 25–35. Amsterdam, Van Gorcum.

Hawkes, C. 1954. Archaeological Theory and Method: Some Suggestions from the Old World. *American Anthropologist* 56, 153–68.

Hodge, R. and Kress, G. 1988. *Social Semiotics.* Cambridge: Polity Press.

Leach, E. R. 1966. Ritualisation in Man in relation to conceptual and social development, *Philosophical Transactions of the Royal Society of London* 251, Series B (772), 403–8.

Liénard, P. and Boyer, P. 2006. Whence collective rituals? A cultural selection model of ritualized behaviour. *American Anthropologist* 108 (4), 814–27.

Miller, D.1985. *Artefacts as Categories. A Study of Ceramic Variability in Central India.* Cambridge, Cambridge University Press.

Moore S. F. and Myerhoff, B. G. 1977. Introduction. Secular ritual: forms and meanings, in S. F. Moore and B. G. Myerhoff (eds). *Secular Ritual,* 3–24. Amsterdam, Van Gorcum.

Pearson, M. 1998. Performance as valuation: Early Bronze Age burial as theatrical complexity. In R. Bailey (ed.) *The Archaeology of Value,* 32–41. Oxford, British Archaeological Reports.

Rapoport, A. 1990. Systems of activities and systems of settings. In S. Kent (ed.). *Domestic Architecture and the Use of Space: An Interdisciplinary Cross-Cultural Perspective,* 9–20. Cambridge, Cambridge University Press.

Rappaport, R. A. 1971. Ritual, sanctity and cybernetics. *American Anthropologist* 73, 59–76.

Rappaport, R. A. 1979. *Ecology, Meaning and Religion.* Berkeley: North Atlantic Books.

Renfrew, C. 1985. *The Archaeology of Cult. The Sanctuary at Phylakopi.* London, Thames and Hudson.

Renfrew, C. 2005. Towards a theory of material engagement. In E. DeMarrais, C. Gosden and C. Renfrew (eds). *Rethinking Materiality: The Engagement Of Mind With The Material World.* Cambridge, McDonald Institute for Archaeological Research, 23–31.

Richards, C. and Thomas, J. 1984. Ritual activity and structured deposition in Later Neolithic Wessex, in R. Bradley and J. Gardiner (eds). *Neolithic Studies. A Review of Some Current Research.* Oxford, British Archaeological Reports, 189–218.

Rowlands, M. 1993. The role of memory in the transmission of culture. *World Archaeology* 25 (2), 141–51.

Schechner, R. 1988. *Performance Theory.* New York, Routledge.

Schieffelin, E. L. 1998. Problematizing performance. In M. Hughes-Freeland (ed.). *Ritual, Performance, Media.* New York, Routledge, 194–207.

Shanks, M. and Tilley, C. 1982. Ideology, symbolic power, and ritual communication: a reinterpretation of Neolithic mortuary practices. In I. Hodder (ed.). *Symbolic and Structural Archaeology,* 129–54. Cambridge, Cambridge University Press.

Shaw, R. and Stewart, C. 1994. Introduction: problematizing syncretism, in C. Stewart and R. Shaw (eds). *Syncretism/ Antisyncretism. The Politics of Religious Synthesis.* London, Routledge, 1–26.

Tambiah, S. J. 1979. *A Performative Approach to Ritual.* London, The British Academy and Oxford University Press.

Turner, V. 1967. *The Forest of Symbols.* Ithaca, Cornell University Press.

Ucko, P. J. 1969. Ethnography and the archaeological interpretation of funerary remains. *World Archaeology* 1, 262–90.

Whitehouse, H. 1996. Jungles and computers. Neuronal group selection and the epidemiology of representations. *Journal of the Royal Anthropological Institute* 2, 99–116.

Whitehouse, H. 2000. *Arguments and Icons. Divergent Modes of Religiosity.* Oxford, Oxford University Press.

Chapter 38

THE DYNAMICS OF RITUAL ON MINOAN PEAK SANCTUARIES

Alan Peatfield

In the early days of my peak sanctuary research, I interviewed my mother about her memories of festival visits to the mountain chapel of Prophitis Elias near her village in Cyprus in the 1930s. I was reminded of her account when I recently encountered Psilakis' book of Cretan folk festivals, which includes a section on visits to mountain chapels, including those on the Minoan peak sanctuaries of Kofinas and Jouktas (Psilakis 2005, 278–2799 and 332–336). These accounts are appropriate in archaeological discourse not as analogy, but rather that within our artefact analysis, category definitions, and intellectual theorizing on the nature of religion and ritual, we are in danger of forgetting the human reality, the dynamic activity that went into the deposition of the material. The question therefore is how we can go through the material to approach that human quality, the reality of the human experience. Such an analytical process is difficult enough for secular activities, but there are special difficulties in relation to ritual/cultic activity, involving as it does, not just the complexities of the human mind, but also the complexities of the human spirit.

The first excavated peak sanctuary, Petsophas above Palaikastro in East Crete, remains the site archetype. Situated on a low (only 215 m high) but prominent mountain, Petsophas was excavated in 1903 by John Myres (Myres 1902–3). The site was bounded by a low wall, within which was a small, open building. From here Myres recovered thousands of clay figurine fragments, of three main types: human (male and female), animals (mostly domestic types), and detached models of human body parts, called 'votive limbs'. Chronologically, this material is of the Middle Bronze Age, early second millennium BC, with some overlap into the Late Bronze period.

It was Arthur Evans himself who coined the term 'peak sanctuary' in his report of his investigation of the site on top of Jouktas, the mountain south of Knossos, which visually dominates the whole of north central Crete (Evans 1909, 151–159). He recognized the similarity of Petsophas and Jouktas, and thus the category of Minoan peak sanctuaries entered the archaeological record.

By the late 1970s more than 50 sites were claimed as peak sanctuaries, many on the simple presence of one figurine and/or being somewhere on a hill (Rutkowski 1972; 1986, 96–99). The initial direction of my own research in the 1980s was to bring clarity to the definitive criteria of peak sanctuaries. Based on extensive fieldwork, and influenced by the pioneering work of Bogdan Rutkowski, I argued that the identification of a peak sanctuary requires the intersection of two essential groups of evidence, topography and artifacts (Peatfield 1983; 1990). The definitive artifacts are not just clay figurines, but specifically the *assemblage* of animals, humans, and votive limbs, and in significant numbers, not just a few isolated finds.

The topographic elements by which a peak sanctuary may be recognized are:

1. Placement on or close to the summit of a mountain (altitude range 200–1200 m);
2. Local or regional prominence of the mountain and/or actual peak sanctuary site;
3. Clear lines of visibility between the peak sanctuary and the settlement areas;
4. Accessibility of mountain and peak sanctuary site (i.e. relatively easy to climb);
5. Proximity to settlements (within a journey time of one to several hours);
6. Proximity to areas of human activity and exploitation (i.e. close to upland farming terraces and pastures);
7. Intervisibility with other peak sanctuaries.

Together, such topographic elements may also be regarded as an assemblage of evidence, but, I repeat, it is the presence of both classes of evidence, the topographic and the artefact, which allow for the reliable identification of a peak sanctuary. Of the 50-plus sites identified as peak sanctuaries prior to my fieldwork, there was a close correlation between the assemblage of artifacts and the assemblage of topographic factors on approximately 23 sites (Peatfield 1990). I excluded the other sites from my subsequent discussions of peak sanctuaries, because they did not conform to both sets of evidential factors. Rutkowski's student Nowicki, achieved similar results in his own fieldwork, and our catalogues of 'confirmed' peak sanctuaries substantially overlap (Nowicki 1994; Rutkowski 1988). In the methodological premise behind this analysis I was influenced by Renfrew's analytical framework for the archaeological recognition of cult, based on the fundamental significance of contextual relationships, whereby assemblage is more important that any single object (or topographic element) within it (Renfrew 1983).

Although empirical, this categorization of peak sanctuaries has withstood scrutiny. The recent GIS study of peak sanctuaries by Soetens confirmed its validity (Soetens 2006). But the purpose of this article is not to compare technological modelling with 'traditional' empirical interpretation. Rather what concerns me is how to move beyond the simple categorization of these elements into understanding the dynamic process of a religious landscape, through which people moved, expressed religious ideas, and carried out ritual acts.

Once archaeological categories and their definitive criteria are established, there is always the tendency to fossilize them. However accurate they may be, such categories are still our constructs. When applied to landscape, these topographic elements become viewed as a sort of static geometry. But the incorporation of landscape into a culture's religious life contains the energy of dynamic behaviour. As illustration, I discuss here two themes: 1) peak sanctuaries within the broader context of the Minoan ritual landscape, and 2) the contextual interpretation of ritual behaviour on a peak sanctuary.

Peak sanctuaries and the Minoan ritual landscape

The issue of the peak sanctuary visibility is fundamental to the topographic elements summarised above, including prominence, proximity, placement, accessibility, and intervisibility with other peak sanctuaries. It is clear that the Minoans were sufficiently aware of the significance of this visibility in the way that they exploited mountain views to good effect in their architectural alignments. The palace of Phaistos is aligned through its central court to the horned peak of Mount Ida. So far as we know the Ida summits are not peak sanctuaries, but sacred significance may be attributed to the similarity of this horned shape to the Minoan religious symbol of horns-of-consecration. Knossos is aligned to Jouktas, probably through its Procession Corridor (Peatfield 1990). And arguably the palace of Zakro is aligned to the Traostalos peak sanctuary (Chryssoulaki 2001), and the Petras palace on Sitias to the Prinias peak sanctuary.

Furthermore, in the iconography of the Neopalatial period, the visual impact of the mountain is transformed into a religious symbol associated with palatial authority, as has been argued for the Mountain Mother sealing, the back of the Throne in the Knossos Throne Room, and the Zakro peak sanctuary rhyton (Peatfield 1987; 1990).

Such visual issues are clear enough, but as I noted above, there is a tendency to reduce them to a static pattern of visual relationships. This does not account for perhaps the most important part of a landscape – motion, movement, travel through the landscape. It seems obvious to say this, but in Minoan studies, the point has not yet been made. The process of the journey through the landscape is to experience the ever-changing nuances of visibility – static geometries become dynamic configurations. The abstract pattern may be transformed to account for human experience.

What do I mean by this? One of the issues not yet addressed in discussions of peak sanctuary topography is the broader ritual landscape, incorporating not only peak sanctuaries, but also sacred caves, and the rural sanctuaries, called 'sacred enclosures' in the literature, that are associated with numinous rocks, streams, trees. Even if we assume that they operated with their own distinctive rituals, overall these cult places are still part of the process by which the Minoans configured their sacred landscape. Any journey through that landscape will touch on, to some degree or other, the Minoan spiritual response to it.

One strong example is the route from Knossos to Jouktas (Karetsou 1980; Zeimbeki 2004). The presence of a road linking palace and peak sanctuary was established by Evans. Approaching the mountain from the north, you pass by the hill of Archanes Phourni with its cemetery. On the lower slope you meet the Anemospilia shrine. Ascending to the peak, just before the entrance to the temenos is yet another building complex. Furthermore, on the south slope there is the sacred cave of Chosto Nero, and just below the chapel of Aphendis Christos on the south summit, Minoan sherds are visible beside the spring. In all the discussions of these sites, particularly the notorious human sacrifice at Anemospilia, there has been little or no discussion as to how these cult places may have interacted, visually and functionally, with the peak sanctuary on the summit. Jouktas is unlikely to be unique in this respect of being part of a configuration of sacred sites, a process of ritual geography centred around a peak sanctuary.

GIS should be the tool to facilitate this next step in the study of Minoan ritual topography. The ability of GIS to model the journey through the landscape was amply demonstrated by the study of Stonehenge (Exon, Gaffney, Woodward and Yorston 2000). The application of this methodology, using dynamic viewsheds, to a peak sanctuary case-study would answer many questions, including the changing nuances of visibility of the process of pilgrimage to a peak sanctuary, the possibility of 'chains of visibility' from lower to higher sacred sites, and may even enable some predictions about the settlements and other shrines which interacted with specific peak sanctuaries. Even more significantly if we are able to reconstruct the approach to a peak sanctuary, it should give greater understanding of the operation of the sanctuary itself, how the distribution of material might reflect the process of ritual movement into and around the site.

Atsipadhes Korakias

This issue of the interaction of the distribution of material remains and topography may be illustrated by one of the features of the Atsipadhes Korakias peak sanctuary. I have remarked that part of the definitive topographic elements of peak sanctuaries are good vistas onto the region and settlements from which the worshippers came. But such a downward view should not assumed to be the same, equally good from every part of the sanctuary, especially given the uneven terrain and size of even the smallest peak sanctuary.

In my field surveys in the 1980s I observed that the density of material over each peak sanctuary often varied immensely. Especially notable were instances where the figurine fragments and sherds were mixed with pebbles. A particularly good example was at Kerias in the Ida mountain range. Here the pebble scatter was enclosed on three sides by extrusions of natural rock, just on the south edge of the site. Intuitively, it seemed that these were often associated with the specifics of different views from different parts of the site. I was able to test this notion with the excavation of the Atsipadhes Korakias peak sanctuary in 1989 (Peatfield 1992).

From the beginning, part of the interest of Atsipadhes was that it was a small rural peak sanctuary, rather than one associated with elite, palatial centres. Therefore, it was more typical of peak sanctuaries that were directly associated with peasant communities in the Middle Minoan period. The Korakias peak is a northern spur of Mt. Kouroupas which divides the Ayios Vasilios valley from the south coast plain of Plakias Preveli, south of the Rethymnon, in West Crete. The peak overlooks the aforesaid valley and has striking views north to the palatial peak sanctuary of Vrysinas, east to Mount Ida, and west to the White Mountains.

The peak itself is relatively small, approximately 10 × 20 m, and divided into two terraces, Upper to the west, Lower to the east. Only the east edge of the Upper Terrace produced finds, scattered sherds, figurines fragments and pebbles, set around a feature empty of finds. This feature, and whatever stood in it, seems to have been the main focus of ritual activity, especially libations, to judge by the presence of vessel and animal rhyta. The drop from the Upper Terrace to the Lower Terrace consists of rough rock clefts. Within these clefts we found more than 50% of our 5000-plus figurine fragments, clearly indicating this was the main place of offering activity.

The figurines included the familiar assemblage of human, animal (mostly cattle) and votive limbs. The vases seem to be mainly cups, bowls, jugs, and some bridge-spouted jars, plus so-called Minoan lamps, which were probably also used for burning fragment materials.

Atsipadhes Korakias: densities and viewsheds

The distribution density of the finds on the Lower Terrace was clear. The material was densest towards in the rock clefts immediately below the Upper Terrace and diminished the further away from that area one moved to the east and to the north. Then there was a second density of finds right on the very east edge of the site. This was on a secondary lower terrace, which then fell away to one of the cliffs and steep slopes, which bounded the Korakias summit. How can we interpret this second density? First, it should be noted that this is not a secondary deposit of figurines and pottery. There are no joins between fragments from this edge deposit and the main deposits around the rock clefts. In my initial report of the excavation I suggested that the material here arises from offering activity associated with view down from the peak sanctuary to the east (Peatfield 1992).

Associated with the excavation of Atsipadhes Korakias was the archaeological survey of the Ayios Vasilios valley (Moody, Peatfield and Markoulaki 2000). One explicit purpose of the survey was the identification of settlement sites contemporary with the peak sanctuary. One of the largest scatters of Middle Minoan material was found on the low hills immediately below the peak sanctuary, around the Turkish fortress called the Koule. Some of pottery fabrics identified in the survey are good matches for the fabrics of figurines and vases on the peak sanctuary. Here it seems that there was a cluster of settlements, that are our strongest candidates for the homes of the peak sanctuary worshippers. From the centre of the peak sanctuary, the liturgical area of the Upper Terrace and the rock clefts immediately below it on the Lower Terrace, the Koule and the area of Minoan settlements cannot be seen. By contrast the east edge offers a perfect view onto the Koule. It makes sense therefore to suggest that the east edge deposit of material indeed, and I repeat, arises out of offering activity associated with the view east, specifically with the view onto the settlements from which the worshippers came.

Such an observation allows us to understand in greater depth the topographic element of peak sanctuaries being able to see the homes the worshippers. It is clear that such an interactive view was intrinsic to the Minoan concept of what a peak sanctuary was for. That concept was dynamically acted upon, expressed in the ritual behaviour that resulted in the deposition of the figurines and vases that we recovered.

Dynamics of ritual

It is this issue of the interaction between the material distribution and the dynamics of ritual that brings me to my last point. I referred above to the presence of pebbles and libation vessels on the liturgical area of the Upper Terrace. Stated thus, it is an observation of a distribution pattern, but once we engage the human reality behind the process, dynamic factors come into play: the effort of climbing, and carrying the offerings, the texture of pebble and clay, the awe of the view, the chill and heat of passing night and day, the action of approach and offering, the sound of liquid poured over stone and earth, all carried out amid the chatter and communitas of a peasant society. This transforms the static remains into an intensely sensory experience, and draws out of the ritual process its essentially performative nature – religion less as things believed and more as things felt and things done.

Conclusion

The limits of this paper preclude a presentation of a comprehensive analysis of peak sanctuary ritual. In the few examples presented I hope that I have made the case that one of the directions of the archaeology of religion should be towards the dynamic interpretation of ritual remains. This is surely the context of energy and life that went into their creation and use.

References

Chryssoulaki, S. 2001. The Traostalos Peak Sanctuary: Aspects of Spatial Organization. In R. Laffineur and R. Hägg (eds). *POTNIA: Deities and Religion in the Aegean Bronze Age. Proceedings of the 8th International Aegean Conference, Göteborg, Göteborg University, 12–15 April 2000 (Aegaeum* 22). Brussels, 57–66.

Exon, S., Gaffney, V., Woodward, A. and Yorston, R. 2000. *Stonehenge Landscapes. Journeys through Real-and Imagined Worlds.* Oxford.

Karetsou, A. 1980. The Peak Sanctuary of Mt. Juktas. In R. Hägg and N. Marinatos (eds). *Sanctuaries and Cults of the Aegean Bronze Age: Proceedings of the First International Symposium at the Swedish Institute in Athens, 12–13 May, 1980* (Acta Instituti Atheniensis Regni Sueciae, ser. in 4°; 28). Stockholm, 137–153.

Moody, J., Peatfield, A. and Markoulaki, S. 2000. The Aios Vasilios Valley Archaeological Survey: A Preliminary Report. *Proceedings of the Eighth International Cretological Congress, Sept. 1996, Heraklion.* Heraklion, 359–646.

Myres, J. L. 1902–1903. Excavations at Palaikastro II. The Sanctuary Site at Petsofa. *BSA* 9, 356–387.

Nowicki, K. 1994. Some Remarks on the Pre- and Protopalatial Peak Sanctuaries in Crete. *Aegean Archaeology* 1, 31–48.

Peatfield, A. A. D. 1983. The Topography of Minoan Peak Sanctuaries. *BSA* 78, 273–280.

Peatfield, A. A. D. 1987. Palace and Peak: The Political and Religious Relationship between Palaces and Peak Sanctuaries. In R. Hägg and N. Marinatos (eds). *The Function of the Minoan Palaces: Proceedings of the Fourth International Symposium at the Swedish Institute in Athens, 10–16 June, 1984* (Acta Instituti Atheniensis Regni Sueciae, ser. in 4°; 35). Stockholm, 89–93.

Peatfield, A. A. D. 1990. Minoan Peak Sanctuaries: History and Society. *OpAth* 18, 117–132.

Peatfield, A. A. D. 1992. Rural Ritual in Bronze Age Crete: The Peak Sanctuary at Atsipadhes. *Cambridge Archaeological Journal* 2, 59–87.

Psilakis, Nikos, 2005, *Laikes Teletourgies stin Kriti* [*Folk Ceremonies in Crete*]. Heraklion Crete.

Renfrew, C. 1985. *The Archaeology of Cult: The Sanctuary at Phylakopi* (British School at Athens Suppl. vol. 18). London.

Rutkowski, B. 1972. *Cult Places in the Aegean World* (Bibliotheca antiqua 10). Wroclaw.

Rutkowski, B. 1986. *The Cult Places of the Aegean,* New Haven.

Rutkowski, B. 1988. Minoan Peak Sanctuaries: The Topography and Architecture. *Aegaeum* 2, 71–99.

Soetens, S. 2006. Minoan Peak Sanctuaries: Building a Cultural Landscape Using GIS. Unpublished dissertation University of Louvain-la-Neuve.

Zeimbeki, M. 2004. The Organization of Votive Production and Distribution in the Peak Sanctuaries of State Society Crete: A Perspective Offered by the Juktas Animal Figurines. In G. Cadogan, E. Hatzaki, and A. Vasilakis (eds). *Knossos: Palace, City, State: Proceedings of the Conference in Herakleion Organised by the British School at Athens and the 23rd Ephoreia of Prehistoric and Classical Antiquities of Herakleion in November 2000 for the Centenary of Sir Arthur Evans's Excavations at Knossos (BSA* Studies 12). London, 351–361.

Chapter 39

IN WHAT CONTEXT? COMPETING AND COMPLEMENTARY APPROACHES TO CONTEXTUAL ANALYSIS IN THE STUDY OF MINOAN RELIGION

Matthew Haysom

The terms context and contextual are used to refer to multiple scales of analysis in and approaches to archaeology – from a grand scale project concerning the nature of meaning in archaeology to approaches that are more focused on excavation methodology and on the interpretation of elements of material culture on the basis of their immediate surroundings (Barrett 1987; Papaconstantinou 2006). The unifying principle of contextual approaches, however, is that any piece of archaeological evidence can be understood only through its relationship with the rest of the archaeological record (compare Hodder 1991, 121–55 with DeMarrais 2005). This paper aims to explore some of the issues arising from applying three approaches that could be called contextual to the study of religion in Minoan Crete in the Neopalatial period (c.1640–1450 BC). It is impossible in the space available here to give the fully rigorous details of an in depth contextual study. The arguments outlined here are based on some of the results of my DPhil thesis (Haysom 2005) and are a fragment of the work conducted for a forthcoming monograph. I would refer those interested in the more detailed underpinnings of the arguments outlined here to the former work.

One of the biggest problems facing Minoan archaeologists is the complexity of the architectural record (McEnroe 1982; Preziosi 1983; Hershenson 2000; Palyvou 2005). There is constant variation in Minoan architecture. No two buildings are the same. Although some buildings are much bigger and more impressive than others, between the simplest building and the most impressive there is only a smooth line of constant variation and individual architectural features can appear at multiple positions along the line (Haysom 2005, 117–26; for just one particularly striking example see Hitchcock's comments in Hägg 1997, 135). These phenomena raise substantial barriers to attempts to produce clear typologies. This means that the kind of everyman contextual analysis that has always been conducted by archaeologists, whereby a norm is established,

assigned the value domestic, and special buildings are ring-fenced in opposition to the norm and their special functions discussed, is extremely difficult. Meanwhile, the complexity and wealth of the material record makes the idea of attempting contextual analysis by building up a complete network of connections between every object, feature and space and every other object, feature and space off-putting to say the least.

In response to these problems Minoan archaeologists have tended to start from those things that seem to be special or especially meaningful, because of some feature such as elaboration or impracticality, in tracing contextual associations. This approach tends to privilege contextual associations between multiple special things, which in turn leads to the special things appearing to be a group – a group that often receives labels like ritual or religious. The vases known as rhyta can be taken as an example of how this type of analysis works in practice. The term rhyton covers a range of vase shapes that are united by having a hole in the bottom so that a liquid poured in the top would come out through the hole (Koehl 1981). This, with its air of impracticality, marks them out as special and contextual associations are traced between them and other things that appear to be special. Rhyta are a regular find at Peak Sanctuaries the special status of which derives from their very particular assemblage of artefacts and their distance from other types of site (Jones 2000, 10–11; Kyrakidis 2005, 138–9). They are occasionally found with other objects or in other spaces that seem to be special because of some air of impracticality. Rhyta can be extremely elaborate and they can be decorated with scenes which seem to depict special places or events. Added together, these associations make a nice pattern and tend to lead to rhyta being regarded as religious, as libation vessels, or, at the very least, to be labelled more nebulously as ritual vases (Gesell 1985, 3–4; Hägg 1990,183). This, in turn, allows other things to be identified as ritual or religious on the basis of contextual associations with them – indeed the presence of rhyta plays a significant role in the identification of many Minoan shrines (Gesell 1985).

At a larger scale a similar method applies. The palaces are the only buildings that clearly stand out in the architectural record because of their large size and their being surrounded by a number of open courts. They also contain lots of the special-looking things, and the congruence of these two phenomena makes the majority of scholars happy with seeing either large parts of the palaces or even all the palaces as being devoted to the practice of ritual or religion (Hägg and Marinatos 1987; Driessen, Schoep, Laffineur 2002). Following the method of contextual analysis by which one starts from associations between special things, when special things that are found in the palace are also found in other buildings they carry their special status with them. And in the case of architectural features they commonly also carry with them the adjective palatial (see for example Driessen 1989-90; Rehak and Younger 2001, 397).

This kind of analysis has led to two reconstructions of Minoan society and the place of ritual and religion in it. On the one hand, the special things in the palaces led to the view that the palaces were the seat of a priestly-monarchy, both residences and religious centres, and that the special things in other buildings marked these out as also combining the religious and residential role so that they were labelled the homes of priests (Evans 1928, 284, 779; Graham 1962; Alexiou 1969, 36–8, 81–5; Hood 1971, 116). On the other hand, a more recent view, partly because of the lack of alternative candidates for temples and a lack of incontrovertible royal imagery, and partly because it finds there to be so many special things in the palace, excises the residential role, calling the palaces temples, ritual or cosmological centres depending on the scholar. Meanwhile, the special things in the palace when found in other buildings increasingly tend to lead to these buildings also being given a special function: as the ritual or religious meeting places of competitive groups who reproduced elements of the palatial rituals (this model emerged as a major theme of Driessen, Schoep, Laffineur 2002 with many of the papers proposing elements of this view or reacting against it).

The problem with this approach, however, derives from it privileging, in interpretation, a proportion of the contextual associations manifested by an element of material culture – those associations that seem special to the investigator – over the full body of that element's contextual associations, interpreting any non-special associations on the basis of the conclusions derived from the special associations. This means that if one instead starts from those non-special associations of an element of material culture a very different interpretation can emerge. The case of the rhyta can again serve to demonstrate how this works in practice.

In the vast majority of cases rhyta are found in otherwise unremarkable circumstances. They are not found in all buildings, but there is no correlation between their presence and the presence of other special things or even the overall size or wealth of the building. Rhyta's only consistent contextual associations are with pithos store-rooms and with the storage of cups (for some valuable general observation and the case study of Akrotiri see Koehl 1981; Koehl 1990; for a detailed examination of rhyta in Cretan sites see Haysom 2005, 138–44, 161–7, 174–6). Cups are also common finds at the special sites, the Peak Sanctuaries, at which rhyta are found (Jones 2000, 51–2; Kyriakidis 2005, 128–33). Working from these contextual associations towards the special associations of rhyta it might be possible to imagine that they were vases involved in something like normal social practices of, for example, hospitality (see also Rehak 1995; Rehak 2000; McGovern, 2003: 274). Their special contextual associations could be seen as a result of this. That, like the wine mixing bowl in Classical Greece, importance in a common social practice led to the rhyton being occasionally monumentalised or left in special places as, for example, a votive.

A similar thing, reversing the special to non-special contextual, can be done on a larger scale with the function of the palaces. As already mentioned, the architectural record of Neopalatial Crete is extremely complex, variation is on a gradual line of increasing complexity, and supposed palatial features can appear at multiple points along this line. This pattern, with the wide distribution of palatial features, allows the picture of their significance to be turned on its head. Instead of viewing them as being vectors, allowing a palatial special function – ritual or religion – to be traced in other buildings, they could be seen as a sign that the palaces were not so greatly distinct and that in many ways they operated as other buildings (lets say for the sake of argument houses) at least wished to operate, only on a larger scale (for a more extensive discussion of the relationship between the palaces and the rest of archaeological record in the Neopalatial period see Haysom 2005, 239–74; for the Protopalatial background see Schoep 2006).

These two approaches to contextual analysis are in competition. The first gives greater interpretive value to contextual associations that seem to the investigator special while the second gives greater value to the more numerous, apparently not-special, associations of an element of material culture. The first approach has the great drawback that, taken to its logical conclusion, always interpreting apparently non-special associations in the light of conclusions from special associations will inevitably lead to the wide attribution of special status, because all elements of material culture are, by some degree of separation, contextually related to something that archaeologists find special (the comment of Dickinson 1994, 276 is interesting in this light). It may appear, meanwhile, that the second approach is more methodologically sound because it is based on a greater number of contextual associations. This, however, is deceptive. The frequency of a contextual association is not necessarily very relevant to the meaning attached to an element of material culture. To take just one easy example there are almost certainly far more crucifixes in cars or houses in modern Greece than there are in churches. But the majority of crucifixes, those found in cars and houses, reference the minority found in churches. There is, therefore, no *a priori* reason to privilege either the top down, special to not special or the bottom up, not special to special, contextual approach and the competition between the two arrives at an impasse.

Both of the contextual approaches outlined so far take as their starting point an individual element of material culture, tracing vectors of association radiating from it. One way to circumvent the impasse, therefore, may be to move the focus of attention away from individual elements of material culture and to look for more generalised patterns in the material record.

In the case of Minoan Crete one such generalised pattern is that although the kinds special-looking objects and architectural features that archaeologists have tended to identify as religious are widely distributed through the buildings of Neopalatial settlements they do not cluster. Overall, no matter what sample one takes different types of special objects do not show a tendency to be found together (for the detailed examination of the evidence underpinning all the statements in this paragraph see Haysom 2005, 127–274). Most special objects and features obey their own quite separate contextual patterns. Many, for example, are most often found with other non-special objects of the same material suggesting the formative logic of the context was to do with storage or exchange. Interestingly the objects which many people might most readily identify with religion are also the furthest from showing correlations with other special objects. Female figurines, for instance, are hardly ever found with any other type of 'special' object. They are rare in settlements, but their closest correlation seems to be with food preparation areas and they can be found in this kind of context in buildings at various points on the line of increasing architectural complexity. Meanwhile, the very rare faience plaques are more closely correlated with administrative documents than any other object type, and may have been the decorations of the boxes in which such documents were kept, rather than votives as is sometimes suggested. On the few instances where there is a tendency for special objects to be found together this can be seen to be part of a wider contextual pattern. So, while most chalices are found with rhyta, only a minority of rhyta are with chalices. But rhyta are extremely common in association with all types of cup.

Archaeologists have missed this general pattern partly because they were chasing individual instances of associa-

tion between objects so the broader pattern, or unexpected patterns of association with non-special objects never appeared, and partly because they wanted to find shrines and other religious spaces. Building Nu at Palaikastro provides a good example of this process because it was excavated by one of the most precise and most cautious of all Minoan scholars Mervyn Popham. He identified a shrine on the upper floor by combining a rhyton, a pair of stone objects commonly called double-axe stands and a set of Horns of Consecration all of which he said fell from above (Sackett and Popham 1965, 257). But this is only true of the Double-Axe stands, the horns of consecration were found in a space under the stairs overlain by the stair slabs and the rhyton was sheltered between and below two pithoi so that it was found hardly damaged. Moreover, each of these objects is quite happy with its own individual contextual associations – rhyta are with pithoi, Horns of Consecration are frequently found in association with staircases (Haysom 2005, 19–20), and it is not unusual to find double axe stands are nearly always found on their own in big empty rooms (Rutkowski 1985).

At this point in order to proceed with assessing the relative contribution of the three contextual approaches to interpretation it is necessary to become more precise about the types of question that archaeologists are asking of the archaeological record and the link between these questions and the ultimate interpretation of that record. Probably the greatest step forward in archaeological thinking about ritual and religion in the last fifteen or twenty years has been the recognition that they are not discreet spheres of activity but are deeply embedded in everyday life. All activities may be influenced by elements of world-view that as outsiders we could label religious. The widespread acknowledgement of this has served to make prehistory a much more realistic place. But it remains true that in many societies certain activities are demarcated in time or space from the rest of life as especially and specifically relevant to those elements of world view that we might characterise as religious. It is these activities that archaeologists have tended to mean when they talk about the archaeology of cult or religion and it is the demarcation combined with the fact that the activities relate to elements of world-view that are specific to the society and, therefore, inexplicable to outsiders that has usually provided the starting point from which discussion of the archaeology of religion begins.

It is important to note that both of the prevailing views of the role of religion in Minoan society are dependent not on the identification of embedded or even of only temporally demarcated activities but on the identification of specific spaces within Minoan settlements as shrines, temples, cosmological centres or clan ritual centres. So one type of question we could ask is whether there really were such temporally and spatially demarcated activities in the towns and cities of Minoan Crete. In combination the conclusions of the latter two contextual approaches – the wide distribution of special elements of material culture and their failure to cluster, combined with each manifesting its own quite separately understandable contextual associations – strongly suggest that there were no such spatially and temporally marked activities within the settlements of Minoan Crete. This conclusion, however, does not necessarily impact on the interpretation of any individual element of material culture. The combination of the two contextual approaches only suggests that no space within Minoan settlements was specifically demarcated for religious activities. This categorically does not mean that no space, such as the streets and courts, was used occasionally for temporally demarcated religious events. And it does not argue against the identification of any individual object as used in ritual or religion.

To conclude, this paper has examined three contextual approaches to the study of religion in Minoan Crete. The first two of these took as their starting point individual elements of material culture, searching for vectors of contextual association radiating from these elements. The third contextual approach moved the focus away from individual elements of material culture looking instead for more generalised patterns. The difference between these three approaches should obviously not be envisaged as hard and fast but is rather one of scale and emphasis. The first two approaches are in competition with one privileging associations between elements that modern archaeologists find special and the other privileging more numerous contextual associations with elements that archaeologists do not find special. The third approach is complementary to these two. Although the third contextual approach cannot resolve the impasse between the first two when it comes to deciding the degree and nature of religious meaning attached to any individual element of material culture, it does to some extent circumvent such problems by reframing the question. In combination with them it can help resolve certain types of question, such as the degree to which there were spatially as well as temporally demarcated religious activities. The negative elements of this conclusion should not detract from the importance of this issue: answering why certain societies dedicate space as well as time to religion is of fundamental importance to any archaeology of religion.

References

Alexiou, S. 1969. *Ancient Crete*. London.

Barrett, J. 1987. Contextual archaeology. *Antiquity* 61, 468–73.

DeMarrais, E. 2005. Holistic/contextual archaeology. In C. Renfrew and P. Bahn (eds). *Archaeology: the Key Concepts*. Oxford, 141–6.

Dickinson, O. 1994. *The Aegean Bronze Age*. Cambridge.

Driessen, J. 1989–90. The proliferation of Minoan palatial architectural style: (1) Crete. *Acta Archaeologia Lovaniensia*, 28–9, 3–23.

Driessen, J., Schoep, I. and Laffineur, R. (eds). 2002. *Monuments of Minos. Rethinking the Minoan Palaces*. Aegaeum 23, Liège.

Evans, A. J. 1928. *The Palace of Minos at Knossos II*. London.

Gesell, G. C. 1985. *Town, Palace and House Cult in Minoan Crete*. Studies in Mediterranean Archaeology 67, Göteborg.

Graham, J. W. 1962. *The Palaces of Crete*. Princeton.

Hägg, R. 1990. The role of libations in Mycenaean ceremony and cult. In R. Hägg and G. C. Nordquist (eds). *Death and Divinity in the Bronze Age Argolid*. Stockholm, 177–84.

Hägg, R. (ed.) 1997. *The Function of the 'Minoan Villa'*. Stockholm.

Hägg R. and Marinatos, N. 1987. *The Function of the Minoan Palace*. Stockholm.

Haysom, M. C. 2005. *An Archaeology of Minoan Religion in the Neopalatial Period. Oxford,* Unpublished DPhil thesis Oxford.

Hershenson, C. R. 2000. Continuity of Syntax in Minoan Vernacular Complexes. In *Πεπραγμένα του Διεθνούς Κρητολογικού Συνεδρίου*. Herakleion, 563–76.

Hodder, I. 1991. *Reading the Past*. 2nd edition. Cambridge.

Hood, M. S. F. 1971. *The Minoans: Crete in the Bronze Age*. New York.

Jones, D. W. 2000. *Peak Sanctuaries and Sacred Caves in Minoan Crete: a Comparison of Artefacts*. Studies in Mediterranean Archaeology pocket-book, Jonsered, 156.

Koehl, R. B. 1981. The function of the Aegean Bronze Age rhyta. In R. Hägg and N. Marinatos (eds). *Sanctuaries and Cults in the Aegean Bronze Age*. Stockholm, 179–88.

Koehl, R. B. 1990. The rhyta from Akrotiri and some preliminary observations on their functions in selected contexts. In D. Hardy (ed.). *Thera and the Aegean World III.1*. London, 350–62.

Kyriakidis, E. 2005. *Ritual in the Bronze Age Aegean: the Minoan Peak Sanctuaries*. London.

McEnroe, J. 1982. A typology of Minoan Neopalatial houses. *American Journal of Archaeology* 86, 3–19.

McGovern, P. E. 2003. *Ancient Wine. The Search for the Origins of Viniculture*. Princeton.

Palyvou, C. 2005. *Akrotiri Thera: an Architecture of Affluence 3,500 Years Old*. Philadelphia.

Papaconstantinou, D. (ed.). 2006. *Deconstructing Context: a critical approach to archaeological practice*. Oxford.

Preziosi, D. 1983. *Minoan Architectural Design: Formation and Signification*. Approaches to Semiotics 63, Berlin.

Rehak, P. 1995. The use and destruction of Minoan stone bull's head rhyta. In R. Laffineur and W.-D. Niemeier (eds). *Politeia: Society and State in the Aegean Bronze Age*. Aegaeum 12, Liège, 435–46.

Rehak, P. 2000. Fragmentation in Minoan Neo-palatial art: stone relief rhyta, bull's head rhyta, and triton shells. *Bulletin of the Institute of Classical Studies*, 44, 215.

Rehak, P. and Younger, J. G. 2001. Neopalatial, Final Palatial, and Post Palatial Crete' in Cullen, T. (ed.). *Aegean Prehistory: a Review*. AJA suppl. 1, Boston, 383–465.

Rutkowski, B. 1985. Minoan Double-Axe Stands. *Archeologia* 36, 7–14.

Sackett, L. H. and Popham, M. R. 1965. Excavations at Palaikastro VI. *Bulletin of the British School at Athens* 60, 248–315.

Schoep, I. 2006. Looking beyond the first palaces: elites and the agency of power in EM III–MM II Crete. *American Journal of Archaeology* 110, 37–64.

Chapter 40

BROKEN POTS AND SEVERED HEADS: CULT ACTIVITY IN IRON AGE EUROPE

Sarah Ralph

Amongst the Celts the human head was venerated above all else, since the head was to the Celt the soul, centre of the emotions as well as of life itself, a symbol of divinity and of the power of the other-world. (Jacobsthal 1944)

Introduction

The body has been a topic of debate and discussion in the humanities and social sciences, much under the influence of works by theoreticians such as Foucault, Bourdieu and Douglas. It is only relatively recently that the topic has entered archaeology (e.g. Hamilakis 1999; Kus 1993; Yates 1993). The notion of embodiment is based on the idea that our subjectivity is defined by our sensory experiences – we exist in and attend to the world through our bodily encounters with the world (Hamilakis 2002, 122). One of the most important aspects of human embodiment is the act of incorporation taking place during food consumption.

Embodied material culture is a special class of material objects produced specifically for immediate destruction, but destruction through consumption by ingestion into the human body. Due to its close association with the body, this kind of material culture has a heightened symbolic and affective resonance in the construction of the self. Moreover, given that eating and drinking are social acts that must be repeated virtually every day for biological survival, they occupy a salient place among the various routinised practices that inculcate *habitus* (Bourdieu 1990) – that is, the set of embodied dispositions that structure action in the world and that unconsciously instantiate social roles and cultural categories and perceptions of identity.

This paper considers the importance of the head in Iron Age Europe (800 BC to AD 100), the contexts in which they appear and their association with feasting. What and how we consume is socially, culturally, economically and politically motivated. Issues of embodiment and the consuming body are investigated during this paper in order to understand the representation of the body, how it was

approached and manipulated in these feasting contexts.

The Iron Age head

Within Iron Age studies, any discussion of the role of the head is often considered alongside the activity of headhunting. Although it has traditionally been linked with 'Celtic' peoples, the magical and social use of heads is widespread, both in space and time (Rosaldo 1980). Literary and archaeological evidence for the Iron Age would suggest that the human head was held in high regard in Iron Age society. Laing (1981) has suggested that the cult of the severed head pervaded Celtic superstition and Powell (1958) viewed headhunting as a horrifying Celtic custom proposing that it originated in cult practices to do with fertility.

The importance placed upon the head and headhunting is not a recent phenomenon for there are detailed Classical literary descriptions of headhunting among the Iron Age peoples; often referred to as the 'Celts'. Strabo described the activity, based on the writing of Poseidonius who visited southern Gaul in *c.* 90 BC and appears to have witnessed the act:

> In addition to their witlessness they [the Celts] possess a trait of barbarous savagery which is especially peculiar to the northern peoples, for when they the leave the battlefield they fasten to the necks of their horses the heads of their enemies, and on arriving home they nail up this spectacle at the entrances to their houses…they embalmed the heads of distinguished enemies with cedar oil, and used to make a display of them to strangers, and were unwilling to let them be redeemed even for their weight in gold. (Strabo, *Geographia* IV,4,5; translation from Tierney 1960)

From this, it would appear that there was no religious or spiritual motivation for headhunting amongst Iron Age peoples. It suggests that it was simply a by-product of warfare (Collis 2003, 215–6) and certainly for Collis, and most probably Poseidonius and his Greek and Roman contemporaries, headhunting was essentially a secular activity connected instead with social display and insulting one's enemies (Collis 2003).

Anthropological work from Southeast Asia would appear to validate assertions of secular headhunting in Iron Age headhunting. Hoskins (1996a, 2) has defined headhunting as an organised and coherent form of violence in which the severed head is given a ritual meaning and the act of head taking is consecrated and commemorated. However, this definition excludes the associated, but non-violent possession of heads as part of secondary funerary rites such as head veneration (e.g. Barth's 1987 work on the Mountain Ok of Inner New Guinea). The human head is an important symbol and therefore at certain times and places it may be violently hunted, revered, depicted in art and iconography, placed on display, removed and hidden and manipulated by particular interest groups (Armit 2006, 2).

Anthropological studies show that the human head can be a potent symbol related to notions such as power, fertility, rites of passage, and acquisition of status. The control and use of this symbol has the potential to inform about social relationships and practices.

Evidence from Iron Age Europe

During the Iron Age there is a profusion of skeletal evidence for the special treatment of the head, often in the context of complex post-mortem treatments of the body, e.g. excarnation or structured deposition (Hill 1995). A re-analysis of human remains from Danebury revealed the presence of weapon-related injuries, suggesting that the remains were the result of violent deaths and the exhibition of the dead (Craig *et al.* 2005). At the Late Bronze Age and Early Iron Age settlement of All Cannings Cross in Wiltshire, Cunnington (1923, 40) interpreted the dispersed remains of thirty-two skull fragments in a midden deposit as evidence of headhunting. This was despite the absence of any other human remains.

In northern France, a large number of sanctuaries have been excavated which have deposits of human bones (Figure 40.1). At Gournay-sur-Aronde, as well as containing 2000 broken weapons and 3000 animal bones in its enclosure ditch, human remains (skull fragments, teeth and vertebrae) were found almost exclusively in the ditch south of the entrance. Long bones also formed vague concentrations at

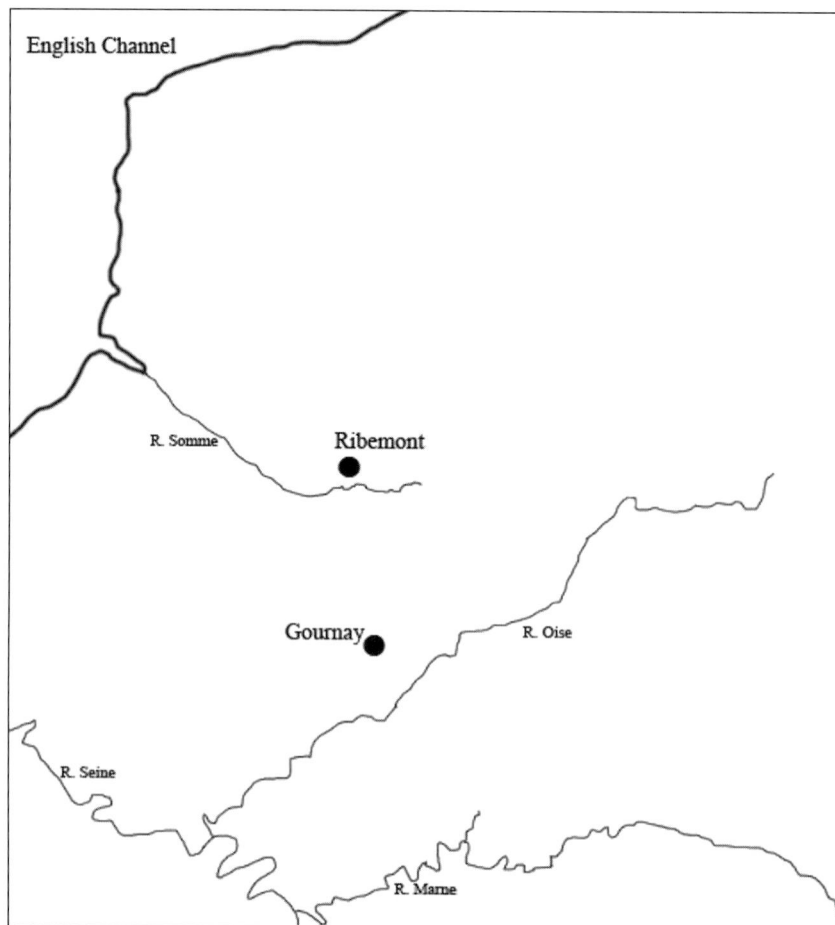

Figure 40.1. Map of sanctuary sites mentioned in text in Northern Gaul.

the north-east and south-east corners of the enclosure. There is evidence for decapitation in the form of multiple, incised cut-marks and chop-marks to the cervical vertebrae, and a mandibular fragment. In some cases, these decapitating blows were delivered from different directions using both a knife and a heavier instrument, indicating that these crania were probably removed after death (cf. Duday 1998; Boylston *et al.* 2000).

The site of Ribemont-sur-Ancre has an immense collection of cult structures. The earliest feature is a ditch dating to *c.* 250 BC, which contained human remains, metal accoutrements and weapons (Fercoq du Leslay 1996). This ditch was followed by a square palisade enclosure, which had scatters of fragmented and crushed human bones and two square ossuaries located in its north-east and south-east corners. These ossuaries, dating to just after 200 BC, comprised *c.* 2000 human long bones, 246 humeri and 501 femora, all mixed with weapons. A post-hole with a funnel-like channel leading to it, occupied the centre of the north-eastern construction with a floor of human iliac bones surrounding it. A mass of splintered and burnt human remains filled the post-hole itself.

Within the sanctuary there were a series of burials of individuals between which were the remains of a decapitated male. Lying along the right side of this individual were a sword and the point of a lance. This combination of a decapitated individual with weapons was witnessed at Stanwick, Yorkshire (Wheeler 1954), the exception being that the head was not found at Ribemont.

The excavated extent of the ditch outside the south-east corner of the palisade contained the remains of 75 adult males. Analyses revealed that these individuals had been decapitated after death. Further examples are known in northern France, for example at Montmartin (Brunaux and Méniel 1997) there is evidence for decapitation and display of crania, as well as dismemberment and defleshing.

The area of southern France, particularly the Lower Rhône Valley, has produced important skeletal and iconographic evidence regarding the human head (Figure 40.2). The majority of finds come from sanctuaries, which are located predominantly in oppida. The motifs that dominate are the images of the warrior and the severed head. Several of the sites with statuary have also produced modified skeletal remains, including crania with embedded iron nails at Entremont (Mahieu 1998), Glanon (Roth Congès 2004) and La Cloche (Chabot 2004), showing that the iconography of headhunting was reflective of real violence. This is also the area in which Poseidonius travelled in the early first century BC, and to which Strabo's comments relates (see above).

Among the earliest of the sculptures is a group displayed in a sanctuary at Roquepertuse (Lescure 2004). The key elements comprised several near life-sized warriors sitting cross-legged, a Janus-head, and several pillars and lintels with niches carved to accommodate skulls. No doubt influenced by the accounts of Poseidonius and others, some researchers have interpreted these features as war trophies. It has also been suggested that the incorporation of the

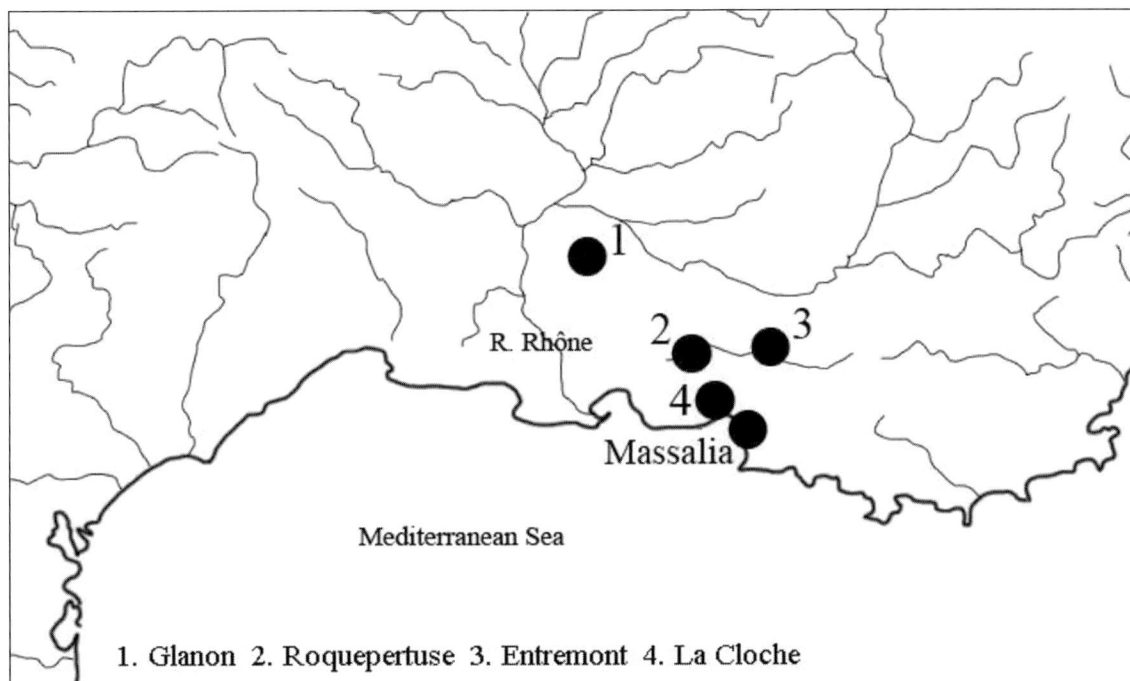

Figure 40.2. Sites mentioned in text in Southern France.

heads into elaborate porticos on a religious site may be more resonant of an ancestor cult (e.g. Arcelin *et al.* 1992).

From the mid-second to the mid-first centuries BC, there was an amplification of the trends seen at Roquepertuse. The main entrance road of an oppidum at Entremont was, according to hypothetical reconstructions, bordered by shelters housing numerous life-sized stone sculptures of heroised male warriors (seated and standing), many holding severed heads (Arcelin and Rapin 2003). These heads, as well as being in the grasp of an individual, are individualistic themselves. This suggests that the identities of both the trophy heads and the warrior were important. Nearby was a hypostyle hall, dating to the last quarter of the second century BC, which contained reused fragments from an earlier portico structure. This included a stone pillar and lintel with engraved representations of severed human heads and carved niches for skulls (Figure 40.3). The pillar depicts twelve virtually identical and stylised heads, all vertically arranged. This 'piling up' of the heads is suggestive of a war trophy and analogous to the skull trees of East Sumba in Indonesia observed in the nineteenth century (Hoskins 1996b). There is no sign of the warrior responsible for such conspicuous success and instead, this object it seems to embody community rather than individual prowess. Twenty-two human skulls were also found in the street near this structure, of which six had traces of having been affixed (Salviat 1993).

A number of finds from *Gallaecia* (modern day Portugal) have produced representations of severed heads, similar to the Gaulish têtes coupées of Gaul (Rapin 2003), particularly in the northern area (*Conventus Lucensis*). These objects are characterised by simple and crude representations of human heads, often in bas-relief, with 'owl faces'. Two pieces from Armeá (Ourense) show the features of a dead person: the most naturalistic element is the swollen, half-closed eyes (Figure 40.4). Two examples, A Graña (A Coruña, Galicia) (Braciela and Rey 2000, 135–136) and San Cibrán de Las-Lansbrica (Ourense, Galicia) (Pérez Outeiriño 1985, 246, plate. IV, 2), came from near the monumental gate or entrance of their associated oppidum.

We are told that after a victory the Celts stripped their dead, but the spoils were not viewed as belonging to them. It was considered important to render them to the divinities and that could explain deposits found at many of the sanctuaries, particularly in northern Gaul. González-Ruibal (2004) proposes that sculpted heads were either apotropaic or ritualistic. The latter could be correct for classical authors inform about the Gaulish custom of putting heads in house doors and the practice of severing their enemy's head in war (Strabo, *Geographia* V, 29, 5; Polybius, *Hist.* II, 28; Livy, *Hist.* X, 26 and 23, 24; Diodorus Siculus, *Hist.* V, 29, 4–5). This textual evidence would suggest that the body of the dead belonged to the warrior and that it was their privilege to take its head. For Brunaux (1988), in killing

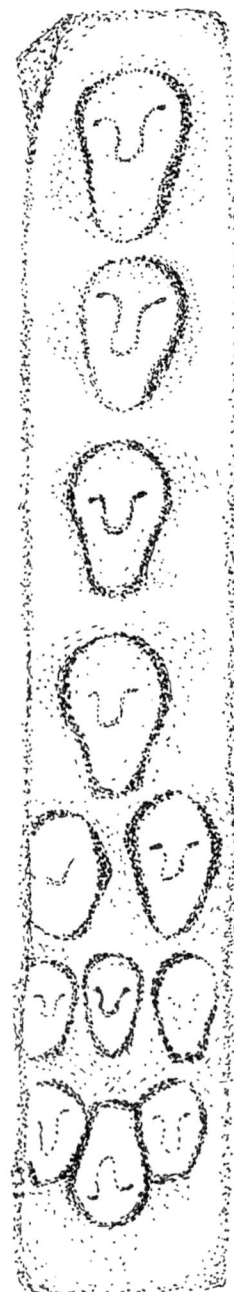

Figure 40.3. Pillar depicting an arrangement of severed heads. Re-used as a lintel in a hypostyle at Entremont.

someone, one appropriated the deceased's spirit and qualities. Thus, it was important that the head remained in the hands of the warrior, who alone had need of their virtues. Diodorus' description indicates that these heads were proof not only of the death of an enemy, but also of their identity and evidence of the warrior's courage and strength (Diodorus Siculus, *Hist.* V, 29, 4–5).

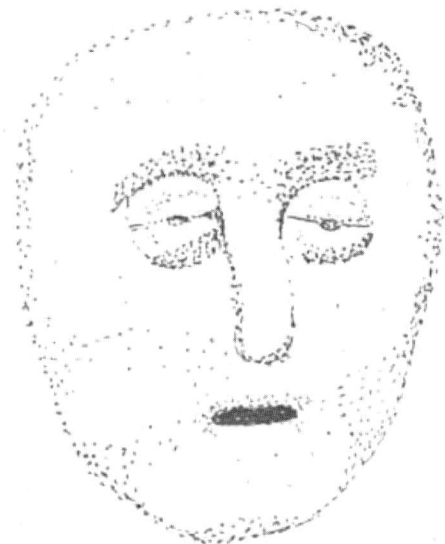

Figure 40.4. Severed head from Armeá.

In Celtiberia, warrior initiation rites included cutting off the heads and hands of the defeated (Strabo, *Geographia* III, 3, 6) in order to show their valour and skill as warriors (García Riaza 2002, 227–230; Sopeña 1995, 149–154). This is seen in the reliefs of Binéfar, Huesca (Sopeña 1995, figures 46–47) and in the 'equine' figure, Herrera de los Navarros, which shows a horse with a man's head under the animal's muzzle (Almagro-Gorbea and Torres 1999, 77–78).

Of broken pots

Pots are closely related to people and lend themselves to thinking about the human form. The terms applied to different parts of vessels are derived from descriptions of the human body, e.g. mouth, lip, neck, shoulder and foot. Pots provide two of the essential requirements of human life, food and water, and these are introduced into the body. The connection between vessels and the human body suggests that pottery might be a powerful indicator of how to understand social, economic and political change, particularly in Iron Age Europe.

It is not just food and drink that are important; it is also their consumption as a social event. Commensality – the social context of sharing the consumption of food and drink – is one of the most profound ways of establishing social connections. Food consumption acquires an immense significance and power in societies because it involves the human body (Hamilakis 1998). The sensory feelings and emotions generated and exchanged in contexts such as funerary feasts or other social gatherings and celebrations, would have constituted the political economy of the body and of bodily memory on the basis of which power

dynamics, competition and negotiation of social roles operated (Hamilakis 1999, 49). Food and drink are incorporated directly into the body and become a part of the person. Power processes and mechanisms operate through the consuming body and thus, the human body acts as a vehicle for cultural discourse. The body can produce and reproduce cultural meanings, and these representations of the body can create and define social ideologies.

Work by Poux (2000; 2004) has investigated the consumption of wine in Iron Age France and considered the types of material culture associated with its consumption, how and where it is consumed, and how the resulting debris is deposited. Of interest is the use of amphorae and their associated treatment.

The above-mentioned deposits of human remains are often associated with evidence of collective consumption, particularly within sanctuaries. Amphorae sherds have been found at some of these sites and the deposition of amphorae appears to have resulted from ritual and cult activity, e.g. the deposition of complete or nearly complete amphorae in pits and wells. The relationship between amphorae sherds and votive offerings is clear at Ribemont where a deposit (dated to the middle of the first century BC) of several hundred amphorae sherds was made in the enclosure ditch. The deposit was associated with metal offerings, animal (particularly pig) and human bones. The amphorae also carried traces of burning.

However, the most interesting form of deposition, particularly in light of the importance of the head during the Iron Age, is the decapitation of amphorae at many of these sites. The 'severing' of amphora, witnessed by the discovery of corked necks and blade impacts, evokes a symbolic decapitation ritual of the vessel. The amphorae had their necks severed with a sword and then the necks were separated from the main body of the amphorae, e.g. Corent (Poux *et al.* 2002), Lyon (Mandy *et al.* 1989) and Clermont Ferrand (Vernet 1997). Wine would have poured down the sides of the amphorae, much like blood down the neck of a human decapitation victim. There are frequent associations of severed amphorae necks and these particular parts of animals and humans, e.g. Mouron, Aulnot and Bâle-Gasfabrik. In fact at the latter site, in certain ditches humans and amphorae were given the same form of decapitation.

Amphorae could have been used as substitute humans for sacrifice, which could involve burial alive, decapitation or cremation (Poux 2000). At Lyon Verbe-Incarné, a human skull of a young female was associated with a body of an amphorae and a collection of cut amphorae necks (Mandy *et al.* 1989). At Bâle-Gasfabrik, the skeleton of a young girl whose head had been removed was deposited in the centre of a deposit of amphorae body sherds (Jud and Spichtig 1994).

The separation and meticulous selection of bodies and necks could be paralleled with dismemberment rituals known at sanctuaries in northern Gaul. This is reinforced by the combined deposition, in certain sanctuaries, of neck bones and skulls from a decapitated body being found in association with a decapitated amphora. Pots have human-like attributes and thus the anthropoid form of amphorae could inspire these deposits of amphorae and human bone.

Amphorae vessels were consciously manipulated after consumption and before deposition. Some had been deliberate broken or burnt whilst still whole vessels or as sherds. It is difficult to explain these phenomena in terms of normal domestic debris, especially given their association with deposits of human bone. Excavations at Corent revealed a large quadrangular area paved with amphorae sherds (Poux *et al.* 2002). There were votive objects including mutilated weapons, brooches, coins, human skulls and the remains of animals. Ritual damage is often present on metal offerings found in sanctuaries and fragments of amphora and pieces of weaponry often display the same traces of blade impacts or striking (see Poux 2004, figure 149; Brunaux 1988).

In Britain, there are potential similarities. For example, the funerary chamber at Welwyn Garden City contained five amphorae, of which one was complete and the remaining four may have had their neck broken (Stead 1967). At the late Iron Age burial at Hertford Heath, one complete Dressel 1B and one neck and rim were found nearby (Hüssen 1983). Further evidence of the breaking of amphorae necks is known from similar graves at Dorton, Buckinghamshire and Mount Bures, Essex. At the former there were parts of three amphorae, all with their necks removed (Farley 1983). The latter is believed to have contained at least five amphorae, possibly six. All that remained were the bodies of the vessels; their necks and handles had been removed (Smith 1911–12).

It is clear that there is a symbolic link between wine and blood. The textures of food and their containers may be significant. The close physical proximity of food and drink to the corpse is a further sensual aspect of feasting and sacrifice. Substances associated with the body are often regarded as dangerous and polluting, but through touching and incorporating food intended for sharing with or sacrificing to the dead, and by handling and interring objects linked to the funerary feast, eating and drinking emphasise the intimate links with the corpse.

Many rites involve the use of wine and for the Iron Age a parallel could be drawn with rituals performed by the Scythians (Herodotus *Hist.* IV, 70). The 'Oath of Friendship' is founded on the sharing of a bowl or a cup of wine mixed with several drops of blood, in which the warriors, one by one, dipped their weapons before drinking it.

Diodorus speaks that during the third century BC, a Greek tyrant Apollodorus wanted to assure the loyalty of his guards, so he sacrificed a young boy whose blood was mixed with wine and shared with his future warriors, among whom were 'Celts'. (*Hist.* XXII, 5) This ritualised sharing of wine was considered to represent the devotion of the warrior and therefore this may be what is represented in the archaeological record.

Conclusion

There has been much discussion regarding perceptions and experiences of the body in past societies (e.g. Hamilakis *et al.* 2002). The retention and display of human heads would seem to suggest that certain parts of the body were thought to retain power and meaning after death. It is conceivable that some part of the soul, essence or spirit of a deceased individual can be captured by the removal and retention of the head. In some societies, care must be taken to free the soul from the decomposing physical body in order to restore balance to the community and prevent the lingering presence of malevolent spirits. Interventions of various sorts may be necessary either to maintain the integrity of the body or to ensure its appropriate processing, e.g. cremation, mummification or inhumation. The appropriation of the head hinders or prevents their incorporation into the spirit world or realm of ancestors. The head may also act to transfer control or ownership of the spiritual force from one group to another.

I am interested in the relationship between the importance of the head and the treatment and use of food and drink, i.e. understanding the nature of the consuming body and its metaphoric and symbolic use in differing contexts. Amphorae can act as substitutes for the body – the human soul is released through decapitation and its neck removed, much like the human body.

Food, pots and politics are intimately linked. Ceramic vessels serve in the mediation of political power and one can consider the relationship between pottery and food in articulating, defining and negotiating identity and power. As shown, the incorporation of food intended for the deceased or sacrificed heightens the bond with the corpse

The condition of embodiment and incorporation is responsible for the power and multiplicity of meanings attributed to food: the mnemonic character of food, the bodily experience of the sight, smell and the taste of food which evokes the senses and generates remembering. Thus, food is constantly used in the generation, maintenance, legitimation and deconstruction of authority and power. Feasting and the sacrifice of vessels with food and drink make an event memorable as well as evoke the remembrance of previous feasting events. The mixture of sacrifice, consumption and intoxication may emphasise vitality and regeneration in the face of the chaos and disorder threatened by death.

It is important to understand how we embody food and drink and how our own bodies are manipulated and used in social, political and economics contexts in both life and death. The consuming body operates through the sensory interactions of eating and the ways in which the physiological body is managed and presented is largely a reflection of broader social concerns. In comprehending these relationships, we can understand Iron Age attitudes towards the body and consumption (in all its forms) and how the body becomes a receptor for change in social, political and economic contexts.

References

Almargo-Gorbea, M. and M. Torres. 1999. *Las fibulas de jinete y de caballito. Aproximación a las elites ecuestres y su expansion en la Hispania céltica.* Zaragoza, Institución Fernando el Católico.

Arcelin, P. and Rapin, A. 2003. L'iconographie anthropomorphe de l'Age du Fer en Gaule Méditerranéenne. In O. Büchsenschütz, A. Bulard, M-B. Chardenoux and N. Ginoux (eds) *Decors, Images et Signes de l'Age du Fer Européen: XXVI Colloque de l'Association Française pour l'Etude de l'Age du Fer, Paris et Saint-Denis, 2002.* Tours, Fédération pour l'édition de la revue archéologique du centre de la France, 183–220.

Arcelin, P., Dedet, B. and Schwaller, M. 1992. Espaces publics, espaces religieux protohistoriques en Gaule méridionale. *Documents d'Archéologie Méridionale* 15, 181–242.

Armit, I. 2006. Inside Kurtz's compound: headhunting and the human body in prehistoric Europe. In M. Bonogofsky (ed.). *Skull Collection, Modification and Decoration.* BAR International Series 1539, 1–4.

Barth, F. 1987. *Cosmologies in the Making.* Cambridge, Cambridge University Press.

Bourdieu, P. 1990. *The Logic of Practice.* Stanford, Stanford University Press.

Boylston, A., Knüsel, C. J., Roberts, C. A. and Dawson, M. 2000. Investigation of a Romano-British rural ritual in Bedford, England. *Journal of Archaeological Science* 27, 241–54.

Braciela, P. and Rey, E. 2000. *Xacementos arqueolóxicos de Galicia. Guía práctica para visitar e coñecer o patrimonio arqueolóxico galego.* Vigo, Xerias.

Brunaux, J-L. (trans. D. Nash). 1988. *The Celtic Gauls: Gods, Rites and Sanctuaries.* London, Seaby.

Brunaux, J-L. and Méniel, P. 1997. La residence aristocratique de Montmartin (Oise). *Doc. D'Arch. Française* 64.

Chabot, L. 2004. *L'Oppidum de la Cloche: Les Pennes-Mirabeau, Bouches-du-Rhône. Protohistoire Européenne. Vol. 7.* Montagnac, Mergoil.

Collis, J. R. 2003. *The Celts: Origins, Myths and Inventions.* Stroud, Tempus.

Craig, C. R., Knüsel, C. J. and Carr, G. C. 2005. Fragmentation, mutilation and dismemberment: an interpretation of human remains on Iron Age sites. In M. Parker Pearson and N. Thorpe (eds). *Warfare, Violence and Slavery in Prehistory.* Oxford, BAR International Series 1374, 165–180.

Cunnington, M. E. 1923. *The Early Iron Age Inhabited Site at All Cannings Cross Farm, Wiltshire.* Devizes, Simpson and Co.

Duday, H. 1998. Le charnier gaulois de Ribemont-sur-Ancre (Somme). *Etudes et Documents Fouilles* 4, 113–19.

Farley, M. 1983. A mirror burial at Dorton, Buckinghamshire. *Proceedings of the Prehistoric Society* 49.

Fercoq du Leslay, G. 1996. Chronologie et analyse spatiale à Ribemont-sur-Ancre (Somme). *Revue Archéologique de Picardie* 3/4, 189–208.

García Riaza, E. 2002. *Celtíberos y lusitanos frente a Romano: diplomacia y derecho de Guerra.* Anejos de Veleia, Series minor 18, Vitoria-Gasteiz.

González-Ruibal, A. 2004. Artistic expression and material culture in Celtic Gallaecia. *E-Keltoi* 6, 113–166.

Hamilakis, Y. 1998. Eating the dead: mortuary feasting and the politics of memory in the Aegean Bronze Age Societies. In K. Branigan (ed.) *Cemetery and society in the Aegean Bronze Age.* Sheffield, Sheffield Academic Press, 115–32.

Hamilakis, Y. 1999. Food technologies/technologies of the body: the social context of wine and oil production and consumption in Bronze Age Crete. *World Archaeology* 31(1), 38–54.

Hamilakis, Y. 2002. *Embodiment and Experience: Introduction.* In Hamilakis *et al.* 2002, 99–103.

Hamilakis, Y., Pluciennik, M. and Tarlow, S. (eds). 2002. *Thinking Through the Body: Archaeologies of Corporeality.* New York, Plenum.

Hill, J. D. 1995. *Ritual and Rubbish in the Iron Age of Wessex: a study on the formation of a specific archaeological record.* Oxford, BAR British Series 242.

Hoskins, J. (ed.). 1996a. *Headhunting and the Social Imagination in Southeast Asia.* Stanford, Stanford University Press.

Hoskins, J. 1996b. *The heritage of headhunting: history, ideology and violence on Sumba 1890–1990.* In J. Hoskins (ed.). *Headhunting and the Social Imagination in Southeast Asia.* Stanford, Stanford University Press, 216–248.

Hüssen, C-M. 1983. *A Rich Late La Tène Burial at Hertford Heath, Hertfordshire.* British Museum Occasional Paper No. 44.

Jacobsthal, P. F. 1944. *Early Celtic Art.* Oxford, Clarendon Press.

Jud, P. and Spichtig, N. 1994. *Basel-Gasfabrik: Ausblick auf neue Grabungen und Forschungen.* Bâle, Coll. de Bâle, 56–71.

Kus, S. 1993. Towards an archaeology of body and soul. In J-C. Gardin and C. S. Peebles (eds). *Representations in Archaeology.* Bloomington, Indiana University Press, 168–95.

Laing, L. 1981. *Celtic Britain.* London, Paladin.

Lescure, B. 2004. La statuaire de Roquepertuse et ses nouveaux indices d'interprétation à l'issue des fouilles récentes. *Documents d'Archéologie Méridionale* 27, 45–47.

Mahieu, E. 1998. L'anthropologie d'Entremont. *Documents d'Archéologie Méridionale* 21, 62–65.

Mandy, B., Sandoz, G., Krausz, S., Genin, M., Godard, C., Thirion, Ph. and Monin, M. 1989. Les fosses du plateau de la Sarra. *Doc. D'Arch. en Rhône-Alpes* 3/2, 37–95.

Pérez Outeiriño, B. 1985. Informe sobre las excavaciones arqueológicas de "A Cidade" de San Cibrán de Las (San Amaro-Punxín, Orense). Campaña de 1982. *Noticiario Arqueológico Hispánico* 22, 213–259.

Poux, M. 2000. Banquets et rites de libation en contexte de sanctuaries et d'enclos. *Revue Archeologique de Picardie* 1–2, 217–32.

Poux, M. 2004. *L'Âge du Vin: Rites de boisson, festins et libations en Gaule indépendante*. Montagnac, Mergoil.

Poux, M., Deberge, Y., Foucras, S., Pasquier, D. and Gasc, J. 2002. L'enclos cultuel de Corent (Puy-de-Dôme): festins et rites collectives. *Rev. Arch. du Centre de la France, T.* 41, 57–110.

Powell, T. G. E. 1958. *The Celts*. London, Thames and Hudson.

Rapin, A. 2003. De Roquepertuse à Entremont, la grande sculpture du Midi de la Gaule. *Madrider Mitteilungen* 44, 223–246.

Rosaldo, R. 1980. *Ilongot Headhunting 1883–1974: A Study in Society and History*. Stanford, Stanford University Press.

Roth Congès, A. 2004. Le context archéologique de la statuaire de Glanon (Saint-Rémy-de-Provence, Bouches-du-Rhône). *Documents d'Archéologie Méridionale* 27, 23–43.

Salviat, F. 1993. La sculpture d'Entremont. In D. Coutagne (ed.). *Archéologie d'Entremont au Musée Granet*. Aix-en-Provence, Association des Amis de Musée Granet, 165–239.

Smith, R. A. 1911–12. On late Celtic antiquities discovered at Welwyn, Herts. *Archaeologia* Second Series. Vo. XIII (Vol. 63).

Sopeña, G. 1995. *Ética y ritual. Aproximacíon al estudio de la religiosidad de los pueblos celtibéricos*. Zaragoza, Institución Fernando el Católico.

Stead, I. M. 1967. A La Tène burial at Welwyn Garden City. *Archaeologia* 101.

Tierney, J. J. 1960. The Celtic ethnography of Poseidonius. *Proceedings of the Royal Irish Academy* 60, 189–275.

Vernet, G. 1997. *Rapport d'opération préventive de fouille d'évaluation archéologique sur le 'terrain IVECO' (parcelles CN 183a, 185 et 186). Zone industrielle Le Brézet Est (Clermont-Ferrand)*. Rapport inédit, D.R.A.C., S.R.A. Auvergne, Clermont-Ferrand 1997.

Wheeler, R. E. M. 1954. *The Stanwick Fortifications*. Oxford, Society of Antiquaries Research Report 11.

Yates, T. 1993. Frameworks for an archaeology of the body. In C. Tilley (ed.). *Interpretative Archaeology*. Oxford, Berg, 31–72.

Chapter 41

CONTEXTS OF CULT IN *HISPANIA CELTICA*

Silvia Alfayé

I aim to offer an updated overview of the contexts of cult documented through literary, archaeological and iconographical sources within the populations of *Hispania Celtica* in this paper. The focus is on the types of places where cult took place, offering an approach to the different rituals carried out in these spaces, discussing topics such as their communal or private meaning, and their links with the past.

The study of cult in Celtic *Hispania* is problematic. There is a complicated historiography and there are few modern excavations of possible sacred places. Most of the possible cult places were excavated at the beginning of the last century, as a consequence the objects discovered in those campaigns do not have a proper archaeological context making their interpretation and dating extremely difficult. These problems seriously limit our knowledge of past religious systems. Literary accounts of rituals on the Iberian Peninsula are extremely rare. Classical historians wrote about religious practices from an anthropological ethnocentrism, distorting the indigenous reality, adapting it to the paradigm of the barbarian and contributing to the construction of the discourse of the conqueror. The adoption of epigraphy as a votive practice by the people of the peninsular provides direct evidence about cultic practices. This source is not without its problems, inscriptions are relatively late in date, hundreds of inscriptions share the problem of lack of archaeological context, and the highly formulaic character of the Latin does not offer much information beyond the name of the Celtic god (Marco 2002).

Natural places

Natural places, such as woods, mountains, outcrops, rock-shelters, caves and springs, are often advanced as the Celtic cult places *par excellence*, but that does not mean that the peoples of *Hispania* worshipped natural powers directly. The invisible divinities manifested themselves through visible signs like these natural elements, but these places were merely places of interaction between gods and human beings, never entities that were honoured in their own right (Webster 1995, 448–451; Marco 2005, 296). It can be difficult to identify these 'natural', sacred, places in the archaeological record, especially if we think that the rituals performed there, the votive offerings and the possible *temenos* or enclosure, could not have left any archaeological trace (Bradley 2000). Ancient literary and epigraphically sources give us some insight into the features of Celtic-Roman sacred geography, possibly linked to cosmological ideas.

In the Iberian Peninsula the existence of sacred woods is also attested by literary sources, although attempts to locate their actual geographical location are controversial (Marco 1999a, 149–152). The problem is shared by mountains: their sacred importance is testified by ancient literary sources and by numerous inscriptions found in mountains dedicated to gods whose names are connected with them, but no cult structures have been identified or excavated there (Marco 2005, 298–299; Richert 2005). Two metallic hoards (first century BC) discovered in Salvacañete (Cuenca) and Lería (Soria) were related to mountains and sources of water. The composition of these votive deposits (coins, miniaturized objects, torques and so on), and their environmental characteristics (elevated location, close to springs and rivers, near an ancient road) have parallels in similar discoveries throughout the Iberian area and Celtic Europe, linked with watery deities (Arévalo and Marcos 2000). The existence of sacred sites near sources of water in Celtic *Hispania* is also attested by the discovery in their surroundings of Latin inscriptions consecrated to indigenous gods, mainly dated between the first and the third century AD. We do not have any archaeological evidence of the cultic use of these places in the pre-Roman period, perhaps due to the absence of monumental structures and the impermanent character of votive offerings. There are two interpretations: either these places represent the survival of pre-conquest practices, or such sites are a post-conquest phenomenon (Webster 1995, 449–450). Some of these possible indigenous cult sites were Roman spas under the divine protection of traditional deities (the *Matres*), or Roman deities (*Minerva*, *Salus*) assimilated with indigenous ones (Díez de Velasco 1998; Gómez Pantoja 1999).

Crags, or rock outcrops, with carved steps, basins, seats, channels or cup-marks have been identified as stones for human sacrifice and rock-altars (Figure 41.1) (Almagro and Jiménez 2000). This interpretation originated in Europe during the eighteenth and nineteenth centuries and was nourished by romantic ideas that identified the megaliths as altars where the druids celebrated ceremonies. The systematic identification of rock structures as open-air Celtic cultic sites persists amongst Spanish scholars, even though the revision of the context of some of these stones forces us to rethink, not only their supposed pre-Roman dating, but also their ritual use (Alfayé, forthcoming b). It does not imply that we should completely deny their ritual purpose. The rock-altar of 'Ulaca' (Solosancho, Ávila) was a communal ceremonial site integrated in a *temenos* measuring 16 × 8 m and located at the axis of the settlement (Figure 41.1). It is very difficult to know exactly when this space was designed as it has not been excavated, despite this most scholars argue that it was probably used for libations and animal sacrifices in the period from the third to the first century BC.

In the Callaico-Lusitanian area, rock outcrops with carved votive inscriptions, such as Cabeço das Fráguas (Sabugal), can be identified as open-air ceremonial sites, probably reflecting earlier traditions, but dating to the Roman Period (second century AD). The epigraphs could be interpreted as manifestations of collective rituals dedicated to indigenous and Roman deities, which included sacrifices of bulls, lambs and pigs (Vaz 2002; Marco 2005, 313–314).

The use of rock-shelter as a context of cult is recorded through the votive Palaeohispanic and Latin inscriptions carved on their walls. No archaeological materials are associated with these places, so it is difficult to determine the kind of rituals celebrated there. The cliff of Peñalba de Villastar (Teruel) is the most important sanctuary of this type because of its size (1.5 km long) and the richness of its carvings and rock epigraphy. Some of the inscriptions document that the Celtic gods *Cornutus Cordonus*, *Eniorosei*, *Tiatumei* and *Equeisos* were worshipped on that mountain during the first century AD (Jordán 2004, 375–393; Beltrán *et al.* 2005). An earlier cultic use is possible because I believe that the adoption of epigraphy as a votive practice by the worshippers in Peñalba allows us to visualize archaeologically previous ritual activities which did not leave any material trace. It is difficult to say exactly what kind of rituals took place at the cliff, due to the absence of material finds, but some of the inscriptions offer some information. From the so-called 'Gran Inscripción' we

Figure 41.1. The indigenous rock-altar of 'Ulaca', at Solosancho (Ávila).

know that a peregrination, or a religious meeting (*comeimu*), took place in Peñalba, which included the construction of an enclosure for the gods. No ancient building has been discovered, but I think that some of the holes carved on the rock could belong to that Celtic-Roman sacred structure. The location, appearance and function could have been very similar to those of the medieval rock-hermitages of the Iberian Peninsula (Figure 41.2). Although their ancient date is controversial, it is possible that some of the carvings had a cultic purpose, and I do not think it is accidental that some of them depict horses and deer, both animals related with the theonyms worshipped in Peñalba (*Equeisos* and *Cornutus Cordonus*), which could have been sacrificed there (Beltrán *et al.* 2005, 936; Alfayé 2005, 229–330).

With a few exceptions, the sacred use of caves is documented through the existence of votive rock inscriptions and not through archaeology (Abascal 2003; Alfayé 2005, 230–231). The most striking cave-sanctuary is 'La Griega' (Pedraza, Segovia), a cave used as a sacred place from Prehistory onwards. More than a hundred Latin inscriptions, carved close to Palaeolithic drawings and concentrated in the deepest parts of the cave, demonstrate its intense religious occupation throughout the first three centuries AD, linked to the worship of the Celtic deities *Nemedus*, *Deva*, *Munidus* and *Deus Moclevus* (Figure 41.3). The archaeological evidence is several mud-figures and rock carvings, possibly tied to Celtic-Roman religious practices (Corchón 1997).

Sacred sites inside settlements

Contrary to traditional opinion (Burillo 1998, 214), the archaeological record documents the existence of spaces within settlements where cult practices took place. Some of these intramural spaces seem to be tied to a communal willingness to create a monumental structure for the celebration of collective rituals. A third century BC monumental building with a columned porch in the centre of the settlement of 'La Hoya' (Laguardia, Álava) was identified as a temple (Llanos 2002, 74). At the highest point of the *oppidum* of 'Castrejón de Capote' (Higuera la Real, Badajoz) a unique structure was built open to the main street, and organized around an altar surrounded by benches (Figure 41.4). This altar-room was used for animal sacrifices and communal consumption of meat and alcohol, from the fifth to the second century BC. This type of structure concerned with 'the Archaeology of the Feast' has parallels in the *Viereckschanzen* of Central Europe, in the insular *bruidne*, in some Gallic structures and in Iberian buildings used for cult activities and communal banquets (Alfayé 2006, Berrocal 1994).

Inside *Numantia* (Garray, Soria) a communal sanctuary could have existed where painted vessels and ceramic *askoi* were deposited. This would be a model of cultic space with parallels in Iberian, such as the 'Departamento 14' at the settlement of *Edeta* (San Miquel de Llíria, Valencia). The absence of archaeological data about the contexts of these ceramics does not allow us to reach definitive conclusions. The room at *Numantia* (first century BC) housing a stone monument and a vessel containing human remains, could have been a *heroon*, a collective sacred space tied to the

Figure 41.2. A view of the rock-sanctuary of Peñalba de Villastar (Teruel).

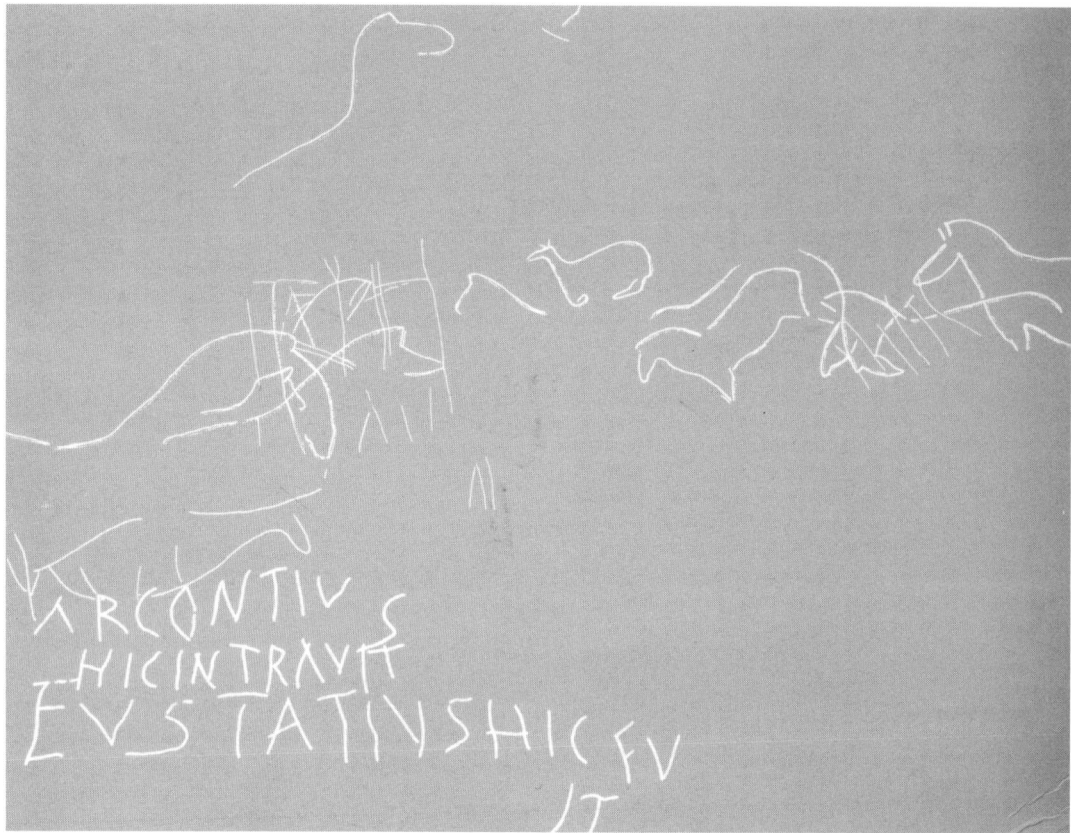

Figure 41.3. Palaeolithic carvings and Latin inscriptions in the cave of 'La Griega', Pedraza (Segovia). Corchón et alii *1997.*

magical protection of the city (Alfayé 2005, 232). This shrine design has parallels in Gallic structures identified as *heroa* (fourth to second centuries BC), which were also terraced to the wall and contained cremated human remains, and in which the community celebrated occasional rituals (Arcelin and Brunaux 2003, 254–256).

An important sanctuary could have been located inside the settlement of Garvão (Ourique) (fourth to the third century BC). The presence of an intramural *favissa* with rich votive materials suggest this, unfortunately we do not know the exact location or the plan of that sacred space (Beirào *et al.* 1985). It is also possible that a monumental sacred building existed in the centre of *Mirobriga* (Santiago de Caçêm), although the archaeological record is inconclusive. This problem is shared by the ruins situated at the highest point of *Tiermes* (Montejo de Tiermes, Soria), identified as a Celtiberian temple, but with uncertainty surrounding its date (Almagro and Berrocal 1997). Turning to the possible existence of monumentalized intramural sanctuaries, several scholars identify depictions on vessels from the settlements of *Numantia*, *Arcobriga* and *Pintia* as representations of indigenous temples. It is difficult to decide if they are depictions of real structures or only artistic, idealized, stylisations (Alfayé 2005, 233).

The kind of communal rituals that took place in buildings, and possibly in the open-air plazas, is a matter of debate. Animals were sacrificed according to sex, age and skin-colour. Occasionally human sacrifice was performed: in times of warfare, during crises, or on special religious occasions (Marco 1999b). Images on pottery and the literary sources (Strabo 3.4.16) attest to religious dances, including fancy dress simulating horses or bulls (Sopeña 2005, 355–356). The ritual banquet was an important ceremonial context governed by strict norms of conduct and rank, it involved specific equipment: metallic instruments related to fire, *simpula*, vessels decorated with human heads (Horn 2003), *oinochoes*, and so on. Collective banqueting was tied to religious preparations for war, the exaltation of victory, the distribution of booty, the celebration of periodic religious festivals, and the sanctioning of agreements and oaths, linked in this case to hospitality. Feasting could also have a private character, motivated by the celebration of personal events, although sometimes the familiar feast could have had a communal meaning as it is illustrated in the wedding banquets offered by the Lusitanian chief *Viriathus* (Alfayé 2006).

Private rituals of sacrifice and commensality took place in domestic spaces in the settlements of Reillo (Guadalajara)

Figure 41.4. The altar-room of 'Castrejón de Capote', at Higuera la Real (Badajoz). Berrocal 1994.

and Cuéllar (Segovia) (fifth century BC). These were rooms within private houses organized around a central fireplace surrounded by benches, which did not have any external sign of monumentality. In their interior metallic cooking instruments have been discovered, with eating and drinking implements, and objects of ritual character such as *aspergillus*, terracotta figures and zoomorphic firedogs. These rooms have been identified as domestic sanctuaries dedicated to banqueting between aristocrats, which included the performance of rituals (Barrio 2002; Moneo 2003, 370–372). Rooms in which clay figurines have been discovered have been interpreted as possible domestic sanctuaries, although others prefer to link them with the existence of a familiar altar in a multifunctional room. In my opinion, most of these figurines had a symbolic meaning, although their typological and technological variety suggests that they were used for different functions (Alfayé forthcoming, a).

The best documented ritual activity in a domestic context is the sacrifice of animals and their burial under or near the house (Figure 41.5). Most of these ritual deposits were very simple (a single animal or parts of it), although some of them were quite complex (e.g. the deposits at *Pintia*). Animal sacrifices were probably propitiatory rituals, maybe

with a foundational character, or they could be linked to closing rituals (Sanz and Velasco 2003, 125–141). Vessels with food or animal offerings inside were also ritually placed under the walls or the floors of houses at several settlements, such as 'El Raso' (Candeleda, Avila) and *Uxama* (Osma, Soria).

Other domestic ritual practice, limited to the Celtiberian and Vaccean areas, is infant burial, a funerary custom which does not seem linked to infanticides or ritual sacrifice (Filloy 1995). Inside the houses people also burnt aromatic substances in special containers, perhaps related to some kind of fire cult. The intentional conservation of human skulls in domestic contexts is documented in the settlement of 'La Hoya' and in the city of *Numantia*, where four male skulls were discovered in a first century BC cellar (Taracena 1943). Possibly they were trophies kept by a warrior in his house, but some scholars suggest that the skulls belonged to ancestors worshipped in a domestic chapel or a communal cult space (Sopeña 1995, 240–241).

Roman sanctuaries to indigenous deities

Archaeology and/or epigraphy reveal the existence of some sanctuaries consecrated to indigenous deities that reflect

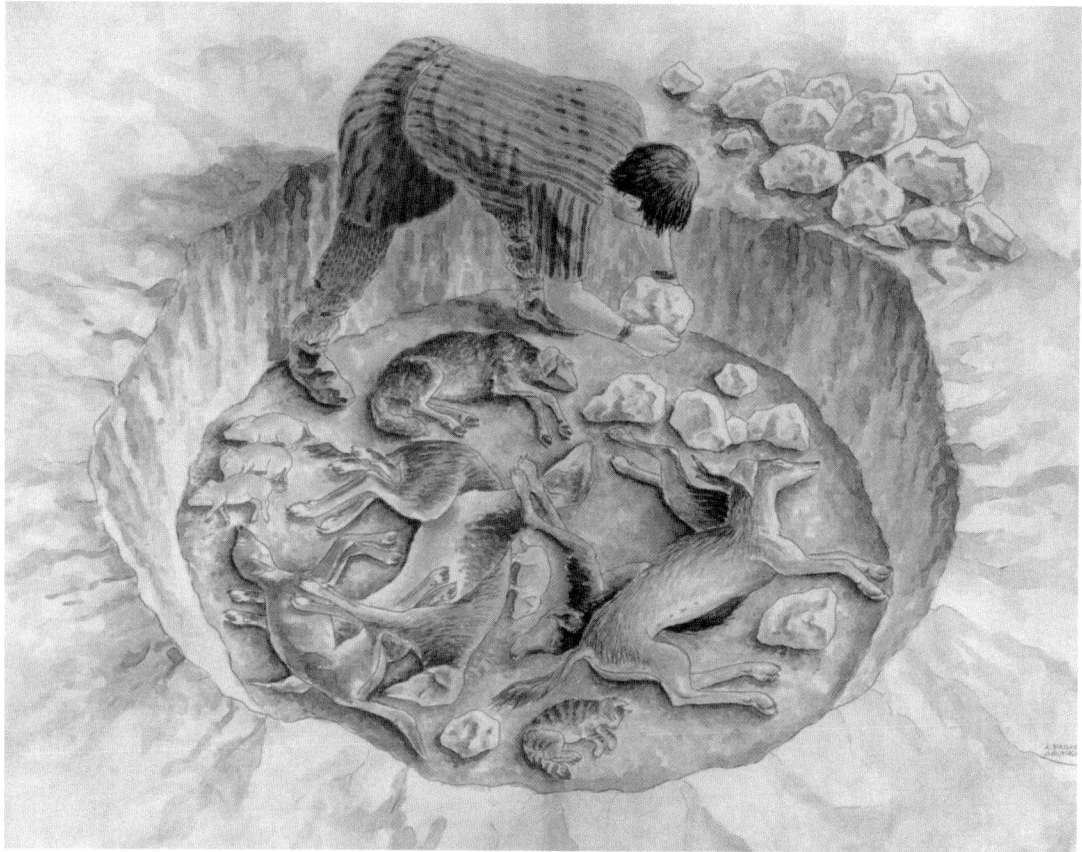

Figure 41.5. Animal deposit at Pintia, *Padilla de Duero (Valladolid). Sanz and Velasco 2003.*

an earlier tradition, but date from the Roman Period, such as the sanctuary of *Endovellicus*, in San Miguel da Mota (Alandroal). Some were located at the crossroads of various ethnic groups, becoming ritual spaces of convergence, 'frontier' sanctuaries (Raposo 2002; Marco 2005).

Cemeteries as sacred places

Ritual practices took place in cemeteries. Weapons were destroyed, pottery was broken, animals were sacrificed, offerings of food and drink were made and funerary banquets consumed (Marco 2005, 327–334). Some studies suggest that the layout of some Celtic cemeteries, such as 'La Osera' (Chamartín de la Sierra, Ávila), 'El Ceremeño' (Herrería, Guadalajara) and 'Carratiermes' (Soria), were carefully planned according to astronomical measurements (connected with cosmological ideas), which determined their location and internal organization, and required the performance of rituals linked to the inauguration and closing of those sacred spaces (Baquedano and Escorza 1998; Argente *et al.* 2001, 241–250; Rodríguez *et al.* 2006).

Several rectangular structures situated close to cemeteries could have been cult sites. One measures 120 ×

75 m, located on the outskirts of the Vaccean cemetery of 'Las Ruedas' (Padilla de Duero, Valladolid) (Sanz and Velasco 2003, 62–63); and another, 7 × 4.4 m, discovered between two chronologically different sections of the Celtiberian graveyard at 'El Pradillo' (Pinilla-Trasmonte, Burgos) (Moreda and Nuño 1990, 174–176). The circles of stone situated near the cemetery of Numantia may also have had a ritual function, possibly as excarnation structures – a Celtiberian warriors' funerary practice attested by literary and iconographical sources – although their chronology is insecure (Jimeno *et al.* 2004, 36–37; Sopeña 2005, 366–368).

Religious use/reuse of ancient cult places: a conscious link with the past?

Several discoveries document the continued use, or the reuse, of prehistoric cultic places, particularly rock-shelters, through the Celtic-Roman period. Carvings, paintings and/ or votive inscriptions were located near or over previous prehistoric art (Alfayé, forthcoming a). In the rock-shelter of 'Covachón del Puntal' (Valonsadero, Soria) a bird-figure, similar to others depicted on Celtiberian pottery, was painted on a wall with pre-existing Bronze-Age paintings (Jimeno and Gómez 1983). The same phenomenon of 'symbolic recycling' is recorded in the rock-shelter of 'La Vacada' (Castellote, Teruel), where a warrior, a horse, a bull-head and an amphora were painted (second or first century BC) near pre-existing Levantine paintings (Martínez Bea 2004). In the cave of 'San García' (Santo Domingo de Silos, Burgos), an indigenous person carved a Palaeohispanic inscription over Bronze Age schematic carvings, this has been interpreted as evidence of the sacred character of the cave in the Celtiberian period (Mouré and García-Soto 1986). In the cave of 'La Griega' Roman votive inscriptions were situated near to Palaeolithic carvings of horses and other prehistoric figures, integrating the previous iconography in their Celtic-Roman religious discourse (Figure 41.3) (Bradley 2002, 116–123). This religious phenomenon of reuse of ancient sacred spaces has been recorded in the Iberian area (e.g. in a rock-shelter at Cogul, Lérida) (Moneo 2003, 308–311). Another example of this ritual link with the past could be the first century AD votive deposit of clay figurines placed at the foot of the wall of the Celtic *oppidum* of 'Castrejón de Capote', which had been abandoned a century before (Berrocal and Ruíz 2003).

This data prompts a number of questions about the character and purpose of this ritual use / reuse. Can we say that the peninsular peoples consciously decided to reuse (or continue the use) of those ancient cult places as a deliberate link with the past, as a way to reinforce their own memory during a period of considerable socio-political changes? In scholars' opinion (Olmos 2005, 258; Marco forthcoming), the religious occupation of these old cultic places could not be accidental in a period of political and territorial reformulations, it could have been tied to the necessity (and the conscious desire) to remember and strengthen their indigenous roots in a time of change.

Final considerations

This synthesis does not imply the existence of a timeless religion in *Hispania Celtica*: the ritual practices and cultic places must be temporally, spatially and historically contextualized, taking into account the changes, transformations and reactions provoked by the impact of the Roman conquest of the Iberian Peninsula. Under a general religious *koine* in Celtic *Hispania*, there existed differences within those populations in their types of sacred spaces, their deities, the kind of rituals carried out and the artefacts used in them, which illustrates the existence of religious peculiarities in each cultural area (Alfayé forthcoming a).

A number of questions about cult and its context in Celtic *Hispania* are still unanswered. What part was played by religion in the construction of these peoples' identity?

Could we talk about religious resistance against the Romans, and of movements of indigenous revitalization in *Hispania*? What was the process of formation of the provincial Hispano-Celtic religious system? I hope that future systematic fieldwork and the revision of old materials will enable a re-evaluation of the effects of Romanization on the religions of *Hispania Celtica* (Curchin 2004), and improve our knowledge of the sacred places and ritual practices of those populations, which is still frustratingly patchy and provisional.

Acknowledgements

I would like to thank William Nash, and David A. Barrowclough for his help with my English.

References

Abascal, J. M. 2003. La recepción de la cultura epigráfica romana en *Hispania*. In L. Abad (ed.). *De Iberia in Hispaniam. La adaptación de las sociedades ibéricas a los modelos romanos*. Alicante, Universidad de Alicante, 241–286.

Alfayé, S. 2005. Santuarios celtibéricos. In A. Jimeno (ed.). *Celtíberos. Tras la estela de Numancia*. Soria, Diputación Provincial de Soria, 229–234.

Alfayé, S. 2006. Sacrifices, banquets and warfare in Indo-European *Hispania*. In M.V. García Quintela *et al.* (eds). *Anthropology of the Indo-European World and Material Culture*. Budapest, Archaeolingua, 139–162.

Alfayé, S. Forthcoming a. *Santuarios y rituales en la Hispania Céltica*. Oxford, Archaeopress.

Alfayé, S. Forthcoming b. Imagined Sanctuaries: stones for human sacrifices and rock-altars in *Hispania Celtica*. In G. Tregidga and L. Cripps (eds). *21st Century Celts*. Cambridge, The Cambridge Scholar Press.

Almagro, M., and Berrocal, L. 1997. Entre íberos y celtas: sobre santuarios comunales urbanos y rituales gentilicios en *Hispania*. *Cuadernos de Prehistoria y Arqueología Castellonense* 18, 567–588.

Almagro, M. and Jiménez, J. L. 2000. Un altar rupestre en el Prado de Lácara (Mérida). Apuntes para la creación de un parque arqueológico. *Extremadura Arqueológica* 8, 423–442.

Arcelin, P. and Brunaux, J. L. 2003. Sanctuaires et pratiques cultuelles. *Gallia* 60, 243–247.

Arévalo, A. and Marcos, C. 2000. Sobre la presencia de moneda en santuarios hispánicos. In B. Kluge and B. Weisser (eds). *XII Internationaler Numismatischer Kongress*. Berlin 1997. Berlin, 28–37.

Argente, J. L., Díaz, A. and Bescós, A. 2001. *Tiermes V. Carratiermes. Necrópolis celtibérica*. Valladolid, Junta de Castilla y León.

Baquedano, I. and Escorza, C. M. 1998. Alineaciones astronómicas en la necrópolis de la Edad del hierro de La Osera (Chamartín de la Sierra, Ávila). *Complutum* 9, 85–100.

Barrio, J. 2002. El santuario de culto doméstico en el poblado prerromano de Cuellar (Segovia). *Madrider Mitteilungen* 43, 79–120.

Beirao, C. *et al.* 1985. Depósito votivo da II Idade do Ferro de Garvão. Noticia da primeira campanha de escavaçoes. *O Arqueólogo Português* 4,3, 45–136.

Beltrán, F., Jordán, C. and Marco, F. 2005. Novedades epigráficas en Peñalba de Villastar (Teruel). *Paleohispanica* 5, 911–956.

Berrocal, L. 1994. *El altar prerromano de Capote. Ensayo Etnoarqueológico de un ritual céltico en el Suroeste Peninsular.* Madrid, Universidad Autónoma de Madrid.

Berrocal, L., and Ruíz, C. 2003. *El depósito altoimperial del Castrejón de Capote (Higuera la Real, Badajoz).* Mérida, Junta de Extremadura.

Bradley, R. 2000. *The Archaeology of Natural Places.* London-New York, Routledge.

Bradley, R. 2002. *The Past in Prehistoric Societies.* London-New York, Routledge.

Burillo, F. 1998. *Los Celtíberos. Etnias y Estados.* Barcelona, Crítica.

Corchón, M. S. (coord.) 1997. *La Cueva de la Griega de Pedraza (Segovia).* Zamora, Junta de Castilla y León.

Curchin, L. A. 2004. *The Romanization of Central Spain. Complexity, Diversity and Change in a Provincial Hinterland.* London – New York, Routledge.

Díez de Velasco, F. 1998. *Termalismo y religión. La sacralización del agua termal en la Península Ibérica y el Norte de África en el mundo antiguo.* Madrid, Universidad Complutense.

Filloy, I. 1995. Los enterramientos infantiles. Los depósitos rituales. In E. Gil, *Atxa: memoria de las excavaciones arqueológicas 1982–1988.* Vitoria-Gasteiz, 171–193.

Gómez Pantoja, J. 1999 Las Madres de *Clunia.* In *VII Coloquio de Lenguas y Culturas Paleohispánicas.* Salamanca, Universidad de Salamanca, 421–432.

Horn F. 2003. Les céramiques pré-romaines à décor de têtes plastiques en Péninsule Ibérique. Leur lien avec le rituel de la tête coupée. *Mélanges de la Casa de Velázquez* 33, 1, 275–314.

Jimeno, A., and Gómez, J. A. 1983. En torno al 'trisceles' del 'Covachón del Puntal' (Valonsadero, Soria) y la cronología de la pintura esquemática del Alto Duero. *Zephyrus* 36, 195–202.

Jimeno, A. *et al.* 2004. *La necrópolis celtibérica de Numancia.* Salamanca, Junta de Castilla y León.

Jordán, C. 2004. *Celtibérico.* Zaragoza, Departamento de Ciencias de la Antigüedad.

Llanos, A. 2002. *Gentes del Hierro en privado.* Vitoria, Museo de Arqueología de Álava.

Marco Simón, F. 1999a. El paisaje sagrado en la *Hispania* indoeuropea. In *Religión y magia en la Antigüedad.* Valencia, Generalitat Valenciana, 147–165.

Marco Simón, F. 1999b. Sacrificios humanos en la Céltica antigua: entre el estereotipo literario y la evidencia interna. *Archiv für Religiongeschichte* 1, 1–15.

Marco Simón, F. 2002. Hispano-Celtic Gods. Methodological problems and geography of the cult. *Études Luxembourgeoises d'Histoire et de science des Religions* 1, 127–148.

Marco Simón, F. 2005. Religion and Religious Practices of the Ancient Celts of the Iberian Peninsula. *E-Keltoi* 6, 287–346.

Marco Simón, F. Forthcoming. A lost identity: Celtiberian Iconography after the Roman conquest. In R. Häussler and T. King (eds). *Continuity and innovation in the North-Western Provinces.* Birmingham.

Martínez Bea, M. 2004. Un arte no tan levantino. Perduración ritual de los abrigos pintados: el ejemplo de La Vacada (Castellote, Teruel). *Trabajos de Prehistoria* 61, 2, 111–125.

Moneo, T. 2003 *Religio iberica. Santuarios, ritos y divinidades (siglos VII–I a.C).* Madrid, Real Academia de la Historia.

Moreda, J. and Nuño, J. 1990. Avance al estudio de la necrópolis de la Edad del Hierro de 'El Pradillo', Pinilla-Trasmonte (Burgos), in F. Burillo (dir.), *Necrópolis celtibéricas.* Zaragoza, Institución Fernando el Católico, 171–181.

Mouré, J. A. and García Soto, E. 1986. Los grabados de la Cueva de San García, Santo Domingo de Silos (Burgos). *Numantia* 2, 193–213.

Olmos, R. 2005. Iconografía celtibérica. In A. Jimeno (ed.). *Celtíberos. Tras la Estela de Numancia.* Soria, Diputación Provincial de Soria, 253–260.

Raposo, L. (ed.) 2002. *Religiôes da Lusitania. Loquuntur saxa.* Lisboa, Museu Nacional de Arqueología.

Richert, E. A. 2005. *Native religion under Roman Domination. Deities, springs and mountains in the north-west of the Iberian Peninsula.* Oxford, Archaeopress.

Rodríguez, G. *et al.* 2006. Observaciones topoastronómicas en la Zona Arqueológica de El Ceremeño (Herrería, Guadalajara). *Complutum* 17, 133–143.

Sanz, C. and Velasco, J. (eds) 2003. *Pintia*: un *oppidum* en los confines orientales de la región vaccea. Valladolid.

Sopeña, G. 1995 *Ética y ritual. Aproximación a la religiosidad de los celtíberos.* Zaragoza, Institución Fernando el Católico.

Sopeña, G. 2005. Celtiberian Ideologies and Religion. *E-Keltoi* 6, 347–410.

Taracena, B. 1943. Cabezas-trofeo en la España Céltica. *Archivo Español de Arqueología* 16, 157–171.

Vaz, J. 2002. Tipologia dos santuarios rupestres de tradicâo paleohispânica em Territorio Portugués. In L. Raposo (ed.). *Religiôes da Lusitânia. Loquuntur saxa.* Lisboa, Museu Nacional de Arqueología, 39–42.

Webster, J. 1995. Sanctuaries and Sacred Places. In M. Green (ed.). *The Celtic World.* London, Routledge, 445–464.

Chapter 42

THE ROLE OF VOTIVE OBJECTS IN ROMAN RELIGIOUS PRACTICES BETWEEN THE FOURTH AND SECOND CENTURIES BC

Letizia Ceccarelli

Introduction

This contribution will focus upon the phenomenon of mid-Republican religious practices and cults (fourth to second century BC). In the identification of religion, in a framework of practices with repeated actions connected with belief and social identity, the most suitable contexts are sanctuaries where features of the deliberate deposition of objects and offerings, such as votive deposits, can be identified. The site of Ardea in *Latium vetus* combines many of the themes important for the discussion.

Ardea lies 40 km south of Rome and 5 km from the coast (Figure 42.1). It was a city of Rutuli, as is attested by Cato "(Cato Origines Frag. 58)", an important member of the Latin League, both politically and religiously. In the late sixth century (509 BC), in the First Treaty between Rome and Carthage, Ardea is mentioned as a city that should be spared, evidence that Rome was already by some means controlling, or had influence over, the territory. In 442 BC Ardea became a Latin colony having been weakened by the war with the Volscians (Livy 4.11). It

Figure 42.1. Map of Latium vetus *with Ardea.*

therefore formed part of the expansion of early Republican Rome, in which selected cities in strategic locations were settled in order to control the landscape. After 338 BC the political power of Ardea declined, but its religious importance remained, as in 217 BC the Romans offered great sacrifices in the forum (Livy 22.1.19). The end of the third century BC appears to have been a difficult period for the city, illustrated by the fact that in 209 BC Ardea was unable to provide military support to Rome during the Second Punic War (Livy 37.9.7). However, archaeological evidence reveals a different situation regarding cults, which witnessed a continuity despite the political upheaval, between the fourth and the second centuries BC.

Archaeology of religion

The archaeology of religion is a field of research that has a significant role in the exploration and understanding of past activities. The subject is theoretically and methodologically complex and it is permeated by sociological, anthropological, ideological and philosophical theories. The cognitive approach, championed by Renfrew (1994, 47–54), considers religion as a structural component of past societies and emphasizes the reconstruction of ancient religious belief through the analysis of symbolic systems, involving cults practices and rituals. He suggests sixteen indicators of ritual divided into the categories of places, symbols reflecting the presence of the deity, participation and offerings, which emphasise the ritual and symbolic dimensions of the material culture. However, a criticism that has been levelled at the cognitive approach to religion is the lack of interest in the ritual objects deliberately deposited (Osborne 2004).

Within the post-processual approach the analysis of religion is marginal, suggesting that complex meaning of religion cannot be reconstructed, and when attempts are made they are biased by the archaeological interpretation. However, here there is a risk of circular argument, as without the archaeological interpretation of material culture and its context there is insufficient evidence for the recognition of cults. In a recent contribution to this discussion, Insoll (2004, 148–149) identifies eight theoretical issues and research questions to identify religion through archaeological evidence. The archaeology of religion has to consider the physical location where rituals take place, their repetition over time and how they can be explained with belief, in a mythological framework and how they are related to the identity of the believers.

One aim of this research is the attempt to prove that the application of a cross cultural theory to religion can be misleading, and that the crucial concept is the context. In considering complex societies and their religious belief, historical, epigraphic and archaeological sources will be used in the analysis. A hermeneutic approach will be taken

(as argued by Hodder 2004, 28); data will be interpreted in their historical framework, taking advantage of the written sources and the classification method (the objective data). The interpretation of their religious significance will be built against a reconstruction of religious perception (the theory and the prejudgments). Material culture, the objects of dedication and the context of action, the sanctuary, forms an important part in the process of creation of a population identity. In the identification of religion in a framework of practices with repeated actions connected with belief and social identity the most suitable contexts are the ones of the deliberate deposition of objects, such as votive deposits. They constitute a valid example that permits the bringing together of the indicators of ritual identified by Renfrew (1994, 51), the types of ritual objects suggested by Whitehouse (1996, 13–26) and the theory proposed by Insoll (2004, 148–149).

Religion in context

Roman religion has been accurately defined an 'orthopraxy' (see Scheid 2003, 18; Ando 2003, 10): a scrupulous performance of a set of rules. It can be further seen as a ritualistic religion, where rituals and sacrifices aimed to maintain order between the state and its gods, the *pax deorum*, and to restore that order when it was disrupted. Therefore, the *cognitio deorum*, the knowledge of the gods and their will, is a crucial concept to understand the need to perform the correct operations, hence rituals, to maintain proper relations with them. Another important feature of Roman religion was its votive character. It was customary at all social levels to make a vow to a deity in return for the fulfilment of a request or prayer.

When discussing the interpretation of the practices of Roman cults the literary sources provide a wealth of information. They were, however, commenting retrospectively on the formation process of different rituals in a time of political and social change, between the end of the second and the first half of the first century BC. They are therefore a form of antiquarian literature, 'fossilised elements of archaic religious practices' (Bispham 2000) attempting to construct a Roman religious identity, projecting contemporary ideas on the past. Texts can be seen as an idealised set of externally perceived aspects of past religion. Their bias emphasises the importance of the archaeological record in forming an understanding of past practices.

The stage of the action: the sanctuary

Society expresses religious experience through culture and ideology, which have their materialisation in physical realities such as rituals, symbols and monuments across the landscape.

The various excavations carried out in Ardea since the late nineteenth century revealed the existence of three sanctuaries within the city (Figure 42.2), which suggest a period of intense building activity in the first half of the fifth century BC (Colonna 1995, 1), which is further supported by new unpublished data currently the subject of research by the author. The three urban cult places, the deity or deities of which are not know, have been named after their location:

The Acropolis temple, excavated in 1930 (Boëthius 1931, 5), has been reconstructed as Tuscanic with three *cellae* or with a central *cella* and *alae*. Several phases of decoration have been identified, which date the structure as the oldest temple of the city. Andren (1940, 438) attributed the earlier phase to the end of the sixth – beginning of fifth century BC. The last identified phase is of first century BC (Manca di Mores 1993, 313).

The second Temple of urban cult was located at Colle della Noce; the ground plan is again Tuscanic with three *cellae* (Crescenzi, Tortorici 1983, 35). The recent discovery of an Etruscan inscription, in a structure connected with the sanctuary, dated the temple to the colonial period, and provides a concrete chronological reference (Colonna 2003, 347). The structure has several decorative phases, the last of which is in the middle second century BC (Manca di Mores 1993, 313).

The third urban temple at Casarinaccio, the Forum temple, has a moulded podium, however its ground plan cannot be defined. The foundation of the temple is dated to the beginning of the fifth century BC on the evidence of the earliest terracotta revetments found. A votive deposit has been excavated (Di Mario 2003, 182) in a cavity underneath the portico of the basilica which is located to the north-west of the temple, in which were discovered over 1500 objects, some of which will be discussed below.

What is of note is that all three temples reveal continuity in building activities and in cults until the end of the 2nd century BC (Morselli and Tortorici 1982, 39, Di Mario 2003, 184). The attribution of the deities to these temples is still subject to much discussion, due to the fragmented nature of the archaeological data. Historical sources have attributed several deities to the temples in Ardea. Traditionally, the Acropolis temple is attributed to Juno, on the basis of Pliny's account (N.H. 35.17), the Casarinaccio temple to Hercules on the basis of an inscription (Stefani 1954, 12) and the Colle della Noce temple to the Castores, whose cult in Ardea is attested by Servius (Aen 1.44).

Figure 42.2. The settlement of Ardea and the location of the three urban sanctuaries: A – temple of the Acropolis, B – temple at Casarinaccio, C – temple at Colle della Noce. The base map is derived from Morselli and Tortorici 1982.

Votive offerings

Votive offerings are a category of objects that allow us to explore the process by which people constructed their identity, both socially and religiously. Votive objects, as well as having cultural value, also acted as interlocutors between the human and the divine, and in this role they can be meaningfully explored as objects of agency, as proposed by Gell (1998). Offerings were displayed in a sanctuary for a long time before being ritually discarded, and whilst on display they '...spread agency over time' (Hodder 2004, 33). Indeed, to the contemporary worshipper these objects portrayed a meaning that archaeology is now attempting to reconstruct.

Moreover, the study of a closed context of a votive deposit permits the analysis of the objects network of relationships. Everyday objects along with precious objects acquire significance through their context. Therefore, the materiality of votive offerings can be addressed through several different points of view: their meaning within the ritual, the expression of individuality and the value of the inscriptions which they carry.

In 1999 at the temple of Casarinaccio, a deposit of objects was excavated (Di Mario 2005). It was a rock-cut cylindrical cistern of 3.6 m in diameter and 3 m depth which contained cult equipment, offerings, non-functional items, such as miniature vessels, imported pottery and organic sacrificial remains, dating from the mid-fourth century to the early second century BC, when it was deliberately sealed in association with a restructuring of the sanctuary. The objects dedicated became the deity's property and thus had to remain within the sanctuary, as is attested by a sacred law at the temple of Marica at Minturnae, where it was forbidden to take away anything that was taken inside the sanctuary (Maras 2005, 44).

Ritual

The equipment involved in a cult can be difficult to identify, as it could also be dedicated and not easily discernible from the other offerings (for Greek sanctuaries see Baumbach 2004, 2). Less problematic is the interpretation of the presence of over 400 coarseware cooking jars, which constitute 56% of the class, ranging chronologically between the fifth to the third centuries BC, some of which were discovered still containing animal sacrifice remains (Arena 2005). Moreover, the deity dedicatory inscriptions are mostly on these vessels, reinforcing the interpretation as cult equipment. However, even among these vessels are miniature examples which do not present burning marks and therefore most likely contained offerings. The vessels which are connected with the ritual preparation of food are the mixing bowls *impasto chiaro sabbioso mortaria* (Merlo 2005).

Faunal remains attest mostly the offering of pigs (40.9% of the total with 214 fragments), sheep (37.3% of the total with 195 fragments) and cattle (12.2% of the total with 64 fragments), all of a young age, a minority of which had butcher marks (Betetto 2005). The sacrifice of these animals attests the rite of *suovetaurilia,* as has also been noted in other votive deposits of this period such as at Satricum (Bouma 1996, I: 443–444). More unusual offerings found were two cockerels, a stag, birds, a heron, and a tortoise. The limited number of sacrificed animals, with a predominance of pigs, generally used for expiations and for funerary cults (Scheid 2003, 81), suggests an expiatory ritual connected to the disposal of sacred objects and the obliteration of the deposit due to the construction of portico's area connecting the temple with the basilica, a complex that constituted the focal point of civic and religious identity of Ardea.

The interpretation of other rituals is a more complex problem, as following the animals sacrifice, was a consumption of the meat along with bread and wine by the celebrants, although not necessarily shared with those present at the sacrifice. Functional vessels connected with wine consumption found in the deposit were 61 amphorae, dated between the end of the fourth and beginning of the third century BC imported from Etruria, Magna Graecia and Sicily, as well as the unusual presence of Punic amphorae, which formed 44% of the total number of fragments. The wine drinking vessels, kylikes and skyphoi in black-glaze, black-glaze over painted and red-figured are limited in number compared with the 197 black-gloss ware bowls (Ceccarelli and Di Mento 2005), whose function could either have been for drinking liquids or for solid offerings. Rituals are characterised by formality and repetition, which can be seen by the high occurrence of these types of pottery (Type Morel 2783–2784). Moreover, the stratigraphic excavation of this deposit revealed the peculiar breakage of these bowls, incompatible with its interment in the cistern, suggesting a ritual of a deliberate breakage.

Offerings

As previously observed, vessels in a votive assemblage can be divided into several categories: cult equipment, functional pottery for ritual dining, and offerings. Within the latter it is possible to identify two categories, as defined by Morel (1992) *'ex-voto par destination'*, objects purposely created as offerings and *'ex-voto par trasformation'*, items transformed into votives through the action of dedication.

Vessels that were made specifically for dedication are the miniaturised non-functional items that represent a symbolic offering, thus attesting that it was the action of offering that was important insomuch as the actual content.

Another class of material whose function was specifically related to ritual is Genucilia plates, which date from the third quarter of the fourth century BC through to the beginning of the third century BC. They are characterised by a repetitive decoration of either a female profile or a geometrical pattern. In the deposit a unique example with a male head was discovered, shedding new light on the possibility of a special commission of objects prior the actual dedication. Moreover, it suggests the existence of a local workshop (Ceccarelli 2005).

Also found were offerings that may not have had their primary destination and function in the religious sphere, and that their secondary use is within the ritual, such as 35 loom weights (Piergrossi 2005).

Individuality – inscribed religion

In a sanctuary context inscriptions played an important role as part of the ritual, as they can be seen as a ritual act in itself, connected with permanence (Wilkins 1996, 124). In the deposit of Ardea were discovered 129 dedicatory inscriptions either incised or painted, of which 42 were on black-gloss ware bowls and 87 on coarseware jars and lids, classes that, as previously noted, fulfilled an important role in the performance of the ritual. The interpretation of the inscriptions can sometimes be ambiguous, as it is unclear whether they refer to the deity or to the worshipper, the latter category seems predominant, shifting the focus from the deity to the worshipper and attesting the religious individual experience as taking an active role in the ceremonies. As regards the deity to whom these objects were dedicated, the Greek inscription HP was interpreted by Acconcia (2005) as possibly being a reference to Heracles or Hera. Comparisons with the dedicatory inscriptions to Hera from sanctuaries in western Greece and the mainland

(Baumbach 2004), where the full name was incised (HPA) suggest that the subject of dedication is likely to be Heracles (see also Cristofani 1985, 21–23). In Roman religion the cult of Hercules can be considered under the category of *rituus Graecus,* a Roman ritual form to emphasise the gods Greek origins (Scheid 2003, 37).

The sacred nature of a sanctuary made it a suitable centre for trade and economic exchange and political and diplomatic relations. In this temple on the forum the presence of foreigners is attested by Greek and Punic inscriptions on vessels, offerings that are representing a *intepretatio*, a cultural interpretation of a deity according to his or her functions equated to a homeland deity. For instance, two impasto lids, dated between the middle of the fourth—beginning of third century BC, have a Punic inscription with the name of the worshipper: Magon. In 348 BC Ardea is mentioned in the second treaty between Rome and Carthage (Polybius 3.24.16). The purpose of these treaties was fundamentally concerned with trade and commercial relationships (Palmer 1997, 15).

Further evidence of private ritual is offered by the discovery of a lead tablet with a curse inscription, dated to the middle of the fifth century BC, which was found in a rectangular structure built with tufa blocks connected to the temple of Colle della Noce (Di Mario 2003, 338). It can be interpreted as a late Archaic open-air shrine or altar preserved alongside the temple. The tablet represents the ritual practice of *defixio*, a binding spell, which vowed a personal enemy to the gods of the underworld. The tablet, measuring 13.6 cm, was folded and pierced by nails (Figure

Figure 42.3. The lead tablet of the defixio.

42.3). The two line inscription, in the Etruscan language, is a curse against a member of the aristocracy (Colonna 2003, 345). It could have been a sort of appeal to justice, as suggested by Mastrocinque (2005, 27) that the fifth century BC *defixiones* were a plebeian practice in the sanctuaries of Demetra-Cerere. Therefore the context in which this magic rite was performed was the socio-political contrast between the patricians and plebeians, as accounted by Livy (4.9–10), and as also found in contemporary Rome (Cornell 1995, 258–268). The inscription not only demonstrates that in Ardea there existed a complex religious system with different cultural components, but also reinforced the importance of writing within the cult. An inscription had a component of eternally perpetuating a ritual and validating the ritual itself.

Conclusion

The detailed analysis of the votive context at the Forum temple in Ardea permits the examination of the important function of sanctuaries in the process of the construction of social and religious identity in the pre- and post-colonial period, and the political interaction between different cultures. The votive material was explored also to detect the characteristics of cults. However, the objects themselves are rarely self-explanatory, except those with the deities name inscribed. There are some difficulties in attempting to argue that objects always have an embedded social meaning (Hodder 2004, 37–38). The reconstruction of the social nature of material culture lies within the context of its discovery; in sacred contexts it is also necessary to take into account other evidence such as architectural features and literary sources.

References

Acconcia, V. 2005. Iscrizioni. In F. Di Mario (ed.). *Ardea. Il deposito votivo di Casarinaccio. Soprintendenza per i Beni archeologici del Lazio*. Roma, Eurografica.

Ando, C. 2003. Introduction: Religion, Law and Knowledge in Classical Rome. In C. Ando (ed.). 2003. *Roman Religion*. Edinburgh, Edinburgh University Press, 1–15.

Andren, A. 1940. *Architectural Terracottas from Etrusco-Italic Temples*. Lund-Leipzig, Acta Instituti Romani Regni Suegiae VI.

Arena, A. 2005. Ceramica di impasto. In Di Mario, F. 2005. (ed.) *Ardea. Il deposito votivo di Casarinaccio. Soprintendenza per i Beni archeologici del Lazio*. Roma: Eurografica, 51–150.

Baumbach J. D. 2004. *The Significance of Votive offerings in Selected Hera Sanctuaries in the Peloponnese, Ionia and Western Greece*. Oxford, Archaeopress. BAR International Series 1249.

Betetto E. 2005. Reperti faunistici. In Di Mario, F. (ed.). *Ardea. Il deposito votivo di Casarinaccio. Soprintendenza per i Beni archeologici del Lazio*. Roma, Eurografica, 369–374.

Bispham, E. 2000. Introduction. In E. Bispham and Smith, C.

(eds). *Religion in archaic and republican Rome and Italy: evidence and experience*. Edinburgh, University Press, 1–18.

Boëthius, A. 1931. *Ardea*. Bullettino di Studi Mediterranei II, 2, 1–18.

Bouma, J. W. 1996. *Religio Votiva: The Archaeology of Latial Votive Religion*. Groningen.

Carbonara, V. 2005. Anfore. In F. Di Mario (ed.). *Ardea. Il deposito votivo di Casarinaccio. Soprintendenza per i Beni archeologici del Lazio*. Roma, Eurografica, 301–315.

Ceccarelli, L. 2005. Ceramica a figure rosse. Piattelli Genucilia. In F. Di Mario (ed.). *Ardea. Il deposito votivo di Casarinaccio. Soprintendenza per i Beni archeologici del Lazio*. Roma, Eurografica, 151–174.

Ceccarelli, L., Di Mento M. 2005. Ceramica a vernice nera. In F. Di Mario (ed.). *Ardea. Il deposito votivo di Casarinaccio. Soprintendenza per i Beni archeologici del Lazio*. Roma, Eurografica, 195–258.

CIL: Corpus Inscriptionum Latinarum.

Colonna, G. 1995. Gli scavi del 1852 ad Ardea e l'identificazione dell'Aphrodisium. *Archeologia Classica* XLVII, 1–67.

Colonna, G. 2003. Ardea, Rivista di Epigrafia Etrusca, Studi Etruschi LXIX: 342–347.

Cornell, T. J. 1995. *The Beginnings of Rome. Italy and Rome from the Bronze Age to the Punic Wars (c. 1000–264 BC)*. London and New York, Routledge.

Crescenzi, L., Tortorici, E. 1983. *Ardea Immagini di una ricerca*. Roma.

Cristofani, M. 1985. Altre novità sui Genucilia, in Contributi alla ceramica etrusca tardo-classica (Atti del seminario di Roma 1984), QuadAEI 10. Roma, Consiglio nazionale delle Ricerche, 21–24.

Di Mario, F. 2003. Ardea, i risultati delle nuove ricerche archeologiche in area urbana e nel territorio. In J. R. Brandt, X. Dupré Raventós, and G. Ghini (eds). *Lazio e Sabina 1*. Roma: De Luca, 181–84.

Di Mario, F. 2005. (ed.). *Ardea. Il deposito votivo di Casarinaccio. Soprintendenza per i Beni archeologici del Lazio*. Roma, Eurografica.

Gell, A. 1998. *Art and Agency*. Oxford, Clarendon Press.

Hodder, I. 2004. The "Social" in Archaeological Theory: An Historical and Contemporary Perspective. In L. Meskell and R. W. Preucel (eds). *A Companion to Social Archaeology*. Oxford, Blackwell, 23–42.

Insoll, T. 2004. *Archaeology, Ritual, Religion*. London, Routledge.

Manca di Mores G. 1993. Terrecotte architettoniche dai templi di Ardea, Archeologia Laziale XI, 2 (QuadAEI 21), Roma, Consiglio Nazionale delle Ricerche, 311–314.

Maras, D. F. 2005. L'iscrizione di Trivia e il culto del santuario alla foce del Garigliano. *Archeologia Classica* 56, 6, 2005, 33–48.

Mastrocinque, A. 2005. Lex sacrata e teste votive. In A. Comella and S. Mele (eds) *Depositi votivi e culti dell'Italia antica dall'età arcaica a quella repubblicana*. Bari, Edipuglia, 25–30.

Merlo, M., Ten Kortenaar, S. 2005. Impasto chiaro sabbioso. In F. Di Mario (ed.). *Ardea. Il deposito votivo di Casarinaccio. Soprintendenza per i Beni archeologici del Lazio*. Roma, Eurografica, 21–43.

Morel, J. P. 1981. *Céramique Campanienne. Les formes*. Paris.

Morel, J. P. 1992. Ex-voto par trasformation, ex-voto par destination. *Ex-voto par trasformation, ex-voto par destination*. Mélanges Pierre Leveque (Annales Litterairies de l'Université de Besançon, 463). Paris, 221–232.

Morselli C. and Tortorici, E. 1982. *Ardea, Forma Italiae*, Regio I – Volumen XVI, Firenze, Leo S. Olschki.

Osborne, R. 2004. Hoards, votive offerings: the archaeology of dedicated objects. In R. Osborne (ed.). The object of dedication. *World Archaeology* Vol 36 (1). London, 1–10.

Palmer E. E. A. 1997. *Rome and Carthage at Peace*. Stuttgart, Franz Steiner.

Piergrossi, A. 2005. Pesi da telaio. In F. Di Mario (ed.). *Ardea. Il deposito votivo di Casarinaccio. Soprintendenza per i Beni archeologici del Lazio*. Roma, Eurografica, 289–300.

Renfrew, C., Zubrow, E. B. W. (eds) 1994. *The Ancient Mind*. Cambridge, Cambridge University Press.

Scheid, J. 2003. *An Introduction to Roman Religion*. Edinburgh, Edinburgh University Press.

Stefani, E. 1954. Ardea. (Contrada Casalinaccio). Resti di un antico tempio scoperto nell'area della città, Notizie degli Scavi di Antichità 1954, 6–30.

Whitehouse, R. 1996. Ritual Objects. Archaeological Joke or Neglected Evidence? In J. Wilkins (ed.). *Approaches to the Study of Ritual: Italy and the Ancient Mediterranean*. London, Accordia Research Centre, 9–30.

Wilkins, J. (ed.) 1996. *Approaches to the study of ritual. Italy and the Ancient Mediterranean*. London, Accordia Research Centre.

Chapter 43

'TOTEMS', 'ANCESTORS', AND 'ANIMISM'. THE ARCHAEOLOGY OF RITUAL, SHRINES AND SACRIFICE AMONGST THE TALLENSI OF NORTHERN GHANA

Timothy Insoll

Introduction

'Totems', 'ancestors', and 'animism' are all seemingly familiar terms, applicable across wide geographical and temporal contexts to describe religious phenomena. Yet in reality they are not as straightforward as they might initially appear either as regards definition or archaeological application. This paper seeks to briefly explore the utility of these terms in relation to the results of an archaeological project begun in 2004 and focussed upon the Tallensi people, subsistence agriculturalists who speak a Gur language of the Oti-Volta group (Naden 1998,12), and who live in the Upper East Region of northern Ghana in West Africa (Figure 43.1). In so doing attention will be primarily given to the archaeology of ritual, shrines, and sacrifice in the Tongo Hills, the area inhabited by one of the two main groups of clans forming the Tallensi, the Hill Talis. This is because in concentrating upon these aspects what is immediately clear is that the conceptualisation of religious phenomena such as 'totems', 'ancestors' or 'animism' in the singular is flawed and instead interpretive plurality is required. A premise which it will be suggested is probably equally valid for archaeological contexts elsewhere.

The Tallensi of Northern Ghana are well-known via the seminal anthropological studies of Fortes (e.g. 1945; 1949; 1987). Fortes provides a wealth of detail on, for instance, kinship and aspects of Tallensi religion and ritual practice in relation to ancestor worship and to a lesser extent shrines. However, his functionalist approach means that Tallensi material culture is comparatively neglected as is the historical dimension of their existence, though the latter has been redressed recently (Allman and Parker 2005). Thus until the start of the current research project in 2004 (Insoll, Kankpeyeng, and MacLean 2004; 2005; in press a) no archaeological research had been completed in the Tongo Hills, the epicentre of Tallensi settlement, beyond an

ethnoarchaeological study of Tallensi house compounds (Gabrilopoulos 1995), and an inventory of cultural heritage completed by one of the project co-directors (Kankpeyeng 2001).

Potentially, Tallensi derived material provides a way of beginning to examine religious phenomena and definitions, and their material signatures and archaeological implications for the majority of the Tallensi remain followers of traditional religion. This, however, is complex and Tallensi religion has as central elements both ancestral and earth cults. Ancestral worship functions on various levels. Each segment of a Talis composite clan has a lineage shrine to distinguish it from other segments (Fortes 1949, 6), to which they sacrifice individually (Fortes 1950, 253). Contrasting with this, groups of maximal lineages belonging to different clans (but not necessarily united by ties of clanship) collaborate, 'in the cult of their collective ancestors' (Fortes 1949, 6) via joint sacrifice. Materially, the ancestral cult is represented by the ancestral shrine or *ba'a* (Allman and Parker 2005, 43) which can be manifest in various ways, as a household shrine, or in an external shrine such as a sacred grove or cave (Kankpeyeng 2001), but involving ritual practices which have no specialist priests (Fortes 1987, 150).

The latter, however, are specifically involved in the earth cult, for this is linked with a class of specialist priest, the *Tendaana*, the 'Custodian of the Earth' (Fortes 1987, 43), and is materially manifest through sacred places, ten, within which are located the earth shrines, *tengbana*, which the priests serve. Secondly, it also differs in the beliefs it reflects being, obviously, connected with the sacred aspect of the earth, which is personified, and which is envisaged, according to Fortes (1987, 135–6), as 'a living force... complementary to the collective ancestors'. To the ancestral and earth cults must also be added totemism, as another

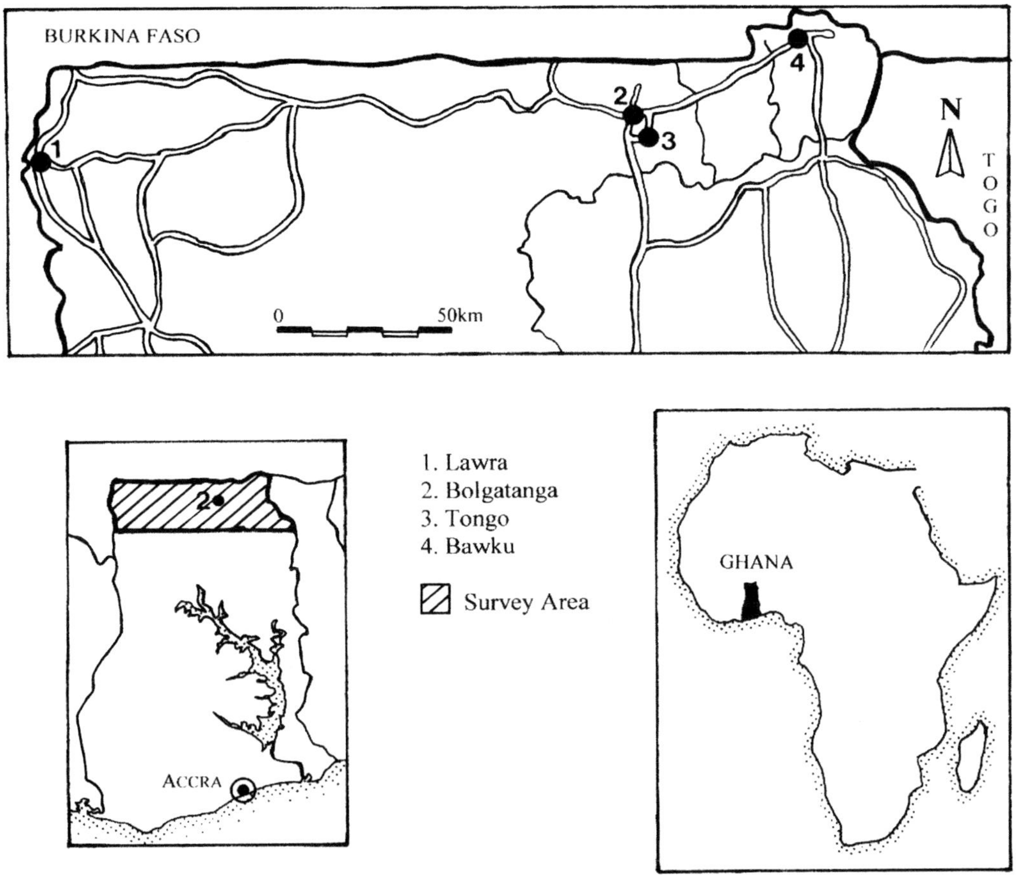

Figure 43.1. Map of Northern Ghana.

element of Tallensi religion. All these components, however, form the ultimate whole which is Tallensi religion, and the existence of a metaphysical upper 'tier' to Tallensi religion must also be acknowledged (see Fortes 1987).

The archaeology of ritual and shrines

Materially, Tallensi religion in all its varied forms is manifest via shrines which exist in a bewildering range of configurations. Moreover that these are not static as a strictly typological approach might suggest (Insoll in preparation a) is clearly indicated via archaeology, i.e. that both shrines and the ritual practices they sustain and generate can instead be adaptive, dynamic, and flexible. Part of the problem here in relation to shrines lies in defining exactly what constitutes a religious place, a focus of devotion, for this is not always best served by the English terminology which is often used within the context of describing relevant material associated with either contemporary traditional religions or in prehistoric archaeological contexts, i.e. 'shrine'. The primary reason for this being that 'shrine' is ultimately derived from the Latin *scrinium* – meaning 'box' or 'receptacle', as in

'containers of sacred meaning and power' (Courtright 1987, 299). This being a term, which it can be suggested, that singularly fails to describe the range of structures included within its boundaries (Insoll 2004, 105). For simply stated, the shrine can contain shrines, as with sacred groves – shrines – that contain standing stones therein – shrines – which are in turn associated with sacred pots – shrines – as can be seen at Nyoo. Hence in the attempt to 'typologise' shrines complexity could easily be lost and an unwarranted degree of uniformity instituted instead.

Innumerable shrines exist in the Tongo Hills, but three shrines dominate, Tonna'ab/Yaane, Bonaab, and Nyoo. Of these Nyoo is perhaps of primary interest to the archaeologist being a large 'sacred grove' functioning as an earth shrine and of further significance in being used annually as a dancing ground at some point from late February to early April during the pre-agricultural Gologo or Golib festival (Fortes 1987, 34; Kankpeyeng 2001, 26). That Nyoo was not a natural sacred grove was immediately indicated by archaeological survey. For far-spreading archaeological vestiges visible on the surface clearly showed that this was in fact an extensive enshrined archaeological site divided into a series of different zones. These included a 'field' of standing stones, an area of stone arrangements with an associated spread of pottery covering some 300 m east to west, and an active sacrificial area lacking such overt archaeological features (Figure 43.2). Furthermore, test excavations completed in 2005 confirmed that this was not a 'natural' sacred grove with, for example, the pottery spread seen to be formed of both complete pottery vessels and sherds which had been forced into the ground to a maximum depth of 30 cm, and thus seemingly representative of an act of structured 'ritual' deposition (Insoll, Kankpeyeng, and MacLean 2005). Hence Nyoo was made the focus of excavation in July 2006 during which two units were opened.

NYOO 06 (A)

The first of these units was assigned the code NYOO 06 (A) and measured 8 m × 4 m. Only shallow archaeological layers were encountered with a maximum depth of c.15–20 cm before sterile deposits were reached. This noted, the matrix that was removed was densely filled with archaeological material, predominantly sherds, many from complete vessels apparently broken in-situ, but also containing an assemblage of 35 lithic objects comprising largely stone grinder/pounder/rubbers, both fragmentary, and complete, but also lumps of quartz (Insoll, Kankpeyeng, and MacLean in press b).

Interspersed amongst the pot filled deposits were seven stone arrangements (Figure 43.3). Originally, it was thought that these might represent cairns, but this idea was discarded on the basis that the stone arrangements were almost entirely composed of a single layer of stones. Similarly, there was apparently no significance in the numbers of stones composing the arrangements which ranged between 16 and 51. However, care had definitely been taken in the arrangements of the stones, possibly with some concern evident as to the colour patterning of the aplite (fine-grained granite), Bongo granite, and schist present. The colours red, pink, black, and grey were noted, with white represented by smaller fragments of quartz frequently found, as well as by the banding in some of the granite. In so-doing perhaps providing a further manifestation of the oft-noted red-white-black colour symbolism evident in sub-Saharan Africa (Turner 1985; Jacobsen-Widding 1979). Removal of the stone arrangements produced very little material, and it would seem that the

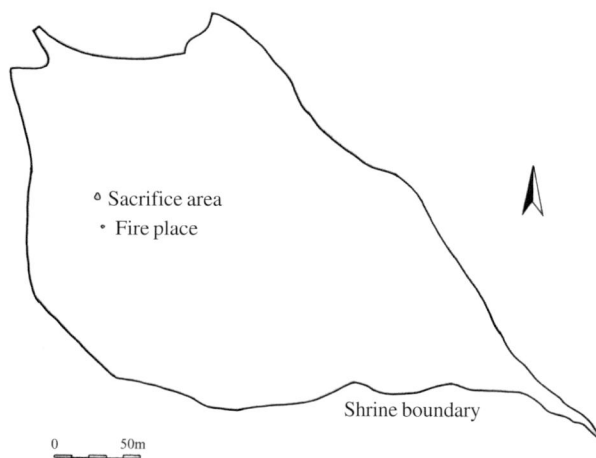

Figure 43.2. Plan of Nyoo.

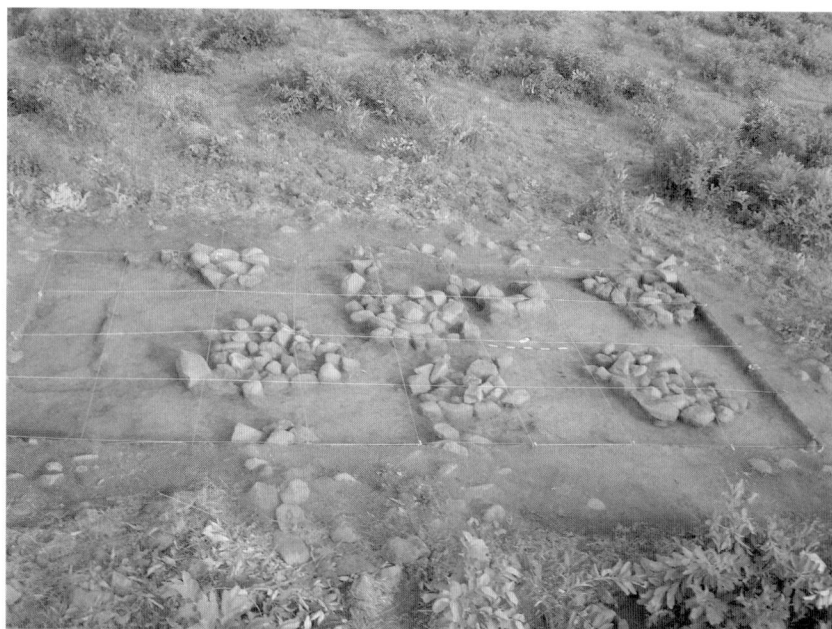

Figure 43.3. NYOO 06 (A) indicating the stone arrangements and pot filled deposits in-situ (all photos T. Insoll).

pots represented by the pot filled layers were deposited after the stones had been arranged (Insoll, Kankpeyeng, and MacLean in press b).

Dates from this and the other excavation completed are in progress, but it is not unreasonable to suggest that perhaps one deposition event involving a lot of people and pottery is represented, rather than a build-up of material over some length of time involving multiple deposition events. This suggestion can be made based upon pre-liminary indications with regard to the pottery assemblage which indicate little variability present, but rather a standard range of vessel types found (Ashley 2006). The absence of any contextual difference also supports this idea of a single, or at least a rapid, deposition event. Though the gradation in density of pottery present indicates that a simplistic uniform infilling around the stone arrangements did not take place.

What the deposition of the pot and other materials might represent, or be associated with, is unclear. Various suggestions can be made, with perhaps the most compelling being that it might broadly function within the framework of commemorating or supplicating the ancestors or deceased. Though the absence of funerary remains precludes a direct link with the dead (similarly absent in the other unit as well). This interpretation would seem plausible based upon broad parallels elsewhere, less so, perhaps, with Tallensi practices today, but certainly reminiscent of, for instance, the Akan *Asensie*, or 'place of pots' (Bellis 1982). A point qualified with the proviso that direct Akan connections are not being proposed, just generic

parallels suggested. The deliberate destruction of some of the pots, with holes forced, bored, or chipped in their bases for example, might support this association with the ancestors or deceased. An interpretation lent further weight by the results of the excavations in NYOO 06 (B) discussed below.

Although it is unwise at this preliminary stage to advance too far in interpretation, it can again tentatively be suggested that based on contemporary parallels what might also be represented by the stone arrangements at Nyoo is the residue of performance or movement, perhaps dance. Again, during the ritual activities observed at Nyoo Biil, dance around and between the stone arrangements was seen to be a key part of the Golib festival (Figure 43.4). That such activities might also have occurred in the area of stone arrangements excavated in Nyoo would not seem inconceivable considering the contemporary parallels with Tallensi practices which exist.

NYOO 06 (B)

The second unit excavated reinforced this image of Nyoo as a complex archaeological site rather than a 'natural' sacred grove. This excavation was completed within the area of Nyoo most densely filled with standing stones. In total 12 clusters of either paired or single standing stones were recorded (Figure 43.5). Almost immediately upon excavating groups of iron bracelets and other artifacts such as points which had been placed adjacent to the standing stones were recorded. Ultimately, eight complete iron

Figure 43.4. Dance in progress in Nyoo Biil.

Figure 43.5. NYOO 06 (B) indicating the standing stones and associated ritual pots in-situ.

bracelets, seven iron bracelet fragments, one iron finger ring, five iron points, and two fragments of iron strip were recovered. The bracelets were almost uniformly of simple design and their presence was described as representing the interring of 'personal gods' associated with the dead, i.e. intimate personal possessions, possibly following the instructions of diviners to carry out such actions (R. Yin pers. comm.).

This would broadly concur with Fortes (1987, 267) description of the notion of *sii* and its links with concepts of the person – personhood – and personal possessions. Specifically, to quote (Fortes 1987, 267), '*sii*, therefore, in one of its aspects, is the focus, one might almost say the medium, of personal identity which is objectively represented in possessions characteristic of a person's sex and status'. Such possessions as described by Fortes (1987) included the individuals clothing, and for a woman her personal ornaments such as brass bracelets and beadwork, and for a man, his tools such as the hoe and axe, or bow and arrow. Iron bracelets would and could certainly constitute such a category of intimate personal possessions, of precise ontological status and association, even if we cannot go so far as to interpret which gender and/or age or initiation status might have been linked with these artefacts.

Considering the evidence from both units it would appear that distinct differences in ritual practice are manifest in Nyoo, both in the excavated materials recovered and the surface features recorded. This notion of differential ritual practices across Nyoo is lent further support by thirteen complete, and one partially complete, pots which were recovered below and slightly adjacent to the standing stones. The ritual nature of the deposits in this area of Nyoo was thus firmly indicated by the discovery of these pots and by two pear-shaped clay objects, broken, but still conjoining, which were uncovered in association with one of these complete pots from NYOO 06 (B). These clay objects (or object, as they had been joined) had a hole in each of the two pear-shaped segments (Figure 43.6). Again, providing a precise interpretation as to what this object was used for is impossible, and opinions sought from community members varied though generally consensus existed in that it was:

a) A ritual object.
b) Probably offered libation and/or sacrifice (hence the holes).
c) Functioned as a 'Personal God'.

That this object might have functioned within the context, perhaps, of fertility concerns or rituals would be entirely plausible, if unproven. Their actual shape, 'pear-

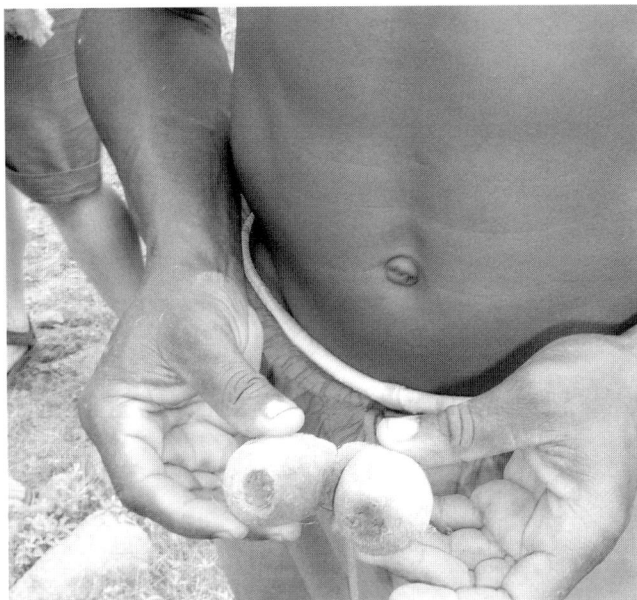

Figure 43.6. The clay ritual object.

shaped' being a somewhat neutral description, is reminiscent of a pair of testicles, and if correct, a fertility association would thus not seem unwarranted. Direct parallels have not been found, though Preston Blier (1987, 48) refers to small earthern balls which are produced by the Batammaliba midwife following the birth of a child. These are made around the infant's birth sack 'as a symbol of the creative process' (Preston Blier 1987, 119). No such meaning is proposed for the Nyoo object, and the latter is not even a ball shape, but it does indicate the ritual use of clay to produce generically similar ritual objects by a linguistically related group from Togo.

As to the meaning of the standing stones, bracelets, pots, clay objects or stone arrangements and their associated rituals in totality, precise information from the Tallensi was not forthcoming – it was seemingly lost. Rather, their general meanings were understood, namely that this material was linked into negotiating destiny via the agency of the aforementioned 'personal gods' and hence functioned within the framework of ancestral worship. Moreover, general consensus existed in that Nyoo should be considered as the great shrine for all the Tallensi, where worship started and spread from (J. B. Zuure pers. comm.). It could thus in effect be called a reservoir or nucleus of ritual practice, and is broadly analogous to the notion of 'symbolic reservoirs' as discussed by Sterner (1992, 171–172; and see MacEachern 1994), but 'symbol' would here be translated into 'ritual'.

The archaeology of sacrifice and the senses

The practice of sacrifice could be indicated archaeologically by many of the categories of material recovered, the broken pottery or the iron bracelets already described, for through their deposition it is possible that they too underwent 'sacrifice'. The shedding of blood, however, is more usually equated with sacrifice in Africa (see De Heusch 1985) and the almost total absence of faunal remains in either of the excavations is of interest in this respect for two primary reasons. Firstly, for totemic observances in relation to the consumption of certain species are a key element of Tallensi belief and social structure today (see Fortes 1987, 136 and 249). And secondly, for the simple reason that blood sacrifice of domestic animals such as chickens, dogs, donkeys, sheep, goats, and cattle is one of the primary acts of ritual practice by the Tallensi, either undertaken individually or collectively (Insoll 2006). How then do we account for the absence of sacrificial residues in the archaeological record – perhaps as an absence of blood sacrifice in earlier, but as yet undated ritual practice as manifest in Nyoo? This is very unlikely, rather it is possible to look to the ethnographic present again to provide possible explanations. Specifically, that such remains disappear for sacrifice is only the act and the residues are not wasted. Instead they are carefully divided according to strict criteria which reflect clan association and social structure. Moreover, what is left; blood, or stomach contents for instance, is soon consumed by scavengers such as dogs, vultures, and dung beetles.

Hence the sacrifice remains are distributed throughout the landscape rather than clustered in one place to enter the archaeological record as at Nyoo. But this is significant for the absence of faunal remains is again reflecting ritual practice, but here seemingly in accord with what occurs among the Tallensi today, rather than at variance with it as is represented by much of the evidence from Nyoo. It is also notable that where faunal remains are distributed in the landscape they can also take on dimensions inaccessible to the archaeologist. This is especially so with the powerful objects formed of blood, fat, skin, bones, and fur which are sometimes attached to the exterior of the house shrine or ritual structure, the *Zong*, which is associated with ancestral worship (Gabrilopoulos 1995, 70).

The example in Figure 43.7 is slowly rotting but is placed adjacent to the main entrance of a Tallensi chief's house in the Tongo Hills. These objects give off a powerful smell and are still accorded a highly prominent position in the house of a prominent individual. They provide a true sensory experience, of smell, often lacking in archaeo-logical contexts but which would have been represented at places of sacrifice by the all-pervading smell of blood, as is immediately apparent in sacrificial areas today. It is not improbable, if unproven, that the excavated areas in Nyoo could also have been used for sacrifice. Hence besides the

Figure 43.7. Tallensi powerful objects formed of fat, skin, bone etc. on Zong.

recognition of sound as a sense potentially of interpretive relevance in relation to dance and performance as already described, smell might also have been a significant, but missing element of our elusive sensory archaeology as well.

Conclusions

It is thus evident that both 'shrines' and 'sacrifice' are evident archaeologically but indications of 'totemism', 'ancestors', and 'animism' are not. Or is such a simple statement warranted? It is not, for all these aspects and none are represented if such a contradiction is possible. This is because what is structuring all the elements present is complexity; i.e. defining shrines is problematic, sacrifice might be evident in terms of pottery vessels but not faunal remains, whereas 'ancestors' are potentially placated by the deposition practices evident, whilst 'animism' or at least 'animistic' concepts may be ascribed to materials such as rock (Insoll 2006), and totemic affiliation could be represented, in the absence of any other discernible patterning, via the use of the stone arrangements by different clans. All of this is of course supposition, but this is the key point. For attempting to generate singular interpretations of religious phenomena based upon archaeological material be it in relation to 'totemism', 'ancestor cults', 'animism' or the current vogue,

'shamanism' (Pearson 2002; Insoll 2004) is nearly always implausible for these are usually based upon supposed 'clear-cut' modern definitions which bare little resemblance to the complex entities which exist in reality (Levi-Strauss 1991; Bowie 2000; Insoll in press a).

Instead what is apparent is that the one aspect so far missing from this concluding discussion but included in the title, 'ritual', is actually the most clearly discernible archaeologically. But not ritual as some sort of vague catch-all category for the otherwise not understood, rather ritual as repeat action of a religious nature in relation to material culture (Bell 1992; Insoll 2004). Here we perhaps have a window into the dynamic nature of Tallensi or 'proto'-Tallensi ritual via archaeology. The specifics of these rituals might be blurred, even with the existence of supporting analogies drawn from extant practices available, but what is recurrent is the importance both of performance and the sensory dimension. The latter potentially manifest in relation to dance, and by association sound. Another associated sensory feature which has been briefly explored is smell, whilst vision could be similarly considered and both are significant in Tallensi ritual today.

This research project, and hence its interpretations, are still at an early stage. Nonetheless, it is hoped that as research proceeds further insights will be gained into the archaeology of ritual and religion in the Tongo Hills.

However beyond this West African context, the potential interpretive relevance of this material is already clear be it for the Neolithic of the British Isles (Insoll 2006) or the Bronze Age of southern England (Insoll in preparation b). For what is immediately apparent is that complexity in religious definition and configuration must, seemingly, be invoked and singular phenomena discounted as more akin to contemporary western conceptualisation of what 'traditional' religions are rather than, potentially, a more accurate configuration of the complexity of past religions.

References

Allman, J. and Parker, J. 2005. *Tongnaab*. Bloomington, Indiana University Press.

Ashley, C. 2006. Unpublished Ceramics Field Notes from Tengzug, 2006. Department of Archaeology, University of Manchester.

Bell, C. 1992. *Ritual Theory, Ritual Practice*. Oxford, Oxford University Press.

Bellis, J. O. 1982. The 'Place of the Pots' in Akan Funerary Custom. Unpublished Report. African Studies Programme, Indiana University.

Bowie, F. 2000. *The Anthropology of Religion*. Oxford, Blackwells.

Courtright, P. 1987. Shrines. In M. Eliade (ed.). *The Encyclopedia of Religion*. London, Macmillan, 299–302.

de Heusch, Luc. 1985. *Sacrifice in Africa*. Manchester, Manchester University Press.

Fortes, M. 1945 [1969]. *The Dynamics of Clanship among the Tallensi*. Oosterhout, Anthropological Publications.

Fortes, M. 1949 [1967]. *The Web of Kingship among the Tallensi*. Oosterhout, Anthropological Publications.

Fortes, M. 1950. The Political System of the Tallensi of the Northern Territories of the Gold Coast. In M. Fortes and E. E. Evans-Pritchard (eds). *African Political Systems*. London, Oxford University Press, 238–71.

Fortes, M. 1987. *Religion, Morality and the Person. Essays on Tallensi Religion*. Cambridge, Cambridge University Press.

Gabrilopoulos, N. 1995. *Ethnoarchaeology of the Tallensi Compound*. Unpublished MA Thesis, University of Calgary.

Insoll, T. 2004. *Archaeology, Ritual, Religion*. London, Routledge.

Insoll, T. 2006. Shrine Franchising and the Neolithic in the British Isles: Some Observations based upon the Tallensi, Northern Ghana. *Cambridge Archaeological Journal* 16, 223–38.

Insoll, T. In Press a. *Archaeology. The Conceptual Challenge*. London, Duckworth.

Insoll, T. In Preparation a. Natural or Human Spaces? Tallensi Sacred Groves and Shrines and their Implications for Phenomenological Interpretations of the Past (submitted to *Norwegian Archaeological Review*).

Insoll, T. In Preparation b. Negotiating the Archaeology of Destiny. Observations from the Tallensi of the Tongo Hills, Northern Ghana.

Insoll, T., Kankpeyeng, B., and MacLean, R. 2004. An Archaeological Reconnaissance in the Tong Hills, and Garu Area, Upper East Region, and Nakpanduri, Northern Region, Ghana. *Nyame Akuma* 62, 25–33.

Insoll, T., Kankpeyeng, B., and MacLean, R. 2005. Excavations and Surveys in the Tongo Hills, Upper East Region, Ghana. July 2005. Fieldwork Report. *Nyame Akuma* 64, 16–23.

Insoll, T., Kankpeyeng, B., and MacLean, R. In Press a. Excavations and Surveys in the Tongo Hills, Upper East Region, Ghana. July 2006. A Preliminary Fieldwork Report. *Nyame Akuma*.

Insoll, T., Kankpeyeng, B., and MacLean, R. In Press b. The Archaeology of Shrines among the Tallensi of Northern Ghana: Materiality and Interpretative Relevance. In A. Dawson and P. Shinnie (eds). *Shrines in African Societies*. Calgary, The University of Calgary Press.

Jacobson-Widding, A. 1979. *Red-White-Black as a Mode of Thought*. Uppsala, Almqvist and Wiksell.

Kankpeyeng, B. 2001. The Cultural Landscape of Tongo-Tengzuk. Traditional Conservation Practices. In Anon, *Traditional Conservation Practices in Africa*. Nantes, CRATerre-EAG, 23–31.

Lévi-Strauss, C. 1991. *Totemism*. London, Merlin Press.

MacEachern, S. 1994. 'Symbolic reservoirs' and Inter-group Relations: West African Examples. *African Archaeological Review* 12, 205–224.

Naden, T. 1988. The Gur Languages. In M. E. Kropp Dakubu (ed.). *The Languages of Ghana*. London, Kegan Paul, 12–49.

Pearson, J. L. 2002. *Shamanism and the Ancient Mind*. Walnut Creek, Altamira.

Preston Blier, S. 1987. *The Anatomy of Architecture. Ontology and Metaphor in Batammaliba Architectural Expression*. Cambridge, Cambridge University Press.

Sterner, J. 1992. Sacred Pots and 'Symbolic Reservoirs' in the Mandara Highlands of Northern Cameroon. In J. Sterner and N. David (eds.). *An African Commitment*. Calgary, University of Calgary Press, 171–79.

Turner, V. 1985. Colour Classification in Ndembu Ritual. In M. Banton (ed.). *Anthropological Approaches to the Study of Religion*. London, Tavistock, 47–84.

Chapter 44

TOWARDS AN ARCHAEOLOGY OF PERFORMANCE

Jon P. Mitchell

Another view from a different bridge

This paper resurrects a tradition. Thirty years ago, a volume emerging from another Cambridge Conference carried a 'comment' chapter by Edmund Leach (Spriggs 1977; Leach 1977). Although given the title *Archaeology and Anthropology,* the volume was primarily concerned with the promise that new directions in Anthropological theory – Marxism, Structuralism and Structural Marxism – might hold for Archaeological analysis. It marked the beginnings of a theory-led rapprochement between the disciplines, which had become estranged following the arrival of Malinowskian Functionalism in the early twentieth century.

This volume is different. Not explicitly focusing on Archaeology and Anthropology, it nevertheless embodies a next stage in this rapprochement; further evidence of the growing convergence between the two disciplines that Gosden, among others, has identified in the last two decades of the twentieth century (Gosden 1999, 7–8). Much of this convergence is down to the strength of Material Culture studies as it emerged in the late twentieth century (Buchli 2002, 10). Material Culture studies built upon Marxism and Structuralism, to develop a 'post-structural' and 'post-processual' discipline, which highlights the fluidity of practice and performance rather than the fixity of system and structure. It emphasises the 'social life of things' (Appadurai 1986), the creative and active practices of consumption (Miller 1995), and the 'agency' of material objects as they are embedded in systems of social relatedness that they are both constituted by and constitute (Gell 1998). It is these themes that I wish to trace in my reading of the papers collected in this volume.

The breadth and quantity of these contributions prevent an approach that addresses every paper and every theme. I have chosen, therefore, to focus on the contributions to the Archaeology of Malta – which were prominent in the Cambridge Conference, and which complement my ethnographic material on contemporary Maltese ritual (Mitchell 2002; 2004). Before addressing these issues in Maltese Anthropology and Archaeology, I will outline what I see as the main features of what one might describe as a Material Culture approach to ritual performance – summarizing an earlier piece I wrote on this theme (Mitchell 2006).

Cult in practice – ritual performance

Like the study of Material Culture, the Anthropological study of religion has moved away from an emphasis on system, structure and ideology towards practice. This has brought the theorization of ritual to the forefront of our understanding of human conceptual systems. For Archaeology, it is an appropriate move. The Archaeological record consists of evidence drawn from the results of human practice – and in the cult context, the results of ritual practice.

This is not the place to survey the various definitions of ritual that have emerged over the years. Catherine Bell (1992) argues that ritual is characterized by action that is 'set aside' from everyday life; but all too often rituals are treated as if they are literally separate from the everyday. To do so not only reproduces a tendency within Judaeo-Christian contexts to separate sacred from profane as domains of meaning – a separation that is inappropriate to most ritual contexts – it also, significantly, mistakes a strategy of ritualization for a property of ritual. Whilst ritual action is strategically 'set aside' in order to make it 'special', it is not its separation from the everyday which makes it significant, but rather the opposite – its ability to influence, or even transform, the everyday.

I have argued that ritual performance should be seen above all as transformative – capable of producing major long-term transformations within the persons, objects and spaces of ritual action (Mitchell 2006). These transformations take place within ritual performance but are then brought back into the everyday context as permanent features of the ritual participants, their paraphernalia and the ritual site. At the same time these 'objects' of ritual action are transformed, in and through performance, from being objects of the material culture of ritual, into ritual subjects – endowed with the power to act; with agency.

I use three key examples to explain this process: initiation in Highland Papua New Guinea; West African masquerade; and the Orange Parades of Northern Ireland. In each case I rely on a range of secondary ethnographic sources, the key ones being Bloch 1992, Poole 1982 and Whitehouse 1996 (for initiation); McNaughton 1988 and Nunley 1987 (for masquerade); and Bryan 2000 and Jarman 1998 (for parades).

The case of initiation involves the transformation of the person, through the agency of the experiencing body. This body-agency generates salient memories in the initiand of the terrifying practices to which they are subjected during the ritual itself. These memories endure within the initiand after their initiation, to become part of their permanent transformed selves, endowed with the power of ancestral spirits. The case of masquerade involves a double transformation – of wood into mask and then mask into an object of power; a conduit for the powerful forces which govern the universe. Through this transformation, the mask itself acquires agency through the careful craftsmanship of the maker, the deployment of correct and powerful combinations of 'medicine', and performance of the mask itself. This object-agency increases with each performance and remains as potential power even when the mask resides in its shrine. The case of the Orange Parades involves the transformation of space, from the relatively neutral space of a lived environment to the symbolically and politically charged space of performance. Parading along particular routes not only reproduces 'traditional' practice, but actively constitutes tradition, configuring and constituting the political geography of sectarianism. Parade routes become furnished with permanent symbols of Orangeism – originally, triumphal arches in wood, then iron; latterly murals and curb-stone markings of red, white and blue, which mark out territory as Protestant and Unionist. The markings are not merely mnemonic. They generate a space which itself 'remembers' its sectarian identity, as the body of the initiand remembers the terror of initiation and the mask of masquerade remembers the power of its medicine and performance. Moreover, it is a space with agency; a space-agency which marks out effective 'no-go areas' for Nationalists, legitimizing Unionist violence against those who transgress.

Performance and Maltese festa

The example of Maltese *festa* brings together the three themes of transformation and agency intrinsic to the argument: the transformation and agency of space; the transformation and agency of objects; and the transformation and agency of persons, in the context of

competition and conflict over power. The Maltese saint's feast – *festa* – is rooted in such conflict. There are 65 parishes in the predominantly Catholic Maltese islands, each of which celebrates at least one *festa* each year. Many of these *festi* directly compete with one another to produce the best *festa*, with the most innovative forms of ritualisation: procession, street decorations, brass band marches, fireworks etc. *Festa partiti* – competing *festa* factions – are also political factions, such that contest between *festi* is political contest (Boissevain 1993). Moreover, *festa partiti* themselves are divided between the often antagonistic authorities of clergy and laity, which means that the *festa* is rooted in the struggle for both secular and spiritual power.

My own ethnographic research in Malta centres on the *festa* of St Paul, held every year in February in Malta's capital city, Valletta (Mitchell 2002). The *festa* itself is opened some two weeks before *festa* day, 10th February, when the monumental statue of St Paul – some ten feet tall and made of solid wood – is taken out of its normal home in a niche in the parish church, and placed on a pedestal in the main body of the church. From that day onwards, the parish streets are elaborately decorated with flags, banners and bunting. The five days leading up to *festa* day see a combination of solemn liturgical functions inside the church and more playful, ludic celebrations outside – including processions, brass band marches, fireworks displays, discos. On *festa* day itself, the statue is taken into the streets in procession around the parish, accompanied by both lively brass bands and a formal liturgical procession.

Conceptually, the *festa* is divided into 'inside' festivities and 'outside', which are the respective responsibilities of the clergy and the lay organisation in charge of *festa* – the *Ghaqda tal-Pawlini* (Association of Paulites). This division is mediated by the statue of St Paul, particularly during the final procession, which involves taking the statue – which belongs to the Church and is normally inside – outside. Whilst outside it is the responsibility of the *Ghaqda*, which takes a contractual responsibility for its safety during the procession. In taking the inside outside, the outside is transformed – from mundane, everyday space into transcendent, ritual space (see Mitchell 2004). In the process, the divisions which exist between the different 'ritual constituencies' (Baumann 1992) involved in *festa* – clergy and laity; younger and older *Ghaqda* members; higher and lower status participants – are mitigated in a moment of Durkheimian effervescence that informants themselves describe as genuinely unifying (Mitchell 2002).

This transformation of space is not limited to the duration of the procession. The procession ensures the enduring patronage of St Paul over the parish, and is like the Orange Parades governed by a significant spatial 'ruling' that for example frames the way the statue should be carried – swaying from side to side as though the saint himself is walking the streets – and requires that where the procession passes streets down which it will not travel, the statue is turned around so that the saint looks down the unwalked streets. Above all, though, the ruling dictates that the procession must, if possible, take place. The mitigating factor is the weather, and where this prevents the procession, there is always conflict and controversy, followed by anxiety – even depression – among parishioners until the procession can be expedited at a later date.

The key to understanding the procession as not merely a symbolic act but a substantive transformation of parish space – and its spiritual rejuvenation – is to recognise that the statue itself is more than a symbol (Mitchell 2004). Like the West African masks, it is more than a representation of the saint, but is rather a substantive embodiment, with its own agency. During the period of the *festa,* when the statue is in the Church, parishioners engage with it as with an actual person – they will talk to it directly, and apologise when turning their back on it. During the procession, the statue is animated by the 'walking' action of the statue-carriers, and its spiritual agency confirmed by its 'looking' down the streets it patronises. The *festa* therefore involves not only a transformation of space, but also a transformation of the object – and like the West African masks, this is a double transformation: from wood into statue, and from statue into saint.

The final transformation is that of the body. Bodily transformation during *festa* reconfirms the agency of the statue-saint not merely as a spiritual agency that ensures patronage and the promise of intercession, but as a felt agency that is inherent in the bodily experience of proximity to the saint himself. This agency is most felt by the statue-carriers or *reffiegha,* for whom the physical trauma of bearing the statue's incredible weight is seen as a kind of penance but also a status-enhancing, status-changing experience that constructs a particular form of masculinity (Mitchell 1998). The trauma is marked on the body in the form of large calluses that develop on the shoulders of a *reffiegh* as bodily manifestations of their proximity to and experience of the saint's agency. This transformation of body and person is particular to those chosen as *reffiegha* – who must be not only physically able, but also morally appropriate for the job. The experience, however, is 'democratised' at the end of the procession, when the *reffiegha* leave the statue and allow other men to experience proximity to the saint. This enables a union of performer and audience; performing unity through the transformation of space, object, body and person.

This analysis demonstrates the multiple transformations brought about by and through ritual performance, demonstrating the fluidity of ritual as practice. Each transformation involves an intersection/interaction of the material and the conceptual; but the material things: bodies, things and space; are not treated here as *objects,* but as *subjects* within the performative process; and as *agents* of power. I see this concern with the interaction between the material and the conceptual, and the resultant trans-formations, as rooted in the tradition of Material Culture studies that has developed through the rapprochement of Archaeology and Anthropology. It focuses not on entities, but on relationships between persons and things, where those things can equally be bodies or spaces as things *stricto facto.*

An archaeology of performance

Within the Archaeology of religious cults, one is always 'reading backwards' from the material evidence into ritual performance. In the framework offered here – of performative transformation – one is seeing the evidence 'post-transformation'; the interpretive art being to understand the contexts through which this material evidence has come to be. Where the tendency within Structuralist-influenced Archaeology has been to interro-gate the evidence to ascertain its meaning, what I am suggesting here, in a 'post-Structuralist' Material Culture mode is that we move away from a search for meaning, towards an understanding of the kinds of *agency* acquired by things through the performative process. This approach makes the stuff of archaeology – landscape, artifact, organic remains, as traces of performative space, object and body – not redolent with meaning and symbolism, but powerful agents within the cult context.

A focus on body-agency demands a move towards a phenomenologically-informed analysis, exemplified in this volume by Robin Skeates's paper on the Maltese hypogea, which were not only sites for placing the dead, but were also multi-sensory experiential environments for the living. Skeates emphasizes the sensory disorientation of ritual participants as they descended into this underworld, where vision, touch and smell were given heightened saliency, generating emotions of shock, stress and terror. Stoddart's evidence from a similar period suggests an orientation to ancestral genealogy, through the annihilation of individuality at burial. One might suggest, then, that like the Melanesian initiands of the ethnographic record – who are placed in the liminal space of the bush and subjected to terrifying ordeals which constitute within them the experience of proximity to powerful ancestral spirits which they subsequently come to embody – so too the participants in hypogeum rituals were transformed through their experience of the underworld. The body-agency of experiences of terror would have constituted within them long-lasting memories, sedimented in their bodies (Connerton 1989), which in turn made them agents of the power of the ancestors. This agency was then re-doubled at death, when their bodies became both locus and conduit of power.

As such, human remains took on the object-agency of the artifact, and were perhaps utilized in ritual alongside the range of other objects – figurines, ornaments, tools, vessels and animal bones – that Caroline Malone documents. She emphasizes the placement of these objects in relatively prominent or concealed locations, according to their relative magical 'potency'. This play of concealment and exposure might equally have informed the performative process through which such objects acquired their potency; their object-agency. As with the West African masks, the performance of an object might have given it greater power. Viewing such objects as agents within a performative process potentially extends analyses such as that presented by Andrew Townsend, of Maltese prehistoric ephebism. Where he focuses on a symbolism of vitality, one might suggest that the artifacts he examines were substantive embodiments of vitality – endowed with power, as counterpoint to the power of morbidity inherent in the Maltese death cult.

Finally, I shall cite the well-developed theme of space-agency within the Maltese material here presented. Caroline Malone focuses on the significance of vision and sight-lines within the temples and hypogea, whilst Michael Anderson and Simon Stoddart attempt to quantify and empirically map this process of concealment and exposure. It is Reuben Grima and Anthony Bonanno who in complementary fashion demonstrate the extent to which a transformed landscape is a landscape with power – an agent in contemporaneous and subsequent peoples' engagement with the world they occupy. This transformed landscape is also a performed landscape and one which, through performance, acquires the power inherent within it.

References

Appadurai, A. (ed.). 1986. *The Social Life of Things*. Cambridge, Cambridge University Press.

Baumann, G. 1992. Ritual Implicates 'Others': rereading Durkheim in a plural society. In D. de Coppet (ed.). *Understanding Rituals*. London, Routledge.

Bell, C. 1992. *Ritual Theory, Ritual Practice*. Oxford, Oxford University Press.

Bloch, M. 1992. *Prey into Hunter: the politics of religious experience*. Cambridge, Cambridge University Press.

Boissevain, J. 1993. *Saints and Fireworks: religion and politics in rural Malta*. (Second edition.) Malta, Progress Press.

Bryan, D. 2000. *Orange Parades: the politics of ritual, tradition and control*. London, Pluto.

Buchli, V. (ed.). 2002. *The Material Culture Reader*. Oxford, Berg.

Connerton, P. 1989. *How Societies Remember*. Cambridge, Cambridge University Press.

Gell, A. 1998. *Art and Agency: an anthropological theory*. Oxford, Oxford University Press.

Gosden, C. 1999. *Anthropology and Archaeology*. London, Routledge.

Jarman, N. 1998. *Material Conflicts: parades and visual displays in Northern Ireland* Oxford, Berg.

Leach, E. 1977. A View from the Bridge. In M. Spriggs, ed. *Archaeology and Anthropology*. Oxford, British Archaeological Reports.

McNaughton, P. R. 1988. *The Mande Blacksmiths: knowledge, power, and art in West Africa*. Bloomington, Indiana University Press.

Miller, D. 1995. *Acknowledging Consumption: a review of new studies*. London, Routledge.

Mitchell, J. P. 1998. Performances of Masculinity in a Maltese *Festa*. In F. Hughes-Freeland and M. Crain, (eds). *Recasting Ritual: Performance, Media, Identity*. London, Routledge.

Mitchell, J. P. 2002. *Ambivalent Europeans: ritual, memory and the public sphere in Malta*. London, Routledge.

Mitchell, J. P. 2004. Ritual structure and ritual agency. 'Rebounding violence' and Maltese *festa*. *Social Anthropology* 12(1), 57–75.

Mitchell, J. P. 2006. Performance. In C. Tilley, W. Keane, S. Kuechler, M. Rowlands and P. Spyer (eds). Handbook of Material Culture. London, Sage.

Nunley, J. 1987. *Moving with the Face of the Devil: art and politics in urban West Africa*. Urbana, University of Illinois Press.

Poole, F. J. P. 1982. The Ritual Forging of Identity: aspects of person and self in Bimin-Kuskusmin male initiation. In G. H. Herdt, (ed.). *Rituals of Manhood: male initiation in Papua New Guinea*. Berkeley, University of California Press.

Spriggs, M. (ed.). 1977. *Archaeology and Anthropology*. Oxford, British Archaeological Reports.

Whitehouse, H. 1996. Rites of Terror: emotion, metaphor and memory in Melanesian initiation cults. *Journal of the Royal Anthropological Institute* (n.s.) 2, 703–715.

INDEX

References to figures are given in italics.